A Birder's Guide
to
Washington

ABA Birdfinding Guide Series

2003

Taking his post at the edge of his territory, a male Spotted Owl confronts an intruder as his mate broods their young in the darkening depths of the old-growth forest.

A BIRDER'S GUIDE TO WASHINGTON

by
Hal Opperman

with contributions

from members of the

Washington Ornithological Society

Illustrated by

Tony Angell

Library of Congress Control Number: 2003111802

ISBN Number: 1-878788-20-5

First Edition
   1   2   3   4   5   6   7   8

Printed in the United States of America

Publisher
  American Birding Association, Inc.

Editors
  Cindy Lippincott and Hal Opperman

Maps
  Cindy Lippincott and Virginia Maynard; using CorelDRAW, version 8

Cover Photograph
  Bud Anderson; *Gyrfalcon, second-year female, February, Whatcom County*

Illustrations and Captions
  Tony Angell

Distributed by
  American Birding Association Sales
  P.O. Box 6599
  Colorado Springs, CO 80934 USA
  phone: 800-634-7736 or 719-578-0607
  fax: 800-590-2473 or 719-578-9705
  email: *abasales@abasales.com*
  website: *www.americanbirding.org/abasales*

For
TERRY AND DENNIS
and for the
FUTURE BIRDERS OF WASHINGTON

PREFACE AND ACKNOWLEDGMENTS

The present book was originally conceived as an updating of *A Guide to Bird Finding in Washington*, by Terence R. Wahl and Dennis R. Paulson—the birdfinding classic first distributed in mimeographed form at the annual meeting of the American Ornithologists' Union in Seattle in 1971. The first commercially available edition, published the following year by the Whatcom Museum in Bellingham, was succeeded by numerous revised editions through 1991. In 1996, the authors donated their book to the Washington Ornithological Society (WOS), which has kept it available through several small reprintings. Thanks to the "Wahl and Paulson," thousands of residents and out-of-state visitors have found their way to Washington's best birding spots for more than three decades.

As the authors well appreciated, however, the state's habitats, land use, and associated birds were changing rapidly, even as understanding of the birds' status, distribution, and ecological relationships grew ever more sophisticated. The guide needed to keep pace or risk losing its edge. The WOS board quickly determined to undertake a new edition. Planning began in 1997; talks with the American Birding Association (ABA) were under way soon thereafter. The project ramped up through 1998, with initial chapter assignments made and site lists drawn up. By 2000, as fresh fieldwork and writing reached cruising altitude, the realization dawned that we were embarked not on a makeover but on an essentially new book. Although the general editorial concept, the division of the state into nine birding regions, and the core site selection remain largely unchanged, almost all of the specific site descriptions and other features have been written anew, from scratch. It was simply easier that way. Here and there, a felicitous turn of phrase or a telling passage has been retained in tribute to our indebtedness—just often enough, we hope, to elicit a smile of approval from readers who remember their Wahl and Paulson fondly. It was (and is) an exemplary book.

Work on the new guide proceeded under three WOS presidents: Marcus Roening, Scott Morrison, and Kraig Kemper. They have stood behind it at every step, keeping the board well informed of the book's progress and urging us on. ABA's interest in adding the Wahl and Paulson title to the ABA Birdfinding Guide Series dates back to 1991, but because a revision of the guide was about to go to press when the inquiry was made, another nine years elapsed until the partnership was sealed. We are grateful to ABA's Publications Committee and several ABA staff members, who retained their enthusiasm for a Washington guide during those years. Particularly helpful was Allan Burns, ABA Director of Publications, for his unwavering support of the book and the resources he committed to it. At a time when drafts of several chapters appeared at ABA in quick sucession, Virginia Maynard applied her considerable mapmaking skills to keep us moving forward. Bob Berman worked many technical wonders, including his signature bar graphs that convey so much information so gracefully.

Like the Wahl and Paulson guide before it, ours is a collaborative venture. It has been a pleasure and a privilege to work with 30 birders and naturalists who have contributed signed subchapters or other sections: Jim Acton, Jim Alt, Tom Aversa, Dave Beaudette, Thais Bock, Wilson Cady, Lee Cain, Richard Cannings, Jim Christensen, MerryLynn Denny, Mike Denny, Bob Flores, Bryan Gates, Donald Haley, Randy Hill, Mark Houston, Barbara Jensen, Kraig Kemper, Bob Kuntz, Bill LaFramboise, Nancy LaFramboise, Joe Lipar, Bob Morse, Bob Norton, Dennis Paulson, John Roberson, Bill Shelmerdine, Dan Stephens, Andy Stepniewski, and Wayne Weber. We revel in the drawings of Tony Angell, Washington artist-naturalist—a marvelous complement to the prose. Mark Goering, Jeff Lewis, and George H. Taylor were instrumental in providing maps of Washington's ecoregions and precipitation upon which our maps inside the front cover are based. Washington raptor biologist Bud Anderson provided the perfect touch for the cover with his striking Gyrfalcon photograph. Thank you, one and all. This book is your book.

Many persons have generously shared their birding knowledge, responded to requests for information about routes and access, ground-truthed birdfinding chapters, and reviewed portions of the text. Thanks go to Kevin Aanerud, Jim Acton, Chuck Adams, Juli Anderson, Janet Anthony, Tom Aversa, Brian Bell, Bob Berman, Fred Bird, Gary Bletsch, Thais Bock, Bob Boekelheide, Mike Boryaewicz, Keith Brady, Marv Breece, Leslie Brown, Dorsey Burger, Sally Butts, Michael Carmody, Rafe Carroll, Kelly Cassidy, Chris Chappell, Eric Cummings, Mike Donahue, Scott Downes, Rose DuBois, Kas Dumroese, John Edison, JoLynn Edwards, Jim Erckmann, Bruce Fisher, Ron Friesz, George Gerdts, Steve Gerstle, Henry Gilmore, Larry Goldstein, Jessi Gonzalez, Denny Granstrand, Gavin Gray, Jason Guthrie, Donald Haley, Neal Hedges, Rich Hendrix, Randy Hill, Michael Hobbs, Scott Horton, Eugene Hunn, David Hutchinson, Hugh Jennings, John Jensen, Curt Johnson, Richard Johnson, Jack Kintner, Ken Knittle, Lisa Langelier, Rachel Lawson, Chuck Lennox, Cindy Lippincott, Chris Loggers, Mike Lohr, Phil Mattocks, Faye McAdams, Kelly McAllister, Jim Miller, Steve Mlodinow, Judy Mullally, John Roberson, Mike Patterson, Dennis Paulson, Greg Pelletier, Anne Peterson, Ted Peterson, Scott Price, Pam Pritzl, Robert Michael Pyle, Barbara Rasch, Allan Richards, John Roberson, Larry Robinson, Marcus Roening, Russell Rogers, Tom Schooley, Michael Schroeder, Carol Schulz, Brenda Senturia, Jan

Sharkey, Greg Shirato, Terry Sisson, Shelly Snyder, Meredith Spencer, Bob Steelquist, Dan Stephens, Willie Stephens, Zach Stephens, Andy Stepniewski, Ellen Q. Stepniewski, Patrick Sullivan, Bob Sundstrom, Dave Swayne, Colin Thoreen, Rob Thorn, Bill Tweit, Tom Van Buren, Carole Vande Voorde, Maurice Vial, Terry Wahl, Diane Weber, Tom Weber, Bart Whelton, Gary Wiles, Bob Woodley, and Max Zahn. Your hundreds of additions, corrections, and insights have made this a far more interesting and useful book.

Andy Stepniewski has given beyond measure. As founding editor, he laid out the plan of the book and recruited many of its authors. As the project evolved, he continued as content editor/coordinator for the five Eastside chapters, working with various contributors to identify routes, craft site descriptions, and determine editorial shape. His authorship is acknowledged from one end to the other of the book: in the Introduction, the birdfinding chapters, the Annotated Checklist. Editorial responsibility for compilation of the non-avian faunal lists also fell to Andy. On top of these tasks, he found time to drive nearly all of the routes, walk most of the trails, and bird just about every site mentioned in the book—often more than once, and usually in the company of Ellen Quiring Stepniewski. Ellen's careful schematic maps, sketched in the field with mileages noted, proved indispensable in assuring the reliability of our maps and route-finding directions. As if this were not enough, Andy and Ellen reviewed and corrected every map and every line of text. Hats off to you both: without you, *A Birder's Guide to Washington* would not exist.

Cindy Lippincott
Colorado Springs, Colorado

Hal Opperman
Medina, Washington

30 June 2003

TABLE OF CONTENTS

xi

INTRODUCTION

by Hal Opperman and Andy Stepniewski

Washington perches at the northwest corner of the conterminous United States—and birders know by instinct that corners are always good. Unlike the Southwestern borderlands, however, or South Florida, or the bottom prong of the Lone Star State, Washington has no particular group of target species that occur nowhere else. Instead, our state is an ecological crossroads, offering year-round birding in settings of great natural beauty where an outstanding diversity of species can be found in a manageably small area.

Washington is the smallest of the 11 Western states, yet the state bird list stands at over 475 species, surpassing all but a few of the others. How can this be, for a state that covers just 3°20' of latitude? One answer is the great variation in relief across its 350-mile width. Another is the 3,000 miles of saltwater shoreline (thanks to Puget Sound and all those islands). Then, too, the state lies between the valleys of the Columbia and Fraser Rivers—two sea-level cuts across the Cascade Range that funnel birds between the interior and the coast. Both rivers have their origins in the British Columbia mountains and are among the largest on the continent.

Five of Washington's nine terrestrial ecoregions stretch north far into British Columbia, six extend south into Oregon or even California and Nevada, two reach eastward through the Rocky Mountains, while to the west lies the open Pacific. Have a look at the Ecoregions map inside the front cover and you will understand why 10 loons and grebes, 10 tubenoses, 12 woodpeckers, and 23 native sparrows and allies occur regularly every year in Washington, along with 30 species of shorebirds and 34 of waterfowl. Thirty-two species of gulls, terns, and their kin have been seen in the state, of which 24 occur regularly. What other state gives you a reasonable chance for 15 owls for your year list (yes, it has been done)? Where else can you count on both Lesser Goldfinch and Boreal Chickadee? Equally revealing is a sampling of records of vagrants from the last four years: Arctic Loon, Shy and Short-tailed Albatrosses, Greater Shearwater, Wilson's Storm-Petrel, Brown Booby, White Ibis, Bean Goose, Falcated Duck, Eurasian Kestrel, Eurasian Hobby, Mountain Plover, Eurasian Dotterel, Lesser Black-backed Gull, Long-billed Murrelet, White-winged Dove, Costa's Hummingbird, Black Phoebe, Vermilion Flycatcher, Dusky Thrush, Yellow and Black-backed Wagtails, Bay-breasted, Yellow-throated, and Mourning Warblers, Summer Tanager, Rustic and Painted Buntings, Hooded Oriole. These and many others arrive from all the compass points.

Some of the best birding locations in Canada lie right across the border in British Columbia—seamless continuations of the habitats on the Washington side. Many birders include Victoria and Vancouver in their Pacific Northwest visits, devising loop trips with various combinations of ferries. The British Columbia Cascades and Okanagan country are just as alluring. By popular demand, and following the example of the Wahl and Paulson guide, we have included a few pages on some of the most productive sites in these areas, generously contributed by members of the province's fine birding community.

This Introduction presents information on topography, habitats, conservation, the birding year, getting around, the birders' information network, and the changing scene, selected and organized to help you find and enjoy Washington's birds.

TOPOGRAPHY

Washington has a particularly complex, and fascinating, geological history. While you don't need to know your geology to bird the state successfully, an understanding of the basics can be helpful. Birds, after all, are tied to specific habitats, determined largely by climate. Climate is a function of topography—and topography is a consequence of geological events. Three great forces shaped the Washington landscape: plate tectonics, volcanism, and glaciation. Together they account for just about all of the distinctive birding regions of the state.

The western coastline of the primeval North American continent was once situated in Eastern Washington, not far from the present-day Idaho line. Moving gradually westward, the North American plate collided with two microcontinents. The Okanogan and Cascade terranes were successively annexed in this way. Tremendous pressures forced the ocean floor upward, tipping and folding the earth's crust into coastal mountain ranges that became the Selkirks and the Cascades. The Columbia Valley at Kettle Falls, the Okanogan Valley, and Puget Sound are remainders of the subduction trenches and former coastlines resulting from the meeting of these plates. Pushing westward, the continental plate next overrode an oceanic plate along a trench off the Washington coast, creating the Olympic Mountains and the Willapa Hills—a process that continues today at the rate of two or three inches a year. Raised up by subduction forces, the continental shelf slopes gradually to its edge 25–30 miles off the Olympic Peninsula—the destination of the Westport pelagic trips—before plunging steeply to the trench where the Juan de Fuca plate is slowly disappearing beneath the continent.

Plate collisions and crustal stresses have made Washington an area of intense volcanic activity for tens of millions of years. The most visible evidence is the High Cascades volcanoes—part of the "ring of fire" along the Pacific Rim—and the multiple outpourings of lavas in the Miocene epoch that left the Columbia Basin buried beneath basalt layers several thousand feet deep. Traces of volcanic activity are everywhere: pillow basalts, mudflows, layers of ash. The massive granite dome of the Okanogan Highlands results from an ancient volcanic event. Still farther back in time, the Blue Mountains trace their origins to an arc of volcanic islands off the coast of the old North American continent.

For the last two million years a succession of continental ice sheets advanced into Washington, then retreated. The most recent glaciation bulldozed its way across the northern third of the state beginning about 20,000 years ago, rounding off mountaintops, deepening valleys, gouging out future lake basins, and leaving behind great quantities of glacial debris when it withdrew 9,000 years later. The present physiognomy of Puget Sound is a textbook case of these processes at work. The glacial sheet was some 6,000 feet thick at the U.S.-Canada border; the site of Seattle lay beneath 3,000 feet of ice. Outwash from the melting glaciers created the gravelly soils of the South Sound Prairies at the southern extremity of glaciation, from Tacoma to Tenino. The Puget Basin is so filled with glacial crud (3,000 feet deep in places) that the nature of the underlying bedrock remains a matter of speculation for geologists. On the Eastside, surges of glacial meltwater known as the Spokane Floods carved the Grand Coulee and many lesser but no less impressive channels, stripped topsoils to create the Channeled Scablands, steepened the Columbia Gorge, and deposited deep layers of silt in the beds of temporary lakes as far west as Vancouver/Portland. About 40 such floods occurred when periodic failures of ice dams released the impounded waters of Glacial Lake Missoula in western Montana.

Our book is organized into compact regions along county lines that artificially cut across the big topographic divisions more often than not. The following directory will help you to line up the topography with the associated birdfinding chapters (in plain italics).

Oceanic. Pelagic and inshore waters and coastline of Pacific Ocean and Strait of Juan de Fuca east to about Port Angeles. *Strait of Juan de Fuca and Pacific Coast*.

Olympic Peninsula. North of the Chehalis River floodplain, bordered by Hood Canal, Strait of Juan de Fuca, Pacific Ocean. Dominated by Olympic Mountains. High-precipitation zone of western slopes contrasts markedly with rainshadowed northeastern portion. *Strait of Juan de Fuca and Pacific Coast, Puget Sound*.

Willapa Hills. Low coastal range south from the Olympic Peninsula to the Columbia River, including the Black Hills. *Strait of Juan de Fuca and Pacific Coast, Puget Sound, Southwest*.

Puget Trough/Willamette Valley/Georgia Depression. Lowlands between the coastal ranges and the Cascades. Includes the Georgia Depression northward from the San Juan Islands, inland marine waters eastward from Port Angeles and Victoria, Puget Sound, and a northern extension of the Willamette Valley of Oregon around Vancouver. The central Westside landform though not the largest, it figures in all four Westside chapters: *Strait of Juan de Fuca and Pacific Coast, Northwest, Puget Sound, Southwest.*

Cascade Range. High, wide mountainous belt separating Western from Eastern Washington. Wet west slopes, dry east slopes offer distinctively different habitats and birdlife, as do the Cascades north and south of Snoqualmie Pass. *Northwest, Puget Sound, Southwest, South Central, Okanogan.*

Columbia Basin. Central, dominant landform of Eastern Washington, relatively low-lying basin sloping from northeast to southwest and watered by the Columbia River and its tributaries. Core is in *Columbia Basin* chapter, periphery in all four of the other Eastside chapters: *South Central, Okanogan, Northeast, Southeast.*

Okanogan Highlands/Selkirk Mountains. Mountains and plateaus east of the Okanogan River and north of the Columbia Basin. *Okanogan, Northeast.*

Blue Mountains. South and east of the Columbia Basin, extending south into Oregon. Part of the Middle Rocky Mountains. *Southeast.*

WASHINGTON HABITATS

Few states show more dramatic contrasts in their environment than Washington. Elevations range from sea level to over 14,000 feet. Precipitation varies from over 200 inches annually on the Olympic Peninsula, nurturing a temperate rain forest and mountaintop glaciers, to a mere six inches in parts of the Columbia Basin, where near-desert conditions prevail. The primary reason for these contrasts is the Cascade Range, which runs from north to south the entire length of the state. Pacific storms slam into Western Washington for much of the year. The *Wet Side* is often cloudy and enjoys moderate temperatures at all seasons. East of the Cascades, Washington's *Dry Side* has a rainshadow climate. Summers are hot, winters cold; clear skies are the norm. Between these extremes, an array of precipitation and temperature regimes supports a remarkable variety of aquatic and terrestrial communities with a rich diversity of bird species. The most prevalent of these habitat types are summarized in the following pages.

Pelagic. Birding in Washington's pelagic zone is as good as anywhere in North America. Marine life of many kinds concentrates 25–30 miles offshore, near the edge of the continental shelf where upwellings are strongest. Typical birds include Black-footed Albatross, Northern Fulmar, Pink-footed, Buller's, and Sooty Shearwaters, Fork-tailed Storm-Petrel, Red-necked and Red Phalaropes, South Polar Skua, Pomarine, Parasitic, and Long-tailed Jaegers, Sabine's Gull, Black-legged Kittiwake, Arctic Tern, Common Murre, Cassin's Auklet, and Tufted Puffin.

Inshore Marine Waters. There is great variability in this habitat due to depth, bottom configuration and substrate, currents, and effects of tides on the water column and its animals. Thus all open salt water isn't equal when it comes to finding birds: different local conditions appeal to different species. The outer coast is exposed directly to the full power of the wind and waves of the Pacific Ocean; life here must be adapted to extremes, and many invertebrates are attached to the bottom. Eastward along the Strait of Juan de Fuca oceanic influences gradually diminish. The complex of protected basins and channels comprising greater Puget Sound is bathed twice daily through tidal action with an abundance of nutrients. Birds to expect in one place or another off Washington's coastlines include Red-throated, Pacific, and Common Loons, Horned, Red-necked, and Western Grebes, Sooty Shearwater (oceanic), Brown Pelican, Double-crested, Brandt's, and Pelagic Cormorants, Surf, White-winged, and Black Scoters, Red-breasted Merganser, Parasitic Jaeger, Heermann's, Mew, California, Thayer's, Western, and Glaucous-winged Gulls, Common Tern, Common Murre, Pigeon Guillemot, Marbled and Ancient Murrelets, Rhinoceros Auklet, and Tufted Puffin.

Sandy Beaches and Dunes. Sandy beaches backed by dunes characterize much of Washington's South Coast. Birds to look for near the water's edge include Brown Pelican, Merlin, Peregrine Falcon, Black-bellied Plover, American and Pacific Golden-Plovers, Snowy and Semipalmated Plovers, Whimbrel, Ruddy and Black Turnstones, Red Knot, Sanderling, Western, Least, Baird's, and Pectoral Sandpipers, Dunlin, Heermann's, California, Herring, Western, and Glaucous-winged Gulls, and Caspian and Common Terns. Shorebirds feed on the abundant California Beach Fleas, a nocturnal crustacean, and on many other invertebrates. Huge numbers of shorebirds may roost along the beach at high tide. The unstabilized dunes closest to the beach are colonized mostly by introduced European Beachgrass. Birds seen here include Northern Harrier, American and Pacific Golden-Plovers, Snowy and Short-eared Owls, Horned Lark (*strigata*), Savannah Sparrow, Lapland Longspur, and Snow Bunting.

Rocky Shores. This habitat occurs mainly along the Outer Olympic Coast and the Straits of Juan de Fuca and Georgia, including the San Juan Islands. An exceptionally diverse fauna of marine organisms, including dozens of species of worms, snails, and other invertebrates, inhabits the intertidal zone. Sea stacks along the coast from Point Grenville north to Cape Flattery have large, but virtually inaccessible seabird colonies (Fork-tailed and Leach's Storm-Petrels, Common Murre, Cassin's Auklet, Tufted Puffin). Other typical birds of rocky shores include Double-crested, Brandt's, and Pelagic Cormorants, Harlequin Duck, Bald Eagle, Peregrine Falcon, Black Oystercatcher, Wandering Tattler, Black Turnstone, Surfbird, Rock Sandpiper, Heermann's,

Western, and Glaucous-winged Gulls, Black-legged Kittiwake, Pigeon Guillemot, and Northwestern Crow.

Estuaries and Tidal Flats. The Puget Sound system is a giant estuary fed by numerous rivers, many with tidal flats. So, too, are two large, protected coastal bays—Grays Harbor and Willapa Bay. Rivers deposit sand and silt, providing an exceptionally rich substrate for burrowing invertebrates. Mudflats, salt marshes, tidal sloughs, and the littoral zone teem with loons, grebes, geese, dabbling ducks, shorebirds, gulls, and terns. Other typical birds found here include Double-crested and Pelagic Cormorants, Great Blue Heron, Osprey, Bald Eagle, Merlin, Peregrine Falcon, Parasitic Jaeger, Pigeon Guillemot, Belted Kingfisher, Purple Martin, and American Pipit. The spring shorebird stopover at Grays Harbor National Wildlife Refuge is of international significance, especially for Black-bellied Plover, Western Sandpiper, Dunlin, and Short-billed Dowitcher.

Westside Ponds, Lakes, and Wetlands. This low- to mid-elevation family of freshwater habitats ranges from large, deep lakes to ponds, sewage lagoons, marshes (including brackish marshes), streambanks, and wet fields. Characteristic seasonal residents and migrants in environments with emergent vegetation and/or shallow edges include Pied-billed Grebe, Double-crested Cormorant, American Bittern, herons, waterfowl (other than diving ducks), Osprey, Bald Eagle, Northern Harrier, falcons, Virginia Rail, Sora, American Coot, Sandhill Crane, shorebirds (Killdeer and Spotted Sandpiper breed), gulls, Belted Kingfisher, Tree, Northern Rough-winged, and Cliff Swallows, Marsh Wren, Common Yellowthroat, and Red-winged Blackbird. Deeper, open waters attract loons, grebes, and diving ducks, although usually in lesser numbers than on salt water.

Westside Broadleaf Forests. Stands of hardwood trees blanket river floodplains, encircle ponds and wetlands, and crowd streambanks from the lowlands to the mountain passes. Red Alder and Bigleaf Maple dominate, with Black Cottonwood, Oregon Ash, Garry Oak, and various species of willows present locally. Broadleaf trees also appear following the removal of conifer forests by fire or clearcutting. The regenerating conifer forest eventually closes its canopy and shades them out, but small stands of hardwoods may persist even then in openings, near wet places, or on steep slopes. Bird species associated with broadleaf and mixed forest include Cooper's Hawk, Ruffed Grouse, Western Screech-Owl, Downy Woodpecker, Hutton's, Warbling, and Red-eyed Vireos, Black-capped Chickadee, Swainson's Thrush, Cedar Waxwing, Yellow, Black-throated Gray, and Wilson's Warblers, Black-headed Grosbeak, and Bullock's Oriole.

Westside Woodland/Prairie Mosaic. Pockets of grasslands dotted with brush and stands of Garry Oak, pines, and Douglas-fir occupy some of the driest parts of the Western Washington lowlands. Quite locally distributed, this unique habitat type occurs on the fast-draining glacial outwash soils of the

South Sound Prairies and upper Chehalis River basin; south along the trough of the Cowlitz River to the plains around Vancouver; and in the lee of the Olympic Mountains from Sequim northeast to the San Juan Islands (the area of lowest rainfall in Washington west of the Cascades). Typical breeding species found much more commonly in one or more of these locales than elsewhere in Western Washington include Northern Harrier, American Kestrel, Common Nighthawk, Cassin's Vireo, Western Scrub-Jay, White-breasted Nuthatch (*aculeata*, now virtually extirpated), House Wren, Western Bluebird, Chipping and Vesper Sparrows, Western Meadowlark, and Purple Finch.

Westside Coniferous Forests. In terms of area, this is by far the largest habitat category in Western Washington. Forest types are differentiated into several zones in consequence of elevation and precipitation. All have been impacted in varying degrees by 150 years of commercial timber harvest.

Bathed in copious moisture, the luxuriant, moss-draped forest of the *Sitka Spruce zone* constitutes a narrow belt just up from the outer coastal beaches. Characteristic bird species of this rather uniform rain-forest habitat include Spotted Owl (scarce and declining), Rufous Hummingbird, Steller's Jay, Chestnut-backed Chickadee, Winter Wren, Golden-crowned Kinglet, Varied Thrush, Townsend's Warbler, and Red Crossbill.

Farther east, in the rainshadow of the Olympic Mountains, the original forest of the low-lying *Puget Sound Douglas-fir zone* has been all but completely logged off. The present-day landscape away from the burgeoning cities is characterized by fragmented second-growth conifer forest interspersed with broadleaf woodlands, semi-rural residential development, farmlands, prairie, wetlands, and glacier-carved lakes. Avian diversity and numbers are higher in this varied landscape than in the Sitka Spruce zone. Familiar breeding species include Northern Flicker, Pacific-slope Flycatcher, American Crow, Violet-green and Barn Swallows, Black-capped Chickadee, Red-breasted Nuthatch, Swainson's Thrush, European Starling, American Robin, Orange-crowned and Wilson's Warblers, Western Tanager, Spotted Towhee, Song and White-crowned Sparrows, Brown-headed Cowbird, Purple Finch (declining), and American Goldfinch, along with several of the common coastal rain-forest species.

Forests of the *Western Hemlock zone* extend up the slopes of the Cascades and Olympics from just above the Sitka Spruce and Puget Sound Douglas-fir zones to mid-elevations, including all of the Willapa Hills. This is the most widespread forest type in Western Washington, dominated by Western Hemlock (the climax species), Douglas-fir, and Western Redcedar. Most of this zone is occupied by industrial tree farms, but significant stands of the original forests remain uncut—for example, in Mount Rainier National Park. Breeding birds more likely here than in the lower-elevation forest zones are Sharp-shinned Hawk, Band-tailed Pigeon, Northern Pygmy-, Barred (increasing), and Northern Saw-whet Owls, Vaux's Swift, Red-breasted Sapsucker,

Hairy and Pileated Woodpeckers, Olive-sided and Hammond's Flycatchers, Common Raven, Brown Creeper, American Dipper, Yellow-rumped and MacGillivray's Warblers, Dark-eyed Junco, and Evening Grosbeak.

The *Silver Fir* zone occupies slopes of the Olympics and west Cascades at middle to high elevations. Silver Fir and Western Hemlock are the dominant tree species. These lichen-festooned forests receive abundant precipitation, much of it in the form of snow. Indicator bird species include Northern Goshawk, Gray Jay, Hermit and Varied Thrushes, Townsend's Warbler, and Pine Siskin.

Above the Silver Fir zone is the *Mountain Hemlock zone*, an excessively snowy subalpine belt extending to the upper limit of closed forests. The most typical breeding species—all of which also occur in lower-elevation forest zones—are Olive-sided Flycatcher, Gray Jay, Red-breasted Nuthatch, Winter Wren, Golden-crowned Kinglet, Hermit Thrush, American Robin, Yellow-rumped Warbler, Western Tanager, Dark-eyed Junco, and Pine Siskin. Red-naped Sapsucker and several other Eastside species breed locally in small numbers in the Mountain Hemlock zone.

Alpine/Parkland. Clumps of Mountain Hemlock and Subalpine Fir, with some Whitebark Pine (drier sites), alternate with lush, herbaceous meadows. Blue Grouse, Clark's Nutcracker, Common Raven, Mountain Chickadee, Mountain Bluebird, Hermit Thrush, American Robin, American Pipit, Slate-colored Fox Sparrow, Dark-eyed Junco, and Pine Siskin are the typical breeding birds. Dwarf alpine vegetation occupies a narrow, treeless strip between these subalpine parklands and the permanent ice and snow of the highest peaks. White-tailed Ptarmigan, Horned Lark (*alpina*), and Gray-crowned Rosy-Finch breed here. In late summer and early fall many raptors and passerines take advantage of the food resources of these high-elevation habitats.

Eastside Coniferous Forests. The *Subalpine Fir zone* is the interior complement of the Westside's Mountain Hemlock zone. Dominated by Subalpine Fir and Engelmann Spruce, it occurs mainly on the east slopes of the Cascades and eastwards, but also on high, east slopes of the Olympics and at the summits of some of the drier ranges in eastern Skagit and Whatcom Counties. Typical birds are much the same as for the Mountain Hemlock zone, with the addition of Spruce Grouse (mostly Okanogan and Northeast), Boreal Owl, Three-toed Woodpecker, Boreal Chickadee (adjacent to the Canadian border), Ruby-crowned Kinglet, Townsend's Solitaire, Chipping Sparrow, Pine Grosbeak (mostly Northeast), Cassin's Finch, and White-winged Crossbill (irregular).

The *Interior Western Hemlock zone*, the wettest Eastern Washington forest habitat, has Western Hemlock and Western Redcedar as its principal tree species. It occurs mainly at mid- to upper elevations along the east slopes of the Cascades, and reappears at low to middle elevations of the Selkirk Mountains (the "Interior Wet Belt"). The typical birds are as for Western Washington wet forests.

The *Grand Fir zone* is a dense-forest type dominated by Grand Fir with a secondary component of Western Larch, Western White Pine, and Douglas-fir, often with an open understory. It occurs at lower middle elevations, below the Interior Western Hemlock and Subalpine Fir zones and above the drier forest habitats that edge the Columbia Basin. With few exceptions, the list of typical bird species resembles one for the Westside Western Hemlock and Silver Fir zones, e.g., Northern Goshawk, Spotted Owl, Hairy and Pileated Woodpeckers, Olive-sided Flycatcher, Gray and Steller's Jays, Mountain and Chestnut-backed Chickadees, Red-breasted Nuthatch, Golden-crowned Kinglet, Hermit Thrush, American Robin, Yellow-rumped and Townsend's Warblers, Western Tanager, Dark-eyed Junco, Red Crossbill, Pine Siskin, and Evening Grosbeak.

Downslope from the Grand Fir forests, at the point where the *Interior Douglas-fir zone* begins, much of the moisture from Pacific storms has been wrung from the clouds. This rainshadow climate results in a relatively open forest characterized by Douglas-fir and some Western Larch and Grand Fir. Birds are much the same as those of the Grand Fir zone, with the addition of Calliope Hummingbird, Williamson's Sapsucker, Western Wood-Pewee, Hammond's Flycatcher, Cassin's Vireo, Townsend's Solitaire, Nashville Warbler, Chipping Sparrow, and Cassin's Finch.

An open forest dominated by Ponderosa Pine forms a broad ring around the Columbia Basin, with tongues up the Methow, Okanogan, and other river valleys. Fires are frequent in this tinder-dry habitat and are succeeded by extensive brushlands. This *Ponderosa Pine zone* has many birds of interest, including Flammulated Owl, Northern Pygmy-Owl, Common Poorwill, Lewis's, White-headed, and Black-backed (rare) Woodpeckers, Gray and Dusky Flycatchers, White-breasted and Pygmy Nuthatches, House Wren, Western and Mountain Bluebirds, Spotted Towhee, and Slate-colored Fox Sparrow. Several of the common species of the Interior Douglas-fir and Grand Fir zones can also be found here.

Eastside Oak/Pine Woodlands. This small zone characterized by savannahs and woodlands of Garry Oak and Ponderosa Pine with a bunchgrass understory occurs at low elevations in the Southeastern Cascades. Transitional between the Ponderosa Pine zone and steppe-sagebrush habitats, the Oak/Pine Woodlands zone represents the northern extension of an ecoregion that stretches along the eastern base of the Oregon Cascades to California's Modoc Plateau. Some of the typical bird species found here are Turkey Vulture, Golden Eagle, Wild Turkey, Anna's Hummingbird, Lewis's and Acorn (rare) Woodpeckers, Western Wood-Pewee, Say's Phoebe, Ash-throated Flycatcher, Western Scrub-Jay, Bewick's and House Wrens, Western Bluebird, Chipping and Vesper Sparrows, Black-headed Grosbeak, Lazuli Bunting, and Lesser Goldfinch.

Eastside Broadleaf Forests. Another bird-rich habitat is the fringe of Black Cottonwood, Quaking Aspen, White Alder, and other broadleaf trees along streams, ponds, lakes, and wetlands in the dry conifer-forest zones, reaching out into the shrub-steppe in places. Most of the species mentioned above for Westside broadleaf forests are also found in this Eastside riparian zone (Hutton's Vireo being a flagrant exception), together with Great Horned and Long-eared Owls, Black-chinned Hummingbird, Lewis's Woodpecker, Red-naped Sapsucker, Western Wood-Pewee, Pacific-slope Flycatcher, Eastern Kingbird, Bewick's Wren, Veery, Gray Catbird, Nashville and MacGillivray's Warblers, Northern Waterthrush (boggy areas, Okanogan and Northeast), American Redstart (mainly boggy areas, Northeast), Yellow-breasted Chat, and Song Sparrow. Aspen groves—widely distributed across conifer-forest openings, bottomlands, and mountain slopes—appeal to cavity-nesting birds, especially woodpeckers.

Shrub-steppe. Shrub-steppe was once Eastern Washington's most extensive habitat type; it is now the most seriously threatened ecosystem in the state due to wholesale conversion for agricultural uses and to various other development pressures. Where it survives, the original landscape of the Columbia Basin might appear homogeneous to the passer-by, but this is hardly so. Grouped from wettest to driest are the following three major communities.

Almost all deep soils of the *Palouse and Blue Mountain Steppe* communities of Southeastern Washington have been converted to dryland wheat farming, hospitable to a limited range of species, including Gray Partridge and Horned Lark. The tiny remaining parcels of native vegetation are hillside Ponderosa Pine groves with scattered clumps of Quaking Aspen and thickets of Black Hawthorn, Common Snowberry, Nootka and Woods Roses, Western Serviceberry, Common Chokecherry, and Red-osier Dogwood, adjacent to grasslands with a high herbaceous cover. These harbor a riparian-like breeding avifauna including Northern Harrier, Eastern Kingbird, Black-billed Magpie, House Wren, Gray Catbird, MacGillivray's Warbler, Yellow-breasted Chat, Spotted Towhee, Vesper and Song Sparrows, and Bullock's Oriole. Most of the typical steppe birds have vanished along with their habitat.

Occurring mainly on higher, north- or northeast-facing ridges of the northern and eastern Columbia Basin, the *Three-tip Sagebrush/Idaho Fescue* communities are characterized by dwarfish mats of sagebrush with vigorous stands of Idaho Fescue and other tall bunchgrasses that attract shrub-steppe obligates such as Swainson's Hawk, Greater Sage- and Sharp-tailed Grouse (both rare, local), Short-eared Owl, Common Nighthawk, Say's Phoebe, Common Raven, Horned Lark, Sage Thrasher, Clay-colored (rare), Brewer's, Vesper, and Grasshopper Sparrows, and Western Meadowlark.

The *Central Arid Steppe* is situated in the lowest, hottest part of the Columbia Basin. In pristine form it is swathed with a combination of Big Sagebrush and Bluebunch Wheatgrass. Native grass cover is now much reduced through livestock grazing, however, and much of the area has been invaded by Cheatgrass, an exotic. Typical breeding birds include Red-tailed Hawk, American Kestrel, Greater Sage-Grouse, Long-billed Curlew, Burrowing Owl, Common Nighthawk, Say's Phoebe, Loggerhead Shrike, Common Raven, Horned Lark, Sage Thrasher, Brewer's, Lark, and Sage Sparrows, and Western Meadowlark.

Eastside Cliffs and Talus Slopes. Coulees and canyons throughout the Channeled Scablands of the Columbia Basin and elsewhere at lower elevations in Eastern Washington provide a niche for nesting raptors and a host of other species. Among the most typical are Red-tailed and Ferruginous Hawks, Golden Eagle, American Kestrel, Prairie Falcon, Chukar, Rock Dove, Barn and Great Horned Owls, Common Poorwill, White-throated Swift, Common Raven, Violet-green and Cliff Swallows, Rock and Canyon Wrens, European Starling, and Gray-crowned Rosy-Finch (winter night roosts).

Columbia Basin Wetlands. Widespread irrigation in the Columbia Basin has caused the water table to rise, expanding historical wetlands and creating new ones—a boon for many species of birds. A sample of the long list of breeding birds of Columbia Basin wetlands includes Eared, Western, and Clark's Grebes, Double-crested Cormorant, Great Blue Heron, Great Egret, Black-crowned Night-Heron, Canada Goose, dabbling ducks (several species), Redhead, Ruddy Duck, Virginia Rail, Sora, American Coot, Sandhill Crane (migration), Killdeer, Black-necked Stilt, American Avocet, Spotted Sandpiper, Wilson's Snipe, Wilson's Phalarope, Ring-billed and California Gulls, Caspian, Forster's, and Black Terns, Belted Kingfisher, Willow Flycatcher, Tree, Northern Rough-winged, and Bank Swallows, Marsh Wren, and Red-winged and Yellow-headed Blackbirds. Seep lakes, river deltas, ponds, and marshes offer excellent shorebirding, especially in fall migration.

Eastside Lakes and Reservoirs. Birds such as loons, grebes, waterfowl, and gulls have benefited greatly from the damming of the Columbia and Snake Rivers. Especially in fall, the migration of many species usually more associated with marine waters has been stopped in its tracks by the lure of the deep, wide reservoirs. Huge flocks of ducks remain as late into winter as ice-free conditions permit. Other Eastern Washington lakes and adjacent wetlands have a similar effect on a smaller scale. American White Pelicans now breed on two islands in Eastern Washington and are being seen in increasing numbers along the Columbia in all seasons. Common Loon, Horned (rarely) and Red-necked Grebes, Bufflehead, Common and Barrow's Goldeneyes, and Black Tern nest on natural lakes in forested parts of the Okanogan and Northeast.

Shrubby Thickets. This widespread family of habitats exists in a variety of situations at all elevations statewide—for example, forest edges and clearings (such as regenerating clearcuts); mountain slopes, including avalanche chutes; fencerows, dikes, and irrigation ditches; power-line and transportation corridors; free-standing patches of brush and small trees in open landscapes; and mature shrubbery in parks and gardens. Among the many birds that exploit these habitats for cover, nesting, or foraging are quails, Rufous Hummingbird, Willow Flycatcher (and other flycatchers), Black-capped Chickadee, Bushtit, Bewick's, House, and Winter Wrens, kinglets, Hermit Thrush, American Robin, Gray Catbird, Cedar Waxwing, Orange-crowned, Nashville, Yellow, MacGillivray's, and Wilson's Warblers, Common Yellowthroat, Yellow-breasted Chat, Green-tailed (rare, local) and Spotted Towhees, American Tree, Fox, Song, Lincoln's, Swamp, White-throated, Harris's, White- crowned, and Golden-crowned Sparrows, Dark-eyed Junco, Lazuli Bunting, House Finch, Lesser and American Goldfinches, and House Sparrow.

Farmlands. Washington contains large areas of pasture and agricultural land, often inhabited by species of native grasslands, although many of the latter are not able to switch to the simpler habitats produced by human endeavor. For example, extensive wheat fields are used by only one species, the Horned Lark, out of many that existed in the original grasslands. Barn, Short-eared, and Great Horned Owls, White-tailed Kite (Southwest and South Coast), Northern Harrier, and Red-tailed Hawk are among the raptor species that exploit high rodent densities of hay fields and pasturelands at any season, joined by Rough-legged Hawk in winter. Swainson's and Ferruginous Hawks have adapted to hunting over Columbia Basin croplands in spring and summer. In Washington, Bobolinks nest only in irrigated hay fields in the Yakima Valley, the Okanogan, and the Northeast. Dairies, feedlots, and grain-storage facilities may draw Gray Partridge, California Quail, Rock and Mourning Doves, and thousands of starlings and blackbirds, along with the hawks and falcons that prey on them. Certain Westside and Eastside farmlands are famous for their large winter concentrations of waterfowl, raptors, cranes, and shorebirds, providing some of the best birding in the state. Orchards and vineyards, on the other hand, offer relatively few birds other than those species commonly associated with mankind.

CONSERVATION

Throughout this guide, birding information intertwines with discussion of conservation concerns for birds and their habitats. By good fortune and foresight, large tracts of Washington lands are preserved in a natural or near-natural condition. However, economic pressures and the state's population growth are such that practically no land is 100 percent invulnerable to human exploitation, even when it has been set aside for wildlife. The future of birding as we know it depends on the continued protection of important breeding, foraging, and migratory bird areas and on the increasing awareness and activism of birders themselves. Volunteer opportunities abound where birders can put their birding skills to use at every level—from saving the local marsh or tidelands from development to participating in projects of hemispheric importance.

Washington has always been a conservation-minded state, and information about how you may become involved is readily available from scores of sources. Check the web sites of the large national conservation organizations, all of which have a strong Washington presence. Many parks and refuges have "friends of" membership groups: ask about these when you visit. Consider supporting some of the state and regional organizations that unite people of diverse interests in a common cause, for example, Washington Environmental Council, Washington Wilderness Coalition, People for Puget Sound, Kettle Range Conservation Group. For a true hands-on experience, join in the restoration of your neighborhood watershed: what's good for native vegetation is also good for water quality, spawning salmon, and birdlife. Most important, activities such as these build community understanding. Wherever you go, be an ambassador for birding. Wear your binoculars proudly; show this book. Patronize local businesses and tell people why you've come to their part of the state. There is no better way to recruit partners for habitat stewardship.

THE BIRDING YEAR

Washington is a year-round birding destination. However, most birds are strongly responsive to the seasonal cycle. Seasons are well marked, especially east of the Cascades. Precipitation is heavier in the winter and spring, summers generally being dry in all regions. In Western Washington winters are very wet, with overcast skies and light rain an almost constant condition in some years (before complaining, remember that overcast weather allows the best viewing because you do not have to contend with the low northern-latitude sun). This is interspersed with short periods of northeasterly winds that bring dry and cold air from the interior, resulting in clear skies and unsurpassed views of the mountains. Snowfall in the lowlands usually occurs at these times, when cold interior air meets moist coastal air. Above a thousand feet in elevation, snow remains on the ground all winter, lasting at the 5,000-foot level into July or even August. Summers west of the Cascades are warm with the amount of rainfall variable from year to year; some summers are entirely dry and quite warm, others are cool and rainy. East of the mountains, winters are cold, and snow may stay on the ground throughout colder winters, even at the lowest elevations. In warmer winters, many ponds in the Columbia Basin remain open, and snow cover melts in a few days. Summers are very dry and hot in Eastern Washington. The desert areas remain green into June, but by July the general impression is one of death, many of the organisms having finished their annual life cycles and gone into a dormant state. Much of the vegetation is dry, and even birds are not particularly in evidence, except around water.

In four-month groupings, here are some of the highlights of the birding year. The bar graphs and the Annotated Checklist at the back of the book will help you fine-tune the specific destinations and the timing of your visits.

Spring and Early Summer (late March–early July). Spring shorebird migration is outstanding along the coasts, with highest numbers at Grays Harbor near the end of April (Western Sandpiper, Short-billed Dowitcher, Red Knot). In the Columbia Basin, Greater Sage-Grouse strut their leks in March–early April, about the same time that Sandhill Crane migration peaks. Forest owls are vocal and territorial. Prolonged and mostly low-key, spring passerine migration takes place over a broad front, with occasional weather-provoked fallouts and concentrations at headlands, along drainage corridors, or in riparian oases. May is the month of greatest species diversity. Westside Big Day record counts cluster toward the end of the first week of the month and about two weeks later east of the Cascades. June is the heart of the nesting season in most of the state's habitats—a good time to look for White-headed Woodpeckers and Gray Flycatchers in Ponderosa Pine woods; grebes, herons, waterfowl, rails, and terns in wetland habitats; or Pelagic Cormorants, Black Oystercatchers, Pigeon Guillemots, Rhinoceros Auklets, and a few Tufted Puffins on the Protection Island boat trip.

Late Summer and Early Fall (late July–early November). Roads in the Okanogan high country are snow-free—an invitation to look for Spruce Grouse, Great Gray and Boreal Owls, Three-toed and Black-backed Woodpeckers, and Boreal Chickadee. This time of year is also your window to look for White-tailed Ptarmigan and other species of alpine habitats. Or try the Blue Mountains for owls and woodpeckers. Mid-summer to early fall hawkwatching can be decent on clear days along Cascade ridges—for example, Red Top Mountain, Cooper Ridge, or Slate Peak. In late August–early September, passerine migrants concentrate in Eastside riparian corridors in open country. Hotspots such as Washtucna, Vantage, Tri-Cities parks, and Lyons Ferry and Palouse Falls State Parks are as close as Washington comes to true vagrant traps. Late summer offers the greatest diversity on the Westport pelagic trips and the possibility of sought-after species such as Laysan Albatross, Flesh-footed Shearwater, and South Polar Skua. Shorebirding on the coast also peaks at this season, with American and Pacific Golden-Plovers, Bar-tailed Godwit, Sharp-tailed Sandpiper, and Ruff occurring regularly. Unusual gulls may turn up among the Bonaparte's at the Everett sewage ponds.

Late Fall and Winter (late November–early March). Southwesterly winter storms and timing of the tidal cycle severely limit pelagic birding possibilities, but protected marine waters welcome great numbers of loons, grebes, waterfowl, and other waterbirds. Chances are good for Ancient Murrelet (November–December best) and there's usually a Yellow-billed Loon around someplace. Black Oystercatchers, Black Turnstones, Surfbirds, and Rock Sandpipers patrol rocky shores, breakwaters, and jetties. Raptors and wintering waterfowl abound on Westside river floodplains, with prizes such as

Emperor Goose, Gyrfalcon, and Snowy Owl. Raptors, including the last two named, work the snowy fields of Eastern Washington as well. Lapland Longspurs and Snow Buntings infiltrate Horned Lark flocks on the high plateaus. Northern Hawk Owls (rare), Bohemian Waxwings, Gray-crowned Rosy-Finches, and Common Redpolls visit Eastside cliffs, weedy roadsides, orchards, and ornamental plantings in towns. Sage Sparrows and other shrubsteppe breeders return as early as February.

GETTING AROUND

For better or worse, the only practical way to bird Washington is by automobile. All of our route descriptions presume that you will be traveling in a private vehicle. Mileages are point-to-point rather than cumulative. In other words, you must reset your trip-odometer to zero at each new mileage indication (or keep track mentally). Weather and road conditions vary considerably from one part of the state to another and from season to season. Particulars concerning driveability and safety are included at the head of each regional chapter. Do have a look at these before setting out for an unfamiliar destination.

Maps. This guide is intended for use in conjunction with a state highway map. An excellent free map published by the Washington State Department of Transportation (WSDOT) is available at state-line tourist kiosks and various other outlets; visit *www.wsdot.wa.gov* to have one mailed to you. Or buy a commercial map. Insets on any of these maps should be sufficient to steer you through all but the largest cities. For birding in and around Seattle, Spokane, or Tacoma, however, purchasing a detailed street map may save you time and anguish. The *Washington Atlas and Gazetteer* (DeLorme) is nearly indispensable if you are venturing off the main highways (but useless in cities). The *Washington Road and Recreation Atlas* (Benchmark Maps) covers the same ground at a slightly smaller scale in attractive relief maps, with a few additional nuances such as regional climate information. These commercial maps and atlases are widely available at booksellers, convenience stores, and newsstands across the state. Birders going to Victoria or Vancouver will definitely want to buy street maps of these populous metropolitan areas.

Some of the best birding in Washington is in the seven national forests: Olympic, Mount Baker-Snoqualmie, Gifford Pinchot, Wenatchee, Okanogan, Colville, and Umatilla. Superb, large-scale maps of each forest, published by the U.S. Forest Service, may be obtained at any forest headquarters, visitor center, or ranger district station, and at many outdoor stores. These maps show the road systems and also the main trails. Birders hiking in the Cascades or Olympics will appreciate the reliability and usefulness of the Green Trails maps, which can be purchased at outdoor and map stores: visit *www.greentrails.com* for specifics.

Roads. Washington's extensive road system is administered by several jurisdictions. Many (but far from all) roads are numbered. We rely on these numerical designations wherever possible, with assorted abbreviations: "I" for the interstate highway system (example: I-90), "US" for federal highways (US-12), "SR" for state routes (SR-20), "FR" for U.S. Forest Service and certain other numbered forest roads (FR-25), "CR" for county roads (rarely used). The first three categories are straightforward enough; you will find these roads on any decent highway map.

Forest Service nomenclature takes a little getting used to. Each national forest has its own numbering system, so road numbers are often repeated from one forest to another. Trunk roads typically have two-digit designators (e.g., 25) and are wide, all-weather thoroughfares, hard-surfaced or well-graded gravel—easily passable by any passenger car unless closed by snow (few forest roads are plowed). As you drive along one of these roads you may notice that it has suddenly acquired a couple of extra zeros (e.g., 2500). This means that although you are still on the main road it has now dropped to a lower standard of engineering and maintenance (unpaved for sure, more dips and curves, maybe narrower and rougher). Secondary roads branching from trunk roads have four-digit numbers, the first two digits being those of the parent road (e.g., 2517). Generally speaking, all of these four-digit roads are suitable for regular passenger cars although you should be on the lookout for rocks, potholes, and severe washboarding in places. The lowest category of forest roads consists of spurs, usually indicated by vertical brown signposts where they branch off. These signposts display three digits reading top to bottom (e.g., 063 or 228). The number of the road from which a spur branches also appears on the spur signpost in small print, and technically is part of the spur's designator (e.g., 2517-063)—but forest maps usually show just the three digits (and so do we in this guide). However, three-digit designators sometimes get reused within the same forest's road-numbering system, so only the full seven-digit number is guaranteed to be unique—important to consider for reporting a problem or for record keeping. Maintenance of spur roads varies from adequate to none, depending on their current use status. Many are for high-clearance vehicles only. Note, too, that forest roads of all categories are subject to washouts, so be prepared to stop with little warning. *Be wary of log-truck traffic.* It is always a good idea to inquire about logging activity and local road conditions at ranger district stations.

Some county roads in Washington used to be numbered, and you will still occasionally see old number signs on roadside posts. Today, however, counties have moved away from numbers in favor of road names. Naming systems and signage standards vary widely from county to county and are not without an element of whimsy. Moreover they seem to be constantly changing, so that names on the ground may not correspond to those on the most recent, otherwise trustworthy maps. Road names in this guide are those visible on actual road signs. Although we have pointed out some of the most egregious instances of nomenclatural conflict involving signs and maps, many others lie waiting to confuse the unwary birder. Pay attention, weigh the evidence, and trust your pathfinding instincts.

Ferries. The Washington State Ferries are part of the state highway system. Visit *www.wsdot.wa.gov/ferries* for full, up-to-date details of routes, fares, and schedules. Basic information on some of the runs is given in the appropriate birdfinding chapters: page 192 for Fauntleroy–Southworth, Seattle–Bremerton, Seattle–Bainbridge Island, and Edmonds–Kingston; page 79 for Mukilteo–Clinton; page 28 for Port Townsend–Keystone; and page 95 for Anacortes–San Juan Islands–Sidney, B.C. Other operators provide ferry service between Port Angeles and Victoria, B.C. (page 37) and between Tsawwassen, B.C. and Victoria (page 144). If your itinerary involves travel by ferry, plan carefully to avoid delays.

Canada. The border crossing seems so routine that it is easy to forget you are moving to different legal, monetary, and measurement systems. You will need proper proof of identity and citizenship. With current security concerns, nothing beats a valid passport, especially for re-entering. Non-U.S. nationals should check in advance with immigration officials of both countries about visa restrictions. Automobile registration and insurance papers must also be in order. You will surely need some Canadian money: a little foresight will net you a more favorable exchange rate. Don't forget Canadian pocket change for parking meters and the like. Think metric: kilometers per hour, liters of fuel at the pump. Allow ample time in your travel plans for immigration and customs clearance, including the possibility of a full vehicle search. Two-hour backups in either direction are not uncommon at the main highway crossing at Blaine.

Fees. "Pay to play" is increasingly a fact of life on many public lands in Washington. The sale of parking and user permits generates millions of dollars in revenues each year that are pumped directly back into maintaining wildlife habitat and providing public access—critical functions in these times of strapped state and federal budgets. Don't neglect to do your homework and acquire the necessary permits *before* your birding visits (most government offices are closed on weekends). Patrolling is aggressive and the fines are substantial.

For national parks you may either pay a day-use fee or purchase the *Golden Eagle Passport* ($65) that grants driver and passengers system-wide access for one year. The one-time purchase of the *Golden Age Passport* ($10) gives seniors (age 62 and over) and their one-carload party lifetime access. A day-use fee ($5) or the *Northwest Forest Pass* ($30)—valid for one year from date of purchase in national forests in Washington and Oregon, at the Mount Saint Helens National Volcanic Monument, and in the Columbia River Gorge National Scenic Area—is required to park at designated trailheads, rustic campsites, picnic areas, and other designated sites. If you already have one of the

Golden Passports, however, it will be honored at all Northwest Forest Pass sites and at national wildlife refuges that charge entrance or parking fees. Visit *www.fs.fed.us/r6* and poke around to obtain fuller information about any of these passports and passes. They can be purchased on-line or at various administrative offices, outdoor stores, and ranger stations.

Many Washington State Parks are good birding sites. The state park system has recently implemented a vehicle parking permit program known as *A Natural Investment*. Count up the number of park visits you might want to make in a year and do the math: the fees are $5 daily, $50 annual, legislated to jump to $7 and $70 in 2007. Daily tickets can be purchased from on-site vending machines, but you have to go to a certain amount of trouble to obtain one of the annual permits. Visit *www.parks.wa.gov* for details.

The Washington Department of Fish and Wildlife (WDFW) maintains over 800,000 acres of Wildlife Areas, offering some of the state's finest birding. Many of these areas require a *Vehicle Use Permit* valid for one year (1 April–31 March), available at sporting goods stores. You get one free if you buy a hunting or fishing license, or you can buy it separately for a $10 fee. Another option, available only through the WDFW web site (*www.wa.gov.wdfw*), is to make a *Conservation Patron Donation* of $20 or more. You will receive your sticker by mail and your contribution will benefit fish and wildlife stewardship efforts; the amount above $10 is tax deductible.

Field Hazards. The only poisonous snake, the Western Rattlesnake, is confined to lower elevations east of the Cascades, usually in rocky terrain. Typically it is not aggressive. If you meet one, give it space and it will likely retreat. There are bugs in Washington, though the good news is there are no chiggers. Mosquitoes and biting flies can be bothersome in the warm months, especially in the mountains and wetlands. Repellent should make your visit tolerable. Wood Ticks abound in some of the drier forests and sagebrush areas of Eastern Washington. The best way to avoid them is not to brush up against vegetation, especially in spring. Tucking pantlegs into socks and dousing both with repellent may help. Poison Oak is locally abundant in interior southwestern parts of the state and eastward through the Columbia Gorge, and Poison Ivy is common in many parts of lowland Eastern Washington. It is a good idea to learn these plants ("leaves of three, let them be") before you head off into the bush. Black Bears can be met in forested regions. Heed the advice of "Bear Aware" pamphlets, particularly if you are in a campground. Out on the trail, troublesome encounters with either bears or Mountain Lions are very rare.

The summer sun can be intense, brutally so on snowfields and on the water. Protect yourself with broad-brimmed hat, long-sleeved shirt, long pants, and sunblock. If hiking at higher elevations, be alert for bad weather. A clear and calm morning can quickly change to cold rain and winds. Hypothermia is a definite hazard, even in summer. Carry the Ten Essentials (extra clothing, extra food, compass, map of the area, flashlight with spare bulb and batteries, knife, sunglasses, firestarter such as a candle stub, first-aid kit, matches in waterproof container). Water may not be available on high trails, especially late in the season. Assume all untreated water is contaminated.

BIRDERS' INFORMATION NETWORK

The following resources are available to those planning a birding trip, looking for details on the current status of a particular species, seeking to report an interesting observation, or just generally interested in the birds of Washington.

Washington Ornithological Society. WOS publishes a bimonthly newsletter (*WOSNews*) with birdfinding articles and other valuable features, a journal (*Washington Birds*), the *Field Card of Washington Birds*, and a membership directory; sponsors numerous field trips to all corners of the state; and hosts monthly meetings in Seattle and an annual conference. See page 612 for information on membership and activities.

ABA members. About 600 Washingtonians are members of the American Birding Association. Many of them have indicated that they are willing to guide visiting birders or respond to telephone or written queries. Codes used in the annual ABA membership directory enable other ABA members to contact these generous people. See page 614 for information about how you can become an ABA member and receive this helpful directory.

Audubon chapters. Washington has 25 chapters of the National Audubon Society. Visit *http://wa.audubon.org/new/audubon* for links to chapter web sites, many of which offer detailed information on local birding areas.

Washington Birder. This quarterly newsletter, published by Ken and Laurie Knittle (2604 NE 80th Street, Vancouver, WA 98665, *washingtonbirder@hotmail.com*), caters to the keen field birder and lister. It is noteworthy for its detailed site guides and well-researched county checklists.

Washington Field Notes. This ongoing record of consequential bird observations appears five times a year in *WOSNews*. Report your sightings by e-mail (*fieldnotes@wos.org*) or by mail to the compiler (currently Tom Aversa, 305 NW 75th Street, Seattle, WA 98103), who will share them with the *North American Birds* editors (see next item).

North American Birds. Bird observations of regional significance are documented in the quarterly *North American Birds*, published by the American Birding Association. These may be reported to the Washington Field Notes compiler or to one of the regional *North American Birds* editors (currently Steven Mlodinow, 4819 Gardner Avenue, Everett, WA 98203, *SGMlod@aol.com*; and Bill Tweit, P.O. Box 1271, Olympia, WA 98507, *Sebnabgill@aol.com*).

Washington Bird Records Committee (WBRC). Observations of species on the Washington Review List (those with names italicized on the Annotated Checklist in the back of the guide or not listed there at all) should be reported to the WBRC with written details and any supporting evidence such as photographs and sound recordings: see page 613 for addresses and an outline report form. Committee determinations are published in *Washington Birds*.

Tweeters. The Burke Museum at the University of Washington hosts this e-mail list on the birds of Cascadia. Some 1,200 subscribers make Tweeters a lively forum for discussion and a great place to learn about the latest interesting bird sightings. In fact, the Tweeters list has become the principal reporting venue for most Washington birders. Coverage centers on Washington—particularly Western Washington—but many postings concern Oregon and British Columbia. To subscribe, visit *www.scn.org/earth/tweeters*. Or you may read postings on-line in digest form at this same web site (with a 24-hour delay).

Inland Northwest Birders. Here is a list devoted to birding in Eastern Washington and adjacent parts of Oregon and Idaho. To subscribe, visit *www.lists.uidaho.edu/mailman/listinfo/inland-nw-birders*.

Oregon Birders On-Line (OBOL). Washington-related bird observations and discussion occasionally figure on this e-mail list, especially in regard to the southwestern part of the state. Visit the Oregon Field Ornithologists web site at *www.oregonbirds.org* for subscription information.

Washington BirdBox. Sponsored by WOS, the BirdBox is a voice mailbox where you may leave reports of unusual sightings or listen to the most recent reports from other birders. (Password for reporting: Washington has four chickadee species.) Coverage is statewide. Call 206-281-9172 and follow the prompts. Transcripts are posted to Tweeters, usually a couple of times a month.

Regional Rare Bird Alerts. For Washington sightings, call the BirdBox (see preceding item). You can also call the following numbers to record a report for the administrator or listen to a tape summarizing recent reports for the areas they serve. Transcripts for most are posted to the Tweeters or Inland Northwest Birders lists.

Lower Columbia Basin (Tri-Cities) — 509-943-6857

Southeastern Washington/northern Idaho — 208-882-6195

Victoria, British Columbia — 250-592-3381

Vancouver, British Columbia — 604-737-3074

Okanagan, British Columbia — 250-491-7738

Oregon — 503-292-0661

LOOKING AHEAD

Washington and its birding profile are changing with phenomenal rapidity. At the time of the publication of our predecessor guide the state checklist stood at about 375 species. In the intervening 30 years the list has grown by about 100 species. The rate of growth has been remarkably steady, averaging 10 new species every three years over the whole period and also over the most recent decade. We can confidently predict that the state list will break the 500 barrier before the current decade is up in 2010.

The lengthening of the list is driven primarily by the fact that more and more people are looking for birds, spending longer hours in the field than before and covering far more territory. Over the same 30-year period since the Wahl and Paulson guide came out, the state's population has grown from about three and a half million to about six million inhabitants—an increase of over 75 percent—and is projected to reach seven million by 2015. Even more important: skilled, committed birders constitute a greater proportion of the population now than then, as witnessed by the growth of membership in birding organizations such as ABA and WOS, and by the number of birders who report their findings to field notes editors. Not only are there more of us, we are more mobile than we used to be. In the 1960s, Washington counted one automobile per two inhabitants. Today there are twice as many vehicles per capita, meaning that registered vehicles actually outnumber licensed drivers in the state. The curve of annual miles driven continues steeply upward with no abatement in sight. Birders, we suspect, are in the vanguard. No wonder the guide has doubled in size!

The birding landscape is changing, too, so extensively and quickly that we could not keep up. An editorial decision was made to freeze the book to reflect conditions as they existed at the end of 2002. Since then, the last known pair of Crested Mynas has disappeared from Vancouver, B.C., and the Snohomish sewage ponds have been closed to visitors (to name just two events). These and no doubt many other changes will have to wait for the next revision.

Birders are a diverse lot—beginners and experts, residents who bird two full days a week and one-time visitors from out of state, listers and those who just like to look. Satisfying their sometimes-competing needs in a single volume has proved to be a real balancing act. We have stuck with a menu of tried-and-true locations for specialties and for a broadly representative range of habitats with their associated bird species, complemented by a certain number of less-well-known sites of local importance or with strong potential. Regrettably but inevitably, tough choices had to be made because of space limitations. Far too many deserving sites have been squeezed out. We welcome corrections, appraisals, updates, and suggestions for new sites or routes, and will consider them all for future editions. Please send yours to Allan Burns, Director of Publications, American Birding Association, P.O. Box 6599, Colorado Springs, CO 80934.

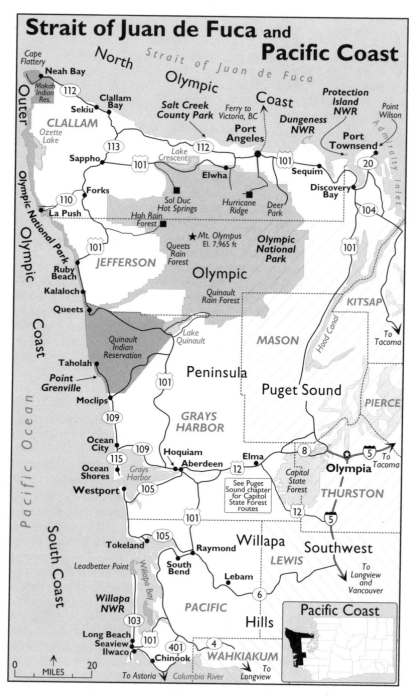

Strait of Juan de Fuca and Pacific Coast

North Olympic

Strait of Juan de Fuca

Coast

Cape Flattery

Neah Bay

112

Makah Indian Res.

Clallam Bay

Sekiu

CLALLAM

Ozette Lake

Salt Creek County Park

Ferry to Victoria, BC

Port Angeles

Dungeness NWR

Protection Island NWR

Point Wilson

Port Townsend

Admiralty Inlet

113

112

Lake Crescent

Elwha

101

Sequim

20

Sappho

101

Discovery Bay

104

Forks

110

La Push

Sol Duc Hot Springs

Hoh Rain Forest

Hurricane Ridge

Deer Park

101

Olympic National Park

JEFFERSON

Queets Rain Forest

★ Mt. Olympus El. 7,965 ft

Olympic

Olympic National Park

Olympic National Park

101

KITSAP

Ruby Beach

Kalaloch

Queets

Quinault Rain Forest

Lake Quinault

MASON

Hood Canal

To Tacoma

Quinault Indian Reservation

Peninsula

Puget Sound

PIERCE

Taholah

Point Grenville

101

Moclips

109

GRAYS HARBOR

Ocean City

109

Hoquiam

Aberdeen

Elma

12

8

5

To Tacoma

Olympia

Ocean Shores

115

Grays Harbor

Westport

105

12

Capitol State Forest

See Puget Sound chapter for Capitol State Forest routes

THURSTON

12

5

101

Tokeland

105

Raymond

Willapa

Southwest

Leadbetter Point

South Bend

Lebam

LEWIS

To Longview and Vancouver

Willapa NWR

Willapa Bay

6

PACIFIC

Pacific Coast

Long Beach
Seaview
Ilwaco

103

101

401

4

WAHKIAKUM

Hills

To Astoria

Chinook

Columbia River

To Longview

0 ———— 20
MILES

Outer Coast

Olympic National Park

Olympic

Coast

Pacific Ocean

South Coast

STRAIT OF JUAN DE FUCA AND PACIFIC COAST

The seacoast of Washington stretches some 250 miles, from Point Wilson at the east end of the Strait of Juan de Fuca to Cape Flattery at the west end, then south along the Pacific Ocean to the Columbia River and the state of Oregon. The coast, including more than 800 offshore islands and rocky outcroppings, offers a variety of habitats and exciting birding opportunities in four rather different subregions: the interior of the Olympic Peninsula, the North Olympic Coast, the Outer Olympic Coast, and the South Coast. The whole area has a maritime climate. Winters are wet and relatively warm, but the damp air and a breeze can make it seem much colder than the thermometer indicates. It is wise to have raingear available. Summers frequently do not start until July and come close to drought with day after day of near-perfect weather through at least early September. Hot spells are infrequent.

The rugged, snow-capped peaks of the Olympic Mountains dominate the interior of the Olympic Peninsula, topped by 7,965-foot Mount Olympus. The mountains and the prevailing storm paths have created a rain-forest ecosystem on the west-facing slopes, with moderate temperatures, fog, and lots of rain—upwards of 200 inches per year. On the opposite side of the mountains, a rainshadow effect brings low rainfall to the area from Port Angeles to Port Townsend, which frequently enjoys blue sky on days when the rest of Western Washington is socked in. Dungeness, near Sequim on the North Olympic Coast, has just 15 inches of rainfall yearly. The South Coast has no high mountains to the east. Climate is similar to that of the Outer Olympic Coast, but rainfall is less abundant.

The North Pacific Ocean at this latitude tends to have a covering of stratocumulus clouds. With prevailing airflow from the west this leads to a lot of foggy mornings with the fog burning off during the day. It also means that it may be drizzling in the lowlands but bright sunshine on Hurricane Ridge in Olympic National Park at an elevation of 5,200 feet. Heavy snows are infrequent except in the high Olympics where they can be a problem. A more regular winter problem is light snow, freezing rain, or frost making the roads very slippery in the morning, especially on the North Olympic Coast.

Surface soils on the Olympic Peninsula are mainly composed of loose glacial debris. In exceptionally rainy years the earth slides in places, closing roads sometimes for long periods until repairs can be made. Large areas of subsidence may continue to move for months, but there is little danger of getting caught by a slide as it is usually more of a creep. Waterside bluff slides are more abrupt and do cause loss of life but present minimal danger to birders— the big ones mostly occur at night.

Information on road closures can be obtained by calling the Olympic National Park Visitor Center in Port Angeles (360-565-3130) or, for the western portion of the peninsula, the Olympic Park-Olympic National Forest Information Center in Forks (360-374-7566). A Northwest Forest Pass is necessary to park at many trailheads. Car prowls do occur, even near towns. It is prudent to lock valuables in your trunk.

Campgrounds are numerous, but some are closed in the winter months and the most popular ones can be crowded during the short summer season. Restaurants, motels, gas stations, and other services are many and varied in larger communities such as Port Townsend, Sequim, Port Angeles, Forks, Ocean Shores, Hoquiam, Aberdeen, Westport, and the Long Beach-Seaview strip. Smaller communities also offer accommodations for travelers, although availability varies seasonally. Some coastal Washington localities have been hard hit by the simultaneous crash of fish stocks and timbering, so some local businesses may be shuttered. The political process of natural-resource management results in great pressure from the involved interests, and there has been no end of scapegoats for the collapse of both industries, among them the Spotted Owl, the Marbled Murrelet, and more recently the Caspian Tern. However, visiting birders are invariably well received.

PORT TOWNSEND AND VICINITY

by Bob Norton

Port Townsend is situated at the mouth of Admiralty Inlet, where the protected waters of the Puget Sound estuary meet the oceanic waters of the Strait of Juan de Fuca. Currents run strong when tides are changing, creating tidal rips that bring "bait" fish, krill boils, and attendant feeding frenzies. Rips are most extreme when large volumes of water are moving through, between the highest high and the lowest low tides of the day (or month). Seabirds float past feeding in the swift currents, then fly upstream and float past again. At slack tides there is little feeding activity. Tidal rips flow relatively close to shore at Point Hudson, Point Wilson, and Marrowstone Point, making these places especially attractive to birds and birders. Any saltwater rarity farther south in Puget Sound almost surely passes by here entering and leaving. During the nesting season, the daily flights of Rhinoceros Auklets commuting between feeding grounds and Protection Island are one of the impressive avian spectacles of the state.

INDIAN AND MARROWSTONE ISLANDS

From the east end of the Hood Canal Bridge (page 194), follow SR-104 westward for 6.6 miles, then turn north toward Chimacum on SR-19. Continue 9.1 miles to a stop sign at Chimacum Road. Turn right here and travel 1.5 miles to the intersection with Oak Bay Road (SR-116). Turn right again. In 0.8 mile, where SR-116 turns left, continue straight ahead on Oak Bay Road, and in another 0.6 mile turn 90 degrees left onto Portage Way (*do not* make the sharper left turn onto Cleveland Street), which leads in 0.2 mile to **Oak Bay County Park**. The jetty offshore often hosts Black Turnstones, Surfbirds, and occasionally Rock Sandpipers. The lagoon is tidal and the exposed flats are attractive before high tide and immediately after for shorebirds, gulls, and terns. The beach on the Admiralty Inlet side has good numbers of Brant and other waterfowl in the winter months.

Return to the intersection with SR-116 (Flagler Road) and go right. In 0.6 mile a bridge crosses the channel to Indian Island. The island is U.S. Navy property and off-limits except for the road across the south end. Cross the bridge to a small public park immediately on the right; its few old apple trees and hedgerows of brambles can be productive for passerines. The best overwater viewpoint is from **Indian Island County Park**, marked by a brown *Day Use* sign 0.8 mile beyond the bridge at a side road to the right. The park looks toward the jetty and channel from a different direction and gives you another chance to pick up rocky shorebirds. Harlequin Ducks can often be found here as well as the usual loons, grebes, scoters, and alcids. There is also a small estuary and marsh. A further 1.2 miles east on SR-116 brings you to the Indian Island-Marrowstone Island causeway with adequate parking on the right side of

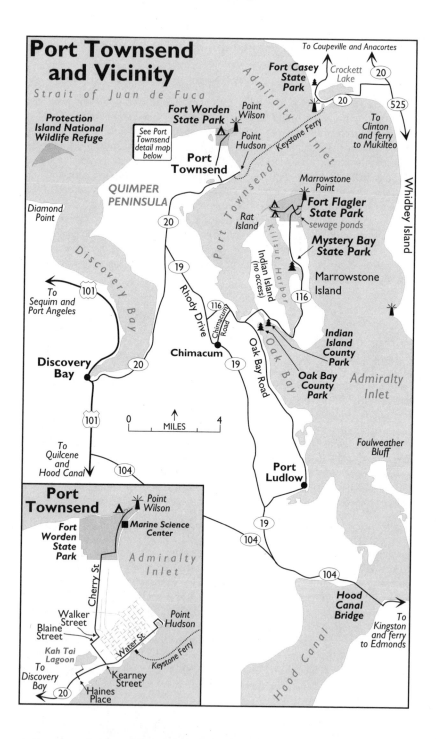

the highway. This low-lying land bridge sometimes has shorebirds and dabbling ducks when the tide is fairly high.

Mystery Bay State Park, 3.3 miles up Marrowstone Island from the causeway on SR-116, offers the only public viewing point for scoping the main portion of Kilisut Harbor, between the two islands, which often has impressive flocks of waterbirds, including high numbers of Eared Grebes in fall.

Fort Flagler State Park is reached at the end of SR-116 in 1.9 miles, and another 0.5 mile brings you to the only important intersection in the park. All three choices are worth exploring. By going left (west) 1.4 miles to the end of the road, you reach the campground and an excellent viewing area of the waters of Port Townsend and the entrance of Kilisut Harbor. A 600-yard spit extends west toward Rat Island, a sandbar lying between the two islands. Here Harlequin Ducks congregate close to shore, three species of cormorants can be compared, and various shorebirds rest and forage. Black Turnstones and Black Oystercatchers are frequently found when the tide is low enough to expose the rocks at the tip of the spit. A good view of Rat Island can be obtained with a scope (this is where displaced birds go if a dog or a jogger sends them fleeing before you reach the end).

Back at the intersection, the spur to the east (straight ahead) leads in 0.3 mile to a parking lot in a partly open area with two sewage treatment ponds surrounded by small trees and brush—good for ducks and landbirds.

Return to the intersection again and turn right (north) to reach the old lighthouse at **Marrowstone Point**, just inside Admiralty Inlet, in 0.7 mile. The road goes right immediately after the first group of former barracks. You will have to walk from the top of the steep bluff if the road is closed to vehicles in periods of heavy winter rains. There are seasonal ponds to the left of the lighthouse and a small parking lot to the right. Marrowstone Point is one of the best places for obtaining close views of feeding seabirds, including Ancient Murrelets in November and December. A good tidal rip will usually have a wealth of birds on the conveyer belt and is worth a thorough scan. In summer Rhinoceros Auklets and Pigeon Guillemots as well as gulls and terns fish it, and in winter loons, grebes, ducks, gulls, and alcids can be abundant. Look too for sea lions and seals.

PORT TOWNSEND

Retrace the route to the mainland, turning right with SR-116 at the stop sign at Oak Bay Road. Follow SR-116 for 2.0 miles from here to the junction with SR-19 (Rhody Drive), turn right (north), and continue on SR-19 as it flows into SR-20 in 3.5 miles. Another 4.2 miles north and east along SR-20 brings you to a traffic light at Kearney Street in Port Townsend. Turn left here and follow the signs to Fort Worden. The entrance is at the end of Cherry Street, in 1.7 miles.

Fort Worden State Park is a major park and is open the year round. Walking the south end of the campground, at the base of a bluff, can be good for landbirds. Check out the grass, dunes, and patches of windblown trees on **Point Wilson**, north from the campground. This sandy point of land has a minor concentrating effect on migrating landbirds. From the parking lot by the Point Wilson lighthouse you can walk a short distance to the left to scan the Strait of Juan de Fuca or to the right to scan Admiralty Inlet, and watch birds passing in review for hours. Gray and Killer Whales, Harbor Porpoises, and California and Northern Sea Lions occur on occasion. The tidal rips off the point are close enough in for good scope views of Pelagic Cormorant, Heermann's Gull, Pigeon Guillemot, Marbled Murrelet, Rhinoceros Auklet, and Tufted Puffin (scarce) in summer, and Brandt's Cormorant and Common Murre in winter. Three species of loons fly past (Pacific is sometimes common), Harlequin and Long-tailed Ducks are regular visitors, and the big migrating flocks of Bonaparte's Gulls in spring and fall may contain unusual gulls as well as Parasitic Jaegers. This is an excellent spot for Ancient Murrelets in late fall and winter (November is the best month). They tend to work the tide rips farther offshore in groups of 6–20, flying low and single-file and diving into the water suddenly and simultaneously. Marbled Murrelets are usually pairs or singles; they and the other local alcids typically land on the water and then dive.

It is possible at low tide to walk around the lighthouse. But if it looks at all foggy, be aware that the foghorn is automatic and it is *loud*. In fall migration and early winter the dunes and beach are good places to look for Horned Lark, American Pipit, Lapland Longspur, and Snow Bunting. The Port Townsend Marine Science Center has a small yet interesting and informative facility on pilings on the Admiralty Inlet side of the beach.

Return to the traffic light at SR-20 and turn left onto Water Street, continuing east 0.5 mile to the Washington State Ferries dock on the right. The trip to Whidbey Island on the **Keystone Ferry** crosses the mouth of Admiralty Inlet. When strong tidal currents are running you may enjoy close-up views of feeding alcids and other waterbirds. Passenger fares are inexpensive. The crossing takes about 30 minutes; you may return on the same boat or disembark to bird Fort Casey and Crockett Lake, both of which are within walking distance (pages 81–83).

From the Port Townsend ferry dock, go northeast along Water Street—the center of the tourist district—to the marina at end of the street (0.4 mile). Jog left for 0.1 mile, right for another 0.1 mile to a stop sign, and right onto Hudson Street. Park where you can. **Point Hudson**, just past the marina at the end of the city's shoreline, is a hotspot, with large numbers of birds congregating virtually at the beach. Aside from the Keystone Ferry, this is probably the best place to see Ancient Murrelets in season. The spit is rocky at low tide, attracting shorebirds and gulls, and the sheltered bay to the left usually has an array of waterbirds.

On your way back out of town, a right turn onto Haines Place at the traffic light by the Safeway (0.5 mile past Kearney Street), followed by another right at the stop sign onto the road behind McDonald's restaurant, and finally a left turn onto the first gravel road, brings you quickly to a parking lot for **Kah Tai Lagoon**. The main lagoon is excellent for ducks, including Ruddy Duck, which is unusual on the North Olympic Coast. Careful scoping of the shoreline may reveal herons, rails, or shorebirds.

From the traffic light, continue west and south on SR-20 for 11.6 miles to the base of Discovery Bay at the junction with US-101. Turn right toward Sequim. (A left turn here will take you south along the west side of Hood Canal, page 222.)

DISCOVERY BAY TO PORT ANGELES

by Bob Norton

The distinctive character of birding on this stretch of the North Olympic Coast comes from a combination of features: the oceanic influence of the broad Strait of Juan de Fuca; the narrow coastal plain (the farthest edge of the Puget Basin) with freshwater streams and tidal lagoons, wooded areas, and large tracts of agricultural land; and the close-by Olympics and resultant dry climate from the rainshadow effect. Prior to the arrival of Euro-American settlers, the Sequim-Dungeness area had many open, grassy places due to the low rain and frequent fires. Fertile soils and availability of water from the Dungeness River led to extensive farming. Wandering birds from drier, more sunny areas are attracted to this landscape. The good weather is also a magnet for retirees, and the farmland is being rapidly replaced with suburban houses.

The following accounts are laid out as a non-summer birding route along the shores of Juan de Fuca. Summer landbirding is better away from the coast, particularly for forest species. Waterbird diversity is low in summer, although a summer trip should yield Pigeon Guillemot, Marbled Murrelet, and Rhinoceros Auklet. Tufted Puffins are often seen at Diamond Point during their nesting season; a boat trip around Protection Island to inspect the seabird nesting colonies may turn up a few as well. After 1 July there will be increasing numbers of shorebirds at favored locations. The North Olympic Coast has provided an abundance of unusual Western Washington records in all seasons, and the described route will take you through the best vagrant hotspots.

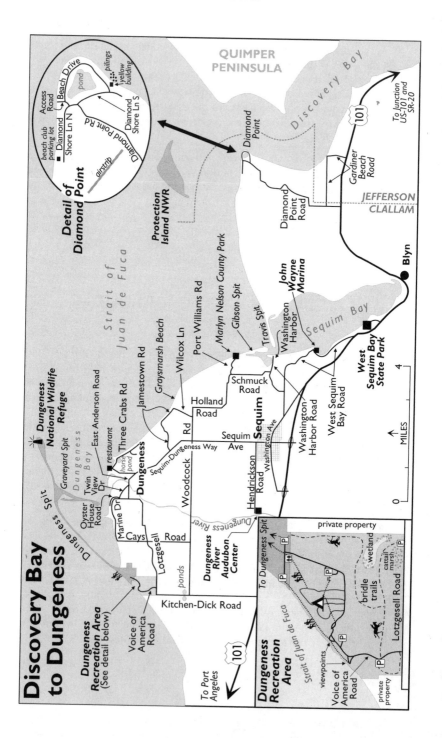

Discovery Bay to Dungeness

DISCOVERY BAY AND PROTECTION ISLAND

From the junction with SR-20 at the foot of Discovery Bay, take US-101 toward Sequim. At 6.5 miles turn right onto Gardiner Beach Road and continue downhill, with a slight left jog, to **Gardiner Beach** on the shore of Discovery Bay (0.5 mile). Park here, where the road bends sharply to the left. An excellent tidal lagoon is on the right, while out on the bay there is usually a flock of Pacific Loons during the winter and lesser numbers of alcids and other waterbirds. The road parallels the bay for about a short city block to a boat ramp, then heads west inland to a T-intersection with Diamond Point Road in 1.6 miles (watch for trolls).

Turn right (north). It is 3.4 miles from here to the freshwater pond at **Diamond Point**. At the fork above the pond stay right on Diamond Shore Lane South and drive counterclockwise around the pond. As you swing left onto Beach Drive, look for a small, weathered yellow building immediately on your right and some old pilings out in Discovery Bay. This is the site of the quarantine station where sailing-ship passengers were made to wait to be sure they were free of dread disease before proceeding to Seattle, a century ago. You can legally park in the little lane and walk to the shore. Gulls and cormorants use the pilings most of the year, as do Pigeon Guillemots during the nesting season. This is the best place in Washington to see Tufted Puffins away from the outer coast. Look for them from May through July, preferably when the tide is running. Continue along Beach Drive to a public viewpoint at Access Road (0.6 mile), looking north to Protection Island, two miles out in the Strait of Juan de Fuca. Back at the stop sign, turn right onto Diamond Shore Lane North and go to a small beach-club parking lot at the end (0.2 mile). Scope the waters offshore. Puffins can frequently be seen quite close in, and other good birds as well. This seems to be a favorite area for jaegers (late summer and early fall). On still, overcast days, you can even make out marine mammals and larger birds such as eagles on Protection Island.

During the summer, spectacular numbers of birds nest on **Protection Island**, a 364-acre national wildlife refuge at the mouth of Discovery Bay. These include hundreds of Pelagic Cormorants, some Black Oystercatchers, Glaucous-winged Gulls, Pigeon Guillemots, and a few Tufted Puffins. The high, sandy bluffs are the main nesting area in Washington for Rhinoceros Auklets, with an estimated 17,000 pairs; some may be seen during daylight around the island, but much larger numbers occur in Admiralty Inlet and other feeding areas in Rosario Strait, the Strait of Juan de Fuca, and San Juan Channel. Entry to this island refuge is strictly controlled. Visitors circling the island by boat must follow regulations that require vessels to be at least 200 yards offshore to avoid disturbance. An excellent way to see the island in spring and fall is from the boat trips that leave from the Point Hudson Marina in Port Townsend. The trips usually also go to the area off Rat Island where the boat can get closer. If the seas are exceptionally calm, the cruise will go around Smith Island (page 86–87)—ten miles to the north—quite closely. The boat is stable, with open decks and a comfortable cabin with generous window area. The on-board naturalist provides commentary on the island's bird population, geology, weather, and history. Details may be had by phone from the Port Townsend Marine Science Center (360-385-5582), or visit them on-line at *www.olympus.net/ptmsc/*.

SEQUIM BAY

Take Diamond Point Road back to US-101 (4.0 miles). Turn right toward Sequim and drive 5.5 miles to the entrance to **West Sequim Bay State Park**. Go through the campground and down to a boat ramp (left) and a moorage (right) offering good views of the bay (Barrow's Goldeneyes in winter). Songbirds may be found in trees and scrubby growth in the campground and along park trails; in particular, the old railroad-grade trail near the entrance is a good spot for Townsend's Warbler year round. Continue west 0.5 mile on US-101 to West Sequim Bay Road (opposite the Sequim Bay Lodge). Turn right here to the **John Wayne Marina** in 1.2 miles. (On the way, a tidal marsh on the left at 0.9 mile frequently has Hooded Mergansers and other ducks as well as Marsh Wrens and other passerines around the margins.) The marina, built on property originally owned by the actor's family, has a north and a south parking lot. Both are worthy of stops. The south lot looks out on a small bay favored by White-winged Scoters, Hooded Mergansers, and alcids. Yellow-billed Loons have appeared there on several occasions (late fall and winter). Black Oystercatchers, a few sandpipers, and American Dippers (winter) are sometimes seen where a small stream empties into the bay. This is a favorite gull roost, particularly attractive to the smaller gull species.

Drive past the main marina building to the north parking lot, and walk to the north outlet of the marina. This is the best vantage point on Sequim Bay to see a Yellow-billed Loon if one is around (beware the many light-billed Common Loons). Marbled Murrelet pairs are here year round (usually far out), as well as Pigeon Guillemots, Rhinoceros Auklets (less common in winter), and small numbers of Common Murres. During the winter, a group of 50 to 100 Pacific Loons is usually loafing straight out at scope distance. In the early fall there can be many Common Terns, and there is a good chance of satisfyingly close looks at Parasitic Jaegers. Long-tailed Ducks, Barrow's Goldeneyes, and Hooded Mergansers favor this area of the bay along with the more common bay ducks. Viewing is best when the tidal flows are greatest.

Go back to the stop sign just past the marina building and turn right to West Sequim Bay Road. Turn right again and continue north and west for 1.8 miles, then right onto Washington Harbor Road, which ends in 1.3 miles at the gate to the Battelle Laboratory at Washington Harbor (no visitors). Park outside the gate and scan tidal channels, which can be excellent for ducks and shorebirds, especially on a rising tide before the flats are completely covered.

Go back 0.4 mile and at the stop sign turn right onto Schmuck Road. After climbing the bluff, you will be in an area of seed (mainly grass) fields. In the winter these hold flocks of waterfowl and gulls; look, too, for Northern Shrikes. Trumpeter Swan is regular. Less predictable are Tundra Swan, Greater White-fronted Goose, and Sandhill Crane; more birds are present when high tides force them off the bay. In 1.3 miles Schmuck Road ends at a T-intersection with Port Williams Road. Turn right and go 0.5 mile to the end of the road at **Marlyn Nelson Park**. Scan the strait from here for loons, grebes, Brant, bay ducks, and alcids. This is a fairly dependable spot to find Eared Grebe, which is uncommon in Western Washington.

One can walk south (to the right) the length of **Gibson Spit**, except on the highest tides. This location seems to produce more than its share of unusual sightings, and the 2.5-mile round-trip can be very rewarding. The tip of the spit provides a fine view of Travis Spit and the north end of Sequim Bay. The bay's narrow outlet makes for great tidal flows and is a favorite feeding spot for Pigeon Guillemots, Rhinoceros Auklets, and grebes. The first part of the hike is along the beach next to a steep, sandy cliff where Pigeon Guillemots sometimes nest. Beyond the cliff the base of the spit is heavily vegetated. Part way down is an old east-west dike. From here, you can continue down the beach or on a grassy trail inside the driftwood and then alongside broad Pickleweed flats. The tidal lagoon to the west, on private land, is attractive to ducks and shorebirds. For excellent views, walk the causeway that crosses the lagoon toward the south end of the spit. From October to January you should confine your walk to the beach if hunters are present.

DUNGENESS

The prairies, wetlands, coastline, and offshore waters between Sequim Bay and Dungeness Spit, on both sides of the Dungeness River north of Sequim, are one of Western Washington's best birding spots. Among areas of comparable size, only Ocean Shores-Westport can rival Dungeness in number and variety of regularly occurring species and for its long (and growing) list of rarities. The many exceptional sightings include species as diverse as Falcated Duck, King Eider, Red-shouldered Hawk, Upland Sandpiper, Bar-tailed Godwit (several records), White-rumped and Curlew Sandpipers, Black-headed and Iceland Gulls, Horned Puffin, Sky Lark, Tennessee and Black-and-white Warblers, Lark Bunting, and Rusty Blackbird. The Sequim-Dungeness Christmas Bird Count regularly tallies the greatest number of species for the state (record 146 in 2002).

Leaving Marlyn Nelson Park, go west on Port Williams Road 0.8 mile and turn right onto Holland Road. This road winds north and west and in 1.7 miles becomes Woodcock Road. The next road to the right (a further 0.2 mile) is Wilcox Lane. Turn right and follow Wilcox to its end at the Strait of Juan de Fuca (0.6 mile). **Graysmarsh Beach** is to the right. However, you may not park here as of this writing. Turn left onto Jamestown Road, drive one long block, and turn left onto Serpentine Road. Park here and walk back. Graysmarsh is a large estate owned by the Simpson timber family. The first half-mile is open to the public except when the family is in residence; a sign-board gives current status and a map. This can be a very rewarding walk, especially if you follow the beach one way and the inland fence the other. Try to have the sun behind you on the beach leg. The marsh at the far end of the inland leg is one of the few places where Short-eared Owls are often seen on the North Olympic Peninsula, and birding for passerines is frequently excellent along the fenceline during migration and in winter.

On leaving the public access, go north along the beachfront on Jamestown Road, which in 0.5 mile turns west away from the beach and goes past some large dead cedars on the right (0.3 mile). These are the Jamestown Snags—a favorite place for Bald Eagles and other raptors to perch (even a Gyrfalcon, if you should be lucky enough to visit when one is passing through). At an intersection in 0.6 mile, turn right onto Sequim-Dungeness Way, which goes right again in 1.3 miles at a fork marked by a sign for the Three Crabs Restaurant. It is 0.6 mile to Dungeness Bay and the restaurant parking lot.

Dungeness Bay, framed by Graveyard and Dungeness Spits to the west and north, is one of the most important habitats on the Olympic Peninsula for eelgrass-associated waterfowl—Brant and wigeons. A large portion of the wintering flock of thousands of American Wigeons is often close in, and Eurasian Wigeons can almost always be picked out. Shorebirds are sometimes present on the beaches and at the little creek to the west. The best spot for shorebirds and other marshbirds is the nearby "horse pond." Go left (southeast) onto **Three Crabs Road** as you leave the restaurant parking lot; the pond is 0.2 mile along on the right, just beyond the big horse barn. *Do not park on the pond side of the road!* It is not safe and raises the ire of the owner who will denounce you in a loud and colorful manner. Shorebirds are most numerous here when high tides force them off the saltwater beaches (although the pond may dry up in late summer). Sharp-tailed Sandpiper, Ruff, and Wilson's Phalarope have been seen in migration.

During the winter it is worth birding the length of Three Crabs Road, which dead-ends a mile past the horse pond. The land to the right is low-lying and marshy. Golden Sands Road branches off about two-thirds of the way down, giving access to several other short streets. This area has a number of canals dug long ago by a developer in an attempt to provide waterfront housing. The entire area is attractive to birds, and the canals, in particular, host American Bittern, ducks, and Virginia Rail most of the year. Recently, conservation-minded persons have bought up much of the marshland to improve it for wildlife and to prevent development.

Return along Sequim-Dungeness Way and turn right onto East Anderson Road at the stop sign (0.6 mile). In 0.4 mile turn right again onto Twin View

Drive after crossing the Dungeness River. At the next stop sign (0.6 mile) take the small lane on the right (Oyster House Road) down to the waterfront. The view of Dungeness Bay is good from here, and shorebirding is often excellent on a rising tide. Check the shoreline both right and left from the **Oyster House**. The mouth of the river, on private property to the east, can have huge concentrations of ducks, gulls, and other birds, visible from the parking lot with a scope.

Return up Oyster House Road to the stop sign and go right onto Marine Drive. In 1.3 miles the road turns left and becomes Cays Road, intersecting Lotzgesell Road in another 0.9 mile. Go right (west) on Lotzgesell 1.5 miles and turn right on Voice of America Road into the **Dungeness Recreation Area**, site of a large broadcasting facility during the Cold War. The recreation area is worth exploring for its mix of grasslands, ponds, and shrubby woods. A bridle trail (open to foot traffic), marked by white posts across the road from a parking area 0.2 mile inside the entrance gate, leads eastward to a large wetland with nesting ducks, coots, Marsh Wrens, and Common Yellowthroats. American Bitterns are common during spring and summer. The trail is closed on posted days from October to January when pen-raised pheasants are released for public hunting. Farther along the road, picnic areas offer views over the Strait of Juan de Fuca from the high bluff; the seaside bushes may hold interesting passerines.

The road continues through the nicely wooded campground to the parking lot for **Dungeness National Wildlife Refuge**, about a mile from the entrance gate. The 631 acres of the refuge include sandspits, tidelands, and forested uplands, accessible only on foot or on horseback. This is a spot of great natural beauty. Dungeness Spit is one of the longest natural sandspits in the world. The nine-mile round-trip out to the lighthouse is perhaps the best saltwater beach hike in the state. The sheltered waters and mudflats inside Dungeness Spit, on both sides of Graveyard Spit, provide outstanding habitat for waterfowl and shorebirds. However, these areas are closed to the public and set aside as a Research Natural Area to protect birds, marine mammals, and the unique vegetation. Although birders may have difficulty obtaining close views, the 1,500 Brant that winter in the area (peaking at up to 8,000 in spring migration) and the thousands of other ducks and geese are an impressive sight. Most of the Brant are on the tidal eelgrass beds around Graveyard Spit. The trail to the beach leaves from the parking lot (entrance fee required). The first half-mile is through coastal forest to a platform with dramatic views of the strait, and down a steep bluff trail to the beach. The 4.5-mile walk from here to the lighthouse on an exposed, sloping sand-and-pebble beach is strenuous exercise. Expect loons, grebes, sea ducks, gulls, alcids, and a few shorebirds including Sanderlings; Gyrfalcon and Snowy Owl are seen fairly regularly in winter. Bring a scope, drinking water, and protection against the elements.

Return to the entrance on Lotzgesell Road and turn right. In 0.1 mile the road turns left (south) and becomes Kitchen-Dick Road. In 0.7 mile ponds on both sides of the road often hold a good variety of ducks and sometimes American Bitterns. US-101 is reached 2.4 miles after leaving the ponds. Turn right (west) for Port Angeles, or left for Sequim.

The **Dungeness River Audubon Center**, northwest of the Sequim business district, offers information and displays about the birds and natural history of the north Olympic Peninsula as well as excellent streamside and mixed-forest birding. Take the Sequim Avenue exit from US-101 and drive north into town. In 0.6 mile, cross Washington Avenue (the main drag) and continue north for another 0.6 mile to Hendrickson Road. Turn left here; the Audubon Center is at the road's end in about two miles. Take the former railroad-grade trail across the Dungeness River. Watch for American Dipper from the bridge (especially in winter) and for Red-eyed Vireo in the riparian woodlands in late spring. Along the wide trail westward for about the next half-mile you may find Red-breasted Sapsucker, Downy Woodpecker, Olive-sided Flycatcher, Western Wood-Pewee, Pacific-slope Flycatcher, Hutton's Vireo, Black-capped and Chestnut-backed Chickadees, Red-breasted Nuthatch, Brown Creeper, Golden-crowned and Ruby-crowned Kinglets, Orange-crowned, Black-throated Gray, and Wilson's Warblers, sparrows, Black-headed Grosbeak, Bullock's Oriole, Purple Finch, and Red Crossbill, depending on the season.

PORT ANGELES

At the intersection with Kitchen-Dick Road west of Sequim, drive west on US-101 to Port Angeles. As you enter the downtown district, a moderate hill descends to an intersection (11.8 miles), where US-101 turns south (left). You will drive straight ahead on Front Street if going to Ediz Hook or right on Lincoln Street if going to the Victoria ferry.

Ediz Hook—a natural sandbar formed from the erosion of cliffs between Port Angeles and the Elwha River and now reinforced by a massive seawall—forms the north margin of Port Angeles Harbor. To get there continue straight on Front Street, which soon becomes Marine Drive and skirts the south side of the harbor. In 2.0 miles you come to the Daishowa America plant that manufactures paper for telephone Yellow Pages. The road runs right through the complex with one stop sign and emerges at the west end of the spit; drive carefully and obey the speed limit. Ediz Hook is an excellent location for shorebirds, gulls, and other waterbirds most of the year, with the summer months being the low period. Harlequin Duck and Marbled Murrelet (irregular) may be present at any time. There are many spots to pull off to scan. Scope the old log booms and other floating structures for shorebirds, especially at high tide. In winter, Black-bellied Plover, Dunlin, and Black Turnstone are the most numerous. Rock Sandpiper is present every year, but, as elsewhere in the Lower 48, numbers are gradually diminishing. Especially in the fall, both golden-plovers, Wandering Tattler, and Surfbird may be found. During the Snowy Owl flight-year of 1996–1997, the first Washington bird showed up on a Port Angeles Harbor log boom and stayed for over a week.

The public road ends in 1.8 miles at the gate for the Coast Guard Air Station that occupies the tip of the hook. A break in the seawall rocks just east of the public restrooms, near the end of the road, allows you to go down conveniently to view the Strait of Juan de Fuca. Different species from those that frequent the harbor may be found in the offshore kelp or farther out. This is the best spot to find Red-necked Phalarope and Ancient Murrelet. The protective log boom at the Pilot House, on the harbor (south) side of the spit, is unusually good for shorebirds as is the adjacent beach (a favorite of Rock Sandpiper and Whimbrel). Check these from outside the gate. Entrance policy for visitors is set by the base commander, and in recent years only active-duty and retired Uniformed Services personnel and their guests have been permitted to enter. But the base has been open to birders in the past and may be again. You can always ask. If access is allowed, be sure to sign in and *stay off the runway*.

The **Coho Ferry** is a popular way to get to Victoria, British Columbia (page 107). Service is frequent in summer, less so in winter. Be sure to check schedules in advance, on-line at *www.northolympic.com/coho* or by phone at 360-457-4491. No reservations are taken, and in peak summer season waits are common for cars to get on board. The crossing takes about an hour and a half. The most windfree area—and also the best viewpoint for birds—is right at the bow. Stake out your spot early as this location is also popular with the nonbirding majority. Of the many possible ferry trips in Washington, this one certainly has the greatest chance for pelagic species, but it also can be disappointing. A trip during fall migration or following a storm out on the Pacific, however, may feature ocean birds such as Northern Fulmar, Sooty or Short-tailed Shearwaters, storm-petrels, phalaropes, Parasitic Jaeger, and Black-legged Kittiwake. The ferry terminal is located a block north and a block west of Front and Lincoln in downtown Port Angeles.

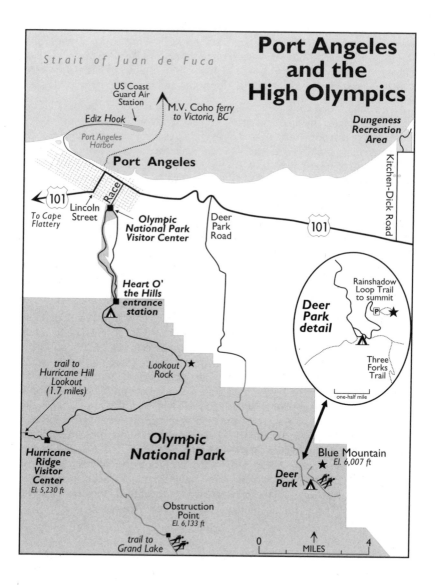

THE HIGH OLYMPICS

by Bob Norton

Several roads follow river valleys up to mid-elevation trailheads around the perimeter of Olympic National Park, but the interior of the park is managed as a roadless wilderness area. Just two roads offer easy, extensive access to subalpine elevations, climbing the ridges above Port Angeles to Hurricane Ridge and Deer Park.

The main attraction of these areas for birders is the good possibility of seeing Blue Grouse. This species is widespread at all elevations in the park, but is far more frequently encountered in the meadows of the subalpine. Blue Grouse are most evident in spring and early summer when they are booming and displaying, and through the summer when hens are wandering about with their young. Early mornings are best, before hikers and campers are stirring. Northern Goshawk, Black Swift, Clark's Nutcracker, Gray-crowned Rosy-Finch, and Pine Grosbeak do occur in the Olympics, but there are better places in Washington to find them unless you are in for extensive backcountry hiking. Rufous Hummingbird, Northern Flicker, Gray Jay, Common Raven, Horned Lark (the breeding subspecies is very pale with little or no yellow), Golden-crowned Kinglet, Hermit Thrush, American Robin, Varied Thrush, American Pipit, Yellow-rumped Warbler, Dark-eyed Junco, Red Crossbill, and Pine Siskin are likely. Northern Harrier, American Kestrel, and Townsend's Solitaire are less common. Several pairs of Golden Eagles breed in the park. September migrants include American Pipit and Savannah Sparrow, among other species.

During the ice ages, the Olympic Mountains stuck out above the glaciers and were a refugium for plants and animals. Several forms unique to the Olympics evolved in consequence of their isolation. One of the most obvious to visitors is the Olympic Marmot, a close relative of the more widely distributed Hoary Marmot. The Olympic Arctic (Oeneis chryxus valerata), one of the most restricted-range butterflies in North America, can be found only on Hurricane Ridge and a few other high ridges close by.

In summer, the high country is usually above the stratocumulus layer. Overcast skies in Port Angeles are not a reliable indicator of weather at the top. Weather reports are available on the park visitor information tape (360-565-3131) and on AM radio at 530 (only in the immediate Port Angeles area). Conditions can change suddenly in late spring and fall with snowstorms sweeping in and whiteouts developing. From July through September, however, weather in the high country is usually boringly perfect, although mornings may be a little cool. Winter is characterized by heavy snowfall. It is not without reason that the Olympics have the lowest-elevation glaciers in the Lower 48.

HURRICANE RIDGE

Hurricane Ridge is the main tourist attraction in Olympic National Park, heavily used during the warmer months. In the snow season the road is usually kept open Fridays through Sundays to access the rope-tow ski and tubing area, but it may be closed for weeks on end in years when snowfall is too heavy for the plows to handle. During the winter you will mainly see snow banks higher than your eyes, Gray Jays, Common Ravens, and hordes of people enjoying the snow.

From US-101 in Port Angeles turn south onto Race Street (seven blocks east of Lincoln Street) and follow the signs about one mile to Olympic National Park Visitor Center on the right (good selection of books and maps). Turn right as you leave the visitor center and in 0.1 mile take Heart O' the Hills Parkway to the right. Heart O' the Hills entrance booth (fee) is another 5.2 miles ahead. The road is almost always open to this point even in winter. Birding in the large campground is typical of the heavily wooded areas of the Peninsula—strong on Chestnut-backed Chickadee, Winter Wren, and Golden-crowned Kinglet, with an unusually high concentration of Varied Thrushes most of the year. Species diversity is greater in the edge habitat than in the deep woods. One of the most accessible populations of Marbled Murrelets in Washington nests in the old-growth forest within the campground. Listen for them flying overhead at dawn during spring and summer.

Hurricane Ridge Visitor Center (snack bar) is 11.7 miles farther up, at an elevation of 5,230 feet. A stop here to look over Big Meadow is recommended, and a short hike on the paved trails to isolated patches of Subalpine Fir may turn up Blue Grouse. The road continues west another 1.4 miles to the Hurricane Hill trailhead. Gray Jays and juncos always seem to be around the picnic area along this road. The 1.7-mile walk to the summit of Hurricane Hill is recommended to see and hear subalpine breeders such as Horned Lark, American Pipit, and Townsend's Solitaire.

Return to the Hurricane Ridge Visitor Center. At the far east end of the parking lot a narrow gravel road drops off to the right (southeast), ending in 7.8 miles at Obstruction Point. This road provides good access to subalpine and alpine habitats in the north Olympics, but in most years the Park Service does not finish plowing the snow off until sometime in July. In late spring and early summer, before it is open to cars, the road can be walked with good birding prospects; a staff or ice axe may be helpful to get over the remaining snow banks. An array of trails is accessible from the parking lot at Obstruction Point (elevation 6,133 feet). The trail along the ridge going south toward Grand Lake is good for Horned Lark and American Pipit. Golden Eagles sometimes soar over these ridges from their nest sites in the high Olympics, keeping an eye out for unwary Olympic Marmots. A backpacking trip from here to the peaks and glaciers of the northeastern Olympics may turn up Clark's Nutcracker and Gray-crowned Rosy-Finch.

Stopping at the pullouts on the return trip down Hurricane Ridge Road may yield some additional species. The viewpoint at Lookout Rock, down a short trail just beyond the tunnels, is fairly dependable during the song period for Townsend's Warbler, which well may be at eye level at this spot.

DEER PARK

Deer Park is a smaller area than Hurricane Ridge, but offers the same birds with fewer people, no entrance fee, and at least as good a chance of seeing Blue Grouse. It also has the only drive-in campground in the subalpine, on the south slope of Blue Mountain. Most years the road is open to autos all the way to the top from about early July until the first major snowfall in early October. The rest of the year it is usually open most of the way, and you can hike the final two miles over snow if need be (boots and staff recommended; check conditions first by calling the visitor center, 360-565-3130). About five miles east of downtown Port Angeles, turn south from US-101 onto Deer Park Road. On the lower part of this drive, stop to look for birds in open areas and along edges where habitat is varied. The road becomes gravel at the Olympic National Park boundary, 8.8 miles from US-101. The rest of the road, though steep, curvy, and a bit rough, is perfectly suitable for ordinary autos. The undisturbed forests for most of the remainder of the ascent have comparatively few birds until the trees begin to thin out in the subalpine. In 7.6 miles you reach a short loop road to the Deer Park Ranger Station; stay on the upper road, toward the campground and Blue Mountain. Bypass the campground by bearing to the left and continuing uphill to a small parking lot on the northwest shoulder of Blue Mountain, 8.9 miles from the park boundary. Park here and walk the half-mile Rainshadow Loop Trail to the summit (elevation 6,007 feet). Clumps of trees near the summit are good for Blue Grouse and other birds. During their breeding seasons, Horned Larks and American Pipits can be found on the exposed southern slopes all the way down to the campground. Walk or drive slowly through the campground to an old burn at the south edge. Another exposure to this burn may be obtained by hiking the first quarter-mile of the Three Forks Trail from the trailhead on the east side of the campground. This area has produced a good selection of high-country forest birds.

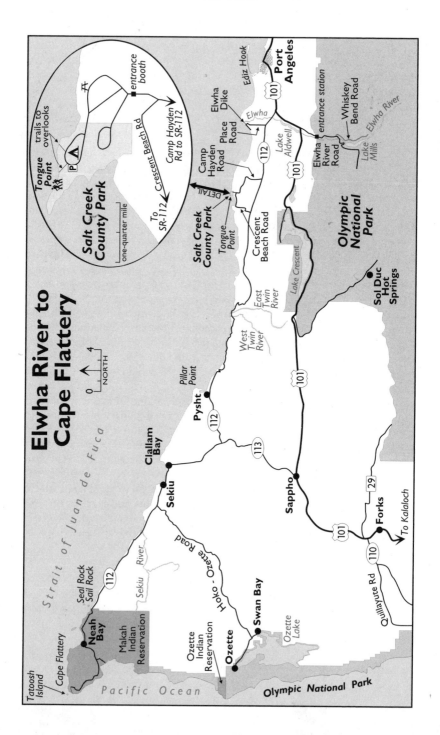

Elwha River to Cape Flattery

ELWHA RIVER TO CAPE FLATTERY

by Bob Norton and Bob Morse

This is mostly a saltwater route, offering greater avian diversity in migration and the colder months and, in spring and summer, important nesting seabird sites. As one moves westward, the terrain becomes increasingly rugged. The coastal plain narrows and eventually disappears. The oceanic influence increases, as does rainfall; forests are dense and fast-growing. At low to mid-elevations Western Hemlock, Western Redcedar, and Douglas-fir dominate. Sitka Spruce becomes increasingly noticeable after Clallam Bay, and is the dominant species of the coastal forest from Cape Flattery south. Areas outside Olympic National Park are managed for timber production, and most have been cut over at least once. The usual lower-elevation forest birds can be found throughout in appropriately-aged timber stands, so no particular sites for these have been singled out.

ELWHA RIVER

Spotted Owls nest in declining numbers in old-growth forests in the Olympics. It is never easy to find one, and in recent years they seem to be retreating higher up the drainages. On the north side of the Olympic Peninsula, night-time owling up the **Elwha River** offers a fair chance of success. To get there from downtown Port Angeles, follow US-101 westbound 5.6 miles from the corner of Front and Lincoln to the intersection with SR-112. Continue left 3.0 miles on US-101, and turn south (left) onto Elwha River Road. The entrance booth for Olympic National Park is in 2.0 miles. Continue past a campground and a seasonal ranger station, and in 2.0 miles turn left onto **Whiskey Bend Road** (unpaved and narrow), which climbs about four miles up the east side of the Elwha Valley through magnificent forest to a trailhead parking lot (elevation 1,205 feet). The most likely owl spots are this parking lot, the area around the ranger station and campground, and the meadow on first entering the park. The best time is late February through April or May when they are calling. Be aware that Barred Owl—a relatively recent arrival—has been favored by the clearcuts outside the park, and occasional hybrids ("Sparred" Owls) are encountered at lower elevations, even in the park.

Return to the intersection of SR-112 and US-101 and head west. In 2.1 miles, turn right onto Place Road after crossing the Elwha River bridge. At 1.9 miles, turn right at the **Elwha Dike** sign and park where you can in the next 0.2 mile. The vegetation on both sides of the road is excellent for landbirds. Follow the short trail for about 175 feet from the end of the road, then left to the end of the dike. A small lake on the left often has a variety of ducks. The sandbars on the east side of the river at its mouth are a favorite roosting and bathing place for gulls, including Thayer's, the abundant Glaucous-winged X Western hybrids, and the occasional Glaucous. Unusual species are regularly found here (including the rare Slaty-backed Gull in winter), so take time to sort through the gull flock carefully. Black Scoters favor the waters off the beach, to the east. A good selection of waterbirds should be seen from the end of the dike, and the short walk across the beach to the west will reveal more on Freshwater Bay.

TONGUE POINT

Returning from the Elwha Dike, turn right onto SR-112 and continue west for 5.0 miles to Camp Hayden Road. Turn right, and stay right at the fork in 3.5 miles (signed *Salt Creek Recreation Area Campground*) to the entrance to **Salt Creek County Park**. This gem of a park contains Tongue Point, one of the best tidepool and diving areas in Washington. In the warmer months it receives busloads of students, especially on weekends when there is a minus daytime low tide, but most of the year it is uncrowded. In fall, a long-running study tracks migrating Turkey Vultures here as they cross the strait from Vancouver Island. Where the road forks after the entrance booth, stay right and drive north to the picnic area at the edge of the bluff. Park shortly after the road turns left, before the trees start, to view the extensive kelp beds—a good place for Harlequin Duck and Marbled Murrelet. Other waterbirds may be present, especially when the tide is running; check the offshore rip with a scope. Continuing west through the wooded portion of the campground leads to a small parking area at the end, where the road loops back. To the right are two overlooks and stairs offering access to Tongue Point, marked by interpretive displays. The point is well worth exploring at low tide, especially if you have an interest in creatures of the intertidal zone. (A walking stick and calf-high rubber boots are recommended for those past the peak of youth and agility.) You may see Black Oystercatchers in some numbers, the occasional flock of Black Turnstones, and very occasional Surfbirds. River Otters are common. The more-westerly overlook offers scope views of Crescent Bay. Long-tailed Ducks stay here surprisingly late into spring.

CLALLAM BAY TO NEAH BAY

Return to the park entrance, turn right onto Crescent Beach Road, and then west onto SR-112. The first sight of the Strait of Juan de Fuca after leaving the park comes in about 10 miles as one winds down the long hill to the Twin Rivers. In about another 18 miles SR-113 turns off to the left. Continue northwestward here on SR-112 to downtown Clallam Bay. Just as SR-112 makes a sharp left bend (6.3 miles), turn right into a parking area (brown sign indicating *Clallam Bay Community Beach Entrance*). This is **Clallam Bay County Park**. A trail on the left offers access via a footbridge to the beach and the Clallam River mouth. Scoping the bay, lagoon, and river from the high beach is frequently productive for alcids, waterfowl, and gulls. A line of kelp starting at the east side of the bay near the lighthouse and extending toward the west as far as you can see from this vantage point may attract Marbled Murrelets and a variety of other waterbirds. The footbridge affords a good look at the riverbanks which have yielded many good birds, particularly in migration.

The turnoff for the picturesque fishing village of **Sekiu** (pronounced C-Q) is 1.9 miles farther along SR-112, on the right. Check the protected waters of the jetty and marina for grebes, cormorants, scoters, and gulls. One crosses the **Sekiu River** at 5.1 miles farther west, a good place to scope for wintering gulls. From here to Neah Bay the scenic, winding road hugs the coast and travel is slow. In winter the waters hold large numbers of loons, grebes, diving ducks, and alcids, but parking along this stretch of the highway is limited and logging trucks roll by at amazing speeds. Use the pullouts and park well off the road. At high tide, rocks just off shore in the early part of the route may hold Surfbirds. Gray Whales summer along this portion of the strait and Sea Otters live in the nearshore kelp beds—the farthest east on the strait that this reintroduced species has penetrated and probably close to the edge of its historic range. (River Otters are frequently encountered in the salt water of the strait from Neah Bay east to Port Townsend.) The best viewpoint for **Seal and Sail Rocks**, the only seabird nesting islands along this shoreline, is at 9.2 miles from the Sekiu River, on an outside curve just before the commercial sign for the Snow Creek Resort. Scope the rocks and surrounding waters for marine mammals and a variety of birds, including Tufted Puffins.

Once you pass the boundary of the Makah Indian Reservation, just ahead, you are on private land. The Makah, like most tribes, have mixed feelings about visiting strangers. Many tribal members welcome them, but others regret that economics requires allowing their presence. All sites described below are freely accessible to the public, but remember that you are a guest. Continue ahead to the community of **Neah Bay**. At the boat basin and around town look for Bald Eagles, which are especially abundant in March and April. Rocks on both sides of the harbor entrance are favorites of Black Oystercatchers. Check the basin and the water of the bay for loons (including Yellow-billed in winter), grebes, all the diving ducks, gulls, alcids, Northern and California Sea Lions, and Harbor Seals. Foul weather sometimes forces pelagic birds to seek shelter or wreck in the bay, especially Black-legged Kittiwakes. Good vantage points are the Old Fish Dock (turn right at 2.9 miles onto the first paved road after coming down the hill into Neah Bay, at the sign for the Makah Housing Authority, and continue on the gravel driveway along the left side of the large white metal building), and the Makah Senior Center (the last large building on the waterfront, 1.3 miles farther west on the main road). Turkey Vultures circle overhead in April and May as they prepare for their flight north over the Strait of Juan de Fuca. Many surprising sightings come from Neah Bay, even though this corner of the state is so remote from population centers that it is not birded much.

CAPE FLATTERY

Follow the road west through Neah Bay. After the Senior Center, the road turns left. Turn right at the second intersection (0.1 mile), just past the Makah Health Center. At the fish hatchery sign, half a block ahead, turn left. The road continues through Red Alder woods and then parallels the **Waatch**

Seeming to walk over the ground swells, Leach's Storm-Petrels watch for amphipods in the near-surface waters, out of view of land off Cape Flattery.

River (pronounced *wy-atch*), a very short river system that is really a tidal grass estuary, unusual in that it has not been diked. If you visit at one of the higher tides, you will feel you are out on a bay. As an island of open grass along the coast, the valley is attractive to many species unusual to wooded, wet Western Washington. Do not take the fish hatchery road that branches off to cross a bridge on the left (2.5 miles), but keep straight toward Cape Flattery. Farther along (0.3 mile), a small dirt track on the left opposite the last Makah Tribal Center buildings leads to the mouth of the Waatch (very rough driving, but an easy walk). This spot frequently has shorebirds and, in migration, impressive flocks of thousands of California Gulls.

The graded gravel road to the **Cape Flattery** trailhead traverses mixed deciduous and coniferous forests and shrubby thickets where you can find birds appropriate to those habitats. The parking lot, on the left in 4.6 miles, is heavily used and does not have a history of vandalism, but it is a simple precaution not to leave valuables in plain sight. Take your scope down the well-designed three-quarter-mile trail, with boardwalks across the wet places, to four viewing platforms with spectacular overlooks of the Pacific Ocean and the Strait of Juan de Fuca at the northwestern tip of the Lower 48. The seabird watching can vary from fair to excellent (usually better when there is a good tidal flow). Pigeon Guillemots nest immediately below the overlook in large caves at the base of the 100-foot cliffs. Search for all species of loons as well as Sooty Shearwater (offshore in summer and fall), Peregrine Falcon, Black Oystercatcher, Black-legged Kittiwake, Rhinoceros Auklet, and Black and Vaux's Swifts (summer; unpredictable). Marine mammals include Gray Whale, Northern Sea Lion, Harbor Seal, Harbor Porpoise, and Sea Otter.

Tatoosh Island, one-half mile offshore and viewable with a spotting scope, supports a variety of breeding seabirds, including Fork-tailed and Leach's Storm-Petrels and Cassin's Auklet (all three highly pelagic during daylight hours, visiting their nest burrows only at night), Pelagic Cormorant, Glaucous-winged x Western Gull, Pigeon Guillemot, Rhinoceros Auklet, and Tufted Puffin (probably the easiest place in Washington to see the latter species). Except in El Niño years, Tatoosh Island has an important nesting colony of Common Murres, but nest predation by the burgeoning Bald Eagle population has become a significant threat. Tatoosh Island is a landbird migrant trap, and numerous rarities have been recorded there, among them White-winged Dove, Brown Thrasher, Blackpoll Warbler, Lark Bunting, Dickcissel, and Common Grackle. The island is now a biological research station and access is restricted. However, the same vagrants could just as well show up at nearby seldom-birded coastal locations, and regular birding forays during migration would probably repay the effort.

The adventurous and experienced can rent a skiff in Neah Bay to explore the hazardous waters around the Cape—a few lucky boaters have seen Leach's Storm-Petrels near their island nests at dawn. A less perilous approach is a charter trip from Neah Bay with Steve Boothe of Puffin Adventures (*www.olypen.com/puffinadventures*; 888-305-2437 toll-free; or inquire in person at Shipwreck Point RV Park and Campground at Chito Beach, just outside Neah Bay). During the seabird nesting season (April–September), his 35-foot boat, the *Puffin,* takes up to six passengers on a three-hour tour that includes Tatoosh Island and Cape Flattery.

To continue down the outer coast, return 24 miles from the reservation to SR-113, then go south another 21 miles via SR-113 and US-101 to the intersection with SR-110 near Forks.

Outer Olympic Coast

by Bob Morse

igh, rocky bluffs and offshore islands that are home to over a dozen species of nesting seabirds dominate the Outer Olympic Coast from Cape Flattery to Point Grenville. Storm-petrels, auklets, and puffins nest in burrows dug into grassy hillsides, while cormorants and murres nest on the high, open cliff ledges. The world's finest temperate rain forest stretches from the water's edge to the mountains of the Olympic National Park and is home to nesting Blue Grouse, Marbled Murrelet, Spotted Owl, and Varied Thrush. Douglas-fir, Western Hemlock, Western Redcedar, Sitka Spruce, and Bigleaf Maple, luxuriantly draped with mosses, fungi, and lichens, form a sensuous landscape with the richly carpeted forest floor. The following itinerary offers opportunities to sample the birds of managed and old-growth forests at several spots, including the Hoh River country and Lake Quinault.

La Push

From US-101, turn west on SR-110. In 7.8 miles the Mora Road branches off on the right. Keep left on SR-110 toward the fishing village of La Push on the Quileute Indian Reservation. The road travels through Douglas-fir, Western Hemlock, and Sitka Spruce forests and crosses into the Olympic National Park as it nears La Push. The 1.3-mile Third Beach Trail, on the left in 3.8 miles, leads to a wilderness beach. It may be possible to hear or see a Spotted Owl along the first part of the trail; with a flashlight it can be safely walked in the dark. Farther along (1.4 miles), Second Beach Trail, on the left, leads in 0.7 mile through spruce woods (check for Red Crossbills) down to a beach where cormorants, Tufted Puffins, Sea Otters, and Harbor Seals may be seen. Peregrine Falcons nest at Second Beach. The Quillayute Needles, offshore, host thousands of nesting seabirds, including the state's largest colony of Leach's Storm-Petrels.

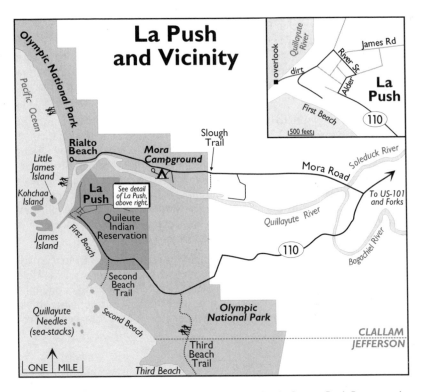

On the outskirts of La Push, just after the La Push Ocean Park Resort cabins, turn right onto Alder Street (0.8 mile) and then left onto River Street. At the T-intersection, go left and veer right onto a dirt road that leads to a rocky overlook (0.2 mile), where good views are possible of the Quillayute River and First Beach to the south, with the Quillayute Needles and the open ocean beyond. The largest offshore islands to the west are James Island (far left) and Little James Island (far right). The larger of the two islands in the middle is called Kohchaa, which in the Quileute language means "gathering place for gull eggs and seafood." Peregrine Falcons nest on James Island. Tufted Puffins nest (May through early August) in burrows on Kohchaa Island and may be seen with a spotting scope. Gray Whales occur in large numbers off First Beach during their spring migration (especially April).

La Push is notable for the gull roost on the gravel bar in the Quillayute River, easily viewable from several points in town. Ring-billed and California Gulls are numerous in August and September. Pick out pure Western and Glaucous-winged Gulls among the far more common hybrids. In winter, check for Mew, Herring, Thayer's, and Glaucous (rare) Gulls, and Black-legged Kittiwakes. Brown Pelicans, Heermann's Gulls, and Caspian Terns are here in summer and fall. Harlequin Ducks, all three scoters, goldeneyes, Buffleheads, and Common and Red-breasted Mergansers are usually in the river channel. Peregrine Falcons and Bald Eagles constantly stir up the gull flocks. Northwestern Crow is common here. Check for Wandering Tattlers (spring and fall) and Black Turnstones (fall through spring) on the rock jetty, and for loons and grebes in the boat basin. The area is attractive to unusual species, but underbirded. Washington's only record of Great Knot is from La Push, and in 1996 an Emperor Goose spent the month of January here.

Retrace your route to Mora Road and turn left. Just as the road enters the Olympic National Park (2.7 miles), the Slough Trail leads off to the left through coastal forest to the Quillayute River. A small parking area is nearby. Along the trail, look and listen for Varied Thrush, Red Crossbill, and other characteristic birds of the rain forest. Bald Eagles have nested where the trail meets the river. **Mora Campground**, just inside the park entrance (fee in warmer months), is situated in old-growth forest with similar birding possibilities. Naturalist programs (summer) explain the ecology of a healthy forest and other elements of the natural and human history of the area.

The road ends at the **Rialto Beach** parking area, 2.2 miles from the park boundary. This is the point of departure for beach hikers heading for the Hole in the Wall, Ozette Lake, and other points north. To the south, a one-mile spit parallels the Quillayute River and ends near the rock outcroppings visible from La Push. Walking may be difficult if winter storms have damaged the protecting jetty.

HOH RIVER VALLEY

Return to US-101 and turn right, reaching Forks in a few minutes. Watch for the National Park Service/U.S. Forest Service Information Center on the left, at the corner of US-101 (Forks Avenue) and E Street. Reset your trip-odometer to 0.0 here and continue south out of town. In 12.0 miles, turn left from US-101 onto FR-3200 (Willoughby Ridge Road; watch for a small road-number sign after you turn). Following this road to its end in 11.2 miles gives easy access to higher-elevations forests and their spring and summer birdlife, along with nice views of the Hoh River valley, the peaks of the Olympic Mountains, and the Pacific Ocean in the distance. The road is suitable for all but low-clearance vehicles. Traffic is minimal since logging in the area was halted in an effort to protect the remaining old-growth forests. For the first 1.9 miles the road proceeds eastward through relatively flat, commercial forest plantations of a variety of ages. It then climbs up the south slope of **Willoughby Ridge**, the divide between the Hoh and Bogachiel drainages, into islands of old-growth Western Hemlock and Silver Fir that have been fragmented by logging over the last 30 years. Search clearcuts, edges, and second growth for Pacific-slope Flycatcher, Hutton's Vireo, Wilson's Warbler, Spotted Towhee, and Song Sparrow. Pullouts look onto the canopy of downhill trees and clearcuts below the road, providing chances for seeing Vaux's Swift and Red Crossbill at eye level. Booming Blue Grouse are common from

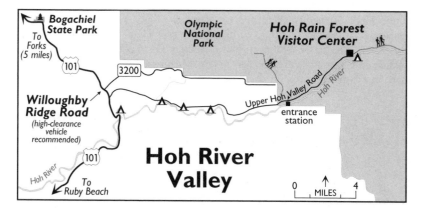

mid-April through June and can often be closely approached with a vehicle. This is also a good place to see and hear a Marbled Murrelet flying about its nesting site in the top of the old-growth trees before daybreak. At night, listen for calling Great Horned, Northern Saw-whet, and other owls (Spotted, if you're lucky).

Return to US-101. Drive south, and in 0.7 mile turn left onto the Upper Hoh Valley Road to reach the Olympic National **Hoh Rain Forest**. The park entrance booth is in 12.6 miles (fee). The road passes through various phases of managed forests, from recent clearcuts to mature stands of Western Hemlock and Western Redcedar. There are many opportunities to pull over to look for species typical of these habitats, including Northern Goshawk, Northern Pygmy-Owl, Vaux's Swift (overhead, May through July), Hairy Woodpecker, Willow and Pacific-slope Flycatchers, Hutton's Vireo, Chestnut-backed Chickadee, Brown Creeper, Winter Wren, Golden-crowned Kinglet, Varied Thrush, Orange-crowned and Wilson's Warblers, and Spotted Towhee. Stop at the alder grove at the parking lot on the right just before the entrance booth, where Downy Woodpecker, Hammond's Flycatcher, Warbling Vireo, Black-capped Chickadee, and Black-throated Gray Warbler are common from May through July. On the other side of the road, and a few hundred feet back west, a footbridge crosses a bog to a trail, good for birds of the coniferous forest from mid-May through mid-July. Continue to the visitor center in about another six miles. Loop trails with interpretive signs lead through moss-draped maples, providing a good introduction to this classic temperate rain-forest ecosystem. In the nearby campground, search for Gray and Steller's Jays and Northwestern Crow, which has moved into this area from its traditional coastal range. Barred Owls may call at night in the spring.

Return to US-101 and turn left. The road follows the Hoh River, reaching the ocean at **Ruby Beach** (13.9 miles), and runs south through the coastal section of Olympic National Park for the next ten miles. There are several well-signed access points to the beach, where Black Oystercatchers may be found in rocky places. Records of Tropical Kingbird and Tennessee and Black-throated Blue Warblers at Ruby Beach give a hint of the vagrant potential of this stretch of seldom-birded coastline. Destruction Island—a major seabird nesting site—is visible four miles offshore. Kalaloch Lodge is on the right in 7.5 miles.

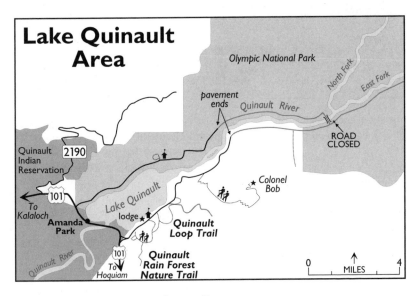

LAKE QUINAULT

After crossing the Queets River (5.0 miles), US-101 heads inland, running east and south through the Quinault Indian Reservation to Lake Quinault. This four-mile-long freshwater lake, fed by the Quinault River and other mountain streams, lies in the southwest corner of Olympic National Park. The adjoining dense conifers, lush broadleaf forests, and lakeside shrubby thickets provide a number of opportunities to sample the birds of this part of the Olympic Peninsula. Much of the better birding is along the south shore of the lake. Turn left about 26 miles from the Queets River bridge onto the Lake Quinault South Shore Road, then right in 1.4 miles into the **Quinault Rain Forest Nature Trail** parking lot (Northwest Forest Pass required; available here from a self-service pay station). Take time to enjoy the half-mile, self-guided walk through magnificent old-growth temperate rain forest with its rich association of ferns, lichens, mosses, and Vine Maples. Colossal specimens of Douglas-fir, Western Redcedar, Western Hemlock, and Sitka Spruce dominate the trail and the gorge; you may see American Dippers in the cascades.

Continue on to the **Lake Quinault Lodge** in 0.7 mile. Built in 1926 in the heyday of the national-park style, the rustic lobby, expansive grounds, and dining room overlooking the lake are a "must see" for visiting birders. After staying here in 1937, President Franklin D. Roosevelt recommended that much of the north shore of the lake be included in Olympic National Park. The equally magnificent south shore was excluded, but the U.S. Forest Service has protected some of it to date. The Quinault National Recreation Trail System, which starts across the road from the lodge, offers a series of hiking trails through the towering coniferous forests. Birds of these habitats include Blue Grouse, Spotted and Northern Saw-whet Owls, Hairy and Pileated Woodpeckers, Steller's Jay, Common Raven, Chestnut-backed Chickadee, Red-breasted Nuthatch, Brown Creeper, Winter Wren, Golden-crowned Kinglet, Varied Thrush, Townsend's Warbler, and Dark-eyed Junco. Check around the lodge, other lakeside buildings, gardens, and along the shoreline trail through broadleaf forests and shrubby thickets, for Red-breasted Sapsucker, Downy Woodpecker, Northern Flicker, Olive-sided and Pacific-slope Flycatchers, Hutton's and Warbling Vireos, swallows, American Dipper (in streams entering the lake, especially at the east end in winter), Swainson's Thrush, Orange-crowned, Yellow, Black-throated Gray, and Wilson's Warblers, Common Yellowthroat, Western Tanager, Fox (winter), Song, and White-crowned Sparrows, and Black-headed Grosbeak. The lake hosts Common Loon, wintering Trumpeter Swan, Hooded and Common Mergansers, and occasional Marbled Murrelets (summer), which nest in the old-growth trees in the hills. Around the lake, check for Osprey nests in snags, and Bald Eagle (especially in winter).

Just east of the lodge is the Quinault Ranger District Station, where you can obtain trail maps, a local bird list, and trailhead parking permits. The South Shore Road continues east, then leaves the lakeshore and meanders through open farmlands bordered by alders and maples to the **Upper Quinault Valley**. In winter, these fields may have herds of Elk. In 3.9 miles, the trailhead for the steep Colonel Bob Trail is on the right. Spotted Owls have been seen along this trail in the past; they call in late winter and early spring from the neighboring hills. Remember that the Northern Spotted Owl is threatened with extinction and is already stressed by legitimate studies to aid its conservation. The playing of taped calls is discouraged. In 1.9 miles, the South Shore Road becomes a dirt road and parallels the Quinault River. Watch for Harlequin Duck (spring), and large numbers of Bald Eagles feeding on dead salmon in January along the river and creeks.

POINT GRENVILLE

Return to US-101 (stay left at the fork after the lodge) and go left (south). At 5.5 miles, turn right (west) onto the Moclips Highway, a 20-mile stretch of road through second-growth forest. At the T-intersection with SR-109, turn right (north) toward Taholah. The entrance to Point Grenville is at milepost

37.7, on the left 5.8 miles ahead. Access to the paved, one-lane road is restricted by a locked gate. For permission to visit and a key to the gate, make arrangements ahead of time with Mike Mail of the Quinault Indian Nation (home phone 360-276-4315) or the Quinault Department of Natural Resources (360-276-8211). A donation of $5 per person is customary, and is used to support tribal youth recreational activities.

Once through the gate, follow the paved road to the spot where dilapidated buildings of the former Coast Guard station stand. Park here. During its use by the military, the area around the buildings was cleared and lawns planted. The facility was abandoned in the 1970s, and the fields have reverted to tall grass interspersed with shrubby thickets. Blue Grouse nest in the narrow corridor of mixed coniferous and broadleaf forest habitat along the entrance road. Migrant songbirds use the California Wax-myrtle, other bushes, and forest edges. The Sooty Fox Sparrow has its southernmost known nesting location here, and is most abundant in the winter in bushes to the southwest of the buildings. Walk north from the buildings, then west on a dirt track across an open field leading to an overlook facing west. In the past, Tufted Puffins have nested in the bluff just below the cliff face across from the offshore sea-stack. Pigeon Guillemots nest in the rock cliffs to the north and Pelagic Cormorants on the whitewashed, open cliff ledges to the south. On the offshore rock formations, Glaucous-winged and Western Gulls (and the more common hybrids of these two species) nest in the grassy areas near the top. Peregrine Falcons may be visible on these rocks or hunting nearby. A second viewing area requires a short walk to the south side of the point. From the old buildings, follow a dirt road to the southwest. Where it appears to end, a small trail leads through thickets of alder, huckleberry, and Salal to a steep overlook. Black Oystercatchers are often seen below, on the rocky shoreline. Cormorants, gulls, and puffins nest on the second islet to the south. The waters below often have loons, Western Grebes, Surf and White-winged Scoters, and Common Murres.

Depending on tides, time of year, and weather, birding at Point Grenville can be outstanding or it can be dreary. May or early June are the best times, but other seasons have much to offer. During migration and winter, seabirds and waterfowl pass the tip in good numbers. Point Grenville can be a great migrant trap and is almost always an excellent seawatch location. Unusual birds such as Horned Puffin, Palm Warbler, Vesper, Lark, and Black-throated Sparrows, and Chestnut-collared Longspur have been seen here. The beauty of the point makes the trip a success no matter what birds are seen or missed.

The spectacular cliffs that characterize the Outer Olympic Coast end here, giving way to a broad coastal plain. Travel south on SR-109 to reach Ocean Shores and other birding sites of the South Coast.

SOUTH COAST

by Bob Morse

The South Coast has a gentler, more open terrain than the mountainous Olympic Peninsula. The seaboard consists of wide, sandy beaches, grasslands, intermittent timber stands, extensive rivers, tidal marshes, and two great estuaries—Grays Harbor and Willapa Bay. The backcountry stretches from the broad Chehalis Valley south over the rolling Willapa Hills to the lower reaches of the Columbia River. Nearly all of the ancient forests are gone, but trees grow quickly in this damp, mild climate (about 100 inches of rainfall annually). In some places, impressive second-growth stands with characteristics of the original forests are being nurtured through sound conservation management. These habitats attract a great diversity of avian species. Hundreds of thousands of shorebirds stop each spring to refuel on the 1,500 acres of mudflats at Grays Harbor National Wildlife Refuge. Nearby Ocean Shores—a magnet for rarities—is perhaps the premier birding hotspot in the state. Regularly scheduled boat trips out of Westport offer birders the opportunity to see albatrosses, shearwaters, petrels, jaegers, auklets, and other pelagic specialties. The 11,000-acre Willapa National Wildlife Refuge hosts a wide assortment and high numbers of wintering waterfowl. Willapa Bay is one of the most pristine, productive estuarine ecosystems in the United States.

OCEAN CITY

To reach the Grays Harbor area from Point Grenville, go south about 20 miles along SR-109 through Moclips, Pacific Beach, and Copalis Beach to the intersection with Second Street in Ocean City. Turn right to the seashore a few hundred yards ahead. Long stretches of the wide, hard-packed, sandy **ocean beach** can be driven between Ocean City and Point Brown at the south end of Ocean Shores. The next access point is four miles south, at the end of Damon Road—the first of five in Ocean Shores. The speed limit is 25 mph, and parts of the beach may be closed to vehicular traffic at certain times. It is illegal to drive over the razor-clam beds exposed at low tide. Stay on firm sand and keep an eye on incoming tides; careless motorists can easily get stranded. During spring and fall migration, large mixed-species flocks of shorebirds are common along the beach, especially at high tide. Carefully check all long-legged waders; Bristle-thighed Curlews were seen here in May 1998. The beach is good for close studies of gulls including Heermann's (summer and fall), Mew (fall through spring), Ring-billed, California (fall), Herring (fall through spring; uncommon), Thayer's (winter; rare), Western, Glaucous-winged, Glaucous-winged x Western, and Glaucous (winter; rare). Loons, Sooty Shearwaters (fall migration), Brown Pelicans (late spring through fall), scoters, and gulls can be seen flying by off shore.

To reach Ocean Shores by conventional highway, continue south 2.0 miles on SR-109 from Ocean City and turn right onto SR-115. The mixed forest and

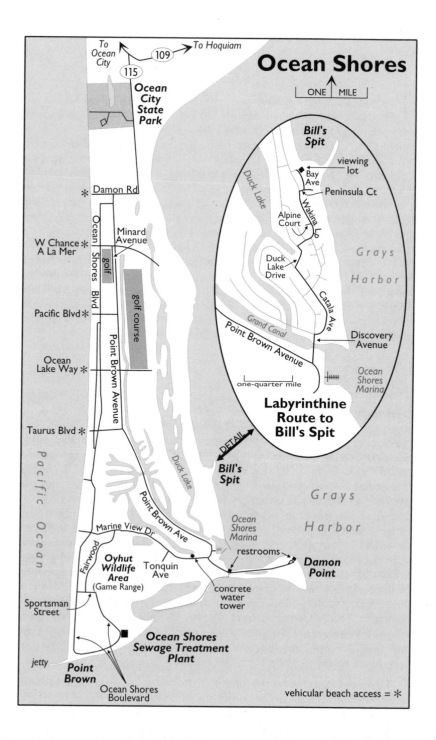

Ocean Shores

ONE | MILE

To Ocean City
To Hoquiam
109
115

Ocean City State Park

Damon Rd

Ocean Shores Blvd

W Chance A La Mer

Minard Avenue

golf

golf course

Pacific Blvd

Ocean Lake Way

Point Brown Avenue

Taurus Blvd

Duck Lake

Pacific Ocean

Point Brown Ave

Marine View Dr

Fairwood

Oyhut Wildlife Area (Game Range)

Tonquin Ave

Sportsman Street

jetty

Point Brown

Ocean Shores Boulevard

Ocean Shores Sewage Treatment Plant

concrete water tower

Ocean Shores Marina

restrooms

Damon Point

Grays Harbor

Bill's Spit

DETAIL

Bill's Spit

viewing lot

Bay Ave

Peninsula Ct

Wakina Lp

Alpine Court

Duck Lake Drive

Catala Ave

Grays Harbor

Grand Canal

Point Brown Avenue

Discovery Avenue

Ocean Shores Marina

one-quarter mile

Labyrinthine Route to Bill's Spit

Duck Lake

vehicular beach access = ✳

shrubs at **Ocean City State Park**, on the west side of the highway just north of Ocean Shores (0.8 mile), have a good selection of typical Western Washington lowland songbirds. Myrtle Yellow-rumped Warblers winter in good numbers in the California Wax-myrtle here and throughout Ocean Shores. Check the freshwater ponds along both sides of the entrance road for Pied-billed Grebe, Great Egret (rare, summer and fall), Green Heron (late spring and summer), ducks, Sora (summer), and yellowlegs (in migration). American Bittern and Virginia Rail have nested here, and Tundra or Trumpeter Swans may be present in winter.

OCEAN SHORES

Upon leaving the state park, turn right onto SR-115 and continue south. The road soon bends right (west). At 1.3 miles you can go straight ahead on Damon Road to a beach access. Otherwise, turn left (south) here and pass through the town gate on Point Brown Avenue, the main artery of Ocean Shores. If undisturbed by golfers, the **golf course** fairways on both sides of the avenue south from the intersection with W Chance A La Mer (0.7 mile) may host flocks of Canada and occasional Greater White-fronted and Snow Geese, ducks, and shorebirds. Buff-breasted Sandpipers may rest here during fall storms. Solitary and Sharp-tailed Sandpipers have been found in the ditch along the fairways behind Linde's Landing Motel. Most of the golf course is easily viewed from neighboring roads. Three of the better vantage points are along Point Brown Avenue, Ocean Shores Boulevard, and Minard Avenue. Generally, golf-course birding is best early in the morning and at high tide. During stormy weather this may be the best place in Ocean Shores to find golden-plovers, curlews, and godwits.

Travel west one long block on W Chance A La Mer, then turn left (south) onto Ocean Shores Boulevard to reach the **Point Brown Jetty** (5.7 miles), best visited in the morning to avoid the glare of the afternoon sun. From the beach on the north side, scan the breakwater rocks for Wandering Tattler (mid-April through May, late July through mid-October), Black Turnstone (late July through May), Surfbird (late July through April), and Rock Sandpiper (early October through mid-April). Look also for Brandt's, Double-crested, and Pelagic Cormorants, and Mew (late August to May), Herring (September to May), Western, and Glaucous-winged Gulls. The shorebirds are often seen on the rocks close to shore on an incoming tide. A scope is helpful. Walking out on the jumble of huge, tilted rocks that compose the jetty (treacherous) may be necessary to get good views of them. At high tides, or when big swells are coming in from the ocean, waves can break over the top of the jetty. At such times, stay off.

Weather permitting, the top of the jetty is a great place to set up a scope for a seawatch, as far out toward the end as you feel comfortable scrambling. Wear warm clothing if you plan a prolonged stay during fall, winter, or spring.

Scan south and west across the channel and ocean for passing birds of the same species mentioned for the ocean beach, plus cormorants, Black-legged Kittiwake (fall through spring), Caspian Tern (spring through fall), Common Murre, and Rhinoceros Auklet. Migrating flocks of Common Terns (May and mid-August through mid-September) often attract a Parasitic Jaeger. Patient observers have been seeing Manx Shearwaters (rare) from the jetty with increasing frequency. Harbor Seals and California Sea Lions are common in the waters south of the jetty. Gray Whales migrate off the coast and are sometimes visible from the jetty, especially from March through May.

The **Ocean Shores Sewage Treatment Plant**, located 0.8 mile farther along on Ocean Shores Boulevard as it curves to the east, is open from 8:30AM to 4:30PM, Monday through Friday. Park off Ocean Shores Boulevard near the fence. The three ponds provide shelter during storms as well as a high-tide refuge for ducks and gulls. Scope the edges closely for shorebirds, especially at high tide. Sharp-tailed Sandpipers have been seen here in fall. Red-necked Phalaropes are regular in fall migration, and Red Phalaropes are possible after severe storms. Lapland Longspurs can usually be found from mid-September to mid-November in the short grasses between the fence and the jetty wall. Paths along the side fences provide access to the tidal mudflats and marshes of the Oyhut Wildlife Area (known as the **Game Range** to birders and natives alike). Pectoral and the rarer Sharp-tailed Sandpipers are most often seen from late September to mid-October in the Pickleweed marsh east and north of the entrance paths. The best birding is one or two hours before or at high tide. Calf-high waterproof boots will increase your enjoyment of this habitat. Continue on Ocean Shores Boulevard, which curves northward and becomes Sportsman Street. Go right on Fairwood Drive (0.8 mile), then right (east) onto Marine View Drive (1.1 mile). In 0.7 mile, turn right onto Tonquin Avenue, a poorly maintained road that dead-ends at a parking lot near a radio facility. Walk around the gate, through an opening in the wax-myrtle to the right of the structure, and out into the salt marsh at the north edge of the Game Range. During fall migration, Pectoral Sandpipers (and far less often, Sharp-tailed) shelter in the Pickleweed on a rising tide; rubber boots are helpful if you want to look for them.

Return to Marine View Drive and continue east. Across from the concrete water tower (0.4 mile), a pullout up a four-foot embankment provides a good scope view of the tidal mudflats and surrounding saltwater marshes of the east end of the Game Range where Whimbrels, other shorebirds, gulls, and terns often roost, especially on a rising or falling tide. Some summers Elegant Terns are numerous here. Proceed east 0.3 mile along Marine View Drive to reach the road to Damon Point, on the right. Access to the eastern end of the Game Range is from the restroom parking area at the beginning of the road. Cross the road and walk south to the water's edge, then back west to the Game Range along a narrow sandspit. (A few pairs of Snowy Plovers nest nearby at their northernmost breeding location on the Pacific Coast; stay out of this clearly posted area from 15 March to 31 August.) Bird the sparsely vegetated flats and the water edges for Black-bellied Plover, American and Pacific Golden-Plovers (uncommon late August through early October), Semipalmated Plover, yellowlegs, Whimbrel, Marbled Godwit, Red Knot, Western, Least, and Baird's (fall; uncommon) Sandpipers, Dunlin, Buff-breasted Sandpiper (fall; rare), dowitchers, Horned Lark, American Pipit, and Lapland Longspur (fall). The saltwater bay on the south side of the sandspit typically hosts loons, Brown Pelican (late spring through fall), cormorants, and all three species of scoters. Long-tailed Duck and jaegers occasionally appear. Rough-legged Hawk (winter), Merlin, Peregrine Falcon, and other raptors hunt the Game Range. Rarities regularly turn up here, among them a Eurasian Dotterel that stayed for two weeks in fall 1999—the most recent of three records for this species at Ocean Shores.

Damon Point (aka Catala Spit, Protection Island) is a long sandspit extending east into Grays Harbor at the southeastern tip of Ocean Shores. The saltwater bay on the north side normally has Common Loon, Western Grebe, and other seabirds. In the fall, Baird's Sandpiper may be found feeding along the kelp-line. The Damon Point Road is subject to washouts by winter storms and high tides, so you may have to walk the 1.3 miles to the tip. The road crosses a culvert about 0.2 mile from the restroom parking lot. Follow the natural depression from the culvert to a long, narrow pond on the right (another path leads across the dunes to the pond from a small parking area a bit farther ahead on the left). The pond attracts a variety of waterfowl and its edges often host shorebirds at high tide. This is a good place to check for American and Pacific Golden-Plovers and Baird's and Buff-breasted Sandpipers in fall, and Red Phalarope in winter. Walking through areas of bare ground and sparse vegetation near the pond is probably the best way to find Buff-breasted Sandpiper in Ocean Shores. Look especially at the west end, along the southeast edge, and southward from the pond toward the channel. The road ends at a vantage point of Grays Harbor with restrooms and nearby picnic tables. The open area west of here between the shoreline and the road is another good place for golden-plovers and Buff-breasted Sandpiper in fall. Set up a scope at the point and enjoy the many seabirds; action is especially good if there is tidal rip off the end of the spit. Walking the beach to the right (south) may produce Baird's Sandpiper and other shorebirds. Gray Whales are occasionally seen from this location between March and May and in summer. At the far southeast tip of Damon Point, two Long-billed Murrelets were observed in early August 1999.

At the **Ocean Shores Marina**, located along Marine View Drive just north of the base of Damon Point, birders get close-range looks at loons (three records of Yellow-billed), grebes, cormorants, turnstones, gulls, and sometimes Common Murre and other alcids. Birds may seek protection here from winter storms. Watch for Purple Martin from late spring to late summer. The Scot's Broom thickets around the intersection of Discovery Avenue and

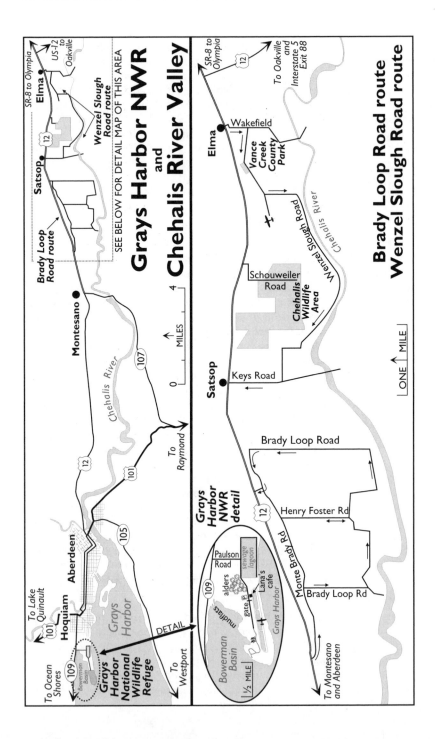

Point Brown Avenue, a couple of hundred yards north, are one of the best spots in the state to find Palm Warbler in the fall and winter.

The best birding site on the Grays Harbor North Bay, north of the marina, is **Bill's Spit**. Geese, ducks, curlews, godwits, small sandpipers, and gulls congregate here, especially one to two hours before or after high tide. Bill's Spit and Tokeland are probably the two most reliable places in the Lower 48 for Bar-tailed Godwit in the fall. A wildlife-viewing lot, reached from the marina in 1.1 miles by a labyrinthine route, offers an excellent vantage point and access to the spit. (See inset map, page 56.) Go north on Discovery Avenue, then turn right onto Catala Avenue, right onto Duck Lake Drive, right onto Wakina Loop, right onto Peninsula Court, and left onto Bay Avenue. The lot is a few houses ahead on the right after number 720 Bay Avenue. The base of the spit can also be approached on foot from a poorly marked public easement at the Peninsula Court cul-de-sac; please avoid flushing the resting birds. Woodlot birding is good along Wakina Loop from Peninsula Court to Alpine Court. When you head back, check the area from the Harbour Pointe Shores retirement community on Catala Avenue southward to the marina for Tropical Kingbird (rare) and Palm Warbler in late fall. Turn right onto Point Brown Avenue, which will take you north through downtown Ocean Shores to the town gate in a bit more than five miles.

BOWERMAN BASIN

From Ocean Shores take SR-115 back to SR-109, reset your trip-odometer to 0.0, and turn right toward Hoquiam. In 14.7 miles, just before entering Hoquiam, take a right onto Paulson Road at the wildlife refuge and airport signs. At the T-junction (0.5 mile) go right on Airport Way along a sewage lagoon. Continue to the airport and park across from Lana's Cafe (0.6 mile). Walk around the gate, go west along the airport pavement, then take the Sandpiper Trail to the **Grays Harbor National Wildlife Refuge** shorebird-viewing areas on Bowerman Basin.

The Grays Harbor estuary is one of eight sites in North America to be designated a Western Hemisphere Shorebird Reserve Network site of hemispheric importance. The extensive mudflats and the high concentration of invertebrates they support (reportedly up to 55,000 per cubic meter) provide a rich resource for the hundreds of thousands of shorebirds that stop here to feed and rest before continuing their 7,000-mile journey from South America to their nesting grounds in the Arctic. The peak of spring migration occurs in late April and early May. At high tide ten or twenty thousand shorebirds, or more, may be feeding at your feet or swirling low in vast clouds you can almost touch. Conversely, when the tide is out few birds remain as they spread out to feed in other parts of the estuary. The most prevalent species are Western Sandpiper, Dunlin, and Short-billed Dowitcher. Black-bellied and Semi-palmated Plovers, Greater Yellowlegs, Red Knot, and Least Sandpiper are usually present but in much smaller numbers. Merlins and Peregrine Falcons regularly hunt here, providing a fascinating spectacle as flying balls of shorebirds maneuver to elude them. The annual Grays Harbor Shorebird Festival is timed to coincide with the peak of spring migration (for information visit *www.blackhillsaudubon.org/bowerman/*). In fall, migrating shorebirds and waterfowl are present in lesser numbers. Large flocks of Dunlins may be found on the mudflats in winter. Greater White-fronted, Snow, and Ross's Geese, Sandhill Crane, Snowy Egret, and American White Pelican have put in an appearance in the saltwater marshes.

On the way out, drive around the sewage lagoon to check for grebes (rarely, Eared in winter), Cinnamon Teal (early to mid-spring) and other waterfowl, phalaropes (Red can occur after winter storms), and gulls (Franklin's is rare in migration). South of the lagoon, the grassy areas and the Chehalis River estuary mudflats are also worth a look.

CHEHALIS RIVER VALLEY

Return to SR-109, zero your trip-odometer, and turn right into Hoquiam. The highway flows into US-101 southbound, which will take you through Hoquiam to Aberdeen. At the east edge of downtown Aberdeen (5.4 miles) you can turn right with US-101 toward Westport (page 65). Or, you can opt for a side trip to explore the wooded and wetland habitats of the lower Chehalis River valley, in which case you should continue straight ahead (east) onto US-12 at this intersection. In 12.7 miles, turn right onto the Montesano Brady (Monte Brady) Road. At 0.8 mile, turn right again onto the **Brady Loop Road**. This seven-mile itinerary crosses open farmlands on the floodplain of the Chehalis River, where shallow ponds host good numbers of wintering waterfowl. Raptors regularly hunt these fields, including Bald Eagle, Cooper's, Red-tailed, and Rough-legged Hawks, Gyrfalcon (rare), Peregrine Falcon, and Short-eared Owl. Check the weeds, fencelines, and brushy patches along the road for Spotted Towhee, sparrows, and warblers in season. In 1.0 mile, the road takes a left turn beside thickets with large stands of alder (flycatchers and songbirds). At 0.7 mile there is a public fishing access to the Chehalis River. In another 0.5 mile the Brady Loop Road turns right while the Henry Foster Road continues straight ahead to meet the Monte Brady Road a mile farther north. Drive part way up Foster Road, then turn around and come back to continue eastward along the Brady Loop, scanning ponds, bordering trees, and fields for waterfowl (swans on the larger ponds), raptors, and Western Meadowlarks. Short-eared Owls sometimes perch on fenceposts, and Western Scrub-Jays should be searched for around the farmhouses. Turn right at the Monte Brady Road (3.8 miles) to return to US-12 a hundred yards ahead.

The 527-acre **Chehalis Wildlife Area** is a haven for waterfowl, shorebirds, and passerines in a mosaic of open wetland, riparian shrub, and meadow/field habitats, with some open water. However, the wildlife area is prone to flooding and may be inaccessible from late fall through spring. To reach it, turn right (east) onto US-12 and travel to the intersection with Schouweiler Road (3.4 miles). Turn right (south) here, then left at the stop sign and follow the 65010 Road to its end in front of a metal gate (0.4 mile). Park out of the way, go around the gate, and walk straight ahead (south) on the dirt road. Birding the paths along weedy edges and thickets usually produces a good mixture of sparrows. Raptors hunt the fields, and American Bitterns, geese and ducks, and Virginia Rails can be found in the sloughs and ponds. Green Herons favor two larger ponds reached by walking east from the gate along a gravel berm.

Return to US-12, continue east 2.0 miles, and take the Third Street Elma exit. Turn right (south) at the stop sign onto Wakefield Road. In another 0.2 mile, turn right again at the county park and airport signs onto **Wenzel Slough Road**. A 10-mile loop westward from here through more fine floodplain habitat is at its best in winter and early spring when fields are flooded, but can be good in any season. Pull into the main parking lot of Vance Creek County Park, on the right in 0.5 mile, and bird the path across the footbridge, riparian habitat, and the long pond west of the parking lot for grebes, waterfowl, and gulls, as well as passerines (especially in migration). Fields near the airport, just ahead, sometimes have shorebirds in migration. Stop frequently anywhere along the route to check ponds, open fields, riparian vegetation, thickets, and brushy patches, and keep a watch for Bald Eagle, Northern Harrier, and Red-tailed Hawk. Swans and other waterfowl may winter in flooded fields and on small ponds. Waterfowl are skittish during hunting season, and you will get better views if you use your car as a blind. Do not enter fields without permission. At the intersection of Wenzel Slough Road and Keys Road, turn right to rejoin US-12. Turn right here and head east to bird Hood Canal (page 219), the Olympia area (page 213), or the South Sound Prairies (page 209). A left turn will take you back to Aberdeen and the road to Westport in about 17 miles.

GRAYS HARBOR SOUTH BAY

At the intersection with US-101 and SR-105 in Aberdeen, reset your trip-odometer to 0.0, turn left (south) toward Westport, and cross the high bridge over the Chehalis River. Just after the bridge, where the two highways divide, stay right on SR-105 toward Westport. In 11.6 miles, turn left to a parking area for the **Johns River Wildlife Area** (WDFW permit required). Beyond the gate, trails lead for over a mile to coniferous and broadleaf forests, shrubby thickets, and fresh- and saltwater marshes. Look for Wood Ducks, other waterfowl, and Wilson's Snipe in the wetland habitats. Typical woodland and edge-loving species found here include Ruffed and Blue Grouse, Band-tailed Pigeon, Northern Flicker, Hutton's Vireo, Black-capped and Chestnut-backed Chickadees, Bewick's and Winter Wrens, Golden-crowned and Ruby-crowned (winter) Kinglets, Yellow-rumped Warbler, Spotted Tow-

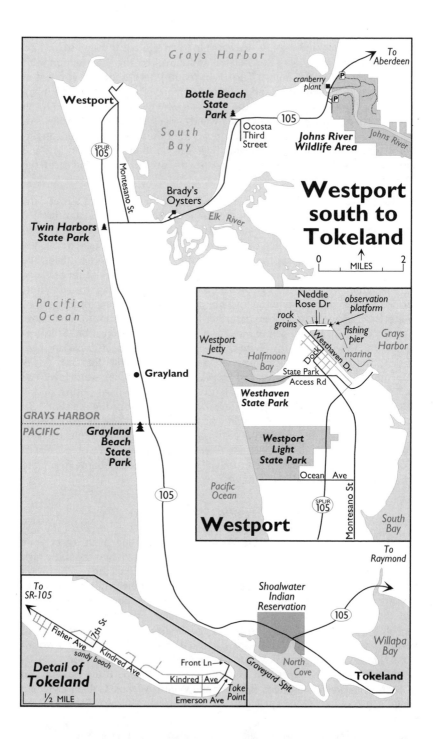

Grays Harbor

To
Aberdeen

cranberry
plant

Westport

**Bottle Beach
State
Park**

Ocosta
Third
Street

105

**Johns River
Wildlife Area**

Johns River

*South
Bay*

SPUR
105

Montesano St

Brady's
Oysters

Elk River

**Westport
south to
Tokeland**

0   2
MILES

**Twin Harbors
State Park**

*Pacific
Ocean*

● **Grayland**

GRAYS HARBOR
- - - - - - - - - - - -
PACIFIC

**Grayland
Beach
State
Park**

105

Neddie
Rose Dr

*observation
platform*

*rock
groins*

Westhaven Dr

*fishing
pier*

Grays
Harbor

*Westport
Jetty*

*Halfmoon
Bay*

Dock

marina

State Park
Access Rd

**Westhaven
State Park**

**Westport
Light
State Park**

Ocean   Ave

SPUR
105

Montesano St

*Pacific
Ocean*

Westport

*South
Bay*

To
Raymond

**Shoalwater
Indian
Reservation**

105

*Willapa
Bay*

To
SR-105

Fisher Ave

75th St

sandy beach

Kindred Ave

**Detail of
Tokeland**

½ MILE

Front Ln →

Kindred Ave

Emerson Ave

Toke
Point

Graveyard Spit

*North
Cove*

Tokeland

hee, Golden-crowned Sparrow (winter, in brush along the dike trail), and Dark-eyed Junco. To reach another portion of the wildlife area, continue southwest on SR-105 past the cranberry plant. In 0.7 mile, turn left onto Johns River Road just after the Johns River bridge. Bear left at the fork with the *Welcome to Johns River* sign, left at the stop sign (0.1 mile), and right down the hill in 200 yards to a parking area (WDFW permit required). Habitats here consist of open farmlands and fresh- and saltwater marshes, adjoining the Johns River. A half-mile walk along the paved river-dike path to a blind should produce ducks, hawks, and occasionally a Short-eared Owl (at dawn); the trail continues unpaved for another mile or so past the blind. Elk sometimes browse in the open pastures.

Continue west on SR-105 for another 2.3 miles from the south entrance of the wildlife area. As the highway curves left, look for a prominent green sign for Ocosta Third Street, on the left. Immediately after the sign, pull off on the *right* side of the highway onto an unmarked, barricaded gravel spur. This is the entrance to **Bottle Beach State Park** on the Grays Harbor South Bay. When developed, the 70-acre park will have a parking area, kiosk, viewing platforms, and a trail through the nearby spruce woods. In the meantime the site is open to birders. Walk around the barricade, clamber across a small bridge, and follow the path to the beach. Shorebird viewing (including Red Knot, Western Sandpiper, and Short-billed Dowitcher) can be quite good during spring migration, especially an hour and a half on either side of high slack tide. The mudflats here are some of the last on the estuary to be covered by the incoming tide. Continuing west on SR-105, Brady's Oysters at the west end of the Elk River bridge is worth a stop (turn right onto Oyster Place at 3.0 miles). Scan the river for loons, grebes, ducks, and if the tide is out, shorebirds. Great Egret is regular in fall. Northern Saw-whet Owls may be calling from conifers to the west in the pre-dawn hours.

WESTPORT

One mile farther west, turn right and travel north on Montesano Street into Westport, the charter-boat fishing capital of the Pacific Northwest. In 3.6 miles, the road swings right and becomes Dock Avenue. At the stop sign in 0.1 mile, take Westhaven Drive (the main street along the docks) left to the rock breakwater, then go right onto Neddie Rose Drive (0.3 mile). Park at the end of the road (0.3 mile) and walk up onto the observation platform next to the public restroom. Gray Whales summer in the surrounding Grays Harbor channel. Throughout the year, scan for Common Loon, Red-necked and Western Grebes, cormorants, Surf and White-winged Scoters, gulls, and Black-legged Kittiwake (fall through spring). Parasitic Jaegers have been seen here, chasing kittiwakes and Common Terns during migration. When strong winds blow in from the ocean, Black Turnstones, Surfbirds, and Rock Sandpipers—normally out on the jetties—may seek protection on the leeward side of the rock groins to the west of the viewing platform. Wandering Tattler is also present in fall. The nearby walkway next to the Harbor Resort leads to the docks of the Westport Marina and, at the end, to a fishing pier, which offers good views of grebes, cormorants, and gulls. The pier pilings sometimes host Black Turnstones and Surfbirds. Look around the docks for Common and Yellow-billed (rare; winter) Loons, Western Grebe, Long-tailed Duck, Barrow's Goldeneye, Heermann's Gull (fall and winter), and Harbor Seal. When returning on Neddie Rose Drive, check the waters off the breakwater and rock groins for Common Murre (winter), Pigeon Guillemot, and Marbled Murrelet. Glaucous Gull is uncommon in winter; a scan of gulls on the roofs of the seafood processing plants or nearby fields may produce one.

Since the mid-1960s, the **Westport Pelagic Trips** have gone offshore to deep oceanic waters, looking for seabirds unlikely to be seen from shore. The Westport trips are well-known among birders for the reliability of Black-footed Albatross (seen on virtually every trip reaching outer continental shelf habitats) and Fork-tailed Storm-Petrel (seen on almost all trips between May and October). Trips are run during all seasons, but most take place from late spring into early fall. Probable for the July–October period are Black-footed Albatross, Northern Fulmar, Pink-footed, Buller's, and Sooty Shearwaters, Fork-tailed Storm-Petrel, Red-necked and Red Phalaropes, Pomarine, Parasitic, and Long-tailed Jaegers, Sabine's Gull, Black-legged Kittiwake, Arctic Tern, Common Murre, Pigeon Guillemot, Marbled Murrelet, and Cassin's and Rhinoceros Auklets. Laysan Albatross, Flesh-footed Shearwater, Leach's Storm-Petrel, South Polar Skua, and Tufted Puffin are possible. Most trips go about 30 miles offshore to the edge of the continental shelf. One or two trips annually head for oceanic waters 65–70 miles out, looking for *Pterodroma* petrels (Murphy's, Mottled) and other intriguing possibilities. Expert spotters accompany each trip. For current schedule and other details, contact Westport Seabirds, P.O. Box 665, Westport, WA 98595, phone 360-268-5222, or on-line at *www.westportseabirds.com*.

The **Westport Jetty** offers similar birding possibilities to the Ocean Shores jetty across the channel, but the walk out is even more difficult and treacherous. The base of the jetty is accessible from Westhaven State Park (day use only). Turn right (west) at the park sign a short distance along Montesano Street as you head back south from town. In winter, Harlequin Ducks may be off the end of the jetty rocks at the entrance to Halfmoon Bay.

SR-105 Spur turns right from Montesano Street 1.2 miles south of the park entrance. Take this route south 3.1 miles, where it joins SR-105, and continue straight ahead 11.7 miles to the sign for Tokeland, on the right.

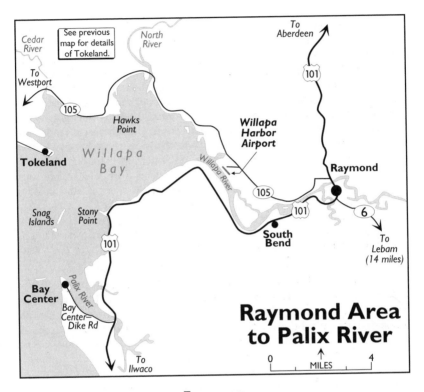

TOKELAND

Tokeland, at the mouth of Willapa Bay south of Westport, is famous for long-legged shorebirds such as Greater Yellowlegs, Willet, Long-billed Curlew, and Bar-tailed (rare in fall) and Marbled Godwits. Follow the signs from SR-105 through the Shoalwater Indian Reservation (map on page 64). Obey the 25-mph speed limit—it is strictly enforced. Where the arterial turns left 1.7 miles from the highway, continue straight ahead on Fisher Avenue and park by the rock wall where the road makes a left turn (0.2 mile). Walk out to the sandy beach and search the offshore sandspit and nearby beaches for Brown Pelican (late spring through fall), shorebirds, and gulls. This is one of the most reliable spots in the state for Willet and Long-billed Curlew in winter. In late summer and fall, huge flocks of Sooty Shearwaters sometimes enter Willapa Bay and can be seen from this and other vantage points. Continue left (north) on Seventh Street, then right in about 75 yards onto Kindred Avenue, which runs east into town. Take a right at Emerson Avenue (hidden street sign on left in 1.0 mile). This dirt road ends in a short distance at Toke Point. Scan the beach, rocks, and pilings for cormorants, Willet, Black Turnstone, Herring (winter), Glaucous-winged, and Western Gulls.

Return to Kindred Avenue, turn right, and continue a couple of hundred yards until the road ends at the Public Fishing Dock. Park and check the bay for seabirds, including Brant (winter, spring), or watch people tending their crab pots. Stretching west from here along Front Lane, the Tokeland Marina—and especially the long rock breakwater beyond the marina—are a favored high-tide godwit roost from late August through the winter. Very often one or more Bar-taileds can be picked out among 200–500 Marbleds, but the Bar-taileds usually disappear by October. Though much rarer, Hudsonian Godwit has been seen here, too. At low tide, the godwits can be anywhere in the Tokeland area including the shoreline at the marina or far out in the bay. Watch for Purple Martin (uncommon) in the marina from mid- to late summer. For direct access to the rock breakwater and the surrounding saltwater marsh, drive west on Front Lane to My Suzie's Store and RV Park. Park out of the way and ask the managers for permission to bird the area (they are birder-friendly). Walk down the stairs at the west end of the RV park and on out to the marsh and breakwater. This is another good place to find Willet (winter).

Many rare landbird vagrants have appeared in Tokeland, among them White-winged Dove, Tropical Kingbird, Northern Parula, Black-and-white Warbler, Lark Bunting, Chestnut-collared Longspur, and Hooded Oriole. Walk the short, dead-end residential streets in fall to see what you can see.

WILLAPA BAY

SR-105 continues east along the north shore of Willapa Bay. The mouths of the Cedar (2.4 miles) and North (5.7 miles) Rivers can be checked for waterfowl in migration and winter. Turn west on Airport Road (5.9 miles) to the **Raymond Airport** (officially, Willapa Harbor Airport) on the floodplain at the mouth of the Willapa River. Occasionally, large Elk herds graze nearby. The fields and small freshwater ponds and sloughs along SR-105 near the airport support many wintering ducks and raptors. Watch for roosting shorebirds at high tide, and Palm Warbler in dense brush in fall and winter. In the past, White-tailed Kites nested here and were often seen on the tops of evergreen trees near the runway, but recently they have been more reliable along Chinook Valley Road (page 74) or Elk Prairie Road (turn south from SR-6 two miles east of Lebam).

Continue east into the town of Raymond (watch for Western Scrub-Jays in residential areas). Turn right at the T-intersection with US-101 (4.5 miles). Drive southwest along the Willapa River toward South Bend, the "Oyster Capital of the World." Purple Martins can be found in season along the river. Beyond South Bend, Cattle Egret and Tropical Kingbird have occurred (rarely) in the open farmlands from late fall to early winter. The road parallels the shoreline of Willapa Bay and crosses the Palix River in about 16 miles from Raymond. Turn west (right) onto the **Bay Center-Dike Road**, just after the bridge. When flooded in winter the fields to the south of the road have waterfowl (including Eurasian Wigeon among the flocks of American Wigeon), Dunlin, and Mew Gull. Large flocks of shorebirds, especially Black-bellied Plover and Dunlin, may be here during spring migration (late April). Loons, grebes, and diving ducks use the three-mile stretch of the river from its mouth to the bridge, and Virginia Rails are common along reedy banks and slough edges. Look for Great or even Snowy Egrets (rare in fall and winter). The best river birding is usually an hour or so before or after high tide.

Continue south on US-101, winding through managed forests interspersed with freshwater creeks that enter the saltwater marshes of Willapa Bay. At the stop sign for SR-4 in 13.5 miles, turn right with US-101 toward Long Beach. Here the road follows the Naselle River across open, expansive marshes. Headquarters for the **Willapa National Wildlife Refuge** are located on the left in 4.6 miles. Those with a boat can launch it across the road to gain access to nearby **Long Island**, the largest estuarine island along the Pacific Coast with 5,000 acres of saltgrass tidal marsh, intertidal mudflats, and mostly second-growth forest. A 274-acre Western Redcedar grove is one of the last remnants of the old-growth coastal forest once prevalent in this area. Woods host Bald Eagle, Ruffed and Blue Grouse, Red-breasted Sapsucker, and Pileated Woodpecker, as well as Elk, Mule Deer, Beaver, and a high concentration of Black Bears. Nesting Band-tailed Pigeons can usually be seen from May through September. Eelgrass beds off the west side of Long Island provide an important food source for large flocks of wintering and migrating Brant. Near the refuge headquarters, at dawn, Marbled Murrelets can be heard passing overhead during the breeding season (best during the first three weeks of July).

The entrance to the **Lewis Unit** of the Willapa National Wildlife Refuge is on the right in another 5.5 miles, just past the Bear River. Turn right and travel 0.8 mile to the parking lot at the end of Jeldness Road. Two gated trails depart downhill from here. The one straight ahead leads in a few hundred yards (stay right at the fork) to an extensive freshwater marsh. The trail to the right from the parking lot goes out on a long dike to the south end of Willapa Bay, offering excellent views; part way out, a spur dike on the left crosses the freshwater marsh. Water levels inside the main dike are controlled to provide freshwater habitat for amphibians, waterbirds, and other wildlife. This habitat and the saltwater and mudflat habitats outside the dike support many species of wintering waterfowl, including large numbers of Brant and occasional Trumpeter Swans. Greater White-fronted and Snow Geese pass through in early May. American Bitterns nest here, and large numbers of migrating shorebirds can be seen from the dike in spring and fall. West from Porter's Point the refuge is managed as a sanctuary, and the dike trail is closed to all public entry. Some other areas may be used by hunters during the hunting season.

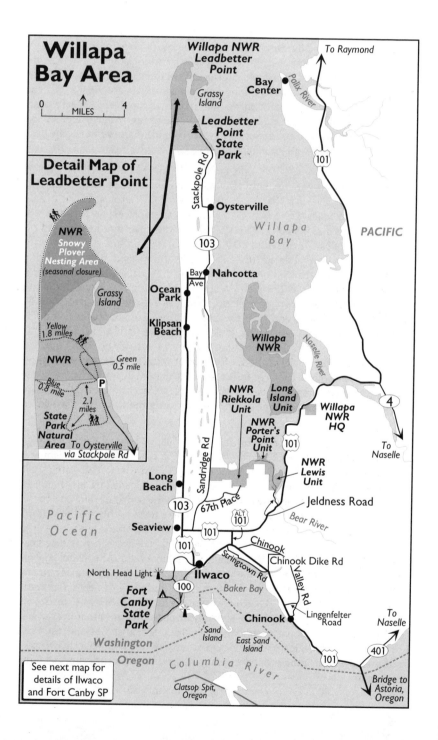

LONG BEACH PENINSULA

Continue west on US-101 toward Ilwaco (do not use Alternate 101). To reach the Long Beach Peninsula, turn right onto Sandridge Road in 4.7 miles (sign for Willapa National Wildlife Refuge) and head north. A right turn onto 67th Place (1.6 miles) takes you past cranberry bogs and mixed forest to the parking area and gated entrance of the refuge's **Riekkola Unit**, in 2.3 miles. In winter, check the large flocks of Canada Geese in the fields here for different subspecies including Western, Cackling, Dusky, Vancouver, Taverner's, Least, or the rarer Aleutian. Return to Sandridge Road and turn north. Turn right at 273rd Street (10.4 miles) in **Nahcotta**, famous for its oysters: one of every six oysters eaten in the U.S. comes from Willapa Bay. Check the oyster-shell piles, marina, oyster plants, rock jetty, and nearby waters for Common Loon, Red-necked and Western Grebes, Ruddy and Black Turnstones, Surfbird, Herring Gull (winter), and Glaucous Gull (rare in winter). Also check the waters around the boat basin at the end of 275th Street. Farther north along Sandridge Road, bear right at Territory Road (3.0 miles) to visit the National Historic District of Oysterville with original houses from the 1860s and 1870s. Turn left onto the Oysterville Road (0.4 mile), which goes westward across the peninsula. At 0.3 mile turn north (right) onto Stackpole Road to reach the upper end of the peninsula.

The parking lot for Leadbetter Point State Park, a day-use natural area, is located at the north end of Stackpole Road (4.3 miles). The land from here up to the end of the peninsula—part of the Willapa National Wildlife Refuge—is **Leadbetter Point**. Sandy trails lead westward, traversing an interesting succession of plant communities on the way to wide beaches fronting the Pacific Ocean. At the parking lot, mature Sitka Spruce forest with a dense and varied understory prevails; next comes a belt of Lodgepole Pine on sandy soils, and then a shrubby zone with many wax-myrtles—very attractive to wintering Myrtle Yellow-rumped Warblers. Approaching the ocean, introduced European Beachgrass grows in the unstable dunes, just above the high-tide zone. You may walk the outer beach northward all the way to the tip of the peninsula.

On the east side of the point, a rich salt marsh of Pickleweed and Arrowgrass floods and drains twice daily with the change of tides. The marsh and adjacent intertidal zone are an important feeding and resting habitat for Brant, especially during April and May when thousands stop here on their northward migration. There is no trail to **Grassy Island**, a thicket of willows, alders, and shrubs near the inner tip of Leadbetter Point that can have unusual passerines in migration. Walk the path to the beach on the east side of the point, then follow along the shore north to the tip and on to Grassy Island. It is a long trek. Attempting to take shortcuts may mean backtracks and futile detours to get around the tidal channels in the marshes. The area is prone to flooding at high tide, especially from October to April. Rubber boots are recommended.

While Leadbetter Point is an excellent site for shorebirds, long experience by birders has shown that Ocean Shores and Tokeland provide much easier access for viewing virtually all Washington shorebird species. However, if you want an opportunity to immerse yourself in a wilderness experience, Leadbetter Point is the place for you. With preparation, proper tides, and a willingness to walk, you may encounter shorebirds in great variety and number. Many records of state rarities come from here, including Gray-tailed Tattler, Upland Sandpiper, Little Curlew, Bristle-thighed Curlew, Hudsonian and Bar-tailed Godwits, and Curlew Sandpiper. Two specific areas are worth mentioning—the salt marsh west of Grassy Island (for American and Pacific Golden-Plovers, and Pectoral and Sharp-tailed Sandpipers), and the ocean beach and flats at the outer point and northwestern shore (for Snowy Plover, but stay out of the clearly marked, restricted nesting area of this state-endangered species). Impressive shorebird roosts may be encountered anywhere along the outer beach at high tide.

Return to Oysterville and continue south on Sandridge Road. Follow SR-103 where it turns westward on Bay Avenue (8.7 miles), then southward for about 20 miles through the towns of Ocean Park, Klipsan Beach, Long Beach, and Seaview, offering a profusion of motels, restaurants, galleries, and amusements. In Seaview, take US-101 south to the town of Ilwaco at the southern end of the Long Beach Peninsula (1.8 miles to the only traffic light in town, at Spruce Street).

COLUMBIA RIVER MOUTH

Go west from the traffic light at Spruce Street in Ilwaco and proceed counterclockwise on SR-100 Loop. In 2.1 miles turn right to the **North Head Lighthouse**. Park in the small lot (0.4 mile) and walk 350 yards to the scenic lighthouse. Migrant passerines are common, spring and fall, on the southwest-facing slope of shrubby thickets and mixed coniferous and deciduous woods. Gray Whales (spring), Brown Pelicans (late spring through fall), and Sooty Shearwaters (fall and spring) swim in offshore waters or fly by the lighthouse, along with scoters, other diving ducks, and Pigeon Guillemots. Black Oystercatchers and Surfbirds may be on nearby rocks.

Return to SR-100 Loop, turn right, then right again at the main entrance to **Fort Canby State Park** (1.1 mile). The 1,666-acre park, located at the mouth of the Columbia River, offers a wide variety of habitats including open salt water, rock jetty, rocky cliffs, sandy ocean beach, saltwater marsh, Sitka Spruce forest, freshwater lakes, Red Alder swamp, shrubby thickets, and park-like settings. Drive ahead past the entrance booth, then turn right into the campground. Freshwater Lake O'Neil and McKenzie Lagoon, in the center of the park, usually have Pied-billed Grebe, Green Heron (summer), and waterfowl (Trumpeter Swan in winter). Virginia Rails are numerous year round in the sedge marshes. Varied Thrushes patrol the lawns in winter.

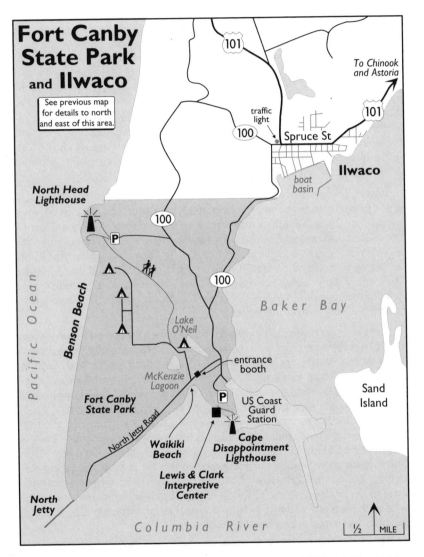

Fort Canby State Park and Ilwaco

See previous map for details to north and east of this area.

101

101

traffic light

100

Spruce St

To Chinook and Astoria

Ilwaco

North Head Lighthouse

boat basin

100

Baker Bay

100

P

Pacific Ocean

Benson Beach

Lake O'Neil

Sand Island

McKenzie Lagoon

entrance booth

Fort Canby State Park

P

US Coast Guard Station

North Jetty Road

Waikiki Beach

Cape Disappointment Lighthouse

Lewis & Clark Interpretive Center

North Jetty

Columbia River

½ | MILE

Check the trees and bushes here, and along the trail to the North Head Light-house (trailhead a bit farther along on the right) for passerines, including Or-ange-crowned, Black-throated Gray, and Wilson's Warblers from spring through fall, and Red Crossbill at any season. Brushy patches hold winter sparrow flocks. Come back out and drive right to the end of the North Jetty Road (0.8 mile). Along the way, isolated conifers on the south side often have interesting passerines during migration.

The **North Jetty** of the Columbia River is subject to constant winter storms that change access, cut away beach front, and deposit logs along access roads and parking lots. Pick your way out the rock jetty to view Pacific and Common Loons, long strings of passing Sooty Shearwaters in fall and spring, flying Surf and White-winged Scoters, and Black-legged Kittiwakes (uncommon). Search for Common and Arctic (rare) Terns during migration. Watch for jaegers, with Parasitic being the most likely, in fall and spring migration. Wandering Tattlers (spring and fall), Black Turnstones, Surfbirds, and Rock Sandpipers inhabit the jetty rocks. Stay off the jetty when winds and high or incoming tides create dangerous conditions with breaking swells, extreme spray, tidal wash, and treacherous footing.

Return toward the entrance booth. The parking lot for Waikiki Beach, across from the campground entrance road, is an excellent place to observe the cliffs of **Cape Disappointment**, where Brandt's and Pelagic Cormorants, Glaucous-winged Gulls, and Pigeon Guillemots nest. Turn right at the stop sign after the booth to a parking lot for the Cape Disappointment Lighthouse (the oldest lighthouse still in use on the West Coast) and the Lewis and Clark Interpretive Center, reached by short, steep trails. Both offer great views of the huge swells as the Columbia River meets the Pacific Ocean. Use caution and stay behind the fence.

Return to the traffic light in Ilwaco and go straight ahead on Spruce Street (US-101 southbound). Before you leave town, the waters off the boat basin (three blocks south) are worth a look. Purple Martins nest in the pilings. **Stringtown Road** turns off to the right from US-101 in 2.0 miles (easy-to-miss sign). This road goes south past a small airport (Lapland Longspur fall and early winter), then turns east along the shore of Baker Bay. Here, on 18 November 1805, a member of the Lewis and Clark Expedition killed "a buzzard of the large kind" measuring 9.5 feet from wingtip to wingtip—an early record of the California Condor, once a regular visitor to the Columbia River. Check roadside vegetation and feeders at houses for hummingbirds and passerines. In 2.6 miles Stringtown Road rejoins US-101. Turn right a short distance to the bridge over the Chinook River. The river mouth has shorebirds in fall and hundreds of ducks in fall and winter on an incoming tide, although they may be scarce during hunting season.

At the Stringtown Road intersection, drive straight across US-101 onto the Chinook Dike Road. Continue by open fields lined with brush (winter sparrows). At the T-intersection (1.2 miles), turn right onto **Chinook Valley Road**. This road is good for geese and ducks, especially during and after rainstorms, and is an important wintering area for raptors. Look for White-tailed Kite, Bald Eagle, Red-tailed and Rough-legged Hawks, and Northern Shrike. At the next T-intersection (2.7 miles), turn left with Chinook Valley Road (Lingenfelter Road, straight ahead, is also good).

In 0.8 mile Chinook Valley Road reaches an intersection with US-101 in Chinook. Turn left here. Encouraged by the Army Corps of Engineers and wildlife agencies, Caspian Terns have recently begun nesting on **East Sand Island** in the Columbia River (actually in Oregon, but visible to the southwest from the Port of Chinook turnoff a short distance ahead). Historically, Caspian Terns nested in Willapa Bay and Grays Harbor. But as the terns lost habitat to vegetation growth, predatory birds, erosion, and human actions, they settled at Rice Island, another dredge-spoil island 12 miles up the Columbia, forming perhaps the largest Caspian Tern colony in the world. There, terns devoured an estimated 11 million salmon smolts in 1998. In 1999 and 2000, workers cleared vegetation from East Sand Island in an attempt to draw the nesting terns away from high concentrations of migrating smolts at Rice Island. The birds appear to have found East Sand Island to their liking. Food sources are more varied at this location, and the terns take far fewer salmon smolts.

Four miles farther east, US-101 crosses the Astoria to Oregon, and SR-401 heads east along the Washington side of the Columbia River toward Cathlamet (page 234).

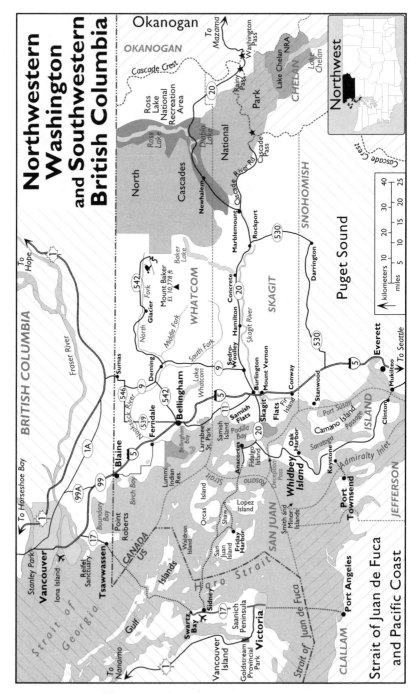

Northwestern Washington and Southwestern British Columbia

Okanogan

Strait of Juan de Fuca and Pacific Coast

Puget Sound

Northwest

NORTHWEST

Belying its size (the smallest of the nine regions in the book), Washington's Northwest enjoys an exceptional richness of birdlife in an exceptional geographic setting. Here the inland marine waters of Puget Sound, the Strait of Juan de Fuca, and the Strait of Georgia meet and mix. Here, too, are the deltas and estuaries of several rivers—the Skagit, the Samish, the Nooksack/ Lummi, and just north of the border, the Fraser. Adding to the bounty, the state's best cross-mountain birding route ascends the Skagit Valley from floodplain through forested foothills to alpine meadows amidst the jagged, glacier-clad peaks of the North Cascades.

Tidal exchange between the Straits of Georgia and Juan de Fuca makes the San Juan Islands a choice seabird location. The Victoria waterfront and Point Roberts near Vancouver stand out among many other fine seabird vantage points. The coastal mainland and Whidbey and Fidalgo Islands offer numerous land- and waterbirding sites, from Drayton Harbor and Rosario Strait south to Puget Sound.

This region has the most important estuaries of the Puget Trough/Georgia Depression. The discharge of the Skagit is far greater than that of any other stream flowing into the basin south of Canada, while the discharge of the Fraser exceeds the total flow of *all* the Washington rivers reaching the basin. The deltas of the Fraser, Skagit, Samish, and Lummi Rivers are famous for wintering raptors and waterfowl. Gyrfalcon is dependable. So, usually, is Snowy Owl. Discrete subpopulations of Snow Goose and Brant winter here in their entirety. More Trumpeter Swans winter on the Skagit and Samish Flats than anywhere else in the conterminous United States. The estuaries attract shorebirds as well—the Fraser delta, in particular, is a world-class shorebird site.

Vast, contiguous portions of the North Cascades are publicly owned and protected within North Cascades National Park, Mount Baker and Ross Lake National Recreation Areas, Mount Baker-Snoqualmie National Forest, and three designated wilderness areas. The North Cascades and Mount Baker Highways traverse several forest zones—Puget Sound Douglas-fir, Western Hemlock, Silver Fir, Mountain Hemlock, Interior Douglas-fir, and Subalpine Fir—on their way to trailheads for the Alpine/Parkland zone above treeline. High-elevation trails provide some of the best access in the state for alpine specialties such as White-tailed Ptarmigan and Gray-crowned Rosy-Finch.

Temperatures average two or three degrees cooler than farther south on Puget Sound (Bellingham mean temperature 37 degrees in January, 62 degrees in July). On the mainland coast, precipitation is about the same as in Seattle or Everett. Whidbey Island, the San Juans, and southeastern Vancouver Island receive less precipitation due to the rainshadow effect of the Olympic Mountains. Vancouver, however, receives noticeably more (47 inches annually at the airport and 62 at Stanley Park, compared to 36 in Bellingham). Eastward up the Cascade slopes annual precipitation increases approximately one inch per mile, reaching 92 inches at Newhalem.

Roads may be icy in the winter months. Snow is infrequent in the lowlands, but troublesome if it accumulates. Of the two mountain highways, SR-542 is kept open all winter to the Mount Baker ski area, but SR-20 is closed most years above Newhalem from December into April.

The main line of communication is Interstate 5 (Highway 99 in Canada). Traffic is usually free-flowing except in Vancouver, which experiences the rush-hour congestion of any large city. Ferry queues and the border crossing can be serious bottlenecks. Be sure to allow plenty of time for these in your travel planning.

Restaurants, lodging, gas, and other services are available in the larger communities and along the I-5 corridor. Campgrounds are fairly numerous in both lowlands and mountains, but demand for campsites often exceeds supply on weekends and in the summer season. Many campgrounds close for the winter. Whidbey Island and the San Juans are popular get-away destinations for mainlanders. Consequently, birders will find a wide selection of accommodations there, from basic motels to charming B&Bs and upmarket resorts, but these are often booked far in advance. Lodging reservations on the islands are highly recommended, especially during summer months.

WHIDBEY ISLAND

by Kraig Kemper

Whidbey Island offers fine Western Washington birding in a magnificent setting at the top of Puget Sound, about 25 miles north of Seattle and 50 miles south of the U.S.-Canada border. With its many twists and kinks, the island has 148 miles of shoreline and stretches 50 road miles from end to end, but averages a mere three miles in width. From some vantage points it is possible to see at one time both bodies of water that flank it. The terrain is low and rolling, with the highest elevations reaching not much more than 550 feet above sea level.

The moderating effects of surrounding water and sheltering mountains provide a mild, temperate climate. Influenced by the Olympic Mountains' rainshadow, average annual rainfall varies from 18 inches at the central part of the island to 26 and 30 inches at the north and south ends—half to three-quarters the rainfall of Seattle or Everett.

Whidbey Island's rich saltwater habitats include open water bringing swells from the Pacific; sheltered passages and bays; rocky and sandy shoreline; and tidal mudflats and salt marsh. Early on, the island was commercially logged, then cleared for farming by settlers. Although little remains of the old-growth Douglas-fir forests that once cloaked the uplands, significant stands of mature second-growth coniferous and mixed forest can be found in some places. Other upland habitats include freshwater lakes, ponds, and wetlands; remnant prairies; pastures and croplands; parks and gardens; and shrubby thickets. This wide variety of habitats supports nearly 250 resident and migrant bird species.

Although Whidbey birding is interesting all year, the most productive times are winter (November through mid-March) and during spring (late April through May) and fall (late July through September) migrations. The main birding areas can be covered adequately in a day.

There are three means of automobile access: by ferry from Mukilteo (just south of Everett) to Clinton, by ferry from Port Townsend to Keystone, or by highway over the Deception Pass bridge at the north end. The itinerary described here begins at the ferry terminal in Clinton, on the southeast side of the island. To get there from I-5, take Exit 189 and proceed west on SR-526 past the Boeing assembly plant, then right (north) on SR-525 to Mukilteo and the ferry landing; the route is well signed. The crossing of Possession Sound to Clinton takes 20 minutes and is usually not very birdy.

SOUTH WHIDBEY STATE PARK

From the Clinton ferry ramp, travel along SR-525 northwestward for 10.6 miles. Turn left (west) onto Bush Point Road (becomes Smugglers Cove Road). At 2.3 miles, where the access road for Bush Point turns off to the left, stay straight ahead on Smugglers Cove Road and proceed north 2.6 miles to

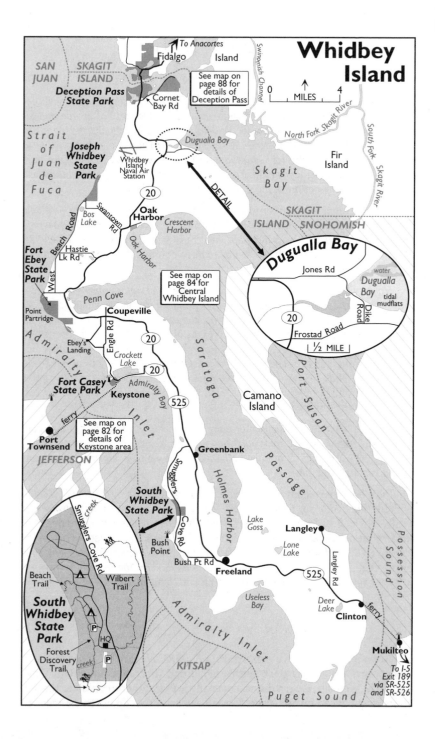

Whidbey Island

To Anacortes

Fidalgo Island

SAN JUAN ISLANDS

SKAGIT ISLAND

Swinomish Channel

0 — MILES — 4

Deception Pass State Park

See map on page 88 for details of Deception Pass

Cornet Bay Rd

North Fork Skagit River

South Fork Skagit River

Strait of Juan de Fuca

Joseph Whidbey State Park

Dugualla Bay

Whidbey Island Naval Air Station

Fir Island

Skagit Bay

SKAGIT ISLAND · SNOHOMISH

DETAIL

20

Oak Harbor

Crescent Harbor

Swantown Rd

Bos Lake

Fort Ebey State Park

Hastie Lk Rd

West Beach Road

Oak Harbor

See map on page 84 for Central Whidbey Island

Dugualla Bay

Jones Rd

water

Dugualla Bay

tidal mudflats

20

Dike Road

Frostad Road

½ MILE

Penn Cove

Point Partridge

Coupeville

Admiralty

Ebey's Landing

Engle Rd

20

Crockett Lake

Saratoga

Camano Island

Port Susan

20

Fort Casey State Park

Keystone

Admiralty Bay

525

Passage

ferry

Port Townsend

JEFFERSON

See map on page 82 for details of Keystone area

Inlet

Greenbank

Holmes Harbor

Lake Goss

Lone Lake

Langley

Possession Sound

South Whidbey State Park

Smugglers Cove Rd

Bush Point

Bush Pt Rd

Freeland

525

Langley Rd

South Whidbey State Park

Smugglers Cove creek

Beach Trail

Wilbert Trail

P

HQ

P

Forest Discovery Trail

creek

Useless Bay

Deer Lake

Clinton

ferry

KITSAP

Admiralty Inlet

Mukilteo

To I-5 Exit 189 via SR-525 and SR-526

Puget Sound

the South Whidbey State Park entrance, on the left. This 348-acre park (gated November–February, but you can walk in) has heavily wooded uplands and an open, wave-washed beach with spectacular views across Admiralty Inlet to the Olympic Mountains. Trails through old Douglas-firs and Western Redcedars are edged by ferns, Red Elderberry, Salmonberry, and Stinging Nettle. Year-round residents include Hutton's Vireo, Steller's Jay, Chestnut-backed Chickadee, Red-breasted Nuthatch, Brown Creeper, Winter Wren, Golden-crowned Kinglet, and other Puget Lowlands forest species. The Beach Trail leaves the campground and parking area and wanders through the forest down a high bank of glacial sediments to the beach. The shore is of gently sloping sand, giving way to cobbles and rock at low tides. Look for loons, cormorants, and mergansers on the open water, and check the beach for Great Blue Heron, Bald Eagle, Sanderling, and other shorebirds. The mile-long Forest Discovery Trail, at the south end of the park, traces a pair of loops along the top of the bluff through Red Alder and conifers; bridges cross creeks and wet areas, bright with Skunk Cabbage in spring. The Wilbert Trail, which begins on the east side of the highway opposite the park entrance, is a 1.5-mile loop through a 255-acre forest of old-growth Western Redcedar and Douglas-fir, with many snags where Osprey, Bald Eagle, and Pileated Woodpecker nest.

CROCKETT LAKE AND KEYSTONE HARBOR

Crockett Lake—a brackish 250-acre marsh and shallow lake formed by the long gravel bar of Keystone Spit—is located three miles south of Coupeville, adjacent to the Keystone ferry terminal. The lake is noted for migrant shorebirds; gulls and terns; a good variety of ducks (many of which winter); raptors; and passerines around the marsh-edge habitat. From the South Whidbey State Park entrance, turn left onto Smugglers Cove Road and continue 4.4 miles to SR-525. Turn left (north), and in 4.7 miles go left (west) onto SR-20 (Wanamaker Road) toward the ferry landing. After descending a hill the arterial makes a 90-degree turn to the left (1.2 miles), then another to the right (0.4 mile). SR-20 now runs along Keystone Spit, paralleling the shores of Crockett Lake on the right (north) and Admiralty Bay on the left. For the next mile and a half you may park anywhere along the wide shoulder and walk out to bird the marsh and lake. Shorebirding is best when water levels are relatively low, exposing extensive mudflats. However, birds can then be a long way out, across wet grass and soft mud. You will need a spotting scope and rubber boots to bird effectively. Proceed with caution. The mud is deep and hazardous in places.

Crockett Lake is ounstanding for shorebirds in fall (mid-July through September). Common species include Black-bellied and Semipalmated Plovers, Killdeer, both yellowlegs, Spotted, Semipalmated (July–early August), Western, Least, Baird's (August), and Pectoral (September) Sandpipers, Dunlin, both dowitchers, Wilson's Snipe, and Red-necked Phalarope (August).

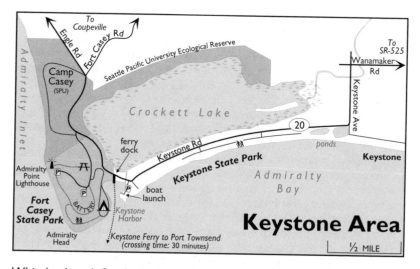

Whimbrel and Sanderling are fairly common. American and Pacific Golden-Plovers, American Avocet (has nested), Solitary Sandpiper, Black Turnstone, Red Knot, Sharp-tailed and Stilt (August–September) Sandpipers, Ruff, and Wilson's Phalarope are uncommon to rare. Black-necked Stilt, Willet, Hudsonian and Marbled Godwits, and Buff-breasted Sandpiper have each been recorded once. Grass and water edges may have American Pipit, Savannah Sparrow, and Lapland Longspur seasonally, or rarities such as Snowy Egret, Little Blue Heron, and White Wagtail (one record of each). Northern Harrier, Bald Eagle, Red-tailed and Rough-legged Hawks, Merlin, and Peregrine Falcon hunt over the marsh and along Keystone Spit. A major portion of the spit, with freshwater ponds and a saltwater shoreline on Admiralty Bay, is open to the public (several parking lots at intervals on your left). Scope the ponds for ducks and shorebirds.

Just before the ferry terminal, turn left into a parking lot on the east shore of **Keystone Harbor** (1.6 miles). The state park boat launch is one of the best on the island, with a good drop-off and excellent protection by breakwater and rock jetty. The jetty, and pilings of the old Army quartermaster dock immediately to the east, are now an underwater state park—the most popular spot on Whidbey Island for snorkeling and scuba diving. Black Oystercatcher has been seen on the rock jetty, and cormorants (all three species) rest on the old platform and pilings. Heermann's Gulls may be here from July to September. Scan Admiralty Bay for Red-throated and Common Loons, Horned and Red-necked Grebes, Harlequin Duck, Pigeon Guillemot, and Rhinoceros Auklet. The 30-minute ferry ride to Port Townsend (page 28) can be excellent for waterbirds. Marbled Murrelet, Rhinoceros Auklet, and other species are sometimes present in Keystone Harbor near the ferry slip.

FORT CASEY AND EBEY'S LANDING

From the ferry terminal and SR-20, continue northwest on Engle Road 0.4 mile to the **Fort Casey State Park** entrance on the left. Along with Fort Flagler and Fort Worden across Admiralty Inlet, Fort Casey was part of a century-old coastal defense system that guarded the entrance to Puget Sound. These fixed-gun fortresses became obsolete after World War I, and the fort is now a 137-acre historic state park. Bird the wooded areas of the park (especially the picnic area) for species of the Puget Sound Douglas-fir zone, including summer visitors such as Pacific-slope Flycatcher and House Wren (local in Western Washington). Spring migrants may include Western Wood-Pewee and Yellow-rumped and Wilson's Warblers. The campground (open year round) is another good vantage point for Keystone Harbor and the ferry dock. Walk out to the lighthouse on the bluff overlooking Admiralty Inlet. Nutrient-rich upwelling draws large numbers of gulls and Rhinoceros Auklets to feed offshore in summer and fall. Common Murres are abundant from fall through spring.

From Fort Casey, turn left (north) onto Engle Road, then left onto Hill Road (1.8 miles), which runs along the south edge of Ebey's Prairie, bends right, and drops down from the bluff edge to a small parking area and beach access at **Ebey's Landing** (1.2 miles). This site has recently been acquired by The Nature Conservancy. The plant community along the bluff is a rare remnant of a coastal prairie ecosystem that has largely disappeared from Western Washington because of development and conversion to agriculture. A robust population of Golden Paintbrush here is one of only about ten in the world. A pleasant beach hike goes northward in about a mile to a large lagoon surrounded by driftwood. In migration, watch for shorebirds and for songbirds in the brushy vegetation at the base of the bluffs. Harlequin Ducks are regular close to shore along with many other waterbirds, especially in winter.

PENN COVE

Turn left from the parking lot at Ebey's Landing. Ebey Road runs uphill (northeast) onto the prairie, bends left, and continues north to Coupeville. From the stop sign in 1.3 miles, continue straight ahead and proceed through the intersection with SR-20 (0.2 mile), where the road changes name to Broadway. In 0.5 mile, turn right onto Madrona Way and follow the arterial downhill to the left (becomes Coveland Street) to NW Alexander Street (0.2 mile). Turn left, travel one short block to NW Front Street, and park. From the **Coupeville Wharf**, take in the view of Penn Cove, a large bay that almost cuts across Whidbey Island from the east. Many loons, grebes, and other waterbirds winter on Penn Cove, including all three species of scoters (thousands of Surf and White-winged, just a few Black); some are present through summer. This is also an excellent location to observe both Common and Barrow's Goldeneyes.

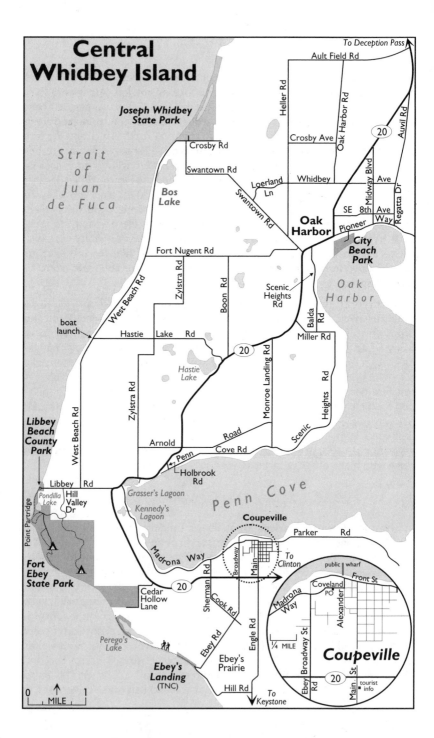

Central Whidbey Island

Strait of Juan de Fuca

To Deception Pass

Ault Field Rd

Heller Rd

Joseph Whidbey State Park

Crosby Rd

Crosby Ave

Oak Harbor Rd

20

Auvil Rd

Swantown Rd

Loerland Ln

Whidbey

Midway Blvd

Bos Lake

Swantown Rd

Regatta Dr

SE 8th Ave Way

Oak Harbor

Pioneer

City Beach Park

Fort Nugent Rd

West Beach Rd

Zylstra Rd

Boon Rd

Scenic Heights Rd

Oak Harbor

boat launch

Hastie Lake Rd

Balda Rd

Miller Rd

20

Hastie Lake

Zylstra Rd

Monroe Landing Rd

Heights Rd

Libbey Beach County Park

West Beach Rd

Arnold

Road

Cove Rd

Scenic

Penn

Holbrook Rd

Libbey Rd

Grasser's Lagoon

Penn Cove

Point Partridge

Pondilla Lake

Hill Valley Dr

Kennedy's Lagoon

Coupeville

Parker Rd

Fort Ebey State Park

Madrona Way

To Clinton

public wharf

Broadway

Main

Coveland

Front St

PO

Cedar Hollow Lane

20

Sherman Rd

Cook Rd

Madrona Way

Alexander

Perego's Lake

Ebey Rd

Engle Rd

¼ MILE

Ebey Broadway St

Coupeville

Fort Ebey State Park

Ebey's Landing (TNC)

Ebey's Prairie

Hill Rd

To Keystone

Ebey Rd

Main St

20

tourist info

0 MILE 1

Return west to the intersection of Broadway and Madrona. Follow Madrona Way westward along the edge of the high bluff. Pull off on the right at a wide spot on the gravel shoulder at 0.3 mile, and a second spot in a further 0.8 mile, to scope the waters of the cove for scoters and other diving birds, including Harlequin Ducks in summer. Black Turnstones, Dunlins, and other shorebirds often roost on the mussel platforms. The road swings north around the end of the cove. **Kennedy's Lagoon**, on the left side of Madrona Way 1.5 miles from the last pullout, may host ducks and a few shorebirds. Park at any of several pullouts on either side of the road for the next half-mile, north to the intersection with SR-20. The west end of Penn Cove has a rocky and sandy shore that is one of the most accessible examples of this habitat type left within the inland marine waters of Washington. Rock-foraging shorebirds are present much of the year: Black Turnstone (most numerous) and Surfbird are common, Ruddy Turnstone is fairly common in migration, and Rock Sandpiper occurs occasionally. Scoters and other waterbirds are often fairly close to shore. Small flocks of Eared Grebes, very local in Western Washington, are seen here throughout the winter.

Look for yellowlegs at **Grasser's Lagoon**, at the northwest corner of Penn Cove. Migrating shorebirds sometimes shelter amidst the low vegetation on the pebbly spit that separates the lagoon from the bay. Turn right onto SR-20 from Madrona Way, then right again at a gravel pullout at the east end of the lagoon (0.2 mile), for another vantage point. Grasser's Hill, north of the highway, is popular with raptors, including Rough-legged Hawk (winter) and American Kestrel. Continue right 0.4 mile on SR-20 and turn right into a gravel lot beside the Penn Cove Pottery store. Walk across Penn Cove Road to the base of the pier (posted; stay off). The shoreline in both directions often hosts flocks of rocky shorebirds.

FORT EBEY AND POINT PARTRIDGE

Go back west on SR-20, which bends left at a junction 0.1 mile past the Madrona Way intersection. Turn right here onto Libbey Road. **Fort Ebey State Park** is reached by turning south (left) onto Hill Valley Drive in 0.9 mile and following signs 0.7 mile to the entrance. Day-use facilities are open year round; the campground is closed November–February. The park offers excellent birding on 644 acres of coniferous and mixed woods, driftwood beach, grassy bluffs, and fresh- and saltwater habitats. Park near the restrooms and walk west 100 yards to the **Point Partridge** overlook. A panoramic view extends southeastward down Admiralty Inlet; south and southwest to Point Wilson, Port Townsend, and the snow-capped Olympic Mountains; west along the Strait of Juan de Fuca; northwest to Victoria and the southeast coast of Vancouver Island; and north to Vancouver and the San Juan Islands. A trail leads down from the bluff to a 1.5-mile sandy beach with shore- and marine birds. Black Oystercatchers forage on rocky outcroppings where the point meets the sea. This is also one of the island's best locations for Harlequin Duck.

The park is an outstanding example of kettle topography, characterized by depressions where huge chunks of ice remained behind as the continental glacier withdrew at the end of the last ice age. From the other side of the restrooms, a short trail leads to Pondilla Lake, a kettle filled with fresh water. Dabbling ducks can be found here, and Bald Eagles often roost in nearby snags. Many resident and migrant forest birds are evident along the park's three miles of hiking trails. Five species of woodpeckers, and typical Westside songbirds such as Hutton's Vireo, Red-breasted Nuthatch, Winter Wren, and Spotted Towhee, are here all year. Migrants and summer visitors include Pacific-slope Flycatcher and several warblers (Orange-crowned, Black-throated Gray, Townsend's, Wilson's). This is the most reliable location for Red Crossbill on Whidbey Island, and good numbers of Varied Thrushes and Sooty Fox Sparrows can be found in winter.

The other side of Point Partridge is reached from **Libbey Beach County Park**. Return to Libbey Road, turn left, and go 0.3 mile to the road's end. Many seabirds associated with the kelp-forest habitat of the open shoreline can be seen here—Horned and Red-necked Grebes, Pelagic Cormorant, Harlequin Duck, and Pigeon Guillemot. Loons (Red-throated, Pacific, and Common), scoters (Surf and White-winged), Long-tailed Duck, Red-breasted Merganser, Black Oystercatcher, Heermann's Gull, and Common Murre also frequent these waters or the shoreline at the eastern end of the Strait of Juan de Fuca. A beach walk south around Point Partridge leads to connecting trails from Fort Ebey State Park, half a mile away. To the north are six miles of public tidelands beneath 200-foot sandy bluffs. Don't get trapped by incoming tides.

WEST BEACH AND SWANTOWN

Return east 0.6 mile on Libbey Road, turn left onto West Beach Road, and proceed north 2.3 miles to the intersection with **Hastie Lake Road**. A parking area and boat launch on the left is another excellent point from which to view the eastern Strait of Juan de Fuca and the many seabirds associated with the Bull Kelp groves that thrive just beyond the low-tide line. Rarities such as Yellow-billed Loon and King Eider have been seen here. Black Oystercatchers sometimes use the cobble-and-boulder beach.

West Beach Road continues north and descends a hill to beach level at a spot called **Swantown**, with a small lake and salt marsh on the right. Park on the wide gravel shoulder on the left (beach) side of the road (2.5 miles) and look out over the eastern end of the Strait of Juan de Fuca. There is a high probability of seeing seabirds year round—especially large numbers of loons, grebes, and ducks (including Harlequin and Long-tailed). Gulls and alcids frequent the channel and feed near shore during the winter. Look for Sanderlings on the beach and Caspian Terns offshore. Navigational lights on Smith and Minor Islands four miles to the west are important landmarks for boats traveling between Puget Sound and the San Juans. The two islands are part of a national wildlife refuge established in 1914 to protect Brant wintering on the neighboring eelgrass beds from slaughter by market hunters. Minor Island has a large breeding colony of Harbor Seals; Smith Island is an important nesting site for Pelagic Cormorant, Black Oystercatcher, Pigeon Guillemot, and Tufted Puffin.

Bos Lake and the surrounding salt marsh (aka Swantown Lagoon), east of the road, are notable for migrating shorebirds, gulls, and terns, and for wintering waterfowl, waders, and raptors. In fall migration (mid-July through September) Bos Lake is an important shorebird stopover, second on the island only to Crockett Lake for numbers and species diversity. However, water levels vary throughout the year, and in fall the mudflats can be extensive and birds a long way out. You may scope from the edge of the road or, for closer views, pull on rubber boots and walk toward the exposed flats. Look for a log crossing over the slough, and beware of deep, sticky mud.

Continue on West Beach Road, turning right to the intersection of West Beach, Crosby, and Swantown Roads (1.0 mile). The entrance to 112-acre **Joseph Whidbey State Park** is just ahead on the left (day use only; closed October–March). Paths lead from the picnic area to the broad sand-and-gravel beach. Expect the same waterbirds as at Point Partridge and the other Juan de Fuca overlooks. Another access can be found next to the first residence on the south side of the park (on the left in 0.7 mile when coming from Bos Lake). Here is a graveled parking lot for a few cars and a trail that leads directly to the beach. Trails through the beach grass just above the driftwood line follow the beach north out of the park property. Just before leaving the park, a half-mile trail through a freshwater wetland offers good views of migrating and nesting waterfowl and marshbirds.

OAK HARBOR AND DUGUALLA BAY

Birding possibilities at **Oak Harbor City Beach Park** are similar to those at Penn Cove, including rocky shorebirds on the beach. This is a good place to see gulls unusual elsewhere on the island (Thayer's, Glaucous). From Joseph Whidbey State Park, follow Swantown Road south and east 2.9 miles to an intersection with SR-20. Turn left onto SR-20 and continue east into the city of Oak Harbor. In 0.5 mile, where SR-20 turns north at a traffic light, stay straight ahead on SE Pioneer Way. Take the next right on SE City Beach Street (0.3 mile) to the day-use area just ahead.

Return to the light at SR-20. Drive north (right) on SR-20 to the intersection with Frostad Road (5.0 miles); turn right, continue 0.9 mile, and turn left onto Dike Road. (See inset map on page 80.) A gravel pullout on the right (0.3 mile) provides a view of **Dugualla Bay**, an indentation on the west side of Skagit Bay. Look for grebes, cormorants, and scaups on the bay, and herons, yellowlegs, dowitchers, and other shorebirds on the beach. The head of Dugualla Bay drains to a quarter-mile-long mudflat at low tide. Optimal viewing is on an incoming or receding tide. Continue about 450 yards farther along the dike to another gravel pullout and viewpoint for bay and beach, on the right. Look also for waterfowl on the impounded lake and surrounding agricultural fields on the left (west) side of the road. This is the most reliable location for swans on Whidbey Island, and large numbers of Canvasbacks may be present in late winter. Watch for raptors, including Peregrine Falcon, and for a variety of passerines in the hedgerows and brush along the dike. Continue 0.2 mile to Jones Road. Turn left to reach SR-20 in 1.0 mile.

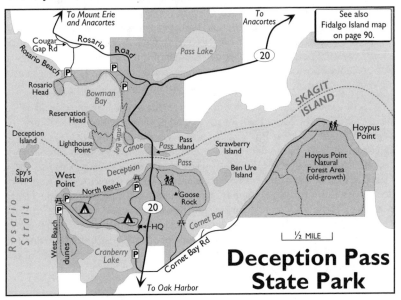

DECEPTION PASS STATE PARK

From Jones Road, continue north 3.4 miles on SR-20 and turn into the main entrance of picturesque **Deception Pass State Park**, on the left. Straddling the narrow, rocky channel separating Whidbey and Fidalgo Islands, the park offers 3,000 acres of old-growth Douglas-fir forest, saltwater beaches, tidepools, and freshwater lakes and marshes. A variety of overnight, day-use, recreational, and educational facilities are available at Cranberry Lake and West Beach, North Beach, Cornet Bay, and Rosario Beach. Most facilities are open year round, but some are closed in winter. Deception Pass State Park is the most heavily used state park in Washington. Due to high summer visitation birding is best in early morning or evening, or in the off-season.

Turn left at a fork in 0.4 mile, near the park office, following signs to the **West Beach** parking lot (0.8 mile). The largest of the park's freshwater lakes, Cranberry Lake, is on the left along the way. Pied-billed Grebe, Wood Duck, Mallard, Bufflehead, Hooded Merganser, and other waterbirds are sometimes present. Also watch for the resident River Otters. Sand dunes separate the lake from West Beach, which has both rocky and sandy shoreline. Loons (especially Red-throated and Pacific), Horned and Red-necked Grebes, cormorants (all three species), sea ducks, and gulls may be seen offshore. Pigeon Guillemots and Marbled Murrelets are regular all year, and Rhinoceros Auklets are frequent in summer. Look for Black Oystercatcher, Black Turnstone, and Sanderling on the beach. The rest of the park is dominated by coniferous forest, and the large trees and edge habitat will yield a list of typical lowland species similar to those found at South Whidbey and Fort Ebey State Parks, including Varied Thrush in winter. The other branch at the fork near the park office leads to **North Beach** and excellent water-level views of the mouth of Deception Pass, where Red-throated Loons can be numerous in winter on the right tide.

To reach **Cornet Bay** on the more sheltered east side of the park, return to the main park entrance, cross over SR-20, and proceed east onto Cornet Bay Road. From 0.9 to 1.4 miles the road overlooks the bay with opportunities for waterbirds. Continue another mile into the Hoypus Point Natural Forest Area, to a beach parking lot at the road's end. This area has an Osprey nest and foot trails through mature Douglas-fir forest. Return to SR-20, turn right, and continue north 0.9 mile to a small parking lot on the left at the south end of the Deception Pass Bridge. The bridge (actually, two bridges that cross Deception Pass and Canoe Pass) is a National Historic Monument. When tides are changing, turbulent waters pour through the chasm between Skagit Bay and Rosario Strait, across a shallow (40-foot) sill. Looking down from the bridge you may see feeding Pigeon Guillemots. Good numbers of Bald Eagles winter here. (In summer this site has heavy visitor traffic and is best avoided.)

Rosario Beach, another portion of the park, lies across Canoe Pass near the southern tip of Fidalgo Island. Take SR-20 north over the bridge. Turn left onto Rosario Road (1.0 mile from the south end of the bridge). Angle left onto Cougar Gap Road in 0.8 mile; at the bottom of the hill turn left onto the park entrance road. This can be a very busy place on summer weekends. Walk out to Rosario Head (a five-minute walk) for views of Bowman Bay—a fine place for alcids (Common Murre, Pigeon Guillemot, Marbled Murrelet, and Rhinoceros Auklet) at all seasons, although late fall through winter is the best time. Ancient Murrelets are often present from November through January. In winter, huge numbers of Red-throated Loons may congregate here. Offshore rocks may have Brandt's Cormorants alongside Double-crested and Pelagic. Search the rocks to the north of the head for Black Oystercatchers and Black Turnstones, and keep an eye out for Wandering Tattlers (rare).

Return to SR-20 and drive north 5.1 miles to a major junction where SR-20 continues right (east) toward Burlington and SR-20 Spur goes left to Anacortes and the San Juan Islands ferry terminal (page 93). Eastbound, it is 5.3 miles to the Farmhouse Inn corner (page 117) and access to birding sites on the Skagit and Samish Flats, or 11.6 miles to join I-5 at Exit 230 at Burlington.

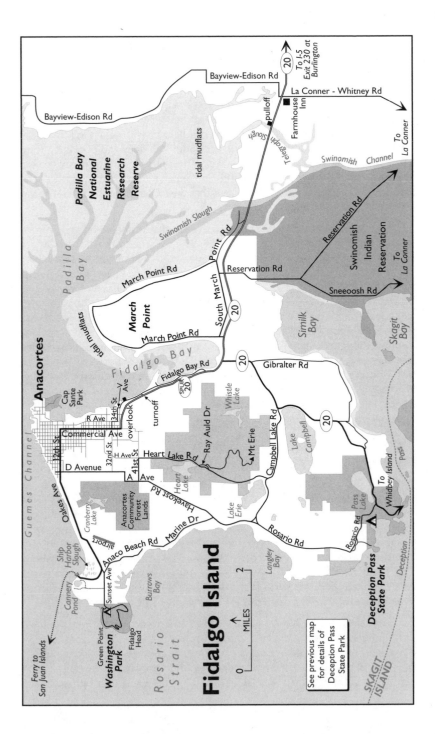

Fidalgo Island

FIDALGO ISLAND

by Bob Kuntz

Fidalgo Island is perhaps best known as the home of the Anacortes ferry terminal—the jumping-off place for the San Juan Islands and Victoria, British Columbia. Birding cognoscenti, however, recognize the island as a fine and varied birding destination in its own right. Any or all of the sites described here are often included on a visit to Whidbey Island or to the Skagit and Samish Flats.

TELEGRAPH AND SWINOMISH SLOUGHS

In fall, winter, and spring, up to 15,000 shorebirds congregate at **Telegraph Slough**, just east of Fidalgo Island. Most are Dunlins and Western Sandpipers, but Baird's (fall; uncommon) and Least Sandpipers are regular, too. Go 0.6 mile west on SR-20 from the traffic light at the Farmhouse Inn corner (page 117) and pull off on the north edge of this four-lane highway. The dikes are off-limits, but you can get good looks from the north side of the railroad embankment an hour or so before or after high tide when the birds are pushed in close. Merlins and Peregrine Falcons hunt the flats in winter.

Continue west on SR-20 for two miles. This will take you across the Swinomish (pronounced *SWIN-ih-mish*) Channel bridge onto Fidalgo Island. You are now on the Swinomish Indian Reservation. Turn right at the exit for March (or March's) Point and then immediately right again onto S March Point Road. At 0.1 mile you can pull off on the left (north) side of the road along **Swinomish Slough**, best viewed at low tide, to look for Semipalmated Plover, both species of yellowlegs, and other shorebirds. Return to a stop sign, turn right, and continue 0.8 mile to a sign reading *March's Point Road*. Turn right onto this road (called E March Point Road on some maps), cross the railroad track, and pull off immediately on the right to check the several dredge-spoil islands, home to a colony of Glaucous-winged Gulls; Caspian Terns are regular summer visitors.

MARCH POINT AND FIDALGO BAY

A peninsula between Fidalgo and Padilla Bays, **March Point** is home to two major oil refineries. The tank farms and cracking towers at your back form an odd contrast with the spectacular natural scenery of Padilla Bay, Mount Baker, and the Cascades. Drive up the road along the eastern shoreline to the tip of the point, pulling off often to scope the waters. Loons, grebes, cormorants, and several species of diving ducks are common here, especially from November through April. March Point is another good place to view Gray-bellied Brant (see page 119). Sanderlings and Black Turnstones are regular on the pebbly beaches; American Pipits and Snow Buntings occur occasionally. Continuing around the point, W March Point Road completes the loop back south to SR-20 in 5.7 miles.

Turn right and continue west about one-half mile. Here SR-20 turns left (south) toward Deception Pass and Whidbey Island (page 89). Stay straight onto SR-20 Spur, travel 1.8 miles, and turn off right onto Fidalgo Bay Road. From the stop sign go straight (northwest) for 0.4 mile. Double-crested and Pelagic Cormorants rest on a series of pilings in **Fidalgo Bay**. This is also a good place to look for all three species of scoters (Black is rare) and Long-tailed Duck. Continue 0.1 mile and turn right onto V Avenue, then left onto 34th Street. Go 0.2 mile on 34th Street to R Avenue. Jog right here for 0.1 mile, turn left onto 32nd Street, and go 0.1 mile to Commercial Avenue (SR-20 Spur). Turn right and continue into the Anacortes business district. At 1.2 miles, turn left with SR-20 Spur onto 12th Street.

MOUNT ERIE

If you are tempted by a panoramic view of the entire area covered by this chapter, with some good forest-birding possibilities thrown into the bargain, an excursion to Mount Erie will well repay the one-hour round trip (to maximize your investment, choose a sunny day). Turn left from 12th Street onto D Avenue (0.8 mile), and follow this arterial south as it bends right, then left, onto A Avenue (1.6 miles). At 0.3 mile, turn left (east) from A Avenue onto 41st Street, then right in another 0.5 mile onto H Avenue, which continues south as Heart Lake Road. The turnoff for **Mount Erie Park** (Ray Auld Drive) is on the left in 1.4 miles. The 1.8-mile road through the 1,400-acre park ends at the 1,273-foot summit. Along the way, species to look for are similar to those for the wooded habitats of Washington Park (see below). There are four vista points, and by visiting each one you can see south the length of Whidbey Island and Puget Sound to Mount Rainier in the distance; southwest to the Olympic Mountains and the Strait of Juan de Fuca; northwest and north across Rosario Strait to the San Juan Islands, Vancouver Island, and the Coast Mountains of British Columbia; and east to the Cascades, Mount Baker, and the Skagit and Samish Flats.

WASHINGTON PARK

Return to the intersection of D Avenue and 12th Street, turning left onto 12th Street, which soon becomes Oakes Avenue. In 2.3 miles, at a right turn for the ferry terminal, continue straight ahead on Sunset Avenue to the entrance to **Washington Park** (0.6 mile), an excellent seabird viewing site from late September through mid-April. The one-way, two-mile loop road through this popular park starts just past the camping area. If you are driving, pull off on the left at Green Point, about 0.7 mile from the park entrance, to scope Rosario Strait and the west entrance to Guemes Channel. However, the loop road is reserved for walkers, runners, and bicyclists up to 10AM, when it opens to automobile traffic. Naturally, the best viewing times are from early to mid-morning before the crowds arrive and with the sun at your back.

At these times, the third-to-half-mile walk to Green Point from the parking area is worth the small effort. Take your scope. Three species of loons (Red-throated, Pacific, and Common) and three of grebes (Horned, Red-necked, and Western) are seasonally common, as are Common Murres, Pigeon Guillemots, and Marbled Murrelets. Rhinoceros Auklets are present in large numbers from July through October. In November and December, this is a good location to seek Ancient Murrelets. Harlequin Ducks and Black Oystercatchers are frequently seen along the rocky shoreline. At dawn, hundreds of Brandt's, Double-crested, and Pelagic Cormorants move up Rosario Strait to feeding areas. Another good pullout is 0.2 mile ahead. Farther along the loop road (0.3 mile), a set of stairs leads to a rocky beach and more oystercatchers. The road weaves its way through a typical low-elevation forest of Western Hemlock, Douglas-fir, and Madrone—the beautiful understory tree with old, red peeling bark and young, smooth chartreuse bark. Stop often to walk the numerous trails, looking and listening for year-round resident species such as Red-breasted Sapsucker, Hutton's Vireo, Steller's Jay, Chestnut-backed Chickadee, Bewick's and Winter Wrens, Golden-crowned Kinglet, Spotted Towhee, and Purple Finch. During migration and summer these may be joined by Rufous Hummingbird, Pacific-slope Flycatcher, Black-throated Gray and Townsend's Warblers, and Western Tanager. The loop road ends back at the main parking and picnic areas.

SHIP HARBOR SLOUGH

Go back out from the park along Sunset Avenue and turn down toward the Anacortes ferry terminal and the adjacent Ship Harbor Slough. Scan marine waters and the wetlands on each side of the terminal building. One good viewing area can be reached by going to the first parking lot to the right as you approach the terminal's entrance station. Drive past the reserved parking spots to park at the far end of the lot. You may see a seasonal variety of waterfowl (among others, Eurasian and American Wigeons, Cinnamon Teal, Long-tailed Duck, both goldeneyes, Hooded Merganser) and gulls (Bonaparte's, Heermann's, Mew, Thayer's, Glaucous-winged) as well as Sora, Violet-green Swallow, Marsh Wren, and Common Yellowthroat. Look in the saltwater channel for loons (Yellow-billed recorded), grebes, cormorants, scoters, and Pigeon Guillemot. The ferry ride to the San Juans and Vancouver Island is described in the following section.

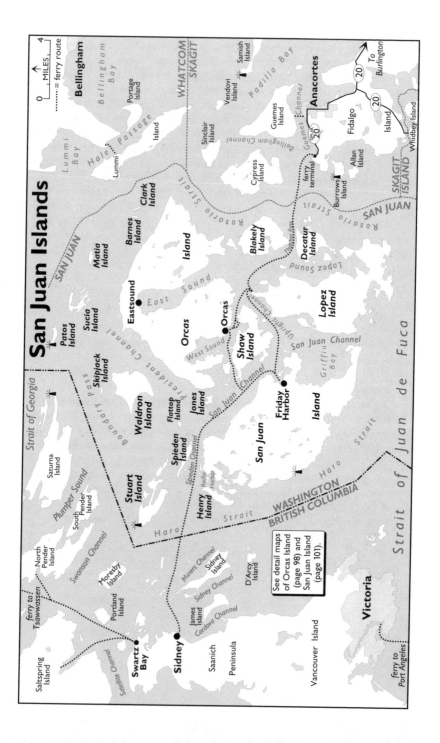

San Juan Islands

See detail maps of Orcas Island (page 98) and San Juan Island (page 101).

SAN JUAN ISLANDS

by Barbara Jensen

The marine waters surrounding the San Juan Islands are the richest in the Puget Basin, abounding with plankton, the primary producers in the food chain. The many large bays, wide channels with fast-moving currents, and quiet harbors are prime locations to observe seabirds in winter and migration, Killer Whales, and Bald Eagles—whether by boat or from shore. Landward, habitat variety is extensive, with forest, prairies, wetlands, rocky shoreline, and sheltered coves all in close proximity. Lying in the lee of the Olympic Mountains, the islands receive around 25 inches of rainfall a year, compared to 35–40 inches along the mainland to the east. The drier conditions exclude certain plant species common in the damp forests and valleys of Western Washington (for example, Vine Maple, Devil's Club, Deer Fern, Evergreen Huckleberry) while favoring other, more drought-resistant species such as Douglas Maple, Garry Oak, and Lodgepole Pine. House Wrens—more usually associated with the dry, open woodlands of Eastern Washington—breed here abundantly. Golden Eagles nest on the three largest islands, Orcas, Lopez, and San Juan. During migration, Lewis's Woodpeckers, Mountain Bluebirds, Townsend's Solitaires, and other species island-hop to and from Vancouver Island and the mainland.

The following accounts describe ferry birding possibilities as well as representative sites on Orcas Island and San Juan Island. Allow a full day to bird either. If you have time for only one island, choose San Juan. Even without the small population of Sky Larks, which now appears to be extirpated, this is a major all-round birding destination with the most diverse array of upland and saltwater habitats in the archipelago. Island road systems are confusing at best, and it is helpful to stop by one of the many real estate offices for a free map.

Four of the islands are served by ferry from Anacortes. Some boats continue to Sidney, British Columbia, 17 miles north of Victoria, and Sky Lark country (page 107). The trip to Sidney takes two to three hours, depending on intermediate stops. If your interest is in birding from the boat as a foot-passenger, the round-trip ferry ride takes all day and requires going through customs. Contact Washington State Ferries at 888-808-7977 for schedules and information about travel to Canada. Vehicle reservations to and from Canada may be made no later than 7:30PM the day prior to sailing, and are recommended. Be sure to arrive at the Anacortes terminal at least one hour before the scheduled departure time (90 minutes in Sidney).

Vehicle reservations are not taken for U.S. routes. Auto spaces fill quickly, and long waits for the next boat are common at certain days and times. It is wise to check the schedules carefully and to arrive early at the terminals. For automated information on fares, schedules, and expected wait times, phone 206-464-6400 in Seattle or 800-843-3779 toll-free statewide, or visit on-line at www.wsdot.wa.gov/ferries.

Follow SR-20 Spur through Anacortes to the ferry terminal; the route is clearly signed. Birding right around the terminal will make the wait seem shorter. Washington's only record of Blue-winged Warbler was found in trees at the edge of the ferry parking lot.

SAN JUAN ISLANDS FERRY

Birding from the ferry is best in fall, winter, and spring. Most common marine species can be seen on this trip, though some are much scarcer or absent in summer. Expected are Pacific and Common Loons, Horned, Red-necked, and Western Grebes, Brandt's (less common in spring, abundant otherwise), Double-crested and Pelagic Cormorants, Surf and White-winged Scoters, Long-tailed Duck, Red-breasted Merganser, Mew and Glaucous-winged Gulls, Common Murre, Pigeon Guillemot, Marbled and Ancient (fairly common to common November–February) Murrelets, and Rhinoceros Auklet (common March–September, fairly common to uncommon fall–winter). Many other species occur in smaller numbers or less predictably, among them Red-throated and Yellow-billed Loons. Notable rarities recorded in these waters include King Eider (February and October), Black-headed Gull (September), Thick-billed Murre (December), Long-billed (August) and Kittlitz's (January) Murrelets, and Horned Puffin (July).

The ferry heads westward across broad Rosario (pronounced roe-ZERRY-oh) Strait. Search here for diving birds, especially alcids. The route then passes among the islands, through narrow channels—sometimes with fast-moving water—and quiet bays. Check calm waters where birds shelter during windy weather. Look along tidal rips or lines on the water for concentrations of feeding birds ("bird balls"), especially cormorants, Red-necked Phalaropes, gulls, and alcids in spring and fall. Northern and California Sea Lions and Harbor Seals fish these areas, too. Bald Eagles and Peregrine Falcons perch in the trees along the shoreline. On the way from Friday Harbor to Sidney, Spieden Channel can host large bird balls, especially at the tide change. Haro Strait marks the international boundary. During the summer look for Killer Whales feeding on migrating salmon. Before reaching Sidney check the channels and bays for flocks of Brant, Harlequin Ducks, and Common Goldeneyes.

ORCAS ISLAND

Giant, horseshoe-shaped Orcas Island is home to Moran State Park—the first state park in Washington—and to the highest point in the islands, Mount Constitution. The shoreline is mostly private, but there are a few marine viewpoints accessible to the public. The routes described below take you through some of the best examples of forest, field, and wetland habitats. Woodland birding is good, especially in spring, for typical Puget Lowlands species such as Rufous Hummingbird, Olive-sided, Willow, and Pacific-slope Flycatchers, Cassin's, Hutton's, and Warbling Vireos, Chestnut-backed Chickadee, Red-breasted Nuthatch, Black-throated Gray, Townsend's, and Wilson's Warblers, and Western Tanager. Black-capped Chickadee is notably absent, having thus far failed to colonize the San Juans after the last ice age. Trumpeter Swans and many ducks are common in winter. Bald Eagles are nu-

In winter, a small flock of Black Turnstones erupts from a stony beach on Lopez Island in a dazzling pattern of blacks and whites.

merous all year. The island is overrun with Black-tailed (Mule) Deer, so drive cautiously, especially at night.

From the Orcas Island ferry landing turn right onto Killebrew Lake Road. Check forest and fields along the 2.2-mile drive to **Killebrew Lake**. Scan the lake for Pied-billed Grebe, Wood Duck, and mergansers. Nearby marshes are home to Virginia Rail and Sora. At a junction at the end of the lake, stay left onto Dolphin Bay Road, which soon becomes gravel. Make another inspection in 1.2 miles at **Diamond Lake** and then continue 4.2 miles to Orcas Road. Follow this road north to Main Street (2.9 miles) and turn right into the town of Eastsound. After passing through the business district, Main Street becomes Crescent Beach Drive. Stop at **Crescent Beach**, just ahead, for waterfowl and for Bonaparte's, Mew, and Glaucous-winged Gulls. At the stop sign in 1.2 miles, turn right onto Olga Road. The entrance archway to **Moran State Park** is in 3.1 miles. Drive carefully through this popular park. The narrow road follows the shoreline of Cascade Lake, where you may see Ospreys.

In 1.3 miles, turn left toward **Mount Constitution**. Stop at the Cascade Falls trailhead in 0.3 mile, on the right, and walk to a series of falls along the creek to look for American Dipper. From the Mountain Lake turnoff, on the right in another 0.6 mile, a level, 3.9-mile trail circles the lake (nesting mergan-

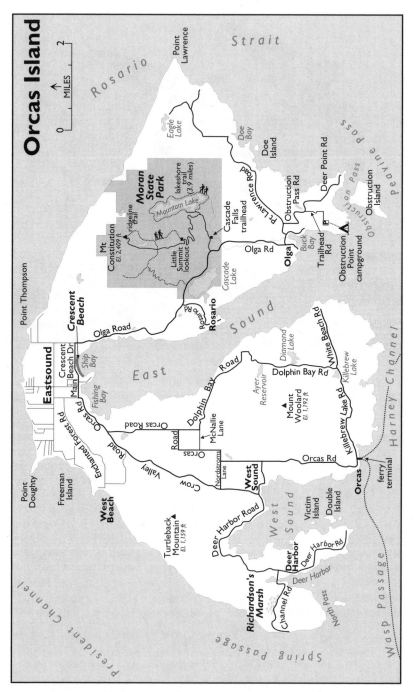

Orcas Island

MILES

0 1 2

Rosario Strait

Point Lawrence

Eagle Lake

Doe Bay

Doe Island

Pt Lawrence Rd

Obstruction Pass Rd

Deer Point Rd

Obstruction Pass

Obstruction Island

Moran State Park

ridgeline trail

lakeshore trail (3.9 miles)

Mountain Lake

Mt Constitution El 2,409 ft

Little Summit lookout

Cascade Falls trailhead

Olga Rd

Olga

Buck Bay

Trailhead Rd

Obstruction Point campground

Cascade Lake

Point Thompson

Rosario Rd

Rosario

Olga Road

East Sound

Crescent Beach

Crescent Beach Dr

Ship Bay

Eastsound

Main

Fishing Bay

Orcas Rd

Enchanted Forest Rd

Diamond Lake

Dolphin Bay Road

White Beach Rd

Dolphin Bay Rd

Killebrew Lake

Ayer Reservoir

Mount Woolard El 1,192 ft

Orcas Road

McNallie Lane

Orcas Road

Nordstroms Lane

Crow Valley Road

West Sound

Orcas Rd

Orcas

ferry terminal

Harney Channel

Point Doughty

Freeman Island

West Beach

Turtleback Mountain El 1,159 ft

Deer Harbor Road

West Sound

Victim Island

Double Island

Richardson's Marsh

Deer Harbor

Deer Harbor Rd

Deer Harbor

Channel Rd

North Pass

Spring Passage

Wasp Passage

President Channel

sers and forest birds). Continue the winding, steep grade toward the summit. A turnout on a hairpin curve in 1.1 miles, on the left, and another on the right just around the bend, have magnificent views of the surrounding islands. The rocky south-facing slopes are open and grass-covered. Look for Blue Grouse and Chipping Sparrow along the forest/grass edges. Similar habitat can be explored from two more turnouts 0.6 mile ahead, or from the parking area for Little Summit (elevation 2,040 feet), on the right in a further 0.1 mile. The road ends at the summit parking lot in 1.6 miles. Coniferous forests on the steep, north-facing slopes have Hairy and Pileated Woodpeckers, Golden-crowned Kinglet, Swainson's and Varied Thrushes, Yellow-rumped Warbler, Purple Finch, and Red Crossbill.

Climb the stone lookout tower, built in the 1930s by the Civilian Conservation Corps, for a 360-degree view of the San Juans, 130 miles south to Mount Rainier, east to the North Cascades, 50 miles north to Vancouver, British Columbia, west to Vancouver Island, and southwest to the Olympic Mountains. Look for Turkey Vultures, raptors, swifts, and Common Ravens. The 2,409-foot summit is at the north end of an exposed, stony plateau with subalpine-like vegetation dominated by Lodgepole Pines (one of the largest forests of this species in Western Washington) parasitized by Dwarf Mistletoe. Brown Creepers and Townsend's Warblers may be seen close-up as they forage in the pines. Common Nighthawks nest on bare ground among the scrubby understory of Hairy Manzanita and Salal. Plants such as Rocky Mountain Woodsia, Rosy Pussy-toes, and Dwarf Mountain Daisy that grow here and nowhere else in the islands are outliers of populations in the Olympics and Cascades. To experience this unique habitat (and jaw-dropping views to the east across Rosario Strait and Bellingham Bay), walk the first half-mile of the ridgeline trail that leaves from behind the restrooms at the south end of the parking lot. The trail continues to Little Summit (2.2 miles from the parking lot), intersecting another trail that drops steeply down the mountain to Cascade Lake.

Return to Olga Road and turn left. The park's south boundary is in 0.4 mile, marked by an arch on a narrow bridge. Travel another 1.5 miles to the intersection with Point Lawrence Road, on the left. Straight ahead, the road ends in 0.2 mile in the village of **Olga**, where a public dock provides a vantage point at the mouth of East Sound (waterbirds). Go east on Point Lawrence Road, which descends to the shoreline of **Buck Bay** in 0.2 mile. Gulls bathe in the freshwater outflow of a small creek that enters the bay, and feed on the bay or on the oyster beds and tideflats. Northwestern Crows are common along the shoreline. In migration, a few shorebirds may be present on the beach at high tide. About 0.3 mile after leaving Buck Bay, turn right from Point Lawrence Road onto Obstruction Pass Road, then bear right onto Trailhead Road at a junction in about 0.8 mile. This potholed road passes through fine deciduous forest and a freshwater marsh (rails), ending in 0.8 mile at the trailhead parking lot for **Obstruction Point Campground** (Washington

Department of Natural Resources). A half-mile trail leads first through dense mixed woodlands, then open, dry forest of Douglas-fir and Madrone on steep slopes, to the 80-acre walk-in campground and beach park. The site hosts a cohort of lowland forest birds including Hutton's Vireo, Steller's Jay, Chestnut-backed Chickadee, Red-breasted Nuthatch, Brown Creeper, Golden-crowned Kinglet, Dark-eyed Junco, and Black-headed Grosbeak. When the tide is running, Marbled Murrelets and other seabirds feed along the tidal rips where Obstruction Pass meets East Sound, affording good scope views from the beach.

Return to Eastsound and turn left from Main Street onto Orcas Road. In 1.1 miles turn right onto Crow Valley Road and continue to the village of West Sound and a T-intersection with Deer Harbor Road, turning right (4.1 miles). Turn right onto Channel Road in 3.6 miles, stopping in 0.2 mile by the bridge across the channel between **Deer Harbor** and the lagoon on the right to check for wintering Common and Barrow's Goldeneyes, Black-bellied Plover, Black Oystercatcher, Black Turnstone, and Northwestern Crow. On the right in another 0.6 mile is the start of **Richardson's Marsh**, one of the most impressive freshwater marshes in the islands. Find a place to pull completely off. Walk the road for the next 500 yards, peeking through and over the bordering vegetation where you can. Though not very productive in winter, the open waters and extensive growth of cattails and other emergent vegetation can be excellent in spring and early summer. Look and listen for Pied-billed Grebe, Wood Duck, teals, Hooded Merganser, raptors, Virginia Rail, Sora, Rufous Hummingbird, Willow Flycatcher, Tree and Violet-green Swallows, Marsh Wren, Common Yellowthroat, and Red-winged Blackbird. Go back to Deer Harbor Road, turn left, and continue through West Sound to Orcas Road (0.8 mile past the junction with Crow Valley Road). Turn right; it is 2.4 miles to the Orcas ferry dock.

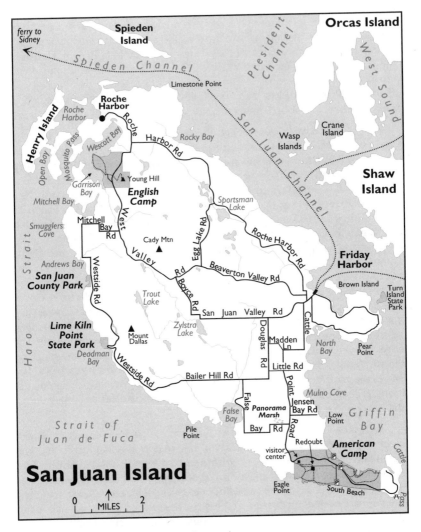

SAN JUAN ISLAND

Almost as large as Orcas but gentler in relief and less sprawling, San Juan Island offers a more complete set of habitats and excellent birding access. In one day of intense birding (two days is better) you may find a large variety of birds along dry, rocky coastlines with stands of Garry Oak and Madrone; in mixed forests of Douglas-fir, Bigleaf Maple, and other species that thrive in moister places; in extensive farmlands, open fields, freshwater marshes, and other wetlands; in saltwater habitats of protected bays, mudflats, and channels with swift tidal currents; and on windswept grasslands overlooking the Strait of Juan de Fuca where a few Sky Larks are still reported now and then. Killer Whales and other marine mammals are easily seen from shore in the proper seasons. Numerous records of passerine rarities include Brown Thrasher, Red-throated Pipit, Tennessee Warbler, Ovenbird, and Indigo Bunting. With more consistent coverage, San Juan Island would probably be revealed as a standout songbird vagrant trap. The following itinerary visits a selection of sites in a clockwise loop from, and back to, Friday Harbor.

From the Friday Harbor ferry ramp, turn right onto Front Street, then left onto Spring Street, and continue through town. Spring Street becomes San Juan Valley Road, turning westward across the broad, open **San Juan Valley**. This is a productive area for raptors, but stopping along the narrow, busy road is dangerous. Turn left onto Douglas Road (1.6 miles) and drive south. You may safely stop and set up your scope at the corners of Madden Lane (0.7 mile), Little Road (0.7 mile), and Bailer Hill Road (0.2 mile) to check the fields and wetlands for Golden Eagle and many other species. Backtrack along Douglas and turn right onto Little Road. In 0.4 mile, turn right onto Cattle Point Road, which passes through impressive stands of Garry Oak on dry, rocky outcroppings, intermixed with stands of Douglas-fir, open pastures, wetlands full of willows, and Madrone along the shoreline. Traffic makes stopping difficult, so turn left onto the less busy **Jensen Bay Road** (1.2 miles) and pull off occasionally to walk or to scan these habitats. Olive-sided Flycatchers, Western Wood-Pewees, and Pacific-slope Flycatchers nest in the forests. The edge between pasture and forest can be good for Rufous Hummingbird, House Wren, and Orange-crowned and Black-throated Gray Warblers. The end of the road faces Griffin Bay and San Juan Channel, yielding scope views of loons, grebes, ducks, and alcids. Check treetops for Bald Eagles as they search the beaches for food.

Return to Cattle Point Road and turn south. It is 1.5 miles to the visitor center entrance at **American Camp**, one unit of the San Juan Island National Historical Park. Drive in and park to bird woodlands and prairie. Bald Eagles nest within sight of the visitor center, and the nearby forest is good throughout the year for the usual flocks of chickadees, nuthatches, creepers, and wrens. Conifers on this end of the island are gnarled from the fierce winds that rip and snap off branches and treetops. This is a notable landfall for birds in migration. Possibilities in fall and spring are Lewis's Woodpecker, Red-breasted Sapsucker, Mountain Bluebird, Townsend's Solitaire, and MacGillivray's Warbler. Breeders include Rufous Hummingbird, Hutton's Vireo, Swainson's Thrush, Townsend's Warbler, and Red Crossbill. Water-stressed glacial soils are covered in extensive grasslands. American Golden-Plovers, Whimbrels, and Snow Buntings can be here in the fall. Winter birding can be a challenge due to strong winds. Take a late afternoon walk eastward to the top of the Redoubt, which overlooks the whole prairie. Spring flowers are abundant. Great Camas colors the area deep purple from April to June. The bulb of this lily was an important food item of the Native peoples, who regularly burned extensive areas of the islands to keep the woody plants in check and camas prairies open. Scan toward the water for Northern Harrier, Short-eared Owl, and Northern Shrike. European Rabbits—introduced in the middle of the 19th century—draw Golden Eagles.

Continue east on Cattle Point Road for 1.4 miles and turn right toward South Beach. At the crest of the hill a road on the right leads to the Redoubt. Continue straight and park about a hundred yards farther on. Sky Larks—offshoots of the ones on southern Vancouver Island—once nested on these prairies. There is a good chance that the colony has been eradicated by predation from introduced foxes and feral cats, but a few birds may still be found occasionally. They could be anywhere; the area just west of this spot was once quite good. Listen for their high-pitched, trilled song and buzzy call-note, and watch for their towering courtship flight in the spring. A walk across the prairie may yield some hidden birds, but be mindful of the numerous rabbit holes.

Continue down to **South Beach** to look for Vesper Sparrows—the uncommon, local, and declining Westside subspecies (*affinis*)—in nearby dunes on the left. The beach is made of smooth, surf-polished stones. The upper beach is piled high with driftwood thrown there during winter storms. The Olympic Mountains dominate the southern horizon 20 miles across the Strait of Juan de Fuca. Native peoples have used this area for thousands of years as prime fishing grounds. Heat-shattered rocks can still be found from the days of smoking salmon on the beaches. Check the waters for Killer Whales fishing for salmon. Filter-feeding Minke Whales are also a possibility. Scope the water from fall to spring for Pacific Loon, Horned and Red-necked Grebes, Surf and White-winged Scoters, Long-tailed Ducks, Common and Barrow's Goldeneyes, Red-breasted Merganser, Common Murre, Pigeon Guillemot, and Marbled Murrelet (usually found in pairs). Summer is a poor time for marine birds except for breeding Pigeon Guillemots and Rhinoceros Auklets. In late summer Cassin's Auklets can sometimes be seen, and there is even a small possibility of Tufted Puffins. In the fall look for Horned Larks and American Pipits in the dunes by the beach.

Return to Cattle Point Road, turn right, and drive 2.1 miles to the picnic area at **Cattle Point**. This is one of the best places in Washington for wintering seabirds. Turbulence resulting from the high-volume tidal exchanges (at times, 12 vertical feet in one tidal cycle) in the narrow (mile-wide) **Cattle Pass** keeps sediments suspended throughout the water column. This provides food to the abundant zooplankton, which in turn feeds the small fish upon which the seabirds prey. Pelagic Cormorant, Harlequin Duck, Black-bellied Plover, Black Oystercatcher, Black Turnstone, Surfbird, and Rock Sandpiper (uncommon) can be seen on the rocky shoreline and on Goose Island just off shore. Scope the rafts and single seabirds feeding mid-channel. Northern Sea Lions feed in the area and haul out on Whale Rocks to the southeast, where their golden-colored bodies are fairly easy to find with a scope. Listen for the roar of the 2,200-pound males from September to May. Nearby pocket beaches are places to find migrating sandpipers or birds trying to stay out of the wind. Raptors work the shoreline. Belted Kingfisher and Northern Rough-winged Swallow nest in the sandy cliffs. The rocky headland here is covered with deep glacial striations—a reminder of the massive, mile-thick ice sheet that passed over the islands during the last ice age.

Go back along Cattle Point Road and turn left onto False Bay Road, 1.2 miles past the visitor center entrance. On the right within a few hundred feet, **Panorama Marsh** is worth a look. Trumpeter Swans winter here, as do Gadwall, Northern Shoveler, Green-winged Teal, Ring-necked Duck, Bufflehead, and Hooded Merganser. Pied-billed Grebe and Wood Duck breed in the wetland, which is also good for breeding songbirds. Continue on through open farmland interspersed with mixed forests of Red Alder, Bigleaf Maple, and Douglas-fir, with views across the strait to the Olympics. In 2.5 miles, stop at the head of **False Bay**, a biological preserve owned by the University of Washington and one of the few large, muddy bays in the islands. At low tide, when this shallow bay empties out for about a mile, the smell of sulphur from algae can be powerful. Be sure to pass by at almost high tide when the birds are relatively close—even then, a spotting scope is useful. A freshwater stream from the San Juan Valley enters the bay a couple of hundred yards to the west. Large numbers of American Wigeons feed here in the winter along with many other ducks. This is the most reliable place on the island for shorebirds in migration (Sharp-tailed Sandpiper has occurred in fall) and for Great Blue Herons and wintering Dunlins. Bald Eagles are numerous, as feeding is good and nest sites are plentiful around the bay. Check willows along the shoreline for songbirds.

Continue on False Bay Road as it heads north, and turn left in 0.8 mile onto Bailer Hill Road. The next mile, to Ranchos Road, is good for wintering raptors. Bailer Hill Road continues west, then swings north along the coast, becoming Westside Road. Turnouts provide spectacular views across **Haro Strait** to Vancouver Island. The channel can be full of birds or seemingly empty, much depending on the wind direction. From spring to fall, Killer Whales concentrate here to feed on salmon heading back to the Fraser River to spawn. **Lime Kiln Point State Park** (4.8 miles from False Bay Road) and **San Juan County Park** (2.4 miles) are excellent whalewatching points. Look also for marine birds and Black Oystercatchers. Harbor Seals feed in the Bull Kelp forests along the shore as does the occasional Northern Sea Lion or River Otter. Pillow basalts (resulting from underwater lava flows) and sediments raised up from the deep ocean floor by colliding continental plates are exposed along the coastline between the two parks.

Drive north 1.8 miles from San Juan County Park, turn right onto Mitchell Bay Road, and in another 1.3 miles go left onto West Valley Road. Travel north to the visitors' entrance for **English Camp**, the other unit of San Juan Island National Historical Park, on the left in 1.5 miles. The parking lot has mixed maple/coniferous forest on one side and Red Alder stands on the other. In the conifer woodlands, look for Pileated Woodpecker, Chestnut-backed Chicka-dee, Brown Creeper, Bewick's and Winter Wrens, and Varied Thrush. The alder is productive for spring birds such as Rufous Hummingbird, Olive-sided and Pacific-slope Flycatchers, Hutton's Vireo, and Swainson's Thrush. Some of the oldest and largest known specimens of Bigleaf Maple grow near the bar-racks building and around the parade grounds. Check these for a possible spring fallout of warblers—Orange-crowned, Yellow-rumped, and Townsend's are the most common species. Walk down to the blockhouse and turn around to see the Osprey nest perched on a snag at the top of the hill. Swallows work the parade grounds and Rocky Mountain Junipers (an-other botanical curiosity for Western Washington). Sheltered **Garrison Bay** is good for wintering waterbirds, Black-bellied Plovers, and Black Turn-stones. The trails here are easy and are sometimes productive for eagles and forest birds. From the parking lot, hike up **Young Hill**. Douglas Maple—a dry-site species—thrives here and elsewhere on the islands, where it replaces the ubiquitous Vine Maple of the damper mainland. The view from the 650-foot hilltop offers the overall essence of the San Juans: grassy hills and oak forest, narrow channels and quiet bays, with the immensity of Vancouver Is-land in the distance.

Turn left from English Camp and continue north on West Valley Road, which ends in 1.3 miles at Roche Harbor Road. Turn left and continue 2.2 miles to **Roche Harbor Resort** (pronounced *roach,* like the bug), an old company town turned resort in the 1950s. Some of the purest limestone west of the Mississippi was quarried and burned in the kilns here to produce lime. The highly groomed grounds are not highly productive for birding, but the flower gardens are beautiful and are a good place for hummingbirds. It is fun to walk the docks where you may see all sorts of boats, from old wooden classics to the latest in ostentatious pleasure vessels. The bay has all three cormo-rants, Bald Eagles, and Pigeon Guillemots. Walk trails through the fairly young second-growth forest around the periphery of the resort to look for flycatch-ers, vireos, thrushes, warblers, and the Cooper's Hawks that chase them. Turning back, it is 10 miles to Friday Harbor via Roche Harbor Road (becomes Tucker Avenue in town), passing by more forests, fields, lakes, and wetlands. Finding a safe place to stop is difficult, but keep an eye out for any of the spe-cies that might be found in these habitats.

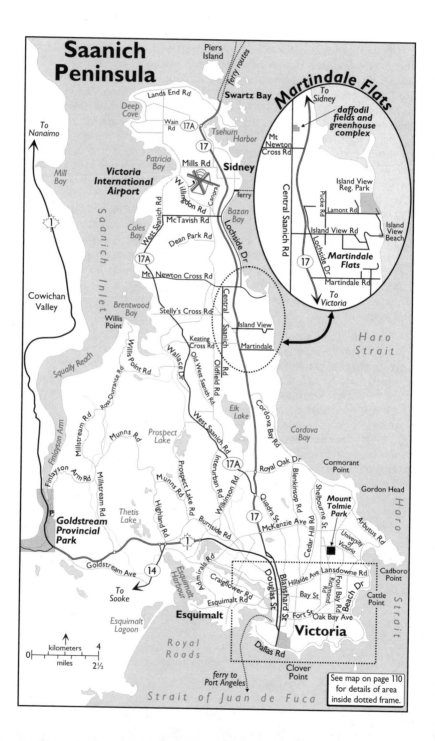

Saanich Peninsula

Piers Island

To Nanaimo

Ferry routes

Lands End Rd

Deep Cove

Swartz Bay

Martindale Flats

To Sidney

daffodil fields and greenhouse complex

Wain Rd

17A

17

Tsehum Harbor

Mills Rd

Sidney

Mt Newton Cross Rd

Patricia Bay

Victoria International Airport

W Willingdon Rd

Canora Rd

ferry

Bazan Bay

Central Saanich Rd

Island View Reg. Park

Pucke Rd

Lamont Rd

Mill Bay

Coles Bay

McTavish Rd

Dean Park Rd

Lochside Dr

West Saanich Rd

Island View Rd

Island View Beach

17A

Mt Newton Cross Rd

Lochside Dr

Martindale Flats

Saanich Inlet

Brentwood Bay

Stelly's Cross Rd

Central Saanich Rd

Island View

17

Martindale Rd

Willis Point

Keating Cross Rd

Martindale

To Victoria

Cowichan Valley

1

Wallace Dr

Old West Saanich Rd

Oldfield Rd

Haro Strait

Squally Reach

Willis Point Rd

Ross-Durrance Rd

West Saanich Rd

Elk Lake

Cordova Bay Rd

Finlayson Arm

Millstream Rd

Munns Rd

Prospect Lake

17A

Royal Oak Dr

Cordova Bay

Cormorant Point

Finlayson Arm Rd

Millstream Rd

Munns Rd

Prospect Lake Rd

Interurban Rd

Wilkinson Rd

Quadra St

Blenkinsop Rd

Shelbourne St

Mount Tolmie Park

Gordon Head

Arbutus Rd

Haro

P

Goldstream Provincial Park

Thetis Lake

Highland Rd

Burnside Rd

17

McKenzie Ave

Cedar Hill Rd

University of Victoria

Goldstream Ave

14

1

Admirals Rd

Craigflower Rd

Douglas St

Blanshard St

Lansdowne Rd

Hillside Ave

Foul Bay Rd

Richmond Rd

Beach Dr

Cadboro Point

To Sooke

Esquimalt Harbour

Esquimalt Rd

Bay St

Fort St

Oak Bay Ave

Cattle Point

Esquimalt

Victoria

Strait

Esquimalt Lagoon

Royal Roads

Dallas Rd

Clover Point

ferry to Port Angeles

0 kilometers 4

miles 2½

Strait of Juan de Fuca

See map on page 110 for details of area inside dotted frame.

VICTORIA (BRITISH COLUMBIA) AND VICINITY

by Bryan Gates

*V*ictoria, the capital city of British Columbia, lies within a splendid setting on the Saanich Peninsula at the southeast tip of Vancouver Island and enjoys what many agree is the most pleasant year-round climate in Canada. Its 350,000 residents welcome birders, just as they do the other 3.6 million visitors who arrive each year. Birders often include a trip to Victoria on their Pacific Northwest itinerary. The big lure is the Sky Lark, which can sometimes be found rather quickly, leaving time for a leisurely exploration of this agreeable city and its broad spectrum of land- and seabird possibilities.

Remember that Canada is metric. Speed limits are in kilometers per hour (km/h). As a general guide, 30 km/h equals 20 mph (schools and playgrounds); 50 km/h equals 30 mph (city traffic); 80 km/h equals 50 mph (most highways); and 100 km/h equals 62 mph (some freeways). Drive safely and err on the side of caution.

SKY LARK SITES

The Sky Lark was introduced by English settlers at the beginning of the last century. This drab Eurasian species has a flight song that is anything but drab. It has done well here—a success story as far as exotic introductions are concerned. It has never expanded its range far out of the Greater Victoria area, does not appear to have displaced native birds, and still survives even though much of its preferred farmland habitat has fallen victim to urban expansion. There are three primary sites where this bird is most likely to be found. From south to north, these are the Martindale Flats (the farm fields between Martindale Road and Island View Road in Central Saanich); the nearby daffodil fields on Central Saanich Road; and the Victoria International Airport.

Those who arrive on the ferry *Coho* from Port Angeles (page 37) will disembark and turn left onto Belleville Street in the Inner Harbour, near the Parliament Buildings and the Empress Hotel. (See map on page 110.) Northwestern Crows (so far the only crow confirmed on Vancouver Island) and Glaucous-winged Gulls will be there to greet you. If you are seeking the Sky Lark, drive east four blocks past the Parliament Buildings and the Royal British Columbia Museum (both are worth a visit) to the end of Belleville. Turn left up the hill onto Blanshard Street, which becomes Highway 17. This will take you to all three Sky Lark habitats as well as to the Washington State Ferry terminal at Sidney and the B.C. Ferry terminal at Swartz Bay. Those who arrive on Vancouver Island by ferries from Anacortes (page 95) or Tsawwassen (page 144) can interpret the following directions in reverse.

Stay on Highway 17 north for 11.0 miles from the *Coho* terminal and turn east (right) onto Island View Road. Park at the red Farmers Market at this intersection and explore **Martindale Flats**. Walk east on Island View Road and its side roads, or south on Lochside Drive (the blacktop road at the market) and then east again on Martindale Road. In spring and summer (and occasionally as early as February) Sky Larks can be heard in their dramatic flight song over the fields. Stop and listen, searching high for the source of the song. In fall and winter concentrations of 10 to 40 or more occur here. Getting a close view is not easy, but by walking slowly through weedy, shortgrass or fallow fields, scanning ahead, or watching a singing bird land, you may be lucky. As a bird flushes, listen for its rattling *chir-y-rup* and twitter. Birders are welcome to walk most of the fields of Martindale Flats throughout the year, but are reminded to remain along the edges of planted fields, to leave all gates as they were, to stay away from livestock, and to say hello to the owners and farm workers. Birders and the general public are fortunate to have a good relationship with the landowners in this area.

All of Martindale Flats from south of Martindale Road to north of Island View Road provides excellent year-round birding and has produced choice records, such as Gyrfalcon, both golden-plovers, Upland and Sharp-tailed Sandpipers, Loggerhead Shrike (September), Ash-throated Flycatcher, Tropical Kingbird, Yellow Wagtail (September), and Indigo Bunting. Trumpeter Swans and other waterfowl are abundant through fall and winter. Look for Eurasian Wigeons among the American Wigeons.

To reach the second Sky Lark site—the daffodil fields—continue north on Highway 17 for 1.5 miles and turn west (left) onto Mount Newton Cross Road, then right in 0.2 mile onto **Central Saanich Road**. Stop beyond the large greenhouse complex on the right side (0.8 mile) and walk the fields to the east or west, staying on the edges or on the farm-vehicle lanes between the bulb fields. This area also holds American Pipits and Western Meadowlarks in fall and winter, and has produced September and October sightings of Red-throated Pipits.

Those traveling by air in or out of Victoria may not need a vehicle to see Sky Larks. The shortgrass areas between runways and ramps at the **Victoria International Airport** attract this species, and the airport authority has worked with the Victoria Natural History Society to encourage its nesting. Continue north 2.7 miles on Highway 17 and turn left onto McTavish Road (a right at this intersection, then an immediate left onto Lochside Drive, brings you to the Sidney ferry landing in one mile; north on Highway 17, it is 4.9 miles to the ferry terminal at Swartz Bay). From McTavish Road turn north immediately onto Canora Road. At the fork in 0.2 mile, go left onto Willingdon Road. In 0.8 mile, just before the airport terminal, turn left with Willingdon and pull off as soon as you safely can. Walk along the airport's perimeter fence, on the right. This is probably the easiest place to see a Sky Lark in spring and summer. Watch and listen through the fence; you may find one just a few feet away. Sky Larks are seen less often on the opposite (left) side of Willingdon Road—inspect the fields from any of three access points 200–300 yards apart. Or continue driving the airport perimeter roads (Willingdon on the south and west, Mills on the north). The airport is generally not productive for Sky Larks in late fall and winter, however.

DALLAS ROAD WATERFRONT

Victoria's shoreline along the Strait of Juan de Fuca provides excellent birding. Two blocks east of the *Coho* terminal, turn south onto Douglas Street where you will reach the water in 0.8 mile at a large sign marking *Mile Zero* of the Trans-Canada Highway. Park and walk west along the shoreline path and out onto the **Ogden Point Breakwater** (0.8 mile). Wandering Tattlers may be found here in August–September and less often in May. Rock Sandpiper is rare but possible from October through early May. Check both sides of the breakwater, especially around the pilot-boat docks. Black Turnstone and Surfbird are often here from late July to March, and Black Oystercatcher is present throughout the year. Offshore, search for Pigeon Guillemot and Marbled Murrelet (both year round) and Rhinoceros Auklet (primarily May through September). Flocks of five to 20 or more Ancient Murrelets can be seen crashing into the water from October through January. Red-necked Phalaropes (August to early September), and jaegers and Common Terns (late August to early October), are also seen here. You may get very lucky and see a Red Phalarope, Cassin's Auklet, or Tufted Puffin from the breakwater. Canada's first Kittlitz's Murrelet stayed here from November 1985 to April 1986, and there are records of South Polar Skua (November) and Ivory Gull (February). Through the winter, check all loons—Pacific and Common Loons are almost always here, and Yellow-billed is possible.

Beacon Hill Park is immediately northeast of Mile Zero and includes ponds that usually hold Eurasian Wigeons through fall and winter. Check the ornamental pine trees in winter for Red-breasted Sapsucker. Barred Owls often roost near the band shell or in the thickets between Dallas Road and the water. This park and the adjacent waterfront have good vagrant potential, and did attract the city's first Sage Sparrow.

Traveling along Dallas Road one mile east from Mile Zero find **Clover Point**, an excellent place to sit and watch the waters of the strait. Most of the species noted for Ogden Point can be expected here, particularly Rock Sandpiper in fall and winter. Search through the Bonaparte's Gulls from July to November for a possible Little or Black-headed Gull, and in the same months watch for a rare appearance of Elegant Tern. A Ross's Gull was seen off Clover Point with Bonaparte's and Mew Gulls in October and November 1966, and there is a March record of Slaty-backed Gull. Walk around the point to check the rocks for shorebirds (Bar-tailed Godwits have appeared here) and to scan the waters for distant shearwaters, Northern Fulmar, and Fork-tailed Storm-Petrel, September through November. This is the best spot in Victoria

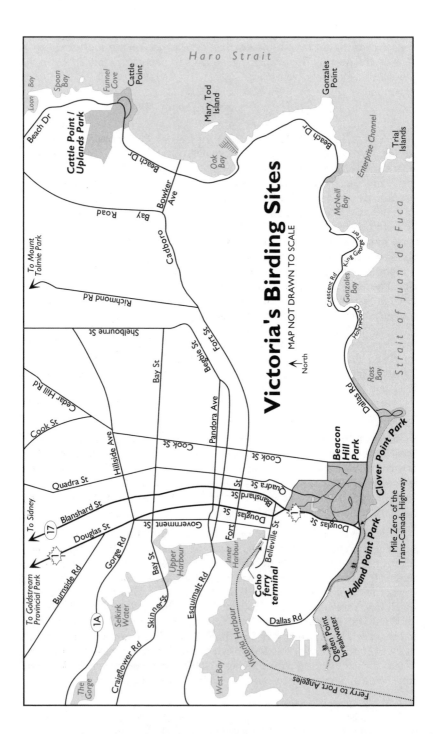

for easy studies of Heermann's (mid-July to late November) and Thayer's (mid-September to March) Gulls.

One can drive the shoreline to the east and north (with several changes of road name), stopping along Beach Drive at the east end of **McNeill Bay** (2.7 miles) to scope the rocks for Rock Sandpiper and Wandering Tattler. Three species of cormorants are often together on the same rock here. In winter scope the open habitat of the closer of the Trial Islands for Bald Eagle, Peregrine Falcon, and in some winters even a Snowy Owl. In another 2.0 miles (past the Oak Bay Marina), turn right onto **Bowker Avenue** and park at the end (one block) to search the rocks in fall for shorebirds, gulls, and terns. Head north once more on Beach Drive to **Cattle Point/Uplands Park** (0.7 mile). Stop at the launching ramps and check the rocks, and walk out beyond the geographical marker in fall and winter for a possible Lapland Longspur or Snow Bunting. A stroll inland through this oak-forested park will produce songbirds.

MOUNT TOLMIE PARK

A spring (April–early June) migrant songbird trap, Mount Tolmie lies just southwest of the University of Victoria. (See map on page 106.) From Mile Zero, drive north on Douglas Street, east on Fort Street, north on Richmond Road, and east on Mayfair Drive to the park lookout (4.5 miles). Walk the trails, especially on the north and east slopes, watching for fallouts of mixed songbirds. Black-throated Gray, Townsend's, and MacGillivray's Warblers should appear, as should Western Wood-Pewee, Pacific-slope Flycatcher, Cassin's Vireo, Western Tanager, Golden-crowned Sparrow, and Black-headed Grosbeak. Band-tailed Pigeon, Townsend's Solitaire, Lazuli Bunting, and Bullock's Oriole usually show up each spring, and Vaux's Swift may pass over. Unusual sightings have included Lark and Black-throated Sparrows, Smith's Longspur, and Indigo Bunting. Present year round are Anna's Hummingbird, Chestnut-backed Chickadee, Bushtit, and Spotted Towhee.

GOLDSTREAM PROVINCIAL PARK

If you arrive between late October and mid-January, visit Goldstream Provincial Park. (See map on page 106.) Take Douglas Street north from Mile Zero and follow the Trans-Canada Highway (Highway 1) north and west through the city and suburbs for 13.3 miles, past the campground, to a parking area off the right side of the highway beside the Goldstream River. A major spawning run of Chum Salmon, with a few Coho and Chinook Salmon mixed in, will be in the river and will have attracted hundreds of gulls, perhaps 200 Bald Eagles, and mixed waterfowl. Look for a Glaucous Gull among the birds scavenging salmon carcasses, and test your skills at identifying the various age classes of Mew, Glaucous-winged, and possibly Thayer's, Herring, and Western Gulls. American Dippers will be dipping under for salmon eggs, and in the ancient, streamside forest you will find woodpeckers (including possibly a Red-breasted Sapsucker), Brown Creeper, wrens, kinglets, and Varied Thrush. An excellent nature house located a few hundred yards downstream maintains feeders for hummingbirds, sparrows, and finches, while Common and Barrow's Goldeneyes will be among the many ducks and mergansers on the estuary. Check with the park naturalists to see if a Western Screech-Owl, Northern Pygmy-Owl, or other owls are present. Western Screech-Owl numbers continue to decline on Vancouver Island, presumably as a result of the fairly recent appearance and build-up of Barred Owl. While here, take time to enjoy the magnificent Western Redcedars in this wet, old-growth forest, and to watch the interactions between the spawning salmon and the many birds seasonally dependent on this abundant food source.

SKAGIT FLATS

by Bob Kuntz

The Skagit Flats and the adjacent Samish Flats (page 117) form a floodplain where fertile soil and ample rainfall provide for a thriving farming industry. Potatoes, carrots, corn, winter wheat, barley, and a variety of other vegetables and grains grow bountifully. These farms are one of the world's largest producers of vegetable seeds and flower bulbs. A wide variety of habitats, mild temperatures, and a profusion of food make this area home to nearly 300 resident and migrant bird species. Although birding is interesting all year, the best seasons are during spring (mid-March through May) and fall (mid-July through September) migrations and particularly winter (November through mid-March) when hundreds of thousands of swans, geese, ducks, and shorebirds can be found. The abundant waterfowl, small mammals, and salmon (spawning in the Skagit and Samish Rivers and their tributaries) attract raptors. Fifteen species of eagles, hawks, and falcons, and 13 species of owls, have been documented in the area—most of them annually.

FIR ISLAND

Bounded by the North and South Forks of the Skagit River and ringed by dikes, low-lying Fir Island is the heart of the Skagit delta. From I-5 Exit 221 (Conway/La Conner), go west about 0.2 mile to the intersection of Pioneer Highway and Fir Island Road in Conway, and turn right onto Fir Island Road. A bridge in 0.5 mile crosses the South Fork onto the island. In winter, several hundred Trumpeter and Tundra Swans can usually be seen somewhere along the five-mile length of Fir Island Road between the South and North Fork bridges. This is a busy road, and the swans are a popular attraction, so be sure to pull completely off the roadway. Birders have been ticketed for blocking traffic and causing a road hazard. If you do not find the swans, try driving some of the other roads on Fir Island, particularly Moore, Polson, and Skagit City Roads. Fir Island and neighboring areas are also the winter home of 20,000 or more Snow Geese. The near-totality of a distinct nesting population of this species, from Wrangel Island in the northeastern Russian Arctic, winters on the Fraser and Skagit–Stillaguamish River deltas. On Fir Island, they may be seen foraging in the farm fields from late fall through April. The best viewing areas are along Fir Island Road, particularly at the Fir Island Farm/Hayton Reserve and at the Snow Goose Produce Market. Fir Island is not a bad place to find Harlan's Hawk or even Gyrfalcon. Wetlands, brushy edges, and woodlots attract many other birds, including rarities, with one record each for Jack Snipe and Magnolia Warbler (September), Yellow Rail and Vermilion Flycatcher (November), and Rusty Blackbird (December).

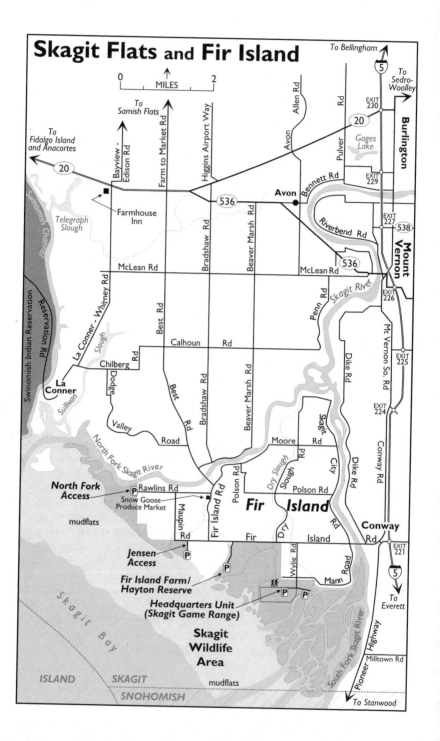

Skagit Flats and Fir Island

SKAGIT GAME RANGE

The Skagit Wildlife Area, a 12,000-acre marsh, tideland, and estuarine pre-serve, offers several access points for viewing Skagit specialties. After crossing the South Fork from Conway, continue 1.3 miles along Fir Island Road and turn left (south) onto Wylie Road. In late fall and winter check for gulls, espe-cially when farm fields have recently been plowed. Among the common Mew, Ring-billed, and Glaucous-winged Gulls you may find the occasional California or Western, and Glaucous Gull has been sighted here. In about a mile from Fir Island Road you come to the wildlife area's Headquarters Unit, locally known as the Skagit Game Range (WDFW permit required to park). From a fork just inside the boundary (check the treetops for a Merlin) the right branch leads to the office (no visitor center), main parking area, and usually very unclean toi-lets; the left branch goes to a boat launch and a second parking area with even worse toilets.

The Game Range consists of a series of dikes, fields, and marshes inten-sively managed for waterfowl and upland gamebirds. A two-mile loop trail fol-lows the dikes from both parking areas, weaving through hedgerows, deciduous forests (mostly mature alder, birch, and cottonwood), fresh- and saltwater marshes, and farm fields. In March, when the Red-flowering Currant and Salmonberry blossom, Rufous Hummingbirds return and set up territo-ries over the densest patches of bloom. In April, Greater and Lesser Yellow-legs, Western and Least Sandpipers, Dunlins, and both dowitchers are com-mon in the wet fields. Solitary, Semipalmated, and Baird's (fall) Sandpipers are seen annually. Yellow-rumped Warblers return in late March; Myrtle may be as common as Audubon's through April. May is an excellent month for mi-grants and residents. Look for American Bittern, Green Heron, Wood Duck, Cinnamon Teal, Virginia Rail, Sora, Band-tailed Pigeon, Bushtit, Swainson's Thrush, and several species of warblers and sparrows. The Game Range is great for migrant *Empidonax* flycatchers—mostly Willow and Pacific-slope, but Least, Hammond's, and Dusky are also possible. Fall passerine migration (mid-August to mid-September) is as good as anywhere in Western Washing-ton. A dozen species of sparrows can be seen in winter: Spotted Towhee, American Tree (uncommon), Savannah, Sooty Fox, Song, Lincoln's, Swamp (uncommon to rare), White-throated (uncommon), Harris's (rare), White-crowned, Golden-crowned, and Oregon Dark-eyed Junco (Slate-colored is uncommon). The best place to look for them is in the hedgerow adjacent to the boat-launch parking area and the first field to the south. Green-tailed To-whee has been recorded here, and Northern Waterthrush has been seen in fall and winter almost annually for the past several years along the slough to the east of this parking area.

TIDELANDS ACCESS POINTS

Return to Fir Island Road, turn left (west), and go 1.5 miles to a public access road on the left. Turn off, park along the road edge, walk back to Fir Island Road, and continue left (west) less than 0.1 mile to a wetland on the south side of the road. Here you can view a Black-crowned Night-Heron day roost that has been active during winter for many years. There are usually a half-dozen or more birds at this site. Return to your car and drive south down the gravel road less than a half-mile to a parking area for the new **Fir Island Farm/Hayton Reserve**, a unit of the Skagit Wildlife Area (WDFW permit required to park). In the near future, a platform is planned for visitors to view the wintering Snow Geese. A dike separates farm fields from salt marsh. Check the fields for Black-bellied Plover, American and Pacific Golden-Plovers (both rare), and the same assortment of sandpipers as can be seen at the Skagit Game Range.

Return to Fir Island Road and go left (west) for another 0.5 mile to where it makes a 90-degree right turn. Jog left here onto Maupin Road. Continue west 0.5 mile and turn left onto a gravel road leading to the **Jensen Access** of the Skagit Wildlife Area. Fields at this intersection, and along the access road, are excellent for shorebirds and American Pipits in spring (April–May) and fall (mid-July through September). Park by the dike at the end of the road (WDFW permit required), from which one can access the dike and salt marsh to the south. Among other species of shorebirds, Pectoral, Sharp-tailed (rare), and Stilt (uncommon to rare) Sandpipers have been seen in the marsh. Optimal viewing is on an incoming or receding high tide. Otherwise, the exposed mudflats are extensive and birds can be a long way from the dike. Check the large driftwood for perched raptors (Bald Eagle, Northern Harrier, Merlin, Peregrine Falcon). Exercise caution if venturing into the marsh. The mud is deep and hazardous in places.

Back on Maupin Road, turn left and continue west and north for 1.3 miles to Rawlins Road. Turn left again and drive one mile to a dead end at a dike. Park along the edge of the road, making sure not to block other cars from leaving. You are now at the **North Fork Access**. This is an excellent place to look for Short-eared Owl (at dusk). Turn back, go 1.7 miles east to Fir Island Road, and turn right. Park at a pullout on the left in 0.1 mile, across from the **Snow Goose Produce Market**. Fields to the east often hold thousands of foraging Snow Geese and several hundred Trumpeter and Tundra Swans.

NORTHERN AND EASTERN FLATS

Swans, Snow Geese, and other waterfowl also winter in agricultural fields on the Skagit Flats north of Fir Island, as do many raptors, including Snowy Owls during flight years. From the produce market, turn back north and go 0.4 mile on Fir Island Road to the intersection with Best Road, on the left. Turn here and continue over the North Fork bridge for 4.5 miles to a traffic light at the intersection with McLean Road. Bird the flats from a grid of roads east to Mount Vernon, north to SR-20, and west to La Conner and the Swinomish Channel. In April, enjoy the tulip fields with Mount Baker and the Cascades Range in the background. Turning left (west) from Best Road onto McLean Road, then right onto La Conner-Whitney Road (1.3 miles), brings you to the Farmhouse Inn and a Texaco station at the SR-20 intersection (1.8 miles). It is about six miles east on SR-20 to I-5 at Exit 230. Or you may turn west on SR-20 toward Fidalgo Island and Anacortes (page 91). Crossing over SR-20 and continuing north will bring you to the Samish Flats.

SAMISH FLATS

by Bob Kuntz

The Samish Flats are one of the best locations in the state for winter raptor viewing. A dozen or more diurnal raptor species are recorded annually, the most common being Bald Eagle, Red-tailed Hawk (including Harlan's), Rough-legged Hawk (dark and light morphs), and Northern Harrier. Five falcon species occur here almost every winter (American Kestrel, Merlin, Gyrfalcon, Peregrine Falcon, and Prairie Falcon)—but just try finding all five on a single outing! Ten species of owls have been observed on the flats or in the adjacent forested foothills, including Barn, Great Horned, Barred, Great Gray (winter; rare), Long-eared (rare), Short-eared, and Northern Saw-whet. Snowy Owls can be common in a good flight year. Abundant winter rains form ephemeral pools in fallow fields, attracting shorebirds, Trumpeter and Tundra Swans, and 25 other species of waterfowl. Washington Department of Fish and Wildlife's "Barley for Birds" program provides food for thousands of ducks. Corn, potatoes, and carrots left from fall harvest also provide resources for waterfowl.

The area is intensively covered by birders, so it is no surprise that many unusual records have occurred here, including Falcated and Tufted Ducks, Iceland Gull, Tropical Kingbird, Clay-colored Sparrow, Rusty Blackbird, Orchard Oriole, and a Brambling in Sedro-Woolley. More records of Cattle Egret (fall–early winter) come from the Samish Flats than from any other Western Washington locality. In fall 1999 a Eurasian Kestrel hung out for a time near Blanchard, and a few ecstatic birders scored a six-falcon day.

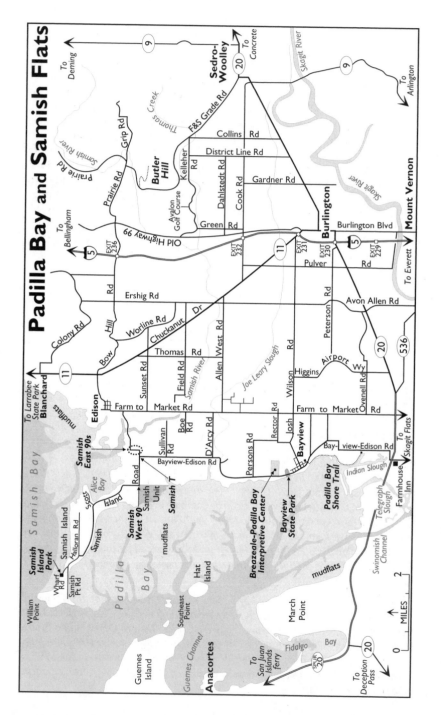

The best way to bird the Samish Flats is to drive all the roads, looking for shallow pools with flocks of foraging or roosting birds, and checking fenceposts, power poles, the ground, and other perches for raptors. Several locations that seem to draw the birds more consistently, and that are on public property or provide adequate parking, are singled out below. Please make sure to pull your vehicle completely off the road when stopping, and observe private-property signs. Local residents are generally well-disposed toward birders. Good manners will further this rapport.

PADILLA BAY

The Samish Flats may be accessed directly from I-5 Exits 231 (Chuckanut Drive) or 232 (Cook Road), north of Burlington. However, if you are also visiting the Skagit Flats, as most birders do, a convenient connection is from SR-20 at the Farmhouse Inn corner (see page 117). At the traffic light there go north across SR-20 and a railroad track and jog right, then left, onto Bayview-Edison Road. The south end of the **Padilla Bay Shore Trail** is on the left (west) in 0.9 mile (limited parking). The trail follows a dike northwestward along Little Indian Slough and the southeast shore of Padilla Bay to the north trailhead (to park here, turn north from Bayview-Edison Road onto Second Street and go 0.1 mile north). The 2.1-mile walk (one way) can be productive for waterfowl and shorebirds in migration and winter. The road distance between trailheads is also 2.1 miles.

Continue north on Bayview-Edison Road, respecting the speed limit through the town of Bayview, to the entrance to **Bayview State Park** (0.6 mile). Turn off right, then go immediately left and under the road to a beach and picnic area along the east shore of Padilla Bay. In winter, this is an excellent place to study Gray-bellied Brant, a form that nests on Melville Island in the Canadian High Arctic. The near-totality of the world population, estimated at perhaps 8,000 birds, winters on the rich eelgrass beds of Padilla and Samish Bays and the Fraser River delta; many come near shore here to preen and forage. Go back through the underpass and check the camping loop for lowland forest birds such as Band-tailed Pigeon, Barred Owl, Hutton's Vireo, Steller's Jay, Chestnut-backed Chickadee, Bewick's Wren, Spotted Towhee, and Red Crossbill.

Travel north another half-mile on Bayview-Edison Road and turn right into the visitors' entrance of the **Padilla Bay National Estuarine Research Reserve** (360-428-1558). The 64-acre site provides a hiking trail through upland and forested habitats and a viewing platform overlooking Padilla Bay. Birds are similar to those found at Bayview State Park. The Breazeale Visitor Center, open 10AM to 5PM Wednesday through Sunday, has excellent interactive exhibits describing the estuary and its aquatic and terrestrial wildlife resources.

WEST 90 AND SAMISH ISLAND

The Samish Flats begin about two miles farther north, where Bay-view-Edison Road meets D'Arcy Road. Continue north past D'Arcy Road for 2.1 miles to the spot known to birders as the **Samish T**, where Bay-view-Edison Road turns right. Go left (west) here onto Samish Island Road, which provides excellent birding. Scan the power poles in winter for falcons (Gyr, Peregrine, Prairie). At dusk, look for Short-eared Owls. At 0.7 mile, where the road makes a right-angle turn to the right, is the recently acquired Samish Unit of the Skagit Wildlife Area, long known to birders as the **Samish West 90** (WDFW permit required to park). In the fields southwest of this corner, state wildlife managers have created a series of shallow ponds that show great promise for waterfowl and shorebirds. Walk west along the field edge, then south along a dike that provides views of some of the ponds and of Padilla Bay. From the West 90, continue north on Samish Island Road. There are several places to pull off and walk up onto the dike on the right side to look over **Alice Bay**, one of the last corners of Samish Bay to fill at high tide. The hour before and after high tide is the best time to visit. At high slack tide, most birds roost or forage in the nearby farm fields. Black-bellied Plover and Dunlin are abundant in winter; Western, Least, Baird's (rare), and Pectoral (rare) Sandpipers have all been seen during fall migration. Look for Semipalmated Plover in Alice Bay. An American Kestrel can often be found on the power lines or a fencepost. Eurasian Wigeons reach their highest density in the contiguous United States in the fields to the west, between Alice Bay and Padilla Bay, where some American Wigeon flocks contain five percent or more of this species.

An intersection with Scott Road is at 1.5 miles from the West 90. You are now on **Samish Island**. Turn right onto Scott Road and park in the church lot, on the left. The field to the west of the church has been productive for sparrows and other songbirds. Great Blue Herons fly back and forth between the bay and a rookery on the hill to the north. Check the treetops for a Merlin, particularly across the street from the church. Go back to Samish Island Road, turn right, travel 1.8 miles, and turn left onto Halloran Road, which becomes Samish Point Road. In another 0.6 mile, turn right onto Wharf Road. Samish Island Park is 0.2 mile ahead. This small park overlooking Samish Bay is excellent for viewing Red-throated, Pacific, Common, and Yellow-billed (rare) Loons; Horned, Red-necked, Eared (uncommon), and Western Grebes; Brant, Harlequin Duck, all three scoters (Black is rare), Long-tailed Duck, and Red-breasted Merganser; and several species of alcids (Pigeon Guillemot and Marbled Murrelet are the most common).

FARM TO MARKET ROAD

Return to the Samish T and go east (straight ahead) on Bayview-Edison Road. A right-angle turn to the left in 0.3 mile, followed by another to the right in 0.3 mile, have been dubbed the **Samish East 90s** by birders. This is another good place to look for Gyrfalcon, Peregrine Falcon, and Prairie Falcon. A further 0.6 mile brings you to the Samish River bridge. Cross, park on the left, and check the slough and adjacent fields on both sides of the road. In irruption years, this is a good location for Snowy Owl. Greater White-fronted Geese can sometimes be seen to the south in April.

The intersection with **Farm to Market Road** is 0.5 mile farther east along Bayview-Edison Road. Turn right (south) here. The next three miles offer unobstructed views of the flats on both sides. Be extra cautious when you stop; this is a busy road. Also drive the first two side roads to the east—Sunset Road (0.7 mile) and Field Road (0.7 mile)—over to Thomas Road, about a mile and a half east. In recent winters this rectangle has been the most dependable place on the flats to find a Gyrfalcon, sitting on one of the posts in the middle of the fields or on a large dirt clod along a field edge. A good vantage point is the spot where Field Road makes a right-angle jog to the south. **Chuckanut Drive** (SR-11), though heavily traveled, goes through fields where swans can usually be seen. You will reach this road in a mile or less by continuing east across Thomas on either Sunset or Field. From Chuckanut, drive east on Field to Ershig Road (0.5 mile) and turn south to another intersection with Chuckanut (0.9 mile). The triangle formed by these three roads can also be good; check the treetops for raptors.

BUTLER FLAT AND BUTLER HILL

The **Butler Flat** area, isolated from the rest of the flats by the unnatural barrier of I-5, is too often neglected by birders. Many raptors (including Gyrfalcon) winter here in fields along both sides of Cook Road, and side roads, from the freeway east to Sedro-Woolley. This is also an excellent place to look for Trumpeter and Tundra Swans from late November through early January when they are foraging in the cut corn fields. From the corner of Ershig, go southeast 0.8 mile on Chuckanut Drive to Cook Road and turn left (east). Cross over I-5 at Exit 232 (1.3 miles). Then turn left from Cook onto Green Road, 0.1 mile after the interchange. Drive north 1.2 miles on Green. When flooded, a marshy field on the right managed by the Skagit Land Trust offers fine waterfowl viewing. In winter, Ring-necked Ducks can be common, and Canvasbacks and Redheads are sometimes present as well. In spring, all three teal species can be found here, as can American Bittern, Virginia Rail, and Sora. The field west of the road may have a winter wigeon flock with several Eurasian Wigeons. At the T-intersection a short distance ahead, turn right onto Kelleher Road. Go 0.4 mile to the entrance to Avalon Golf Course.

Park on the north side of Kelleher where you can pull completely off. From here you can walk a short distance up the golf course entrance road for a closer look at the marsh, or east on Kelleher to bird the hillside and slough edge. About 250 yards east, a lane crosses the ditch to a good vantage point on a dike (beyond the dike, however, the lane is private, so keep out). Black and Vaux's Swifts have been seen here in early May. Alders on the hillside host a good assortment of spring migrants and summer residents, among them Rufous Hummingbird, Warbling Vireo, Bushtit, Swainson's Thrush, Orange-crowned and Wilson's Warblers, Black-headed Grosbeak, and Lazuli Bunting.

Drive east on Kelleher Road to an intersection in 1.9 miles where District Line Road comes in from the right. In late April and early May, migrating Whimbrels stop on Butler Flat to forage for insects in the freshly mowed winter wheat and hay fields. You may find a loose flock with as many as 300 Whimbrels anywhere inside the 0.5-by-1.5-mile rectangle bordered by District Line, Cook, Collins, and Kelleher Roads.

To swell your day list with a bit of woodland birding, continue east along Kelleher Road to F and S Grade Road (0.5 mile). Turn left and drive two miles. Bird the mixed lowland forest along the base of **Butler Hill** for another half-mile, to a gated road on the right, which you can walk up to the top of the hill (elevation 886 feet). These woods are best from spring migration into summer, with the possibility of Pacific-slope Flycatcher, Cassin's (nesting in deciduous woods near the base of the walk-up road), Hutton's, and Warbling Vireos, Steller's Jay, Chestnut-backed Chickadee, Brown Creeper, Bewick's and Winter Wrens, Yellow, Audubon's Yellow-rumped, Black-throated Gray, and Wilson's Warblers, Western Tanager, Spotted Towhee, Golden-crowned Sparrow (April–May), Black-headed Grosbeak, and Purple Finch.

NORTH CASCADES HIGHWAY

by Bob Kuntz

From near sea level on the floodplain farmlands west of Sedro-Woolley, the North Cascades Highway (SR-20) follows the Skagit River eastward for 95 miles, ascending gradually to 5,477-foot Washington Pass. The route traverses several vegetation zones with a diverse and contrasting birdlife. Lower slopes are famous for damp, old-growth forests of Western Hemlock, Western Redcedar, and Douglas-fir that may reach heights of 200 to 300 feet. Broad swaths of luxuriant deciduous growth line the streams. Higher-elevation forests of Silver Fir give way to parklands with stands of Mountain Hemlock. Above treeline is an area of meadows and jagged, glacier-laden peaks that has been called North America's Alps.

The best times to visit are from May through October. During spring, summer, and fall, some of the many species to be found along the way are Barrow's Goldeneye, Golden Eagle, Blue Grouse, Northern Pygmy-Owl, Black and Vaux's Swifts, Hammond's Flycatcher, Cassin's and Red-eyed Vireos, Gray Jay, Clark's Nutcracker, American Dipper, Mountain Bluebird, Townsend's Solitaire, Black-throated Gray, Townsend's, and MacGillivray's Warblers, American Redstart, Slate-colored Fox and Lincoln's Sparrows, Lazuli Bunting, Gray-crowned Rosy-Finch, Pine Grosbeak, and Red and White-winged (irregular) Crossbills. In most years the highway closes around the first of December and does not reopen until April. However, it is open year round below Newhalem. From mid-December through January, when Chum and Coho Salmon are spawning, the Skagit River between Rockport and Newhalem provides food and shelter to 300–500 Bald Eagles.

No gasoline or other services are available between Marblemount and Mazama, approximately 70 miles. For much of the itinerary described here the highway corridor passes through the North Cascades National Park. Park information is available on-line at www.nps.gov/noca. For updates on camping reservations, backcountry travel, and road closures, call 360-856-5700 or stop by any of several visitor centers and ranger stations along the route.

SEDRO-WOOLLEY TO MARBLEMOUNT

A stop at the National Park Service/U.S. Forest Service office in Sedro-Woolley to pick up maps and a North Cascades National Park bird checklist is an excellent way to begin your trip. From I-5 Exit 232 north of Burlington, follow Cook Road east 4.4 miles to its intersection with SR-20 (North Cascades Highway). Turn left, and proceed 1.1 miles to the intersection with northbound SR-9. The office is on the left just before this intersection (open 8AM to 4:30PM Monday through Friday year round, and Saturday and Sunday from Memorial Day weekend through Columbus Day).

Continue east for 9.2 miles on SR-20 and turn right onto Hamilton Cemetery Road (0.2 mile past milepost 75). At the stop sign in 0.2 mile, continue

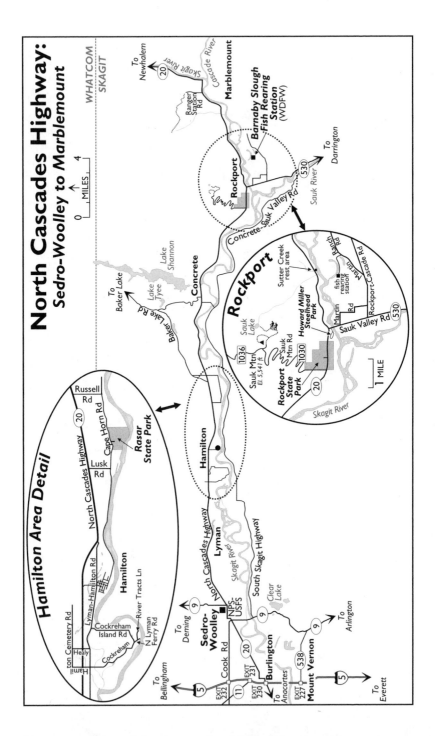

North Cascades Highway:
Sedro-Woolley to Marblemount

Hamilton Area Detail

Rockport

0 — MILES — 4

WHATCOM
SKAGIT

To Newhalem

Skagit River

Cascade River

Marblemount

Ranger Station Rd

Barnaby Slough Fish Rearing Station (WDFW)

Rockport

To Darrington

530

Sauk River

Concrete-Sauk Valley Rd

To Baker Lake

Lake Shannon

Lake Tyee

Baker Lake Rd

Concrete

Sutter Creek rest area

Martin Ranch Rd

fish rearing station

Martin Rd

Rockport-Cascade Rd

Sauk Valley Rd

530

Sauk Lake

Howard Miller Steelhead Park

1036

Sauk Mtn El 5,541 ft

Sauk Mtn Rd

Rockport State Park

1030

20

1 MILE

Skagit River

Russell Rd

Cape Horn Rd

North Cascades Highway 20

Rasar State Park

Lusk Rd

Hamilton

Hamilton Cemetery Rd

Lyman-Hamilton Rd

Hamilton

River Tracts Ln

N Lyman Ferry Rd

Cockreham Island Rd

Cockreham

Healy

Hamil

North Cascades Highway

Lyman

Skagit River

South Skagit Highway

Clear Lake

To Deming

9

Sedro-Woolley

NPS-USFS

20

Cook Rd

9

Burlington

9

To Arlington

538

Mount Vernon

To Bellingham

5

EXIT 232

11

EXIT 231

EXIT 230

To Anacortes

EXIT 227

5

To Everett

straight for another 0.7 mile (you are now on **Cockreham Road**) and check the farm pond on the right for shorebirds in spring. In another 0.9 mile, turn right onto N Lyman Ferry Road. Park at the boat launch in 0.2 mile and walk back to the intersection with River Tracts Lane, birding the deciduous forest for Red-breasted Sapsucker, Hammond's Flycatcher, Red-eyed Vireo, and Bullock's Oriole. Return to Cockreham Road and turn right. A pond on your right in 0.2 mile can have waterfowl, shorebirds, and swallows. In another 0.2 mile Cockreham Road makes a 90-degree left turn, becoming Cockreham Island Road. A pair of Western Kingbirds has nested on a power-line transformer at this corner for the past several years. In 1.1 miles, turn left onto Lyman-Hamilton Road, then right onto Healy Road in another 0.6 mile, and finally right (east) onto SR-20 in 0.2 mile.

Travel 5.2 miles (0.8 mile past milepost 80) and turn right onto Lusk Road. In 0.7 mile, turn left onto Cape Horn Road, then right in 0.8 mile into the **Rasar State Park** entrance. This 128-acre park, situated on the north bank of the Skagit River in a mixed-forest habitat, is best visited from May through September. Look for Ruffed Grouse, Barred Owl, Red-breasted Sapsucker, Downy and Hairy Woodpeckers, and resident/migrant passerines, including Pacific-slope Flycatcher and Cassin's Vireo. Turn right onto Cape Horn Road for 1.3 miles, then left (north) onto Russell Road to return to SR-20 in 0.8 mile.

The town of Concrete is about six miles farther east along SR-20. Be careful; this is a notorious speed trap. In another mile, east of Concrete where power lines cross the Skagit River (0.8 mile past milepost 89), note the Osprey nest-platform on the south side (birds present mid-April through mid-September). Continue east for 6.3 miles and turn left onto **Sauk Mountain Road** (FR-1030), an improved gravel road that winds upward to the Sauk Mountain Trailhead. At 1.6 miles, park at a gated logging landing and check the brushy hillside for Rufous Hummingbird, MacGillivray's Warbler, and Black-headed Grosbeak. In 1.4 miles, at the three-mile post, stop to look for Townsend's Warbler. In 4.5 miles turn right onto FR-1036. In May and June, the last stretch of road to the trailhead (0.3 mile) is a good place to look for Gray Jay and Slate-colored Fox Sparrow. The 2.1-mile trail leads to alpine meadows on Sauk Mountain (summit 5,541 feet, elevation gain 1,040 feet). Watch for Blue Grouse, Olive-sided Flycatcher, Hermit Thrush, and several species of warblers, sparrows, and finches. In July, the wildflower display is spectacular on these slopes.

Return to SR-20, turn left, and go 0.5 mile to **Rockport State Park**, on the left (open 1 April to 15 November). Hike any of the five miles of trails through the park's ancient Douglas-fir forest to see or hear Blue Grouse, Band-tailed Pigeon, Barred Owl, Vaux's Swift, Pileated Woodpecker, Pacific-slope Flycatcher, Steller's Jay, Chestnut-backed Chickadee, Brown Creeper, Winter Wren, Golden-crowned Kinglet, Swainson's and Varied Thrushes, Townsend's Warbler, Western Tanager, and Spotted Towhee.

Continue east on SR-20 for 1.1 miles and turn right onto SR-530 (Sauk Valley Road). The entrance to **Howard Miller Steelhead Park**, along the north bank of the Skagit River, is on the right in 0.2 mile. You may find Ruffed Grouse (drumming in spring), Band-tailed Pigeon, and Vaux's and possibly Black Swifts flying overhead. Cross the Skagit River on the SR-530 bridge and turn left onto **Martin Road** (0.3 mile from the park). At 0.2 mile is a small wetland with Willow Flycatchers, Warbling and Red-eyed Vireos, and an assortment of warblers, sparrows, and finches in spring and summer. A public river access 0.2 mile farther along Martin Road offers similar species. In the shrubby areas beside the road, look for Western and Eastern Kingbirds and Lazuli Bunting. Rarities are possible: Sage Thrasher and Yellow-breasted Chat have been found here. At a T-intersection in 1.3 miles, turn left onto Rockport-Cascade Road, then left again in 0.9 mile onto Martin Ranch Road. In 1.2 miles, turn left onto Barnaby Slough Road (gravel) and drive a quarter-mile to a building and an interpretive display. Park out of the way and walk left down a road to the **Barnaby Slough Fish Rearing Station** (WDFW) through a mosaic of habitats that provides excellent spring and summer birding (keep out November–February when the area is closed to provide sanctuary for waterfowl). In addition to the usual lowland forest birds, the area has been good for vagrants, including Chestnut-sided and Black-and-white Warblers (June).

Retrace your route to SR-20 and turn right. **Sutter Creek Rest Area**, on the right in 2.4 miles (at milepost 100), is a great place to watch wintering Bald Eagles close-up (best before 10AM when they are foraging and interacting). The meadows between 2.5 and 3.0 miles farther east at **Corkindale Creek** often swarm with swallows (six species possible and the best place in Skagit County to find Bank Swallow). Watch also for Willow Flycatcher, Western and Eastern Kingbirds (rare but annual), Lazuli Bunting, and Bullock's Oriole.

Just over two miles from Corkindale Creek, turn left onto Ranger Station Road and continue 0.5 mile to the intersection with **Powerline Road**. Check along this road for a quarter-mile in both directions. Eastern Kingbird and Lazuli Bunting are dependable here. Ranger Station Road ends in 0.3 mile at the National Park Service's Backcountry Information Office. Return to SR-20 and turn left (east) toward Marblemount.

CASCADE RIVER TO WASHINGTON PASS

A side trip up the **Cascade River Road** to the Hidden Lake and Cascade Pass trailheads offers good birding in summer and fall, and magnificent scenery. Allow one full day for this trip. Note that the last few miles of the road are usually not clear of snow until the beginning of July. In Marblemount, where SR-20 makes a 90-degree turn to the left (north), stay straight onto Cascade River Road across the Skagit River bridge. As you drive the 23-mile road to the parking area at Cascade Pass Trailhead, watch for Barred Owl, Common

Nighthawk, Red-breasted Sapsucker, Black-throated Gray Warbler, Varied Thrush, and other lowland forest species. Views from the trailhead are breathtaking. You are in a U-shaped trough, glacially over-deepened, with steep valley walls, waterfalls, swift streams, and avalanche chutes grown to Sitka Alder thickets; similar terrain stretches north through the Coast Mountains of British Columbia and Southeast Alaska. Listen for the roar of falling ice as you view a series of hanging glaciers on Johannesburg Mountain.

Cascade Pass Trail winds along a series of switchbacks to Cascade Pass, a 3.7-mile hike that gains about 1,800 feet to an elevation of 5,392 feet. In summer near the trailhead you may find Blue Grouse, Black and Vaux's Swifts, Olive-sided Flycatcher, Hermit Thrush, Yellow, Yellow-rumped, Townsend's, MacGillivray's, and Wilson's Warblers, and Slate-colored Fox Sparrow. At the pass, look for Clark's Nutcracker, as well as Hoary Marmot and Pika. To reach the alpine zone, cross the pass and continue down the other side for about 100 yards. Here the rough **Sahale Arm Trail** branches off to the left and goes north for about a mile and a half, following the ridgeline that marks the Cascade crest (Columbia River drainage to the east, Skagit River to the west). The first mile is steep and rocky. The trail becomes more gentle upon reaching Sahale Arm, a widening of the ridge, beginning at 6,300 feet elevation and ending at about 7,000 feet. "Sky gardens" along the way have many colorful wildflowers; Blue Grouse are common in this habitat. Look for White-tailed Ptarmigan, American Pipit, and Gray-crowned Rosy-Finch on the broad, heather-covered slopes of Sahale Arm.

Another good place for Gray-crowned Rosy-Finch (and spectacular scenery) is **Sibley Pass**, reached by turning east from Cascade River Road onto Sibley Creek Road (FR-1540) about ten miles above Marblemount (13-plus miles if coming down from Cascade Pass, on the right). Drive another 4.5 miles to the trailhead. Take the Hidden Lake Peak Trail, which for the first mile climbs through forest and then breaks out into the meadows of Sibley Creek basin. The saddle to the east is Sibley Pass. Take the switchbacks for about another mile until you reach an area where the trail straightens, traversing along a series of meadows and talus slopes. Leave the trail here and make your way a final mile up to the pass. In September, several hundred Gray-crowned Rosy-Finches have been observed foraging along the steep cliffs. Be watchful for Golden Eagle.

Six miles northeast of Marblemount, SR-20 enters the North Cascades National Park Service Complex. In about four more miles, look for the Whatcom County line sign (0.5 mile east of milepost 116). Park here, taking care not to block the gate, and walk south to the **Skagit/Whatcom County Line Ponds** and access to the Skagit River. This attractive riparian area consists of a mixture of deciduous (mostly Black Cottonwood and Red Alder) and conifer forest. In late spring and summer, Hammond's and Pacific-slope Flycatchers, Red-eyed Vireo, Swainson's Thrush, and Yellow-rumped, Townsend's, and Black-throated Gray Warblers can be heard and seen. American

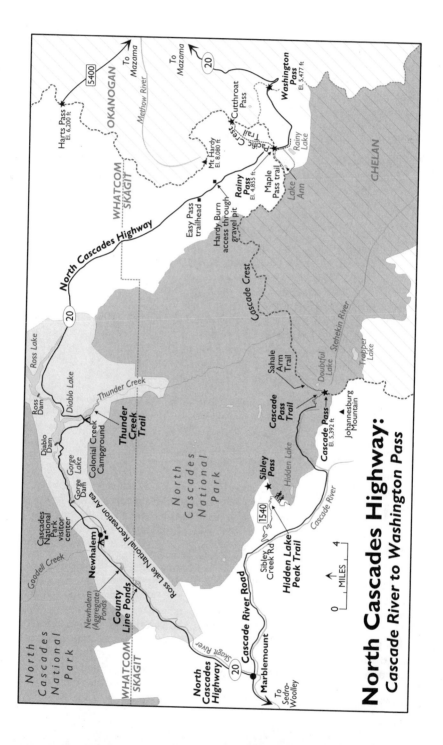

North Cascades Highway:
Cascade River to Washington Pass

Redstarts nest here—their only confirmed breeding site in Western Washington. In winter, Bald Eagles congregate along the river and ponds to feed on salmon that have spawned and are dying. Check the ponds for Hooded Mergansers and other waterfowl. This is a good place to compare Common and Barrow's Goldeneyes. American Dippers can be seen swimming under water, plucking salmon eggs off the bottom of the pond and bobbing to the surface to swallow them, then submerging again to repeat the process.

Drive another 1.7 miles and turn off right onto a gravel service road (0.1 mile east of milepost 118). Park here, again making sure not to block the gate. (Do not drive through the gate even if it is open. You might get locked in.) The **Newhalem (Aggregate) Ponds** can be reached by walking west along the road until it crosses a spawning channel. Go left, then right to get to the main pond, a second pond, and the Skagit River, or continue straight to the north edge of the main pond. Waterfowl and Bald Eagles use the ponds in winter. During the breeding season, woodpeckers, flycatchers, vireos, thrushes (including Veery), warblers (including American Redstart), Western Tanagers, and finches are abundant in the riparian growth between the spawning channel and SR-20.

East on SR-20, stop in 1.7 miles at the Goodell Creek bridge for American Dippers (present all year). On the right in another 0.1 mile is Newhalem Campground and the main visitor center for the park complex, well worth a visit. Back on SR-20, turn right and in another 0.5 mile enter the town of **Newhalem** (no services, except for a general store). Check the steep hillside and brushy area on the left for Violet-green Swallow, Orange-crowned, Nashville, MacGillivray's, and Wilson's Warblers, Western Tanager, Pine Siskin, and Evening Grosbeak.

Colonial Creek Campground, on Diablo Lake, is ten miles east of Newhalem on SR-20. Turn right into the south unit of the campground and drive the one-way loop to the amphitheater and the Thunder Creek Trailhead. MacGillivray's Warblers nest in the shrubs adjacent to the restrooms, across from the amphitheater, and a pair of Barred Owls is resident here. Hike the first mile of trail along the lake to the bridge over Thunder Creek. Check the excellent riparian habitat at the creek mouth for Red-breasted Sapsucker, Olive-sided Flycatcher, Western Wood-Pewee, and a variety of songbirds. Barrow's Goldeneyes nest here, and Harlequin Ducks are seen occasionally.

For the next 29 miles the highway climbs steadily through superb alpine scenery to Rainy Pass. Stop often at the many pullouts to look and listen for Blue Grouse, Black Swift, Hammond's Flycatcher, Townsend's Solitaire, Hermit Thrush, Townsend's and Yellow-rumped Warblers, Western Tanager, and Lincoln's Sparrow. Red-naped Sapsucker, Pine Grosbeak, and White-winged Crossbill (erratic) are often seen at the Easy Pass Trailhead in about 21 miles (0.5 mile past milepost 151). In another 1.6 miles (0.1 mile past milepost

153), turn left into a gravel pit and park so as not to block truck access. Walk to the uppermost edge of the gravel pit, and follow a steep, poorly marked trail uphill through the woods. Spruce Grouse nest along the edge where the trail emerges from the trees at the lower end of the **Hardy Burn**, below Mount Hardy. The burn has been good for Northern Goshawk, Golden Eagle (flying along the ridge above), woodpeckers (although the burn now appears to be too old for Three-toed and Black-backed), Clark's Nutcracker, Mountain Bluebird, Townsend's Solitaire, and Red Crossbill. Calliope Hummingbird, Red-naped Sapsucker, Dusky Flycatcher, and Lincoln's Sparrow have been seen by the edge of the gravel pit near SR-20.

The picnic-area parking lot at 4,855-foot **Rainy Pass** (4.6 miles) is a good place to look for Northern Pygmy-Owl. Gray Jays, both species of crossbills, and other mountain finches may be present along the easy first section of Maple Pass Loop Trail 740 and the side trail to Lake Ann (1.8 miles, 700 feet elevation gain). Trail 740 continues steeply after that for 2.2 miles to Maple Pass (6,600 feet); White-tailed Ptarmigan have been found on the slopes above the pass. The trail loops back to Rainy Pass (7.5 miles total). The five-mile hike north along the Pacific Crest Trail to Cutthroat Pass offers the possibility of Spruce Grouse, Mountain Chickadee, Bohemian Waxwing (late summer–early fall), Pine Grosbeak, and crossbills, as well as other mountain species.

It is another 4.8 miles to **Washington Pass** on the divide between the Methow and Stehekin River drainages—the highest point on the North Cascades Highway (5,477 feet). Turn left into the rest stop entrance road 0.3 mile east of milepost 162. The meadow north of the highway is a good place to look for Spotted Sandpiper, Mountain Bluebird, American Pipit, and other alpine nesters. A short, paved trail leads to a scenic overlook of the upper Methow Valley. Look here for Gray Jay, Clark's Nutcracker, Red Crossbill, and an occasional Pine Grosbeak. The highway descends along the east slope of the Cascade Range, giving access to birding sites on the Dry Side (page 432).

MOUNT BAKER HIGHWAY

by Bob Kuntz

Mount Baker is the northernmost volcano in Washington and, at 10,778 feet, the highest peak in the North Cascades Range. A good highway to the 5,000-foot elevation, and numerous trails reaching alpine habitats around 6,000 feet, make this one of the state's most accessible locations for White-tailed Ptarmigan and Gray-crowned Rosy-Finch. Mount Baker is popular with hikers and campers (four Forest Service campgrounds along the highway) on summer and fall weekends. Hit the road and trails early in the morning to beat the crowds. Be prepared for any kind of weather at any season. Ninety-five feet of snow fell on Mount Baker in the winter of 1998–1999, setting a world record. In a normal year, upper-elevation trails are snow-free by the middle or end of July, and the birding season extends to early October. The road to the ski area is kept open all winter but you will not find many birds at this season.

The Mount Baker Highway (SR-542) runs east from I-5 Exit 255 in Bellingham to its end in about 60 miles. If you are coming from the Skagit or Samish Flats, or farther south, you may prefer to leave the interstate at Exit 232. Drive east 4.4 miles on Cook Road, then left 1.2 miles on SR-20 to the intersection with northbound SR-9 in Sedro-Woolley. Turn left here on SR-9, joining SR-542 at the east edge of Deming. This leisurely, scenic, 22-mile route along the valleys of the Samish and South Fork Nooksack Rivers is about 12 miles shorter. Either way, Mount Baker is an all-day trip if you do one of the alpine hikes.

From December to February, one of the best eagle-viewing spots in Washington is east of Deming. Turn right from SR-542 onto **Mosquito Lake Road**, 2.3 miles from the SR-9 intersection, and continue past a fire station to a bridge crossing the North Fork Nooksack River (0.6 mile). As many as 50–60 Bald Eagles can be seen at one time on the exposed gravel bars or in the trees lining the river, where they congregate to feed on spawning and dying salmon. Common Mergansers often float by with the current.

The Glacier Ranger Station, run jointly by the National Park Service and U.S. Forest Service, is located 17 miles farther east on SR-542 (a Northwest Forest Pass is required to park at trailheads beyond this point and you may purchase one here). Shortly after you leave the ranger station (0.6 mile), turn right onto Glacier Creek Road (FR-39), then almost immediately left onto FR-37, which winds upward 12 miles to the Skyline Divide Trailhead (elevation 4,000 feet). The three-mile **Skyline Divide Trail** brings you to superb subalpine meadows (elevation 6,000 feet) that in July are carpeted with wildflowers. Here you may find species such as Golden Eagle, Clark's Nutcracker, American Pipit, and Gray-crowned Rosy-Finch (fall).

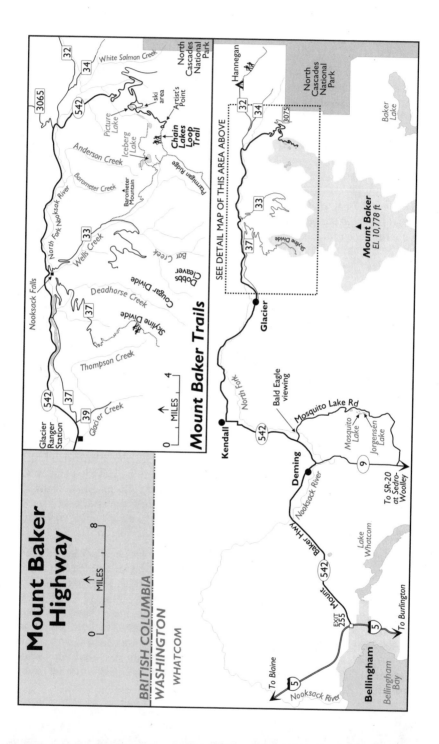

A bit more than six miles east on SR-542, turn right onto **Wells Creek Road** (FR-33). In 0.5 mile, where the road crosses North Fork Nooksack River, look for Harlequin Ducks above and below spectacular Nooksack Falls. One can often see Mountain Goats by stopping at some of the switchbacks and scanning the high slopes as FR-33 winds its way up the side of Barometer Mountain.

Six miles farther east on SR-542, Hannegan Pass Road (FR-32) branches off to the left. Stay left at the first fork in 1.3 miles. The road ends at a campground in another four miles. A fine hike into White-tailed Ptarmigan country begins here, at an elevation of 3,000 feet. The trail passes through conifer forest with many large avalanche paths grown to Sitka Alder and Vine Maple (presumed wintering habitat for ptarmigan), reaching Hannegan Pass in four miles (elevation 5,066 feet). Turn left at the pass and hike uphill along a ridge across open forest for about a mile to the broadly rounded summit of **Hannegan Peak** (elevation 6,186 feet). Look for ptarmigan on the summit meadows and in patches of meadow along the way.

Continue on SR-542. When you come to a fork in 7.6 miles at **Picture Lake**, stay right. There are many areas to park along this much-photographed lake, rimmed with Mountain Hemlock with Mount Shuksan in the background. Check the Sitka Mountain Ash thickets for Pine Grosbeak and migrant songbirds, especially in fall. At 0.5 mile from the fork, turn right and drive another 1.7 miles to reach Artist's Point (elevation 5,100 feet) near timberline. From here several trails traverse the northeast side of Mount Baker. The best two for birding start from the middle-west edge of the parking area.

The **Chain Lakes Loop Trail** is an easy five-mile hike across alpine meadows past a chain of six lakes, including Iceberg Lake. **Ptarmigan Ridge Trail** follows the Chain Lakes Loop Trail for one mile, then veers left onto Ptarmigan Ridge, reaching Camp Kiser in about seven further miles. Parts of this trail may be under snow until early August. The best place for finding White-tailed Ptarmigan is the first two to three miles of Ptarmigan Ridge. To improve your chances, get up the trail early, before other hikers have spooked the birds. Other alpine species seen along these trails include Golden Eagle, Black and Vaux's Swifts, Horned Lark, Mountain Bluebird (uncommon), American Pipit (more likely on the Chain Lakes Trail), Lapland Longspur (rare in fall), and Gray-crowned Rosy-Finch. Hoary Marmots and Pikas are common. Pay attention to whistling marmots, as they may signal the approach of a Golden Eagle. Mountain Goats are fairly common and often seen along the southeast side of Ptarmigan Ridge.

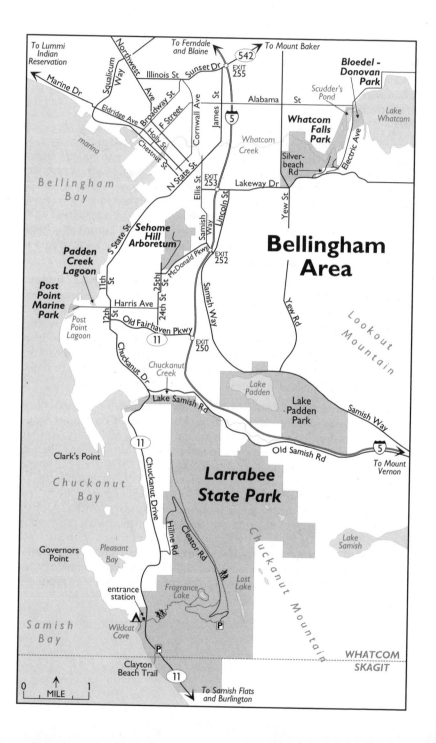

To Lummi
Indian
Reservation

To Ferndale
and Blaine

To Mount Baker

Northwest Ave

Squalicum Way

Illinois St

Sunset Dr

542

EXIT
255

Broadway St.

F Street

Cornwall Ave

James St

Alabama St

Bloedel -
Donovan
Park

Scudder's
Pond

Lake
Whatcom

Marine Dr

Eldridge Ave

Holly St.

5

Whatcom
Falls
Park

marina

Chestnut St.

N State St.

Whatcom Creek

Electric Ave

Silver-
beach
Rd

Bellingham
Bay

Ellis St

EXIT
253

Lincoln St

Lakeway Dr

Yew St

S State St

Sehome
Hill
Arboretum

Samish Way

**Bellingham
Area**

Padden
Creek
Lagoon

11th St

25th St

McDonald Pkwy

EXIT
252

Post
Point
Marine
Park

Post
Point
Lagoon

Harris Ave

24th St

Samish Way

Yew Rd

Lookout
Mountain

12th St

Old Fairhaven Pkwy

11

EXIT
250

Chuckanut Dr

Chuckanut
Creek

Lake
Padden

Lake
Samish Rd

Lake
Padden
Park

Samish Way

11

Clark's Point

Chuckanut Drive

Old Samish Rd

5

To Mount
Vernon

Chuckanut
Bay

**Larrabee
State Park**

Governors
Point

Pleasant
Bay

Hiline Rd

Cleator Rd

Lost
Lake

Lake
Samish

Chuckanut Mountain

entrance
station

Fragrance
Lake

P

Samish
Bay

Wildcat
Cove

P

Clayton
Beach Trail

11

WHATCOM

SKAGIT

To Samish Flats
and Burlington

0 MILE 1

BELLINGHAM AND VICINITY

by Bob Kuntz

The port city of Bellingham is situated some 90 miles north of Seattle and 20 miles south of the U.S.-Canada border, between the Strait of Georgia and the North Cascades foothills. Nearby protected bays, deltas of the Nooksack River and several lesser streams, lowland lakes, and fragmented patches of forestland offer numerous birding opportunities. Migration (late April through May, late July through September) and winter are the most productive seasons. Influenced by outflows of arctic air from Canada's Fraser River valley, the area has several winter records of Northern Hawk Owl and Great Gray Owl. Black Scoter and Snow Bunting are more easily found here than farther south in Puget Sound. Notable records of northern rarities include King Eider (Birch Bay, May; Bellingham Bay, December), Hudsonian Godwit (Semiahmoo Bay, September), Thick-billed Murre (Drayton Harbor, December), and Brambling (Lummi Flats, January).

LARRABEE STATE PARK

Encompassing 2,700 acres of conifer forest with a sprinkling of Madrone and other broadleaf trees, Larrabee State Park clings to the slopes of Chuckanut Mountain along the rocky shore of Samish Bay. Coming from the south on SR-11 (Chuckanut Drive), the park is about five miles north of the Samish Flats (page 117). Coming from I-5, take Exit 250 on the south edge of Bellingham, go west onto SR-11 (Old Fairhaven Parkway), and proceed 1.3 miles to 12th Street. Stay with SR-11 as it turns left, then veers left again in about 200 yards onto Chuckanut Drive. The main park entrance is 5.2 miles south, on the right. After the entrance station, swing left to the parking lot and short trail for the beach. In winter this is a good place to look for Western Grebe, cormorants (all three species), Harlequin and Long-tailed Ducks, Barrow's Goldeneye, and shorebirds on the offshore rocks. At any season you may find Band-tailed Pigeon, Hutton's Vireo, and an assortment of other Westside lowland forest species. Across the highway from the park entrance a stiff hike up the Fragrance Lake Trail will give you additional exposure to forest habitats.

Travel south 0.5 mile on Chuckanut Drive and turn left into the Clayton Beach Trailhead parking area. Walk across Chuckanut Drive and take the half-mile trail to **Clayton Beach**, another good place for species similar to those found at the previous stop. To drive up the side of **Chuckanut Mountain**, return north 1.7 miles on Chuckanut Drive and turn right onto Hiline (Cleator) Road, which ends in 3.7 miles at an overlook from which you may see soaring Bald Eagles or other raptors when winds are favorable. This road can be good all year but is best in spring and early summer. Much of the forest has been logged at different times in the past and habitats are in various stages of succession. Stop often to look for Western Screech-Owl, Northern

Pygmy-Owl, Barred Owl, Band-tailed Pigeon, and nesting flycatchers, vireos, chickadees, thrushes, warblers, sparrows, and finches.

BELLINGHAM

From the corner of Old Fairhaven Parkway and 12th Street, where SR-11 goes east to I-5 and south to Larrabee State Park, drive north three blocks, then turn west onto Harris Avenue. On the right in 0.2 mile, **Padden Creek Lagoon** is a good place in winter to look for saltwater ducks and gulls, particularly Thayer's Gull. Continue another quarter-mile through the historic Fairhaven business district and turn left onto Post Point Road, which ends at **Post Point Marine Park**. Check the waters of **Bellingham Bay** for Red-throated, Common, and even Yellow-billed (several records) Loons, Red-necked and Western Grebes, cormorants, Harlequin and Long-tailed Ducks, scoters, both goldeneyes, Common Murre, Pigeon Guillemot, Marbled Murrelet, and Rhinoceros Auklet (well offshore).

Sehome Hill Arboretum, adjacent to the Western Washington University campus, is reached from I-5 Exit 252. Go west on Samish Way, then turn left in a short distance onto Bill MacDonald Parkway. In 0.9 mile, at 25th Street, turn right into the entrance to the arboretum. There are several pull-outs along the winding road as it climbs the hill to a parking area in 0.8 mile. This is an ideal walker's park, with almost six miles of trails crisscrossing 165 acres of native, mixed-forest hilltop habitat. The best times to visit are spring through fall. Particularly during spring migration, the arboretum can be alive with birds. Walk the trails and look for woodpeckers, Pacific-slope Flycatcher, Hutton's and Warbling Vireos, Black-capped and Chestnut-backed Chickadees, Black-throated Gray and Townsend's Warblers, Western Tanager, Black-headed Grosbeak, and Purple Finch.

For **Whatcom Falls Park**, leave I-5 at Exit 253. Travel east 1.5 miles on Lakeway Drive and turn left onto Silverbeach Road (just past the Bayview Cemetery). An entrance to the park is about 0.2 mile from this intersection, on the left. A second entrance is reached by continuing on Lakeway Drive about 0.2 mile past Silverbeach Road to Electric Avenue. Turn left onto Electric Avenue and left again at the entrance in about 300 yards. Birding is good year round in the woods and along Whatcom Creek, which bisects the park with several wetlands. Look for American Dippers below Whatcom Falls. Nearby **Bloedel-Donovan Park**, at the northwest end of Lake Whatcom, is 0.8 mile north of Lakeway Drive on Electric Avenue. During winter, look for waterfowl and gulls. In spring, Hooded Mergansers nest at **Scudder's Pond**, on the west side of Electric Avenue 0.1 mile farther north. Watch for Beavers and signs of their activities. These and many other Bellingham parks are interconnected by an excellent series of trails, which birders will enjoy exploring.

LUMMI INDIAN RESERVATION

The birding sites described in this section are within the boundaries of the Lummi Indian Reservation and subject to the laws of the Lummi Nation. You are asked to obtain a permit to bird on tribal lands. Permits are free and may be applied for by fax or in person during weekday business hours through the Lummi Tribal Office at 2616 Kwina Road (east of Haxton Way; call 360-384-1489 for details). Be respectful of private property; bird from the roadside.

Drive west on Slater Road from I-5 Exit 260, crossing the Nooksack River in 1.6 miles. Continue another 0.6 mile to the intersection with Ferndale Road, the northeast corner of the reservation. Go left (south) 1.9 miles on Ferndale, then turn right onto Marine Drive. After 0.8 mile, veer to the left from Marine Drive onto **Lummi Shore Drive**. The road soon approaches Bellingham Bay and bends a bit to the right, with a view of the Nooksack River delta on the left. Over the next few miles Lummi Shore Drive follows the northwest shore of the bay. Stop at the many pullouts to look out over the delta and the river mouth. Herons, swans, geese, and Bald Eagles are often abundant, but you will need a scope to get good views. Loons, grebes, saltwater ducks, and gulls are common in Bellingham Bay. At 6.4 miles from Marine Drive, Lummi Shore Drive makes a right and becomes Lummi View Drive, and for the next 1.7 miles follows the shoreline of **Hale Passage** with Lummi Island across the channel. Check along the channel, particularly at Gooseberry Point near the ferry terminal, for loons, Red-necked Grebe, Greater Scaup, scoters (including Black), Common Murre, Pigeon Guillemot, Marbled Murrelet, and Rhinoceros Auklet. This is also a good location to look for jaegers (usually Parasitic) during fall migration.

Lummi View Drive curves right past the ferry terminal and becomes Haxton Way. Continuing north, in 5.9 miles you reach South Red River Road and the edge of the **Lummi Flats**. These low-lying, fertile fields on both sides of the Lummi River—part of the Nooksack delta system—are the single best birding area around Bellingham. Swans, hawks, falcons, and owls, and shrikes and other passerines, are abundant on the flats in winter (the best season). Drive any of the roads (see map on next page) to check wet spots for shorebirds (spring) and blackbirds (Rusty possible fall–winter, Yellow-headed in any season). Gravel-surfaced South Red River Road, with a low volume of traffic, is the most leisurely road for birding. In late evening, Short-eared Owls hunt for mice in the fields along this road. In irruption years, Snowy Owls may be found here and elsewhere on the flats. Winter sparrows use the hedgerows bordering the slough; check finches feeding on the alder cone crop for redpolls (one record of Brambling). Dikes and areas of open ground such as those at the west end of Kwina Road can be productive for Lapland Longspurs and Snow Buntings (one November record of McKay's Bunting).

From South Red River Road, go north on Haxton Way for 0.6 mile to Slater Road. Turn left (west), drive 3.6 miles, and turn left onto Beach Way. In 1.3

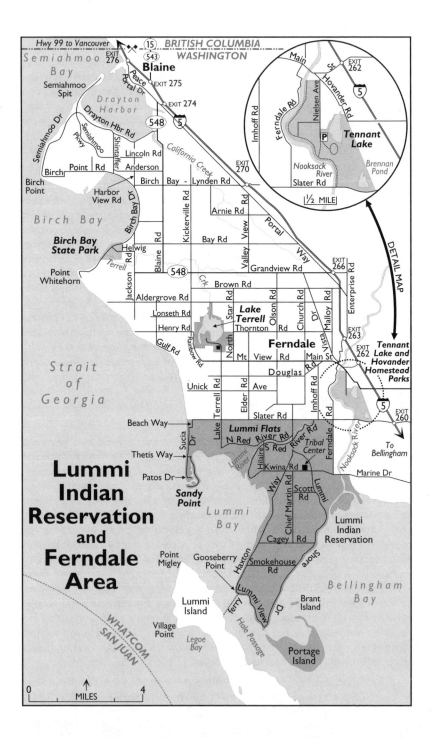

Hwy 99 to Vancouver

Semiahmoo Bay

BRITISH COLUMBIA
WASHINGTON

EXIT 276
EXIT 275
EXIT 274

15
543

Blaine

Main St

EXIT 262

5

Semiahmoo Spit

Peace Portal Dr

Drayton Harbor

548

5

Drayton Hbr Rd

Semiahmoo Dr

Semiahmoo Pkwy

Shintaffer

Lincoln Rd

Anderson

Imhoff Rd

Ferndale Rd

Nielsen Ave

Hovander Rd

P

Tennant Lake

California Creek

EXIT 270

Nooksack River

Brennan Pond

Birch Point Rd

Birch Point

Birch Bay - Lynden Rd

Slater Rd

½ MILE

Harbor View Rd

Birch Bay Dr

Birch Bay

Arnie Rd

DETAIL MAP

Birch Bay State Park

Helwig Rd

Terrell

Bay Rd

Valley View

Portal Way

EXIT 266

Enterprise Rd

Point Whitehorn

Blaine Rd

548

Grandview Rd

Jackson Rd

Ck

Brown Rd

Aldergrove Rd

Star Rd

Olson Rd

Church Rd

Malloy Rd

Lonseth Rd

Lake Terrell

EXIT 263

Strait of Georgia

Henry Rd

Thornton Rd

Ferndale

Vista Dr

EXIT 262

Tennant Lake and Hovander Homestead Parks

Gulf Rd

Rainbow Rd

North

Mt View Rd

Main St

Douglas

5

EXIT 260

Unick

Lake Terrell Rd

Elder Rd

Ave

Imhoff Rd

To Bellingham

Slater Rd

Beach Way

Sucia Dr

Lummi Flats

N Red River Rd

Tribal Center

Ferndale Rd

Nooksack River

Thetis Way

Lummi River

S Red River Rd

Marine Dr

Lummi Indian Reservation and Ferndale Area

Patos Dr

Hilaire Way

Kwina Rd

Sandy Point

Lummi Bay

Chief Martin Rd

Scott Rd

Lummi Indian Reservation

Cagey Rd

Lummi Shore

Point Migley

Gooseberry Point

Haxton Way

Smokehouse Rd

Bellingham Bay

Brant Island

Lummi Island

Lummi View Dr

Hale Passage

Village Point

Legoe Bay

Terry

Portage Island

WHATCOM
SAN JUAN

0   4
MILES

miles, after curving right onto South Beach Way, then left onto Sucia Drive, you reach Thetis Way on **Sandy Point**, a gravel spit at the northwest end of Lummi Bay. Once rich in habitat for birds in migration and winter, Sandy Point has been greatly altered by housing development. A weedy field set aside for wildlife extends along the east side of Sucia Drive for 0.7 mile, from Thetis Way down to Patos Drive, and is still worth a look. Snowy Owl, American Pipit, and Snow Bunting have been seen here.

TENNANT LAKE AND LAKE TERRELL

Tennant Lake, along the Nooksack River south of Ferndale, is at the heart of a 720-acre tract jointly administered as a county park and a state wild-life area. Varied habitats make this an excellent birding site at any time of year. An observation tower and a boardwalk through a cattail marsh to the lake provide opportunities to view Green Herons, waterfowl, and raptors. Other trails run south and west through grasslands, wetlands, and deciduous forest. The boardwalk and the area around the lake are off-limits to all but hunters from mid-September into January. From I-5 Exit 262, go west 0.5 mile on Main Street to Hovander Road. Turn left, drive 200 yards, then take the second right onto Nielsen Avenue and continue 0.9 mile to the parking area for the visitor center, on the left (the first right from Hovander goes to a WDFW boat-launch area on the river). From the Lummi Flats the site is easily reached by following Slater, Imhoff, and Douglas Roads to Main Street.

Lake Terrell Wildlife Area, established in 1947, offers 1,500 acres of open water, marshlands, grasslands, and mixed deciduous-coniferous forest. Hunting is allowed here, so the best times to visit are spring into September when you will find a good variety of waterfowl, marshbirds, swallows, and other songbirds. From Ferndale, head west on Main Street, which becomes Mountain View Road. In 4.5 miles, turn right onto Lake Terrell Road. Continue 0.8 mile to the parking lot (WDFW permit required to park). Or go north from Slater Road on Lake Terrell Road (2.4 miles west of Haxton Way) to reach the parking lot in about three miles. Common Loons nested at Lake Terrell through 1987, and alternate-plumaged individuals are still occasionally observed during the breeding season. Look for Tundra Swans, Wood Ducks (nesting), Redheads (late winter and spring), and Hooded Mergansers. Western Screech- and Northern Saw-whet Owls have nested in Wood Duck boxes around the lake. Lake Terrell regularly attracts unusual passerines in spring and fall, among them Least Flycatcher, Say's Phoebe, Bank Swallow, House Wren, American Redstart, and White-throated Sparrow.

BIRCH BAY

From I-5 Exit 266, follow the signs for **Birch Bay State Park** west along Grandview Road for seven miles, north 0.7 mile on Jackson Road, then left on

Helwig Road 0.6 mile to the park entrance. Or you can work your way north and west from Lake Terrell. Just past the entrance, walk the half-mile Terrell Marsh Trail through some of the park's 193 acres of lowland forest, looking and listening for the usual woodpeckers and passerines. Wood Ducks and Hooded Mergansers can often be found in the fresh- and saltwater marsh habitats at the estuary of Terrell Creek. From the entrance gate continue downhill through the park to **Birch Bay** (0.4 mile). This large, shallow, protected saltwater bay has extensive eelgrass beds and several miles of shoreline looking toward the Canadian Gulf Islands. Follow Birch Bay Road (Drive) north from the park through the town of Birch Bay, stopping often to scan the bay. This is an excellent winter viewing area for Red-throated and Common Loons, Western Grebe, Brant, Harlequin and Long-tailed Ducks, scoters (all three species), Ruddy Duck, gulls and terns (especially on the beaches in town), and alcids. Western Sandpipers and other shorebirds occur in spring migration along the shoreline, and Dunlins winter in good numbers.

DRAYTON HARBOR AND SEMIAHMOO BAY

Drayton Harbor, a large estuarine bay isolated from Semiahmoo Bay by Semiahmoo Spit, is one of the most important winter waterbird sites in the state. If you are coming from I-5, take Exit 270 and go west on Birch Bay–Lynden Road for about four miles, then turn right (north) onto Harbor View Road, which intersects Lincoln Road in 1.0 mile. Turn left and follow Lincoln (becomes Semiahmoo Parkway at Shintaffer Road) to the end to access the spit. If you are coming from Birch Bay, turn right from Birch Bay Drive at the north end of the bay onto Shintaffer Road (3.5 miles from the intersection of Birch Bay Road and the state park road). In 0.6 mile, follow the Semiahmoo sign by turning left onto Semiahmoo Parkway, and proceed as above.

Semiahmoo Spit is feeling the pressure of development; its tip is now occupied by a resort. However, a county park extends about two-thirds of the length of the spit from the base, giving good views of **Drayton Harbor** on the inside and of **Semiahmoo Bay** to the north. There is convenient parking at both ends of the park. In winter this is an excellent place to view loons, grebes, cormorants, Brant, dabbling and diving ducks, Dunlins, gulls, and alcids. Ospreys, Bald Eagles, and Peregrine Falcons use the spit.

At the opposite corner of Drayton Harbor, look through the many ducks at the mouth of California Creek for an occasional Eurasian Wigeon. To get there, backtrack on Semiahmoo Parkway, turning left (east) 0.5 mile past the county park onto Drayton Harbor Road and following it for three miles, bearing left at the two stop signs, to the creek bridge. For a good vantage point on the east side of Drayton Harbor, cross the California Creek bridge and turn left onto Blaine Road (0.1 mile). Go north for 0.9 mile to Peace Portal Drive, just after the Dakota Creek bridge. Turn left here and drive 1.4 miles to the intersection with Cedar Street in Blaine. Park and cross the road. A bluff above

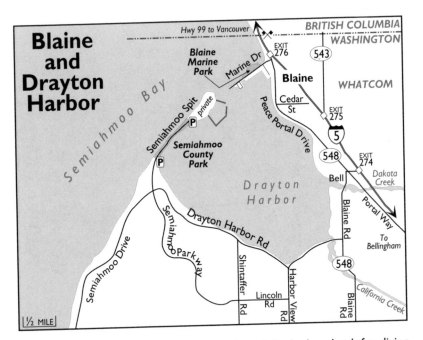

Blaine
and
Drayton
Harbor

Semiahmoo Bay

Hwy 99 to Vancouver

BRITISH COLUMBIA
WASHINGTON

Blaine
Marine
Park

Marine Dr

EXIT
276

543

Blaine

WHATCOM

Cedar
St

Peace Portal Drive

EXIT
275

5

Semiahmoo Spit

private

P

Semiahmoo
County
Park

P

P

Drayton
Harbor

548

EXIT
274

Bell

Dakota
Creek

Drayton Harbor Rd

Blaine Rd

Portal Way

To
Bellingham

Semiahmoo Drive

Semiahmoo Parkway

Shintaffer Rd

Lincoln
Rd

Harbor View Rd

548

Blaine Rd

California Creek

½ MILE

the railroad tracks provides a panoramic view of the harbor. Look for diving birds and Brant. Black Turnstones, Whimbrels (late April–May), and other shorebirds may be present on a fairly low tide. Another good viewpoint is the parking lot behind the Red Caboose, five blocks farther north.

Blaine Marine Park, at the mouth of Drayton Harbor within sight of the Peace Arch and the U.S.-Canada border, affords closer views of the same species as at Semiahmoo Spit. Continue north through the four-way stop to the first traffic light on Peace Portal Drive and turn left onto Marine Drive. (From I-5 northbound, take Exit 276, cross under the freeway, and turn right immediately onto Marine Drive; southbound, turn right at the end of the offramp.) Marine Drive goes out a spit for two-thirds of a mile, terminating at a fishing pier at the entrance to Drayton Harbor. The pier is a good spot for observing cormorants, Harlequin Duck, Barrow's Goldeneye, and (in spring and fall) Common Tern. Across the channel, Harbor Seals haul out onto the concrete breakwater at the end of Semiahmoo Spit. Waterbird viewing from the fishing pier is good at any tide level. The tideflats on the north (Semiahmoo Bay) side of Marine Drive often have impressive numbers of shorebirds, conveniently viewed from a paved promenade atop the low bluff along the edge of the bay. Shorebirding is best near the base of the spit as the incoming tide pushes the feeding birds toward shore. Besides the species expected for Washington's inland marine shorelines, uncommon species and even rarities have turned up here during spring and fall migration.

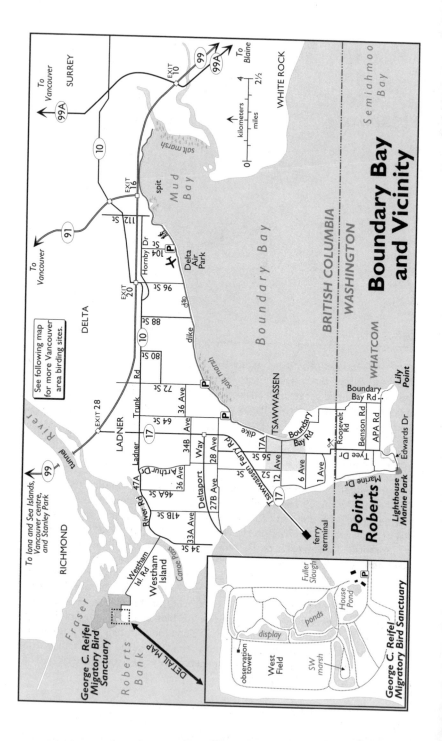

Boundary Bay and Vicinity

See following map for more Vancouver area birding sites.

VANCOUVER (BRITISH COLUMBIA) AND VICINITY

by Wayne Weber

Greater Vancouver, British Columbia, is an outstanding birding area, especially for waterbirds, shorebirds, and birds of prey. This is largely because of its location at the mouth of the Fraser River, one of the largest and most productive estuaries on the Pacific Coast. About 400 bird species have been recorded in the area—more than 80 percent of the number on the British Columbia list. A few Crested Mynas remain, too, although this signature Vancouver species is fast disappearing.* Certain other sought-after species may be found more reliably here than in Washington (e.g., Sharp-tailed Sandpiper, Snowy Owl). The regularity with which unusual shorebirds turn up is legendary. These include Spotted Redshank, Far Eastern Curlew, Red-necked, Little, and Temminck's Stints, and Spoonbill Sandpiper—mega-rarities for which there are no Washington records. No wonder so many visitors include Vancouver on a Washington birding trip!

This account gives only a bare introduction to the marquee sites, with enough information to get you there and keep you busy for a day or two. As you will quickly discover, however, Vancouver is a destination in its own right. Pick up a copy of The Birder's Guide to Vancouver and the Lower Mainland, edited by Catherine J. Aitchison (Vancouver Natural History Society, 2001), and plan a longer stay.

When driving north from Seattle or Bellingham on I-5, you will cross the U.S.-Canada border at Blaine. I-5 then becomes Highway 99, which continues as a freeway until it enters the city of Vancouver. In Canada, exits and other signs are marked in kilometers. However, miles will be used in this section, in conformity with the rest of the book, recognizing that most cars coming from the U.S. will not have metric odometers. Ten miles per hour equals 16 kilometers per hour. Mind the speed limits!

BOUNDARY BAY

Shallow Boundary Bay, bordered on its north side by a dike, offers fine birding in tideflat, saltmarsh, and farm-field habitats. This large area attracts high numbers and a great diversity of shorebirds in migration (over 45 species recorded) and of wintering waterfowl and raptors, including five falcons and Snowy Owl. Access to the dike and bay is by any of several numbered roads running south across the farmlands, which offer the principal raptor-viewing opportunities.

Coming from Blaine on Highway 99, take Exit 20 to Highway 10. Make a left and cross the freeway; you are now on Highway 10 (Ladner Trunk Road) westbound. At the traffic light just ahead (0.3 mile), turn left onto Hornby Drive, which bends back east and follows the south side of the freeway. In 1.3

---

* Now apparently extirpated: see page 151 (Ed.).

miles, turn right onto 104th Street and continue to the parking lot for the Delta Air Park, less than a mile ahead on the right. Parking is in short supply along Boundary Bay and has become a contentious issue. Presently, you may park only in this parking lot or at the ends of 64th and 72nd Streets. From there you may walk, bicycle, or ride your horse along the dike.

One of the best shorebird-viewing spots in the Vancouver area is a spit extending into Mud Bay half a mile east of 112th Street (no parking). Walk east along the dike from 104th Street, then diagonally out across the salt marsh to the spit; the total distance one way is about 1.7 miles. The best season for shorebirds is fall migration (July–October), but you may see many waterbirds in all seasons. Avoid the high and low extremes of the tidal cycle.

Return west on Hornby Drive, and at the traffic light near the Highway 99 interchange, turn left onto Highway 10 westbound. In 2.7 miles, turn left onto 72nd Street. Fields along the road on both sides may have large numbers of roosting gulls, especially Mew, Thayer's, and Glaucous-winged. Iceland and Slaty-backed Gulls (both rare) have been seen here. The turf farm on the west side of the road south of the railroad track may have shorebirds in fall migration, including American and Pacific Golden-Plovers and Baird's and Buff-breasted (rare) Sandpipers. The salt marsh at the end of 72nd Street (2.1 miles) is usually a good location for Snowy Owls, even in a poor flight year (peak numbers mid-November to mid-March).

Go back north about half a mile, turn left onto 36th Avenue, then left again in 1.0 mile onto 64th Street. Park at the end of the street (1.2 miles). The vast salt marsh between the dike and the tideflats has many informal trails that you can walk to look for raptors, shorebirds, and waterfowl, especially in winter.

B.C. Ferry to Swartz Bay

Direct service for autos and passengers traveling between Vancouver and Victoria (page 107) leaves from the Tsawwassen ferry terminal. Coming west along Ladner Trunk Road (Highway 10), turn left onto Highway 17 about half a mile west of 64th Street. In 3.5 miles, note the intersection with 56th Street; you will turn south here to reach Point Roberts, described in the following section. Continue straight (southwest) on Highway 17 to the ferry terminal (3.5 miles) and board the Victoria ferry. The best birding comes after crossing the broad Strait of Georgia, as the boat threads **Active Pass** and continues among several of the Gulf Islands to the terminal at Swartz Bay. Expect the same species of waterfowl, gulls, alcids, and other seabirds as on the San Juan Islands ferry (page 96). Numbers and diversity are high in late fall and winter, but late spring and summer trips can be dull. The crossing takes an hour and a half.

POINT ROBERTS

Point Roberts—actually a peninsula, not a point—is part of Whatcom County, Washington, but can be reached by land only by way of Canada. From the intersection of Highways 17 and 10, proceed southward on Highway 17 as if heading toward the Victoria ferry, until you reach 56th Street (also called Point Roberts Road), marked by a traffic light (3.5 miles). Turn left here and continue through the business district of Tsawwassen for 2.9 miles to the Canada-U.S. border. This is a border crossing like any other (open 24 hours a day), so be sure you have proof of identity, and be prepared for a vehicle inspection in either direction.

Beyond the border crossing, 56th Street becomes Tyee Drive. **Lighthouse Marine Park**, one of the two best birding spots on Point Roberts, is reached by driving south 1.4 miles to the junction of APA Road. From here, Tyee Drive almost immediately swings to the right, skirting the Point Roberts Marina. It eventually becomes Edwards Drive, paralleling the shoreline until it reaches the park ($4 day-use fee for non-county residents, May–September) in 1.1 miles. Here deep waters come close to shore, and strong currents often bring fish or other edibles to the surface, attracting many seabirds. This is one of the best places for seabird rarities in Washington's inland marine waters (and in the Greater Vancouver area), with records for Yellow-billed Loon, Sooty Shearwater, South Polar Skua, Pomarine and Long-tailed Jaegers, Franklin's, Little, Black-headed, and Sabine's Gulls, Black-legged Kittiwake, and Arctic Tern.

Cormorants (Double-crested, Pelagic, and in fall and winter, Brandt's) and gulls (Bonaparte's, Mew, and Glaucous-winged) usually form the nucleus of feeding flocks. Loons (Red-throated, Pacific, and Common) often join such flocks. In fall, Heermann's Gulls and Ancient Murrelets may be seen, sometimes in the large flocks and sometimes by themselves. Common Murres are numerous from September through May. Pigeon Guillemots, Marbled Murrelets, and Rhinoceros Auklets (May through November) are seen in smaller numbers. Harlequin Ducks can be seen all year, mostly along the gravelly beach to the east; all three scoters are present from September through May. At low tide, Black Turnstones and Sanderlings are often on the beach (except in summer). During most of the year, a constant procession of diving ducks and marine birds flies past the point, sometimes affording close views. Besides species already mentioned, these include Brant, Long-tailed Duck, Common Goldeneye, and Red-breasted Merganser, plus Horned, Red-necked, and Western Grebes. In late spring and early fall, Parasitic Jaegers harass Bonaparte's Gulls and Common Terns off the point.

The other outstanding spot is **Lily Point** at the southeast corner of Point Roberts. From Tyee Drive travel straight east for 1.7 miles on APA Road until it dead-ends at a small cemetery. Park your car here, then follow a broad path that leads eastward and southeastward through the forest. (Despite the *No*

Trespassing signs, locals and birders have used this area for years without reproach.) About 0.5 mile along the trail, next to an area of slumping gravel cliffs, a well-used but unsigned path leads down a steep hill to a large, flat beach area (Lily Point itself), where many of the same birds found at Lighthouse Marine Park can be seen. The conifer forest near Lily Point and elsewhere on Point Roberts is good for Barred Owl and for the expected lowland woodpeckers and passerines.

REIFEL SANCTUARY

From the intersection of Highways 17 and 10 north of Point Roberts, proceed west on Ladner Trunk Road until you reach the business district of Ladner at the intersection of Arthur Drive in 1.1 miles (traffic light). Ladner Trunk Road makes a slight jog to the left here and becomes 47A Avenue, then eventually winding River Road. About 2.3 miles from Arthur Drive, at the sign for the Reifel Sanctuary, take a right turn and cross the old wooden bridge over Canoe Pass, an arm of the Fraser River, onto Westham Island. Stay with Westham Island Road through several turns. In about 2.4 miles from the Canoe Pass bridge, make a 90-degree left turn at the sign onto the gravel entrance road for the sanctuary. You will soon reach the gravel parking lot.

The **George C. Reifel Migratory Bird Sanctuary** is operated by the non-profit B.C. Waterfowl Society, which charges a modest admission fee. The Sanctuary is open from 9AM to 5PM daily (no entry allowed after 4PM). A gift shop sells bird checklists, books, etc., and the staff are usually informed about unusual species that have been seen recently.

The Reifel Sanctuary embraces extensive brackish cattail marshes, diked impoundments (good for waterfowl and shorebirds, depending on season and water level), agricultural fields, and wooded dikes that are home to many songbirds. It is the most popular birding spot in Greater Vancouver, especially from September through May, and can be crowded on weekends. Even when the sanctuary is closed, the farm roads of Westham Island offer very good birding (watch for, and yield to, farm vehicles).

From October through April, up to 20,000 Snow Geese winter here and at the Skagit Flats in Skagit County, Washington; some years there are few geese at Reifel in January and February. Several hundred Trumpeter (and a few Tundra) Swans also winter here. Depending on conditions, geese and swans may feed in intertidal areas or in the farm fields, sometimes offering ridiculously close views. Many other waterfowl species stay here in winter; up to 10,000 or more dabbling ducks include mainly American Wigeons, Mallards, Northern Pintails, and Green-winged Teal. Eurasian Wigeon is fairly common; one can find up to 10 or 20 male Eurasians in a large wigeon flock. Small numbers of diving ducks, as well as Pied-billed Grebes, Double-crested Cormorants, Great Blue Herons, and American Coots winter on freshwater sloughs in and near the sanctuary. In willows next to Fuller Slough there is a winter roost of two to six Black-crowned Night-Herons—the only place in British Columbia where this species can be seen predictably. The cattail marshes support American Bittern, Virginia Rail, and Marsh Wren all year.

Many birds of prey are present in winter, including Northern Harrier, Red-tailed and Rough-legged Hawks, Merlin, Peregrine Falcon, and Barn, Great Horned, Long-eared, Short-eared, and Northern Saw-whet Owls. Species occasionally present include Northern Goshawk, Gyrfalcon, and Snowy and Barred Owls. Bald Eagles nest on the island, and dozens are seen some days. A guided bird walk around the sanctuary is offered at 10AM every Sunday, year round, and a special effort is often made to find owls.

The wooded dikes are great in winter for sparrows (e.g., Sooty Fox, Song, Golden-crowned, and White-crowned, and occasionally Swamp, White-throated, or Harris's). Migrating flycatchers, vireos, and warblers are often seen in large numbers in spring and fall.

Reifel is also noted for shorebirds. Wintering species include Black-bellied Plover (common), Killdeer, Greater Yellowlegs, Dunlin, and Wilson's Snipe (less common). In spring and fall, many migrant shorebirds can be seen at high tide in the West Field, Southwest Marsh, and House Pond. Regular shorebird migrants include Semipalmated, Western, Least, Baird's, Pectoral, Sharp-tailed (rare), and Stilt Sandpipers (the last three mostly in fall), and both dowitchers. Species seen less frequently include Black-necked Stilt, Hudsonian Godwit, Ruff, and Red Phalarope. Along with Boundary Bay and Iona Island, Reifel is one of Vancouver's three top spots for shorebird ultra-rarities.

IONA AND SEA ISLANDS

Iona and Sea Islands are part of the Fraser River delta, and Iona is home to the Greater Vancouver sewage treatment plant and to Iona Beach Regional Park. Sea Island, once mainly farmland, is now 80 percent covered by the sprawling Vancouver International Airport. These islands are noted for waterfowl and birds of prey from October through April or May, and for shorebirds all year, but especially in migration. Counting both waterbirds and landbirds, Sea and Iona Islands have produced far more records of out-of-range birds than any other locality in the Vancouver area.

From Highway 99 northbound, take Exit 39 for Vancouver Airport and follow signs for the Main Terminal along Bridgeport Road and Grant McConachie Way until you reach Templeton Drive (1.8 miles). (If you are already at the airport terminal, drive east on Grant McConachie Way until you reach a traffic light at Templeton Drive.) Turn north on Templeton, which swings left and merges onto Grauer Road (becomes Ferguson Road). The road then curves to the right (north), crossing a causeway over McDonald Slough to reach the Iona sewage plant, surrounded by a chain-link fence (3.6

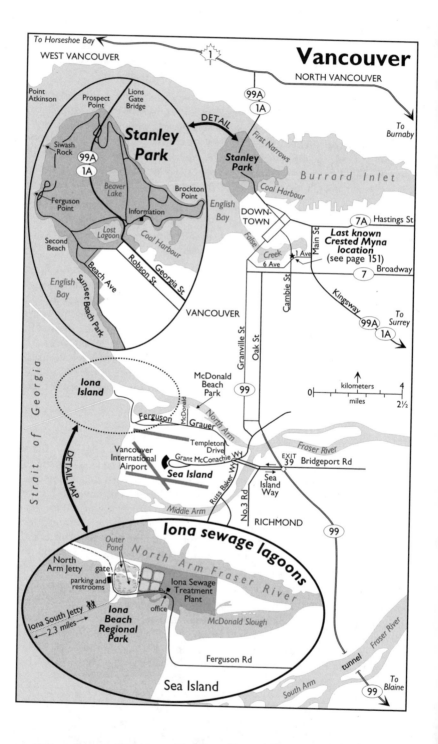

miles). When the plant is open (Monday–Friday, 9AM to 5PM) you may park next to the office. At other times, stay on the road for a couple of hundred yards as it curves to the left, and park next to a locked gate through which birders may visit the sewage lagoon enclosure on foot after entering a code. Obtain the current combination in advance. Instructions are posted to the Vancouver Natural History Society web site at *www.naturalhistory.bc.ca*. Or, to bird the west end of the island or the Iona South Jetty, continue on 0.4 mile from this gate and park at the Iona Beach Regional Park parking area, next to the restrooms.

Shorebirding is the main attraction at the **Iona sewage lagoons**. Only one of the four settling ponds is active (receiving effluent) at any given time. Usually, one or two ponds have a mixture of exposed sludge and water and serve as high-tide roosting areas for shorebirds, often thousands of them. At such times the Iona ponds are unparalleled as a place to get close views. Try to be there within two hours before or after the high tide. Dunlins are abundant in winter, with small numbers of a few other species. In spring (April and May), common species are Black-bellied Plover, Greater Yellowlegs, Western and Least Sandpipers, Dunlin, and Short-billed Dowitcher. Some days, more than 10,000 Western Sandpipers are present. Less-numerous spring migrants include Semipalmated Plover, Lesser Yellowlegs, Whimbrel, Semipalmated, Baird's, and Pectoral Sandpipers, and Long-billed Dowitcher. In fall migration (late June through late October), as well as all the above species, American Golden-Plover, Hudsonian Godwit, Sharp-tailed, Stilt, and Buff-breasted Sandpipers, and Ruff are usually seen from one to several times each year. Shorebird rarities occur at Iona with astonishing regularity. For example, of the 11 securely documented records of Red-necked Stint for the Greater Vancouver area, nine have been from these ponds.

From September to May, the sewage ponds, Outer Pond (outside the sewage plant), and nearby mudflats support many dabbling ducks, Lesser Scaup, Ruddy Ducks, and American Coots. The Outer Pond usually has many diving ducks, including Canvasback, Redhead (rare), Ring-necked Duck (rare), Greater and Lesser Scaups (usually more of Lesser), Common Goldeneye, and Hooded and Common Mergansers. Look carefully for a Tufted Duck (male or female) among the scaups. Blue-winged and Cinnamon Teals are common in summer, and the Outer Pond has nesting Yellow-headed Blackbirds—the only colony in coastal British Columbia.

The **Iona Island South Jetty**, extending southwestward for 2.3 miles from just south of the Iona Beach Park restrooms, has a roadway (closed to private vehicles) on it, plus a huge pipe (atop which you can walk) that carries treated sewage out into the Strait of Georgia. It's a long walk to the end. Although birding the South Jetty is often mediocre at high tide, the intertidal flats are partly exposed at low tide and teem with birds. Except in summer, look for Red-throated and Common Loons, Horned and Western Grebes, Double-crested Cormorants, Great Blue Herons, ducks (including all three scoters), and gulls. Look especially for Thayer's Gull along shorelines and in fields on Sea Island. Many of these species can be seen from shore, but only at high tide. In May there are often thousands of Bonaparte's Gulls on the flats; Little and Black-headed Gulls are rare. Parasitic Jaegers and Common Terns are frequent in May and September, as are Lapland Longspurs and Snow Buntings on the jetty itself in late fall or early spring.

Birds of prey seen at Sea and Iona are similar to those at the Reifel Sanctuary, except for fewer owls. Some species, especially Bald Eagles, Merlins, and Peregrine Falcons, feed mainly on birds, and frighten off shorebirds often enough to be a major nuisance to birders.

Passerine migration is noteworthy on Sea and Iona Islands and has brought a long list of rarities including Tropical Kingbird, Scissor-tailed Flycatcher, Sage Thrasher, Yellow-breasted Chat, Brewer's, Sage, and even Baird's Sparrows, and Bobolink. For one consistently productive area, go back the way you came and turn north at an intersection 2.1 miles from the sewage plant gate. Bird from here to the end of the road at McDonald Beach Park, and along the dike toward the east.

STANLEY PARK

Stanley Park occupies a peninsula jutting out into Burrard Inlet, close to downtown Vancouver. Most of its 1,000 acres are native conifer forest, although windstorms have destroyed or damaged many trees. The eastern and southwestern parts of the park feature extensive lawns and ornamental plantings. A masonry seawall topped by a broad asphalt path extends around the entire shoreline and provides excellent access for birding, but is often crowded. There are many trails in the park's forested interior.

Stanley Park is easily reached by car from downtown Vancouver. For information on bus service, phone TransLink at 604-521-0400, or check their web site at www.translink.bc.ca. The main park road follows the shoreline in a 7.5-mile counterclockwise loop; many of the other park roads are also one way. Parking is available at many locations, but it is all pay parking. Credit cards are accepted, or Canadian change is available at the park information office along the loop road about 0.3 mile east of Lost Lagoon.

Lost Lagoon, a small lake near the Georgia Street entrance, is packed with waterfowl and gulls in winter, partly because of deliberate feeding of birds. Common winter birds include Double-crested Cormorant, Great Blue Heron, Wood Duck, American Wigeon, Canvasback, Greater and Lesser Scaups, Bufflehead, Common and Barrow's Goldeneyes, Hooded and Common Mergansers, Ruddy Duck, American Coot, and Mew and Glaucous-winged Gulls. One or a few Redheads and Ring-necked Ducks are often present, and Tufted Duck occurs every year, with one sometimes staying for weeks.

Anyplace along the Stanley Park seawall can be great for birding from September through May but the **English Bay** (west) side of the park is consistently best, from the Beach Avenue entrance north to Siwash Rock. Regular winter species include Red-throated and Common Loons, Horned, Red-necked, and Western Grebes (Westerns often in rafts of thousands), Double-crested and Pelagic Cormorants, American Wigeon, Greater Scaup, Harlequin and Long-tailed Ducks, Surf Scoter, Bufflehead, Common and Barrow's Goldeneyes, Red-breasted Merganser, Bald Eagle, and Mew, Thayer's, and Glaucous-winged Gulls. Common Murres, Pigeon Guillemots, and Marbled Murrelets are often seen, usually well offshore. At low tide, shorebirds (Black Oystercatcher, Black Turnstone, Sanderling, Dunlin) are sometimes seen on the rocky shore near Ferguson Point.

In the forest, year-round residents include Barred Owl, Hairy and Pileated Woodpeckers, and the usual assortment of lowland conifer-forest passerines. Winter brings Red-breasted Sapsucker, Ruby-crowned Kinglet, Varied Thrush, Sooty Fox Sparrow, and Dark-eyed Junco. In summer the forest is much more lively, with many additional breeding species, among them Olive-sided, Hammond's, and Pacific-slope Flycatchers, Cassin's and Warbling Vireos, Orange-crowned, Black-throated, Townsend's, MacGillivray's, and Wilson's Warblers, Western Tanager, Black-headed Grosbeak, and Purple Finch. In June and July the **Beaver Lake** area has the greatest variety of birds, partly because of the denser forest there (less wind damage). The lake itself is shallow and choked with water lilies, and has breeding Pied-billed Grebes, Wood Ducks, and Mallards.

Large numbers of passerine migrants can be seen some days in April, May, late August, and September. The best areas, especially in spring, are usually the ornamental plantings west of Lost Lagoon and around **Brockton Point**—especially where there are maples, which seem to provide many insects.

Besides the everyday birds, Stanley Park has produced many exciting rarities over the years. Examples include King and Common Eiders, Smew, Black-headed and Sabine's Gulls, Great Gray Owl, Least Flycatcher, Black Phoebe, Philadelphia Vireo, Clark's Nutcracker, Black-and-white Warbler, Ovenbird, and Grasshopper Sparrow.

CRESTED MYNA

Crested Mynas were accidentally introduced at Vancouver in 1897. Numbering over 20,000 birds at its peak, the population declined dramatically after about 1980. As of 2002 only one pair was left, in an industrial area at the intersection of First Avenue and Wylie Street near the south end of the Cambie Street Bridge.* Mynas seen at other locations are usually reported on the Vancouver rare bird alert.

* Killed by traffic in February 2003 (Ed.).

Puget Sound

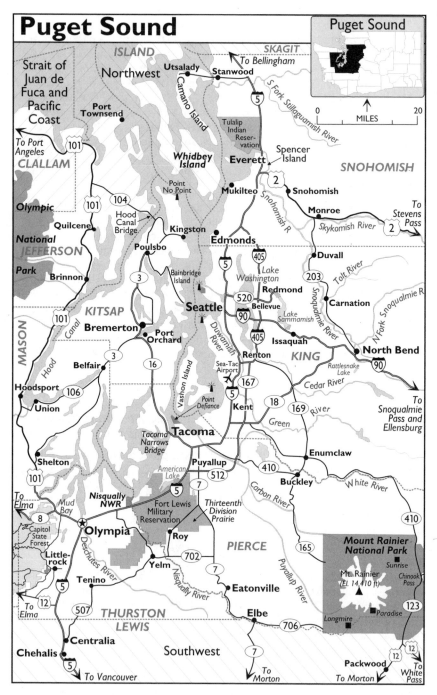

PUGET SOUND

Puget Sound is a region of strong contrasts. Sixty percent of the state's population lives along the east shore of the Sound from Everett to Tacoma, in a narrow, crowded, 70-mile strip undergoing the trials of rapid growth. At the other extreme lie some 1,400 square miles of roadless, uninhabited wilderness, including all or parts of 11 designated Wilderness Areas and two National Parks. In little more than an hour one can move from monumental urban traffic snarls to "difficult hiking over steep forested slopes and along exposed ridges through tangles of huckleberry and thimbleberry . . . a wilderness experience seldom surpassed in primitive solitude and exertion."* Truly there is something here for every birding taste!

The region's greatest glory is the Sound itself, plied by Washington's famous ferries. The open waters and shorelines of the deep Main Basin from Point No Point past Seattle and Tacoma to The Narrows, and of the South Sound, Hood Canal, and the many lesser bays, inlets, and passages, harbor some of the largest populations of marine birds in the U.S. Five major rivers drain into the Sound from the West Central Cascades. The estuaries of the Duwamish (Seattle) and the Puyallup (Tacoma) have been converted to pure industrial landscapes, but the Snohomish estuary at Everett, although much reduced, still has some fine bird habitat. The Stillaguamish and the Nisqually—the smallest of the five estuaries and the least disturbed—are among the state's best birding sites, despite having been partially drained and diked for agriculture.

The low-elevation Puget Sound Douglas-fir zone surrounds the Sound, ringed successively by the Western Hemlock, Silver Fir, Mountain Hemlock, and Alpine/Parkland zones as one moves up the slopes to the permanent ice and snow of Mount Rainier—at 14,410 feet, the highest peak in Washington. Set into the lowland Douglas-fir south of the Sound is the unique Woodland/Prairie Mosaic zone, a landscape of dry grasslands and Garry Oaks. Significant parts of the higher-elevation zones are in protected status, but those at lower elevations are greatly altered. The Puget Sound Douglas-fir forest is mostly gone, and the oak prairies are sadly reduced. The Western Hemlock zone now consists largely of managed forests. And yet, thanks to a good system of urban, suburban, and rural parks and natural areas, each of these zones still retains its characteristic birdlife.

---

* Wonder Mountain Wilderness Area web page:
    www.wilderness.net/nwps/wild_view.cfm?wname=Wonder%20Mountain

The Sound enjoys a favorable climate for birds and for those who wish to find them. At the Seattle-Tacoma airport, the average annual precipitation is 39 inches (the same as Indianapolis, Tulsa, and Washington, DC); 158 days have some precipitation (like Pittsburgh and Cleveland); winters are mild (January average temperature 39 degrees, the same as Raleigh and Little Rock) and summers cool (July average temperature 65 degrees, as at Duluth and Caribou, Maine). Annual precipitation increases as one moves eastward up the Cascade slopes (105 inches at Snoqualmie Pass) or southwestward around the Olympics toward the coast (52 inches in Olympia). Most of the winter precipitation in the mountains falls in the form of snow. Snoqualmie Pass on I-90 is open most of the time, but ice and snow are a common hazard and traction devices may be required. Stevens Pass on US-2 is frequently closed for snow clearance, and Chinook Pass on SR-410 is closed for the entire winter season. Snow is infrequent in the lowlands, but a couple of inches that stick can cause a real mess. Traffic is always a mess in the urban agglomeration, even in nice weather. Monster tie-ups on I-5, I-90, and other major thoroughfares are becoming routine. Drive smart. Try not to be a returning weekender on Sundays or holidays. You'll do fine if you avoid morning and evening rush hours and listen to the radio traffic reports.

Seattle Birding Areas

1 Discovery Park
2 Montlake Fill
3 Washington Park Arboretum
4 Edmonds Marsh / Fishing Pier
5 Alki Beach Park

6 City of Tukwila Shops
7 Marymoor Park
8 Lake Sammamish State Park
9 Cougar Mountain Regional Wildland Park

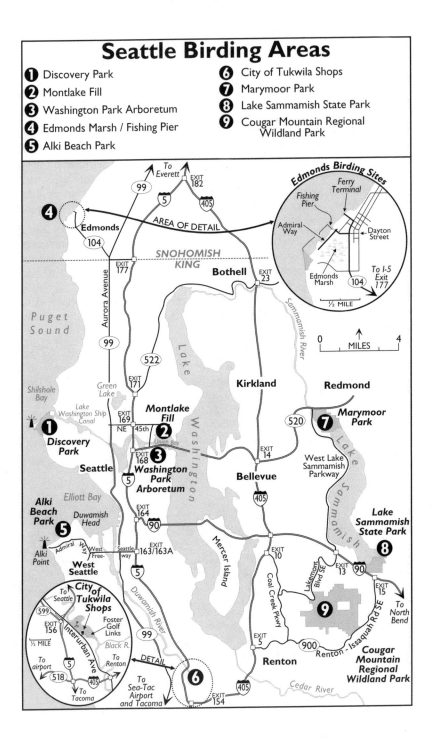

SEATTLE AND VICINITY

by Hal Opperman

Seattle is built around Elliott Bay, at the estuary of the Duwamish River. Two miles east, Lake Washington gathers the flow of the Sammamish and Cedar Rivers from the Cascades and foothills. When the first settlers arrived the surrounding lands were covered with an ancient forest of Douglas-fir and other conifers. The outlet of Lake Washington was the Black River, at its southern end. The Green River, draining the Cascades to the southeast and flowing northward from present-day Kent across a wide floodplain, joined the Black River in Tukwila to form the Duwamish. Vast tidelands occupied the southern end of Elliott Bay at the mouth of the Duwamish, some ten miles farther north.

Today one sees a radically altered landscape. Long ago, the ancient forests found their way to the sawmill. The Duwamish was dredged to deepen and straighten it for port facilities. Railroad yards were built on fill where the tidelands used to be. The opening of the Ship Canal to Puget Sound (1916) lowered the level of Lake Washington ten feet, and the Black River ceased to flow. The flat floodplain valley of the Green River, with its rich alluvial soils, was first cleared for farming, and then succumbed to industrial and commercial development.

Despite the changes, nearly all of the typical Puget Lowlands avian species can still be found easily and enjoyably without leaving the Seattle metropolitan area. Described below are three fine birding sites right in the city—Discovery Park, the Montlake Fill, and the Washington Park Arboretum. Four specialty sites are listed with less detail. The metropolitan area is fringed on the east by a rapidly expanding belt of suburbs along the Sammamish Trough, from Woodinville and Redmond south to Issaquah. Birding opportunities in three large outlying parks will well repay the 20 minutes of freeway driving required to reach them from the city.

DISCOVERY PARK

Seattle's best one-stop birding venue, Discovery Park can be exciting at any season. More than 230 bird species have been recorded in the park—half the number for the whole state. Scattered throughout its 534 acres are representative fragments of most of the habitat types that can be found in the immediate Seattle area, with salt water, beaches, meadows, and mixed forest being the most important. Sixty species of birds breed here, and 80 species might be found on a good day during migration.

From I-5 Exit 169, go west on NE 45th Street through the Wallingford business district. Follow the arterial as it slants right to N 46th, passes under the SR-99 viaduct, bends right again in a few more blocks to become NW Market Street, and angles down the side of Phinney Ridge into Ballard. Continue west on Market to 15th Avenue NW, turn left (south) and cross the bridge over the Ship Canal, then go right on Emerson Street (becomes W Emerson Place) past the

Fishermen's Terminal and railroad yard to the stop sign at Gilman Avenue W. Turn right onto Gilman, following this arterial as it becomes W Government Way, swinging west, south, and finally west again to the park's east entrance, a bit more than five miles from I-5. (*From downtown Seattle* take Western Avenue northwestward above the waterfront; stay with the arterial as it turns north onto

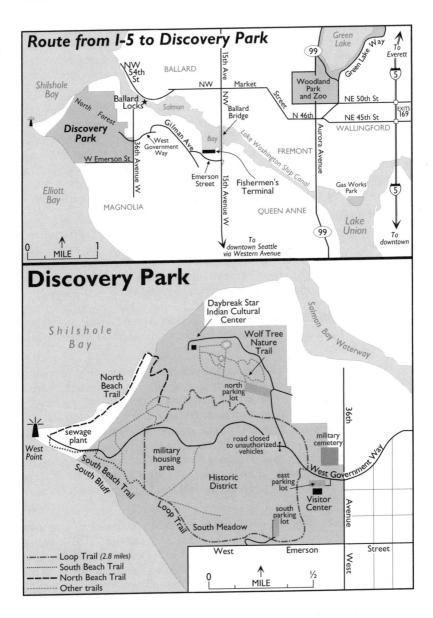

Route from I-5 to Discovery Park

Green Lake
99
To Everett
5
Green Lake Way

NW 54th St
BALLARD
15th Ave NW
Woodland Park and Zoo
NE 50th St

Shilshole Bay
NW Market
Street
N 46th
NE 45th St
EXITS 169
WALLINGFORD

Ballard Locks
North Forest
Salman
Ballard Bridge
Lake Washington Ship Canal
Aurora Avenue
FREMONT

Discovery Park
Gilman Ave
West Government Way
Bay

W Emerson St
36th Avenue W
Emerson Street
Fishermen's Terminal
Gas Works Park
5

Elliott Bay
15th Avenue W
QUEEN ANNE
Lake Union
To downtown

MAGNOLIA
99

0 MILE 1
To downtown Seattle via Western Avenue

Discovery Park

Daybreak Star Indian Cultural Center

Shilshole Bay
Wolf Tree Nature Trail
Salmon Bay Waterway

North Beach Trail
north parking lot
36th

sewage plant
military cemetery

West Point
South Beach Trail
South Bluff
military housing area
road closed to unauthorized vehicles
West Government Way

Historic District
east parking lot
Visitor Center
Avenue

Loop Trail
south parking lot
South Meadow

West
Emerson
Street
West

—·—·— Loop Trail (2.8 miles)
·········· South Beach Trail
— — — North Beach Trail
·········· Other trails

0 MILE ½

15th Avenue W, then exit right to loop across 15th onto Emerson Street, which heads west past the Fishermen's Terminal, as above.)

A short distance inside the park, turn left into the east parking lot by the visitor center (open 8:30AM–5PM daily except holidays). Here you may pick up maps and a bird list, and ask the naturalist about current bird-sightings information, birdwalks, and other programs. Permits are available for senior citizens and those with disabilities to drive down to West Point and park. Otherwise you may leave your car here, or continue along the main park road 0.5 mile to the north parking lot, or drive south from the east entrance on 36th Avenue W, then west on W Emerson Street, to the south entrance and parking lot.

The moderately level **Loop Trail**, 2.8 miles, circles the park, passing through woods, thickets, and grasslands. This leisurely circuit takes two hours; many side-trails lead to beach and wetland habitats. Listen for the insect-like "song" of male Anna's Hummingbirds in clearings. Hutton's Vireo is easy to find in spring by its monotonous zwee...zwee song. Owls may surprise you at any location or season. Bald Eagles survey the shoreline, and sometimes nest in the park. Pigeon Guillemots have nested in the South Bluff.

South Meadow has nesting Savannah Sparrows in summer, and occasionally a few Western Meadowlarks in winter. Raptors are often seen here, especially in fall. Look for Anna's and Rufous Hummingbirds, Willow Flycatcher, Orange-crowned Warbler, and Black-headed Grosbeak in brush or trees around the edges. Parts of the meadow have recently been cleared of Scot's Broom and other invasive growth and replaced by new plantings of Salal, snowberry, huckleberry, Oregon-grape, and other natives, providing excellent habitat for birds. Remnant Scot's Broom (especially near the military housing units) and blackberry tangles are good for sparrows, including Lincoln's and Golden-crowned in fall.

North Forest is a thick belt of mixed woodland with clearings, extending from the visitor center across the north side of the park. In winter, look for a Hutton's Vireo or a warbler in the numerous flocks of small passerines. Accipiters are fairly common. Red-breasted Sapsucker is an uncommon visitor, usually around the beginning of the year. **Wolf Tree Nature Trail** leaves from the northwest corner of the north parking lot and is a good place in summer for Cassin's and Warbling Vireos, Winter Wren, Swainson's Thrush, and Black-throated Gray Warbler. A spur trail leads west to three small ponds where you may find herons, swallows, waxwings, and small numbers of ducks.

West Point, jutting out into Puget Sound, is an outstanding birding spot, with sandy and rocky shorelines and an historic lighthouse (1881). North Beach Trail (prone to mudslide closure: check at the visitor center) descends the bluff to a riprap retaining wall. Loons, grebes, and ducks, including an occasional Long-tailed or Harlequin Duck, can be found on Shilshole Bay, while a long freshwater pond above the beach attracts dabbling ducks and other waterfowl. Look for Wandering Tattler (fall) and Whimbrel (fall or spring) on rocky outcrops exposed at high tide. Songbirds frequent the fringe of small trees, especially in migration. Both the north and south sandy beaches are good for shorebirds. Merlin and Peregrine Falcon are possible. Migrating Brant use the eelgrass beds offshore (January–April). West Point itself is a fine lookout for gulls, terns, alcids, and other waterbirds. Small numbers of Ancient Murrelets are likely in fall (November is best). Careful observation of the large fall flocks of Bonaparte's Gulls may result in a sighting of a rare Little or Sabine's Gull, or a dashing Parasitic Jaeger. Franklin's (rare), Heermann's (uncommon), and Thayer's Gulls may be seen close in. During stormy periods of strong southwest winds there is even a chance of a Sooty or a Short-tailed Shearwater well offshore, especially in late fall. South Beach Trail leads back up to the Loop Trail and South Meadow.

MONTLAKE FILL AND UNION BAY

The Montlake Fill ("the Fill" for short; officially, Union Bay Natural Area) is a popular and productive birding destination on Lake Washington. When the lake level was lowered an extensive marsh emerged from the shallows of Union Bay at the mouth of Ravenna Creek. For the next 50 years the marsh was gradually filled with garbage and converted to shopping malls, athletic fields, and parking lots, until dumping ceased in 1966. The most recent fill was covered with soil, graded, seeded, and left to nature. This 35-acre tract grew up to grass and scattered brush with a few broadleaf trees and remnants of the marsh around the edges. Almost at once, this patch of accidental prairie became a magnet for birds. Over 200 species have been recorded, including state rarities such as Blue-headed Vireo, Chestnut-collared Longspur, and Indigo Bunting. Birds more commonly associated with Eastern Washington stray regularly to this little island of habitat, for example, American Kestrel, Say's Phoebe, both kingbirds, Loggerhead Shrike, Mountain Bluebird, American Redstart, Northern Waterthrush, Brewer's, Vesper, and Sage Sparrows, Lazuli Bunting, Bobolink, Western Meadowlark, and Yellow-headed Blackbird.

Several shallow ponds at the Fill (formed in depressions where the garbage settled unevenly) help compensate for Seattle's poverty of shorebird habitat, attracting a great diversity of species in spring and fall migration—never many birds at a time, but the cast changes daily. In addition to the usual yellowlegs, dowitchers, and peeps, there are records for American and Pacific Golden-Plovers, Black-necked Stilt, American Avocet, Solitary, Upland, Semipalmated, Baird's, Pectoral, Sharp-tailed, and Stilt Sandpipers, and Ruff. American Bittern, Green Heron, Virginia Rail, and Sora are in the marsh much of the year (uncommon to absent in winter). The ponds and adjacent Union Bay host many ducks, including Blue-winged and Cinnamon Teals in summer. In summer and migration, Vaux's Swifts are common, and Black Swifts may forage

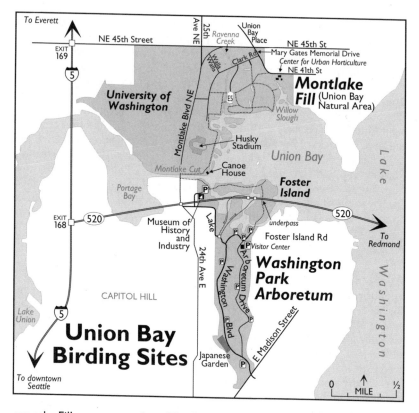

To Everett

NE 45th Street

EXIT 169

University of Washington

Montlake Blvd NE

25th Ave NE

Walla Walla

Ravenna Creek

Union Bay Place

NE 45th St

Clark Rd

Mary Gates Memorial Drive
Center for Urban Horticulture
NE 41th St

Montlake Fill (Union Bay Natural Area)

ES

Willow Slough

Husky Stadium

Montlake Cut

Canoe House

Union Bay

Foster Island

Portage Bay

EXIT 168 520

Museum of History and Industry

Lake

24th Ave E

P

520

To Redmond

underpass

Foster Island Rd

Visitor Center

Washington Park Arboretum

Arboretum Drive

Washington Blvd

CAPITOL HILL

Lake Union

Union Bay Birding Sites

Japanese Garden

E Madison Street

To downtown Seattle

Lake Washington

0   MILE   ½

over the Fill on overcast days. The Fill is actively managed as a mix of habitats, with open grassland, native shrubs, and ponds bordered by plantings or left with open edges. Invasive Scot's Broom, Himalayan Blackberry, and Purple Loosestrife are being brought under control. When you visit, please stay on the paths.

To reach the Fill, go east from I-5 Exit 169 onto NE 45th Street, through the University District, along the north edge of the University of Washington campus, and down a viaduct across 25th Avenue NE to a traffic light. Bear left here, and at the next light go right onto Mary Gates Memorial Drive (Union Bay Place NE on older maps). You may park along this road except where signs say otherwise. To park close to the center of things, take the first right, Clark Road, and drive 350 yards to the fourth turning on the left for University of Washington parking lot E-5 (bring six quarters to purchase ticket from machine; free Saturday afternoon and Sunday). Find someplace else to go birding on football Saturdays.

To explore the other side of Union Bay, you can walk around the end of Husky Stadium, along the Montlake Cut, left over the bridge, then left again down the steps and back east on the other side of the canal to the Museum of

History and Industry; you can also drive to the museum as described in the next paragraph. A footpath (often wet) follows the shoreline on the left (and the roaring traffic of SR-520 on the right) to the tip of Foster Island. Tree Swallow, Marsh Wren, Common Yellowthroat, and other species nest along the path north of the freeway. Union Bay can be packed with waterbirds, especially in winter, and Foster Island is an excellent vantage point. Most of the Union Bay Marsh is inaccessible on foot but birdable by canoe or kayak. Daytime canoe rentals are available from February through October at the University of Washington Canoe House, at the northeast corner of the Montlake Cut: call 206-543-9433 for details.

WASHINGTON PARK ARBORETUM

The neighboring Washington Park Arboretum was designed and installed as part of John C. Olmsted's plan for Seattle parks and boulevards (1903–1936). The 230-acre public park holds the second-largest collection of temperate woody plants in North America. To get there on foot, walk to the north end of Foster Island as described above, then through the highway underpass to the main part of the island (see map). Or you may drive there from the Fill by returning along Mary Gates Memorial Drive to NE 45th Street and turning left (west). Stay in the left lane and follow the road as it curves south, joining Montlake Boulevard NE. You will pass Husky Stadium and cross the bridge over the Montlake Cut. Remain in the left lane, and immediately after the SR-520 overpass, turn left onto Lake Washington Boulevard E. The entrance road to the Museum of History and Industry, with parking for the trail along Union Bay, is on the left a short distance ahead. Lake Washington Boulevard curves right (south), then left, to a stop sign. Turn left at the next stop sign a few hundred feet ahead onto E Foster Island Road, which ends in about 0.2 mile, near the footbridge to Foster Island.

Foster Island woodlands and nearby backwaters of Union Bay are good for small songbirds, including mixed winter foraging flocks of chickadees, nuthatches, and kinglets. Rare vagrants such as Blue-gray Gnatcatcher and Tennessee, Chestnut-sided, and Black-and-white Warblers have been found here. The Seattle area's largest winter roost of American Crows (10,000 or more) is at Foster Island. At dawn, birds stream out to all the compass points, returning in the late afternoon. The rest of the Arboretum stretches south from Foster Island for about a mile, to Madison Street; there are several parking lots. Among its plantings you will find a good assortment of summer and year-round resident edge-loving and forest birds, including Hutton's Vireo and Bewick's Wren, plus others in migration. Western Screech-, Great Horned, and Barred Owls are sometimes found in the Arboretum.

SPECIALTY SITES

To round out the possibilities, here are four places in or on the edges of Seattle that offer specialty birding. (See Seattle Birding Areas map, page 155.)

The **Edmonds Marsh** has birds of saltwater marsh and mudflats, a rare habitat type for the Seattle area (take SR-104 west from I-5 Exit 177 to the Edmonds ferry dock; do not get in the ferry lanes but turn left onto Dayton Street, then left into a parking lot just before the railroad crossing; the marsh is at the back).

The **Edmonds Fishing Pier**, at the north end of the marina, is excellent for seabird viewing (from the Edmonds Marsh, cross the railroad tracks on Dayton Street, park, and walk out).

Alki Beach Park in West Seattle is a fairly consistent place for rocky shorebirds in winter, especially at Duwamish Head on the north end and around Alki Point to the south, and is also a good seabird overlook (take Exit 163A from I-5 southbound, or Exit 163 if northbound, onto the West Seattle Freeway, then SW Admiral Way to 63rd Avenue SW, and turn right one block to the waterfront).

The **City of Tukwila Shops**, on the banks of the Duwamish River adjacent to Foster Golf Links, are known for early-winter congregations of "pink-legged" gulls (Glaucous-winged, Glaucous-winged X Western hybrids, and Thayer's are common; Herring is fairly common; Glaucous is rare but regular). Take Exit 156 from I-5, go south on Interurban Avenue, and turn left onto S 140th Street half a mile from the freeway underpass. Look for gulls on the shop roofs and on the nearby fairways.

LAKE SAMMAMISH

Occupying 640 acres of former farmland, **Marymoor Park** sits at the north end of Lake Sammamish, in the heart of the outer suburban belt. Despite heavy use (over one million visitors a year), the park offers good birding in all seasons, with an eclectic list of over 150 species. Early morning on a weekday is the best time to visit. Travel east from Seattle on SR-520 to the West Lake Sammamish Parkway NE exit. Turn right. The park entrance is 0.2 mile south of the offramp, on the left. In about 0.4 mile, at the third stop sign, turn right and continue to the south parking lot. From the far left corner of the lot, take the short trail to the Sammamish River, and turn left. From here, a 1.5-mile loop on park trails will take you through most of the habitats. For the first half-mile the trail follows the river through riparian habitat inside the dog-exercise area. At the weir (200 yards), swallows and Common Yellowthroats abound in summer. Dog-swimming accesses provide good spots to search the far bank of the river for Green Heron and Spotted Sandpiper. Willow Flycatchers nest along the river; Ruby-crowned Kinglets and Fox Sparrows are numerous in winter. The whole riparian area can be excellent in mi-

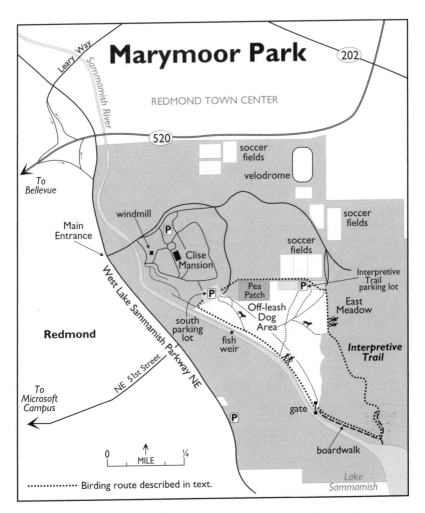

Marymoor Park

REDMOND TOWN CENTER

Leary Way

Sammamish River

202

520

To Bellevue

soccer fields

velodrome

Main Entrance

windmill

P

Clise Mansion

soccer fields

soccer fields

Interpretive Trail parking lot

P

P

Pea Patch

Off-leash Dog Area

East Meadow

Redmond

south parking lot

fish weir

Interpretive Trail

West Lake Sammamish Parkway NE

NE 51st Street

To Microsoft Campus

gate

P

boardwalk

Lake Sammamish

0   ¼
MILE

•••••••••••••• Birding route described in text.

gration for vireos, warblers, tanagers, and orioles. At the other end of the dog area, go through a gate and continue along the Interpretive Trail to a board-walk beside the river. The boardwalk takes you to the north end of Lake Sammamish at the outlet of the Sammamish River where you can scope for waterbirds. Black Swifts regularly forage over the lake on cloudy summer days. Bending sharply left, the trail goes through a marsh on a boardwalk, fol-lowed by a small deciduous woodland and finally wet grasslands lined by wil-lows. You should find Rufous Hummingbird, Red-eyed Vireo, Marsh Wren, Swainson's Thrush, Yellow Warbler, and Black-headed Grosbeak in summer; Orange-crowned Warbler and other migrants; and Black-capped Chickadee, Bewick's Wren, and American Goldfinch year round. The trail approaches the eastern side of the dog area and follows the fence northward for 200 yards to the Interpretive Trail parking lot. East Meadow, on the right, has nesting Savannah Sparrow in summer and may have Short-eared Owl, Northern Shrike, and Western Meadowlark in winter. Walk back west to the south parking lot across the soccer fields or the north end of the dog area. Sparrows gather at the edges of the Pea Patch community gardens in fall. The grass soccer fields can have gulls and shorebirds in winter and American Pipits in fall. The park's open areas attract the occasional Say's Phoebe, Mountain Bluebird, Lazuli Bunting, or other species typical of the open landscapes of Eastern Washington. Barn Owls nest in the windmill by the old mansion.

Lake Sammamish State Park occupies 506 acres at the south end of the lake, at I-90 Exit 15. At a traffic light just north of the interchange, turn left onto NW Sammamish Road. In 0.4 mile, turn right into the park entrance. The park is crowded on weekends and warm summer days. The quietest part is at the back, away from the beach and the freeway. Continue all the way in (north) to the last parking lot and cross the footbridge over Issaquah Creek (look for Wood Ducks and mergansers, and returning salmon in fall and early winter). Turn left and follow the path, bordered by tall trees, to the mouth of the creek. Expect a typical array of lowland-riparian songbirds in the breeding

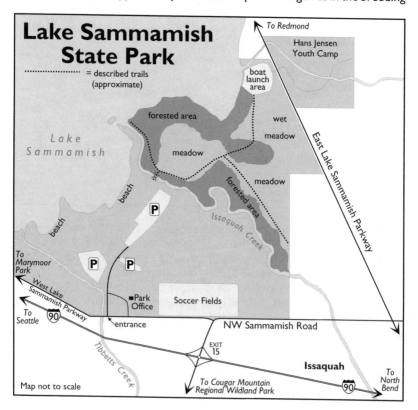

Lake Sammamish
State Park

············· = described trails
(approximate)

To Redmond

Hans Jensen
Youth Camp

boat
launch
area

forested area

wet
meadow

Lake
Sammamish

meadow

meadow

East Lake Sammamish Parkway

beach

P

beach

Issaquah Creek

forested area

P

To
Marymoor
Park

P

West Lake
Sammamish Parkway

To
Seattle

90

Park
Office

Soccer Fields

entrance

NW Sammamish Road

EXIT
15

Issaquah

To
North
Bend

Tibbetts Creek

Map not to scale

To Cougar Mountain
Regional Wildland Park

90

season; look for Green Heron on logs and low branches next to the stream. Lake shoreline and open water have a seasonal variety of ducks, gulls, and other waterbirds. Backtrack and continue on straight ahead without recrossing the footbridge. An open meadow is on the left and the stream on the right, both bordered by willows. Willow Flycatcher, Yellow Warbler, Common Yellowthroat, and Savannah Sparrow nest here. Look for the Great Blue Heron nesting colony in trees to the north, between the meadow and the lake. A broad, mown path (can be muddy in spots) leads across the meadow. At the back of the first meadow, the trail forks; take the left branch through a band of blackberries, willows, and hazelnut brush. The trail traverses a patch of deciduous woods (Oregon Ash, Black Cottonwood), then a tussocky wet meadow (Marsh Wren in summer, Northern Shrike in winter, Lincoln's Sparrow in fall migration), joining the willow-fringed lakeshore and boat launch parking area at the northeast corner of the park in about 0.7 mile. The park can be good in migration, and unusual birds sometimes winter here; Black Swifts forage overhead on summer days when low cloud cover has the mountains socked in. An abandoned railroad right-of-way follows the Lake Sammamish shoreline from the boat launch area north about eight miles to Marymoor Park, and has been acquired by King County for a trail. Birding possibilities are promising, although as yet untested.

COUGAR MOUNTAIN

A lobe of mountains geologically older than the Cascades, with forests of the Western Hemlock zone, reaches from North Bend all the way to Lake Washington. The 3,082-acre **Cougar Mountain Regional Wildland Park,** situated just south of Lake Sammamish, offers fine hiking opportunities and a foretaste of Cascades birding on the westernmost of these "Issaquah Alps." The land has a long history of abuse, from coal mines to logging and Cold War military installations. The present park, with interpretive displays and 36 miles of well-maintained trails, resulted from citizen initiatives when the missile silos were decommissioned in 1965. Maps are available at the Red Town, Wilderness Creek, and Anti-Aircraft Peak trailheads.

Forests are slowly returning to a natural state. Red Alder, Bigleaf Maple, and other deciduous trees are reaching climax in some stands; second-growth conifers (Western Hemlock, Douglas-fir, Western Redcedar, some Sitka Spruce) prevail in other areas. The understory is of Swordfern, Oregongrape, Salmonberry, and other plants of damp, shade-loving places. Some virgin forest remains near the summit of 1,595-foot Wilderness Peak.

The park supports a healthy population of owls (Western Screech-, Great Horned, Barred, Northern Saw-whet). Common Raven and Black Bear are found here—as close to Seattle as these species get. Varied Thrush and Townsend's Warbler nest in the eastern Issaquah Alps, where the conifer forest is more intact, but sometimes occur here as well. Birds of woods and

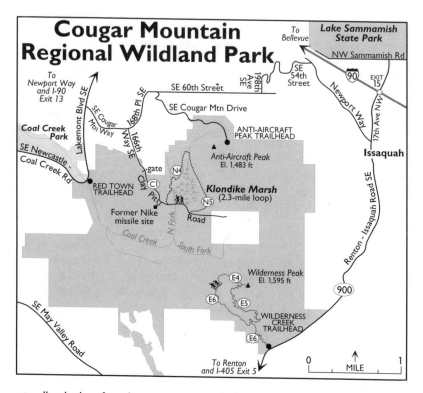

Cougar Mountain Regional Wildland Park

woodland edges found year round include Ruffed Grouse, Band-tailed Pigeon, Red-breasted Sapsucker (stream courses), Downy, Hairy, and Pileated Woodpeckers, Hutton's Vireo, Steller's Jay, Black-capped and Chestnut-backed Chickadees, Bushtit, Brown Creeper, Bewick's and Winter Wrens, Golden-crowned Kinglet, Spotted Towhee, Song Sparrow, Dark-eyed Junco, Purple Finch, and Pine Siskin. These are joined in summer by Rufous Hummingbird, Willow (wetlands and cleared areas), Hammond's (coniferous forest), and Pacific-slope Flycatchers, Cassin's and Warbling Vireos, Swainson's Thrush, Orange-crowned, Black-throated Gray, and Wilson's Warblers, Western Tanager, and Black-headed Grosbeak (mostly along stream corridors).

There are several entrances and approaches to the park. From I-90 Exit 15, go south 3.1 miles on SR-900 (Renton-Issaquah Road SE) to the parking lot for the **Wilderness Creek Trailhead**, on the right (west) side of the road. Trail E6 climbs steeply through the best coniferous forest in the park, past gorges, cliffs, and jumbled blocks of andesite. Where the trail divides take either branch (E6/E4 to the left or E5 to the right) to Wilderness Peak and return by the other route in a 3.5-mile loop (1,200-foot elevation gain).

From I-405 Exit 10 (first exit south of the I-90 interchange), go southeast on Coal Creek Parkway SE. In 2.6 miles, make a sharp left onto SE Newcastle-Coal Creek Road. This road crosses Coal Creek (1.9 miles) and becomes Lakemont Boulevard SE. A parking area for the **Red Town Trailhead**, immediately on the right, gives access to riparian habitat and the historic mining district. Continue along Lakemont Boulevard SE 0.7 mile and turn right onto SE Cougar Mountain Way. In 0.5 mile, turn right onto 166th Way SE. Park near a gate (0.4 mile) at an unimproved trailhead. Walk past the gate along **Clay Pit Road** (Trail C1) about 700 yards to an abandoned Nike missile site (open grassy area on right). Klondike Marsh, a large forest wetland, is on the left in another 350 yards, encircled by Trails N4 and N5 (2.3-mile loop).

Return to SE Cougar Mountain Way. Veer right onto 168th Place SE, and follow the arterial right onto SE 60th Street a total of 0.5 mile. Turn right again onto SE Cougar Mountain Drive. The road ends in 1.1 miles at the park maintenance office on **Anti-Aircraft Peak** (elevation 1,483 feet; views of Lake Sammamish to the northeast, Squak and Tiger Mountains to the east and southeast). Several trails depart from the parking lot.

SNOQUALMIE VALLEY TO EVERETT

by Hal Opperman

At the end of the last ice age, impounded waters burst from a glacial lake east of the present site of North Bend, scouring out a lowland valley extending some forty miles to Puget Sound. Today, three forks of the Snoqualmie River come down from the Cascades to unite at the head of this valley. After plunging over Snoqualmie Falls a few miles downstream, the river meanders across a broad floodplain with ancient oxbows, ponds, marshes, wet meadows, and patches of woods. The Tolt River flows in from the east at Carnation, and the Skykomish joins the Snoqualmie near Monroe to form the Snohomish, with its estuary 15 miles farther on at Everett. Converted to farmland by early settlers, the valley has largely preserved its bucolic character despite intense development pressures. From foothills to tidelands, this riverine ecosystem offers the best all-round birding in the Seattle/Everett metropolitan area.

The route described below follows the river closely, with a representative selection of good birding spots. However, the enterprising will find the same birds practically anyplace in the valley where there is a bit of habitat. Those inclined to leave their cars will enjoy walking or biking along the Snoqualmie Valley Trail, an abandoned railroad grade between Cedar Falls and Duvall that provides many birding opportunities.

For the most part the birds mentioned are those that can be found in migration or the breeding season. Winter birding out in open country is also excellent, although access is regularly disrupted by flooding, and dense morning fog does enshroud the

Snohomish Flats occasionally. Look for raptors perched or hunting—a Golden Eagle or a Gyrfalcon is not an impossibility. Be on the alert for unusual species in winter sparrow flocks along brushy ditches and fencerows, blackberry tangles, and thicket edges. American Tree, Clay-colored, Swamp, White-throated, and Harris's Sparrows are possible among the numerous Spotted Towhees, Fox, Song, Lincoln's, White-crowned, and Golden-crowned Sparrows, and Dark-eyed Juncos. Windbreaks and pine plantations may harbor roosting owls. In wooded tracts, foraging flocks in conifers or among bare branches may include Downy Woodpecker, Hutton's Vireo, and Yellow-rumped or Townsend's Warblers along with Black-capped and Chestnut-backed Chickadees, Bushtit, Red-breasted Nuthatch, Brown Creeper, Bewick's Wren, Golden-crowned and Ruby-crowned Kinglets, and various finches. Winter Wrens frequent the understory, and now and then you may pick up the call-note of a skulking Hermit Thrush.

RATTLESNAKE LAKE

The itinerary begins at the foot of the Cascades at Rattlesnake Lake, southeast of North Bend at an elevation of 900 feet. From I-90, go south at Exit 32 on 436th Avenue SE, which crosses the South Fork Snoqualmie River and changes name to Cedar Falls Road SE, arriving in 2.7 miles at the blue entrance sign for the **Rattlesnake Lake Recreation Area** (despite the name, there are no rattlesnakes in Western Washington). The first of several parking lots is 0.2 mile ahead, on the right. Ospreys patrol the lake in summer; Western Screech-Owls and Barred Owls nest in the surroundings. The John Wayne Pioneer Trail climbs across the Cascades from here to Eastern Washington, following the old Milwaukee Road railway grade. Local trails lead along the lakeshore and through the woods to Rattlesnake Ledge, with a fine overlook. Conifer-forest specialties on the way up may include Hairy Woodpecker, Varied Thrush, and Townsend's Warbler. Peregrine Falcons have nested on the rock face. The road ends at the head of the lake at Cedar Falls, administrative center for the Cedar River Watershed.

The principal source of Seattle's drinking water, the 141-square-mile watershed is managed as an ecological reserve, closed to the public. Common Loons nesting on the reservoir produce half of the state's fledgling loons each year—inquire at the Education Center about special tours to see them. Except for tours, you are limited to exploring the watershed around the edges. For one productive spot, go back to the entrance sign for the recreation area, turn right (east) onto an unmarked gravel road, and continue straight about 150 yards to a closed gate. Park out of the way and walk around the gate. In 100 feet, walk around a second closed gate on the left. Follow the track through mixed forest, primarily big old Red Alders with some second-growth conifers and Black Cottonwoods, with a large wetland on your left. In about a quarter-mile stay right where the track forks, then right again in another 400 feet and continue a short distance to **Christmas Lake**, a shallow lake with much emergent vegetation and drowned-out snags where Tree Swallows nest.

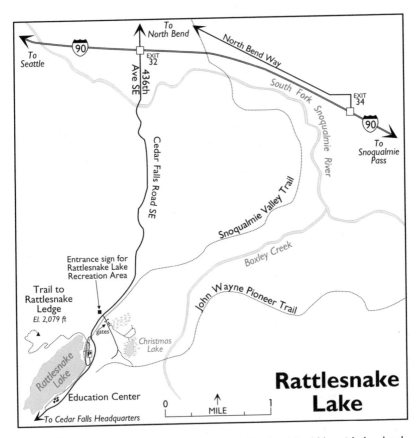

Woods and shoreline offer a fine selection of birds of the Westside lowlands in migration and summer, including Band-tailed Pigeon, Vaux's Swift, Rufous Hummingbird, Red-breasted Sapsucker, Pileated Woodpecker, Western Wood-Pewee, Willow, Hammond's, and Pacific-slope Flycatchers, Hutton's and Warbling Vireos, Red-breasted Nuthatch, Winter Wren, Swainson's Thrush, Cedar Waxwing, Yellow, Black-throated Gray, and Wilson's Warblers, Common Yellowthroat, Spotted Towhee, Song Sparrow, Black-headed Grosbeak, Purple Finch, and Evening Grosbeak.

You may return by the same route, or instead follow the path to the right at the first fork, which soon goes downslope along a fenceline to another fork. Go left here to the next fork where you first turned off to reach Christmas Lake, and continue right back to the gate. A more extensive hike takes you around the south end of Christmas Lake by turning left from the gate rather than right back to your car. Follow the road as it bends to the right. In about 350 yards, look for a utility pole and a small wooden sign indicating a trail on the left. This trail follows a fence, skirts the lake, and climbs the embankment of the railroad-grade trail. Go left; in 0.5 mile the grade crosses Boxley Creek. In the early hours of 23 December 1916 a glacial moraine incorporated into the retaining wall of a reservoir on the Cedar River, to the south, ruptured. The resultant flow of water and debris swept away the railroad embankment and rushed down Boxley Creek to the South Fork Snoqualmie, destroying the settlement of Edgewick and a lumber mill. The scars are still visible on the landscape. One of them is Christmas Lake.

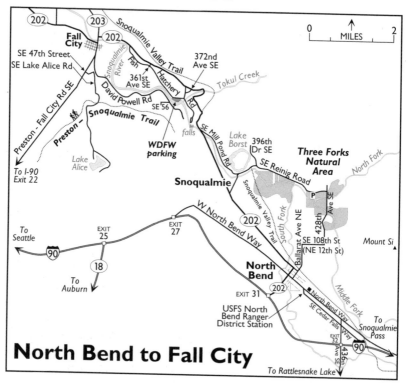

NORTH BEND TO FALL CITY

North Bend is easily accessible from I-90. From North Bend Way in the center of the business district, turn north onto Ballarat Avenue NE (two blocks east of SR-202). Stay on this main road as it changes name and turns right (0.6 mile) toward Mount Si, then left (0.5 mile) in a rural setting where it becomes 428th Avenue SE. The road soon crosses the Middle and North Fork Snoqualmie Rivers a few hundred yards apart. In 1.4 miles turn left (west) onto SE Reinig Road. Pull into a small parking area 0.2 mile farther ahead on the left, at the entrance to **Three Forks Natural Area**. A trail leads to the river through tall broadleaf trees and thickets. The union of North and Middle Forks is close to this spot, and that with the South Fork half a mile downstream. Red-eyed Vireo, locally distributed in Washington and a Snoqualmie Valley specialty, can be found in mature riparian vegetation here and elsewhere along the river. Walk the broad cobble margins looking for swallows and swifts overhead, Spotted Sandpiper on gravel bars, Green Heron in overhanging streamside vegetation, and Common Merganser on the river. Continue driving west on Reinig Road. The river is never far, and there are several places to pull off to bird. At the stop sign in 1.5 miles, where 396th Drive SE comes in from the right, bear left with Reinig Road, and turn right at the fork in 0.3 mile onto SE Mill Pond Road. Lake Borst, in an old river oxbow on the right (0.4 mile), is good for ducks. In another 0.9 mile, Stearns Road branches off to the right. Stay left to the intersection with Snoqualmie-Fall City Road (SR-202), just ahead.

Turn right at the stop sign. On the left in 0.3 mile is the visitor center for 272-foot-high **Snoqualmie Falls**, a popular day-trip destination for residents of Pugetopolis. The falls in full flow are a spectacular sensory experience, but if water is being diverted for power generation, they can be reduced to a trickle. Peregrine Falcons nest beside the falls on rock ledges. Continue along SR-202 and turn left onto 372nd Avenue SE (1.4 miles). In 0.2 mile, turn right onto SE Fish Hatchery Road, then immediately left into the WDFW parking lot (permit required). Scramble down the short trail to the Snoqualmie River where it emerges from the gorge below the falls; Tokul Creek flows into the river just upstream on the left. This is a good place to find American Dipper. Continue downriver (left from the parking lot) along **Fish Hatchery Road**, pulling off frequently to bird streamside trees, open fields, and scattered wetlands. Black and Vaux's Swifts can sometimes be seen overhead. At 0.6 mile, an oxbow on the right supports an extensive marsh, home to Hooded Merganser, Wilson's Snipe, and Marsh Wren. Opposite, the river curves away to the left at the site of historic Fort Tilton (sign). Continue ahead to 361st Avenue SE (0.3 mile) and turn right to rejoin SR-202 in 0.1 mile. Turn left here to the intersection with SR-203 in Fall City (1.6 miles).

Follow SR-202 left over the Snoqualmie River bridge. Do not turn right with SR-202, but instead swing left onto Preston-Fall City Road SE. In 0.3 mile, turn left (east) onto **SE David Powell Road**. Bird your way along the road as it traverses forest, wetlands, and rural homesteads, and in 1.9 miles comes alongside the Snoqualmie River with a pasture on the right. Bullock's Orioles have nested here. The public road ends at the junction with SE 56th Street at Fall City Trees (0.4 mile). Return to the Preston-Fall City Road and turn left. In 0.2 mile, turn left (east) onto SE 47th Street, which in 0.2 mile bends south and becomes SE Lake Alice Road. In another 0.6 mile, turn right into a parking lot where the road intersects the **Preston-Snoqualmie Trail**, a former railroad grade. Park and cross back over the road. The blacktopped trail goes east along a wooded hillside, ending in 1.8 miles at an overlook high above Snoqualmie Falls. On an early morning in June the trees are alive with songbirds. A Pileated Woodpecker may surprise you, or even a Barred Owl.

CARNATION AND VICINITY

From Fall City, drive west on SR-202, the Fall City-Redmond Road. Continue one mile to a junction with 324th Avenue. Turn right onto 324th Avenue NE and follow the paved road down the broad, flat valley as it jogs and changes names several times, eventually becoming West Snoqualmie River Road NE. Breeding species of this open landscape include Savannah and White-crowned Sparrows, Red-winged and Brewer's Blackbirds, House Finch, and American Goldfinch. In winter scan the sodden fields for ducks and other waterfowl,

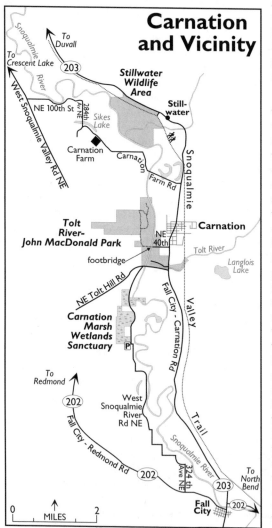

American Pipit, Western Meadowlark, and perhaps a Northern Shrike. Check brushy patches for winter sparrow flocks.

Note the entrance to Tall Chief Golf Course (2.6 miles) and continue past it to a turnout on the left in another 1.3 miles. Here an overgrown trail gives access to one corner of the Seattle Audubon Society's **Carnation Marsh Wetlands Sanctuary**, an unimproved tract extending northward for over a mile. This former river course is impenetrably vegetated and mostly flooded (with help from Beavers), and the road shoulders are narrow, so park at this spot and bird along the road on foot. Ninety-six species have been recorded in the breeding season, including American Bittern, ten species of ducks, Osprey, Ruffed Grouse, Virginia Rail, Wilson's Snipe, five species of woodpeckers (Red-breasted Sapsucker, Downy, Hairy, Northern Flicker, Pileated), Willow and Pacific-slope Flycatchers, four species of vireos, five of swallows, Marsh Wren, and most of the other Puget Lowlands songbird species.

Continue driving north to the intersection with NE Tolt Hill Road in 1.8 miles and turn right (east) onto a bridge over the Snoqualmie River. In 0.7 mile turn left again at the junction with Fall City-Carnation Road (SR-203), and drive north across the Tolt River into the town of Carnation. The main entrance to **Tolt River-John MacDonald Park** is reached by turning left onto NE 40th Street (0.5 mile). Go straight in to the last parking lot. You may walk south through the picnic area to the Tolt River at the point where it joins the Snoqualmie, birding the tall riparian trees, but the best birding is on the west bank of the Snoqualmie, reached by a suspension footbridge. This area of diverse habitats (forest, grasslands, brushy edges, riparian) is served by an extensive trail system. Expect almost any Western Washington lowland species including Cassin's, Hutton's, Warbling, and Red-eyed Vireos, Steller's Jay, Black-capped and Chestnut-backed Chickadees, Orange-crowned, Black-throated Gray, MacGillivray's, and Wilson's Warblers, Western Tanager, and Bullock's Oriole. As elsewhere along the Snoqualmie, swifts often forage overhead. Belted Kingfisher and many swallows can be seen from the bridge.

Return to SR-203. Turn left (north). In 3.3 miles, just past the Stillwater store, turn left into the **Stillwater Wildlife Area** and park (WDFW permit required). Bordered on the northeast by the highway and on the southwest by the river, this section of the Snoqualmie floodplain extends about a mile and a half as the river flows and three-quarters of a mile across. It is managed for hunting, with numerous open fields where grain crops are left to ripen for feed, framed by ditches, dikes, and sloughs. Maples, cottonwoods, alders, and willows flourish along watercourses; blackberries and other dense brush provide winter sparrow cover along field borders; cattails and sedges dominate the marshy places. Birds typical of these habitats can be found readily in the appropriate seasons. Avoid the area during the hunting season (September to January with some variation—the current year's regulations are usually posted at the parking area). The Snoqualmie Valley Trail passes the back end of the parking lot and can be safely walked even during the hunting season, as shooting is prohibited within 300 feet. In the non-hunting months of the year you may wander the area freely. A good cross-section of habitats can be sampled by walking right (northwest) along the trail from the parking lot. A marshy pond between trail and highway has herons and other waterbirds. In about 400 yards, a service road descends the embankment on your left. Follow this road toward the southwest. It turns left along a dike, right to follow a slough, left across the slough, then right again toward the river. At the back of the last field turn right when you reach a row of tall trees. Look for a path on your left going down to a plank bridge across a slough; you may flush Wood

Ducks. This is fine riparian habitat. The river lies just ahead but is difficult to reach through the dense understory.

Return to your car and head back toward Carnation. In 1.9 miles, turn right (west) onto Carnation Farm Road, which soon crosses the Snoqualmie River. The imposing **Carnation Farm** (2.3 miles), once a model dairy farm for "contented cows," is now a center for animal nutrition research operated by the Nestlé Corporation. Long, narrow Sikes Lake, lying in the valley just below the westernmost farm buildings, is good for ducks in winter. In 0.5 mile, 284th Avenue NE turns off to the right (north). A bridge across Sikes Lake is a fine vantage point. Along this and other valley roads hay fields saturated by winter rains host vast flocks of Gadwall, American Wigeon, Mallard, Northern Pintail, Green-winged Teal, and other ducks; Eurasian Wigeon can usually be picked out with a scope. Continue along 284th Avenue as it turns left and morphs into NE 100th Street—a lightly-used road with many places to stop to bird the fields and the river.

Turn right (north) onto West Snoqualmie Valley Road NE (2.0 miles). It is imprudent to poke along on this far busier road, but there are a few places where you can safely pull off to scan the valley. At the Snohomish County line in 6.6 miles the name changes to High Bridge Road. Turn right (east) in another 2.0 miles onto Crescent Lake Road and recross the Snoqualmie River.

CRESCENT LAKE

On the left in 0.4 mile from High Bridge Road is the south entrance to **Crescent Lake Wildlife Area** (also known by its former name, Two Rivers; WDFW permit required to park). The lake is a broken O of water in an old river oxbow, bordered by trees and tangled vegetation. The 360-acre wildlife area includes the land inside the oxbow and west to the Snoqualmie River. About a third of the total area is sharecropped with a part of the grain left standing for wildlife. From the parking lot, a wide track follows the edge of the lake northwestward. Blackberries and other brush provide winter cover for sparrows, and the trees are attractive to woodpeckers, Pine Siskin, and other species (avoid the open fields and lake edges in fall if hunters are present). Farther north, where the lake ends, a path on the right enters an extensive tract of mature maples, alders, willows, and other hardwoods, crisscrossed by a maze of often-muddy trails. This is probably the best chunk of relatively little-disturbed floodplain forest left in the region. In spring and summer, look and listen for Ruffed Grouse, Red-breasted Sapsucker, Pacific-slope Flycatcher, Cassin's, Warbling, and Red-eyed Vireos, Black-capped Chickadee, Swainson's Thrush, Purple Finch, and other woodland species.

Exiting the parking lot, turn left onto Crescent Lake Road, which follows the lake (walking this stretch gives good viewing) to a pullout on the left in 0.3 mile by a closed gate. Here you may walk into the wildlife area across a filled-in piece of the lake; in summer, expect Green Heron, Willow Flycatcher, Yellow

Crescent Lake and Snohomish Flats

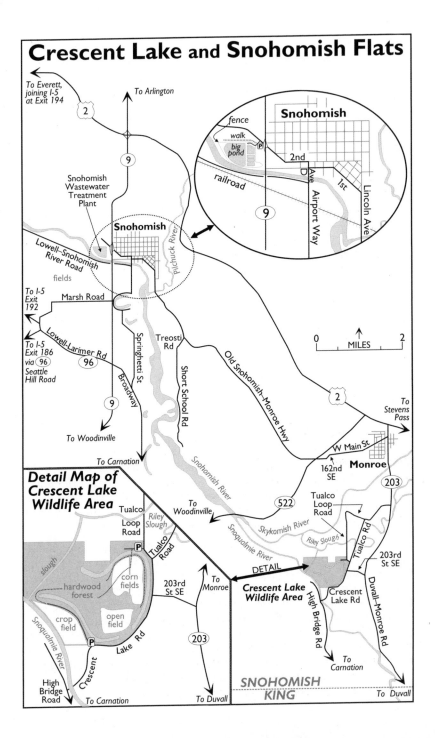

To Everett, joining I-5 at Exit 194

2

To Arlington

9

Snohomish Wastewater Treatment Plant

Snohomish

Pilchuck River

Lowell–Snohomish River Road

fields

To I-5 Exit 192

Marsh Road

To I-5 Exit 186 via 96 Seattle Hill Road

Lowell-Larimer Rd

96

9

Springhetti St

Broadway

To Woodinville

To Carnation

Treosti Rd

Short School Rd

Old Snohomish-Monroe Hwy

Snohomish River

0 MILES 2

2

To Stevens Pass

W Main St

162nd SE

Monroe

203

Snohomish

fence

walk

big pond

P

2nd

Ave

Airport Way

1st

Lincoln Ave

railroad

9

Detail Map of Crescent Lake Wildlife Area

Tualco Loop Road

Riley Slough

To Woodinville

Tualco Road

Snoqualmie River

522

Skykomish River

Riley Slough

Tualco Loop Road

Tualco Rd

203rd St SE

P

slough

hardwood forest

corn fields

crop field

open field

P

Snoqualmie River

High Bridge Road

Crescent Lake Rd

203rd St SE

To Monroe

DETAIL

Crescent Lake Wildlife Area

High Bridge Rd

Crescent Lake Rd

Duvall-Monroe Rd

To Carnation

203

To Duvall

SNOHOMISH
KING

To Duvall

To Carnation

Warbler, Common Yellowthroat, and Bullock's Oriole. At the junction with 203rd Street SE in another 0.4 mile the road becomes becomes Tualco Road. Keep straight 0.3 mile and go left onto Tualco Loop Road. The north entrance to the wildlife area is 500 feet ahead on the left. Park here (WDFW permit required) and walk in along the service road that continues the entrance road, turning left to cross the lake on a culvert. You are now in the hole of the doughnut. Dense trees and blackberries on the perimeter screen the lake from view but provide excellent cover for wintering sparrows. Least Flycatchers have occurred here twice in June. Go either way around the corn fields. By following paths through the hardwood forest at the west end of the second field you can reach the south parking lot and walk a complete loop.

Two-tenths of a mile north of the north parking lot, Tualco Loop Road crosses **Riley Slough**, bordered by tall broadleaf trees and blackberries. Rusty Blackbird has been seen here in winter. At the intersection in 1.4 miles go straight ahead onto Tualco Road, then left in 0.7 mile onto SR-203 (Duvall-Monroe Road), which crosses the Skykomish River in another 0.9 mile and enters the town of Monroe. At a traffic light in downtown Monroe in 0.4 mile, turn left onto W Main Street to continue to the Snohomish Flats. (If you instead go straight and cross the railroad tracks, the next light is at US-2; turn left here to join I-5 at Everett, or right for the Cascades and Stevens Pass, page 407).

SNOHOMISH FLATS

Main Street becomes 162nd Street SE on the west outskirts of Monroe, passes under SR-522 (1.8 miles), and leaves town as the Old Snohomish-Monroe Highway. About 3.6 miles past the SR-522 interchange, the road drops down onto the Snohomish Flats. This open farm country is home to a large population of raptors in winter, including one or two Gyrfalcons in recent years. Along the stretch from here to the Pilchuck River bridge (1.8 miles), scan isolated treetops, fencerows, utility poles, and the ground. Make sure you pull safely off the road; shoulders are narrow in most places. A side trip down Short School Road and back can also be productive.

Just after the bridge and a railway underpass, the road—now Lincoln Avenue—enters the old river town of Snohomish. A short way past the city limits, turn left onto First Street (expect to spend some time here if you have an antiques collector in your party). At Avenue D in eight blocks, go north one block to Second Street and turn left. In 0.6 mile, just past the SR-9 underpass, the entrance to the **Snohomish Wastewater Treatment Plant** is on your left. Pull in and park here, then walk up the gravel road to the entrance gate. Follow a path outside the fence right from the gate and around the corner to the left, which will take you to the large main pond. Walk the borders. Ducks, shorebirds, and gulls can be found here, along with a variety of woodpeckers and passerines in the surrounding vegetation.

Turn right from the entrance to the sewage plant, then right again onto the onramp for SR-9 southbound and the Snohomish River bridge. The fields west of SR-9 between the river and Lowell-Larimer Road (2.2 miles farther south) are worth scanning in winter. There are several informal pullouts along both of these roads, and also along Marsh Road. Raptors and swans can be of interest, as can shorebirds when the fields are partially flooded. Lowell-Snohomish River Road (cross the river on Avenue D and turn right at the south end of the bridge) lies between the diked river and a high railway embankment. For the first mile west of SR-9 it is possible to get a view of the flats in a few places, but *stay off the railroad tracks!* This main line carries frequent, high-speed freight and passenger traffic, and approaching trains can be amazingly silent (especially if you have a falcon in your scope).

The next stops are downriver on the Snohomish delta. To get there, go west on Lowell-Larimer Road, which eventually becomes Junction Road and brings you to the Exit 192 interchange with I-5 at 41st Street SE in Everett, 7.9 miles from SR-9. Or you may travel about six miles westbound on US-2 from the interchange with SR-9 north of Snohomish. In both cases, take I-5 northbound when you reach it.

EVERETT SEWAGE TREATMENT PONDS

Spencer Island and the Everett sewage ponds—two of Puget Sound's finest birding sites—are reached from Exit 195 on northbound I-5. Turn left (north) at the end of the offramp onto E Marine View Drive. At the interchange in 1.5 miles, turn left for the onramp to SR-529 (Pacific Highway) northbound and cross the Snohomish River. Stay in the right lane and turn right at the first road, 28th Place NE, 0.2 mile from the north end of the bridge, indicated by signs for the marina and for Langus Riverfront Park. Immediately after turning off, turn right again onto 35th Avenue NE (small sign for Spencer Island). At the next intersection (0.3 mile from SR-529) turn left onto Ross Avenue. Continue past Dagmars Landing (marina), staying right where 12th Street NE branches off in 0.9 mile (do not cross over I-5). Ross Avenue becomes Smith Island Road at this intersection. You soon come to Langus Riverfront Park along the Snohomish River on your right (restrooms). Pass under I-5. The office of the City of Everett Water Pollution Control Facility is on the right, 1.1 miles from 12th. Pull through the gate and park at the visitor parking lot, on the right.

(From I-5 southbound, take Exit 198 *North Broadway-Port of Everett* onto SR-529 southbound; cross the Steamboat Slough/Union Slough bridges, and watch for the sign to Langus Riverfront Park; exit right at 0.5 mile onto Frontage Road, which turns left in 0.7 mile and passes under SR-529. At the stop sign with 35th Avenue NE, bear right onto Ross Avenue and continue past the marina, as above.)

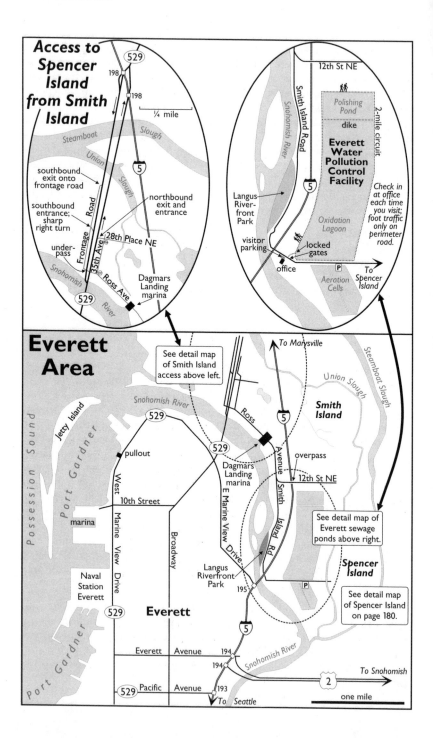

Access to Spencer Island from Smith Island

529
198
198
¼ mile

Steamboat Slough
Union Slough

southbound exit onto frontage road

Frontage Road

southbound entrance; sharp right turn

5

underpass

northbound exit and entrance

28th Place NE
35th Ave

Ross Ave

Snohomish River

529

Dagmars Landing marina

12th St NE

Smith Island Road

Snohomish River

Polishing Pond
dike
2-mile circuit

Everett Water Pollution Control Facility

Langus Riverfront Park

Check in at office each time you visit; foot traffic only on perimeter road.

Oxidation Lagoon

visitor parking

locked gates

office

P

To Spencer Island

Aeration Cells

Everett Area

See detail map of Smith Island access above left.

To Marysville

Union Slough

Steamboat Slough

Possession Sound

Jetty Island

Port Gardner

Snohomish River

529

pullout

West

529

Ross

5

Smith Island

Dagmars Landing marina

overpass

12th St NE

See detail map of Everett sewage ponds above right.

10th Street

marina

Marine View Drive

Broadway

E Marine View Drive

Smith Island Rd

Avenue

Spencer Island

See detail map of Spencer Island on page 180.

Naval Station Everett

529

Langus Riverfront Park

195

P

Everett

5

Port Gardner

Everett   Avenue   194

194

Snohomish River

2   To Snohomish

529   Pacific   Avenue   193

To Seattle

one mile

The strategically located Everett sewage treatment ponds function as part of the Snohomish estuary ecosystem, attracting a great number and variety of birds in all seasons. Birders are welcome. Apply at the office for a permit (free; good for two years). You must register each time you visit. The office and visitor parking lot are open Monday through Saturday during normal operating hours; inquire about closing time when you sign in. If you have special requirements (such as visiting with a large group) it is best to make arrangements in advance by calling 425-257-8821.

Enter the pond area on foot (no cars) through the gate east of the office, across the road. The circuit of the large oxidation lagoon and smaller polishing pond north of it is a bit more than two miles. You may also walk the dike separating the two ponds. In migration and winter, the ponds may be crowded with freshwater ducks or they may be nearly empty. High tides often drive waterfowl to take refuge here, as does hunting pressure during the open season (October to January). The ponds are large, so if you are careful the birds will usually swim away from you rather than taking flight. You will not regret toting your scope.

A flock of 200–300 Canvasbacks often winters; Ring-necked Duck, both scaup species (Lesser breeds almost annually), Bufflehead, Common Goldeneye, and Ruddy Duck are usually present. Look carefully for the occasional Redhead and Eared Grebe (both infrequent but regular west of the mountains) and for Tufted Duck (rare). The odd Long-tailed Duck, or other sea duck, may also show up. Dabbling ducks can be common in winter, with some often present in summer. Gadwall and Mallard are here year round. American Wigeon and Green-winged Teal breed in small numbers. Blue-winged and Cinnamon Teal are common in May–June (Cinnamon also uncommon in other seasons). An introduced American Black Duck population was established here for three decades. No "pure" birds have been seen for a while, but many hybrid individuals can be identified among the resident Mallards in the Everett area. Genuinely wild American Black Ducks are accidental in Washington and should be carefully documented.

The ponds attract hordes of gulls. Glaucous-winged is present all year. Ring-billed and California are uncommon in migration, rare in winter. Herring and Thayer's can usually be found in winter. Western occurs annually. Ranks of Mew (winter) and other species often line the border of the lagoon. Swarms of Mew and Bonaparte's patrol the aeration cells, across the road to the south of the main oxidation lagoon (visitors may not enter the enclosure, but can easily view it through the chain-link fence), and are often in the main ponds, too. Scrutinize these for unusual species such as Franklin's, Little, Black-headed, and Sabine's. Caspian (summer) and Common (migration) Terns are regular; Arctic, Forster's, and Black are infrequent visitors.

Wilson's (uncommon to rare) and Red-necked (fall) Phalaropes use the ponds in migration. Winter high tides may drive Dunlins and other shorebird species to roost around the pond edges. Marshes along the east side of the outer dike can be fabulous for shorebirds in fall, with Semipalmated, Baird's, Pectoral, and Stilt Sandpipers sometimes appearing in good numbers along with the common species. The ponds even have records for Pacific Golden-Plover, Wandering Tattler, and Sharp-tailed and Rock Sandpipers. In migration and summer, all seven species of Washington swallows have been seen around the ponds. Weeds, brush, small trees, and wetlands next to the fences attract sparrows (Swamp uncommon in winter), finches, and other passerines, including species rare for the locality such as Black-throated Sparrow and Lesser Goldfinch.

Directions for returning to the interstate are given following the Spencer Island account.

SPENCER ISLAND

The Snohomish estuary consists of numerous low-lying islands separated by sloughs. Across Union Slough to the east of Smith Island (where the Everett sewage ponds are situated) is 412-acre Spencer Island, diked and converted to farmland around 1930 but now managed for wildlife and non-motorized recreation. In the few years since opening to the public in 1995, Spencer Island has become a premier birding destination. The north end is owned by the Washington Department of Fish and Wildlife and is open to hunting from October to January, while the

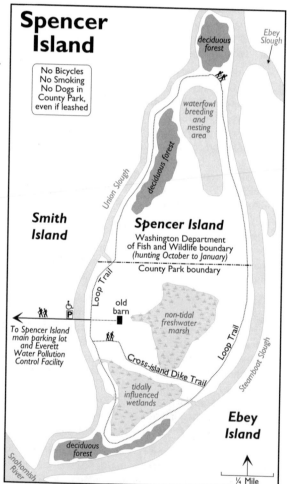

Spencer Island

No Bicycles
No Smoking
No Dogs in County Park, even if leashed

Ebey Slough

deciduous forest

waterfowl breeding and nesting area

deciduous forest

Union Slough

Smith Island

Spencer Island
Washington Department of Fish and Wildlife boundary
(hunting October to January)
County Park boundary

Loop Trail

old barn

non-tidal freshwater marsh

Loop Trail

Steamboat Slough

P

To Spencer Island main parking lot and Everett Water Pollution Control Facility

Cross-island Dike Trail

tidally influenced wetlands

Ebey Island

deciduous forest

Snohomish River

¼ Mile

southern half is a county park where dogs and hunting are not permitted.

Go east along the road at the south end of the sewage ponds; a small parking lot is on the right about 0.2 mile from the office. Walk another 700 yards and cross the old iron bridge over Union Slough. You are on county property at this point; the WDFW boundary is about 450 yards to the north. A well-maintained 3.5-mile dike trail follows the entire perimeter of the island, but most birders visit just the southern part, which has all the habitats, including a fringe of alder woods. The area around the old barn, straight east from the end of the bridge and accessible on a path, is a good place to observe Tree Swallow, Marsh Wren, Common Yellowthroat, and other birds that nest in the marsh. Take the loop trail right from the end of the bridge, then walk left onto the trail that crosses the island on top of a dike. To the south, the perimeter dike has been breached in three places, creating a tidally influenced wetland in the area on the right side of the cross-island trail. The area on the left (north) side of the trail, isolated by dikes, is a large freshwater marsh.

Wetlands (fresh- and saltwater) host migrating shorebirds, including both golden-plovers, yellowlegs, and dowitcher species, Western and Least Sandpipers, Dunlins, and uncommonly Semipalmated, Baird's, Sharp-tailed (one record), and Pectoral Sandpipers. Also here are American Bittern, Vaux's Swift, American Pipit (migration and winter), and a wide variety of ducks. Yellow-headed and Rusty Blackbirds have been recorded, along with the regular icterids. Raptors in marshlands and bordering woods include Northern Harrier, Bald Eagle, all three accipiters (Northern Goshawk a rare winter visitor), and Peregrine Falcon. In winter and migration unusual species such as Swamp and Harris's are regularly found in sparrow flocks along slough edges or in brushy places. Washington rarities seen here include Tufted Duck, Red-shouldered Hawk, Yellow-throated Vireo (October; the only state record), and Red Fox Sparrow. Eastern Kingbird—quite uncommon west of the Cascades—has nested on the island for several years. On certain June mornings when cold, cloudy weather forces them down from the mountains, hundreds of Black Swifts may forage at eye level over the wetlands and nearby sewage lagoons.

A right turn at the far end of the cross-island dike will take you along Steamboat Slough and back around the south end of the island to the iron bridge, with woodland birding opportunities.

To reach I-5 *northbound* (see Access inset map, page 178), retrace your route past Langus Riverfront Park and the marina to the intersection with 35th. Turn right here and continue 0.3 mile to 28th Place NE, turn left, then immediately right onto SR-529. The northbound I-5 onramp exits left in 1.3 miles, after the highway divides. To return to Everett and I-5 *southbound*, retrace your route as above, but at the Ross/35th intersection stay left beneath the underpass and follow Frontage Road north. In 0.5 mile a sharp right puts you onto SR-529 southbound and over the Snohomish River bridge to an exit for Marine View Drive, on the right (0.9 mile). Get off here. At the traffic light at the end of the offramp loop, you may turn left with SR-529 to the Everett waterfront (see below). A right turn will take you south on Marine View Drive to a southbound I-5 onramp in 1.5 mile (stay left at the fork after the first mile).

EVERETT WATERFRONT

A visit to the Everett waterfront is a good way to round out your day list. (See map on page 178.) Turn left at the aforementioned traffic light and follow SR-529 as it swings west onto Marine View Drive. In 1.4 miles a pullout on the right offers great views of the harbor. Scan here for Osprey (a large colony nests on old pilings in the Snohomish estuary) and various waterbirds. In 0.4 mile, turn right onto 10th Street (signs for *Port of Everett*) to the public boat launch, another good viewing spot. The parking area often has a lot of gulls, and Purple Martins nest in pilings to the north. Just offshore to the west is **Jetty Island**, a dredge-spoil barrier separating Port Gardner—the natural harbor at the river's mouth—from Possession Sound. The two-mile-long, 200-yard-wide island is served by a free ferry operated Wednesday through Sunday by Everett Parks and Recreation, from after the Fourth of July to before Labor Day. Sandy beaches and a small salt marsh provide nesting habitat for gulls; shorebird migration beginning in July is another attraction. A few pairs of Arctic Terns were discovered nesting on Jetty Island in 1977. Arctic Terns have returned to the Everett port area in small numbers and nested with varying success ever since, at what is still their southernmost known nesting site on the West Coast. In 1990, a few Caspian Terns showed up, and by 1994 a rapidly expanding breeding colony fledged some 2,500 young Caspians. This colony has been displaced by construction of the new naval base. Efforts to reestablish it nearby have not been successful to date.

To reach I-5 northbound, continue south on SR-529 past the marina and turn left onto Everett Avenue. For I-5 southbound, go four blocks farther south, then follow SR-529 left onto Pacific Avenue.

STANWOOD AND CAMANO ISLAND

by Hal Opperman

The Stillaguamish River discharges into two tidal channels south of Stanwood: West Pass, joining Skagit Bay, and South Pass, joining Port Susan. Like a miniature version of the Snohomish estuary, the sloughs and alluvial deposits at the mouth of the river have been diked to create dry land for crops and dairying. Taken as a whole, this is a major site for waterfowl and shorebirds from late fall to early spring, and supports a large population of wintering raptors. It is an area of hemispheric significance for Snow Geese and Dunlins. To the west lies Camano Island, reached by a high bridge over West Pass. The Camano shoreline offers several fine viewpoints for scoping Skagit Bay, Saratoga Passage, and Livingston Bay—highly productive waters for loons, grebes, waterfowl, and alcids, especially in the colder months.

STILLAGUAMISH DELTA

For a tour of the Stillaguamish delta, go west from I-5 Exit 208 toward Silvana on Pioneer Highway. The road turns northwest, enters the town of Silvana, turns north, and crosses the Stillaguamish. Immediately after the bridge, turn left onto **Norman Road** (3.6 miles from I-5). The river is on the left and open fields on the right. When partially flooded in spring, these fields can be excellent for migrating shorebirds; look them over from Norman Road or from any of the connecting roads running north to Pioneer Highway. At the junction with Miller Road stay left on Norman, which crosses the river once more, to a stop sign at Marine Drive (4.7 miles from the beginning of Norman Road). Go straight across onto **Boe Road**, with the Hat Slough dike on your left. The main attraction along this road is waterfowl (sometimes thousands of Snow Geese) and shorebirds in the fields, especially on high tides. Look, too, for Merlin and Peregrine Falcon. In winter, Short-eared Owl may be seen here or elsewhere on the delta—primarily at daybreak or in late afternoon—and Snowy Owl at any time of day during an invasion year. Boe Road dead-ends in 1.4 miles at the levee along Port Susan. In late 2001, The Nature Conservancy acquired 4,000 acres of tidelands across the levee. Visits to this new Port Susan Bay Preserve will be by permission only until parking and other access issues have been worked out. Go back to Marine Drive and turn left. In 0.8 mile turn left onto **Thomle Road**, which ends in about two miles at a food-processing plant. The winter possibilities are similar to those along Boe Road, including American Pipit and Western Meadowlark in the fields and a good diversity of sparrows in brushy spots.

Return to Marine Drive. Turn left (north), cross the river again, then turn left onto 267th Place NW at the Stanwood city limits just before the SR-532 underpass, and continue to the traffic light (1.1 miles from the Thomle Road junction). Go left onto SR-532, and in another 0.6 mile left again onto 98th Avenue NW. On the left in 75 yards is the entrance to the **Stanwood Waste Water Treatment Plant**. The gate is open on weekdays. Birders are welcome; please park and check in at the administration building. Weekend visitors can arrange in advance for the gate to be opened by calling the plant at 360-629-8041 during normal weekday hours. There are several ponds. Access is on foot only, and birds will inevitably spook as you walk the dikes, but if you move slowly and are patient you should be rewarded with good scope views. Freshwater ducks (dabblers plus scaups and other *Aythya* species) are the most numerous inhabitants, but you may also find an interesting gull or

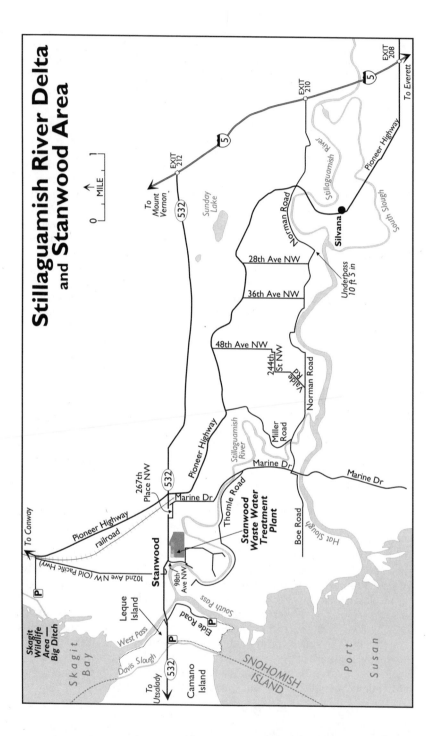

Stillaguamish River Delta and Stanwood Area

shorebird (phalaropes in migration). Unusual passerines have been found along the weedy dikes and fencerows. Swallows can be abundant in migration.

Go back to the SR-532 stop sign, turn left, and head west out of Stanwood, up and over the high bridge. Part way down the embankment on the other side of the bridge, make a hard left onto **Eide Road** (0.9 mile). Turning across heavy approaching traffic can be tricky. Slow down and signal your turn well in advance, *before* cresting the hump of the bridge, and watch your mirrors. You may prefer to drive on ahead, turn around at a less hazardous spot, and approach this intersection from the west. Eide Road follows the levee along the east side of Leque (pronounced *LEK-wee*) Island, formed between Camano Island and the mainland by sediment from the outwash of the Stillaguamish. This is excellent habitat for sparrows and other wintering passerines. Small trees and brush sometimes have flocks of Yellow-rumped Warbler and Purple Finch, and many unusual species have been found here over the years, including Say's Phoebe and Northern Mockingbird. In winter, Short-eared Owls can be numerous at dusk. Snowy Owls are often in the area in a good flight year: look for them on low perches such as fenceposts or farm equipment, or on the ground. A Barn Owl is usually resident in one of the old farm buildings but is rarely abroad in daylight. Bald Eagle, Northern Harrier, and Red-tailed and Rough-legged Hawks are present in winter—sometimes in high numbers—along with less common raptors such as Merlin and Peregrine Falcon.

Drive one mile to the road's end at a WDFW wildlife-area parking lot (permit required). Put on rubber boots (except in summer when the birding is not very good anyway). Large winter sparrow flocks in nearby brushy patches routinely contain unusual species. Walk on out along the dike where you can, but blackberry growth makes this difficult or impossible in some places. The easiest way is to go around the gate to the right and walk along the east edge of the field to its south end (look for wintering Western Meadowlarks), then clamber up onto the dike at a promontory overlooking **Port Susan**. This shallow bay is great for shorebirds an hour or two before and after high tide, when a relatively narrow zone is exposed between land and water's edge. At low tides the birds disperse over vast areas of mudflats extending almost farther than the eye can see. At high tide, viewing can be good for shallows-loving waterbirds. A Snow Goose flock is often at Port Susan in winter, and if something puts them up, 20,000 geese create an impressive snowstorm to the south. From here, you can continue to walk the perimeter of the island clockwise on the dike, in the fields, or along Davis Slough, to another WDFW parking area on the south side of SR-532. Pen-reared pheasants are released for hunting from October to March; stay out of the fields when hunters are present.

Back at SR-532, turn left from Eide Road, dart across traffic, and pull off quickly on the right at the foot of the bridge (0.1 mile). Walk the short road back east alongside the bridge. You may walk out into the fields (often flooded in winter—rubber boots a must) and on the West Pass levee if blackberries haven't taken over. This is the north tip of Leque Island; expect the same birds as on the Eide Road side. Some winters bring unusually large concentrations of Marsh Wren and Savannah Sparrow. Black-bellied Plover and Dunlin may roost in the fields at high tide. Flocks of Snow Goose, Trumpeter Swan, and other species of waterfowl fly freely back and forth from Port Susan to Skagit Bay, especially on an incoming tide. Dunlins rise up in large balls when displaced by the tide or by the Merlins and Peregrine Falcons that pursue them. Up to 50,000 Dunlins winter on Port Susan/Skagit Bay, one of the largest concentrations in North America.

Another pullout on the right in 0.3 mile, on Camano Island just across the Davis Slough bridge, offers similar possibilities. Access to the land between the dike and **Davis Slough** on both sides of the highway is unrestricted, though this area is full of logs and other impediments and is sometimes flooded. Land west of the dike on both sides of SR-532 is private and posted. In winter, many raptors patrol the fields and the salt marsh or avail themselves of handy perches. Bald Eagle, Northern Harrier, and Red-tailed and Rough-legged Hawks are common. Sharp-shinned and Cooper's Hawks are fairly common, and Harlan's Red-tailed Hawk and Gyrfalcon have occurred.

CAMANO ISLAND

Seven miles across at its north end and tapering 15 miles to its south point, Camano Island was completely logged over between 1855 and 1920. Conforming to the typical pattern of Puget Lowlands land-use succession, the level ground was then cleared of stumps and used for agriculture for many decades. Today, the last farm fields and second-growth forest are disappearing beneath a wave of residential development. Most of the shoreline is private. However, a few publicly accessible points provide an opportunity to view the marine environment and its rich birdlife, while remnant woods and other upland habitats can be sampled along the quiet roadsides and in parks. Breeding has been documented for 80 species on the north part of the island, and over 130 species have been found there on the Skagit Bay Christmas Bird Count.

From the pullout at Davis Slough on SR-532, travel west 0.9 mile and turn right onto Good Road, which bends west and becomes Utsalady Road. In 1.9 miles, just past the airport, turn right (north) and follow Moore Road to its end in 0.6 mile, staying right down a narrow two-track to a parking area near the beach. This is **English Boom**, site of a new county park on the southwest edge of Skagit Bay. All that remains of the boom (log-sorting and rafting facility) of the English Logging Company is the forest of pilings offshore, now fitted out with Purple Martin nest boxes. The shoreline to the west is private. To the east a muddy beach stretches all the way to Davis Slough; a small salt marsh cut across by tidal channels lies between it and the bluffs. Some day a boardwalk will facilitate access to this area; until then, pick your way among the

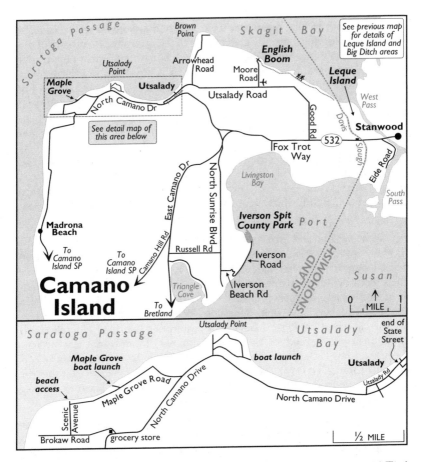

channels, driftwood, and scrubby vegetation. In winter, Green-winged Teal and other dabbling ducks use this habitat, as do shorebirds (mostly Dunlins, with a few Greater Yellowlegs and Least and Western Sandpipers mixed in). Among the resident songbirds, listen for three species of wren (Winter, Bewick's, Marsh). This part of the bay is shallow, and probably best birded on an outgoing tide. Depending on tides, wind direction, and where the hunters happen to be pushing them on a given day, thousands of ducks may be present. Diving birds feed along a deep channel offshore, among them loons (Common and Red-throated common to uncommon, Pacific fairly common, Yellow-billed recorded), grebes (mostly Horned, Red-necked, and Western), Greater Scaup, all three scoters, Common Goldeneye, and Red-breasted Merganser. When the Snow Goose flock is resident on the Fir Island tidelands, you will see a white mass like a snowbank four or five miles across Skagit Bay to the northeast.

Go back out to Utsalady Road, turn right, and drive over to Utsalady. In the heyday of logging, Utsalady could boast of the busiest port and one of the largest mills on Puget Sound, but today it is a sleepy retirement community with one little store. Three open lots on the right side of the road offer lookouts onto **Utsalady Bay**. The first one is in 1.8 miles, opposite the end of State Street. On the leeward side of the island from the prevailing southwest winds, the sheltered bay harbors Red-throated and Common Loons, hundreds of scoters, dozens of goldeneyes (including many Barrow's), and sometimes one or two Eared Grebes or a Thayer's Gull. In calm weather you may see birds of deeper waters farther out on Saratoga Passage. Utsalady Road continues another 0.3 mile, past the other two lots, and bends left to a stop sign at North Camano Drive. Turn right here. In 1.2 miles, turn right onto Utsalady Point Road, which doubles back and drops down to a public boat launch (0.3 mile) where you can scope the west side of Utsalady Bay.

Come back up and turn right onto North Camano Drive. In 0.2 mile take another right onto Maple Grove Road and drive down to the **Maple Grove Boat Launch** (0.4 mile). Saratoga Passage is at its narrowest here—three miles from Whidbey Island—and the deep channel is close to shore. Many birds feed here, and others fly up and down the channel. Practically any Washington gull species is possible. Specialties include alcids (Common Murre irregular fall to spring, Pigeon Guillemot year round, Marbled Murrelet fairly common in winter, Rhinoceros Auklet in summer); loons (especially Pacific—there are a few records of Yellow-billed); Harlequin Duck; and all three cormorants (Brandt's is rare). A winter flock of 1,000–2,000 Western Grebes can often be found far out in the channel. This is an excellent place to set up a scope and do a sea-watch when there is activity.

Continue right from the parking lot rather than going back uphill to the left the way you came. Maple Grove Road ends at Scenic Avenue in 0.3 mile. Park out of the way. The right stub of Scenic Avenue is a beach access. The sand-and-cobble beach may have Sanderlings—local on Camano Island due to limited habitat. Scan the waters; Marbled Murrelets are often here, especially to the left (northwest). Drive a couple of blocks up Scenic Avenue away from the beach to its end at Brokaw Road. Turn left and go to the stop sign at Huntington's Grocery corner (0.3 mile), and left onto North Camano Drive. In 3.8 miles, stay right at the fork onto Sunrise Boulevard to a stop sign with East Camano Drive in 0.2 mile, and continue straight ahead on Sunrise. In 2.6 miles, turn left onto Iverson Beach Road, which meanders 0.4 mile to Iverson Road. A left turn brings you to the road-end parking lot in 0.6 mile.

Iverson Spit, a new 100-acre county park, enjoys a splendid setting at the mouth of Livingston Bay. A one-mile stroll takes you through several different habitats with their typical birds, so Iverson Spit is a popular place to build a quick and varied day list. Walk around a gate onto a wide path that continues the direction of the road you drove in on, and get up onto the dike. Follow the dike path around to the left. Salt marsh is on your right and freshwater marsh on your left. Cross a culvert between the two (look for River Otters). The path soon leads to a wooded area (Red Alder, Douglas-fir, Madrone), bending left and skirting the base of the bluff. When you reach the sign indicating the end of county property, go left to a small clearing surrounded by alders and blackberries. Return the way you came. About 200 yards after the sign take a path to the right that will lead you around the edge of the freshwater marsh and back to the dike (may be impassible in the wet season). Turn right along the dike, recross the culvert, and at a fork in the trail take the right branch that follows the edge of a field back to the parking lot. You may also walk north-ward along the beach and the salt marsh behind it (except when duck hunters are using the beach blinds, October–January).

Go back to East Camano Drive and turn right. In 0.3 mile, swing right onto SR-532. In another 0.6 mile, turn right onto Fox Trot Way, which dead-ends in 0.2 mile. **Livingston Bay**, to the south, can hold thousands of ducks. This is a good vantage point, but the tide runs *waaay* out, so time your visit for a three- or four-hour bracket centered on peak high tide. On sunny days, try for early morning or late afternoon to avoid the glare. You may walk out to the shoreline here. However, beach and tidelands to the east and west are pri-vate. Drive east on SR-532 to reach Stanwood.

BIG DITCH

From SR-532 on the west side of Stanwood, turn north onto 102nd Avenue NW. (See map on page 184.) The name changes to Old Pacific Highway as you travel north out of town. In 2.4 miles, just as the road swings right and is about to cross the railroad track, turn left (west) onto a dirt road signed *Big Ditch Ac-cess*, which ends in 0.6 mile at a parking lot on the right (WDFW permit re-quired). One of several developed access points to the Skagit Wildlife Area, **Big Ditch** is located about a mile south of the mouth of the South Fork Skagit River. Walk up onto the dike above the parking lot, across the big drainage ditch that ends at a tide gate on your left, and through a turnstile beside a steel-pipe gate. You are on a high levee with the ditch on the inside and a vast salt marsh, cut through with sloughs, extending to the tidelands of Skagit Bay to the west. This is primarily a winter birding site. The levee for a mile northward provides a priv-ileged post from which to scan for raptors, including Peregrine Falcon, which hunts over the marsh and mudflats. Even in a mediocre flight year there is usu-ally a Snowy Owl or two at Big Ditch. A wintering Snow Goose flock is some-times out on the intertidal zone. For a closer view of this habitat, put on your rubber boots, go south along the levee, through a fence, and take the famously slippery, muddy trail that follows a slough out to the water's edge.

Drive back out and cross the railroad track to the stop sign at Pioneer Highway. To reach birding sites to the north, turn left and go 4.4 miles to the junction with Fir Island Road in Conway (page 113). If you turn south (right) it is 2.3 miles to SR-532 in Stanwood, and 4.5 miles east from there to I-5.

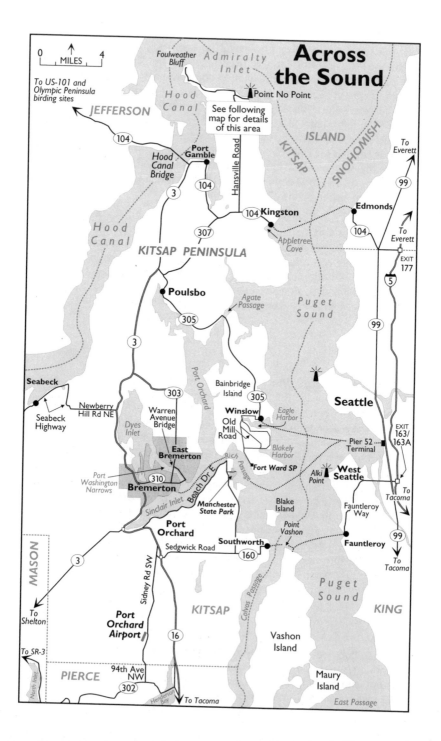

Across the Sound

0 [MILES] 4

To US-101 and
Olympic Peninsula
birding sites

Foulweather Bluff

Admiralty Inlet

Point No Point

Hood Canal

JEFFERSON

104

See following
map for details
of this area

ISLAND

Hansville Road

Port Gamble

Hood Canal Bridge

3

104

104

Kitsap

SNOHOMISH

To Everett

99

104 Kingston

Edmonds

104

Appletree Cove

To Everett

307

Hood Canal

KITSAP PENINSULA

EXIT 177

5

Poulsbo

Agate Passage

Puget Sound

99

305

3

Port Orchard

Seabeck

Newberry Hill Rd NE

303

Bainbridge Island

305

Seattle

Seabeck Highway

Warren Avenue Bridge

Dyes Inlet

Winslow

Old Mill Road

Eagle Harbor

EXIT 163/163A

East Bremerton

Blakely Harbor

Pier 52 Terminal

310

Port Washington Narrows

Bremerton

Sinclair Inlet

Beach Dr E

Rich Passage

Fort Ward SP

Alki Point

West Seattle

To Tacoma

MASON

Manchester State Park

Blake Island

Fauntleroy Way

Port Orchard

Point Vashon

Fauntleroy

3

Sedgwick Road

160 **Southworth**

99

To Shelton

To SR-3

Sidney Rd SW

KITSAP

Colvos Passage

Puget Sound

KING

To Tacoma

Port Orchard Airport

16

Vashon Island

PIERCE

94th Ave NW

302

Henderson Bay

To Tacoma

Maury Island

East Passage

North Inlet

ACROSS THE SOUND (KITSAP COUNTY)

by Hal Opperman

B ainbridge Island and the Kitsap Peninsula, joined together by a highway bridge over Agate Passage, lie between Puget Sound on the east and Hood Canal on the west. Once completely covered by towering lowland forests of the Puget Sound Douglas-fir zone, this area has been 99+ percent logged off and is now a mosaic of second-growth forest, agricultural land, light to medium development (single-family dwellings with parks and other open spaces), and heavy urban/industrial development (around Bremerton). The landscape is endowed with small lakes, ponds, streams, and wetlands (but no large rivers)—and plenty of saltwater shoreline. The area is relatively lightly birded except for one outstanding site—Point No Point—and, incidentally, a few lesser spots along the standard route from Seattle to the North Olympic Coast.

Not that there are few birds! On the contrary, 115 species breed here, and 120 or more are routinely found in any given year on the three Christmas Bird Counts—impressive numbers, considering the county's small size and comparatively uniform habitat. The rural setting offers a good chance to observe the regular Puget Trough landbirds, including Band-tailed Pigeon, Rufous Hummingbird, Red-breasted Sapsucker, Pileated Woodpecker, Olive-sided and Pacific-slope Flycatchers, Hutton's Vireo, Violet-green Swallow, Chestnut-backed Chickadee, Bewick's Wren, Swainson's Thrush, Black-throated Gray and Wilson's Warblers, Western Tanager, Spotted Towhee, Black-headed Grosbeak, and Purple Finch. Owls find the mixture of open forest and clearings to their liking: Western Screech-, Great Horned, Northern Pygmy- (uncommon), Barred, and Northern Saw-whet all nest.

Most visitors arrive by one of the four cross-sound ferry routes. Truth be told, ferry birding is usually dull. Out in the channels you may see alcids, scoters, and gulls as flybys or feeding in tidal rips, but birds are far more numerous in protected waters near the terminals where they may readily be seen from shore. Amazing sightings do occur, especially in migration or a day or two after a major storm along the outer coast. But even if the birding is unexceptional, visiting birders must take a ferry trip to appreciate the lay of the land (and water), which is key to understanding how birds function in the Puget Sound ecosystem.

If you should find yourself docking in Kitsap County on a fine early morning in May, June, or July, drive off the ferry, pick up a map, and take some time to go prospecting for birds on your own. Landbirds tend not to be concentrated at a few favored areas, but instead are widely and rather evenly distributed. You are just as likely to find them along the many quiet roadsides as in the public parks. Although most of the shoreline is privately owned, there are numerous spots to get a peek at bays, coves, inlets, and passages. Waterbirding can be good at any season. Pigeon Guillemots nest in sandbank burrows at several places along the shoreline, and the Warren Avenue Bridge across the Port Washington Narrows in Bremerton has a nesting colony of Pelagic Cormorants.

Here are a few suggestions to get you started. If you arrive on the Kingston ferry, check the viewpoints on the west side of Appletree Cove, opposite the ferry dock. On Bainbridge Island, go around the west end of Eagle Harbor (where the ferry arrives) and bird your way south through woods and orchards along Old Mill Road NE to the abandoned mill site at the west end of Blakely Harbor—a fine, birdy spot—and on to Fort Ward State Park. Seabeck, on Hood Canal about a 15-mile drive from the Bremerton ferry dock, offers mixed woodlands, a saltwater bay, and the productive estuary of Seabeck Creek. Not far from the Southworth ferry landing is forested Manchester State Park, north of Manchester on Rich Passage. From here you can follow Beach Drive E along the shoreline to Port Orchard, with seabird and shorebird possibilities.

Ferries to Bremerton and to Bainbridge Island leave from the Pier 52 terminal at the foot of Madison Street in downtown Seattle. The ferry to Kingston leaves from Edmonds (take Exit 177 from I-5 about 13 miles north of downtown Seattle and follow the signs along SR-104 to the dock). The ferry to Southworth sails from the Fauntleroy terminal in West Seattle (take the West Seattle Freeway exit from I-5 about 2.5 miles south of downtown Seattle, then follow the signs along Fauntleroy Way). Crossing time varies from 30 to 60 minutes. Service is frequent, but waits for auto boarding can be long during commuting hours and on holidays and summer weekends. For automated fare and schedule information, phone 206-464-6400 in Seattle or 800-843-3779 toll-free statewide, or visit www.wsdot.wa.gov/ferries on-line.

KINGSTON FERRY TO HOOD CANAL BRIDGE

Kitsap County's destination birding site, **Point No Point** is conveniently accessed by the ferry from Edmonds. Drive west on SR-104 from the Kingston ferry ramp to the traffic light at Hansville Road (2.5 miles) and turn right (north). Turn right again in 7.3 miles onto Point No Point Road. The small parking lot at the lighthouse (0.9 mile) may be full; if so, come back 0.2 mile to the overflow parking area. Walk past the lighthouse along the sandy beach to the point. Admiralty Inlet, on the left, brings oceanic waters to the entrance of Puget Sound, on the right. Strong currents churn up plankton and small invertebrates when tides are running. Large concentrations of Pacific Sand Lance and Pacific Herring gather in the tidal rips at these rich feeding areas, in turn attracting high numbers of marine birds. Until the dramatic decline of the salmon runs, Point No Point was renowned for its sport fishery, for the same reason.

In fall migration, Parasitic Jaegers attend flocks of Common Terns that sometimes number in the hundreds. Many hundreds or even thousands of Bonaparte's Gulls work the rip tides in fall and winter. Rarities such as Franklin's, Little, Black-headed, and Sabine's Gulls, and Black-legged Kittiwake, are sometimes among them. All the regular Washington alcids occur here seasonally (Ancient Murrelet mostly in November; Cassin's Auklet and Tufted Puffin rare). Western Washington's first record of Arctic Loon was at Point No Point in the winter of 2000–2001, and Yellow-billed Loon has been seen more than once. When tides go slack the feeding frenzy ends and most of these birds disappear, but be sure to check the calmer waters back west toward the boathouse and around the point to the south, which usually have a sprinkling of birds at any tide stage.

To the south and west a lagoon and marsh, edged by brush, are well worth checking, as is the driftwood-lined beach to the south. Point No Point is something of a songbird migrant trap, with several records of out-of-range species, including Blue-gray Gnatcatcher and Black-backed Wagtail. The uplands to the south—cloaked in mature second-growth forest—are in Point No Point County Park, accessible by a trail that starts where the bluff meets the beach.

Return to Hansville Road and turn right. The road bends left at the Hansville Store (0.1 mile), becoming NE Twin Spits Road. Ask to see the bird-sightings log kept in the store, and add your observations to it. Continue westward on NE Twin Spits Road. At 2.7 miles from the store, look for a group of mailboxes on the right (including number 3480) followed by a pullout and unmarked trailhead on the left. Park here; this is the access point for The Nature Conservancy's **Foulweather Bluff Preserve**. A short trail leads through mature conifers and past a quiet lagoon to the beach on Hood Canal. Hutton's Vireo and other lowland forest birds can be found here. The road ends in another 0.7 mile along the waterfront at Twin Spits, with a view across the mouth of Hood Canal.

Attired in winter plumage, a Red-necked Grebe feeds from nearshore waters off the Kitsap Peninsula.

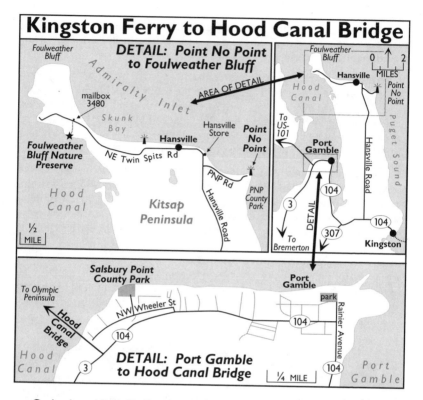

Kingston Ferry to Hood Canal Bridge

DETAIL: Point No Point to Foulweather Bluff

Foulweather Bluff

Admiralty Inlet

AREA OF DETAIL

mailbox 3480

Skunk Bay

Foulweather Bluff Nature Preserve

Hood Canal

NE Twin Spits Rd

Hansville

Hansville Store

Point No Point

PNP Rd

PNP County Park

Kitsap Peninsula

Hansville Road

½ MILE

Foulweather Bluff

Hansville

0   2
MILES

Point No Point

Hood Canal

Puget Sound

Hansville Road

To US-101

Port Gamble

104

DETAIL

3

To Bremerton

307

104

104

Kingston

DETAIL: Port Gamble to Hood Canal Bridge

To Olympic Peninsula

Salsbury Point County Park

NW Wheeler St

Hood Canal Bridge

104

3

Port Gamble

park

Rainier Avenue

104

104

Hood Canal

Port Gamble

¼ MILE

Go back to Hansville Road and south to the traffic light at SR-104. Turn right. Follow SR-104 as it turns right at the next traffic light (1.4 miles) and reaches **Port Gamble** in another 3.5 miles. Pay attention to the speed limit in town. Where the highway takes a 90-degree turn to the left (approximately 0.2 mile) go straight ahead a couple of blocks on Rainier Avenue to a small park in the center of this well-preserved old mill town, founded in 1853 by the Puget Mill Company (later Pope & Talbot), once the dominant lumber company on the Sound. At the time of its closing in 1995, the Port Gamble mill was the oldest continuously operated sawmill in the U.S. You can scope the waters of Hood Canal from the overlook, but the log dumps are off-limits. Park trees may hold passerines in migration. Return to SR-104 and turn right. Just after leaving town turn right onto Wheeler Street (0.8 mile), then right again in 0.2 mile into **Salsbury Point County Park**. The boat-ramp parking lot offers water-level views of Hood Canal, with good seabird possibilities.

Back at the highway, a right turn leads in 0.4 mile to the east end of the Hood Canal Bridge. Here you may turn right with SR-104 to reach Port Townsend and the coast (page 25), or the west shore of Hood Canal (page 222). Continuing straight ahead on SR-3 rather than crossing the bridge will take you down the Kitsap Peninsula toward Bainbridge Island, Bremerton, and points south.

SOUTHWORTH FERRY TO NARROWS BRIDGE

The **Southworth Ferry**—perhaps the most picturesque of the four routes, and often the birdiest—arrives at Southworth in south Kitsap County; most crossings also make an intermediate stop at Vashon Island (see map on page 190). The head of Colvos Passage, off Point Vashon, often has flocks of feeding birds when the currents are favorable. If you are attempting to find Mountain Quail, this is the ferry you will likely take. Introduced long ago and once widespread in Western Washington, this elusive species hangs on in a few scattered populations from the Kitsap Peninsula south and west toward Shelton and Elma. Locations may not be predictable from one year to the next, but Mountain Quail sightings are almost always reported, so it is worth monitoring the BirdBox and Tweeters in advance of your visit. Even if there are current reports, however, your chances of ticking this bird are only fair.

The most reliable place for Mountain Quail since the mid-1990s has been the disused **Port Orchard Airport**. From Southworth, drive west 7.2 miles on SR-160 (Sedgwick Road) to the SR-16 interchange. Keep straight ahead across the overpass. At the next major intersection in 0.5 mile turn left (south) onto Sidney Road SW. The entrance to the airport is on the right in 4.2 miles. Mountain Quail are most often among stumps and Scot's Broom on the hillside west of the airport. A model airplane club has leased the west side of the airport and uses it for flights on weekends after 9AM. Please respect their rights. In any case, the quail are far easier to find in the first two or three hours after dawn, before the model planes are flying. The best season is from March to early May when the males are calling (they can be heard from a great distance and sometimes come in to tapes). Another place is the band of trees between the landing field and the road, to the southeast. A third place is a county highway department gravel quarry much beloved of local dirtbikers, across Sidney Road a short distance south of the airport entrance, behind a steel gate. Park off the road and walk in; make yourself known and ask permission if workers are present. Mountain Quail are in their element on stony ground such as this, among patches of Scot's Broom and other scruffy growth in and around the quarry. Family groups can sometimes be heard clucking in the brush, but they are adept at racing away under cover. Count yourself lucky if you get a brief glimpse.

SR-16 northbound leads back to the Bremerton area. To reach Tacoma via the Narrows Bridge—about a 20-minute drive from the airport—take Sidney Road south (becomes 94th Avenue NW at the Pierce County line) for 3.5 miles, then go left onto SR-302, which joins SR-16 in 3.7 miles. Turn south here toward Tacoma.

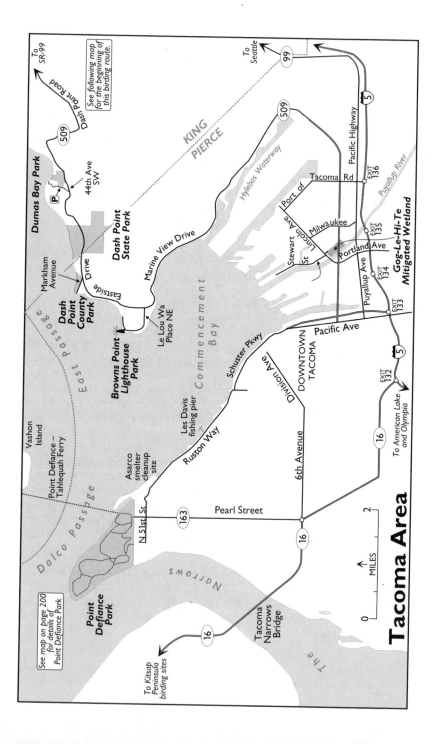

Tacoma Area

TACOMA AND VICINITY

by Bill Shelmerdine and Thais Bock

The logging, shipping, and manufacturing center of Tacoma lies at the southeast corner of the main basin of Puget Sound. Here the Puyallup River (pronounced pew-AHL-up), with its tributaries the Carbon and the White, delivers Mount Rainier's glacial meltwaters to Commencement Bay. Like Seattle, the city is built where ancient forests once stood, and the tideflats and estuary have been dredged, channeled, and filled to create the deepwater port and rail yards. In this intensively urbanized setting, a necklace of viewpoints strung along the shoreline on both sides of Commencement Bay offers fine saltwater birding in fall, winter, and spring. Christmas Bird Count data show that Pacific Loon, Brandt's and Pelagic Cormorants, White-winged Scoter, Bonaparte's and Thayer's Gulls, Common Murre, Pigeon Guillemot, and Rhinoceros Auklet are all many times more abundant in Tacoma than in Seattle (but Seattle is far stronger in Brant, Harlequin Duck, and Black Scoter). Point Defiance Park, at the west end of this chain of viewpoints, is the birding gem of the metropolitan area. Here the waters of the South Sound and those of the Main Basin mix at The Narrows, creating optimal seabird foraging conditions. A splendid swatch of the original forest subsists in the uplands of the park. American Lake, in the nearby suburbs, is a perennial spot for Little Gull.

DES MOINES MARINA TO COMMENCEMENT BAY

A tour of saltwater parks begins at the **Des Moines Marina.** (See map on next page.) Go west from I-5 at Exit 149, following SR-516 to its end at Marine View Drive (1.9 miles). Turn right (north) 0.3 mile to S 223rd Street, then left to the marina's long fishing pier (0.3 mile) and adjacent Beach Park where Des Moines Creek empties into Puget Sound. Gulls line the pier's railings; grebes, wigeons, all three scoters, and both goldeneyes provide close-up viewing. Return to Marine View Drive and continue south 1.7 miles. Turn right onto S 251st Street, then immediately left onto Eighth Place S to the entrance of **Saltwater State Park**, just ahead. Look for Black Scoter in winter, Brant in spring, and a variety of landbirds on forested bluffs. Return to Marine View Drive and continue south to its end (1.0 mile), then double back to the left with the arterial, which becomes Woodmont Drive S. At the traffic light (0.6 mile), turn right (south) onto 16th Avenue S to the next traffic light at S 272nd Street (0.7 mile). Go right here, winding your way downhill (street names change several times) to Redondo Beach Drive S (0.9 mile). Turn left to a fishing pier, boat launch, and boardwalk on Poverty Bay (0.1 mile). Rhinoceros Auklets favor this area.

From Salty's Restaurant, take Redondo Way S uphill (southeast) 1.0 mile to the intersection with SW Dash Point Road (SR-509). Turn right and follow SR-509 for 5.0 miles, with many sharp turns, past a sewage treatment plant and Dumas Bay Family Theatre to 44th Avenue SW. Turn right (north) and go

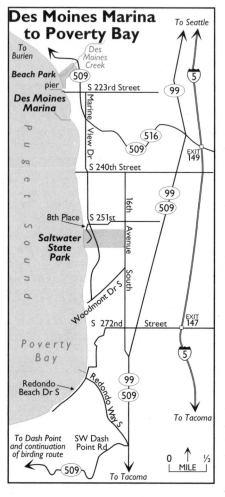

Des Moines Marina to Poverty Bay

To Seattle

To Burien

Des Moines Creek

Beach Park (509)
pier S 223rd Street

Des Moines Marina

(5)

(99)

Marine View Dr

Puget Sound

(516)
(509)
S 240th Street

EXIT 149

(99)
(509)

16th Avenue South

8th Place S 251st

Saltwater State Park

Woodmont Dr S

S 272nd Street

EXIT 147

(5)

Poverty Bay

Redondo Beach Dr S

Redondo Way S

(99)
(509)

To Tacoma

To Dash Point and continuation of birding route

SW Dash Point Rd

(509)

0 ____ ½
MILE

To Tacoma

0.2 mile to a parking lot for **Dumas Bay Park**. (See map on page 196.) Walk downhill through the woods for five minutes to the beach and the large, shallow bay fed by three streams. Loons, rafts of wigeons, and shorebirds are among the seasonal features. Virginia Rail and Sora are summer residents in the freshwater marsh. A few Great Blue Heron nests may be glimpsed through trees lining the road. Return to SR-509, continue west 0.9 mile, and turn right into **Dash Point State Park**. Trails and campgrounds are good for woodland birds such as Hutton's Vireo and Townsend's Warbler. Along the saltwater shore and wide beach look for loons and alcids. Return to SR-509, continue west, and after crossing into Pierce County turn right at Markham Avenue NE and signs for the Lobster Shop (0.6 mile). The short road winds down into **Dash Point County Park**. The fishing pier can be productive for alcids. Ancient Murrelets (November–December) are difficult to find nowadays although Pigeon Guillemots are usual. Parasitic Jaegers appear in September when Common Terns are in migration.

Go back to SR-509 and continue west, then south, 1.5 miles to Brown's Point Shopping Center. Turn right (west) here on Le Lou Wa Place NE (becomes Tok A Lou Avenue NE) and go 0.6 mile to **Browns Point Lighthouse Park**. Marbled Murrelets are fairly reliable in small groups and in June can be seen in breeding plumage.

Return to SR-509 and continue downhill (southeast) to **Commencement Bay** (1.2 miles), at the eastern margin of what used to be the tideflats at the mouth of the Puyallup River. Stop at the first large turnout past Crow's Nest Marina to scan log booms for large flocks of gulls and dozens of herons at high tide, and rafts of Western Grebes. Any of the numerous pullouts can be productive as SR-509 continues southeastward along Hylebos Waterway.

Watch for pilings with Purple Martin boxes, a recent success story. Look for Least and Western Sandpipers (migration), Black Turnstones on log booms (winter), and rafts of ducks during migration. SR-509 bends south and west around the end of the waterway. Bear right at a fork in 5.3 miles at a sign for Port of Tacoma Road, continuing through the traffic light at the top of the overpass. In 1.0 mile, turn right onto Milwaukee Way and travel 0.5 mile to Lincoln Avenue. Turn left and go 0.3 mile to a gravel road on the left, just after a railroad crossing and shortly before the Puyallup River bridge. Turn in here to the **Gog-Le-Hi-Te Mitigated Wetland** (aka Lincoln Avenue Marsh). This rehabilitated garbage dump in the vast wasteland of industrial Tacoma has hosted over 80 bird species since 1990 (a Bar-tailed Godwit visited the new marsh upon its completion). Green Herons nest here. An opening to the river allows daily tidal action on the mudflats. More recently this area has proven to be a hotspot for large gulls in winter. Thayer's occurs in nearly pure flocks, Glaucous is regular, Slaty-backed has appeared almost annually, and a Kumlien's Iceland Gull stayed for over two weeks in January 2000. When searching for gulls, check also the roof of the meat-rendering plant just to the east and other roofs in the vicinity. On leaving, turn left on Lincoln Avenue, then right onto Stewart Street (0.1 mile). Drive down Stewart through the industrial area along the Puyallup River, staying to the left of a guard gate and going under the bridge. Park where the road ends (0.8 mile). A trail next to a chain-link fence leads to the mouth of the river and Commencement Bay. At certain tide stages you may find many more gulls along the river here than at Gog-Le-Hi-Te.

Continue southwest on Lincoln Avenue across the Puyallup River bridge, then turn left (south) onto Portland Avenue (0.2 mile). The I-5 interchange at Exits 134/135 is 0.6 mile ahead. To continue around the other side of Commencement Bay to Point Defiance, turn right (west) onto Puyallup Avenue in 0.4 mile, before reaching the I-5 interchange. In 1.1 miles, turn right (north) onto Pacific Avenue and continue northward through downtown Tacoma for another 1.2 miles, where Pacific Avenue joins Schuster Parkway. Follow the parkway as it curves northwestward along the shoreline. Move to the left lane, and in 1.4 miles take the overpass across the railroad tracks onto **Ruston Way**, lined by a two-mile scenic waterfront park. Several turnouts with parking provide good access. Look for gulls and other waterbirds, and sometimes Black Turnstone. Large rafts of Barrow's Goldeneyes are often present; check around pilings and dilapidated piers. The **Les Davis Fishing Pier** (1.4 miles) provides sheltered viewing and restrooms. Waterfront access ends at the Asarco smelter cleanup site. Continue on Ruston Way as it bends westward and becomes N 51st Street, and turn right in 2.0 miles on Pearl Street (SR-163) to the east entrance to Point Defiance Park (0.2 mile).

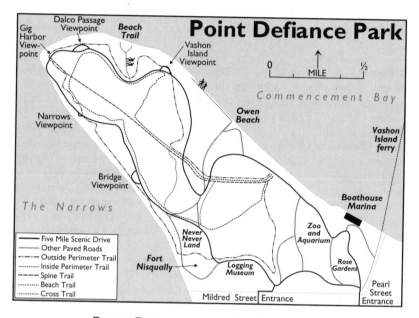

POINT DEFIANCE AND THE NARROWS

A thumb of land projecting into Puget Sound at a mile-wide constriction called The Narrows, Point Defiance is Tacoma's destination birding site. Large volumes of water flow though the passage from the South Sound to the main basin of Puget Sound and back again, across a shallow sill, creating strong currents and tidal rips. Mixing of deep and surface waters here brings an upwelling of nutrients, and consequently ideal feeding conditions for marine birds as well as seals, sea lions, and salmon. The seasonal seabird occurrence at Point Defiance ranks as one of the best in the state. From fall through spring huge numbers of Bonaparte's, Mew, and other gulls, and alcids and other diving birds, feed in The Narrows and surrounding saltwater areas.

All of the birding sites and viewpoints are contained within 698-acre **Point Defiance Park**. Around the end of the point are high bluffs from which one may look down upon the water. Beach trails—especially at the northeast base of the point—allow water-level viewing. Several walking trails in the upland portion lead through beautiful remnants of the Puget Sound Douglas-fir forest. The Point Defiance Zoo and Aquarium, Rhododendron Garden, Fort Nisqually Historic Site, and Logging Museum provide additional attractions for birders and non-birders alike.

The information station (free maps) across from the Rose Gardens near the beginning of **Five Mile Scenic Drive**, just inside the Pearl Street entrance, is a good place to start. Drive the five-mile loop road counterclockwise. Turnoffs near the beginning take you to the boathouse and public marina and (farther ahead) to Owen Beach, providing views of the calm waters of outer Commencement Bay. Scan here for a variety of waterbirds. One can also backtrack along the waterfront to the Point Defiance ferry terminal for further views. From Owen Beach, walk the beach path northwestward. The strata exposed in the bluffs tell the story of the last great advance and retreat of the Puget Lobe of the continental ice sheets (17,000–13,000 years BP). Advancing ice dammed the outlets to the west, creating a large lake. The fine-grained deposits at the bottom are from the bed of this lake. Sand and gravel layers exposed through most of the bluff are outwash deposits from rivers draining the ice front and surrounding upland areas. Near the top is a dense mixture of silt and small boulders deposited at the glacier's base as it overran the earlier deposits. Finally, a thin layer exposed in places at the top represents outwash from rivers draining the retreating ice sheet.

Return to Five Mile Scenic Drive and continue the loop. Walk the trails to explore old-growth conifer forest with the typical suite of tree species of the Puget Lowlands (Douglas-fir association), and mixed forest. Many of the massive trees and snags show signs of active woodpecker work. The common bird species include Steller's Jay, Black-capped and Chestnut-backed Chickadees, Red-breasted Nuthatch, Brown Creeper, Winter Wren, and Golden-crowned Kinglet. Hutton's Vireo (year round) and Townsend's Warbler (winter) are frequently present as are Hairy and Pileated Woodpeckers and many other species. Listen for flocks of Red Crossbill and Pine Siskin overhead. In summer, add Pacific-slope Flycatcher and Swainson's Thrush. In winter, a few Hermit and Varied Thrushes are present.

Scope the water from each of several bluff viewpoints, all the way around the point to Fort Nisqually. The outer portion of the loop road is sometimes gated and requires a walk that is well worth the effort. If on foot, try to check at least **Vashon Island, Dalco Passage**, and **Gig Harbor Viewpoints**. Take the beach trail about a quarter-mile past the Vashon Island Viewpoint for water-level viewing. A few Pigeon Guillemots nest in the north bluff. From fall through spring, Double-crested and Pelagic Cormorants, Common Murres, and Rhinoceros Auklets are common in The Narrows; search also for the occasional Parasitic Jaeger in September (when Common Terns or Bonaparte's Gulls are here in numbers). This is a great place to search for Little Gull among the Bonaparte's, and other rare species as well.

SR-163 southbound from the park entrance brings you to the northbound onramp to SR-16, on the right, in 3.0 miles. Turn here for the Narrows Bridge and Kitsap County (page 195). The southbound SR-16 onramp—on the left in 0.4 mile, after the underpass—will take you to the I-5 interchange at Exit 132 (3.5 miles).

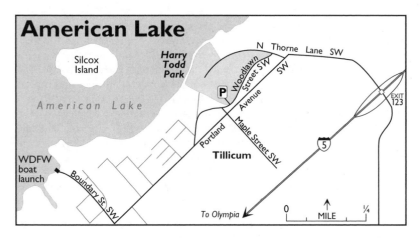

AMERICAN LAKE

A large lake southwest of Tacoma at the north edge of Fort Lewis, American Lake gained attention from birders primarily because of a Little Gull present among Bonaparte's Gulls every winter during the 1990s. Even though the gulls are not always there (presumably they spend a fair amount of time on Puget Sound), potential for a variety of waterfowl and easy access from I-5 make this a popular stop. Take Exit 123 from I-5. At the traffic light, turn northwestward onto North Thorne Lane SW and follow the signs to Harry Todd Park in Lakewood, the traditional Little Gull spot (turn right with Thorne in 0.3 mile, then left onto Woodlawn Street SW in 150 yards, and right into the fee parking lot 0.2 mile ahead). Bring a scope; the gull flock can be quite far out. Another vantage point is from the WDFW boat ramp a bit farther west. Turn right out of the parking lot, then immediately left onto Maple Street for one block and right again onto Portland Avenue SW. Follow signs to *Boat Launch*, turning left at the entrance in 0.6 mile (WDFW permit required).

SOUTH SOUND PRAIRIES

by Bill Shelmerdine

A unique (and shrinking) ecosystem of grasslands, oaks, and conifer woodlands stretches westward across Fort Lewis, southwest of Tacoma, to Littlerock, south of Olympia, marking the southern edge of the Puget Lobe of the last glaciation. Between about 14,000 and 13,200 BP the ice sheet gradually withdrew. Dammed by the retreating glacier and hemmed in east and west by the Cascades and the Olympics, meltwaters formed a huge lake. Runoff was directed westward from the lake's south end into the Chehalis River, depositing gravelly, excessively drained, nutrient-poor soils in plains, channels, and terraces. The prairies that later developed on the glacial outwash occupy the driest spots within the Puget Sound Douglas-fir vegetation zone that surrounds them. The suggested birding route follows the glacial meltwater drainage plain from east to west, through excellent examples of these native prairies.

This Woodland/Prairie Mosaic zone has several habitat types. The dry, treeless grasslands are blanketed with clumps of Idaho Fescue separated by a tight layer of moss and other low herbaceous plants. Bordering forest stands include Lodgepole Pine, Western White Pine, and relict Ponderosa Pine, but are mostly of Douglas-fir and Garry Oak. Salal, Common Snowberry, Indian-plum, and Western Serviceberry are typical of the understory. Numerous swamp and bog communities exist in spots where drainage is poor. Oregon Ash and Garry Oak dominate the riparian areas.

Bird species resident within the South Sound Prairies, but uncommon or highly local elsewhere in Western Washington, include Northern Bobwhite (introduced), Mourning Dove, Common Nighthawk, Horned Lark, House Wren, Western Bluebird, Chipping and Vesper Sparrows, Lazuli Bunting, and Western Meadowlark. Distinctive races of several butterflies are near-endemic to this zone, among them Great Spangled and Zerene Fritillaries, the state-endangered Mardon Skipper, and Edith's Checkerspot. These glacial outwash prairies are also home to the state-threatened Western Gray Squirrel and the seriously declining Mazama Pocket Gopher.

About 4,000 acres of grasslands remain of an estimated 150,000 acres historically. Agriculture and suburban sprawl account for most of the loss. Garry Oak and Douglas-fir are encroaching on much of the rest—an unintended consequence of fire suppression. Prior to white settlement, openings were maintained by fires, including deliberate burning by Native Americans. Modern management interventions such as controlled burns, brush clearing, and selective logging take place periodically on some of the remaining portions.

FORT LEWIS PRAIRIES

Several sites are on Fort Lewis, a U.S. Army training facility. Before birding here you must obtain an access permit (good for 12 months) issued by Range Operations, Fort Lewis Area Access Office (253-967-6277). It is recom-

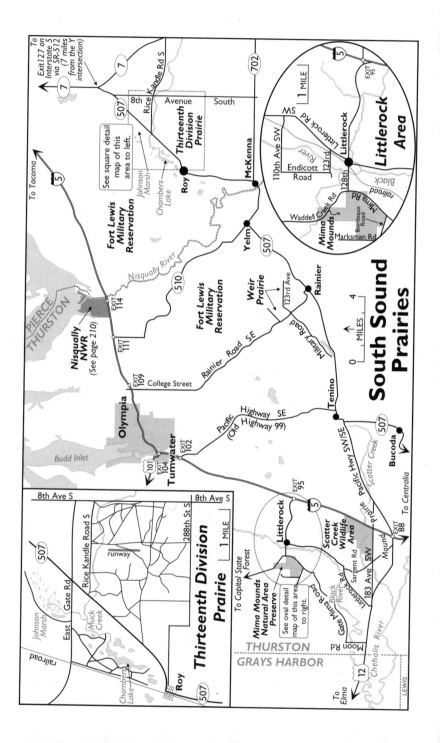

mended that you call ahead for directions to Range Operations (Dupont Gate, I-5 Exit 120). Depending on the installation alert status you may need to enter first at the Main Gate (I-5 Exit 122). At a minimum, you will need your driver's license, current vehicle registration, and proof of insurance. Fort Lewis has numerous training areas, each designated by a number (indicated here by FL AREA #). Areas where training is occurring are closed to the public. To avoid disappointment, call ahead for closure information and current permit requirements; make sure you know the numbers of the areas you want to visit. Hunting (especially for upland birds) is a popular activity in many areas, so use caution.

Fort Lewis birding is best in May. Prairie wildflowers are at their peak then, too, among them Henderson's Shooting Star, Common Camas, Chocolate Lily, Blue-eyed Grass, and the endemic White-topped Aster. Dry Douglas-fir forest edges are particularly good in spring for a variety of bird species favoring lowland conifer forests. In the early 1980s, Fort Lewis began a bluebird nest-box program. There are now about 160 nesting pairs of Western Bluebirds scattered about the fort. In winter things are usually pretty quiet; Northern Shrike can often be found, and Merlin, Short-eared Owl, and other raptors less reliably.

Armed with a valid permit and current access information, drive east on SR-512 from I-5 Exit 127. In about two miles, turn right (south) onto SR-7, and at the fork in 5.1 miles, stay right onto SR-507. Two excellent areas—Johnson Marsh (FL AREA 10) and Chambers Lake (FL AREA 12)—are within the gated, more strictly controlled part of the installation, but well worth visiting if they are open. Travel 3.9 miles on SR-507 and turn right onto East Gate Road. Just past a small outlet creek, go right at 1.0 mile onto an unmarked gravel road that runs through Douglas-fir forest along the west side of **Johnson Marsh** for well over a mile, with many vistas and access points. The zone where the forest meets the marsh supports a great diversity of passerines, including flycatchers, four species of wrens (Bewick's, House, Winter, Marsh), and warblers. Wood Duck, Hooded Merganser, and Purple Martin nest at Johnson Marsh, which is also one of the few places in Western Washington where Yellow-headed Blackbird occurs regularly (has nested).

Return to East Gate Road and turn right (west). Numerous dirt roads—some of them barely driveable—lead into and across the **Chambers Lake** area south of the road; one access point is 0.2 mile farther along, on the left. An easier way is to continue another 0.8 mile west on East Gate Road and turn left onto an asphalt road just before the railroad crossing. This road runs south along the west edge of a large prairie with scattered Ponderosa Pines, to a closed gate on the northern outskirts of Roy. A good graded road turns off to the left in 0.4 mile, crossing the north end of the tract. Look and listen for House Wren, Western Bluebird, and Chipping and Vesper Sparrows. Six-tenths of a mile south of this intersection another paved road branches off to the southeast, crosses the prairie, and runs along the west side of the lake, which is fringed with brush and open stands of Ponderosa Pine, Douglas-fir, and Garry Oak—good for passerines. The lake itself may have Ring-necked Duck, Lesser Scaup, an occasional Redhead, and other ducks. After the lake, the pavement ends and the dirt road swings back north through the forested eastern part of the area.

Go back out East Gate Road, cross SR-507, continue east 2.0 miles to the intersection with Eighth Avenue S, and turn right. [If you are coming down SR-7 from the north and are not visiting Johnson Marsh or Chambers Lake, go right onto SR-507 at the fork and in 1.1 miles veer left (south) onto Eighth Avenue S (*do not* make the sharp east turn onto 208th Street S).] **Thirteenth Division Prairie** (FL AREA 14)—a vast prairie bordered by open, dry Douglas-fir forest and a few scrubby clearcuts—begins just south of Rice Kandle Road S, 2.5 miles from the SR-507 intersection (about half a mile south of East Gate Road). Turn off to the west and drive the maze of dirt roads to likely habitat. Muck Creek runs through the site in a corridor of Oregon Ash; an old landing strip is here as well. Northern Bobwhite, Short-eared Owl, Common Nighthawk, Western Kingbird, Horned Lark, and Vesper Sparrow are among the birds seen at least occasionally. The vegetation along the creek can be good for migrant passerines and riparian species.

Travel south on Eighth Avenue S. Once you cross 288th Street S (2.5 miles from Rice Kandle Road S) you are off the military reservation. Continue 4.0 miles south and turn right onto SR-702. Road edges, open places, and recent clearcuts are worth exploring as you head west toward the intersection with SR-507 in McKenna (5.2 miles). Drive the side roads, and walk in on blocked or unused logging tracks. The area is noteworthy for open-country birds uncommon or absent in most parts of Western Washington—particularly Northern Bobwhite, but also Western Kingbird, Western Bluebird, and Lazuli Bunting. Shrubby thickets following clearcutting are good for these and other species, including MacGillivray's Warbler.

Weir Prairie (FL AREA 21; Tenalquot Prairie on some maps), near Rainier, can be reached by turning left (south) on SR-507 in McKenna. Travel through Yelm to Rainier, and turn right (northwest) onto Minnesota Street (8.4 miles). The road bends left, then right, becoming 138th Street SE and finally Rainier Road SE. In 2.1 miles, turn right (northeast) onto Military Road SE, which in 0.6 mile bends right (east) onto 123rd Avenue SE, running along the southern border of **Upper Weir Prairie**. Turn left through the access gate (1.1 miles from the Rainier Road intersection). This is normally a good place for Western Bluebird and Western Meadowlark. In early spring look also for Mountain Bluebird (rare). Unusual birds, including Least Flycatcher and Clay-colored and Grasshopper Sparrows, have been found here in recent years. The Garry Oaks along much of the west edge of the prairie are a good place to search for passerines, including House Wren.

Go back to Rainier Road SE and turn right (northwest). This stretch of Rainier Road bisects **Lower Weir Prairie**, with well-maintained gravel roads leading off in several directions. The prairie has Northern Bobwhite, Vesper and Savannah Sparrows, and Western Meadowlark. For one reasonably consistent location for Northern Bobwhite, go right from Rainier Road onto a road at the northwest edge of the prairie (0.6 mile from the Military Road intersection); follow this paved though potholed road 0.8 mile to an intersection with a gravel road. Park here and walk southeastward (right) toward some snags, a rise (glacial terrace edge), and shrubby cover in the center of the prairie. House Wren and Western Bluebird are here as well. Roadside forest edges may hold Hammond's Flycatcher, MacGillivray's Warbler, Western Tanager, Chipping Sparrow, and several others.

SCATTER CREEK AND BLACK RIVER

Return to the town of Rainier and drive right (southwest) on SR-507 to Tenino (city limits sign 6.8 miles). If you explore side streets and residential areas north from the main drag you should be able to find Western Scrub-Jay on phone lines or other perches. At the other edge of Tenino (about two miles), turn right (west) onto Pacific Highway SE (Old Highway 99), then bear right (west) onto 183rd Avenue SW (5.2 miles). Soon after crossing over I-5, turn right onto Guava Court (2.0 miles) and continue straight to the large gravel parking lot near the end, on the left (WDFW permit required). This is the main entrance to **Scatter Creek Wildlife Area** at the north edge of Mound Prairie. The site is popular with upland bird hunters and dog trainers and should be avoided in the hunting season, which is not a hardship since the best period for birding is late April though early June. (Gamebird releases occur—don't assume Ring-necked Pheasant, California Quail, or Northern Bobwhite are wild or established, and certainly the occasional Chukar is not part of the countable avifauna.) This is a great place for an early morning walk in spring. Take the trail westward from the parking lot, between the barn and the creek—and for the more ambitious, all the way around the oak grove, fields, edges, and overgrown areas to the west and south. There is a fine riparian area of Oregon Ash with surrounding Garry Oak and understory shrubs. Across the creek are conifers of the typical lowland Douglas-fir association. These varied habitats will produce an excellent list of Western Washington lowland species, in addition to many of the local prairie specialties. When restoration efforts have kept the invasive Scot's Broom at bay, Scatter Creek can be a fabulous spot for prairie wildflowers from May into the summer.

From the parking lot at Scatter Creek Wildlife Area, go back south to 183rd Avenue SW, turn right, and travel west 1.6 miles to Sargent Road SW. Go right (north) to the intersection with Littlerock Road SW in 2.0 miles, and turn right again. The road follows the **Black River**, on the left, which flows south into the Chehalis. The valley's breadth is a reminder of the tremendous volume of glacial meltwater that coursed through this area for centuries, as the last ice age came to an end. There is not much river access on foot but birding is excellent from a canoe or kayak. A gravel pullout 2.2 miles ahead is a good place to launch. To reach other access points, drive north to Littlerock (4.3 miles from Sargent Road), jog right onto 128th Avenue SW, then left, continuing north on Littlerock Road for another 0.5 mile. Turn left onto 123rd Avenue SW to a river crossing. An open wetland here has resident waterfowl, rails, and other marshbirds, and a few shorebirds in migration. Turn right 0.2 mile past the bridge and go north on Endicott Road SW; in 1.3 miles the road turns right and becomes 110th Avenue SW. Another canoe launch is located near the river bridge (0.7 mile). A five-mile stretch of the river upstream from Littlerock to the south end of Black Lake, near Olympia, is the backbone of the new Black River National Wildlife Refuge (under development). The slow-flowing river and dense riparian vegetation, with Oregon Ash, Black Cottonwood, Red-osier Dogwood, willows, and other trees, has been described as having a character reminiscent of rivers in the southeastern United States. Expect Green Heron (common), Bullock's Oriole, and other typical riparian species, including a few small concentrations of Red-eyed Vireos.

MIMA MOUNDS

Birders should not miss visiting the nearby Mima (pronounced MY-muh) Prairie, west and south of Littlerock, to ponder the elusive origins of the strange mounded surface of the ground. Interpretive displays at the 445-acre **Mima Mounds Natural Area Preserve** will help get you started with some of the explanations that have been proposed. Prehistoric pocket gophers are among the more intriguing hypotheses. From the intersection with Littlerock Road in Littlerock, go west on 128th Avenue SW. At the intersection in 0.8 mile, go right (north) onto Waddell Creek Road SW. Proceed 0.8 mile and turn left into the gravel-road entrance to the preserve (easy-to-miss brown sign on the right). Continue to the parking and picnic area, where nature trails lead from conifer woods to the prairie edge. Western Meadowlarks are common on the grasslands. Return to Waddell Creek Road. A left turn brings you in 1.6 miles to the Waddell Creek Entrance to the Capitol State Forest (page 217).

A few White-tailed Kites have been present in recent years, especially along the south and west sides of the preserve. Backtrack on Waddell Creek Road SW until it becomes Mima Road SW at the junction with 128th Avenue SW. Continue south for 0.9 mile, where the forest edge thins. This part of the preserve can be viewed from Mima Road SW on the east, Bordeaux Road SW on the south, and Marksman Road SW on the west (map on page 204). Pullouts are few and traffic presents a hazard. One wide pullout with a sign noting prairie restoration efforts is located a quarter-mile down Bordeaux Road SW. This area is actively managed to control Scot's Broom and other invasives. Species abundance and distribution, and ease of birding, shift with the vegetation.

Return to 128th Avenue SW and turn right (east) to I-5 Exit 95 in 3.7 miles. Take I-5 northbound for Olympia (page 213), or southbound to Centralia, Chehalis, and birding sites of Southwestern Washington (page 236). Or continue down Mima Road to Gate, then left onto Moon Road SW to US-12 (about eight miles). Turn right (west) on US-12 and travel down the Chehalis River Valley to birding sites near Elma (page 63), and on to the South Coast.

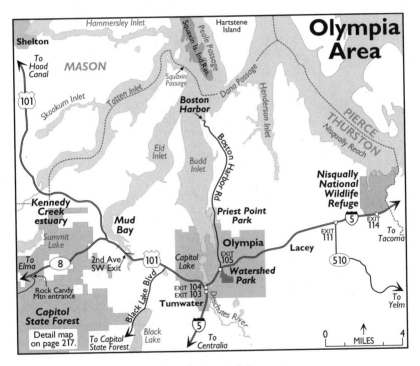

OLYMPIA AND VICINITY

by Bill Shelmerdine

Main routes between Puget Sound, southwestern Washington, the outer coast, and the Olympic Peninsula meet in Olympia, at the southernmost extent of Puget Sound. A few miles east is the Nisqually River delta, the most pristine of the Sound's large estuaries and a significant birding site. The South Sound breaks up into shallow inlets with many interesting birding opportunites, including at the end of Budd Inlet in downtown Olympia. Western Scrub-Jays now nest regularly in the city, at the northern edge of their continuing range expansion. Watershed Park, near the city center, is a fine place to look for lowland forest birds.

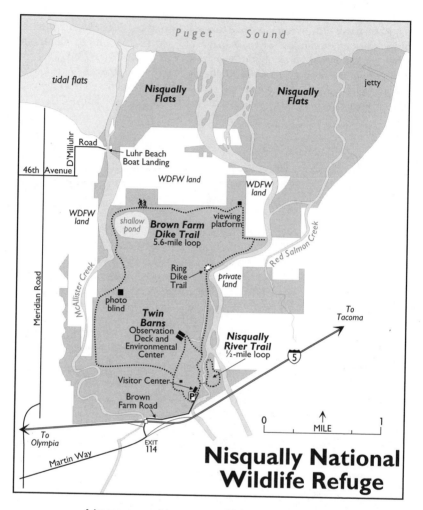

Nisqually National Wildlife Refuge

This is the single best birding location along the South Sound, offering 2,817 acres of open grasslands, tidal flats, freshwater and saltwater marshes, and riparian woodlands at the estuary of the Nisqually River. Well over 200 species of birds have been seen in these diverse habitats. In winter, the refuge supports some 20,000 waterfowl and a large raptor population. Winter is also good for sparrows and finches. High numbers of shorebirds stop to feed in fall and spring, and thousands of Dunlins winter here. Passerine migration can be excellent in the riparian woodlands. Summer is the slow season, but even then the refuge is alive with incredible numbers of Willow Flycatchers, nesting

Tree Swallows, and the songs of Swainson's Thrush and Yellow Warbler. A scope is essential for shorebirding (and useful for raptors and waterfowl).

Take Exit 114 from I-5, between Fort Lewis and Olympia, and follow the signs north a short distance into the refuge (entrance fee). Extensive renovations (1999) include a new parking lot and visitor center, upgraded trails and viewing areas, and a one-mile barrier-free boardwalk. Much of the lower floodplain and estuary was diked for agriculture in pre-refuge days. A gravel road atop the old dike system is now the main public trail, encircling the heart of the refuge. The outer section (three miles) is closed during hunting season (mid-October to late January) to provide a sanctuary for waterfowl. The epicenter of the magnitude-6.8 earthquake of 28 February 2001, was at the mouth of the Nisqually. Some refuge buildings and dikes were weakened, with as yet undetermined consequences for how the refuge is managed.

One of the most productive birding areas is **Twin Barns**, close to refuge headquarters, featuring a large wheelchair-accessible viewing deck. Scan for waterfowl, Short-eared Owl (dawn or dusk), Northern Shrike (fall and winter), and various raptors. (Barn Owls inhabit the barns but are rarely seen.) The woods east of the barns host Rufous Hummingbirds and many passerines. Great Horned Owls live in the large Black Cottonwood trees, and Red-breasted Sapsuckers frequent the Bigleaf Maples. The short cross-over trail east to the river goes through these woods. In spring, Wood Ducks can be found in sloughs here and adjacent to the dike trail north along the river.

The 5.5-mile dike loop is described here in a clockwise direction, but you may walk it either way. From the visitor center west to McAllister Creek the trail crosses open fields with many shrubs, ponds, and cattail-lined sloughs. Marshes have Virginia Rail and American Bittern (uncommon). Fox, Song, White-crowned, and Golden-crowned Sparrows are typical of winter sparrow flocks, Lincoln's is less common, and American Tree, Swamp, White-throated, and Harris's are seen rarely. Marsh Wren, Common Yellowthroat (summer), and Savannah Sparrow (common in summer, uncommon in winter) are also resident.

The dike turns northward along McAllister Creek, bordered by hedgerows of blackberry, Western Serviceberry, wild rose, and low trees—excellent for passerines, including winter sparrow flocks. Check the lower part of the creek for loons, grebes, waterfowl, shorebirds, and gulls. An extensive shallow pond at the inside northwest corner of the dike is one of the best spring shorebird locations on the refuge. You will need a scope. Greater Yellowlegs, Western and Least Sandpipers, and Dunlins are common, sometimes joined by Lesser Yellowlegs, Solitary Sandpiper, and Wilson's Phalarope in early May. This is a good spot seasonally for Greater White-fronted Goose, Eurasian Wigeon, and Blue-winged, Cinnamon, and Green-winged Teal along with many other waterfowl. The pond is normally dry from July through September, but in the wettest years it can be good for fall shorebirds.

The north portion of the dike trail looks out a long distance over salt marsh and tideflats to the open salt water of the Nisqually Reach at the bottom of Puget Sound. Merlins and Peregrine Falcons can often be seen sitting on stranded logs or dive-bombing the shorebird flocks. Brant frequent the marsh edges in early spring and sometimes winter here. Set up a scope on the elevated viewing platform at the east end of the dike. The shoreline near the mouth of the Nisqually River often has many Bald Eagles. Gulls (Bonaparte's is often common), Caspian and Common (fall) Terns, and shorebirds are here in numbers, but viewing at this distance can be frustrating.

The dike trail along the east side of the refuge follows the Nisqually River, passing through a riparian area of Red Alder, Black Cottonwood, and Oregon Ash with a densely vegetated understory. In winter, foraging flocks of chickadees and kinglets will usually have a few Red-breasted Nuthatches and Brown Creepers and perhaps a Hutton's Vireo. Downy Woodpecker, Bewick's and Winter Wrens, and Song Sparrow are common. Cedar Waxwings are abundant at times, Bushtits are uncommon residents, and there are usually flocks of Pine Siskins. Pileated Woodpeckers work this area. Spring and fall migration can be choice, with large, mixed flocks of passerines including a variety of flycatchers, vireos, warblers, Western Tanager, and Black-headed Grosbeak. During summer, Willow and Pacific-slope Flycatchers, Swainson's Thrush, Yellow Warbler, and American Goldfinch are common. The pond at the Ring Dike can be good for American Bittern, Virginia Rail, and occasionally Sora. This is a good spot from which to scan the interior for raptors (including Northern Shrike) in winter.

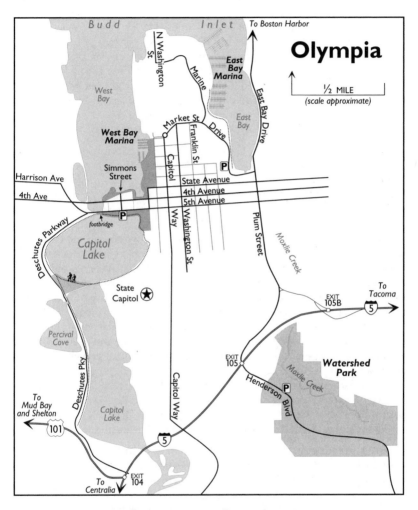

OLYMPIA AND BUDD INLET

Washington's capital offers a variety of waterbirds and passerines right in the center of town. From I-5 southbound turn off at Exit 105B (Exit 105 if north-bound) and follow the signs for the Port of Olympia. Either exit will deposit you on Plum Street. Head north, and in 0.7 mile turn left onto Marine Drive NE. Park on the large gravel shoulder on the left, across the road from the head of **East Bay** and an outfall pipe where gulls and diving ducks often feed. Mudflats exposed at low tide attract small flocks of shorebirds in spring and fall, and Purple Martins use the nest boxes on pilings in the bay. You may follow the footpath along the west side of the bay as far as the marina, or drive, pulling off where shoulders and views allow. If driving, continue on Marine Drive along the shoreline of East Bay, bearing right at the intersection in 0.4 mile where Market Street comes in from the left, to East Bay Marina (Swantown). This deeper (dredged) part of the bay is good in winter for loons, grebes, and bay ducks, including small numbers of Black Scoters. Continue ahead, turn right onto Washington Street, and park between Genoa's Restaurant and KGY radio station, at the tip of the point between East and West Bays (0.5 mile from Market Street). Bonaparte's Gulls and Caspian (summer) and Common (fall) Terns are sometimes here in numbers, along with diving birds, including Rhinoceros Auklet and three species of cormorants.

Backtrack on Marine Drive, turn right onto Market Street, and go 0.2 mile to the roundabout at Olympia's Farmers Market. Directly across the circle and ahead one block is West Bay Marina and parking. Viewing is from the boardwalk along the water or from the observation tower to the north. The water is deeper than in East Bay and may have a different assortment of waterbirds. Check sailboat rigging for Purple Martins. Return to the circle, turn right and take Capitol Way seven blocks south (toward downtown), and turn right onto Fifth Avenue. In four blocks, at Simmons Street, park in the lot on the left to go birding on foot along **Capitol Lake**—noted for diving ducks and a large gull flock that roosts there in the afternoon. Cross the street at the light and walk west two blocks. At low tide, the footbridge next to the KFC is a great spot to view the schools of Chinook Salmon that stage at the mouth of Capitol Lake in August, awaiting entry to the Deschutes River. Bird from the footpath that makes a 1.5-mile loop around the lower (north) lake and goes down the west side of the upper (south) lake, or drive west two blocks on Fifth Avenue and bear left at the fork onto Deschutes Parkway, which parallels the shoreline with many places to park. Check both lakes and Percival Cove for a good variety of waterfowl. Virginia Rail, Marsh Wren, and Red-winged Blackbird nest in the small marshes at the south end. American Dipper is a regular wintering species at Tumwater Falls about a mile farther upstream.

Boston Harbor, about seven miles north of Olympia at the confluence of Budd and Eld Inlets, is a good place to view birds of the deeper, more open waters of Puget Sound. Go back east on Fourth Avenue (one block north of Fifth) through the business district and turn left (north) onto Plum Street, which soon becomes East Bay Drive. A sidewalk provides a good place from which to look for birds on East Bay. Priest Point Park, at 1.5 miles from the Fourth Avenue intersection, is good for forest and waterbirds. Continue on north 5.5 miles (name change to Boston Harbor Road), then go left 350 yards on 73rd Avenue NE to the harbor. Scope the inlet from the vicinity of the boat ramp. Loons, grebes, cormorants, saltwater ducks, gulls, terns, and alcids fly above the channel or feed along current lines when tides are changing, sometimes in good numbers. Oddities may appear after large winter storms.

Watershed Park is a 115-acre wooded ravine a mile south of downtown Olympia. Go south on Plum Street, and at the traffic light just before the I-5 onramps bear right toward the southbound onramp but then stay left and go under the freeway onto Henderson Boulevard. A 1.5-mile loop trail begins at a gravel parking area on the left shoulder 0.3 mile ahead. Douglas-fir, Western Hemlock, Bigleaf Maple, and other large trees shade a lush and varied understory. Snags are numerous. Red-breasted Sapsucker and Pileated and Hairy Woodpeckers have nested. Vaux's Swifts are often overhead. Owls found here include Western Screech-, Great Horned (has nested), Northern Pygmy-, and Barred (roosting along the creek). Many forest birds nest here or are year-round residents; others can be found in spring migration. This is a decent spot to look for Hutton's and Cassin's (spring) Vireos.

ELD AND TOTTEN INLETS

At the upper end of Eld Inlet a few miles west of Olympia, **Mud Bay** is one of the last areas to be flooded by a rising tide. One to two hours before peak high tide, shorebirds and small gulls often concentrate close to the road for excellent viewing. At low tide, birds disperse up or down the bay. Take the Second Avenue SW exit from US-101 (just across the bridge over the bay, if you are coming from Olympia). Turn east (right if coming from Olympia, left if from Shelton) onto Mud Bay Road and park at either end of the concrete bridge spanning Mud Bay (0.2 mile). A good variety of gulls can be found here. Franklin's has been seen with the large Bonaparte's flock in September and October. Shorebirding is good in fall and spring, with all of the typical migrants occurring at least occasionally. Dunlins winter in good numbers, along with the occasional Black-bellied Plover, Greater Yellowlegs, Willet (rare), or Spotted Sandpiper. Sometimes there are large numbers of Hooded Mergansers in fall.

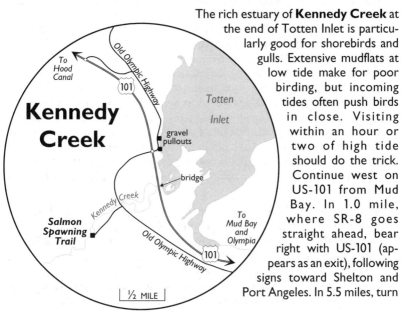

The rich estuary of **Kennedy Creek** at the end of Totten Inlet is particularly good for shorebirds and gulls. Extensive mudflats at low tide make for poor birding, but incoming tides often push birds in close. Visiting within an hour or two of high tide should do the trick. Continue west on US-101 from Mud Bay. In 1.0 mile, where SR-8 goes straight ahead, bear right with US-101 (appears as an exit), following signs toward Shelton and Port Angeles. In 5.5 miles, turn off right onto Old Olympic Highway, just after the Kennedy Creek bridge (traffic is heavy; be careful). The mouth of Kennedy Creek is an important wintering site for Black-bellied Plover and Dunlin. In spring and fall migration, Black-bellied Plover, Greater Yellowlegs, Western and Least Sandpipers, Dunlin, and Long-billed Dowitcher are common. In September, high numbers of the smaller gulls stage here, mostly Bonaparte's, Mew, and Ring-billed. Kennedy Creek has one of the largest remaining Chum Salmon runs in the South Sound, attracting the larger gulls from late October into December to feed on the spent carcasses. One can view the innermost part of the estuary from a gravel parking area just off the highway. The outer part of the estuary can be seen well from a second gravel pullout about 0.1 mile ahead on Old Olympic Highway. Birds often roost just across the creek at high tide. If visiting on a weekend from the first of November through the first weekend in December, check out the salmon spawning trail about one mile upstream. Drive across US-101 and go 0.7 mile on Old Olympic Highway. Turn right onto a gravel road and drive an additional 0.5 mile to the interpretive site.

To reach Chehalis River valley and South Coast birding sites (page 63), return south to SR-8 and turn west. Continuing north on US-101 will take you to Hood Canal (page 219).

CAPITOL STATE FOREST

The 90,000-acre Capitol State Forest, at the heart of the Black Hills southwest of Olympia, is probably the most reliable, readily accessible place in Washington to look for Hermit Warbler. Also found here are Mountain Quail (uncommon) and a lowland population of Gray Jay. This is a working forest—in other words, intensively managed by the DNR for timber harvest. Vegetation is generally young to middle-aged conifers dominated by Douglas-fir and Western Hemlock interspersed with clearcuts in various stages of regrowth. Few large, old forest stands remain. The network of logging roads can be confusing. Some areas are poorly signed; road numbers change; closures may spring up unexpectedly. It is recommended that you pick up a map at the Olympic National Forest headquarters on the southwest corner of US-101 and Black Lake Boulevard in Olympia or through the DNR Photo and Map Sales office near the capitol (phone 360-902-1234). Roads are aggregate-surfaced and usually suitable for passenger vehicles, but beware of logging-truck traffic.

Two convenient access points are the Rock Candy Mountain Entrance from SR-8 on the north side of the forest (4.5 miles west of the US-101 intersection), and the Delphi Entrance on the east side. Take the Black Lake Boulevard exit from US-101 (the first exit west of I-5 in Olympia) and head south (the USFS office is immediately on your right). In 4.3 miles, go left onto Delphi Road. At a fork in 2.1 miles, where Delphi Road goes left, stay straight on Waddell Creek Road to reach the Delphi Entrance in 2.7 miles. Another op-

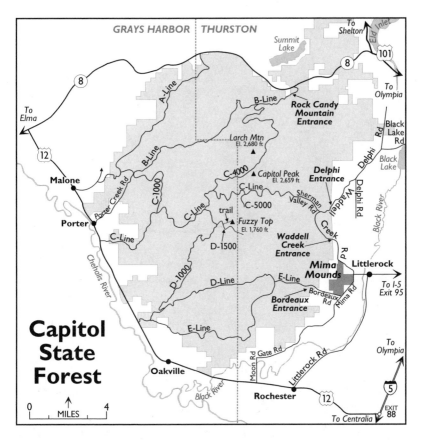

tion is to continue west from Mima Mounds Natural Area Preserve (page 208) on Waddell Creek Road for 1.6 miles to the Waddell Creek Entrance. A good through route starting at the Rock Candy Mountain Entrance follows the B-Line to Road C-4000, thence to the C-Line and out the Delphi or Waddell Creek Entrance.

Some worthwhile areas to search for Gray Jay and Hermit Warbler include along Road C-4000 between Larch Mountain and Capitol Peak (the two highest points in the Black Hills), the trail at Fuzzy Top (accessed from the west on Road D-1500), and along the C-Line between the junctions with Roads C-4000 and C-5000. Mountain Quail have been seen in spring along Road C-4000 near and north of Larch Mountain. Other species of interest in these wet conifer-forest habitats include Northern Pygmy-Owl (uncommon), Hutton's Vireo, and Black-throated Gray (alder patches) and Townsend's Warblers. Search brushy clearcuts and margins for Olive-sided Flycatcher, MacGillivray's Warbler, and Western Tanager. The most common species encountered will likely be Chestnut-backed Chickadee, Winter Wren, and Golden-crowned Kinglet.

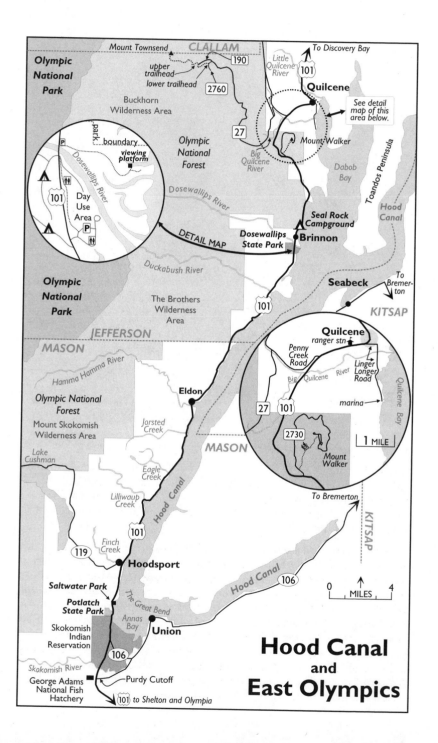

Hood Canal
and
East Olympics

HOOD CANAL AND EAST OLYMPICS

by Bill Shelmerdine

Hood Canal—a beautiful, sheltered arm of Puget Sound—is one of only a few true fjords in the conterminous United States. Its deep waters, steep sides, and narrow, rocky shoreline support comparatively smaller numbers of wintering waterbirds than the rest of the Sound. Birding is primarily from along the edge of US-101, which clings to the west rim of Hood Canal. There are few places to get out and walk, and the shoreline is either not accommodating to foot travel or is privately owned. However, birding can be quite productive at the modest deltas, salt marshes, and shallow waters at the mouths of the principal rivers (from south to north, the Skokomish, Hamma Hamma, Duckabush, Dosewallips, and Big and Little Quilcene) and a few smaller creeks. Such estuarine habitats draw waterfowl and gulls, and most have salmon runs that attract birds in season (usually October–November). Numerous forest roads and wilderness trails reach into the eastern Olympics from US-101. Birders may wish to sample lower-elevation forest habitats on an easy drive up 2,800-foot Mount Walker, or hike through upper-elevation forest zones to alpine parkland at the 6,200-foot summit of Mount Townsend.

GREAT BEND AND ANNAS BAY

From the intersection with SR-8 west of Mud Bay (page 215), proceed north on US-101 about 21 miles to the Purdy Cutoff Road north of Shelton. Turn right here, opposite the George Adams National Fish Hatchery, and descend the lower Skokomish River Valley to the junction with SR-106 (2.8 miles). Turn right toward Union. After another 1.7 miles you will reach the south end of Hood Canal and the mouth of the river at **Annas Bay**, which offer extensive, excellent saltwater habitat and high concentrations of birds, especially in winter. The main drawback is access. Much of the lower Skokomish River lies within the Skokomish Indian Reservation or is in private ownership. Generally, birding—though productive—will be from the edge of the road and a long-distance affair. Find a wide spot along the shoulder and scan the salt water, shoreline, and delta. Common wintering waterfowl include Mallard, Northern Pintail, Red-breasted Merganser, and large flocks of American Wigeons. Farther out in the bay Canvasback (uncommon) and Common Goldeneye are found along with flocks of Surf and White-winged Scoters (and Black Scoter uncommonly). This is a favorite area for loons and grebes. Yellow-billed Loon has been seen here, and Clark's Grebe has been found among the numerous Westerns. Continue 1.7 miles to **Union**, where Hood Canal makes its Great Bend to the east. Pull out on the left, just after the Union Bay Cafe (across from Union Country Store), and scan the open salt water. This is a good spot for birds that prefer deeper, more open waters than those of Annas Bay. In August, Purple Martins may be seen on pilings or boats at the small marina.

Take SR-106 west to US-101 (5.2 miles), and turn right (north) to **Pot-latch State Park** (2.0 miles), at the northwest corner of Annas Bay. The waters here are quite productive from fall into spring. Horned, Red-necked, and Western Grebes are common, as are Red-throated and Common Loons. Scaups, scoters, and goldeneyes also winter here in good numbers. Half a mile back south on US-101, the Skokomish Tribe maintains a small salmon-stocking facility at a paved pullout beside a creek. This can be loaded with gulls. Take the opportunity to walk west along the shoreline at the end of the bay and scan for waterfowl—one of the few chances you will have on Hood Canal to get away from the road and stretch your legs for a bit. Six-tenths of a mile north of the state park on US-101 is Tacoma City Light's **Saltwater Park** and boat ramp. A large gravel parking lot is on the right, across from the power-house. The penstocks and power canal discharge a large volume of cold, fresh water that has been diverted from the North Fork Skokomish River and the Lake Cushman hydroelectric project. Flow, and perhaps feeding conditions, attract a variety of waterbirds, including Harlequin Duck (occasional) and Barrow's Goldeneye.

HOODSPORT TO QUILCENE BAY

The fish hatchery on Finch Creek, at the north end of the town of **Hoodsport** (2.8 miles), is also good for waterbirds. Park at the hatchery and walk through the complex to the creek mouth. Continuing north on US-101, the mouths of Lilliwaup Creek (4.3 miles), Eagle Creek (2.5 miles), and Jorsted Creek (3.2 miles) can have concentrations of waterbirds in fall and winter. All three cormorants (Brandt's uncommon) roost on the pilings of the former log dump and decking area just north of Jorsted Creek, and Purple Martins sometimes use them in late August and early September. The **Hamma Hamma River** (1.5 miles) is a large stream with an estuary and salt marsh. Brant, bay ducks, gulls, and sometimes shorebirds may be seen from a spot on the south side of the Hamma Hamma Oyster Company, at the south end of the estuary. When salmon are running (October–November), look for Bald Eagles in the trees just upstream of the bridge on the far side of the estuary. There is a Great Blue Heron rookery in the large cottonwood trees a bit farther upstream. The **Duckabush River estuary** (9.9 miles) is best known for its small wintering population of Trumpeter Swans. Up to a dozen birds can be anywhere on the estuary, November–March. Pullouts are narrow and the traffic unforgiving, so be careful.

Dosewallips State Park (3.0 miles), at the mouth of the Dosewallips River just south of Brinnon, offers some of the best and most accessible birding on Hood Canal. Diverse habitats include conifer forest in and around the campground, a Red Alder-dominated riparian zone along the river, and thickets, openings, and salt marsh leading to the open shoreline and sloughs at the river's mouth. Turn right off the highway into the day-use area (restrooms), or left to the campground. For the best birding, drive 0.4 mile north across the river on the new highway bridge to the beach-trail parking lot on the right, and walk to the beach through mixed riparian vegetation beneath some large cottonwoods. Vireos, chickadees, kinglets, and warblers may be here in good numbers during migration; Hutton's Vireo and Townsend's Warbler are usually somewhere in the vicinity during fall or winter. The area around the viewing platform can be good for sparrows, with Savannah, Song, Lincoln's, White-crowned, and Golden-crowned present seasonally. From the platform itself, the shoreline, salt marsh, and open-water habitats beyond can be scanned (best at high tide). Harbor Seals haul out at the river mouth. If you walk across the bridge, scan upstream and down. Harlequin Duck (rare), Common Merganser, and American Dipper have all been seen here. Around the end of September you may be treated to the sight of spawning salmon. Seal Rock Campground (1.2 miles), just off US-101, has many of the same birds and is also a delightful place to camp.

Quilcene Bay is a rich winter area for waterbirds. From the Olympic National Forest ranger district office at the south edge of the town of Quilcene (10.2 miles; maps, road and trail information) continue 0.3 mile to a fork where US-101 northbound bends left. Stay straight ahead (east) onto Linger Longer Road. The road soon turns right. Look for a road on the left (1.1 miles from US-101) with a sign for *Day Use Parking Area*. Drive out to the shore of the bay to a bigger sign for the Quilcene Bay State Tidelands. This and a second stop at Quilcene Harbor, an additional 0.6 mile down Linger Longer Road, are good places to scope the bay and shoreline at any tide stage.

MOUNT WALKER AND MOUNT TOWNSEND

The short trip up **Mount Walker** is an excellent way to see birds of the conifer forest. Both Townsend's and Hermit Warblers are found here (and a range of intergrades between the two). The steep sideslopes allow for views into the canopy, which greatly simplifies finding these and other frequently-encountered species such as Hammond's and Pacific-slope Flycatchers, Gray and Steller's Jays, Chestnut-backed Chickadee, Brown Creeper, Winter Wren, Golden-crowned Kinglet, and Varied Thrush. Northern Goshawk, Blue Grouse, and Northern Pygmy-Owl are sometimes seen. Northbound on US-101, turn right onto FR-2730 at the sign for the Mount Walker View Point, 5.6 miles north of Seal Rock Campground (southbound from Quilcene, this turnoff is on the left 4.6 miles from the ranger station). The four-mile road is suitable for passenger vehicles but not recommended for trailers. Birds can be found anywhere from the Mount Walker trailhead, a quarter-mile from the highway, to the summit (elevation 2,804 feet) with spectacular views of Puget Sound, Mount Rainier, and Seattle to the east, and the Olympic Mountains to the west. Those who crave exercise may park at the trailhead and walk the two-mile trail to the top (roughly 2,000 feet elevation gain). The trail climbs steeply through hundred-year-old

Douglas-fir forest with Pacific Rhododendron, Salal, and Oregon-grape understory.

If you enjoy hiking, consider an outing to **Mount Townsend**, about 15 miles north and west of Quilcene. The moderately difficult but well-maintained Trail 839 climbs 3,350 feet over 5.5 miles to the Alpine/Parkland vegetation zone, traversing the Olympic Douglas-fir and Subalpine Fir zones on the way. The 6,200-foot, broadly rounded summit—densely carpeted with Common Juniper, Shrubby Cinquefoil, and boreal lichens—is in the Buckhorn Wilderness Area. Western slopes drain into the Dungeness River and the Strait of Juan de Fuca, while the Big and Little Quilcene Rivers conduct the eastward runoff toward Hood Canal. Snowfall is relatively light on the dry northeast side of the Olympics, so the trail is usually snow-free by June—earlier than on most high-elevation routes in these mountains. The summer wildflower show in the subalpine meadows and along the summit ridge can be fantastic. Birding possibilities are similar to those for Deer Park (page 41), but without the cars and people. Look for Blue Grouse in the open subalpine forest, and Townsend's and Hermit Warblers near the trailhead. From US-101, turn west onto Penny Creek Road (0.9 mile south of the ranger station in Quilcene or 3.7 miles north of the Mount Walker turnoff). After 1.4 miles, turn left onto FR-27 (Big Quilcene River Road) and continue 12.4 miles to FR-2760, then left another 0.7 mile to the lower trailhead, indicated by an obscure sign. Park here at a wide spot in the road (Northwest Forest Pass required). To save a mile of hiking each way and 500 feet of elevation gain (but also skipping deep woods and views of Sink Lake), do not turn off at the lower trailhead but instead continue up FR-27 for another 1.2 miles, then go left on FR-190 to the upper trailhead (0.7 mile).

North from Quilcene, it is about 10 miles to the intersection with SR-104. Go east here to the Hood Canal Bridge, Kitsap County, and the ferry to Edmonds (page 194). Another 2.1 miles farther north along US-101 brings you to the junction with SR-20 (page 29); turn right here to bird the Port Townsend vicinity, or stay straight ahead on US-101 for sites along the way to Sequim and Port Angeles.

MOUNT RAINIER

by Bill Shelmerdine

M any sought-after bird species nest on, or visit, the upper west slopes of the Cascades above Puget Sound, but much of this country is accessible only by backpacking. The three trans-mountain highways run through cut-over forests at relatively low elevations most of the way to the crest, and the species that live in these habitats can usually be found just as well in the lowlands. The best birding these roads have to offer is at the actual summits: Snoqualmie Pass on I-90 (page 267), Chinook Pass on SR-410 (page 325), and Stevens Pass on US-2 (page 407). By visiting these places birders can readily find the common and even some of the uncommon mountain species, but chances of finding any of the true alpine specialties are remote. Fortunately, one high-elevation Puget Sound site has both good birds and ready access. You will have to set aside at least one full day to go there, but even if you miss a target bird or two, you will not regret a trip to Mount Rainier.

A striking feature and major landmark, Mount Rainier is readily visible from many locations around Western and Eastern Washington. It is a composite volcano of massive proportions with an extensive system of glaciers covering roughly 37 square miles—the largest single-peak glacial system in the Lower 48. Currently considered dormant, it has had a history of intense volcanism. One can only imagine the incredible bulk and height of the 16,000-foot ancestral summit, reduced to its present 14,410 feet by violent eruptions, mudflows, and thousands of years of glacial erosion. The mountain and surrounding lush, old-growth forests are included within 235,625-acre **Mount Rainier National Park**, famous for spectacular scenery and subalpine wildflowers (July–August). The fall color change can be just as impressive, with the intense reds of the huckleberry understory set against the deep greens of Mountain Hemlock and Subalpine Fir.

The park is a good place to look for the typical birds of wet conifer forests, but the big treat is easy birding access to subalpine forest and alpine areas. Gray Jay, Clark's Nutcracker, Mountain Chickadee, Hermit Thrush, Cassin's Finch, and Evening Grosbeak are common in the subalpine. Golden Eagle, Blue Grouse, Mountain Bluebird, and Townsend's Solitaire are fairly common, while Black Swift and Pine Grosbeak are seen occasionally. The most sought-after specialties—White-tailed Ptarmigan, Boreal Owl, Gray-crowned Rosy-Finch—are present at certain times and places, but finding them may require intensive searching (and luck). The late season (September–October) is often productive for these species.

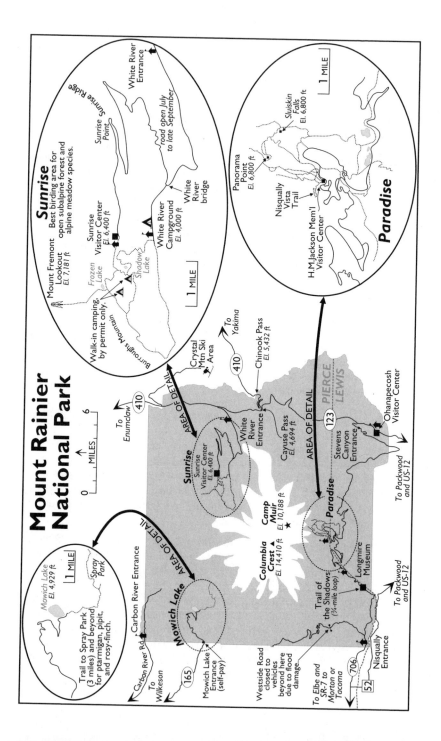

Mount Rainier National Park

0 — MILES — 6

To Enumclaw
410

AREA OF DETAIL

To Yakima

Crystal Mtn Ski Area

Chinook Pass
El. 5,432 ft

410

Cayuse Pass
El. 4,694 ft

Sunrise

Sunrise Visitor Center
El. 6,400 ft

White River Entrance

PIERCE
LEWIS

AREA OF DETAIL

123

Stevens Canyon Entrance

Ohanapecosh Visitor Center

Camp Muir
El. 10,188 ft

Columbia Crest
El. 14,410 ft

Paradise

Longmire Museum

To Packwood and US-12

Mowich Lake

Carbon River Entrance

Carbon River Rd

To Wilkeson

AREA OF DETAIL

165

Mowich Lake Entrance (self-pay)

Westside Road closed to vehicles beyond here due to flood damage.

Trail of the Shadows (¾-mile loop)

To Elbe and SR-7 to Morton or Tacoma

Nisqually Entrance

706

52

To Packwood and US-12

Sunrise

Best birding area for open subalpine forest and alpine meadow species.

Mount Fremont Lookout
El. 7,181 ft

Sunrise Ridge

Sunrise Point

road open July to late September

White River Entrance

White River bridge

Sunrise Visitor Center
El. 6,400 ft

Frozen Lake

Shadow Lake

White River Campground
El. 4,000 ft

Burroughs Mountain

Walk-in camping, by permit only.

1 MILE

Paradise

Panorama Point
El. 6,800 ft

Sluiskin Falls
El. 6,800 ft

Nisqually Vista Trail

H.M. Jackson Mem'l Visitor Center

1 MILE

Mowich Lake

Mowich Lake
El. 4,929 ft

Spray Park

Trail to Spray Park (3 miles) and beyond for ptarmigan, pipit, and rosy-finch.

1 MILE

Mount Rainier is popular with tourists from around the world and also with local day-trippers. Spring and summer—overall, the best seasons to visit—are also the most crowded. Visitor pressure declines after Labor Day, but even then, finding a spot in a designated pullout or parking area is much easier on weekdays and early in the morning.

The park receives a *lot* of snow. Average annual snowfall at Paradise, on the south side of the park, exceeds 50 feet. In typical years, trailheads and trails to alpine habitats will be snow-free and accessible from July into October. The road to Paradise from the Nisqually Entrance is kept open year round (bring tire chains in winter). All other roads are subject to snow closures, especially between late October and early May. If planning a visit early or late in the season, call ahead (360-569-2211) to check access, snow levels, and trail conditions.

There are five summer entrance points. Most visitors—birders included—go in either via the Nisqually Entrance (on the southwest side) to Longmire and Paradise, or via the White River Entrance (on the northeast side) to Sunrise. A loop trip connecting these two entrances around the southeast side of the park is possible, too, but time-consuming. Birders with only a day to spend should consider focusing their efforts at Sunrise, especially if pursuing the higher-elevation species. The Sunrise Visitor Center is about 75 road miles from Tacoma, 90 from Yakima, or 95 from Seattle, mostly on two-lane roads that can be slow going, so count on a long day. Better still, take a couple of days and camp at one of the many campgrounds (reservations essential at the height of the season). In addition to Sunrise, there are visitor centers at Paradise, Longmire, and Ohanapecosh, offering interpretive displays, books, maps, and snacks. Basic maps and information can also be obtained at kiosks where entrance fees are paid. Gasoline is not available inside the park, so gas up before you go in.

Large portions of the park are covered by dense, wet conifer forest. Forests at lower elevations around the park's perimeter are in the Western Hemlock zone. Douglas-fir, Western Hemlock, Western Redcedar, and Grand Fir are the primary large tree species. Several stands of old growth have massive trees over 200 feet tall, and a complex, multi-storied structure. The interiors of these stands are dark, have variable understory vegetation, and are typically covered with downed logs and mosses. Winter Wren is the most conspicuous member of the bird community here, and possibly the only one you will actually see. Other species spend most of their time up in the canopy and out of sight. Pullouts along the road shoulder or at overlooks, especially in some of the younger forest stands, can be good for finding birds of the canopy. Natural openings and forest edges along streams or at developed sites offer some of the best viewing opportunities. As one climbs in elevation one enters the Silver Fir zone, then the Mountain Hemlock zone (around 4,500–5,000 feet), with Mountain Hemlock, Alaska Yellowcedar, and Subalpine Fir replacing the larger true firs and Western Hemlock. Forests become more open above 5,500 feet, transitioning into subalpine parklands and alpine meadows. Bird-viewing is much easier in these habitats.

While some of the bird species change with the forest type, many remain the same. Characteristic species of lower-elevation forests include Ruffed Grouse, Northern Pygmy-Owl (uncommon), Red-breasted Sapsucker (fairly common), Hairy Woodpecker, Pacific-slope Flycatcher, Winter Wren, Swainson's Thrush, and Western Tanager. Species that may be found in both lower- and higher-elevation forest zones include Blue Grouse, Olive-sided Flycatcher (fairly common), Gray and Steller's Jays, Chestnut-backed Chickadee, Red-breasted Nuthatch, Brown Creeper, Golden-crowned Kinglet, Varied Thrush, Townsend's and Wilson's Warblers, Dark-eyed Junco, Red Crossbill, and Evening Grosbeak. A characteristic though uncommon resident of some of the older forest stands is the threatened Northern Spotted Owl. The park staff monitors populations of this species, but known locations are not disclosed. Spotted Owls are sometimes seen or heard in late summer when young birds have left nesting territories and are wandering about. Vaux's Swifts nest and roost in the larger tree stands and can often be seen flying above the canopy or river valleys. American Dippers are fairly common throughout the park from forest zones up to the edge of the snowfields, along rivers, lakes, and alpine streams.

LONGMIRE AND PARADISE

The Nisqually Entrance (elevation 2,003 feet) is 14 miles east of Elbe on SR-706. The 23-mile road from there to Paradise (elevation 5,560 feet) offers an excellent elevational transect of the park's forest types and their associated birdlife. Especially impressive old-growth stands can be found about five miles inside the entrance, as one approaches **Longmire**. Across the road from the National Park Inn (6.4 miles), the Trail of the Shadows offers birds of open, lowland habitats—meadows, Beaver pond, cattail marsh, alder thickets— along a three-quarter-mile loop rimmed by forest. At **Paradise**, trailheads provide easy access into open subalpine parkland and meadows, with fine wildflower displays, plenty of Hoary Marmots, and nesting Horned Larks and American Pipits. White-tailed Ptarmigan are sometimes seen above Paradise Park, at Panorama Point, around Golden Gate, north of Sluiskin Falls on the Paradise Glacier Trail, or west toward the Nisqually Glacier, at elevations ranging from 6,300 to 7,000 feet. However, Sunrise is usually a better bet for this species. Gray-crowned Rosy-Finches also occur in the area, but during the summer they often haunt crags and cliffs high on the mountain, for example at Camp Muir (elevation 10,188 feet)—definitely within the realm of alpine wilderness travel, and not for the inexperienced or unprepared. Weather on the mountain changes suddenly and can be fierce.

MOWICH LAKE

If you are tempted by subalpine meadows on a par with Paradise but without the crowds, head for the Mowich Lake Entrance on Mount Rainier's remote northwest side. Depending on snowpack, the road may not open until late July. Facilities are minimal, and reaching the alpine zone requires an invigorating hike. From SR-410 at the south edge of Buckley, turn south onto SR-165. Keep left at the fork in 1.7 miles, and continue 2.9 miles to Wilkeson (National Park Backcountry Information Center). In 5.9 miles, take the right branch at another fork and go 11.2 miles through managed forests to the park boundary and self-pay fee station. It is another 5.6 miles to the end of the road at Mowich Lake (elevation 4,929 feet). American Dippers are sometimes seen at the lake's outlet. Hike the trail three miles to Spray Park, where the meadows begin. At the high point in the trail, roughly a mile later, an unmarked trail goes south and uphill, traversing extensive alpine habitats. In this landscape of heather and fell field, look for White-tailed Ptarmigan, American Pipit, and Gray-crowned Rosy-Finch, the latter especially higher on the trail near the permanent snowfields and cliffs.

SUNRISE

The White River Entrance (elevation 3,500 feet) is reached by turning west from SR-410 onto a side road 4.6 miles inside the park's north boundary and 3.6 miles north of the SR-123 intersection at Cayuse Pass. The ranger station and entrance kiosk are 1.4 miles ahead. This is big-conifer habitat of the Western Hemlock zone, with birds characteristic of wet lowland forests. The road to the White River Campground (elevation 4,000 feet) branches off to the left in 3.9 miles, just after the White River bridge. Just beyond is the gate for winter closure. Nightly closures can occur anytime after early September: call ahead for status. From the gate the road climbs steeply, and Alaska Yellowcedar, Silver Fir, and Mountain Hemlock become increasing components of the forest stands. Species characteristic of these upper-elevation forests include Ruby-crowned Kinglet, Hermit Thrush, and Yellow-rumped Warbler. In 7.8 miles, a large pullout at **Sunrise Point** (elevation 6,100 feet) provides a fabulous viewpoint, and trailheads to some interesting areas away from roads and crowds. In late summer and fall Elk bugle from the forest edges.

For the next three miles the road traverses large meadows with dense clusters of subalpine tree species. Red-tailed Hawk, American Kestrel, Blue Grouse, Clark's Nutcracker, Common Raven, and Mountain Bluebird are seen along this stretch. The road ends at the **Sunrise Visitor Center** (elevation 6,400 feet), perhaps the single best birding area in the park for species of open subalpine forests and alpine meadows. Trees and edges right around the visitor center have Chestnut-backed Chickadee, Red-breasted Nuthatch, both kinglet species, Chipping Sparrow, Dark-eyed Junco, and Pine Siskin; Gray Jay and Clark's Nutcracker should be nearby, as should Cascade Golden-mantled Ground Squirrel, Yellow-pine Chipmunk, and Hoary Marmot. In September, look for mixed-species flocks including flycatchers, vireos, warblers, and sparrows. Northern Harrier, accipiters (including Northern Goshawk), Red-tailed and Rough-legged Hawks, Golden Eagle, Prairie Falcon, and other raptors are often seen around Sunrise in fall. Boreal Owls have been found in September and October in subalpine stands extending west from Sunrise Point to the walk-in Sunrise Camp beyond the visitor center (between about 5,800 and 6,400 feet elevation). Please do not torment them with excessive tape-playing.

To get the most out of Sunrise birding, obtain a map and hike some of the trails beginning at the visitor center. The high trail to Frozen Lake is the best bet for Townsend's Solitaire and Cassin's Finch, whereas the trail west toward Sunrise Camp and Shadow Lake is better for Blue Grouse (also try the adjacent trails) and Gray Jay. Mountain Chickadees are found throughout the area. Frozen Lake (elevation 6,750 feet), reached in about a mile, is the minimum distance one must go to find some of the true alpine species. Horned

Lark and American Pipit are often here, while Baird's Sandpiper and other shorebirds have been seen along the margins of the lake during fall migration.

From this point and above is the summer range of the White-tailed Ptarmigan. The most reliable location in the park over the last few years has been along the 1.8-mile trail from Frozen Lake to the **Mount Fremont Lookout**. The birds have been found around scree and loose, rocky slopes, and within heather clumps and other low alpine vegetation—especially on the ridge right by the lookout (elevation 7,181 feet). The other traditional location for ptarmigan, in similar habitat, is **Burroughs Mountain** (elevation 7,100 to 7,400 feet), from about a mile to a mile and a half west of Frozen Lake. Gray-crowned Rosy-Finches nest higher on the mountain, well above the areas that hikers and birders usually visit, but they are given to substantial up-and-down movements each day. In summer, you may detect them about late-lingering snowfields near areas of rocks. They are more conspicuous in fall when they gather in post-breeding flocks.

South of the road to Sunrise, SR-410 has a few places to pull off and look out over the forest and valley below. These can be good for Vaux's Swift (often foraging at eye level) and birds of the canopy. From the intersection at Cayuse Pass you may continue eastward on SR-410 to bird Chinook Pass (page 325) and sites in South Central Washington. SR-123 runs south to the Stevens Canyon Entrance (11 miles), where you may turn west on the road to Paradise (21 miles). SR-123 continues south past the Ohanapecosh Visitor Center to the park boundary in three miles and joins US-12 in another 2.5 miles (page 332). A left (east) turn here will take you in about 13 miles to White Pass—another South Central access point. Westbound, US-12 goes to Packwood and southwestern Washington birding sites, including the "back door" route to Mount Saint Helens (page 241).

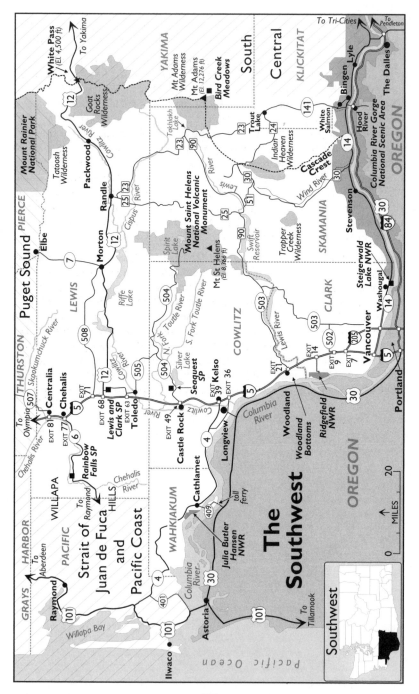

SOUTHWEST

Put simply, southwestern Washington is the Westside's Columbia Basin. Although its northwest and northeast corners are drained by the Chehalis and Nisqually Rivers, all the rest is in the Columbia River watershed. Culturally and economically, this region looks more to Portland/Vancouver than to the Puget Sound megalopolis—especially south of Centralia and Chehalis. Good birds are often reported to the Portland RBA and the OBOL e-mail list before they show up on Tweeters or the Washington BirdBox.

The Southwest was one of the first parts of Washington to be explored and settled by Euro-Americans. Lewis and Clark found few bird species new to science on their 4,100-mile Voyage of Discovery (1804–1806), and none in what is now Washington, even though they obtained several first state records. Fort Vancouver (which you may visit in Vancouver) played a prominent role in the area's early ornithological history. While based here between 1834 and 1836, John Kirk Townsend identified eight new bird species and several other distinct forms, including Vaux's Swift, Chestnut-backed Chickadee, Bushtit, Western Bluebird, Audubon's Yellow-rumped, Black-throated Gray, Townsend's, Hermit, and MacGillivray's Warblers, and Oregon Dark-eyed Junco. John James Audubon depicted all of these, from Townsend's specimens, in his *Birds of America*. No California Condor is better known than the one that served for Audubon's plate, a specimen taken by Townsend near the mouth of the Columbia.

The Southwest is differentiated into five subareas by its topography. On the west are the Willapa Hills, a low coastal range with few summits above 2,500 feet. On the east is the Cascade Range, rugged and remote, topped by Mount Adams at 12,276 feet. Another massive volcano, Mount Saint Helens, sits many miles west of the crest. Interstate 5 runs north and south down the middle of the third subarea—the lowlands between the coastal hills and the Cascades. The fourth subarea is the Columbia River bottomlands, especially those around Vancouver, and the last is the Columbia Gorge east to the Cascade divide.

The Willapa Hills are seldom visited by birders. Abundant rainfall blessed these hills with magnificent forests, but only scattered fragments of old growth have escaped the loggers. Nearly all of these lands belong to timber companies (with a few state forests) and are managed as tree farms, which limits bird species diversity. Gray Jay and Hermit Warbler are among the more interesting species to be found here if one takes the time to explore the hundreds of miles of logging roads.

The central lowlands—unglaciated, in contrast to glacially overriden Puget Sound to the north—consist of level ground or low hills, with few lakes. Much of this area was originally covered with Douglas-fir forests, but the deep alluvial soils prompted early clearing for agricultural use. In the northern part, from Chehalis south to Toledo, prairies and stands of Garry Oak still occupy patches of sandy, gravelly soils deposited by outwash from the melting glaciers farther north. A few White-tailed Kites work the prairies and valley bottoms. Farther south the Cowlitz River flows down to Longview, and the Columbia flows up to meet it, through a relatively narrow trough. Miles of tree farms extend to the east and west.

The plains around Vancouver are a northward continuation of Oregon's Willamette Valley. As the last ice age came to a close (15,000–13,000 BP), each release from the failed ice dams on Glacial Lake Missoula created large, temporary lakes in low-lying basins along the Columbia. The Willamette Valley was thus flooded dozens of times, depositing rich lacustrine soils that grew to prairies when the flooding ended. The original vegetation of these prairies is long gone, plowed under by settlers who arrived on the Oregon Trail. Large tracts of floodplain forest—Black Cottonwood, Oregon Ash, Bigleaf Maple, Garry Oak—still thrive adjacent to the Columbia, notably at Ridgefield National Wildlife Refuge. Diked fields at this refuge and elsewhere in the lowlands support high numbers of waterfowl, raptors, and Sandhill Cranes in migration and winter.

The Cascade Range occupies the eastern half of the area. Most of this territory, with typical Wet Side forests, is in the Gifford Pinchot and Mount Baker-Snoqualmie National Forests and the Mount Saint Helens National Volcanic Monument. Many of the national forest lands are subject to timber sales, but significant parts are permanently preserved in the Tatoosh, Goat Rocks, Mount Adams, Indian Heaven, Trapper Creek, and William O. Douglas Wilderness Areas. Other stands of old growth survive on Forest Service lands—for example, along the Lewis River above Swift Reservoir. Numerous sites around Mount Adams and Mount Saint Helens provide forest birding as good as any in Western Washington.

The ancestral Columbia River maintained its course westward to the Pacific as the Cascades were slowly uplifted, carving the deep Columbia Gorge. The gorge was further widened as powerful floodwater torrents swept through the constriction following the repeated failures of ice dams on Glacial Lake Missoula. The flood crest averaged 1,000 feet high at the east end of the gorge, lessening to 500 feet at the west end. Today the Columbia Gorge is a notable migration corridor for birds and for remnants of the once-epic salmon runs. It is also an important site for wintering waterbirds.

Precipitation varies greatly within the region. Cathlamet, near the ocean, receives an average of 80 inches annually. The central lowlands receive 45–60 inches, rising to 70 inches at higher elevations of the Cascade foothills. Vancouver receives just 39 inches (the same as Seattle), but at the mouth of the Columbia Gorge barely 15 miles east, Washougal averages 84 inches annually. Eastward through the gorge precipitation gradually drops off.

Marine low-pressure systems moving east bring heavy winter rains to the west end of the gorge. High pressure east of the Cascades drives gale-force winds westward through the gorge, bringing hot, dry air in summer and cold, continental air in winter. Sometimes the two opposing systems meet in winter, and when this happens, the west end of the gorge can see ice storms and blowing snow. Strong, steady winds in summer and fall make the gorge a renowned windsurfing site. But they can also hamper birding.

Temperatures are much the same as elsewhere in Western Washington. Means for Centralia and Vancouver are 39–40 degrees in January and 65–66 degrees in July.

The two trans-Cascades highways are open all year, although US-12 across White Pass is subject to snow-clearance closures (usually brief). SR-14 through the Columbia Gorge, and other lowland roads, may be made hazardous by ice and snowfall.

Accommodations and services may be found in the Vancouver/Portland metropolitan area, in cities and towns north along the I-5 corridor, and also in a few communities along US-12 and the Columbia.

FINDING SOUTHWESTERN SPECIALTIES

by Hal Opperman and Andy Stepniewski

F our bird species are closely associated with southwestern Washington. Three of these—White-tailed Kite, Red-shouldered Hawk, and Western Scrub-Jay—are expanding their ranges into the state from western Oregon, while the fourth, Hermit Warbler, is retreating southward as it loses ground to Townsend's Warbler. Birders target these signature species when visiting the region. Since it is sometimes more convenient to look for them at various peripheral localities that do not fit neatly into the chapter plan, we seize this opportunity to describe here several worthy sites that might otherwise have been left dangling.

WESTERN SCRUB-JAY

Western Scrub-Jay is the most widespread of the four species, though rarely numerous. Once confined to the Vancouver Lowlands, for the last 60 years it has been pushing slowly, inexorably northward up the lower Cowlitz Valley and up and down the Columbia. Western Scrub-Jays are now fairly common year-round residents at lower elevations in relatively open land-scapes (towns, open woods, edges) throughout southwestern Washington, north to Olympia, west to the coast, and into the eastern Columbia Gorge. They favor Garry Oaks when available—for example, at Ridgefield National Wildlife Refuge (page 244)—but are not tied to them. These jays are still enough of a novelty that Washington birders look for them when visiting the Southwest.

RED-SHOULDERED HAWK

Although Red-shouldered Hawks have wintered recently in widely scattered parts of the state (for example, Dungeness, Everett, Tri-Cities), this species is dependable only along the lower Columbia River. A Red-shouldered Hawk first wintered at Ridgefield National Wildlife Refuge in 1991, and others (sometimes two or three) have wintered there each year since then. Individuals are now being found with increasing regularity as far upstream as Steigerwald Lake National Wildlife Refuge at the mouth of the Columbia Gorge (page 251).

There are also records of Red-shouldered Hawk far downstream, for example at **Julia Butler Hansen National Wildlife Refuge**, near Cathlamet. This refuge was established in 1972 specifically to protect and manage the endangered Columbian White-tailed Deer. Today, about 300 of these deer live there, and another 300–400 live nearby on private lands. Although distant from the other sites described in this chapter, the refuge is definitely worth a visit if you are on your way to or from the coast. Habitats include tideland Sitka Spruce forest, riparian woodland, tidal and freshwater wetlands, and

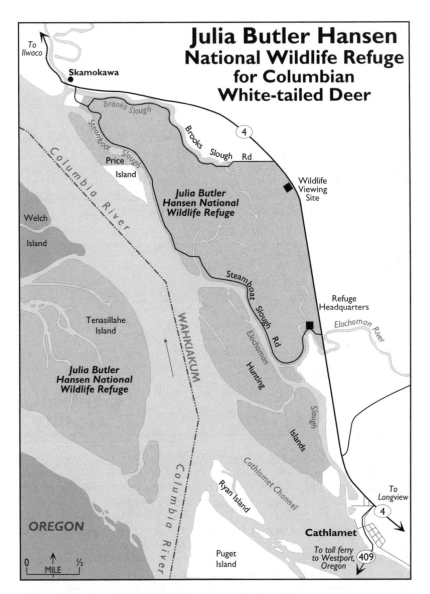

Julia Butler Hansen National Wildlife Refuge for Columbian White-tailed Deer

open fields, making for a diverse and abundant birdlife. Two miles north of Cathlamet, turn west from SR-4 onto Steamboat Slough Road. Here begins a 7.2-mile tour that encircles the refuge with very little traffic, rejoining SR-4 on Brooks Slough Road two miles northwest of the starting point. Especially numerous are Canada Geese (various subspecies), Tundra Swan, and other waterfowl. Bald Eagles are conspicuous, as are Red-tailed Hawks. The riparian woodlands have the usual assortment of wet-forest passerines. Recently created pools and large wetlands, some of which can be seen from the highway, promise to attract waterfowl and shorebirds and to provide even better viewing opportunities.

WHITE-TAILED KITE

White-tailed Kites occur locally in the interior Southwest as well as along the South Coast, and appear to be increasing. A few hunt the rank grasslands at Julia Butler Hansen National Wildlife Refuge, and kites have been seen as far up the Columbia as Steigerwald Lake National Wildlife Refuge. Farther north, they are regularly seen on some of the glacial outwash prairies that dot the lowlands between the Chehalis and the Cowlitz Rivers, from Centralia to Toledo.

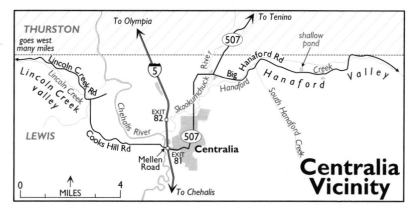

Two good sites are reached from I-5 Exit 81 in Centralia. For the **Hanaford Valley**, go east and north on SR-507 through downtown Centralia. About two and one-half miles north of town, just past the second Skookumchuck River bridge, turn right onto Big Hanaford Road. Drive 3.5 miles to a shallow pond on the left. Scope the open fields from the road for the next three miles as you pass by a steam plant where power is generated from locally-mined coal. Several more ponds and wet fields are along the road after the plant complex. Of interest from fall through spring are American Bittern, geese and other waterfowl (including Eurasian Wigeon), and White-tailed Kite and other raptors. In spring, look for Black-bellied Plover, Greater Yellowlegs, Western and Least Sandpipers, Dunlin, and Long-billed Dowitcher.

The **Lincoln Creek valley** is on the other side of the interstate. From Exit 81, take Mellen Road west (becomes Cooks Hill Road after crossing the Chehalis River). At an intersection in 4.6 miles, turn left (west) onto Lincoln Creek Road and bird the valley bottomlands for the next 10 miles. Open fields, marshes, brushy patches, and weedy grasslands with south-facing slopes provide habitat for waterfowl, raptors (White-tailed Kite, Red-tailed Hawk, American Kestrel), and sparrows, especially in winter. Wild Turkeys have been released in this area in the past and may still be present. Hunting clubs are everywhere, so beware.

White-tailed Kites are occasionally seen north and east of Toledo, hunting over the prairies or perched on treetops along the edges. Go east from I-5 Exit 63 onto SR-505, which continues through Toledo and east out of town onto the **Layton Prairie**. Look for kites for the next four or five miles. Return on SR-505, and about a mile north of Toledo turn right onto Jackson Highway. This is the **Cowlitz Prairie**; explore the roads around the airport. Two or three miles farther north on Jackson Highway, **Lewis and Clark State Park** preserves a 600-acre stand of old-growth conifers, complete with resident Gray Jays—interesting relics of a time when these lowland forests were intact.

HERMIT WARBLER

Hermit Warblers inhabit Douglas-fir forests on the east and south slopes of the Olympic Mountains, on the west slopes of the Cascade Range south of the Cowlitz River, and southward and westward through the Willapa Hills. Their range is contracting as they are being displaced by the competitively superior Townsend's Warbler, which is advancing from the north and east. The two species meet along narrow, moving hybrid zones in the eastern Olympics—for example, near Quilcene (page 221)—and the southwestern Cascades. During the nesting season, use caution in identifying either species anywhere along the west slopes of the Cascades between White Pass and Mount Adams—for example, around Takhlakh Lake (page 262) and Indian Heaven (page 261). Hybrids may be seen farther afield in post-breeding dispersal or fall and spring migration, but rarely east of the Cascade crest or north of Puget Sound.

Most hybrids have yellow faces and therefore are mistaken for Hermits, while the smaller share of hybrids that have black masks are usually called Townsend's. It is important to check multiple characteristics. "Good" Hermits have gray (not green) backs and pure-white underparts with no yellow below the bib, no streaking on the flanks (a touch on the lower flanks is OK), and a white gap between the bib and the back. "Good" Townsend's have a solid-black crown (yellow in Hermits except for a small amount of black approaching the nape), heavily streaked flanks, and a bright yellow breast; the black bib corners reach the green back. Hybrids cannot confidently be separated from either parent species by song.

If you want an identification challenge, drive some of the forest roads north, east, and south of **Packwood**, on US-12 about 20 miles below White Pass. This is smack in the middle of the hybrid zone, and you may see

Townsend's, Hermits, and everything in between. Singing birds often come down to taped playbacks of their songs, affording close looks.

Phenotypically pure Hermit Warblers can reliably be found on the south side of Mount Saint Helens (page 242) and also in the Willapa Hills—for example, at Capitol State Forest just north of the chapter boundary (page 216). Go exploring for Hermits on your own in the lightly birded hills farther south. In past years they were often reported singing high in the canopy in the mature Douglas-fir, Western Hemlock, and Western Redcedar forest at **Rainbow Falls State Park**. From Exit 77 on I-5, take SR-6 west about 16 miles to the park entrance. Western Screech-Owl is also reported in these forests. The rushing waters of the Chehalis River provide good habitat for American Dippers and a scenic spot to picnic.

MOUNT SAINT HELENS

by Wilson Cady and Andy Stepniewski

In May of 1980 the eruption of Mount Saint Helens transformed 230 square miles of forestlands into a barren moonscape now mostly contained within the 110,000-acre Mount Saint Helens National Volcanic Monument. The devastation sent an ash cloud northeast across the continent, blew megatons of logs and avalanche debris into lakes and rivers, and in the process created a laboratory for the study of recolonization by flora and fauna. Vegetation is recovering rapidly as nature rushes to heal this massive insult. As plant communities evolve, so do the bird populations that depend on them. Inside the monument the landscape was left to regenerate unaided, and over 80 species of birds have already been found nesting. By contrast, dead timber outside the boundaries was salvaged and the area replanted, creating an even-aged stand of young trees with little avian diversity.

Within the monument you must stay on the maintained trails, which limits the number of places where you can search for birds. Some of the trails are up to 30 miles in length and are designed for backcountry hiking and camping trips. You will need a Northwest Forest Pass to park at trailheads and other designated areas in the monument and the surrounding Gifford Pinchot National Forest. Higher-elevation roads are closed to auto traffic in winter, usually from late November until sometime in May. Call monument headquarters (360-247-3900) for access information if you are contemplating an early- or late-season visit.

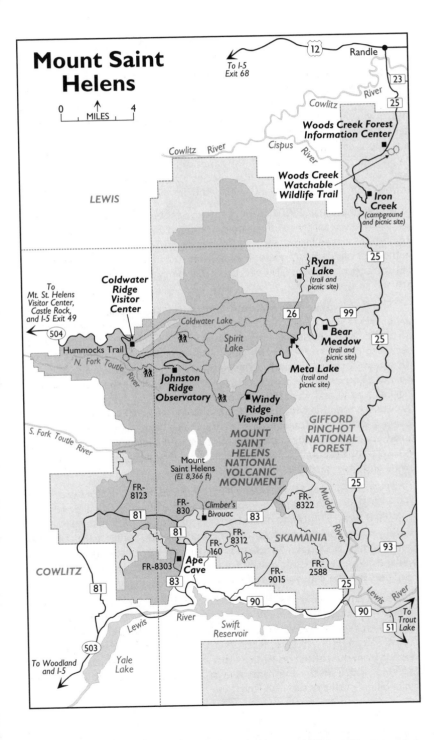

Mount Saint Helens

Northwest Side (Toutle River)

Most of the visitor amenities are found on the western side of the volcano. Take Exit 49 from I-5 at Castle Rock and go east five miles on SR-504 to the **Mount Saint Helens Visitor Center**, where you can purchase your Northwest Forest Pass and pick up maps and a bird checklist. This visitor center is on Silver Lake, a large, shallow body of water formed by a mudflow from a previous eruption that blocked small streams. Along the 0.5-mile Silver Lake Wetlands Trail you can search for American Bittern, Wood Duck, Virginia Rail, and Sora, among many other species. Other spots along the lake have fewer people present and can be birded from the roadside.

Located across SR-504 from the visitor center, **Seaquest State Park** has old-growth forests of the type that existed before these lowlands were converted to tree farms. Spotted Owls once nested here, but the increased number of campers has made them difficult to find. Red-breasted Sapsucker, Hutton's Vireo, Brown Creeper, and other denizens of old-growth conifers are still fairly common.

The **Coldwater Ridge Visitor Center** is located about 38 miles east of the previous stop on SR-504, within the national volcanic monument, where trees and other debris were blown down into the Toutle River. Regrowth of herbaceous plants is rapidly changing these areas. There are many trails in the recovering forests and some of the better birding is found here due to the variety of plants and insects providing food sources. Orange-crowned, Yellow, MacGillivray's, and Wilson's Warblers nest here, and Common Yellow-throats are found in the riparian growth along the creeks. Different, forest-loving species can be found in patches of standing dead trees and in those sheltered areas where ridges blocked the blast and there are still living trees. Western and Mountain Bluebirds nest in stubs, which also are home to Vaux's Swifts and several species of woodpeckers.

The 2.3-mile-long **Hummocks Trail** at the south end of Coldwater Lake loops through a landscape pockmarked by cattail marshes, small ponds, and tree-lined lakes. This is one of the better birding spots, with many passerines nesting in the young alder forest. Pied-billed Grebes, Mallards, Ring-necked Ducks, American Coots, Soras, and Red-winged Blackbirds also nest in the wetlands. Western Meadowlarks are common in the open areas, and Bank Swallows use the cliffs formed of volcanic ash.

The open pumice plains north of the mountain were created by landslides and both pyroclastic and mudflows. Due to the depth of the pumice and ash, this habitat type is recovering slowly. Birds that may be found here include Prairie Falcon, Horned Lark, Rock Wren, and Western Meadowlark. Trails starting from the **Johnston Ridge Observatory**, where the road ends, lead to Windy Ridge on the southeast side of Spirit Lake. Be sure to carry water while hiking in this desert-like landscape.

NORTHEAST SIDE (WINDY RIDGE)

A new road has been proposed that would connect the two sides of the mountain without having to return to I-5. For now, however, it is a four-hour drive. To reach the less frequently visited but no less spectacular east side of the monument (closed in winter), drive east from I-5, Exit 68 on US-12 to Randle (48 miles). Turn south onto FR-25 and continue 5.7 miles to the Woods Creek Forest Information Center where you can obtain maps, books, and a Northwest Forest Pass.

A few hundred feet past the center, on the left, is a parking area for the 1.5-mile **Woods Creek Watchable Wildlife Trail**, which goes through mixed hardwood and conifer forest to Woods Creek Beaver Pond. Many typical Westside lowland species can be found on this loop, including Great Blue Heron, Wood Duck, Ruffed Grouse, Red-breasted Sapsucker, Downy, Hairy, and Pileated Woodpeckers, Western Wood-Pewee, Willow, Hammond's, and Pacific-slope Flycatchers, Warbling Vireo, Tree Swallow, Black-capped and Chestnut-backed Chickadees, Winter and Marsh Wrens, Swainson's Thrush, Orange-crowned, Yellow, Yellow-rumped, and MacGillivray's Warblers, Common Yellowthroat, Song Sparrow, Purple Finch, and Pine Siskin. Just past the pond, the **Old-growth Loop Trail** takes off, returning to this point in one mile. This aptly named trail is excellent for woodpeckers, Varied Thrush, and Townsend's (or Townsend's x Hermit) Warbler. Northern Goshawk and Spotted Owl occur, but are infrequently seen.

Another 3.9 miles south along FR-25 is **Iron Creek Campground**, situated in impressive old-growth forest along the Cispus River. Two-tenths of a mile farther on FR-25, a short interpretive trail at the Iron Creek Picnic Site goes through giant Douglas-firs, Western Hemlocks, and Bigleaf Maples reminiscent of the Olympic rain forests. Another trail follows the river downstream to the campground through similar forest. Birds are not numerous or conspicuous in this habitat, but you should find Chestnut-backed Chickadee, Winter Wren, Golden-crowned Kinglet, and Swainson's and Varied Thrushes.

FR-25 winds south from here, alternating between old-growth and second-growth forests for 11.1 miles to FR-99, gateway to the northeast side of Mount Saint Helens. Climb this paved but twisting road 4.2 miles to **Bear Meadow**, at the edge of the blast zone. One can gain a clearer appreciation of the pre-eruption forest by walking up Boundary Trail 1, which begins north of the picnic site and ascends a sidehill, in a few hundred yards entering dense, old-growth Western Hemlock, Silver Fir, and Noble Fir forest where Hermit and Varied Thrushes and Townsend's (or Townsend's x Hermit) Warblers are common. A quite different habitat and birdlife can be found in the blast zone, below the picnic area.

Continue along FR-99 and turn right in 4.4 miles onto FR-26, reaching **Ryan Lake** in 5.0 miles. Walk the 0.6-mile interpretive trail with signage that explains the near-complete recovery of the lake's waters since the eruption. Return to FR-99, turn right, and drive 0.2 mile to **Meta Lake**. Birding along the short trail to this small lake should reveal many birds typical of the recovering forest, among them Blue Grouse, Rufous Hummingbird, Hairy Woodpecker, Northern Flicker, Willow Flycatcher, Warbling Vireo, Tree Swallow, Winter Wren, Mountain Bluebird, Swainson's and Hermit Thrushes, American Robin, Orange-crowned, Yellow, and MacGillivray's Warblers, Fox, Song, Lincoln's, and White-crowned Sparrows, Dark-eyed Junco, and Pine Siskin.

Windy Ridge lies 6.8 miles ahead. En route, watch for Dusky Flycatchers on the brushy slopes, and Townsend's Solitaires in steep, rocky areas by the roadside. At the parking lot, the long series of steps ascends steeply about 200 feet to a superb viewpoint of Mount Saint Helens and Spirit Lake. Surprisingly, the lake's water chemistry returned to normal by 1985, but waterbirds, by and large, do not seem to have figured this out yet.

SOUTH SIDE (LEWIS RIVER)

Take Exit 21 from I-5 at Woodland and travel east up the Lewis River valley on SR-503 (becomes FR-90). Obtain a map of the Gifford Pinchot National Forest and drive some of the roads on the south and southeast sides of the mountain, to the intersection with SR-25 at the east end of Swift Reservoir. Lush vegetation and old-growth forest in this area were spared as the volcano blew to the northwest. Pure-looking Hermit Warblers can be found in these woods, which lie west of the hybrid zone. Ape Cave, the longest lava tube in the Lower 48, is worth a visit. Turn north from FR-90 onto FR-83 at the west end of Swift Reservoir. In about a mile and a half stay left onto FR-8303 and continue to the cave entrance in another mile and a half. Lanterns are available for rent. Townsend's Big-eared Bats use a part of the cave as a summer roost (inaccessible to visitors).

You may go north on FR-25 to Randle (turning off along the way on FR-99 to visit Windy Ridge), and complete a loop around the mountain by returning to I-5 on US-12. For those who enjoy backcountry exploration, FR-90 follows the Lewis River upstream from Swift Reservoir for many miles (old-growth forest, waterfalls, forest service campgrounds), eventually reaching FR-23 at the edge of the Mount Adams Wilderness Area near Takhlakh Lake (page 262). You may take FR-23 south to Trout Lake or north to US-12 at Randle.

VANCOUVER AND VICINITY

by Wilson Cady

The Columbia River bottomlands north and east of Vancouver, though mostly diked, offer vast freshwater marshes, grasslands, shallow lakes, and some of the densest remaining high-quality floodplain forest in Washington. The mile-wide Columbia is tidal here, and the shoreline is just a few feet above sea level, conveying an estuarine feeling. The most important sites are the Lewis River delta, near Woodland; alluvial deposits from the outwash of the Willamette River, near Vancouver; and the mouth of the Columbia Gorge, near Washougal. Birders come here principally to find waterfowl, raptors, Sandhill Cranes, and gulls, in migration and winter. Birding is also good for typical passerines in all seasons, and the area has had its share of rarities.

WOODLAND BOTTOMS

The Woodland Bottoms are a diked remnant of the former floodplain at the confluence of the Columbia and Lewis Rivers. Nearly all of the land inside the dike has been converted to agricultural use. Crops are rotated yearly. In migration and winter, geese, ducks, and Sandhill Cranes move from field to field depending on what foods are available. The best way to bird this area is by scanning the fields as you drive the road on top of the encircling dike, looking for signs of bird activity. When you see something interesting, drive the crossroads to get closer. The dike road also gives access to riparian forest, beaches, and sandbars along the Columbia River. Bald Eagle, Merlin, and other raptors can be plentiful here, feeding on birds or on salmon and smelt in the Lewis River. In years when there is a smelt run, loons, grebes, and thousands of gulls gather at the river's mouth in March.

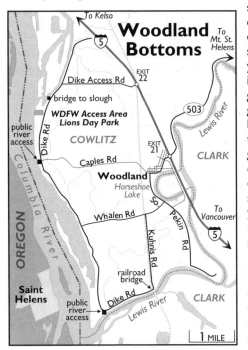

Take Exit 22 west from I-5 onto Dike Access Road and continue for 1.6 miles to the dike. To the right, Dike Road dead-ends in 1.3 miles after paralleling a shallow slough bordered by an extensive willow forest on the far shore. Shorebirds and wading birds use the mudflats exposed when water levels are low. Purple Martins sit on the power lines around the pumping station.

Return to the intersection with Dike Access Road and continue south along the dike for 0.4 mile. Park by a gate; walk across a bridge to a slough with a riparian forest, and on to the Columbia River. Drive another 0.3 mile to a WDFW Access Area and Lions Day Park, on the Columbia River. Obtain a permit (for the park) from the Port of Woodland, 141 Davidson Avenue, Woodland, WA 98674. Public access to the Columbia can be had in another 1.0 mile at the intersection with Caples Road. The wave-protected waters around the offshore sandbars here and for the next three miles harbor loons, grebes, and waterfowl, while geese and gulls roost on the sandbars.

In 3.7 miles, the dike-top road makes a 90-degree turn to the east, following the Lewis River. Check for birds on the pilings. Barrow's Goldeneyes winter near the railroad bridge (1.0 mile). From here, drive north on Kuhnis Road 1.6 miles to an intersection. Turn right on Whalen Road, then bear left on South Pekin Road (which will become Fifth Street as it enters Woodland), skirting Horseshoe Lake and reaching Davidson Avenue in 1.3 miles. Turn right and follow the main road through Woodland to I-5 Exit 21 in 0.6 mile.

RIDGEFIELD NATIONAL WILDLIFE REFUGE

This 5,150-acre refuge was created in 1965 to protect the Dusky Canada Goose, a dark-breasted subspecies that nests mainly on the Copper River delta in south central Alaska. Oak woodland, extensive areas of marsh, and wet fields attract a great diversity of other bird species, including Sandhill Cranes. Much of the refuge is closed to provide sanctuary for Bald Eagles and other nesting species. Two units that are open to the public can be reached by taking Exit 14 from I-5 and driving west on SR-501 (Pioneer Street). Turn left at S Ninth Avenue in Ridgefield (2.5 miles) and drive 0.6 mile to the entrance to the **River "S" Unit**, on the right. The entrance road goes steeply down through a ravine forested with Douglas-fir, Western Redcedar, and Bigleaf Maple where you may find Hutton's Vireo, Varied Thrush (winter), and other passerines. Across Lake River, the refuge is diked and managed through agricultural practices to provide winter food and resting areas for up to 25,000 geese and 40,000 ducks. Tundra Swans are abundant from fall through spring.

Between 1 October and 30 April, you must remain in your vehicle as you travel the 4.2-mile auto tour route. The only exceptions are the entrance parking lot and the observation blind at **Rest Lake**. Birds become accustomed to vehicles and remain close to the roads without flushing, allowing observation and photography. During the rest of the year you may get out and walk anywhere along the tour route. Wheelchair-accessible Kiwa Trail, just past the observation blind, loops through wetlands with nesting rails. A small colony of Yellow-headed Blackbirds nests at the south end of the lake.

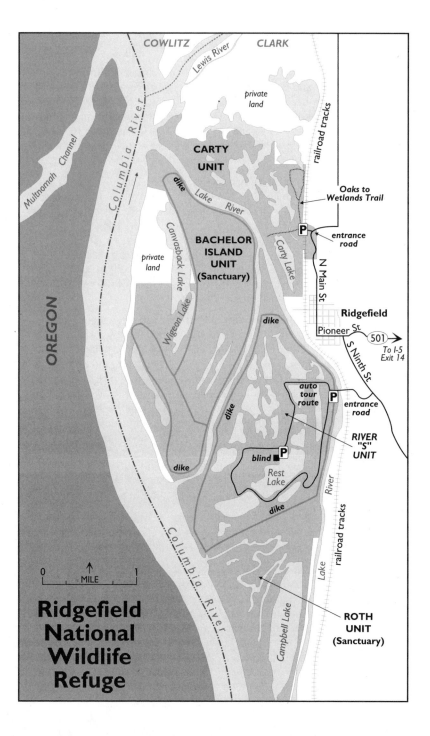

COWLITZ

CLARK

Lewis River

Multnomah Channel

Columbia River

private land

CARTY UNIT

dike

Lake River

railroad tracks

Oaks to Wetlands Trail

P

entrance road

Canvasback Lake

private land

BACHELOR ISLAND UNIT (Sanctuary)

Carty Lake

N Main St

Wigeon Lake

Ridgefield

Pioneer St

501

To I-5 Exit 14

S Ninth St

dike

dike

OREGON

dike

auto tour route

P

entrance road

RIVER "S" UNIT

blind ■ P

Rest Lake

dike

Columbia River

River

railroad tracks

0   MILE   1

Ridgefield National Wildlife Refuge

Lake

Campbell Lake

ROTH UNIT (Sanctuary)

The water level of the many lakes on this unit is controlled to optimize the growth of aquatic plants upon which the waterfowl feed. American Bitterns, Virginia Rails, and Soras are common in these habitats. Recently, a few Black-necked Stilts and Black Terns have attempted to nest. In late summer some of the lakes become mudflats, attracting up to a dozen species of shorebirds. The stands of Oregon Ash, Black Cottonwood, and willows on both this and the Carty Unit are the best place in the state to look for Red-shouldered Hawks, which have wintered here annually for more than a decade.

To visit the **Carty Unit** return to Ridgefield and turn left onto Pioneer Street, then right in 0.4 mile onto Main Street, which leaves town and drops down to cross Gee Creek (brush and trees worth checking for winter sparrow flocks) on its way to the refuge entrance, on the left (1.0 mile). This undiked, non-hunting unit—open year round—preserves a Columbia River floodplain in much the same condition as in 1806, when Lewis and Clark visited the Chinook village of Cathlapotle and its 900 inhabitants near this spot. A visitor center that will highlight the history and wildlife of the refuge is being planned for the area north of the parking lot.

Two trails await you on the other side of the footbridge spanning the railroad tracks. The one to the left goes past the restrooms, down a hill, and along an old road skirting Carty Lake, through cottonwood and willow stands. In winter, Merlins and Peregrine Falcons prey on snipe, ducks, and other birds in the open meadows. The **Oaks to Wetland Trail**, to the right, is a nearly-level, two-mile loop that starts under majestic Garry Oaks. Western Scrub-Jays are common here. This is perhaps the only place in the state where one can still reliably see White-breasted Nuthatches of the subspecies *aculeata*, which once nested fairly commonly from the Vancouver Lowlands north to the Fort Lewis Prairies. This coastal form is still widespread in western Oregon, but the Washington population is close to extirpation. The trail continues over basalt outcroppings forested with Oregon Ash, Garry Oak, and Douglas-fir, with places where you have good views of ponds and wetlands. Many bird species use these mixed habitats.

VANCOUVER LOWLANDS

A diked remnant of the vast floodplain at the confluence of the Columbia and Willamette Rivers, west of the city of Vancouver, the Vancouver Lowlands attract many of the same species as the adjacent Ridgefield National Wildlife Refuge to the north. Birding is best here from early fall through late spring, when wintering species congregate. The large flocks of Canada Geese may contain five or more subspecies and should be carefully checked for other geese—Greater White-fronted, Emperor (casual), Snow, Ross's (rare), and Brant.

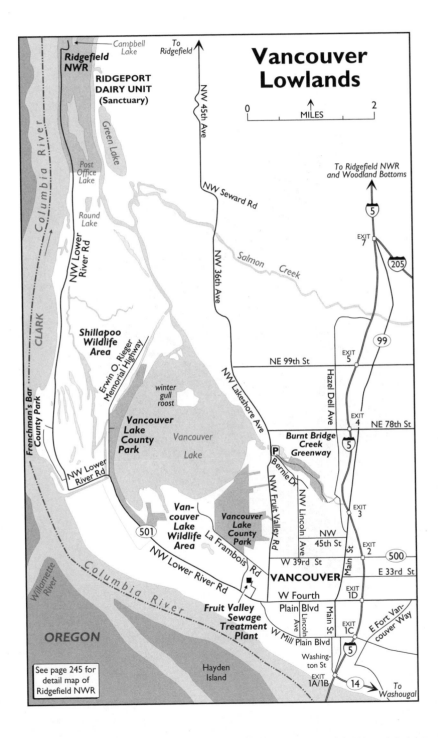

Vancouver Lowlands

Ridgefield NWR

RIDGEPORT DAIRY UNIT (Sanctuary)

Campbell Lake

To Ridgefield

Green Lake

Post Office Lake

Round Lake

Columbia River

CLARK

NW 45th Ave

NW Seward Rd

NW 36th Ave

Salmon Creek

0   MILES   2

To Ridgefield NWR and Woodland Bottoms

5

EXIT 7

205

99

NE 99th St

EXIT 5

Hazel Dell Ave

Shillapoo Wildlife Area

Erwin O. Rieger Memorial Highway

NW Lower River Rd

winter gull roost

Vancouver Lake County Park

Vancouver Lake

NW Lakeshore Ave

NE 78th St

EXIT 4

5

Burnt Bridge Creek Greenway

P

Bernie Dr

NW Fruit Valley Rd

NW Lincoln Ave

EXIT 3

NW Lower River Rd

501

Van-couver Lake Wildlife Area

La Frambois Rd

Vancouver Lake County Park

NW 45th St

EXIT 2

500

W 39th St

E 33rd St

Main St

VANCOUVER

Frenchman's Bar County Park

Willamette River

Columbia River

OREGON

Fruit Valley Sewage Treatment Plant

W Fourth

EXIT 1D

Plain Blvd

Lincoln Ave

Main St

W Mill Plain Blvd

EXIT 1C

E Fort Van-couver Way

5

Washing-ton St

EXIT 1A/1B

14

To Washougal

Hayden Island

See page 245 for detail map of Ridgefield NWR

A consummate avian hunter, a Black Merlin (Falco columbarius suckleyi) pursues its shorebird prey in a brief but intense chase over Columbia River bottomlands in winter.

Take Exit 1D from I-5 and drive west on Fourth Plain Boulevard (SR-501). In 1.3 miles, at the Fruit Valley Road intersection, stay straight ahead onto NW Lower River Road. In another 0.3 mile a road on the right leads to the **Fruit Valley Sewage Treatment Plant**. Turn in here, then bear left onto a gravel road that follows the fence north to a gate on the left. Park without blocking access to the plant. On your right, a dike with a row of utility poles continues northward, paralleling the fence. Climb to the top of the dike and walk north until you reach the last pond. From this vantage you can view diving ducks—mostly Ring-neckeds and Lesser Scaup, with some Canvasbacks and Ruddies. With a spotting scope you should be able to find a few Greater Scaup and possibly a Redhead or even a Tufted Duck (casual).

Continue west on NW Lower River Road, checking the ponds and fields for geese, ducks, Great Egrets, and Sandhill Cranes. In three miles, stop on the right at the parking lot and restroom for the flushing channel that brings water from the Columbia River into **Vancouver Lake**. The influx of fresh water attracts fish and the birds that feed on them. Loons, Western Grebes, and Double-crested Cormorants winter here. Occasionally a Red-necked or Clark's Grebe can be spotted among them. During late summer and at low tide mud-flats in a bay on the right (east) side of the flushing channel attract shorebirds. With a surface area of 2,800 acres, Vancouver Lake was less than three feet deep until it was dredged and the flushing channel constructed. The dredge spoils were used to make an island in the center of the lake that serves as a night-time roost for over 5,000 gulls during the winter months. Check them out when they depart at dawn, or at dusk as they are returning.

Just ahead is an intersection where NW Lower River Road turns left. Stay straight ahead onto Erwin O. Rieger Memorial Highway and continue 0.7 mile to the entrance to **Vancouver Lake County Park**, on the right. Ornamental trees and thick plantings of shrubs throughout the park attract migrant and wintering passerines. At the north end of the park is a trail lined with roses and other thick brush that harbors many sparrows. The trail leads to an Oregon Ash forest that may produce roosting owls or hawks.

Turn right from the park entrance and continue north on Rieger Highway. For the next 1.7 miles, until it ends, the road parallels the shore of Vancouver Lake. The land on the right side of the road is owned by Clark County Parks, and access to the lake is available in several spots. On the left side, the road follows one edge of the **Shillapoo Wildlife Area**, approximately 1,000 acres of grasslands and wetlands around the bed of a drained lake used as a pheasant-release site for hunting purposes. In winter, Short-eared Owls are found in the open fields. Tundra Swans, geese, and Sandhill Cranes can be numerous here when hunters are not present.

Return to Lower River Road and turn right (west). The fields on both sides of the road in 1.5 miles are one of the better spots in the lowlands to find Sandhill Cranes and goose flocks. Opposite the entrance to Frenchman's Bar

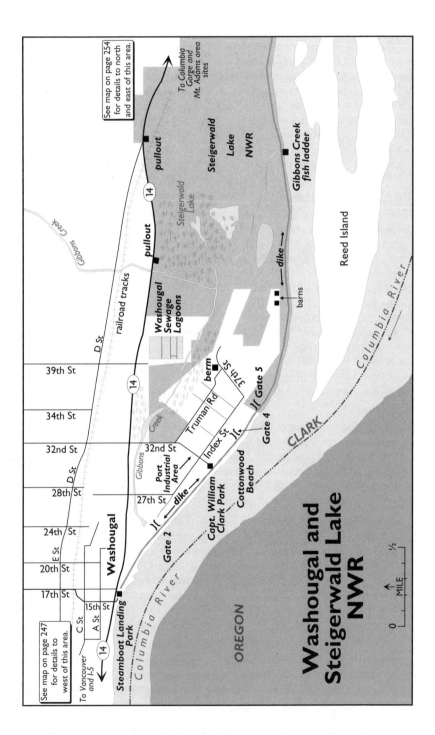

See map on page 254 for details to north and east of this area.

To Columbia Gorge and Mt. Adams area sites

Steigerwald Lake NWR

Gibbons Creek fish ladder

Gibbons Creek

pullout

14

Steigerwald Lake

Reed Island

pullout

Columbia River

railroad tracks

dike

Washougal Sewage Lagoons

barns

D St

39th St

14

berm

37th St

Gibbons Creek

34th St

Truman Rd

Gate 5

32nd St

32nd St

Index St

Gate 4

CLARK

Port Industrial Area

28th St

27th St

dike

Capt. William Clark Park

Cottonwood Beach

D St

24th St

E St

Washougal

Gate 2

20th St

17th St

15th St

C St

A St

Steamboat Landing Park

Columbia River

14

OREGON

Columbia River

See map on page 247 for details to west of this area.

To Vancouver and I-5

Washougal and Steigerwald Lake NWR

0   ½
MILE

County Park (0.3 mile) is a large Great Blue Heron rookery. Continue scanning the fields and ponds as you drive to **Post Office Lake** (4.5 miles), in the south section of Ridgefield National Wildlife Refuge. The fields and lake here, which are closed to hunting, are often swarming with geese and ducks in winter. The road continues another mile past flooded fields where a large share of the 30,000 geese that winter on the refuge sometimes gather. The final section of field is a consistent spot to find Dusky Canada Geese.

Return toward Vancouver and turn left (north) onto NW Fruit Valley Road. In 0.4 mile, La Frambois Road goes left to a parking area and boat launch in the **Vancouver Lake Wildlife Area**—some 500 acres of brush and fields and a stretch of shoreline at the south end of the lake (WDFW permit required to park). During hunting season, when the fields are a pheasant-release site and the boat launch is used by duck hunters, bird from the road.

Go back to Fruit Valley Road and turn left. In 1.9 miles, turn right at the intersection of Bernie Drive, then left into a parking lot for the **Burnt Bridge Creek Greenway**. A splendid, 1.5-mile paved trail meanders eastward from here to Hazel Dell Avenue, passing through mixed forest and along wet, grassy bottomlands where Anna's Hummingbird, woodpeckers, and many passerine species may be seen. Before leaving, check the arm of Vancouver Lake at the mouth of the creek for waterfowl.

WASHOUGAL AND STEIGERWALD LAKE

Upriver from Vancouver, a productive stretch of Columbia River bottomland—now diked and drained—extends eastward for about four miles from the town of Washougal to Point Vancouver, at the mouth of the Columbia Gorge. This is a migration crossroads, as birds following along the Cascade foothills or traveling through the gorge stop to use the ponds, marshes, pastures, riparian woodlands, river beaches, and offshore waters. Over 185 species have been recorded here, including numerous unusual species such as White-faced Ibis, Tufted Duck, Surf Scoter, White-tailed Kite, Red-shouldered Hawk, Gyrfalcon, Black-necked Stilt, American Avocet, Gray Flycatcher, Black Phoebe, Sage Thrasher, Palm Warbler, and Lesser Goldfinch. A substantial part of these lands is within the 1,200-acre **Steigerwald Lake National Wildlife Refuge**, established in 1984 but presently closed to the public pending development of a management plan. For now, one may bird the refuge from a dike-top footpath across the south side or from pullouts along SR-14.

Take Exit 1A/1B from I-5 (or Exit 27 from I-205), drive east on SR-14 to Washougal, and at the stoplight at 15th Street turn off right to **Steamboat Landing Park** (10 miles east of I-205). From the floating fishing dock, scan the Columbia River for loons, grebes, and diving ducks over the rocky reef just downstream. Purple Martins nest in the pilings that once supported the old paddlewheel steamer dock. The park is the west access to the dike separating the Columbia from its former floodplain around Steigerwald Lake. The dike path extends east for about 3.5 miles; do not cross any fences onto refuge or private property.

To shorten the walk to the best birding places, return to SR-14 and drive east to the 32nd Street entrance to the Port Industrial Area, on the right (1.0 mile). Just after turning off, stop at a pullout on the right side of 32nd Street that affords views of a remnant channel of Gibbons Creek. To the west, the creek is lined with trees and brush, good for Green Herons and Wood Ducks. East across the road, the creek goes through a large marsh where bitterns and rails are common. Continue south on 32nd Street to Index Street and the Captain William Clark Park parking lot by the dike (0.5 mile). A trail over the dike leads to sandy **Cottonwood Beach** through an extensive riparian forest of cottonwood, ash, and willow—excellent in migration for passerines. Bullock's Oriole is a conspicuous nester here. Camping is allowed with a permit from the Port of Camas/Washougal, 24 South A Street, Washougal (phone 360-835-2196).

Leave your car in this lot or at either of two other access points (Gates 4 and 5) farther east on Index Street. From Gate 4, a road leads into the forest at Cottonwood Beach farther away from most beach activities. As you walk east on the dike, note **Reed Island** out in the Columbia River—the southernmost spot in the state. This undeveloped state park has a Great Blue Heron rookery. Check the shallow, protected waters between the island and the dike for loons, grebes, and diving ducks, and the open fields for geese, raptors, and cranes. Along the dike, note the white posts with mileage marks. The barns at mile 1.25 often have wintering sparrows around them. A shallow pond just past these barns, at the refuge boundary, is good for nesting American Bitterns and wintering waterfowl. Shorebirds use the mudflats in late summer as the pond level drops. At mile 2.0 is the **Gibbons Creek fish ladder**, recently installed to allow salmon and Steelhead to return to the creek after a 20-year absence. Long rows of cottonwoods parallel to the river mark what were the tops of islands when this area flooded annually, before construction of the dike. Here you may find nesting White-breasted Nuthatches (the declining Westside race), House Wrens, and Lazuli Buntings. Turn back in another half-mile where a fence marking private property crosses the dike.

Return to your vehicle and drive east along Index, which bends left and becomes 37th Street. From the stop sign at Truman Road (0.6 mile) continue through the intersection onto a gravel road. The berm to the north (0.1 mile) overlooks an extensive marsh where bitterns, ducks, and rails nest. Return to Index Street and drive west. Where 27th Street (and the good pavement) turn north, stay straight ahead to the end of the rough road in another quarter-mile. Park and climb up on the dike at **Gate 2**, near the pumping station, and check for shorebirds on the sandbars in the Columbia River exposed during low water. From the dike looking north you can see part of the old creek channel with a bridge-like weir that prevents debris from reaching the pumps that help keep the industrial area dry. Green Herons perch on this weir and can sometimes be seen roosting on the crossbeams beneath it.

Go back to 32nd Street. Drive north to SR-14, turn right, and drive east. On the right in 0.5 mile, the **Washougal Sewage Lagoons** are viewable from the entrance road or from the highway shoulder a few yards ahead. Wood Ducks are numerous here in spring and summer. As you travel east you can safely stop on the wide, paved highway shoulder to view the refuge. A pullout on the right marks the entrance to the proposed refuge visitor center (0.5 mile). When it is completed, trails will lead from here through the wetlands to the dike. The U.S. Fish and Wildlife Service has enlarged what remained of the lake and planted ash and willow trees along the creek and wetlands. Cattail patches have reappeared and Yellow-headed Blackbirds, a species that formerly nested here, are being seen again. Thousands of geese and ducks use these fields and the ponds during winter. You will need a spotting scope at the last viewing spot, just past the railroad overpass (0.6 mile).

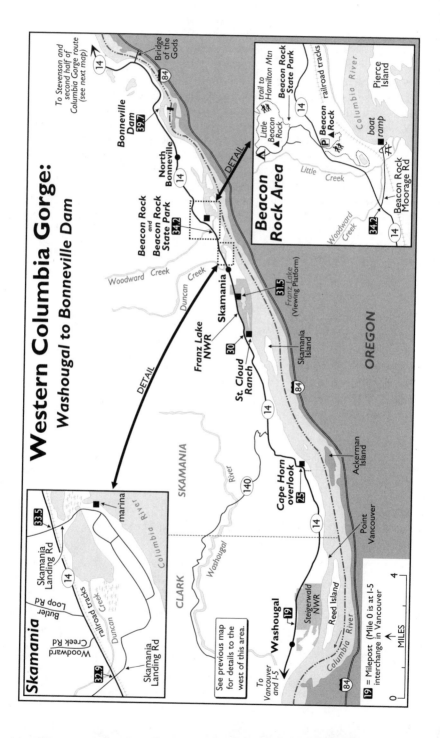

Western Columbia Gorge:
Washougal to Bonneville Dam

To Stevenson and second half of Columbia Gorge route (see next map)

Bridge of the Gods

14

84

Bonneville Dam **39.7**

North Bonneville

14

Beacon Rock and Beacon Rock State Park **34.2**

DETAIL

Woodward Creek

Duncan Creek

Franz Lake NWR

Skamania **31.5**

Franz Lake (Viewing Platform)

Skamania Island

St. Cloud Ranch

30

SKAMANIA

River

140

84

14

Ackerman Island

Cape Horn overlook **25**

Point Vancouver

14

CLARK

Washougal **19**

Steigerwald NWR

Reed Island

To Vancouver and I-5

Columbia River

84

See previous map for details to the west of this area.

19 = Milepost (Mile 0 is at I-5 interchange in Vancouver)

0   MILES   4

Beacon Rock Area

Little Hamilton Mtn

trail to Hamilton Mtn

Beacon Rock State Park

Little Beacon Rock

14

Beacon Rock

railroad tracks

Columbia River

Pierce Island

P

boat ramp

Beacon Rock Moorage Rd

Little Creek

Woodward Creek

14 **34.2**

Skamania

33.5

Skamania Landing Rd

14

marina

Columbia River

railroad tracks

Woodward Creek Rd

Butler Loop Rd

Duncan Creek

Skamania Landing Rd

32.9

OREGON

WESTERN COLUMBIA GORGE

by Wilson Cady

The **Columbia River Gorge National Scenic Area** is a place of outstanding natural, cultural, and scenic interest. Traveling east through this near-sea-level break in the mountains for some 80 miles, SR-14 provides a striking wet-to-dry transect, from Western Hemlock and Douglas-fir forests on the west to Garry Oak and Ponderosa Pine toward the east, and finally grasslands and shrub-steppe. Fifteen species of plants that grow in the gorge are found nowhere else in the world.

Floodwaters released periodically from Glacial Lake Missoula rushed through the narrow gorge, creating the oversteepening of its sides one sees today. One result is the many waterfalls (mainly on the Oregon side). Another is slope instability, provoking large-scale landslides over the millennia since the floods subsided. In some places on the Washington side the road is built atop slide debris.

Prominent mileposts line SR-14 (mile zero is at the I-5 interchange in Vancouver). These offer the most convenient reference points through the gorge; interpolate the tenths from your odometer. The route begins at milepost 19, just past the easternmost viewing pullout at Steigerwald Lake. From here it is about 45 miles to the town of Bingen and south central Washington.

At milepost 24.7, an unimproved trail leads from a parking area on the right through a Bigleaf Maple grove where you may find nesting Red-eyed Vireos. This trail ends at an abrupt cliff overlooking a waterfall. Just beyond, at milepost 25, is the **Cape Horn Overlook**, with one of the best views in the gorge. Peregrine Falcons nest on the cliff face formed by at least five separate volcanic flows, while Turkey Vultures and Cliff Swallows cruise by at eye level.

The only remnant of the **Saint Cloud Ranch**, on the right at milepost 29.9, is the century-old apple orchard on the banks of the Columbia River. The trees while in bloom can be filled with migrant birds feeding on nectar and insects. During fall and winter the fruit attracts many species, and Red-breasted Sapsuckers bore sap wells in the ancient limbs.

Franz Lake National Wildlife Refuge is closed to the public but there is a viewing platform above the lake at milepost 31.5. This large, shallow backwater of the Columbia River is completely covered with Wapato (also known as Indian Potato) in summer. This plant was a food staple of Native Americans and the starchy roots are a favorite food of swans. In winter, if the water level is low enough for them to be able to reach these tubers, over a thousand Tundra Swans may gather here. Across the lake in a large cottonwood tree on the edge of the river is an active Bald Eagle nest.

As you enter Skamania at milepost 32.9, exit to your right onto **Skamania Landing Road**. This one-mile loop crosses the railroad tracks

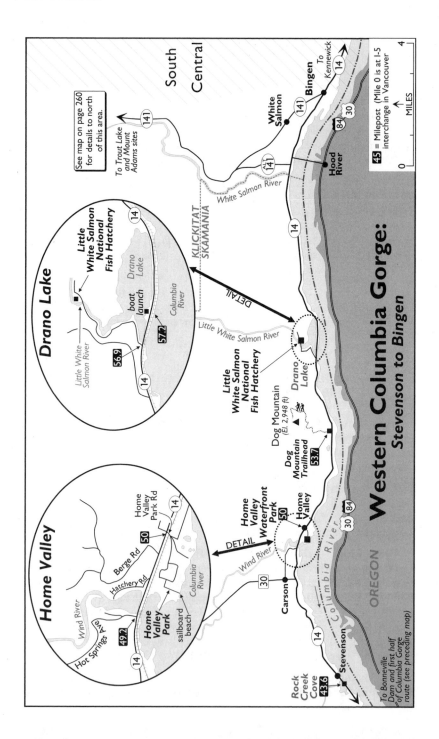

Western Columbia Gorge:
Stevenson to Bingen

Drano Lake

Little White Salmon National Fish Hatchery

Little White Salmon River

boat launch

Drano Lake

Columbia River

56.9

57.2

14

See map on page 260 for details to north of this area.

To Trout Lake and Mount Adams sites

141

141

141

White Salmon River

White Salmon

Bingen

To Kennewick

14

Hood River

84

30

South Central

KLICKITAT
SKAMANIA

DETAIL

14

Little White Salmon River

Little White Salmon National Fish Hatchery

Dog Mountain (El. 2,948 ft)

Dog Mountain Trailhead

53.7

Drano Lake

Home Valley

Home Valley Park Rd

Berge Rd

Hatchery Rd

Home Valley Park

sailboard beach

Columbia River

Wind River

Hot Springs Ave

49.2

50

14

DETAIL

Home Valley Waterfront Park

Home Valley

50

Wind River

Carson

30

84

30

14

Stevenson

Rock Creek Cove

43.6

To Bonneville Dam and first half of Columbia Gorge route (see preceding map)

OREGON

Columbia River

45 = Milepost (Mile 0 is at I-5 interchange in Vancouver

0   MILES   4

and circles a small impoundment on Duncan Creek. The dam is opened and the lake drained during fall and winter to allow passage for spawning salmon and Steelhead. This creates a rare habitat type in the gorge—mudflats that attract shorebirds. Nest boxes at the private marina on the east end of the loop are used by Purple Martins.

Continue east to milepost 34.2 and turn right down Beacon Rock Moorage Road to the picnic area and boat ramp at the base of **Beacon Rock**, a prominent landmark. Watch for the Peregrine Falcons that nest on the south side of this monolithic volcanic plug. Return to SR-14 and continue east 0.8 mile to the parking lot for the trail that leads to the top of the rock, 840 feet above the river. The trail is steep but guarded by railings at all exposed points, and the views are great. Across the road is the entrance to **Beacon Rock State Park** (camping and picnic areas). Trails from here go through the forest to Hamilton Mountain on the north rim of the gorge. Lazuli Buntings nest on the open, shrubby slopes. Use caution, as one of the most common shrubs on the exposed hillsides in the gorge is Poison Oak.

At milepost 39.7 is **Bonneville Dam** with an underwater viewing room where you can observe American Shad, salmon, Steelhead, and other species as they travel through the fish ladder. Walk up the short trail from the upstream end of the visitor parking lot to the viewpoint. Look for loons, grebes, gulls, and rafts of ducks on the calm waters above the dam.

As you enter the town of Stevenson stop at the pullout on the south side of the road at milepost 43.6, just before crossing the bridge over Rock Creek, to scan **Rock Creek Cove**. This shallow, weedy, wind-protected backwater is closed to hunting. Large flocks of waterfowl feed here, including both dabbling and diving ducks. Canvasbacks and Redheads are regular. Climb the trail up the railroad embankment to check the shallow reefs and rocky islands in the Columbia for other diving ducks. At the county fairgrounds across the cove geese and ducks can be observed closely as they feed on the lawn or come for handouts.

Stop at the mouth of the **Wind River** at milepost 49.2. Harlequin Ducks nest higher up the river but may be seen near the mouth in spring and early summer. **Home Valley Waterfront Park** is on your right at milepost 50. As you enter the park take the road to the right toward the sailboard beach, where a small wetland and thick riparian woods are worth a check in migration. There are a few primitive camping spots at the east end of the park, past the ball fields. In fall and winter the bay upstream holds diving ducks—best observed from the highway shoulder just past the park.

Park at the **Dog Mountain Trailhead** at milepost 53.7 and check the rafts of Ring-necked Ducks and Lesser Scaups for Canvasback, Redhead, and Greater Scaup. The trail to the top of Dog Mountain takes you to one of the most spectacular wildflower displays in the gorge. Differences in soil depth, slope, and aspect, and the 3,000-foot elevation gain, create an extended bloom time. Lazuli Buntings nest in brushy patches near the top. Watch for Poison Oak along this trail, which also marks the western limit in the gorge for rattlesnakes.

On the west side of Drano Lake at milepost 56.9 is the one-mile spur to the **Little White Salmon National Fish Hatchery**. Common and Barrow's Goldeneyes winter where the Little White Salmon River enters the lake, along with Hooded and Common Mergansers. The falls at the hatchery are a good spot to find American Dippers, and at the end of the fall salmon run Bald Eagles and gulls gather on the sandbars to feed on the spawned-out fish. Drive back to SR-14, turn left, and park on the wide shoulder on the south side of the highway opposite the boat launch (milepost 57.2). Climb the railroad embankment on the right to check the flocks of diving ducks on the Columbia River. **Drano Lake**—the wind-sheltered impoundment north of the road—usually has Canvasbacks and Redheads in the mixed flocks of ducks. Scan the lake from the shoulder.

When you reach the White Salmon River bridge and Alternate SR-141 in about six miles you are entering South Central Washington. See page 332 for the continuation of the Columbia Gorge route on the Dry Side.

MOUNT ADAMS

by Andy Stepniewski

M ount Adams, Washington's second-highest peak (12,276 feet), is a dormant volcano with numerous glaciers and snowfields. The summit is on the Cascade crest at the west edge of the Yakama Indian Reservation, roughly 30 miles north of the Columbia Gorge, 30 miles south of White Pass, and 30 miles east of Mount Saint Helens. This remote region has been little explored by birders, even though it is scenic, birdy, and eminently birdable with a bit of preparation and care. Make sure you have a Gifford Pinchot National Forest map and a Northwest Forest Pass. Overnight camping expands the possibilities, as there are no motels between US-12 and SR-14, and it is a long drive in and out. Expect birds of wetlands, moist and transitional Wet Side–Dry Side forests, and meadows ranging from lower-elevation zones up to the subalpine. Alpine species such as White-tailed Ptarmigan, American Pipit, and Gray-crowned Rosy-Finch are documented on Mount Adams, but reaching their habitat requires serious hiking, which few birders attempt.

TROUT LAKE

The best access point for the Mount Adams area, and a good base for exploring all parts of it, is the unincorporated town of Trout Lake, which lies in a broad valley between the Indian Heaven Wilderness Area on the west and the mountain on the north. Basic services are available here (gas, cafe, general store). Eastbound on SR-14 in the Columbia Gorge, turn left just after crossing the White Salmon River bridge onto Alternate SR-141, joining the main trunk of the highway in 2.1 miles. From SR-14 westbound, turn right onto SR-141 in Bingen and drive through White Salmon, reaching the intersection with Alternate SR-141 in 4.8 miles. It is about 19 miles north from this corner to the junction with the Mount Adams Recreation Highway in Trout Lake. If you are traveling between Trout Lake and birding sites in the upper Klickitat country (page 338), your connector is Sunnyside Road, which heads east from Mount Adams Recreation Highway 0.3 mile north of SR-141. At an intersection in 3.9 miles where Sunnyside Road turns right (south), stay straight ahead onto Trout Lake Highway, reaching Glenwood in about 12 miles.

SR-141 continues west through Trout Lake, passing in 0.8 mile the USFS Mount Adams Ranger District station (information, maps, passes). In another 0.8 mile, turn north onto Trout Lake Creek Road. Elk Meadows RV Park (0.9 mile) is a heavily forested campground with excellent facilities for tent and vehicle campers, where birders are welcome. From the northeast end of the campground a wide trail goes east and downstream for about a mile along the edge of marshy **Trout Lake** (elevation 1,950 feet). Fifty or sixty species can be observed here on an early-morning walk in June, including Pied-billed Grebe, American Bittern, Hooded Merganser (uncommon), Osprey, Virginia Rail, Band-tailed Pigeon, Common Nighthawk, Belted Kingfisher, Red-

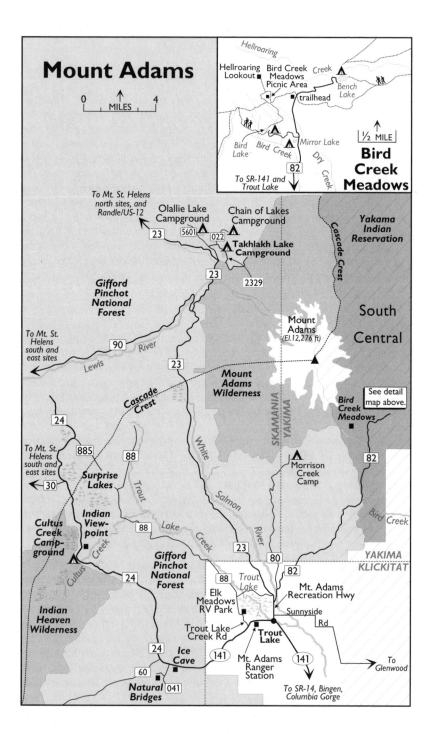

Mount Adams

0 MILES 4

To Mt. St. Helens
north sites, and
Randle/US-12

Olallie Lake
Campground

Chain of Lakes
Campground

Yakama
Indian
Reservation

23 5601 022 Takhlakh Lake
Campground

Cascade Crest

23

2329

Gifford
Pinchot
National
Forest

South

Central

Mount
Adams
(El.12,276 ft)

To Mt. St.
Helens
south and
east sites

90 River

Lewis

23

Mount
Adams
Wilderness

See detail
map above.

Cascade
Crest

White

SKAMANIA
YAKIMA

Bird
Creek
Meadows

24

To Mt. St.
Helens
south and
east sites

885

88

30

Surprise
Lakes

Indian View-
point

Trout

Salmon River

82

Morrison
Creek
Camp

Bird Creek

Cultus
Creek
Camp-
ground

88

Lake

Creek

23

80

82

YAKIMA
KLICKITAT

Cultus Creek

24

Gifford
Pinchot
National
Forest

88

Trout
Lake

Elk
Meadows
RV Park

Mt. Adams
Recreation Hwy

Sunnyside

Rd

Indian
Heaven
Wilderness

Trout Lake
Creek Rd

Trout
Lake

24

Ice
Cave

141

Mt. Adams
Ranger
Station

141

To
Glenwood

60

041

Natural
Bridges

To SR-14, Bingen,
Columbia Gorge

Bird Creek Meadows (detail map)

Hellroaring

Hellroaring
Lookout

Bird Creek
Meadows
Picnic Area

Creek

trailhead

Bench
Lake

½ MILE

Bird
Lake

Bird Creek

Mirror Lake

Dry Creek

Bird
Creek
Meadows

82

To SR-141 and
Trout Lake

breasted Sapsucker, Downy, Hairy, and Black-backed (rare) Woodpeckers, Western Wood-Pewee, Willow and Hammond's Flycatchers, Cassin's and Warbling Vireos, Tree, Violet-green, and Northern Rough-winged Swallows, Veery, Swainson's Thrush, Gray Catbird, Orange-crowned, Nashville, Yellow-rumped, Townsend's, Hermit (uncommon), and MacGillivray's Warblers, Common Yellowthroat, Western Tanager, Purple Finch, and Evening Grosbeak.

INDIAN HEAVEN

The Indian Heaven area is reached by going west from Trout Lake on SR-141, which becomes FR-24 upon entering the Gifford Pinchot National Forest (about four miles past the Trout Lake Creek Road turnoff). In another mile, take time to visit the **Ice Cave**. It is a bizarre experience to leave balmy summer weather and singing Hammond's Flycatchers, Hermit Thrushes, and Townsend's (at least that's what they sound like) Warblers to descend a ladder 30 feet into winter temperatures and snow. Heed the signs advising you to dress up. **Natural Bridges**, just ahead, is another attraction worth a few minutes' detour to visit. Turn left from FR-24 onto FR-041 in 0.8 mile, then right in 0.3 mile onto FR-050. Vine Maples line the lava-tube ravine, with a couple of natural bridges adding a delightful architectural touch.

Another 0.8 mile west on FR-24, keep right at its junction with FR-60. In nine miles, stop at Cultus Creek Campground, on the left, where you may find good-looking Hermit Warblers (but you are still in the hybrid zone). The **Indian Heaven Wilderness Area** (20,650 acres) lies just west of the campground. A trail network visits a few of the 175 small lakes in this plateau landscape, where wet meadows fringed by fir and spruce forests alternate with brushy terrain. Mosquitoes can be fierce, so you may prefer to visit at the end of summer after they have disappeared. Singing will have ceased by then for many bird species, but the huckleberry picking is great. In years of White-winged Crossbill invasions, Indian Heaven often has its share of this enigmatic species. Stop at **Indian Viewpoint** 0.5 mile farther north on FR-24 to enjoy the superb view of Mount Adams and to look for mountain birds in the treetops without having to crane your neck.

The terrain around the **Surprise Lakes**, 2.6 miles ahead, includes numerous boggy ponds and large brush fields (maintained by burning in the past, less so in recent times) of huckleberries, Mountain Ash, and Beargrass, with extensive forest typical of the Mountain Hemlock and Silver Fir zones. Birds of the meadows and bogs include Mountain Bluebird, Hermit Thrush, and Fox, Lincoln's, and White-crowned Sparrows. Forest birds include Black-backed Woodpecker, Gray and Steller's Jays, Mountain and Chestnut-backed Chickadees, Varied Thrush, and Townsend's and Hermit Warblers (and intergrades). Mosquitoes are very bad in the early season. Starting in late July, large flocks of sparrows, warblers, and other small passerines can be found around the meadows; Nashville Warblers are common at that time. Indians camp here in August and September to pick huckleberries.

To reach the south and east sides of Mount Saint Helens, you may turn left from FR-24 onto FR-30 at a fork about a mile farther on, then right onto FR-51 in another ten or eleven miles. In five miles this road joins FR-90 along the Lewis River, about four miles east of Swift Reservoir (page 242).

TAKHLAKH LAKE

The west side of Mount Adams, with several trailheads for the Mount Adams Wilderness, is accessed by taking the Mount Adams Recreation Highway north from Trout Lake, keeping left in 1.4 miles onto FR-23. This road runs upstream (north) along the White Salmon River, crosses the headwaters area of the Lewis River, and enters the Cowlitz River watershed on the northwest side of the mountain. In about 23 miles, where FR-23 goes left, keep right onto FR-2329, which goes right again in about a mile and reaches Takhlakh Lake Campground in another 0.7 mile. Takhlakh Lake (elevation 4,385 feet), amidst tall firs, affords awesome views of the north face of Mount Adams. Many species typical of the higher mountain forests can be found here and at other nearby campgrounds (Chain of Lakes, Olallie Lake), including Gray Jay, Winter Wren, and Varied Thrush. Be sure to look carefully at any Townsend's or Hermit Warblers; this is the heart of the hybrid zone.

BIRD CREEK MEADOWS

Near timberline on the southeast slopes of Mount Adams, Bird Creek Meadows have good subalpine forest birding and beautiful displays of wildflowers. The area is open from 1 July through 30 September (fee, collected by the Yakama Nation; in years of heavy snow the road may not open until later). Go north from SR-141 in Trout Lake on the Mount Adams Recreation Highway. At an intersection with FR-23 in 1.4 miles, keep right onto FR-82. In 0.6 mile, at another fork where FR-80 (the road to Morrison Creek Camp, the base camp for mountain climbers) goes straight ahead, stay right again with FR-82. At the next five-way junction (2.6 miles), make sure to keep on FR-82 (clearly marked). In 5.8 miles, you cross the divide (elevation 4,000 feet) into the Klickitat River watershed and the Yakama Indian Reservation. Mirror Lake is another 4.4 miles over a moderately bumpy dirt road (a large trailer might not make it). Just beyond the lake (0.1 mile), turn left onto a road that leads in one mile to **Bird Lake** and a primitive campground in a forested setting where Gray Jay, Varied Thrush, and Townsend's Warbler are common.

Although a trail to the mountain meadows begins here, perhaps a shorter alternative is to return to the main road and drive north (toward Bench Lake) another 1.1 miles to a trailhead signed *Bird Creek Meadows*, on the left. Park and begin a 2.5-mile loop, returning to this spot. Birds along the way include Gray and Steller's Jays, Clark's Nutcracker (attracted to Whitebark Pines), Mountain Chickadee, Townsend's Solitaire, Hermit Thrush, Yellow-rumped and Townsend's Warblers, and Cassin's Finch. Flocks of migrant warblers and sparrows appear in late summer, along with many other scattered up-mountain migrants. The trail reaches the **Bird Creek Meadows Picnic Area** (elevation 6,100 feet) in less than a mile. The subalpine meadows to the west are a peaceful alternative to the crowds at Paradise on Mount Rainier.

Find a trail leading north from the picnic area up the side of a ridge. Stay right at a junction, and continue up a sandy, bouldery gully for 0.5 mile to **Hellroaring Lookout** (6,350 feet), with spectacular views of the south ridges of Mount Adams and the rocky and meadowed valley below. Look for Mountain Goats on the meadows across the valley. Views to the southeast extend downslope to Glenwood and Conboy Lake National Wildlife Refuge (page 338)—a reminder that you are already in Eastern Washington. To return to your car, follow the steep trail that descends the ridgeline to the east.

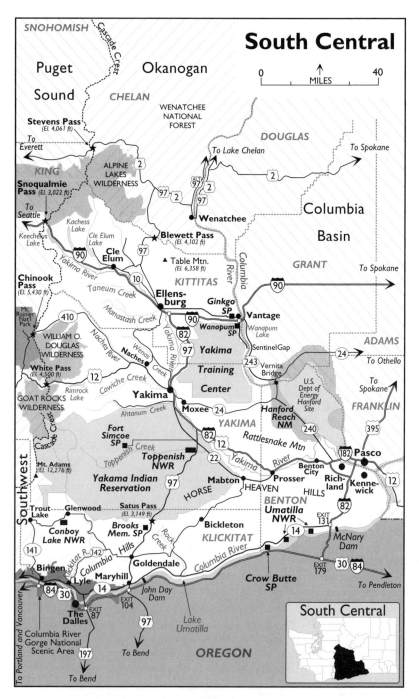

South Central

0 — MILES — 40

SNOHOMISH

Cascade Crest

Puget Sound

Okanogan

CHELAN

WENATCHEE NATIONAL FOREST

Stevens Pass *(El. 4,061 ft)*

To Everett

DOUGLAS

To Lake Chelan

To Spokane

KING

ALPINE LAKES WILDERNESS

2

97 ALT 2

97

Snoqualmie Pass *(El. 3,022 ft)*

To Seattle

Kachess Lake

Cle Elum Lake

Wenatchee

2

Columbia Basin

Keechelus Lake

Yakima River

Cle Elum

Blewett Pass *(El. 4,102 ft)*

97

Columbia River

Chinook Pass *(El. 5,430 ft)*

90

Taneum Creek

10

▲ Table Mtn. *(El. 6,358 ft)*

KITTITAS

GRANT

To Spokane

Mt. Rainier Nat'l Park

Manastash Creek

Ellensburg

90

Ginkgo SP

Vantage

90

Naches River

410

WILLIAM O. DOUGLAS WILDERNESS

82

Wanapum SP

Wanapum Lake

ADAMS

Wenas Creek

Yakima River

97

Yakima Training Center

Sentinel Gap

243

24

To Othello

White Pass *(El. 4,500 ft)*

Naches

12

Cowiche Creek

Vernita Bridge

To Spokane

GOAT ROCKS WILDERNESS

Rimrock Lake

Yakima

U.S. Dept of Energy Hanford Site

FRANKLIN

Cascade Crest

Ahtanum Creek

Moxee

24

Hanford Reach NM

Mt. Adams *(El. 12,276 ft)*

Fort Simcoe SP

Toppenish Creek

82

YAKIMA

240

Rattlesnake Mtn

395

Toppenish NWR

12

Yakima River

182

Pasco

Southwest

Trout Lake

Glenwood

Yakama Indian Reservation

97

22

Mabton

HEAVEN

Prosser

Benton City

Richland

Kennewick

12

Conboy Lake NWR

141

Brooks Mem. SP

Status Pass *(El. 3,149 ft)*

HORSE

Bickleton

KLICKITAT

BENTON

Umatilla NWR

14

EXIT 131

82

HILLS

Bingen

142

Klickitat R.

Columbia Hills

Rock Creek

Goldendale

McNary Dam

Lyle

30

Maryhill

14

John Day Dam

Columbia River

Crow Butte SP

EXIT 179

30

84

To Pendleton

84

30

EXIT 87

The Dalles

EXIT 104

97

Lake Umatilla

Columbia River Gorge National Scenic Area

197

To Bend

OREGON

To Bend

To Portland and Vancouver

South Central

264

SOUTH CENTRAL

One of the two largest regions of the nine in this book, South Central Washington is also one of the most varied in topography, climate, vegetation, and wildlife. Much of the region is within day-trip distance of Puget Sound (one hour to Snoqualmie Pass, two to Ellensburg, two and a half to Vantage or Yakima). Hence, for most birders, this is the gateway to the Dry Side of the state.

Pacific storms drench the west slopes of the Cascades, resulting in the great conifer forests that characterize the Pacific Northwest in the popular imagination. East of the crest, however, precipitation declines. Forests become more open, and instead of firs and hemlocks, there are many Ponderosa Pines. Farther down, precipitation is lower still—too low for any tree growth except along streams. A belt of shrub- and grasslands begins at the lower forest edge. This arid shrub-steppe zone extends across the Columbia River all the way to the eastern boundary of the state.

The region's dominant physical features are the Cascade Range on the west and north, and the Columbia River on the east and south. Secondary in importance is the so-called Yakima Fold Belt—a series of west-east trending basalt ridges emanating from the Cascades and dividing the region into numerous valleys. The many elevations, aspects, slopes, soils, and microclimates of this ridge-and-valley system support a wealth of plant communities and a corresponding diversity of animal life.

About three-quarters of South Central Washington is drained by the Yakima River. Gathering waters from the mountains to the west and north, this stream carves through several high ridges via the Yakima Canyon, then flows south and east across the farms and orchards of the broad Yakima Valley to join the Columbia River at Richland. Numerous minor streams drain the fringe of shrub-steppe on the east and south directly to the Columbia. East of Mount Adams, the Klickitat River waters a unique landscape of meadows, parklands, cliffs, and Garry Oaks, cutting its canyon down to the Columbia Gorge at Lyle.

What do birders come here to find? The perennial draw for Wet Siders is breeding birds of the lower forest zone and adjacent shrub-steppe: Common Poorwill, Calliope Hummingbird, White-headed Woodpecker, Gray Flycatcher, Say's Phoebe, Loggerhead Shrike, Sage Thrasher, and Brewer's, Lark, Black-throated, and Sage Sparrows. But there is much more than that. The

Kittitas County record for a Big Day in May is 150 species (200 possible in theory), while the Tri-Cities Christmas Bird Count tallies 100–110 species routinely. The Garry Oak habitats of the Columbia Gorge and Klickitat country are the only place in the state to find Acorn Woodpecker and Lesser Goldfinch (and the best place for Ash-throated Flycatcher). Chickens are good: Chukar, Gray Partridge, Greater Sage-Grouse, Blue Grouse. So are owls: Flammulated, Burrowing, Spotted, Northern Saw-whet. Parks in Richland and Kennewick are great passerine migrant traps. Waterbirds crowd Columbia River reservoirs in migration and winter, and the Yakima River delta is one of the interior Northwest's best fall shorebird spots.

Temperature and precipitation follow a gradient from northwest (coolest, wettest) to southeast (warmest, driest). July average maximum temperature is 81 degrees in Cle Elum (in the lower mixed-forest zone southeast of Snoqualmie Pass) and 87 degrees in Yakima (in the shrub-steppe zone 50 miles farther southeast). Cle Elum receives 22 inches of precipitation annually, Yakima just eight. Winter temperature is about the same in both places (January average minimum 20 degrees), but it snows a lot more in Cle Elum (81 inches compared to 24 inches in Yakima). These are only examples. Weather patterns are strongly influenced by the region's complex topography, and local variation can be great.

Snowfall is heavy in the mountain passes. Chinook Pass (SR-410) closes for the winter, but Snoqualmie Pass (I-90) and White Pass (US-12) are kept open. So is US-97 across Blewett Pass and Satus Pass. When conditions merit, traction devices may be required on any of these passes, so be prepared. Forest roads on the east slopes of the Cascades close by default when snow accumulates. Snowfall is light in the lowlands, and roads (including SR-14 through the Columbia Gorge) stay open all winter long, except for the occasional storm. Watch for ice, however. In spring, wind may hamper birding in open country (the Kittitas Valley is notorious for this). Strong, steady winds are characteristic of the Columbia Gorge in any season.

There are numerous motels, restaurants, gas stations, and other services in Cle Elum, Ellensburg, Yakima, Toppenish, the Tri-Cities, and across the Columbia in Hood River and The Dalles, Oregon, as well as (less reliably) in smaller communities, especially along the I-90 and I-82 corridors. Campgrounds are plentiful along the various routes traversing national forest lands; elsewhere they are few and far between.

Snoqualmie Pass and Vicinity

by Hal Opperman and Andy Stepniewski

Fifty miles east of Seattle on Interstate 90, Snoqualmie Pass is the most traveled and accessible crossing of the Cascades. The pass is super wet, with about 100 inches of precipitation annually, including an average of 450 inches of snow. Wet, mild conditions prevail eastward from the crest for many miles along the upper east-slope Cascades, favoring development of a once-impressive conifer forest, much of which has been clearcut. More than a century ago, Congress granted alternate one-square-mile sections of land to the Northern Pacific Railroad in a wide corridor on each side of the proposed right-of-way. The railroad was built up the Yakima River valley from the Tri-Cities to the crest at Stampede Pass, then down the Green River drainage on the west slope, reaching Puget Sound in 1887. The checkerboard of remote, rugged timber lands remaining in railroad ownership was left largely unexploited until the 1980s, when a massive clearcutting program was initiated. Even the Spotted Owl crisis of that decade could not slow the rush to "get the cut out." Fortunately, the sections in public ownership have been managed less aggressively, while the forests on the railroad land-grant sections are now slowly regenerating. Areas of beauty with birds and wildlife remain even near I-90. Farther away, up the many side valleys, the landscape is more intact. The higher elevations to the north on both slopes of the Cascades are formally protected in the Alpine Lakes Wilderness Area.

Snoqualmie Pass

Snoqualmie Pass (elevation 3,022 feet) is not high enough to reach the sub-alpine, but the combination of forests, fake "meadows" of ski slopes, and some clearcuts has produced varied habitats. The summit area can be reached from any of three I-90 exits. Coming from the Seattle side the first is Exit 52, signed *West Summit*. (However, there is no offramp for westbound traffic at this exit, so those coming from the Ellensburg side should use Exit 54 or Exit 53 instead.)

If you have time for a hike, the **Commonwealth Basin Trail** goes through an uncut forest of Silver Fir on the west slope of the Cascades, out of range of traffic noise, with decent birding possibilities. Go left from the West Summit offramp onto Alpental Road, passing under the interstate. In a hundred yards turn right and drive a short distance to a large trailhead parking lot (Northwest Forest Pass required). Take the Pacific Crest Trail northbound as it climbs into the Alpine Lakes Wilderness. In 2.5 miles (elevation 4,000 feet), Trail 1033 branches off to the left and drops down into the basin of Commonwealth Creek, then climbs into the subalpine, with a series of switchbacks, to **Red Pass** (2.5 miles, elevation 5,300 feet). Blue Grouse, Hammond's Flycatcher, Townsend's Solitaire, and Hermit and Varied Thrushes nest here, along with most of the familiar species of Puget Lowlands forests. Red Pass lies on the divide between the South and Middle Forks of the Snoqualmie River.

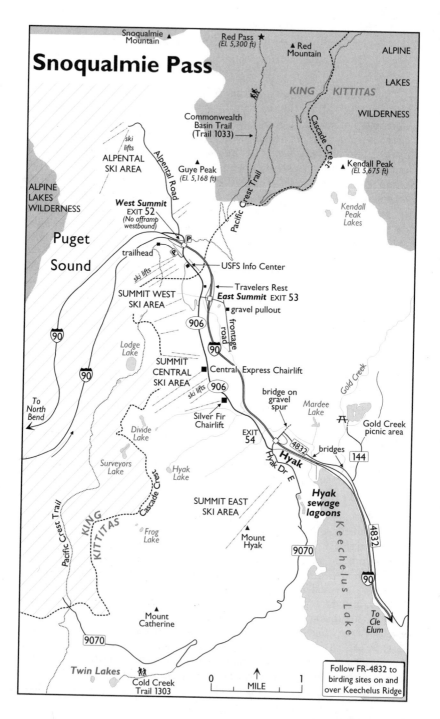

Snoqualmie Pass

Snoqualmie Mountain

Red Pass (El. 5,300 ft)

Red Mountain

ALPINE

LAKES

KING KITTITAS

WILDERNESS

Commonwealth Basin Trail (Trail 1033)

ski lifts

ALPENTAL SKI AREA

Alpental Road

Guye Peak (El. 5,168 ft)

Kendall Peak (El. 5,675 ft)

ALPINE LAKES WILDERNESS

Pacific Crest Trail

Cascade Crest

Kendall Peak Lakes

West Summit EXIT 52 (No offramp westbound)

Puget Sound

trailhead

USFS Info Center

ski lifts

SUMMIT WEST SKI AREA

Travelers Rest
East Summit EXIT 53

906

gravel pullout

frontage road

90

90

Lodge Lake

SUMMIT CENTRAL SKI AREA

Central Express Chairlift

Gold Creek

To North Bend

906

ski lifts

Silver Fir Chairlift

bridge on gravel spur

Mardee Lake

Gold Creek picnic area

EXIT 54

4832

bridges

144

Divide Lake

Hyak Dr E

Hyak

Surveyors Lake

Hyak Lake

Hyak sewage lagoons

4832

KING

Cascade Crest

KITTITAS

Frog Lake

SUMMIT EAST SKI AREA

Mount Hyak

9070

Keechelus Lake

90

Pacific Crest Trail

To Cle Elum

Mount Catherine

9070

Twin Lakes

Cold Creek Trail 1303

0   MILE   1

N

Follow FR-4832 to birding sites on and over Keechelus Ridge

High crags of the Cascades can be seen across the deep valley of the Middle Fork, to the north, with Mount Baker in the distance. Gray-crowned Rosy-Finches nest in rock clefts along steep, treeless slopes in the high country here and throughout the wilderness area, usually well away from trails. An off-trail traverse westward from Red Pass to Lundin Peak (elevation 6,067 feet) and Snoqualmie Mountain (elevation 6,278 feet) may turn up a few, but there are far more comfortable ways to see this species.

Many mountain birds can be found closer to the interstate, although traffic noise can be an unpleasant distraction. A hundred yards right (south) from the stop sign at the end of the West Summit offramp is an entrance sign for The Summit at Snoqualmie, on the right. Turn in, then go right into a large gravel parking lot for the **Summit West** chairlifts. One attraction of Snoqualmie Pass for birders is the possibility of breeding Slate-colored Fox and Lincoln's Sparrows. Both are sometimes present here in wet, brushy spots at the edge of the ski slopes, as are Willow Flycatchers and White-crowned Sparrows. A gravel road out the back of the parking lot swings left to a parking area for the **Pacific Crest Trail** southbound (0.3 mile; Northwest Forest Pass required). A two-mile hike from here to Lodge Lake in the lower subalpine runs through intact forest, brushy ski slopes, and marshes (high point 3,600 feet).

Turn right from the Snoqualmie Summit entrance sign and proceed along SR-906 (the old highway) through the small commercial district. The USFS Information Center on the right (0.1 mile; open seasonally) has maps and parking permits. On the right in another 0.2 mile, across the road from the Travelers Rest, is an entrance to **Village at the Summit**, a small residential community best visited on foot. Be courteous, and stay on the roads; this is private property. Many homes have feeders that attract Rufous Hummingbirds and the occasional Calliope. You may hear Blue Grouse booming in the conifers. Listen, too, for Red Crossbills and other finches. Return to SR-906 and turn right. Roadside brush may have singing Yellow and MacGillivray's Warblers and White-crowned Sparrows. In 0.1 mile, turn left and go under I-90 (this is Exit 53, East Summit). In 0.2 mile, turn right onto the frontage road on the other side of the interstate and park at a gravel pullout on the left in 0.1 mile. Walk the road both ways. The forest is dense, with A-frame bungalows tucked among big conifers. Blue Grouse, Varied Thrush, Townsend's Warbler, and Pine Siskin are usually here in late spring and summer.

Go back under I-90 and turn left onto SR-906, which serves the Summit Central ski area. In 0.9 mile the **Central Express Chairlift**, on the right, operates on summer weekends to take hikers and mountain bikers to a trail system at the Cascade crest, above the freeway din: for current information, visit *www.summit-at-snoqualmie.com* or call 425-434-7669. Fox and Lincoln's Sparrows nest here in subalpine meadows and shrubby growth, and Red-breasted Sapsuckers nest in snags (sometimes in mixed pairs with Red-naped). If you wish to extend the birding possibilities, walk back down along the forested margins of the ski slopes instead of riding the lift.

Drive another 0.3 mile along SR-906 and park at the **Silver Fir Chairlift**, on the right. Cross to the other side of the road and walk to the back of the overflow parking lot and along a gravel service road for a few hundred yards. Tracks on the left (groomed for cross-country skiing in winter) lead away from the noisy interstate into an area of open forest with broken-topped old trees, small pools, and patches of wet meadow. Red-breasted Sapsucker, Winter Wren, Varied Thrush, and Yellow-rumped, Townsend's, MacGillivray's, and Wilson's Warblers may be found here.

HYAK AND GOLD CREEK

Continue along SR-906 for 0.7 mile and turn right onto Hyak Drive E, opposite the Hyak/Gold Creek interchange (I-90 Exit 54). Follow the paved road 0.5 mile through a ski-area parking lot and a residential community to a 90-degree right turn, then a 90-degree left turn in 200 feet. The road follows the fence of the **Hyak sewage lagoons**, on the left—worth a look for ducks (Barrow's Goldeneye in summer), migrating shorebirds, and hordes of swallows. The pavement ends in 0.1 mile at the start of FR-9070, a good gravel road that gives access to the forests and clearcuts of the backcountry. From a trailhead in a switchback on the left 2.6 miles ahead, the easy, though rocky, **Cold Creek Trail 1303** ascends initially through an old clearcut, then into old-growth forest (mostly Western Hemlock and Silver Fir), to the first of the Twin Lakes (0.8 mile, 100 feet elevation gain). In this wilderness setting, look for Barrow's Goldeneye, Spotted Sandpiper, American Dipper, and the usual songbirds associated with wet forest, especially Varied Thrush.

Return to the old highway and cross under I-90 to the other side of the Hyak interchange. In 0.1 mile, where FR-4832 goes right, continue straight ahead a short distance to a creek bridge on a gravel spur. Fox Sparrows may be found in willows and widely spaced small conifers in this vicinity. Go back and take FR-4832 to the left. Look for American Dipper at the creek bridge in 0.4 mile. On the left in another 0.1 mile a track leads down onto gravel flats with willows—another good place for Fox Sparrow. Small trees along FR-4832 for the next 0.2 mile, up to the **Gold Creek** bridge, are often aswarm with Yellow-rumped Warblers, and Barrow's Goldeneyes are sometimes spotted upstream from the bridge. In another 0.1 mile potholed FR-144 turns off to the left. Travel 0.4 mile to the entrance of the Gold Creek picnic area, on the left. A short, paved, interpretive trail leads to several ponds—former gravel borrows used in construction of I-90. Look for Barrow's Goldeneye and other waterfowl, Black and Vaux's Swifts, Willow Flycatcher, Warbling Vireo, Yellow Warbler, and Fox Sparrow (in willow growth on streamside gravel deposits). By scanning the ridgetops you might spy a Mountain Goat.

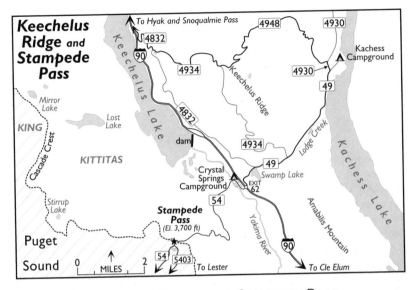

KEECHELUS RIDGE AND STAMPEDE PASS

FR-4832 continues alongside I-90 for another 1.5 miles, where the pavement ends and the road starts to climb **Keechelus Ridge**. By following FR-4832, FR-4934, FR-4948, and FR-4930—good gravel roads—you may drive over the top of the ridge (high point 4,400 feet) and down the other side to Kachess Lake through a landscape of clearcuts and early-successional regrowth with some old forest, meadows, and gorgeous mountain vistas. Birds of these habitats include Olive-sided and Hammond's Flycatchers, Gray Jay, Hermit Thrush, Fox and Lincoln's Sparrows, and the same array of wet-forest species as found at Snoqualmie Pass. FR-49 goes south from Kachess Lake to join I-90 at Exit 62, about 17 miles from the start of the route at the pavement's end on FR-4832.

The road to **Stampede Pass** (FR-54) starts from the south side of I-90 at Exit 62. In 0.2 mile a snag-filled swamp, on both sides of the road, is excellent in summer for Red-breasted Sapsucker, Black and Vaux's Swifts, Willow Flycatcher, Tree Swallow, and MacGillivray's Warbler. Crystal Springs campground, between the Yakima River and the growling freeway another 0.2 mile ahead, has nesting Osprey, Barred Owl, Pileated Woodpecker, American Dipper, and Yellow and Townsend's Warblers. FR-54 and numerous other roads that branch from it give access to mountain forests along the crest, most but not all of them recently logged. Across Stampede Pass (elevation 3,700 feet), FR-54 and FR-5403 drop down the west slope into the basin at the head of the Green River drainage, to the site of the old railroad town of Lester. Birding possibilities are much the same as at Snoqualmie Pass and elsewhere on the Cascade slopes. Be sure to obtain maps with up-to-date road information before attempting to explore these areas; the USFS Cle Elum and North Bend Ranger District maps, and the Green Trails quads for Snoqualmie Pass and Lester, are best.

CLE ELUM AND VICINITY

by Andy Stepniewski and Hal Opperman

Twenty-five miles east of Snoqualmie Pass and a thousand feet lower in elevation, precipitation plummets to roughly 25 percent of that at the crest. Ponderosa Pine and Douglas Maple—both indicators of drier habitats—are increasingly common from Easton to Cle Elum, and the birdlife changes as well. Exploring the Yakima River valley along this stretch, and the Cle Elum River valley from its confluence with the Yakima northward past Cle Elum Lake, allows one to observe a mix of bird species—some characteristic of the Wet Side, several others of the Dry Side, and many that are equally at home in both. Cle Elum, like neighboring Roslyn, became a thriving town after 1884, when Northern Pacific Railroad geologists discovered coal and the company bought up much of the land to mine locomotive fuel. The area has long been popular with weekenders, and a large resort development is underway.

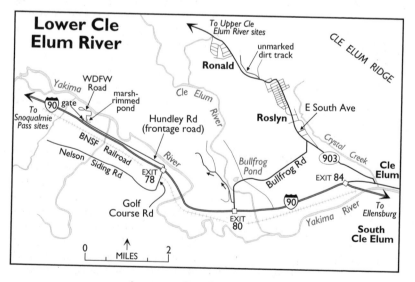

LOWER CLE ELUM RIVER

For a first taste of these Eastside habitats, take I-90 Exit 78, marked *Golf Course Road*. From the north side of the interchange go left (west) onto the frontage road (Hundley Road). After 2.1 miles, note the marsh-rimmed pond below the road on the right. Waterfowl such as Wood and Ring-necked Ducks may be found here, and the willows should have a Yellow Warbler or two. In another 0.1 mile, just before the road ends at a church-camp gate, turn right onto a fishing access road. Continue through more marsh and riparian habitat—birding gets better as you leave the freeway noise behind. The road ends in 0.5 mile at the Yakima River (WDFW permit required). The floodplain gallery forest of mature Black Cottonwoods may have Warbling and Red-eyed Vireos, and Nashville, Yellow, and MacGillivray's Warblers.

Return to I-90 and go east a couple of miles to Exit 80. Head north toward Roslyn on Bullfrog Road. Intermingling of habitats here allows many species of birds to nest in a very small area. Birding is sure to be rewarding in and around the open Ponderosa Pine forests, mixed forests (Douglas-fir and Grand Fir with an understory of Douglas Maple, alders, and willows), brushy thickets, lakes, and marshes—particularly from May through July. However, these lands are at the core of the new Mountainstar Resort development; access to some parts of them will certainly be affected as construction progresses.

In 0.1 mile, take the gravel road going left and up a sidehill into resort property. Go right at the first fork (0.3 mile) then left at the next fork (0.5 mile) to a brushy, semi-open area with Douglas-fir and Douglas Maple growing back after logging (0.3 mile). Currants and other shrubs, and the forest edge, are attractive to an interesting mix of species including Hairy Woodpecker, Calliope and Rufous Hummingbirds, Cassin's and Warbling Vireos, Mountain and Chestnut-backed Chickadees, House Wren, Hermit and Swainson's Thrushes, Nashville, Yellow-rumped, Townsend's, and MacGillivray's Warblers, Western Tanager, Black-headed Grosbeak, Chipping Sparrow, and Cassin's Finch. Black-throated Gray Warbler and Purple Finch—quite locally distributed east of the Cascades—are common here and elsewhere in the Cle Elum River valley in dry habitats at the upper margin of the Ponderosa Pine zone.

Return to Bullfrog Road, turn left, and cross over the Cle Elum River. In 0.4 mile, **Bullfrog Pond** is on the left, behind a guard rail. Pull off on the right 50 yards ahead at a turnoff for a private road, taking care not to obstruct traffic. Walk back and hop over the guard rail. Hooded Merganser, Vaux's Swift, and Common Yellowthroat may be found around the pond, and a small colony of Bushtits was present several years ago at the edges of the marsh. Walk along the old road that goes south through wet woodlands to the river. Look for Warbling and Red-eyed (in the tall Black Cottonwoods) Vireos, Black-capped Chickadee, Veery, and many Yellow Warblers. An American Redstart stayed here one season. North and east from the pond on both sides of Bullfrog Road to its intersection with SR-903 (2.1 miles) are open Ponderosa Pine woods, good for Hairy Woodpecker, Mountain Chickadee, Red-breasted Nuthatch, Western Bluebird, Western Tanager, Chipping Sparrow, and Purple and Cassin's Finches.

Go left (north) on SR-903 to the outskirts of the former coal-mining town of **Rosyln,** which enjoyed a brief revival of its fortunes when the television series "Northern Exposure" was filmed here several years ago. Turn right onto E South Avenue (0.5 mile) and continue one block to a house on a northeast corner with several feeders. All three *Carpodacus* finches (Purple, Cassin's, House) are regular around Roslyn, and these feeders have proven to be a great place to study this sometimes confusing group, along with Red Crossbill, Pine Siskin, American Goldfinch, Evening Grosbeak, and various blackbirds. (If the feeders are not active, drive the residential streets of town searching for ones that are.)

Return to the stop sign at SR-903. Reset to 0.0, turn right, and stay with the highway as it goes through Roslyn, with several turns, and leaves town headed west. At 1.8 miles bear right onto an unmarked dirt track roughly paralleling the highway (do not take the sharper right turn onto the logging road that heads uphill at this same spot).

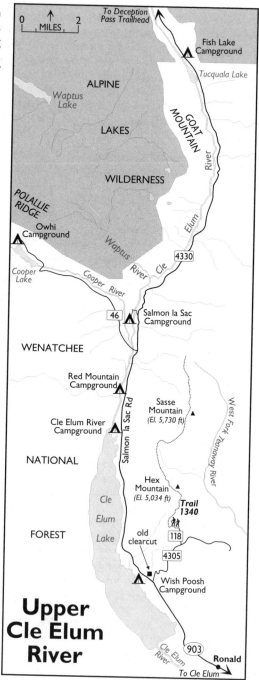

Upper Cle Elum River

Open forest with a brushy understory for the next 0.7 mile should be good for Olive-sided and Dusky Flycatchers, Red-breasted and White-breasted Nuthatches, House Wren, Nashville Warbler, and White-crowned Sparrow. You might find Williamson's Sapsucker, too. Black-throated Gray Warblers haunt a small stream corridor where the road ends.

UPPER CLE ELUM RIVER

Return to SR-903 and turn right. Travel through the town of Ronald and continue north for 5.1 miles (name change to Salmon la Sac Road after entering the Wenatchee National Forest), to an intersection with FR-4305, on the right. This gravel road ascends through clearcuts and second growth to a turnoff (FR-118) on the left in three miles, with a sign for the **Sasse Mountain Trail 1340**, leading to a small parking lot (Northwest Forest Pass required). From there you may hike north 2.6 miles on the high ridgeline between the Cle Elum and Teanaway River drainages to Hex Mountain (elevation 5,034 feet) and another 3.8 miles to Sasse Mountain (elevation 5,730 feet). The rugged trail traverses a pine plantation, recently logged and old-growth forests, grassy hillsides, and bare rock, reaching the subalpine in places—an opportunity to search for birds of higher elevations such as Northern Goshawk, Three-toed Woodpecker, Gray Jay, and Clark's Nutcracker. Unfortunately, the first couple of miles are also open to motorcycle traffic. FR-4305 continues east for about two more miles with good forest birding possibilities (Blue Grouse, Williamson's Sapsucker, Townsend's Solitaire).

On the right side of Salmon la Sac Road 0.2 mile north of the FR-4305 intersection, an unmarked track leads into an old clearcut where Dusky Flycatchers nest. The clearing and its wooded margins, and a small wetland at the back, are also good for hummingbirds, Cassin's Vireo, Spotted Towhee, and Lazuli Bunting. In another 0.1 mile on the left is the entrance to **Wish Poosh Campground** (Northwest Forest Pass or day-use fee required). There is usually a pair of Pileated Woodpeckers in the campground, and the mixed Douglas-fir and Douglas Maple forests around the edges have Black-throated Gray Warbler. Many other birds can be noted on a June or July walk about the marshy terrain toward Cle Elum Lake.

Another 7.9 miles north on Salmon la Sac Road brings you to the **Cooper Lake Road** (FR-46), which immediately crosses the Cle Elum River, on the left. In the afternoon and early evening in summer, the bridge is a good vantage point from which to scan the skies for Black and Vaux's Swifts. Vaux's nest nearby, usually in tall snags among the Black Cottonwoods along the river. Black Swifts evidently breed in the Cle Elum Valley, but to date no nest has been found here or anywhere in the state. Continuing on this road five miles you will come to Owhi Campground, set in moist forest on Cooper Lake, and access to the high-country hiking trails of the Alpine Lakes Wilderness. Though numbers are declining, a few Spotted Owls survive in the managed

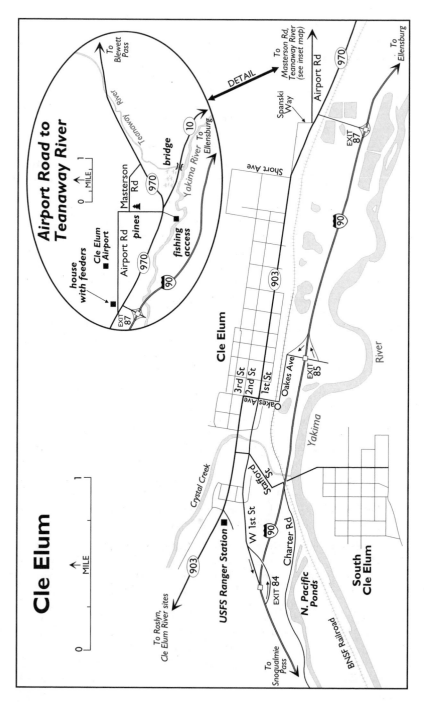

Cle Elum

Airport Road to Teanaway River

forests south of Cooper Lake. This and other old-growth-dependent species are probably more numerous in the lower elevations of the wilderness area to the north.

Back on Salmon la Sac Road and headed upriver, you reach **Salmon la Sac Campground** by turning left at a fork in 1.2 miles and crossing a bridge. Black Swifts forage over the river and campground at treetop level in late afternoon. Trails up Polallie Ridge and the Waptus River valley into the wilderness area leave from here. More good hiking opportunities exist if you take the right branch at the fork onto FR-4330 (unpaved; be prepared for clouds of dust as cars stir up the glacial flour) and travel about ten miles to **Tucquala Lake**. Swifts, swallows, and Common Nighthawks often forage above this shallow lake and marshy meadow. Continue 2.5 miles to the end of the road. From here a gentle trail follows the Cle Elum River about five miles into the Alpine Lakes Wilderness through old-growth forest, then climbs 900 feet in a final mile to join the Pacific Crest Trail at Deception Pass (elevation 4,500 feet). In these lakes, open meadows, and wetter forests you may find most of the same species as lower down the valley, plus Barrow's Goldeneye, Golden Eagle, Gray Jay, Clark's Nutcracker, Winter Wren, Ruby-crowned Kinglet, Varied Thrush, American Pipit, Fox Sparrow, and many Lincoln's Sparrows. Engelmann Spruce is common along the wet bottomlands from Tucquala Meadows up. Dense stands of this tree are attractive to Brown Creeper. In years when spruces are producing a large cone crop, both Red and White-winged Crossbills should be looked for.

AROUND CLE ELUM

Coming from Roslyn on SR-903, the USFS Cle Elum District Ranger Station (509-674-4411) is on the right, 1.5 miles east of the Bullfrog Road corner—a good place to pick up a map and inquire about road and trail conditions. Continue east 0.4 mile to Stafford Street, turn right, cross First Street (0.1 mile), and continue ahead. (If you are coming from the west on I-90, take Exit 84, which enters Cle Elum on First Street; go past the Safeway and turn right onto Stafford at the foot of the hill, following signs for South Cle Elum.) Go 0.4 mile on Stafford to the I-90 underpass, then make an immediate right (west) turn onto Charter Road next to the railroad tracks (one-way traffic regulated by a signal), to the **Northern Pacific Ponds** (0.2 mile). Occupying more than a mile of former streambed cut off when the railroad embankment was built across the floodplain, diverting the Yakima River into a new channel, these ponds have a good fringe of marsh vegetation and sizable cottonwoods. Wood Duck, Hooded Merganser, Osprey, Ruffed Grouse, Virginia Rail, Eastern Kingbird, Tree Swallow, Gray Catbird, and Nashville Warbler all nest here.

Return to First Street, turn right, and drive east through the business district. (Many homes on residential streets north of First Street and parallel to it have feeders and ornamental plantings that attract Bohemian Waxwings and various finches in winter.) In 1.6 miles turn off left, then jog immediately right onto **Airport Road**. In another 0.3 mile, look for a house on the north side (511 Airport Road). A year-round feeding operation here attracts numerous birds—another good spot to study the three finches of the genus *Carpodacus*. Airport Road continues east, then south. At the intersection with Masterson Road (2.4 miles) check the pines to the southeast for Pygmy Nuthatch and Red Crossbill. Continue south on Airport Road 0.8 mile to SR-970. Go straight across the highway into a fishing access at the Yakima River (0.3 mile; WDFW permit required). Here, amidst tall Black Cottonwoods and thick understory vegetation, Warbling and Red-eyed Vireos, many Yellow Warblers, and a selection of other birds characteristic of riparian vegetation may be found.

Return to SR-970 and go right to its junction with SR-10 (0.1 mile). Turn right (east) onto SR-10 and drive one mile to the bridge that crosses the **Teanaway River** just upstream from its confluence with the Yakima River—a popular rafting put-in spot. Look for American Dipper nesting under the bridge, Red-naped Sapsucker, Western Wood-Pewee, Red-eyed Vireo, Veery, Gray Catbird, Nashville and Yellow Warblers, and Western Tanager. Wood Duck, Cinnamon Teal, Hooded Merganser, and Common Yellowthroat are regular on the small pond and marsh just west of the bridge on the north side of the highway. Scenic SR-10 continues on, following the canyon along the Yakima River toward Ellensburg and Kittitas Valley birding sites (page 285).

TEANAWAY RIVER AND SWAUK CREEK

by Andy Stepniewski and Hal Opperman

The Blewett Pass Highway (US-97 from Ellensburg, joined by SR-970 from Cle Elum) provides easy access to the basins of two streams draining the south slope of the Wenatchee Mountains. Sasse Ridge divides the Cle Elum River drainage, to the west, from the Teanaway Basin. The Swauk Basin is the next one east, across Teanaway Ridge; Table Mountain separates it from the Naneum Basin still farther east. Lower elevations have birds of dry Ponderosa Pine forests and riparian habitats. Mixed-conifer forests in the middle elevations are known for their owls. Although logging has been widespread, enough old-growth forest remains to support small populations of Spotted Owl and Northern Goshawk. Fall hawkwatching can be good on some of the higher ridges. Upper elevations have birds of subalpine forests and mountain meadows.

TEANAWAY RIVER BASIN

About seven miles east of Cle Elum, Teanaway Road turns off to the northwest from SR-970, midway between its junctions with SR-10 and US-97. For the next seven miles, up to the intersection where it splits into West Fork Road (left) and North Fork Road (straight ahead), Teanaway Road goes through farmlands in the broad **Teanaway River valley**, flanked by areas of riparian growth and Ponderosa Pine forest. Although this is mostly private land, there are places along the way to pull off the road to bird. In spring and summer look for Turkey Vulture, Osprey (nests along the river), Wilson's Snipe, Common Nighthawk, Vaux's Swift, Eastern Kingbird, swallows, Western and Mountain Bluebirds, Yellow and MacGillivray's Warblers, Savannah and Song Sparrows, Red-winged and Brewer's Blackbirds, Western Meadowlark, and Brown-headed Cowbird around buildings, open fields, brushy fencerows, and ditches and other wet spots. Red-tailed and Rough-legged Hawks hunt the area in fall and winter.

Access to forest and riparian vegetation is better along **West Fork Road**. Go west 0.6 mile and park near the intersection where Middle Fork Road turns off to the right. Bird on foot for half a mile north along Middle Fork Road, then half a mile west along West Fork Road to a gate on the left. You may walk through this gate, cross a bridge over the West Fork Teanaway, and follow a small creek up Carlson Canyon on the north slope of Cle Elum Ridge. Also check the Ponderosa Pines in the campground along the south side of West Fork Road as you walk back to your car. In an hour's birding of this sampler of habitats you may find Ruffed Grouse, Calliope and Rufous Hummingbirds, Red-naped Sapsucker, Hairy and Pileated Woodpeckers, Western Wood-Pewee, Dusky Flycatcher, Cassin's and Warbling Vireos, Black-capped and Mountain Chickadees, Red-breasted Nuthatch, Brown Creeper, House Wren, Golden-crowned Kinglet, Townsend's Solitaire, Veery, Swainson's and Hermit Thrushes, Cedar Waxwing, Nashville Warbler, Western Tanager, Spotted Towhee, Chipping Sparrow, Dark-eyed Junco, Black-headed Grosbeak, Purple and Cassin's Finches, Red Crossbill, Pine Siskin, and Evening Grosbeak.

As you continue north on **North Fork Road** the surrounding forests, especially where unlogged, are home to Spotted Owls. Their populations continue to decline, so nest locations are not disclosed. One good possibility is FR-9738, which branches off to the right in 5.5 miles and runs east up **Jack Creek**, flanked by extensive tracts of old-growth forest. Northern Goshawks are seen fairly regularly along this route. A prime area for Flammulated Owls is at 4.5 miles up FR-9738 on a sidehill to your left where Douglas-fir, Ponderosa Pine, and Deerbrush as a groundcover provide suitable habitat. For the next four miles you pass through mature forest; stopping at night at half-mile intervals might prove a successful strategy for locating Spotted Owls. After crossing Teanaway Ridge, FR-9738 descends the Blue Creek drainage, reaching US-97 in about 15 miles from North Fork Road.

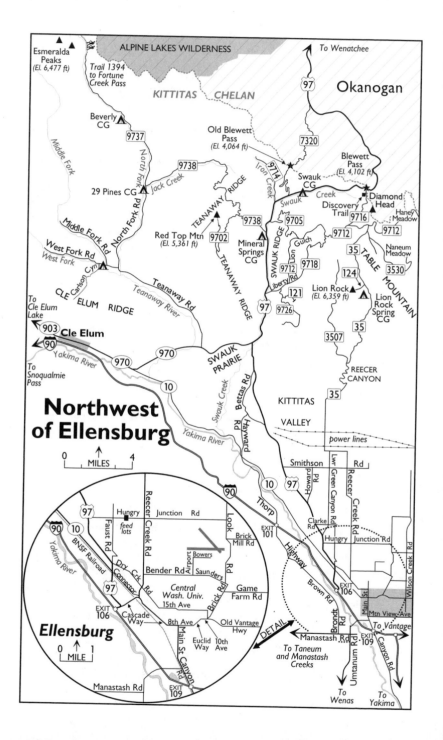

ALPINE LAKES WILDERNESS

Esmeralda
Peaks
(El. 6,477 ft)

Trail 1394
to Fortune
Creek Pass

KITTITAS   CHELAN

To Wenatchee

97

Okanogan

Beverly
CG   9737

Middle Fork

North Fork Rd

9738

Jack Creek

29 Pines CG

Old Blewett
Pass
(El. 4,064 ft)

7320

Iron Creek

9714

Blewett
Pass
(El. 4,102 ft)

Swauk
CG

Swauk Creek

Discovery
Trail   9716

Diamond
Head

Haney
Meadow

9712

Middle Fork Rd

West Fork Rd

West Fork

Carlson Cyn

Red Top Mtn
(El. 5,361 ft)   9702

TEANAWAY RIDGE

9738

9705

Mineral
Springs
CG

SWAUK RIDGE

Lion Gulch

9712

Liberty Rd

9718

35

TABLE MOUNTAIN

124

Naneum
Meadow

3530

CLE   ELUM   RIDGE

Teanaway Rd

Teanaway River

TEANAWAY RIDGE

97

121

9726

Lion Rock
(El. 6,359 ft)

Lion
Rock
Spring
CG

35

To
Cle Elum
Lake

903   Cle Elum

90

Yakima River

970   970

SWAUK
PRAIRIE

3507

3507

REECER
CANYON

To
Snoqualmie
Pass

10

Swauk Creek

Bettas Rd

KITTITAS

VALLEY

35

Northwest
of Ellensburg

0   4
MILES

Hayward Rd

Yakima River

power lines

Smithson   Rd

Howard Rd

Lwr Green Canyon Rd

Reecer Creek Rd

10   97

Thorp

90

97   Hungry
feed
lots

Junction   Rd

10

BNSF Railroad

Faust Rd

Reecer Creek Rd

Dry Crk Connector Rd

Look Rd

Brick
Mill Rd

EXIT
101

Bowers
Airport

Bender Rd   Saunders

Central
Wash. Univ.
15th Ave

Brick Rd

Game
Farm Rd

Clarke
Rd

Hungry   Junction Rd

Highway

Brown Rd

EXIT
106

Yakima River

97

EXIT
106

Cascade
Way   8th Ave

Old Vantage
Hwy

Brndt Rd

Main St

Mtn View Ave

Wilson Creek Rd

To Vantage

Ellensburg

0   1
MILE

Manastash Rd

Main St Canyon Rd

EXIT
109

Euclid
Way   10th
Ave

DETAIL

Manastash Rd

Umtanum Rd

EXIT
109

Canyon Rd

To Taneum
and Manastash
Creeks

To
Wenas

To
Yakima

North from the intersection with FR-9738, North Fork Road becomes FR-9737. There are several branches; be sure you stay on FR-9737. It is about 10 miles to the end of the road at the trailhead (elevation 4,200 feet) for **Esmeralda Basin Trail 1394**. This popular trail traverses forest, subalpine meadows, and the rugged high country of the Wenatchee Mountains—famous for its July wildflowers. Most of the birds can be seen in the first two miles in the lower, lusher part of the basin. An additional 1.5 miles on a rockier tread brings one to Fortune Creek Pass (elevation 6,000 feet), and views to the west of glacier-mantled Mounts Daniel and Hinman at the Cascade crest. Birds that might be seen along this trail include Rufous Hummingbird (warring over the prime patches of Scarlet Gilia in the drier meadows), Hairy Woodpecker, Hammond's Flycatcher, Warbling Vireo, Gray Jay, Clark's Nutcracker, Mountain and Chestnut-backed Chickadees, Winter Wren, American Dipper, Golden-crowned and Ruby-crowned Kinglets, Townsend's Solitaire, Hermit and Varied Thrushes, Yellow-rumped and Townsend's Warblers, Western Tanager, Chipping, Fox, and Lincoln's Sparrows, Dark-eyed Junco, Red Crossbill, and Cassin's Finch. Pikas and Hoary Marmots are frequently encountered mammals.

SWAUK CREEK BASIN

Although fragmentation resulting from logging has affected some species, this forested basin retains its well-deserved reputation for owls— Flammulated, Great Horned, Northern Pygmy-, Spotted, Barred, and Northern Saw-whet. March through early May is best, as calling by most species diminishes later in the season. Other bird species of mountain forests may be found here as well, including Northern Goshawk and Williamson's Sapsucker.

To reach one good owling spot, go north three miles on US-97 from the SR-970 intersection. Turn right (east) onto Liberty Road (FR-9718), then right again in 0.7 mile onto FR-9726. Keep on the main road 0.8 mile to **Pine Gulch Road** (FR-121). Go left here for another 0.7 mile to a sharp bend where the road is blocked. The mature Grand Fir forest in this area has historically been good for Spotted and Northern Saw-whet Owls, although there is evidence that Barred Owl is moving in and replacing its threatened relative.

For another owling route, go back to Liberty Road (FR-9718) and turn right. In 0.7 mile, keep left onto FR-9712 as it goes up **Lion Gulch**. In three miles, keep left onto FR-9705. Beginning in one mile and thereafter for another mile, listen for Flammulated Owls as this road switchbacks up a south-facing slope grown to Ponderosa Pine and Douglas-fir. Another suitable spot for this species is at about three miles from FR-9712. Then the road begins a descent into north-facing ravines with moister forest—habitat for Spotted and Northern Saw-whet Owls—and rejoins US-97 in about 2.5 miles.

Just north of Mineral Springs Campground on US-97 (3.6 miles north of Liberty Road and 0.8 mile south of FR-9705), FR-9738 turns off and follows Blue Creek to the west. At a fork in 2.6 miles, keep left onto FR-9702 (staying right with FR-9738 brings you to the North Fork Teanaway Road in about 12 miles). FR-9702 ends at a small parking lot in 4.7 miles. Take the graded, but steep, half-mile trail to the lookout tower on **Red Top Mountain** (elevation 5,361 feet). Hawkwatching can be good here from mid-August through October, especially on clear days with winds from the north or east. Sharp-shinned, Cooper's, and Red-tailed Hawks are the most common species. Less common, but still regular, are Northern Goshawk, both eagles, Rough-legged Hawk (late fall), American Kestrel, and Merlin. You may also see small parties of Turkey Vultures. There is an extensive agate bed for rockhounds half a mile farther north along the ridge. If you hit the wrong conditions for raptors, the view from Red Top northwest to the granitic ramparts of the Enchantments may be compensation enough.

Continue north on US-97 and in 2.9 miles turn left onto FR-7320, a tortuous section of highway across the Wenatchee Mountains that was decommissioned when US-97 was rerouted. The open, forested slopes and meadows up to and around **Old Blewett Pass** (4.0 miles; elevation 4,064 feet) are known for owls (particularly Flammulated and Northern Saw-whet), Common Poorwill, Williamson's Sapsucker, and Red Crossbill. Many Mule Deer inhabit this area, attractive to Mountain Lions. You would be having extraordinary luck to spot this elusive cat, but Black Bears are seen occasionally.

Half a mile north on US-97 from the FR-7320 turnoff, **Swauk Campground** is in a birdy area with riparian, forested, and meadow habitats all close by. Look for Hammond's Flycatcher, Swainson's and Hermit Thrushes, Nashville, Townsend's, and MacGillivray's Warblers, Pine Siskins, and wandering flocks of Evening Grosbeaks.

Climb 4.1 miles on US-97 to **Blewett Pass** (elevation 4,102 feet; called Swauk Pass on older maps), gateway to birding routes in the Okanogan (page 410). From here, in summer, one can take FR-9716 south 0.5 mile to the **Discovery Trail**, a graded, 2.7-mile interpretive loop through forest habitats in varying states of regeneration after logging. A good selection of montane forest birds should be encountered, including Rufous Hummingbird, Hairy Woodpecker, Olive-sided and Hammond's Flycatchers, Warbling Vireo, Gray Jay, Mountain Chickadee, Red-breasted Nuthatch, Golden-crowned Kinglet, Townsend's Solitaire, Hermit and Varied Thrushes, Yellow-rumped and Townsend's Warblers, Western Tanager, Cassin's Finch, and Evening Grosbeak. Wildflowers are an added bonus. You can shave a mile off by bearing left just after marker 16. However, going the extra mile will reward you with the best views and the largest and oldest trees.

TABLE MOUNTAIN

Continue on FR-9716 for 3.2 miles and turn left onto FR-9712, which follows a valley between the talus-strewn slopes of Diamond Head to the north and Table Mountain to the south. Large, spring-green Western Larches (golden in fall) cling to the steep slopes. In 1.6 miles, at the junction with FR-35, keep straight on FR-9712. As the road climbs, subalpine tree species such as Subalpine Fir, Lodgepole Pine, and Engelmann Spruce become common. **Haney Meadow** is reached in 3.2 miles at about 5,500 feet elevation. Look for Williamson's Sapsucker wherever there are larches, and Black-backed Woodpecker in dense Lodgepole Pine stands. Boreal Owl has been noted in this general area; the best time to look for this reclusive species is September and October, but its status is not fully known. Beyond Haney Meadow, those equipped with four-wheel drive and so inclined can continue on FR-9712 along the ridgeline of the Wenatchee Mountains and down the other side, reaching Wenatchee in about 20 miles. Reasonable persons may prefer to retreat to better roads, however.

Return to the FR-35 junction, turn left, and in 0.1 mile make another left onto FR-3530. In 1.8 miles you reach an overlook of lush, subalpine **Naneum Meadows**, rimmed by Subalpine Firs. Take time to wander. Great Gray and Boreal Owls have been noted here in fall, and Gray Jay, Ruby-crowned Kinglet, and Hermit Thrush are common. One can continue another four miles on FR-3530 to its end at the Howard Creek Trail. En route, a picturesque, lichen-encrusted basalt cliff forms a backdrop to a small grove of willows thick with Warbling Vireos.

Back at FR-35, turn right and make your way back to US-97 at Blewett Pass. Alternatively, turn left onto FR-35 for a memorable drive across Table Mountain to Ellensburg. The roadbed is rough for the first four miles, to a four-way junction. Here the even rougher FR-124 turns off right to **Lion Rock** (0.8 mile; elevation 6,359 feet) on the west side of Table Mountain —another fall hawkwatching site, similar to Red Top Mountain. Continue south on FR-35. In 2.1 miles, the road (now paved) begins a spectacular, seven-mile descent to the Kittitas Valley, with numerous switchbacks and expansive views. The subalpine forest is soon left behind, replaced briefly with a mixed-conifer association, then Ponderosa Pines (fine wildflower show in late spring and early summer), and eventually riparian habitat along Reecer Creek Road (page 286).

If you are traveling from Blewett Pass to Ellensburg via US-97—the conventional route—a slight variant enlarges the birding possibilities. Turn right from US-97 onto **Bettas Road** 1.7 miles south of the SR-970 intersection. Western and Mountain Bluebirds are often numerous around these ranchlands. In 2.7 miles, turn right onto graveled **Hayward Road** (not plowed in winter), which crosses shrub-steppe habitat. More than 280 species of plants are reported from this hill, making it a favorite of botanists. Vesper Sparrows inhabit the grassier parts. As you top a broad hump, stop to enjoy the panorama. To the west are the lower east slopes of the Cascades—the lower margin of the Ponderosa Pine zone is especially apparent. Below, the meandering Yakima River exits from a deep gorge. To the east is the wide Kittitas Valley, bordered on the south by Manastash Ridge with the higher Umtanum Ridge behind it. Raptors soar overhead, taking advantage of the winds that regularly sweep the valley. In 2.8 miles from Bettas Road you reach SR-10 where you may turn east to Ellensburg or west to Cle Elum. Crossing SR-10 and continuing straight ahead onto N Thorp Highway will take you across the Yakima River and through the town of Thorp to I-90 Exit 101 in about five miles, with roadside wetland and riparian birding possibilities along the way.

KITTITAS VALLEY

by Andy Stepniewski and Hal Opperman

Ellensburg is an agricultural and college town in the midst of the Kittitas Valley. (There is no Kittitas River—origins of this Indian name are obscure.) Irrigated farmlands here grow high-quality Timothy hay of worldwide renown. Raptors, including owls, are beneficiaries of hay farming, as these fields support high rodent populations. In addition to the many raptors, Gray Partridge (year round) and Bohemian Waxwing (winter) are major draws for birders. The partridges are rather common in fields and grasslands, although they can be maddeningly difficult to find. The waxwings are usually found at apple and ornamental trees with persistent fruit, or flying from one to the next in large, starling-like flocks, in town as well as around farms. However, their numbers seem to have declined in recent years.

The Kittitas Valley is a notable wintering raptor area. Red-tailed Hawk is the most common species, with usually at least one Harlan's in the local contingent. Northern Harrier, Rough-legged Hawk, and American Kestrel can also be numerous, as can Short-eared Owl some winters. Great Horned Owls roost in willow thickets, sometimes right along the road. Prairie Falcons hunt the fields and shrub-steppe edges. Merlins can be spotted perched atop tall conifers either in town or about farmhouses. Golden Eagles sometimes descend to the valley from the surrounding canyons where they nest, especially when snow cover is heavy. Bald Eagles are opportunists. There are usually a few along the Yakima River all winter, but look for them especially in the late winter and spring calving season when they are attracted to afterbirth and perhaps stillborn calves.

Check livestock ponds for Wilson's Phalarope and Cinnamon Teal in spring and summer, and other waterfowl and shorebirds in migration. Barn Owls are common year round, although you may miss them unless you search the fields at night; in winter they roost in hay sheds. Northern Harriers, Long-billed Curlews, and Short-eared Owls attempt to nest each year in hay fields and grasslands, and some succeed, despite predation and adverse harvest schedules. A few pairs of Swainson's Hawks nest, at the western edge of their Washington range, in the intensively farmed area east of I-82 and south of I-90.

ELLENSBURG

To bird Ellensburg, take Exit 109 from I-90 and proceed north on Canyon Road to the first pull-in on the right. (See inset map on page 280.) A large pond behind the Bar 14 Restaurant is attractive to waterfowl in spring and fall, and usually has a hundred or more Canada Geese, ducks of several species, the occasional swan in winter (Trumpeter and Tundra both possible), and sometimes Sandhill Cranes in migration. Continue north (becomes Main Street) about a mile and a half to the Ellensburg business district. From December through February, Bohemian Waxwings can sometimes be found in the ornamental plantings in the older, residential part of town that begins a few blocks east, generally between First and Eighth Avenues and east of Chestnut (eight blocks east of Main). Continue north on Main to Eighth Avenue (almost two miles north of I-90) and turn right. Follow this arterial eastward past the Central Washington University campus (becomes Euclid Way, then 10th Avenue) to Brick Road (0.9 mile), and go left on Brick to a 90-degree left turn (1.2 miles) in an area with mature ornamental plantings. This neighborhood hosted Washington's first recorded Yellow-bellied Sapsucker and has had Blue Jay, Bohemian Waxwing, and Common Redpoll (all in winter). Bird from the road, or ask for permission to enter yards (usually granted). From this corner proceed another 0.1 mile to Look Road. Turn right (north), checking open fields for raptors. In less than a mile the east end of the airport is on your left. Weedy fields in this vicinity have been fairly reliable for Gray Partridge and Short-eared Owl (winter). Both are easiest to locate at dawn or dusk. At these times of day the partridge utters a scratchy call, betraying its presence. Please do not trespass.

NORTHWEST KITTITAS VALLEY

The valley north and west of Ellensburg has a number of farm and riparian sites that host interesting species. Continue north on Look Road to Hungry Junction Road (1.8 miles from the start of Look Road). Check the stock pond east of the intersection for waterfowl and migrating shorebirds, then turn left onto **Hungry Junction Road**, which runs west to an intersection with US-97. Its entire 4.2-mile length is worth birding. The airport is on the south for over a mile—an excellent place for Gray Partridge and for wintering raptors. Look for Short-eared Owls in the late afternoon. In another mile or so the intersection with Reecer Creek Road is a possible spot for Gray Partridge. They have even been seen in the yard of the house on the southwest corner, along with California Quail. West of this intersection, spilled grain at a big livestock-feeding operation attracts both of these chickens, especially when snow cover limits foraging opportunities in the farmlands. Blackbirds abound in the feedlots. At the next corner (one mile from Reecer Creek Road), turn left onto Faust Road and look for partridges in the fields, down to the house where the road bends left. Turn around and go back north on Faust across

Hungry Junction Road for another mile, to the junction with Clarke Road. This has also been a good partridge area, including the dead-end stub of Clarke to the right. Go west on Clarke for 0.5 mile and turn right onto Lower Green Canyon Road. The fields to the west for the next two or three miles north from here have had nesting Long-billed Curlews. They can be a ways out but if you hear one you can usually track it down.

Three miles north of Clarke Road is Smithson Road. Short-eared Owls have nested, and sometimes winter, in fields on the north side of Smithson, a mile east and a mile west from this corner (between Howard and Reecer Creek Roads). A mile north of Smithson, turn left onto **Reecer Creek Road**, which bends north again in 0.5 mile, leaving the Kittitas Valley bottom and passing under two sets of power lines in the next mile. Wilson's Snipe winnow above the wet fields east of the road in spring, and Long-billed Curlews are sometimes present. After passing a couple of ponds on the right (scope them from the road) and a ranchette development, the road narrows to a single, paved lane (FR-35), bends toward the northeast, and enters the small canyon of Reecer Creek. For about two miles until it hits the hill, switches back, and starts to ascend steeply, the road follows the creek in an area of brush, grassy slopes, and small deciduous trees that can be fantastically birdy. Expect Veery, Nashville Warbler, and Lazuli Bunting in the riparian zone; Cassin's Vireo and Western Tanager in the conifers at the head of the canyon; and Common Poorwill at night. Bohemian Waxwings have been seen here in fall, feeding on the fruits of various berry-producing shrubs and trees (wild rose, Bitter Cherry, Common Chokecherry, Black Hawthorn, Red-osier Dogwood)—a natural habitat that birders now seldom search for this winter visitor. By continuing north up Table Mountain on FR-35 you can reach Lion Rock, Liberty, and Blewett Pass (pages 282–283).

NORTHEAST KITTITAS VALLEY

East of the Ellensburg airport, Brick Mill Road meets Look Road (1.3 miles north of the start of Look Road and 0.5 mile south of the Hungry Junction intersection). Turn east here to bird the northeast part of the valley. Except in summer, raptors should be in evidence in the numerous fields. Gray Partridge is possible, too. In 5.1 miles, No. 81 Road turns off to the right and runs south 3.0 miles through similar habitat to the Old Vantage Highway. Go left (east) here to reach Vantage and the Columbia River (page 289).

A series of canyons coming down into the valley from Naneum Ridge—the eastern extremity of the Wenatchee Mountains—can be reached by driving north a few miles from Brick Mill Road on Naneum Road (to Naneum Canyon, gated at its mouth but you may walk or bike in), Fairview Road (to Schnebly Canyon), Cooke Canyon Road (to Coleman and Cooke Canyons), and finally Colockum Road, the old stage road to Wenatchee. After

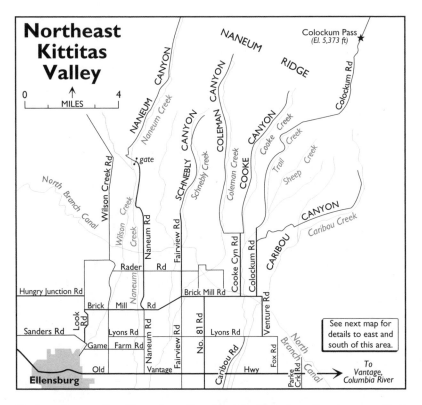

Caribou Canyon Road branches off to the right, Colockum Road runs up Trail Creek and over 5,373-foot Colockum Pass. Any of these canyons offers fine birding of the shrub-steppe/Ponderosa Pine ecotone, and for the adventurous, a transect of other forest habitats as one moves up, reaching the Subalpine Fir zone in several places. Once they leave farm and ranch country these roads are minimally maintained and recommended only for high-clearance vehicles. Areas above 5,000 feet may be snowed in until July.

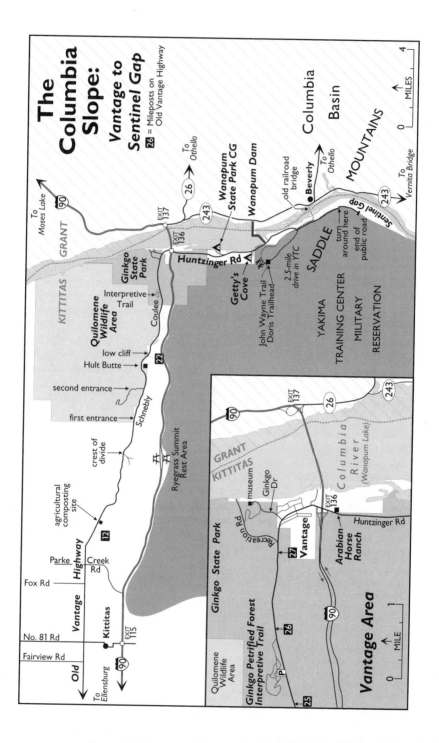

The
Columbia
Slope: *Vantage to Sentinel Gap*

26 = Mileposts on Old Vantage Highway

To Othello

Wanapum State Park CG
Wanapum Dam

old railroad bridge

To Othello

Beverly

To Vernita Bridge

243

Columbia

Basin

MOUNTAINS

Sentinel Gap

243

0   MILES   4

To
Moses Lake

90

GRANT

EXIT 137

EXIT 136

243

Huntzinger Rd

KITTITAS

Ginkgo State Park

Interpretive Trail

Coulee

Quilomene Wildlife Area

low cliff

Hult Butte

second entrance

first entrance

crest of divide

agricultural composting site

12

Parke Creek Rd

Fox Rd

Vantage Highway

Old Vantage Highway

No. 81 Rd

Fairview Rd

Kittitas

EXIT 115

90

To Ellensburg

22

Schnebly

Ryegrass Summit Rest Area

Getty's Cove

John Wayne Trail
Doris Trailhead

2.5-mile drive in YTC

SADDLE

turn around here
end of public road

YAKIMA
TRAINING CENTER
MILITARY
RESERVATION

Vantage Area

GRANT
KITTITAS

EXIT 137

26

243

90

Columbia
River
(Wanapum Lake)

museum
Ginkgo Dr

Recreation Rd

Vantage
27

EXIT 136

Huntzinger Rd

Arabian
Horse
Ranch

90

Ginkgo State Park

26

Ginkgo Petrified Forest
Interpretive Trail

Quilomene
Wildlife
Area

P

25

0   MILE

THE COLUMBIA SLOPE:
VANTAGE TO SENTINEL GAP

by Andy Stepniewski

A scenic, lightly traveled, 28-mile alternate road from Ellensburg to the Columbia River is the former US-10, demoted since the completion of I-90 and now known simply as the Old Vantage Highway. This popular birding route offers the fastest access from Seattle or Tacoma to good-quality shrub-steppe habitats.

OLD VANTAGE HIGHWAY

Go east on Eighth Avenue from the corner of Main Street at the north end of the Ellensburg business district. Stay on this main road as it heads out of town into extensive areas of farmland in the eastern Kittitas Valley. Note the intersection with No. 81 Road (6.5 miles; a right turn here will take you through the town of Kittitas to I-90 Exit 115, the last interchange before the Columbia River). The old highway continues east through irrigated fields, the easternmost of which may have a few Long-billed Curlews in spring. In 5.5 miles, at milepost 12, the road reaches the first hills and enters unfarmed shrub-steppe habitat. An agricultural composting site on the right in 0.6 mile offers an opportunity to observe Horned Larks, swallows, and sparrows, especially in late summer and fall. In spring and summer, look for Loggerhead Shrike and Mountain Bluebird as the winding highway continues to climb for 4.1 miles to a divide (turnoff on the right to radio towers and disposal facility).

Here begins a gradual descent along **Schnebly Coulee** toward the Columbia River through some of the most arid, desert-like terrain in Washington. In 1.8 miles, pull off to the left at a sign for the **Quilomene Wildlife Area**. In spring this is a great spot for Sage Thrasher. A rough road leads away into a vast expanse of largely wild country with some cattle grazing and dryland wheat farming, stretching north for 22 miles and east eight miles to the sheer basalt cliffs of the Columbia. Most of this land—some 134,000 acres—lies within three state wildlife areas (Colockum, Quilomene, and Schaake or Whiskey Dick), which may also be accessed off the Colockum Road. Birding is excellent in varied habitats of rimrock, shrub-steppe, riparian vegetation along several creeks, and Ponderosa Pine at the upper edge. *Motorists should not attempt to enter this country except in a high-clearance, four-wheel-drive vehicle, and fully equipped for wilderness travel.*

Another entrance to the wildlife area is 1.7 miles farther east. Just inside is a dense stand of Bitterbrush and Big Sagebrush with deep Bluebunch Wheatgrass, prime habitat for Sage Thrasher and Brewer's and Sage Sparrows. In April and May the wildflower display can be quite beautiful. Winds are frequently fierce.

The highway soon begins a sweeping curve to the left, dropping down and swinging back to the east around the north base of **Hult Butte** through excellent Sage Sparrow habitat. In 1.9 miles, at milepost 22, Schnebly Coulee narrows and starts to descend more steeply. Stop on the right in 0.2 mile at a low cliff with lichen- and moss-encrusted basalt columns. A Great Horned Owl may be sleeping in a cleft. From here on down the coulee, other birds to look for include Say's Phoebe, Rock Wren, and Sage Sparrow. Brush patches in the moister spots harbor other songbirds, especially in migration. Chukars may be seen or heard along the rimrock in early morning and near sunset.

Driving on downvalley, note the **Ginkgo Petrified Forest Interpretive Trail** entrance at 3.3 miles. The walk among the petrified logs is worth the effort. As a bonus, you might find a few flycatchers and songbirds in spring and fall in the small collection of trees at the parking lot, which constitutes a micro migrant-trap. On the road again, turn left in 2.0 miles onto Ginkgo Drive and proceed to the **Ginkgo Petrified Forest State Park Interpretive Museum** (0.4 mile). During winter closure (Monday noon–Friday noon) you may park outside the gate and walk the short distance in. There is a commanding overlook of the Columbia River (actually a reservoir here, Wanapum Lake) from which waterbirds far below can be scoped. Common Loon, Western Grebe, and Greater Scaup are frequent in winter. In spring and early summer White-throated Swifts zoom by, and Say's Phoebes sometimes nest under the eaves of the building. Isolated trees in the irrigated lawn attract many migrants; you might be lucky and find something unusual.

The I-90 interchange (Exit 136) is a half-mile south of the state park entrance road through the small business district of Vantage.

HUNTZINGER ROAD

The I-90 interchange in Vantage is at the west end of the Columbia River bridge, in a basalt gorge with layer upon layer of solidified lava exposed. Winds often howl in the Vantage area; morning hours are usually calmer, and best for birding. Go south from the interchange onto Huntzinger Road, which follows the river through several excellent sites for birds of the arid shrub-steppe and rocky cliffs. In 0.2 mile, turn in left to the Arabian Horse Ranch and inquire at the home for permission and directions to bird the dense willow and poplar groves along the river a few hundred yards to the east. During migration you will likely get to study gobs of Yellow-rumped Warblers (mostly Audubon's) and many other species. A few rare warblers such as Magnolia and Blackpoll have been found here, especially in late August and early September.

Continue south on Huntzinger Road and turn left into the **Wanapum State Park Campground** (2.5 miles). This irrigated grove of introduced trees is an oasis in the surrounding arid landscape. Spring and fall migration can be productive. Large flocks of wintering songbirds, including Bohemian Waxwings, sometimes congregate in brushy growth along the river on sunny late-winter days. A small colony of Bank Swallows nests in a sandy bank south of the boat launch. In summer the campground is crowded and noisy, especially on weekends and during the Gorge Amphitheatre concert season. At such times try to visit early in the morning.

Huntzinger Road is one of the best in the state for Chukars. Listen for their raucous *rucka rucka rucka* calls, and keep an eye open for them along the roadside or standing motionless on the rimrock. Chukars are most active in early morning. Large winter flocks sometimes forage in sagebrush around the campground, clucking softly.

Once again driving south, stop along the road, on the right, by a gate in a rocky bowl with sparse shrub-steppe vegetation (0.7 mile). This spot has been reliable for Black-throated Sparrows some years (late May through early July). Listen for their simple song coming from the slopes above, less complex and much shorter than that of the Lark Sparrow, the common nesting sparrow in this area.

Farther south on Huntzinger Road is **Getty's Cove**, a private campground (0.7 mile). The impoundment on the right side of the road is worth checking for waterfowl (look closely for Eurasian Wigeon). The road runs right beside Wanapum Lake here, and a scan of the lake from fall through spring might yield Common Loon, Horned and Western Grebes, Greater Scaup, and Common Goldeneye. This is a good spot in October or November for Surf and White-winged Scoters, both rare species in Washington away from the saltwater coast. The west end of **Wanapum Dam** (parking) is in 0.8 mile. Continue another 0.1 mile and turn left below the dam onto a rocky track that leads to the Columbia—a good place from which to scope for waterbirds in winter.

In 0.7 mile, Huntzinger Road goes through a rock cut and crosses a short fill; pull off on the right at either end of the embankment to look for Say's Phoebe and Rock Wren. Set up a scope to inspect the gravel islands in the Columbia, especially in the summer months, for American White Pelican, Double-crested Cormorant, gulls (mostly Ring-billed and California, in fall and winter also Herring and Glaucous-winged), and Caspian and Forster's Terns. In winter, keep an eye out for flocks of Gray-crowned Rosy-Finches along the cliffs. Another good pullout is on the left in 0.3 mile, just before a cattle guard.

The road takes a sharp right in 0.5 mile, crosses the John Wayne Pioneer Trail (the former Milwaukee Road railway corridor, now a state park), then bends back to the left. An entrance to the Yakima Training Center is on the right in 0.1 mile. You may drive in for 2.5 miles without first obtaining a visitor pass from the military police. The wide, graded gravel road passes through arid shrub-steppe vegetation—excellent for Common Poorwill in the first and last hours of darkness.

South from the training center entrance Huntzinger Road crosses more desert-like habitat, approaching the base of the towering cliffs where the Columbia cuts through the Saddle Mountains at **Sentinel Gap**. The gently sloping terrain below the talus slopes typically has a few Black-throated Sparrows in years when this species makes an appearance in Washington. Look for them along the road for the next 1.0 mile, up to the west end of the old railroad bridge where a large apple orchard begins. Continue driving beside the orchard, stopping at pullouts on the left. Cliffs and talus on the right provide habitat for Prairie Falcon, Chukar, Rock Dove, White-throated Swift, Say's Phoebe, Rock and Canyon Wrens, and Lark Sparrow. In some years Golden Eagles nest high on the cliffs. The road jogs left in 1.0 mile and crosses an old railroad grade (Yakima Training Center entrance on the right). This is a good place to turn around; the county road leaves the cliffs here to end in1.2 miles at the orchard office.

Retrace your route to Vantage. Take I-90 eastbound to birding sites of the Columbia Basin (page 351). If you are traveling the interstate between here and Ellensburg, stop at the **Ryegrass Summit** rest area at the top of the ten-mile grade west of Vantage. In spring and early summer this is a good spot for Sage Thrasher and Brewer's Sparrow.

TANEUM CREEK AND MANASTASH CREEK

by Hal Opperman and Andy Stepniewski

S outhwest of the Kittitas Valley, the east slopes of the Cascades are dissected by ravines and canyons with innumerable variations in slope and aspect, creating niches for a wide array of breeding species. The best time to visit is from late May through July; winter snow closes most of the higher elevations. A fine loop through this area goes up Taneum Creek, then south over Taneum Ridge to Buck Meadows, and back out to the east following South Fork Manastash Creek. Coming from the west, take I-90 Exit 93 (Elk Heights). Turn left across the interstate, then right at the next stop sign onto Thorp Prairie Road. At a stop sign in 3.5 miles, turn right onto the I-90 overpass to a junction (0.2 mile), then right onto W Taneum Road. Exit 101 (Thorp) is your access if coming from the east. Go left (south) across the interstate, and in 0.6 mile turn right onto Thorp Cemetery Road, which will take you in 4.8 miles to the foot of the I-90 overpass; continue straight ahead here onto W Taneum Road. No gas or services are available along this loop.

TANEUM CREEK

The valley quickly narrows, as South Cle Elum Ridge rises up on the right and Taneum Ridge closes in from the left. Pull off at a small rock quarry on the right in 1.3 miles, across from a mailbox numbered 6680. Calliope Hummingbird, Vesper Sparrow, and Lazuli Bunting inhabit the brushy, grassy slopes. The county road ends, and FR-33 begins, in 0.8 mile. Steep rock faces overhang the road on the right (nesting Cliff Swallows).

In 0.6 mile is a sign marking the entrance of the **L.T. Murray Wildlife Area**. A track on the left a couple of hundred yards ahead leads down to tall trees along Taneum Creek (Warbling Vireo, Evening Grosbeak). The road then runs beside wet meadows and a cattail marsh, accessible on foot in several places. An excellent riparian area is at 0.9 mile. Park and walk across Taneum Creek on a footbridge where American Dippers have nested. Brush and tall trees along the stream for several hundred yards in both directions (old road running east along the base of the slope to an abandoned orchard; open gallery forest to the west) have nesting Mourning Dove, Western Screech-Owl, Red-naped Sapsucker, Western Wood-Pewee, Pacific-slope Flycatcher, Warbling Vireo, House Wren, Veery, Swainson's Thrush, Cedar Waxwing, Nashville, Yellow, and MacGillivray's Warblers, Western Tanager, Spotted Towhee, Black-headed Grosbeak, and Bullock's Oriole.

In 1.4 miles, primitive Moonlight Canyon Road (high clearance advised) leads up the ridge to the right, where the open, south-facing Ponderosa Pine forest offers Williamson's Sapsucker (higher up), Dusky Flycatcher, Cassin's Vireo, Mountain Chickadee, Yellow-rumped and Townsend's Warblers, Chipping Sparrow, Lazuli Bunting, Cassin's Finch, and Red Crossbill. Back on FR-33, **Taneum Campground** (elevation 2,400 feet), across the stream on a footbridge in 0.8 mile, has a small stand of old-growth Ponderosa Pines. In another 1.4 miles, primitive Cedar Creek Road turns up the ridge to the right, with birding opportunities similar to those along Moonlight Canyon Road.

TANEUM RIDGE

As one continues up FR-33 forests gradually become denser. Ponderosa Pine yields ground to Douglas-fir, and Hermit Thrush replaces Veery. At a fork in 1.4 mile, where FR-33 continues straight, bear left onto FR-3330 (well-maintained gravel), which drops down to cross Taneum Creek, then immediately begins to climb the cooler, wetter, north-facing slope of Taneum Ridge, with many pullouts, side roads, and informal trails. Most of the forest is second-growth, with some recent clearcuts and a few big old trees. Western Larch begins to appear. After 2.9 miles of steady rise, the road levels out temporarily at Gooseberry Flat (elevation 3,500 feet), then twists and turns its way upward for another 3.7 miles to **Gnat Flat** (elevation 4,800 feet), an area of open steppes, aspen groves, and isolated conifer stands. Characteristic species of the habitats here and on the way up include Turkey Vulture, Northern Goshawk, Blue Grouse, Flammulated (local) and Spotted (uncommon) Owls, Rufous Hummingbird, Williamson's and Red-naped Sapsuckers, Hairy, Three-toed, and Black-backed Woodpeckers (the last two rare), Gray Jay, Mountain Chickadee, and Hermit Thrush. Mixed-conifer forests on these flats

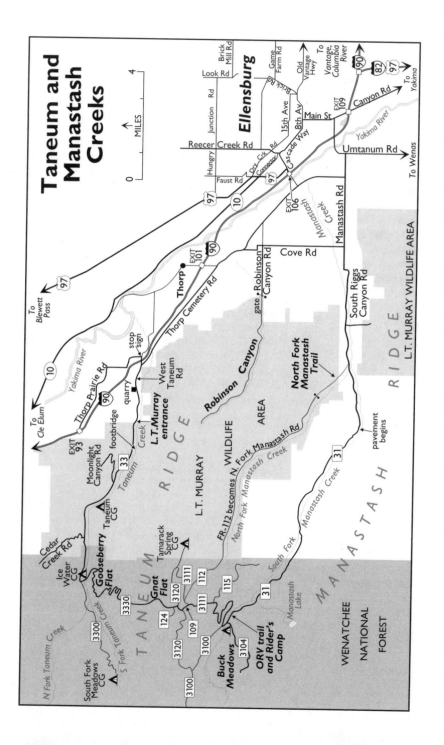

Taneum and Manastash Creeks

are logged in rotation, and the various successional stages attract different sets of birds. Farther south, the flats have large patches of sagebrush, and in 1.5 miles the road reaches its high point of 4,900 feet at an intersection with FR-124 on the right (signboard with map of road system). Continue left with FR-3330 as it begins to drop down into the Manastash Creek drainage.

At a junction in 0.3 mile, where FR-3330 ends, take FR-3120 to the right (signed for Buck Meadows). Then go left in 0.3 mile onto FR-109, a cutoff road that descends through second growth and clearcuts on a drier, south-facing slope with areas of meadow and sagebrush (Yellow-rumped and Townsend's Warblers, Chipping Sparrow). FR-109 ends at another junction in 0.5 mile; bear right here onto FR-3111. Pull off in 0.8 mile, just as the road curves right toward a cattle guard, and walk left out into a clearcut replanted to young pines. Dusky Flycatcher and Mountain Bluebird may be found here and in the large meadow below. In 0.4 mile, where FR-115 turns off to the left, stay straight ahead on FR-3111.

BUCK MEADOWS

For the next 3.7 miles the road winds down through dry, open forests (Mountain Chickadee, Red-breasted Nuthatch, Pine Siskin), meeting FR-31 at Buck Meadows (elevation 4,300 feet). Turn left here on FR-31 across South Fork Manastash Creek, and in 0.3 mile turn right onto FR-3104. In the first half-mile meadows open up on the left. Park and walk down to aspen groves and a small stream to look for Williamson's and Red-naped Sapsuckers, Warbling Vireo, Yellow and MacGillivray's Warblers, Black-headed Grosbeak, Dark-eyed Junco, and other nesting species of these mid-elevation forest wetland openings. A similar area is reached by returning to FR-31 and going right 0.5 mile. Park across from an ORV trail (4W311) and walk around a rail fence on the right side of the road. A meadow extends back for a considerable distance. Ruby-crowned Kinglet, Wilson's Warbler, and Lincoln's Sparrow may be present in trees and brush along the wetland edges on the left. Stands of Lodgepole Pine, Western Larch, and Engelmann Spruce here and on the other side of FR-31, in the Rider's Camp, may have Hammond's and Dusky Flycatchers, Gray Jay, Townsend's Solitaire, Hermit Thrush, Yellow-rumped and Townsend's Warblers, Western Tanager, and Red Crossbill.

MANASTASH CREEK

The drive down the Manastash drainage is a recapitulation in reverse of the birding possibilities along Taneum Creek, but on a grander scale. For the next 6.5 miles FR-31 descends smartly in a canyon with steep basalt cliffs, rockslides, and scattered Ponderosa Pines. Stop from time to time to look for Golden Eagle, American Kestrel, Prairie Falcon, White-throated Swift (uncommon), Common Raven, and Rock and Canyon Wrens. Then the valley broadens out somewhat and a generous riparian zone develops. For about the next six miles you may find Ruffed Grouse, Calliope Hummingbird, Lewis's Woodpecker, Red-naped Sapsucker, Cassin's Vireo, Northern Rough-winged Swallow, Black-capped and Mountain Chickadees, Red-breasted and White-breasted Nuthatches, House Wren, Nashville, Yellow, and MacGillivray's Warblers, Lazuli Bunting, Purple and Cassin's Finches, and typical riparian species. FR-31 ends, and the paved county road begins, at 9.7 miles from the Rider's Camp at Buck Meadows. In 2.7 miles, the two forks of Manastash Creek unite. On the left is a parking lot for the **North Fork Manastash Trail**, which follows an abandoned road. White-headed Woodpeckers and Pygmy Nuthatches have been found in the open pine woods half a mile to a mile up the roadbed.

From this point east the road is called Manastash Road. Continue a further 1.7 miles and scrutinize the weedy roadside on the left for a vertical, two-inch-wide, brown signpost lettered S RIGGS in white, with an arrow pointing across the road. Here you will find the number 10600 next to what looks like a private driveway but is actually the beginning of **South Riggs Canyon Road**, a public right-of-way. The riparian area where this road crosses Manastash Creek, a few hundred feet in, sometimes has nesting Western Screech-Owls and is usually good for Veeries. Manastash Road emerges into the southwest corner of the Kittitas Valley at the intersection with Cove Road, in 3.0 miles. If you continue 3.6 miles east from here to an intersection with Umtanum Road, you may turn left to Ellensburg and easy access to I-90 Exit 109, or right to Wenas.

ROBINSON CANYON

For an interesting side trip from Manastash Road, go north 2.9 miles on Cove Road and turn left onto Robinson Canyon Road. A gate marks the entrance to the **L.T. Murray Wildlife Area** in about two miles, at the mouth of Robinson Canyon. This small drainage has Gray Flycatchers and most of the other characteristic species of the lower Ponderosa Pine zone, although in lesser numbers than the Wenas Creek region to the south. One or more of Flammulated, Western Screech-, Northern Pygmy-, and Northern Saw-whet Owls can usually be found somewhere along the canyon, and Common Poorwills forage from the road at night. The rough road has recently been closed to vehicular traffic, but you can walk along it up the gulch for about four miles (mind the rattlesnakes).

Cove Road ends at S Thorp Highway (1.2 miles); a left turn brings you to the intersection with Thorp Cemetery Road (1.4 miles) where another left turn takes you back to Taneum Creek and the start of this loop; going straight on S Thorp Highway, the I-90 interchange at Exit 101 is 0.6 mile ahead.

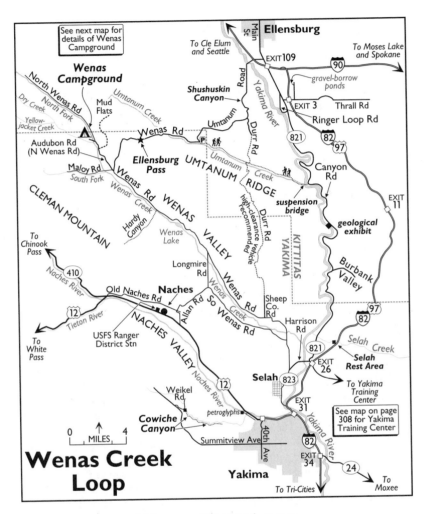

See next map for details of Wenas Campground

Ellensburg

To Cle Elum and Seattle

EXIT 109

To Moses Lake and Spokane

90

gravel-borrow ponds

Wenas Campground

North Wenas Rd

North Fork

Dry Creek

Yellow-jacket Creek

Mud Flats

Umtanum Creek

Shushuskin Canyon

Umtanum

EXIT 3   Thrall Rd

Ringer Loop Rd

821

82

97

Wenas Rd

Audubon Rd (N Wenas Rd)

Maloy Rd

South Fork

Ellensburg Pass

Umtanum Creek

UMTANUM RIDGE

high-clearance vehicle recommended

Durr Rd

Canyon Rd

EXIT 11

suspension bridge

geological exhibit

CLEMAN MOUNTAIN

Wenas Creek

Hardy Canyon

Wenas Lake

WENAS VALLEY

KITTITAS
YAKIMA

Burbank Valley

To Chinook Pass

410

Naches River

Longmire Rd

Wenas Rd

Naches

Allan Rd

So Wenas Rd

Sheep Co. Rd

12

Tieton River

Old Naches Rd

NACHES VALLEY

Harrison Rd

97

82

To White Pass

USFS Ranger District Stn

Naches River

12

821

EXIT 26

Selah Creek

Selah Rest Area

Weikel Rd

Cowiche Canyon

petroglyphs

Selah   823

EXIT 31

To Yakima Training Center

See map on page 308 for Yakima Training Center

0   MILES   4

Summitview Ave

40th Ave

82

EXIT 34

Yakima River

Wenas Creek Loop

Yakima

To Tri-Cities

24

To Moxee

WENAS CREEK LOOP

by Andy Stepniewski and Hal Opperman

The Wenas Creek region, often simply referred to as "Wenas," is situated at the lower forest–shrub-steppe margin. Well known to naturalists, Wenas is an excellent place to observe a wide range of breeding birds within a short distance. Habitats range from arid, low-elevation shrub-steppe to park-like Ponderosa Pine forests and higher-elevation mixed-conifer communities. An added bonus is the presence of several riparian-zone environments along permanent streams draining the Cascades' east slopes. Birding is best from late April into July, with mid-May through June being the peak time.

Camping at Wenas Campground is a popular way to experience the region. For more than 30 years, Audubon Society members from throughout Washington have gathered here over Memorial Day weekend at the height of the spring wildflower and birding seasons, when from 130–150 species of birds are recorded.

The loop begins just off I-90 at Exit 109 (the east Ellensburg exit). Total driving distance is about 90 miles. Allow one day to complete the whole loop comfortably. It is described in four segments: 1) from Ellensburg via Umtanum Creek to Wenas Campground; 2) the campground and vicinity; 3) down the Wenas Valley to Selah, just north of Yakima; and 4) three options for the return leg to Ellensburg, described in the following section (page 304). A portion of the first and second segments is on gravel roads, parts of which may not be passable in winter or during the spring thaw. Once you leave Ellensburg there are no facilities on the loop until you reach Selah. Make sure you have topped up your fuel tank and have all provisions.

UMTANUM ROAD

From I-90 Exit 109 (Canyon Road) in Ellensburg, go north 0.5 mile on Canyon Road. Just north of McDonald's restaurant, turn left (west) onto Umtanum Road. The road crosses the Yakima River (1.0 mile), turns south, passes through flat agricultural fields, and then begins a steep ascent into **Shushuskin Canyon**. A riparian area that attracts migrants is on the left part way through the canyon (2.3 miles). At the top of the canyon, the pavement ends at the junction where Durr Road goes left (1.7 miles); keep straight on Umtanum Road, which bends west almost at once. The landscape alternates between dryland wheat farms and shrub-steppe vegetation. Horned Larks are common on the plowed fields. Mountain and a few Western Bluebirds nest in the boxes set out by the Yakima Valley Audubon Society along the roadside. Farther west along Umtanum Road one enters the **L.T. Murray Wildlife Area** (2.8 miles; sign) and shrub-steppe habitat, composed of Big Sagebrush (grayish-hued shrubs) and Bitterbrush (brownish-green-hued shrubs). In this area, from April through July, look for Horned Lark, Sage Thrasher, Loggerhead Shrike, and Brewer's and Vesper Sparrows. In winter there are few birds in the shrub-steppe, but the farmland may have Red-tailed and Rough-legged Hawks and an occasional Prairie Falcon or Northern Shrike.

The road continues west, then turns south and crosses into Yakima County. The edge of the Ponderosa Pine zone is reached at a mixed pine and riparian area on the right (1.7 miles). There are often many birds here in spring and early summer, including Great Horned Owl and Lewis's Woodpecker. Migrant flycatchers, vireos, kinglets, and warblers may be common in April and May. Continue to a small parking area on the left side of Umtanum Road (0.3 mile). A trail follows **Umtanum Creek** downstream eight miles or so, all the way to the Yakima River. Even a short walk along this stream can be good for migrants. Picturesque Umtanum Falls are encountered in less than a mile.

The road bends sharply westward as you leave the parking lot and changes names—from here on it is shown as **Wenas Road** on most maps. A brushy stretch along the road in 1.1 miles is a good place to look for Ash-throated Flycatchers, a rare breeder this far north. They sometimes nest in the bluebird boxes; in the past, a good spot for these flycatchers has been in the neighborhood of box 63. As the road continues west and higher into the foothills of the Cascade Range, the Ponderosa Pine forest becomes more continuous (1.5 miles), reflecting an increase in precipitation. The open pine woods along this stretch have Gray Flycatchers, a recent arrival in Washington. Look and listen also for White-headed Woodpecker and Red Crossbill. In areas with pines, the nest boxes along the Umtanum/Wenas Road bluebird trail have many Western Bluebirds and House Wrens with the occasional White-breasted Nuthatch and Yellow-pine Chipmunk. Hundreds (one year over 1,000) of Western and Mountain Bluebirds fledge from this and several other trails in the Wenas region each year.

Ellensburg Pass (2.3 miles) in the pines marks the high point on the road. From the pass the road continues west, leaving the Umtanum Creek drainage and descending into the Wenas Creek drainage through Ponderosa Pines and a brushy riparian area flanking the road (1.5 miles). This habitat is good for Lazuli Bunting. At dusk on warm spring or summer nights, Common Poorwills call from the bordering slopes and are often seen on the road. Drive slowly to avoid hitting these remarkable birds.

The pavement begins again at a three-way junction (2.1 miles). Turn right from the main road onto an unpaved road that forks immediately. Stay right onto **Audubon Road** (called North Wenas Road on most maps; the signage here is confusing). Initially, this bumpy road traverses shrub-steppe composed mainly of Bitterbrush and scattered Ponderosa Pines. Lewis's Woodpecker, Western Bluebird, Spotted Towhee, Brewer's (a few) and Vesper Sparrows, and Cassin's Finch should be found along this stretch. As you proceed northwestward, the road gets rougher (but is usually passable to standard automobiles), and soon meets North Fork Wenas Creek (1.7 miles). Water flows over the road in spring, but the bottom is good and one can usually drive through easily. However, go slowly and be especially cautious if the water is high. Fine riparian habitat is skirted here, with tall cottonwoods, willow and alder thickets, and aspen glades. This area has many birds—Vaux's Swift, Red-naped Sapsucker, Western Wood-Pewee, Black-capped Chickadee, Veery, Cedar Waxwing, Yellow Warbler, and Black-headed Grosbeak are common. Turkey Vultures may nest along the steep escarpment above the road. Keep left at a junction (0.5 mile) with a dirt track leading to Mud Flats (four-wheel drive only). The road leaves the riparian zone and continues west through grassy fields and open pine woods to a junction (0.5 mile). Turn left here, across the wooden bridge over North Fork Wenas Creek. A few yards ahead is a large sign marking the entrance to the campground.

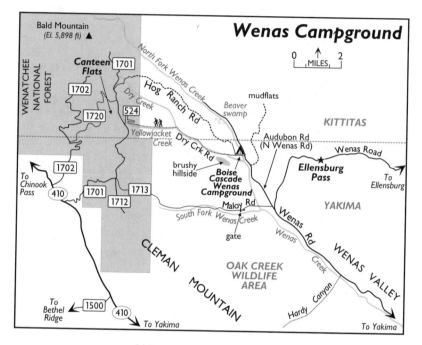

WENAS CAMPGROUND

The **Boise Cascade Wenas Campground** is well known for its variety of breeding species. It is also a popular destination and therefore best visited on weekdays. On weekends during spring and summer you will likely encounter throngs of campers, horseback riders, dirt-bikers, and archery groups from the Yakima area. The campground is primitive and unpatrolled, with no piped water, toilets, hookups, or telephone; if you plan to stay here, bring all your own supplies. The Boise Cascade Corporation selectively logs portions of this area periodically, but it is still a good place find birds of the lower Ponderosa Pine zone.

Four different habitats, each with a distinct complement of breeding birds, occur in proximity. Along the North Fork, in the campground, is a lush riparian community; Vaux's Swift, Red-naped Sapsucker, Downy Woodpecker, Western Wood-Pewee, Pacific-slope Flycatcher, Warbling Vireo, House Wren, Veery, Nashville, Yellow, and MacGillivray's Warblers, and Black-headed Grosbeak are common. The Ponderosa Pine woods in and around the campground have White-headed Woodpecker (scarce in some years), Gray Flycatcher, Mountain Chickadee, White-breasted and Pygmy Nuthatches, Townsend's Solitaire (usually nesting near·a steep bank), Chipping Sparrow, Cassin's Finch, and Red Crossbill (irregular, depending on pine seed crops). Brushy slopes mixed with young pines surrounding the area are excellent for

Blue Grouse, Calliope Hummingbird, Dusky Flycatcher, Nashville Warbler, and Fox Sparrow. Finally, moister forest is encountered a mile or so north from the campground, along with nearby riparian vegetation. Hammond's Flycatcher and Yellow-rumped Warbler are found here.

The campground proper is best visited on foot. Adjacent areas, described below, are partially accessible by car, but hiking is the most rewarding way to experience them if you have the time and the inclination.

From the south entrance sign, a dirt track follows the fenceline west along the north side of **Dry Creek**. A short walk or drive up this track leads to three good areas for birds. In 400 yards, at the intersection with Hog Ranch Road on the right, continue straight ahead on Dry Creek Road for another 250 yards and drive or hop across the creek—usually not difficult, but pay attention when the creek is full in early spring. Immediately after crossing, explore the brushy hillside to your left. Calliope Hummingbird, Dusky Flycatcher, Townsend's Solitaire, Nashville Warbler, and Fox Sparrow should be encountered from May through July in the Deerbrush, which creates a brush field reminiscent of the chaparral found in the mountains from Oregon south through California. Blue Grouse are often heard booming on the slopes above. Look also for Prairie Falcon, which nests in the Yakima Canyon and commutes to these Cascade foothills to forage.

Hikers may wish to continue westward along the sketchy road that follows Dry Creek, a fine riparian corridor with occasional rock outcrops, bordered by drier slopes with Ponderosa Pine habitats and open, grassy ridges. In 2.5 miles, watch for **Yellowjacket Creek** coming in from the left. Turn onto the trail that follows it, and continue another 1.5 miles to a section-line fence. (A short spur road switchbacks steeply from this point to FR-1701 at Canteen Flats, page 323.) This four-mile (each way) hike with a gentle, 1,300-foot elevation gain, offers an excellent transect of east-slope habitats, ending in moister, mixed-conifer forest at 3,900 feet. Among many other species, look for Ruffed Grouse, Western Screech-Owl, Common Nighthawk, Calliope Hummingbird, Pileated Woodpecker, Hammond's and Dusky Flycatchers, Cassin's and Warbling Vireos, Mountain Chickadee, Red-breasted Nuthatch, Brown Creeper, House and Winter Wrens, Veery, Swainson's and Hermit Thrushes, Yellow-rumped, Townsend's, and MacGillivray's Warblers, Western Tanager, Black-headed Grosbeak, Purple and Cassin's Finches, Red Crossbill, Pine Siskin, and Evening Grosbeak.

Return to the spot where Dry Creek Road crosses the creek, backtrack the 250 yards east to the intersection, and turn left (north) onto **Hog Ranch Road**. If you are driving, park here. Walk north along this dirt track for a few hundred yards. The brushy, willow-lined hillside to the west is another good area for Calliope Hummingbird, Dusky Flycatcher, Nashville Warbler, and Fox Sparrow. Farther along, the road deteriorates and then climbs steeply to a higher bench, about one-half mile in from Dry Creek Road. (This area may

also be accessed via a steep dirt track at the northwest end of the campground.) The open pine forests on this bench, with little or no undergrowth
except Pinegrass, are the favored habitat for Gray Flycatcher, first recorded in
the state in 1970 at Wenas Campground. White-headed Woodpecker, Pygmy
Nuthatch, and Cassin's Finch may also be found here.

Those with a four-wheel-drive vehicle may drive beyond this bench and
uphill on Hog Ranch Road, through open pine and Douglas-fir forests interspersed with rocky, treeless balds. Flammulated Owl (local), Common
Poorwill (dusk), White-headed Woodpecker, and Western and Mountain
Bluebirds can be found along this road, which eventually reaches
higher-elevation mixed-conifer and subalpine forests on Bald Mountain. However, the rough jeep track is difficult even with four-wheel drive. Access to
this area is much easier from the southwest, off SR-410 via FR-1701 (Benson
Creek) and FR-1702 (Rock Creek). These graded roads are suitable for ordinary vehicles (page 321).

To explore moister habitats, return to and cross the bridge below the
campground entrance. Turn left onto **North Wenas Road**, which leads to
habitats with Douglas-fir, Grand Fir, and tall riparian vegetation. In about 0.7
mile, the road overlooks a fine Beaver swamp, best accessed by continuing another 0.3 mile north, then turning left onto a dirt track that doubles back and
closely follows the east bank of the creek. Walk downstream to the wetland,
birding along the way. Alternatively, this swampy area can be reached by walking north from the campground and crossing the creek.

WENAS VALLEY

Back at the junction just off Wenas Road, where Audubon Road begins,
take the other branch and head west on **Maloy Road**. This gravel road passes
hay fields at first, then enters fine riparian habitats of cottonwoods and aspens
at the crossing with North Fork Wenas Creek (0.7 mile). *This is private land
and you must bird from the road.* Veery and Swainson's Thrush occur in the
woodlands here. Look also for House Wren, Yellow Warbler, and
Black-headed Grosbeak. The agricultural edge habitat is attractive to Purple
Finch, a local nester east of the Cascade crest. A number of "eastern" vagrants
or spring overshoots have occurred in this area from early June through
mid-July, among them Least Flycatcher (regular; may breed), Ovenbird,
American Redstart, and Rose-breasted Grosbeak. Farther west on Maloy
Road, keep left at the first fork (0.3 mile). At the Cooperative Land Manage-
ment Area (0.4 mile) continue west into the Ponderosa Pine forest. Park and
walk through a gate on your left marked *State Land* (0.3 mile) to explore the
open pine forest, looking (and listening) for White-headed Woodpecker,
Gray Flycatcher, White-breasted and Pygmy Nuthatches, Cassin's Finch, and
Red Crossbill. Maloy Road continues west for about six more miles (becomes
FR-1713), eventually reaching Rocky Prairie and FR-1701 (page 323).

Return to the pavement on Wenas Road. Take a right (southeast) and drive down the Wenas Valley, a mosaic of hay and grain fields and riparian habitats. The **Hardy Canyon** entrance to the Oak Creek Wildlife Area is on the right in 4.0 miles, at a pipe gate that is usually locked. Park, walk through the pedestrian access, cross Wenas Creek on a wooden bridge, and go exploring on foot. This beautiful area is filled with birds associated with riparian, field, and shrub-steppe habitats. In the breeding season look for Cooper's Hawk, Ruffed Grouse, Least and Pacific-slope Flycatchers (along Wenas Creek), Ash-throated Flycatcher (some years present near brush on the sidehill south of the creek), Eastern Kingbird, Warbling Vireo, Tree Swallow, Gray Catbird (a few), Nashville and Yellow Warblers, Yellow-breasted Chat, Spotted Towhee, Black-headed Grosbeak, and Lazuli Bunting. Spring migration (end of April through mid-May) can be impressive. Depending on weather conditions, flycatchers, vireos, warblers, and tanagers can be found in good numbers then. Early May is a good time to look for Golden-crowned Sparrows, after the main northbound push of White-crowneds (race *gambelii*) has gone through.

A five-minute walk south from the bridge brings you to the upper edge of aspen woodlands. From here a rough, seven-mile road heads up Hardy Canyon to the 4,700-foot summit of Cleman Mountain (the ridge between the Naches River and Wenas Creek). Shrub-steppe vegetation in the lower part of the canyon is attractive to Vesper Sparrows. If you continue to climb you will notice a gradual change to coniferous forest.

Return to Wenas Road and turn right (southeast). Look for a sign indicating *Public Fishing Access* on your right (1.5 miles). Take this down to **Wenas Lake** (0.1 mile). High water and hordes of anglers often make Wenas Lake unattractive to birds during spring and early summer. However, lower water levels expose a wide area of mud by late July or August in many years. If and when this happens, Wenas Lake can be good for shorebirding. Common fall migrants include both yellowlegs species, Solitary, Semipalmated, Western, and Least Sandpipers, Long-billed Dowitcher, and Red-necked Phalarope. A number of rarities have been encountered here, including Wandering Tattler (one record), Willet, and Stilt Sandpiper. A fine riparian area can be reached by walking upstream from the parking area along a trail bordering Wenas Creek. From May through July, look for Eastern Kingbird, Bank Swallow, Gray Catbird, Yellow Warbler, Black-headed Grosbeak, Lazuli Bunting, and Bullock's Oriole.

Continue southeast on Wenas Road. At Longmire Road (3.8 miles) stay left on Wenas Road. Anywhere along this stretch of agricultural land keep an eye out for Swainson's Hawk (spring and summer). At **Sheep Company Road** (6.3 miles), turn left (north) and continue to the entrance of the L.T. Murray Wildlife Area (1.3 mile), a large reserve of shrub-steppe and stony ridges. Just south of the entrance sign, look for a pair of Burrowing Owls on the east side of the road. Long-billed Curlews are occasionally seen in spring on the grasslands here.

Three choices for returning to Ellensburg are described in the following section. One of them, Durr Road, goes north across the wildlife area from this spot, but is recommended only for high-clearance vehicles. To access the other two, return along Sheep Company Road to Wenas Road, turn left, and continue east and south to a junction with SR-823 (4.8 miles). Straight ahead, SR-823 (Wenas Road) soon reaches Selah. A left turn at this intersection onto SR-823 (Harrison Road) brings you to SR-821 (1.8 miles). Turn left to follow the Yakima Canyon route to Ellensburg, or turn right to the Exit 26 interchange with I-82. Here you may go south to Yakima, north to Ellensburg, or straight ahead to the Yakima Training Center (page 309).

FROM YAKIMA TO ELLENSBURG

by Andy Stepniewski and Hal Opperman

Take your pick of three routes between these county seats. (Refer to map on page 297.) All three are about 30 miles long, but the time required to travel them differs greatly. Unimproved Durr Road, the oldest, slowest, and most difficult, goes over the top of a high ridge through extensive shrub-steppe with a touch of riparian habitat. The Yakima Canyon—the leisurely, paved, water-level route, featuring steep cliffs and a fine riparian zone—has the most varied year-round birding possibilities. The interstate has some birding potential, too, despite limited access, and of course it's the newest, fastest, and easiest route.

DURR ROAD

Durr Road—the stage road from Yakima to Ellensburg in the late 1800s—begins where Sheep Company Road ends, at the entrance to the L.T. Murray Wildlife Area north of Selah (page 303). This gravel and bare-rock road through Wild West scenery reaches Umtanum Road southwest of Ellensburg in about 15 miles. Do not attempt to drive it except in a high-clearance vehicle with sturdy tires (including a full-sized spare), extra drinking water, and emergency supplies. If you are properly equipped, you may expect to find shrub-steppe species such as Sage Thrasher and Loggerhead Shrike. Brewer's, Vesper, and Sage Sparrows occur commonly in suitable sagebrush stands. A few Greater Sage-Grouse may survive on this side of the Yakima River, but are seldom reported. Horned Lark and Mountain Bluebird are common on the high barrens, where you might also see Bighorn Sheep. A variety of raptors such as Northern Harrier, Red-tailed, Ferruginous (rare), and Rough-legged (winter) Hawks, Golden Eagle, American Kestrel, and Prairie Falcon should be looked for in this huge area.

The road climbs steadily. Stay right at 2.8 miles, then left in 0.1 mile, to reach the top of **Umtanum Ridge** (5.2 miles). The view from the 3,500-foot summit is spectacular, with Ellensburg to the north and Yakima to the south, framed by the snowy Cascade volcanoes to the west and the vast Columbia Basin to the east. Descending northward from the summit, Durr Road reaches **Umtanum Creek** in about three miles. The creek offers great birding for riparian species on rough trails for the adventuresome hiker, west (upstream) three and a half miles to Umtanum Road or east (downstream) four and a half miles to the Yakima River. After fording the creek, Durr Road climbs out of the canyon and continues north about four more miles to Umtanum Road. Look for Lark Sparrow in overgrazed shrub-steppe, before the wheat fields start.

YAKIMA CANYON

If you have at least two or three hours and it's not midday on a summer weekend (when all of Yakima, or so it seems, floats the river on rafts or roars along it on jet skis), by all means take the Yakima Canyon route. This old highway, formerly part of US-97 but since supplanted by the interstate, was built through the canyon in parallel to the historic Northern Pacific Railroad. The river winds along a magnificent gorge cut through three basalt ridges that host a dense breeding population of raptors. Chukar, White-throated Swift (summer), and Canyon Wren are also common. Access to riparian areas along lower Umtanum Creek is another highlight.

Go north onto SR-821 from I-82 Exit 26, four miles north of Yakima. At the intersection with SR-823 a short distance ahead, reset your trip-odometer to 0.0 and continue straight on SR-821. Pull off on the right at the first major wide spot after entering the canyon (3.3 miles). From March through June, watch for Red-tailed Hawk, American Kestrel, and Prairie Falcon, all of which nest on the towering basalt cliffs here and elsewhere in the canyon. In winter, Bald Eagles patrol the river for whitefish and carrion (fish or mammalian). The next pullout (0.5 mile) is around a sharp, blind curve, so slow down and signal as you approach it. Golden Eagle and other raptors nest on the cliffs across the river to the west. Listen for White-throated Swift and Canyon Wren, both of which are common here. In winter, survey the waters and banks of the river below for Common Goldeneye, Common Merganser, and Bald Eagle. Farther up the canyon, a side road comes in from Burbank Valley on the right (3.4 miles). Recreational access points along this stretch allow you to pull off beside the river. After sunset, listen for Common Poorwill on the open slopes and Western Screech-Owl in the riparian groves.

From the Burbank Valley turnoff, stay on SR-821 as it twists and turns along the Yakima until you come to a geological exhibit (4.7 miles) that explains the antecedent nature of the river here. Prior to the regional uplifting of the various east-west trending ridges in the canyon, the Yakima River likely was a mature stream, meandering across a fairly level, low landscape. Uplift of the basalt ridges apparently took place very slowly, permitting the erosive, down-cutting powers of the river to keep pace. Thus, the ancient bends and loops in the river course remain. Looking west across the river, the striking whitish ash layer from the huge Mount Mazama eruption in south-central Oregon 6,600 years ago is visible just above the river. The collapse of Mount Mazama created Crater Lake. The explosion sent 116 cubic kilometers of ash across all the western states and three Canadian provinces, as far eastward as Nebraska. Another favored nest cliff for Golden Eagle is visible from here, high on the shoulder of Baldy Mountain (the highest mountain to the southeast). Look for it to the right of the summit below the west shoulder, on the largest, lichen-coated cliff.

From the exhibit, drive on up the canyon to the Umtanum Recreation Area (3.8 miles). Turn left off the highway and swing right to a parking area. A suspension footbridge crosses the Yakima River to the mouth of **Umtanum Creek**. A trail parallels the creek for eight miles all the way to Umtanum Road (page 298). The lower end of this trail is a favorite in spring for birders and hikers. You may encounter a local population of Bushtits—as yet an uncommon species east of the Cascade crest. Yellow-breasted Chats are also present. Cooper's and Red-tailed Hawks, Golden Eagle, American Kestrel, and Prairie Falcon nest on the canyon walls or in the trees along the creek. Rock and Canyon Wrens are also common. You can't miss Spotted Towhee, except in mid-winter. From mid-April through the end of May a wide array of neotropical migrants (flycatchers, vireos, warblers, Western Tanager, Bullock's Oriole) should be looked for in the riparian zone.

In the warmer months keep an eye out for Western Rattlesnakes, which are frequently encountered along this trail. Watch them from a distance but do not harm them. In general, this species is not aggressive and would rather avoid you, too. Watch the steep slopes for Bighorn Sheep. A sizable herd (250 in 1998) resides in this area. Your first clue to their presence might be the sound of dislodged rocks clattering down the talus slopes. Watch also for Yellow-bellied Marmots, the western equivalent of the Woodchuck.

Continue north toward Ellensburg, pulling off along the river at a widening in the shoulder (4.3 miles). The road embankment has lots of Prickly Pear Cactus. The cliffs across the river should be scanned for Red-tailed Hawk, American Kestrel, Prairie Falcon, and Common Raven. The small caves not far above the river may harbor Great Horned Owls. In winter you are sure to see Bald Eagles along this stretch.

The final stop is reached by turning left from SR-821 at Ringer Loop Road (4.1 miles). Go west over the railway track and drive this road toward the Yakima River. Shortly before the road turns north, a fishing access on the left (0.3 mile) offers a place to park and wander among the tall cottonwoods and other streamside growth (WDFW permit required). Birds of the riparian zone are a feature here. At night, listen for Western Screech- and Long-eared Owls. Ospreys nest in the area, too. Follow Ringer Loop Road as it turns north and crosses a small wetland before rejoining the highway (0.9 mile). Continue north to I-90 (2.4 miles).

INTERSTATE 82

Much of the arid rainshadow landscape in the river valleys of South Central Washington has been converted to irrigated agriculture. Little natural vegetation survives except along the riparian corridors of rivers and major creeks. However, a significant tract of the original shrub-steppe ecosystem occurs along I-82 between Yakima and Ellensburg, much of it within the Yakima Training Center.

Start at I-82 Exit 26 north of Yakima (there is a Great Blue Heron rookery in the large Black Cottonwood grove to the west of the freeway). As you head north on I-82 toward Ellensburg, the Redmon Bridge crosses the deep gorge of Selah Creek in about two and a half miles. Unfortunately, there is no place to pull off from the northbound lanes, but if you are traveling south toward Yakima, stop at the Selah Rest Area (13 miles south of Exit 11). The overlook beyond the restrooms provides a dramatic view of Selah Creek. Especially between April and July, check the basalt cliff at the north end of the parking area for nesting Ferruginous Hawk (rare or absent in recent years), Prairie Falcon, White-throated Swift (which apparently nests in openings in the concrete arches of the freeway bridge), and Violet-green and Cliff Swallows. Say's Phoebe and Rock Wren should also be looked for here. Red-tailed Hawk and American Kestrel are hard to miss.

At Exit 11, signed *Military Area*, shrub-steppe birds such as Sage Thrasher and Brewer's, Vesper, and Sage Sparrows can sometimes be observed beyond the fences on both sides of the interstate (easier to find in early morning when traffic is still relatively light). A pair of Common Ravens often nests under the freeway overpass.

In eight miles, take Exit 3 (Thrall Road) and go east 0.1 mile to No. 6 Road. Turn left (north) and travel 1.3 miles to a gravel road on the left that leads to two gravel-borrow ponds (WDFW permit required). These ponds (a large one on the north and a smaller one to the south) can have many ducks in migration and winter when they are not being used by anglers. In fall, scoters and Long-tailed Ducks regularly visit en route to the ocean. One can also walk the east bank for birds of scrub and marsh.

Back on I-82, it is three more miles to the I-90 junction, and a mile west from there to the east Ellensburg exit.

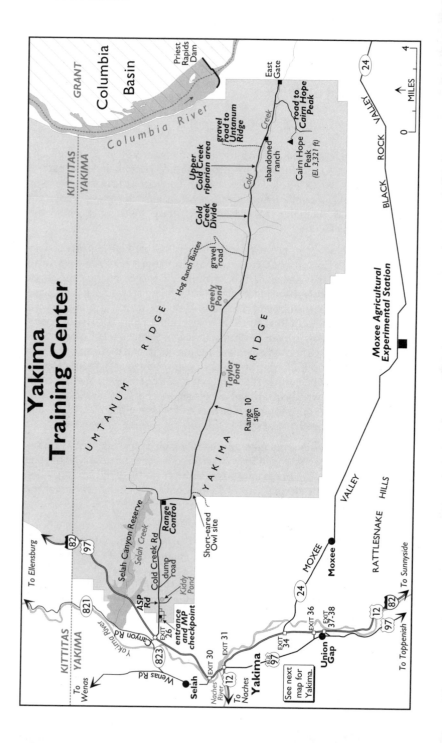

YAKIMA TRAINING CENTER

by Andy Stepniewski

The Yakima Training Center comprises the largest remaining contiguous block of shrub-steppe habitat in Washington—365,000 acres stretching from the Columbia River west to I-82 and from I-90 south to the outskirts of Yakima. This U.S. Army subinstallation (of Fort Lewis) is one of the few areas of the state where the shrub-steppe ecosystem continues to function on a landscape scale. Nearly all bird species characteristic of this zone can be found here, including the declining Greater Sage-Grouse. Birding is superb in riparian areas during migration.

GREATER SAGE-GROUSE LEK TOURS

The Yakima Training Center is one of two sites in Washington where Greater Sage-Grouse still occur in significant numbers. Your best chance to observe them is on one of the organized tours during the peak courtship period in March, offered by center biologists in conjunction with the Yakima Valley Audubon Society (P.O. Box 2823, Yakima, WA 98901) and the Seattle Audubon Society (206-523-4483). At other seasons, you are unlikely to get more than a brief view as birds flush in the distance. The tour will take you to a lek where females gather to observe displaying males, starting well before sunrise. While at the lek site, look for other shrub-steppe species such as Horned Lark, Sage Thrasher, and Vesper and Sage Sparrows.

BIRDING THE CENTER ON YOUR OWN

You may enter the center on your own in any month, although access to some parts of it may be restricted from time to time due to military exercises. Take Exit 26 from I-82 just north of Yakima. Go east from the exit to the Military Police (MP) checkpost at the center's entrance (1.7 miles) and sign in. You will need your current vehicle registration, driver's license, and proof of insurance. You will also be asked to state the purpose of your visit (birdwatching) and your destination. While birding can be productive in many parts of this huge installation, birders are advised to stick to the Cold Creek Road, described below. Access to this area is usually granted. The route goes east from the MP station to East Gate and passes through a variety of shrub-steppe and riparian vegetation communities, giving an opportunity to see many bird species of these habitats. Military activity may be evident in spring and early summer, but most tracked-vehicles remain on a side road paralleling the main road. The round trip is about 60 road miles; excursions to and from Hog Ranch Buttes, Umtanum Ridge, Cairn Hope Peak, and Selah Creek will add another 15 miles. The Cold Creek Road provides a very full day of birding, especially if you take advantage of the hiking possibilities.

Depending on the timing of your visit, the center may be crawling with soldiers and military machinery or it may be a deserted wilderness. In either case it is potentially a hazardous place. Some precautions are in order:

It is wise to carry a cell phone and make sure you have the MP's phone number. Get the current number when you check in (this number has a curious way of changing). The MP will assist you in an emergency.

You will fare better if you drive a high-clearance vehicle (with six-ply tires if possible) and carry a shovel. Make sure your spare tire is in good shape.

Drive gravel roads slowly, especially on curves (to minimize risk of sidewalls of your tires coming in contact with sharp rocks).

Carry extra food and water, especially in summer, and emergency clothing in winter. Be aware that there is often an extreme fire hazard on the installation in summer. Do not drive a low-clearance vehicle over Cheatgrass or other weedy or grassy terrain. A Cheatgrass fire can outpace a vehicle in motion!

COLD CREEK ROAD

Before leaving the MP station, inquire whether Cold Creek Road is gated 0.1 mile east. If the gate is locked, have the MP give you precise directions through the cantonment (developed) area to get you around it.

From the MP station, exit right (east) onto Cold Creek Road. ASP Road is soon passed (0.7 mile). The Kiddy Pond behind a grove of introduced Black Locust trees at this corner has birds of the riparian zone in migration. East on Cold Creek Road, at a road marked *Refuse Collection Site* (0.7 mile), turn right (south) and drive a short distance toward the dump, a good area for Sage Sparrow. Return to Cold Creek Road and turn right. From here to **Range Control** (4.0 miles) is fine shrub-steppe habitat, especially on the south side of the road. If conditions are noisy due to tactical vehicles and other traffic, hurry along. If not, stop occasionally to look and listen for Sage Thrasher and Brewer's, Vesper, and Sage Sparrows. Sagelands along this stretch are home to many Black-tailed and a few White-tailed Jackrabbits—one of the few sites in Washington where these rabbits can still be found. Because of the high rodent and jackrabbit population, this is a good area in which to look for raptors such as Northern Harrier, Red-tailed Hawk, Golden Eagle, and American Kestrel. At Range Control (now closed, but buildings still there), Sage Sparrows are common in the sagebrush on the north side of Cold Creek Road. Grasshopper Sparrows may sometimes be found in the weedy, grassy terrain uphill and south from here.

From the east side of the Range Control complex, turn right (south) and keep on the paved road. Short-eared Owls are often seen on the slopes just to the south of a major bend in the road (1.5 miles), particularly at dawn and dusk. Stop to search for Sage Sparrow, which becomes less numerous eastward from this spot to well beyond the Cold Creek Divide, as increasing moisture induces a grass cover higher than its liking. Continue east to the *Range 10* sign (5.0 miles), where the sagebrush is good for Northern Harrier, Prairie Falcon, Greater Sage-Grouse, Short-eared Owl, Sage Thrasher, and Brewer's and Vesper Sparrows.

Taylor Pond is on the right (south) in another 2.7 miles—not visible from the road but marked by the first riparian-zone vegetation east of Range Control. This sensitive area, protected by fencing, is a magnet for many birds. Enter on foot through an unlocked gate. Northern Harriers are common. Look also for Long-eared Owls and migrant passerines in the trees. An extensive Greater Sage-Grouse conservation area, off-limits to military activity, lies between Taylor Pond and the following site.

Greely Pond (2.6 miles), an isolated stand of riparian habitat, offers excellent birding for migrants in spring and fall. To enter, walk to the east side of the fenced area and downstream. The small pond may have nesting Soras. Great Horned Owls nest here, as do Bullock's Orioles. Dense Big Sagebrush east of the pond once hosted a summering Clay-colored Sparrow. Passerines are often thick in migration.

Continue east from Greely Pond to a well-maintained gravel road (1.7 miles), turn left, and climb four miles to the summit of **Hog Ranch Buttes**, site of several communication towers. *Do not attempt this side trip if there is mud or snow on the road.* Chukar, Gray Partridge, migrant raptors (including Northern Goshawk and Gyrfalcon), Snow Buntings (late fall), and Gray-crowned Rosy-Finches (winter) have all been seen on this route, and good-quality lithosol plant communities attract Horned Larks. The view from the summit (elevation 4,100 feet) extends from Mount Jefferson in Oregon north to Mount Stuart.

Return to the Cold Creek Road, turn left, and climb 1.2 miles to a broad pass, the **Cold Creek Divide**, at an elevation of nearly 3,000 feet. Here you leave the Selah Creek drainage and enter that of Cold Creek. The extensive Threetip Sagebrush/Bluebunch Wheatgrass habitat is a prime foraging ground for nesting raptors such as Northern Harrier, Red-tailed and Swainson's Hawks, and American Kestrel. Watch for Short-eared Owl at dusk and dawn. Fall raptor migration (late August–October) can be exciting, too. Watch for Northern Harrier (61 one September day), Sharp-shinned, Cooper's, Swainson's, Red-tailed, and Rough-legged (beginning in October) Hawks, Golden Eagle, Prairie Falcon, and American Kestrel as they circle and sail south from Umtanum Ridge. Common Ravens also migrate south in large numbers. In fall, listen and look for Lapland Longspur and Snow Bunting. Gray Partridge occurs in these grasslands, but is difficult to spot.

The shrub-steppe community along the north slope of Yakima Ridge (to the south), from the divide east along **Upper Cold Creek**, is in excellent condition. A hike up one of the fire-break roads should produce Sage Thrasher and Brewer's and Vesper Sparrows. In 2.1 miles from the divide, riparian areas with thickets of Black Hawthorn, wild rose, Coyote Willow, and Blue Elderberry, and groves of Black Cottonwood, Peach-leaf Willow, and Quaking Aspen, offer sensational birding for migrants. From late April through early June, and again from late July through September (and even October), the area can be alive in early morning with migrant flycatchers, vireos, kinglets, warblers, tanagers, and sparrows. This is especially so in the fall when hundreds, even thousands of birds can be viewed each hour winging their way west and up the valley on any given morning. In the brushy thickets, abundant fruit attracts Lewis's Woodpecker (early September), Townsend's Solitaire, American Robin, Varied Thrush, and Sage Thrasher. Some species occur in stunning numbers (e.g., 65 Hammond's Flycatchers and 675 Ruby-crowned Kinglets tallied in one two-hour period). Sharp-shinned Hawks (as many as 20 one morning) provide an escort. Unusual migrants noted here include Barred Owl, Gray Flycatcher, Pine Grosbeak, and Purple and Cassin's Finches. Black Swift—almost unknown as a migrant east of the Cascades away from its breeding haunts—has been noted twice in early September. The abrupt eastward bend in the Columbia River at Priest Rapids (five miles north), and the availability of food and shelter along Cold Creek, may prompt many southbound passerines to strike south and west on a direct overland route rather than detouring east around the White Bluffs along the Hanford Reach.

Continue downstream, following the creek. On the left in 2.1 miles is a gravel road leading to the crest of **Umtanum Ridge**. En route, Greater Sage-Grouse, Sage Thrasher, and Brewer's and Vesper Sparrows may be found in the excellent Threetip Sagebrush habitat. The view from the crest is vast. Directly below is Priest Rapids Lake, to the north are the Saddle Mountains and the Stuart Range, and to the east are the many nuclear reactors on the Hanford Site, with Rattlesnake Mountain rising in the southeast.

Return to the Cold Creek Road, turn left (east), and drive to an abandoned ranch on the right (0.4 mile) where riparian habitat hosts many nesting and migrant birds. Continuing downhill, turn right in 2.1 miles onto a road that descends and crosses Cold Creek, then steeply climbs the north flank of Yakima Ridge below **Cairn Hope Peak** (1.0 mile). The Nature Conservancy and the Washington Natural Heritage Program recognize the plant communities on this slope as some of the finest remaining Big Sagebrush/Bluebunch Wheatgrass shrub-steppe vegetation in the state. All of the regularly occurring shrub-steppe passerines can be found here readily (Grasshopper Sparrow is uncommon).

Return to Cold Creek Road and continue downstream to **East Gate** (2.1 miles). In addition to the plants mentioned for Upper Cold Creek, Water Birch (copper-colored trunk and branches) is abundant along these lower stretches—the buds an important winter food source for the now extirpated Sharp-tailed Grouse. Taken in conjunction with the high-quality shrub-steppe vegetation along the ridges south of Cold Creek, this is potentially excellent habitat for Sharp-taileds and a prime site for a reintroduction effort.

Return to the major intersection at Range Control and turn right (north) to a crossing of **Selah Creek** (0.5 mile). A hike downstream on the dirt track on the south side of the stream leads past riparian habitats and, farther on, to cliffs. Many raptors nest in this area—Northern Harrier, Swainson's, Red-tailed, and Ferruginous (at least formerly) Hawks, Golden Eagle, American Kestrel, Prairie Falcon, and Great Horned, Long-eared, and Short-eared Owls. The lower part of the canyon has no trails and reaching it involves a rigorous hike. Watch out for rattlesnakes in the warm months. White-throated Swift, many Violet-green and Cliff Swallows, Rock and Canyon Wrens, Lazuli Bunting, and Bullock's Oriole may also be found along the creek.

Turn in your visitor pass at the MP checkpost on the way out.

After impaling a plump Sagebrush Lizard it has captured, a Loggerhead Shrike prepares to feed in the open shrub-steppe country within the Yakima Training Center.

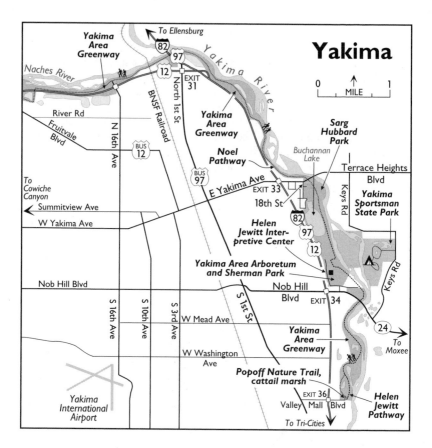

YAKIMA AND VICINITY

by Andy Stepniewski

Yakima is situated at the head of the richly productive Yakima Valley and the foot of the Cascades. This thriving center for light manufacturing, forest products, and (especially) agriculture has 73,000 residents. Parks on the edges of the city offer birding of wetland and riparian habitats in any season. The agricultural land and shrub-steppe of the Moxee and Black Rock Valleys east of the city are known for raptors and for migrating and wintering songbirds. To the south, lower Toppenish Creek hosts species of wet fields and marshes in all seasons, while Fort Simcoe in the upper Toppenish drainage has Lewis's Woodpeckers and other birds of Garry Oak habitats. The lower Naches Valley west of Yakima features birds of cliffs and streamside vegetation.

YAKIMA

Fine birding is available right within the city, principally along the Yakima Area Greenway—a wide, paved path paralleling the Yakima River for nine miles that passes through riparian, marsh, and open-field habitats. There are four main access points, one from US-12 and three from I-82.

At the 16th Avenue exit on US-12 (one mile west from Exit 31 on I-82), go north and immediately find the parking area for the western part of the Yakima Greenway. Walk the path east (downstream), to the base of the railway-bridge abutments. American Dippers descend to winter here from their summer haunts in the Cascades.

From Exit 33 on I-82 (Yakima Avenue/Terrace Heights Boulevard), drive east on Terrace Heights Boulevard 0.3 mile to 18th Street. Turn right (south) and continue 0.1 mile to the **Sarg Hubbard Park** entrance and parking. You can go either north or south from here. The path to the south soon reaches a small, marshy area where Virginia Rail and Wilson's Snipe might be found. Dabbling ducks such as Green-winged Teal are frequent. Farther south is Buchannan Lake, on the west side of the path. In winter this large, deep lake is attractive to grebes and diving ducks. Ring-billed Gulls are common in summer. The Yakima River lies east of the path. Bald Eagles are common here in winter, as are Common Goldeneyes and Common Mergansers.

From Exit 34 on I-82, go east on Nob Hill Boulevard (SR-24) 0.1 mile to the first traffic light. Turn left (north), then immediately right into the parking lot for Sherman Park. The Noel Pathway can be walked either north or south from here. To the north are Black Cottonwood and mature riparian woodlands of the William Schroeder Memorial Wetland, part of the **Yakima Area Arboretum**. This habitat is good in migration and winter for a variety of passerines. Western Screech-Owl is reliable here, as are Downy Woodpecker and Bewick's Wren. To reach brush piles that are excellent in winter for sparrows, walk left on a small path at the *William Schroeder Memorial Wetland* sign about 200 feet to an opening surrounded by brush. Lots of seed is put out here by the Yakima Valley Audubon Society, attracting Fox, Song, Lincoln's, White-throated, Harris's (rare), White-crowned, and Golden-crowned Sparrows. Extensive ornamental plantings are another feature of the arboretum. From the parking lot for Sherman Park head back toward the traffic light at Nob Hill Boulevard but keep straight just before the light to reach the Helen Jewitt Interpretive Center (0.3 mile). In fall and winter, Cedar (and rarely Bohemian) Waxwings, American Robins, and Varied Thrushes feed in the hawthorn plantings just to the north of the center.

Yakima Sportsman State Park can also be reached from Exit 34. From the traffic light 0.1 mile east of I-82, go east on SR-24 to Keys Road (0.8 mile). Turn left (north) and go 0.9 mile to the park entrance. The duck pond in the park is good for Wood Ducks—often more than 100 may be found here.

Western Screech-Owl and Great Horned Owl are common. The riparian woodlands on the west side of the park can be birdy: look for Downy Woodpecker, Black-capped Chickadee, and Bewick's Wren.

From Exit 36 on I-82, go east 0.1 mile on Valley Mall Boulevard to parking on the left for the southernmost access to the Yakima Greenway. On the west side of the parking lot, the **Bob and Helen Popoff Nature Trail** (gravel) makes a short loop north through a cattail marsh where Common Yellowthroat is sometimes found, then past several ponds, and finally groves of Russian Olive trees, swarming in winter with berry-eating birds such as American Robin, Varied Thrush, and Evening Grosbeak (and clouds of European Starlings). The **Helen Jewitt Pathway** begins on the east side of the parking lot. First comes riparian woodland, then a tree-rimmed pond attractive to Ring-necked Duck, Hooded Merganser, and other diving ducks from fall through spring (except when frozen).

MOXEE AND EAST

East of Yakima on SR-24 is the **Moxee Agricultural Experimental Station**, 16.5 miles from I-82 Exit 34. (See map on page 308.) This USDA research facility features ten long rows of conifers and some deciduous trees planted as windbreaks to shelter field crops, and appears as a wooded island in the midst of wide-open country. Long-eared Owls have nested here. Barn, Great Horned, Short-eared, and other owls roost in the trees in winter. Swainson's Hawk also nests. You will see lots of Black-billed Magpies and California Quail, which attract Cooper's Hawk and Northern Goshawk in winter. Migrant passerines utilize this oasis, too. Pull off and park near the caretaker's house between the road and the rows of trees, and obtain permission to enter. The gate may be closed on weekends. Don't neglect the westernmost row of trees that has many ash trees where Purple Finches winter erratically.

In some winters, good hawkwatching can be had along SR-24 in the **Black Rock Valley**, for example in an area of mostly abandoned wheat fields 1.8 miles east of the experimental station. Short-eared Owls forage in these fields, especially in winter, and sometimes roost in the trees. In addition to raptors, look for Gray Partridge (fairly common but elusive resident of the valley) and Long-billed Curlew (April through July). Beginning 2.5 miles farther east on SR-24 and continuing for the next six miles, scan the open country for Northern Harrier, Red-tailed, Ferruginous (mainly March through May), and Rough-legged (November through April) Hawks, Golden Eagle (especially February through April when migrants are moving north), American Kestrel, and Prairie Falcon. Though rare, Gyrfalcon is regularly found here; most records span December through mid-March. Horned Larks by the thousands gather grit on the roadway in winter. Pick through these large flocks carefully for Lapland Longspur and Snow Bunting. If you stop, make sure to park your vehicle completely off the pavement. Traffic moves very fast.

SOUTH TO TOPPENISH CREEK

The **Toppenish National Wildlife Refuge** is a rich birding area situated in the Toppenish Creek bottomlands some 20 miles south of Yakima. Bobolinks and a variety of other species nest on the refuge, while migration and winter bring many waterfowl, raptors, sparrows, and blackbirds. To reach the refuge from Yakima, take I-82 southeast to Exit 50. Turn right onto SR-22 and proceed 3.2 miles to the second light in Toppenish. Go straight through this traffic light (you are now on US-97) to Pump House Road (4.7 miles), also marked *Toppenish National Wildlife Refuge*. Turn right here, then make an immediate sharp right into a parking lot with an information kiosk and short, paved path to a covered, raised observation platform. This is an excellent place in spring and early summer to study a variety of waterfowl, and later on, when waters recede, shorebirds such as Black-necked Stilt and American Avocet. Eastern Kingbird and Gray Catbird nest in riparian thickets in front of the platform.

A road leads from the parking lot to **refuge headquarters** (0.5 mile). Proceed by car if the gate is open; otherwise you may walk. Trees and brush about the headquarters may be teeming with migrants in spring and fall. Great Horned Owls nest in these trees, often mobbed by Black-billed Magpies. A trail goes north, shortly crossing a concrete bridge to seasonally flooded fields and marshes where birding is often good for waterfowl, raptors, shorebirds, Marsh Wren, and Common Yellowthroat, from February to June.

Return to Pump House Road and turn right (west). A good area for shrub-steppe species is reached in 0.7 mile. Park by the road and walk south into the sagelands along the base of Toppenish Ridge. Look for sparrows from April through early August—Sage Sparrow in the densest tracts of Big Sagebrush, Lark Sparrow in the rocky and more arid places nearby, and Vesper Sparrow in areas of dense grass with few shrubs. Common Poorwills can be found at dusk from late April into September. Another patch of shrub-steppe habitat a short distance farther on (0.3 mile) offers similar possibilities. Continue west on Pump House Road and turn right onto **Old Goldendale Road** (1.2 miles from the second sagebrush patch, 2.2 miles from the headquarters turnoff). A marsh on the right side of the road (0.5 mile) has Sora, Virginia Rail, Marsh Wren, and Common Yellowthroat. American Bitterns "pump" here on spring and summer nights.

Return to Pump House Road, turn right, and go 7.0 miles to **Lateral C Road**, checking flooded fields (mainly spring) along the way for waterfowl and shorebirds (especially Long-billed Curlew) and the Greasewood-dominated shrub-steppe for Loggerhead Shrike. Black-tailed Jackrabbit, a declining species in Washington, is common here. At Lateral C, turn right and descend to the bridge over Toppenish Creek (0.4 mile) from which waterfowl and many swallows can often be viewed. Look, too, for Barn, Western Screech-, and Great Horned Owls. Another 0.4 mile on Lateral C brings you to an area of

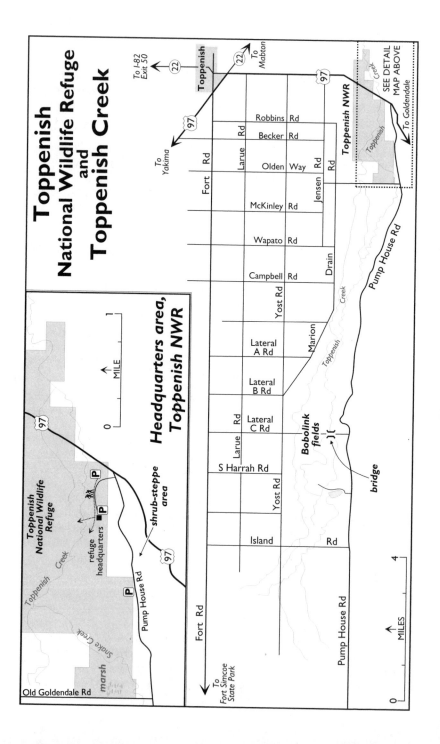

Toppenish
National Wildlife Refuge
and
Toppenish Creek

Headquarters area, Toppenish NWR

wet fields, site of a disjunct Bobolink colony; look and listen for them from late May through July. The nearest other populations are in irrigated hayfields along the northern tier of counties east of the Cascades. Lateral C Road meets Fort Road 3.1 miles farther north. You may turn right here to join US-97 in Toppenish, or left to visit Fort Simcoe.

Fort Simcoe, a historic frontier outpost west of Toppenish and now a state park, is famous for its Lewis's Woodpeckers. Indeed, the planted Garry Oak groves around the grounds are probably the best place to observe this charismatic species in Washington. Most common from April through early September, the woodpeckers may winter in smaller numbers if acorns are available (some years the mast crop fails). Other birds of the Garry Oaks include California Quail, Northern Flicker, White-breasted Nuthatch, and Steller's Jay (mainly winter). Brushy growth by the creek south of the fort usually has a few pairs of Ash-throated Flycatchers in early summer. Migrants are occasionally numerous in both spring and fall in the thick brush, especially around the ranger's residence. Fort Simcoe is reached by driving west from US-97 in Toppenish on Fort Road to Signal Peak Road (19.1 miles). Turn left here, go two miles, and turn right onto Fort Simcoe Road. The park entrance is on the left in five miles. Habitat on the approach to Fort Simcoe appears parched for much of the year, but is enlivened with many colorful wildflowers in early spring (March–April). Check shrub-steppe along the road for Loggerhead Shrike and Brewer's Sparrow.

WEST TO NACHES

Just west of Yakima is scenic, cliff-rimmed **Cowiche Canyon**, protected by a land trust. (See Wenas Creek map on page 297.) Take 40th Avenue south from US-12 to Summitview Avenue (1.5 miles). Turn right and go 7.1 miles to Weikel Road. Make a right here to the signed entrance (0.5 mile). A three-mile gravel trail follows the canyon bottom beside Cowiche Creek. Check the cliffs for Turkey Vulture, Red-tailed Hawk, Violet-green Swallow, and Rock and Canyon Wrens. The thick, brushy riparian vegetation has many resident Black-capped Chickadees. Flycatchers, vireos, and warblers can be numerous in migration. Cedar Waxwing, Yellow-breasted Chat, and Black-headed Grosbeak are a few of the summer residents.

Continuing west on US-12, turn left onto Ackley Road (1.4 miles west of the 40th Avenue exit). A few hundred feet ahead is Powerhouse Road. Stop here to admire the petroglyphs at the **Painted Rocks**, up a short flight of steps, and to view nesting White-throated Swifts and Cliff Swallows (April through July). These imposing cliffs are the terminus of the Tieton Flow, a sinuous andesite lava flow that originated from the Goat Rocks volcano one to two million years ago.

Return to US-12 and turn left, passing Allan Road (8.0 miles), a southern access to the Wenas Creek region (page 303). Continue 1.2 miles on US-12 to the traffic light in the center of Naches (check your gas if headed west to the mountain passes). From here it is 4.5 miles to the junction of US-12 and SR-410. Go right at this intersection onto the **Old Naches Road**. You will soon (0.1 mile) cross a canal where migrants can be thick in spring and fall. In summer, look for Yellow-breasted Chat and Lazuli Bunting. Continue on this road for another 0.5 mile to a WDFW parking lot on your left, in the Oak Creek Wildlife Area. This is a winter feeding station for the Bighorn Sheep that reside on Cleman Mountain, to the north. A Golden Eagle nest—active for years, near the top of the cliffs directly across the river—can be scoped from here, and both eagle species often soar high above. Chukar and Rock Wren utilize the talus.

CHINOOK PASS HIGHWAY

by Andy Stepniewski and Hal Opperman

Beginning 17 miles west of Yakima at an intersection with US-12, the seasonal Chinook Pass Highway (SR-410) ascends northwest, then west, following the Naches, Bumping, and American Rivers to beautiful Chinook Pass, an eastern access to Mount Rainier National Park. The highway is closed for the winter about five miles below the pass (from November through May in an average year). The full altitudinal range of Eastside habitats from Garry Oak and upper shrub-steppe to lower subalpine is present along this route and its many side branches, although lakes and marshes are in relatively short supply.

UPPER NACHES RIVER

At the junction of US-12 and SR-410, go right (northwest) on SR-410. In two miles, a gravel road leads off to the right and climbs steeply to **Mud Lake**. This road is good for Common Poorwill and Common Nighthawk at dusk in the warmer months. Nile Road turns off left from SR-410 in a further 6.0 miles. In 1.4 miles, turn left from Nile Road onto Bethel Ridge Road (FR-1500), then left again in 1.0 mile onto Little Rattlesnake Road (FR-1501), which follows **Little Rattlesnake Creek** for the next 5.2 miles to a junction with FR-1503. Pacific-slope Flycatcher, Warbling Vireo, Veery, Yellow and MacGillivray's Warblers, and other riparian species are common along this stretch. At the junction, keep right onto FR-1503. A marsh-rimmed lake in 1.5 miles has many more birds of riparian and montane-forest habitats.

Return to **Nile Road** and turn left to a bridge over the Naches River (3.3 miles). Streamside vegetation and marsh along the road have many birds, including Black-chinned and Rufous Hummingbirds, Red-naped Sapsucker, Willow and Pacific-slope Flycatchers, Warbling Vireo, Black-capped Chickadee, House Wren, Veery, Gray Catbird, Cedar Waxwing, Yellow and Mac-Gillivray's Warblers, Song Sparrow, Black-headed Grosbeak, Purple Finch, and Evening Grosbeak. Nile Road rejoins SR-410 in another 0.2 mile. Turn left toward Chinook Pass.

In 1.3 miles, **Bald Mountain Road** (FR-1701) takes off uphill to the right, offering quick access to montane dry-forest habitats—excellent for Flammulated Owl in May and June. Drive up this road for 1.6 miles and turn right onto FR-1711. In another 0.8 mile, stop to listen for the owl. Good habitat for Flams continues for another quarter-mile. Several miles farther on, the forest opens up with large patches of Bitterbrush, good for Common Poorwill.

For good daytime birding in open Ponderosa Pine and Douglas-fir forests at the head of the Wenas Creek drainage, travel uphill on FR-1701 from the FR-1711 intersection. Turn right in 2.2 miles onto FR-1712, go 0.1 mile, and

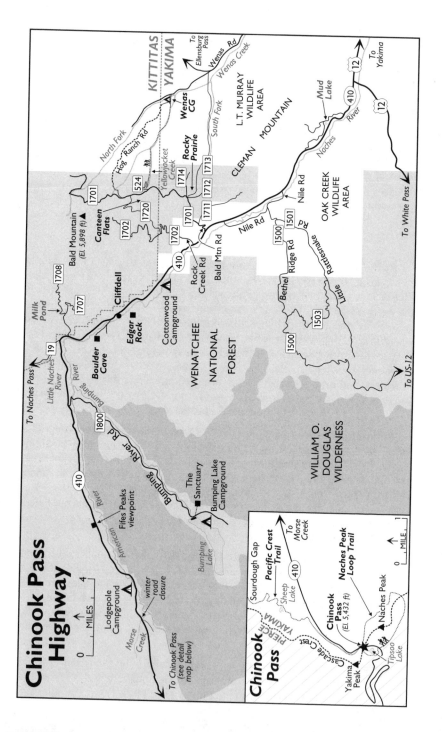

bear left onto FR-1713. **Rocky Prairie** (elevation 3,800 feet) starts in 0.5 mile. Look here for White-headed Woodpecker, White-breasted and Pygmy Nuthatches, Western and Mountain Bluebirds, Townsend's Solitaire, and Cassin's Finch. **Canteen Flats** (elevation 4,400 feet) is reached by continuing on FR-1701 for three miles past the FR-1712 turnoff. The rocky meadows rimmed by open forest have birds similar to those of Rocky Prairie. A short spur road (FR-524; now closed to vehicular traffic, but you may walk it) descends eastward from Canteen Flats to a trailhead for Yellowjacket Creek. From here you may follow along Yellowjacket Creek and Dry Creek to Wenas Campground (hike described on page 301). Several miles farther north on FR-1701, wetter forests of Grand Fir and Western Larch are good for Williamson's Sapsucker, Hammond's Flycatcher, Ruby-crowned Kinglet, and Townsend's and MacGillivray's Warblers.

Nine-tenths of a mile farther up SR-410, a second road (FR-1702) turns off right and ascends **Rock Creek**. Begin checking for Flammulated Owls about five miles up, on a sidehill where Douglas-fir, Ponderosa Pine, and an undergrowth of Deerbrush and other shrubs make for a high density of moths, the owls' preferred food. In April, this area is good for Great Horned and Northern Saw-whet Owls.

Continue west along SR-410. In 5.4 miles, pull completely off the road opposite **Edgar Rock**, which towers above you across the Naches River. Turkey Vulture, Red-tailed Hawk, Peregrine Falcon, and numerous Violet-green Swallows may be seen overhead, while the riparian woodland by the roadside has Warbling Vireo, Veery, and Yellow Warbler. Cliffdell, in another 0.8 mile, offers the last reliable service station for 80 miles.

Seven-tenths of a mile after Cliffdell, turn off left from SR-410 and cross the Naches River, then make an immediate right and go just over a mile to **Boulder Cave** (USFS fee area)—famous for its roost of the rare Townsend's Big-eared Bat. A barrier-free trail allows birding of the open pine forest and passes through an alder-lined slough with Warbling Vireo and Yellow Warbler. Harlequin Duck and American Dipper are regular along the river.

Return to SR-410 and turn left. In 2.7 miles you reach FR-1708, a good owling road that leads to **Milk Pond**. Go two miles up the road to a ravine. By walking about 500 yards up this forested gulch, then ascending a slope to the left for another few hundred yards, you might encounter Spotted Owl. Northern Saw-whet Owl is also a possibility. Hammond's Flycatcher, Hermit Thrush, Townsend's Warbler, and Evening Grosbeak are common in these woods.

LITTLE NACHES RIVER TO NACHES PASS

West again on SR-410, find FR-19, the **Little Naches Road**, on the right (0.7 mile). Near this corner the Bumping River and the Little Naches River unite to form the Naches River. The large Little Naches watershed—heavily clearcut in the last 25 years—now consists of a mosaic of meadows, gallery riparian woodland, and fir forests, favorable to Barred Owls, which have invaded the area fairly recently. Stopping along the road at dawn or dusk, especially near openings in the forest, will often turn up one. Spotted Owls, formerly widespread, have greatly declined, although a few still persist.

The historic Naches Trail—a wagon road to Puget Sound used by early settlers—followed the Little Naches River up across **Naches Pass**, then down the Greenwater and White River drainages on the Westside. FR-19, FR-1914, and FR-70 approximate its route. The actual pass, however, is now crossed by a deeply eroded, seven-mile jeep track. Despite the devastation from no-holds-barred logging and ATV traffic, patches of original forest in the wide vicinity of the 4,900-foot pass still harbor Three-toed Woodpecker, Gray Jay, Ruby-crowned Kinglet, and other montane specialties. White-crowned Sparrow (*gambelii*) breeds at the pass, and there are even fall reports of Boreal Owl. Keen birders occasionally venture here to find Eastside species such as Calliope Hummingbird, Red-naped Sapsucker, Dusky Flycatcher, Mountain Bluebird, and Cassin's Finch at their western range limits. **Government Meadows**, a mile west of the summit, is generally a productive spot. Before setting out to explore this area, make sure you have up-to-date maps and road information and a Northwest Forest Pass. All of these are available at the USFS ranger district stations on SR-410 in Naches and Enumclaw.

BUMPING RIVER TO CHINOOK PASS

Continue west on SR-410 from the Little Naches Road intersection. In 3.7 miles, turn off left onto the Bumping River Road (FR-1800). Lands on both sides of the narrow valley corridor are protected in the William O. Douglas Wilderness, named for the late Supreme Court justice and noted conservationist who made this area his second home. Look for Northern Goshawk and Pileated Woodpecker in the beautiful, mostly unlogged forest that lines the road, although the goshawk is remarkably elusive in the breeding season. Stop off the highway in 6.5 miles to explore a meadow by the river. Spotted Sandpiper and American Dipper are expected here, while Vaux's Swifts zip by overhead. In another 4.6 miles you reach the dam for **Bumping Lake**, a reservoir with nesting Barrow's Goldeneye, Osprey, and Spotted Sandpiper. The picnic area at Bumping Lake Campground (USFS fee area), in 0.2 mile, provides an overlook of the lake.

At the dam, go east from FR-1800 onto an unmarked, sandy, but passable track. Follow the main track through thick Lodgepole Pine woods to its end (0.6 mile). Walk a hundred yards to **The Sanctuary**, a small grove of huge Western Redcedars forming a Westside-type forest—great for Barred Owl, Chestnut-backed Chickadee, and Varied Thrush. Put your identification skills to work sorting out the two species of pine, three true firs, a spruce, two hemlocks, two cedars, Western Larch, and Douglas-fir that occur here, along with Red Alder—almost exclusively a Westside tree.

From the Bumping River Road intersection, SR-410 follows the American River westward the rest of the way to Chinook Pass. Stop at the **Fifes Peaks Viewpoint** (7.0 miles). The forest here is quite moist, reflecting proximity to the Cascade crest. Hammond's Flycatcher, Chestnut-backed Chickadee, Hermit and Varied Thrushes, and Townsend's Warbler are all common. Spy on the volcanic spires of the Fifes Peaks towering above; you may see a band of Mountain Goats. Stop again at **Lodgepole Campground** (4.8 miles). Williamson's Sapsucker is often found in the forest here—a mixture of Lodgepole Pine and Western Larch. The highway is closed for the winter at **Morse Creek** (2.0 miles). Near the winter-closure gate, a track leaves the highway on the left (downhill) side. Forest along this track has been a reliable spot to find Barred Owl and Chestnut-backed Chickadee, while the slopes on the right (uphill) side of the highway are excellent for Blue Grouse.

It is 5.4 miles from Morse Creek to **Chinook Pass** (elevation 5,432 feet), in the subalpine along the eastern boundary of Mount Rainier National Park (page 229). Views of the mountain are superb, especially in early morning. The forest here is composed of Mountain Hemlock and spire-like Subalpine Fir, alternating with lush meadows (best flower display from mid-July through mid-August). Gray Jays and Clark's Nutcrackers panhandle shamelessly among the throngs of visitors. Blue Grouse frequent the meadow edges. Migrant flycatchers, vireos, warblers, and sparrows can be numerous in the thickets in fall. In early evening, watch for a small flight of Black Swifts heading back to their nesting cliffs, presumably in the park. A modest showing of raptors appears over the ridges beginning in late August and continuing through mid-October.

Trails at the pass offer fine birding but are not fully open until the snow melts—usually by late July. The five-mile **Naches Peak Loop** is on the south side of the highway. Look for Horned Lark, Mountain and Chestnut-backed Chickadees, Red-breasted Nuthatch, Winter Wren, Townsend's Solitaire, Hermit and Varied Thrushes, American Pipit, Yellow-rumped and Townsend's Warblers, Chipping and Fox Sparrows, Pine Grosbeak (uncommon), Cassin's Finch, and Red and White-winged (irregular) Crossbills. North from the pass, a two-mile trail leads to Sheep Lake. White-tailed Ptarmigan are occasionally seen by hiking another mile, then descending into the snowy, bouldery terrain below **Sourdough Gap**.

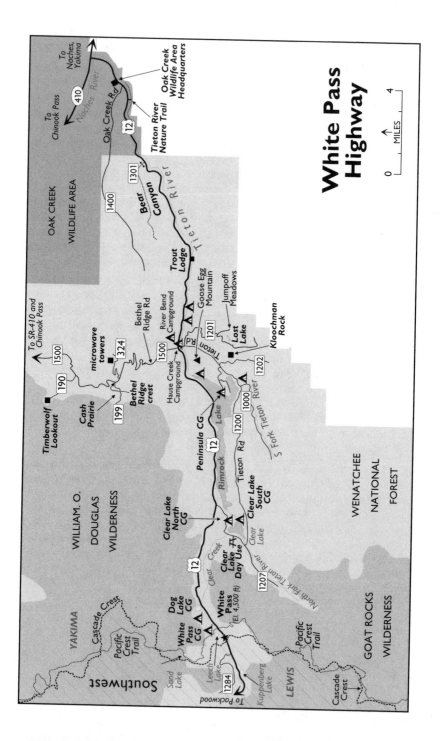

White Pass Highway

WHITE PASS HIGHWAY

by Andy Stepniewski

One of the better Cascades birding routes is the 34-mile stretch of US-12 that ascends the Tieton River to 4,500-foot White Pass, along a transect from arid Garry Oak and shrub-steppe vegetation at the lower end to tall, wet subalpine forest at the Cascade crest southeast of Mount Rainier.

OAK CREEK AND LOWER TIETON RIVER

Turn west with US-12 at the junction with SR-410, about four miles west of Naches. Lewis's Woodpeckers and Bullock's Orioles frequent Garry Oaks at the **Oak Creek Wildlife Area Headquarters** (2.0 miles). An extensive Elk-feeding program makes this a winter tourist attraction; several thousand animals can sometimes be observed. Nearby, an out-of-view carcass dump for road-killed animals attracts numbers of Turkey Vultures (summer) and Bald (winter) and Golden Eagles. Watch for them overhead.

West on US-12 another 0.2 mile is **Oak Creek Road**, on the right. This gravel road runs uphill alongside the creek into the heart of the 42,000-acre wildlife area, passing through Garry Oaks, Ponderosa Pines, and riparian vegetation. For the first four miles, look for Golden Eagle, Common Poorwill, White-throated Swift, Lewis's Woodpecker, Western Wood-Pewee, Least Flycatcher (rare but regular in aspen groves), Rock and Canyon Wrens, Veery, Nashville Warbler, Yellow-breasted Chat, Western Tanager, Black-headed Grosbeak, Lazuli Bunting, and Bullock's Oriole. Western Gray Squirrels still occur here—one of the relatively few places in the state where this declining species may be seen.

Another access to the wildlife area is one mile farther along US-12, on the left. Park here (WDFW permit required) and take the path leading right toward the river. Cross the swinging bridge to the **Tieton River Nature Trail**, which follows the river beneath towering cliffs of andesite for several miles both up- and downstream. Habitats include riparian woodland, Garry Oak and Ponderosa Pine groves on slightly drier sites, and finally a zone of Bitterbrush on yet drier slopes. Look for Blue Grouse, Lewis's Woodpecker, and Nashville Warbler, among many other species. At times in migration the trees here are filled with birds, especially on mornings following a storm.

Another 3.4 miles west on US-12—just beyond the Wenatchee National Forest boundary sign—turn off right onto gravel FR-1301 and park at the gate (Northwest Forest Pass required). A good walk goes uphill from here into cliff-rimmed **Bear Canyon**. The slopes are grown to picturesque Garry Oak, Ponderosa Pine, and Douglas-fir, while the canyon bottom has tall cotton-woods and willows. Bear Canyon is one of Washington's premier spots to observe butterflies (more than 60 species have been noted here) and is also good for bird species typical of the lower east slopes of the Cascades, such as Golden Eagle, Common Poorwill, White-throated Swift, Dusky Flycatcher, Cassin's Vireo, Violet-green Swallow, Canyon Wren, Townsend's Solitaire, Nashville Warbler, and Western Tanager.

Continuing west, US-12 parallels the rushing Tieton River. Check for Harlequin Duck (best mid-April–early June), Prairie Falcon (nesting on cliffs), and American Dipper. **Trout Lodge** (5.9 miles) has a small restaurant with several hummingbird feeders visible from the dining room, attracting Calliope and Rufous Hummingbirds. Please offer a word of thanks to the owners for providing this service. Between three and five miles west of the lodge on US-12, several forest service campgrounds are set in Ponderosa Pines, Black Cottonwoods, and willows along the Tieton River. All offer the chance to see White-headed Woodpecker.

BETHEL RIDGE

Continuing west on US-12, watch on the right for FR-1500, the **Bethel Ridge Road** (4.7 miles from Trout Lodge). This graded, though often washboarded gravel road steeply ascends the south slopes of Bethel Ridge, the eroded remnant of an ancient volcano. After gaining over 3,500 feet in elevation and passing through various types of colorful volcanic rock (tuffs and breccias, mainly) and a succession of forested habitats (Ponderosa Pine to mixed-conifer to subalpine), the road tops out in 7.5 miles at over 6,000 feet elevation. It is open in summer only. Species to be found along the way include Flammulated and Northern Pygmy-Owls, Common Poorwill, Williamson's and Red-naped Sapsuckers, White-headed Woodpecker, Cassin's Vireo, Cassin's Finch, and Red Crossbill.

Check the Ponderosa Pine woods in the general vicinity of the fork in 0.3 mile for White-headed Woodpecker. Two areas of wet montane meadow— the first 1.5 miles from the fork, the second in another half-mile—have Red-naped Sapsucker, Warbling Vireo, and MacGillivray's Warbler. Higher yet, FR-1500 leaves the Ponderosa Pine zone. Stop in 3.5 miles at a narrow band of mixed-conifer forest where Western Larch attracts Williamson's Sapsucker. Cold, snowy subalpine habitats with Subalpine Fir, Mountain Hemlock, and Lodgepole Pine begin abruptly in another 1.0 mile. Turn right here on FR-324 to reach the **microwave towers** atop Bethel Ridge. The dark, dense forests on the north aspects of the ridge harbor a few Spruce Grouse, although they are rarely seen. The promise of a tough slog through the nearly impenetrable vegetation is enough to deter all but the most sure-footed hikers. Easier to spot are Gray Jay and Clark's Nutcracker.

The Bethel Ridge crest is another 0.7 mile up FR-1500. Turn left onto FR-199 to reach **Cash Prairie** (1.1 miles), a beautiful subalpine meadow where Ruby-crowned Kinglet is common and the Lincoln's Sparrow bubbly song emanates from the tall, corn-like False Hellebore—a poisonous member of the lily family. Among the many raptors that soar over this meadow from late summer through fall, look especially for accipiters, Red-tailed and Rough-legged Hawks, Golden Eagle, American Kestrel, and Prairie Falcon. The road ends in another 1.0 mile at a trailhead for the William O. Douglas Wilderness from which views extend to Mount Adams, the Goat Rocks, and the summit of Mount Rainier. The exposed, steep south-facing slopes have a few shrub-steppe plants such as Big Sagebrush and Scarlet Gilia; look for Rock Wren here. Only a few yards away are equally steep, north-facing slopes mantled in snow-forest species such as Mountain Hemlock, Subalpine Fir, and Lodgepole Pine, plus scattered Alaska Yellowcedar, Engelmann Spruce, and Whitebark Pine. Golden-crowned and Ruby-crowned Kinglets and Townsend's Warbler breed in these cold forests. Pine Grosbeak and White-winged Crossbill are rare wanderers.

Return to FR-1500 and turn left. Descend 3.5 miles to FR-190, turn left, and climb 2.6 miles to **Timberwolf Lookout**, at 6,400 feet. A small band of Mountain Goats is often seen on the nearby cliffs. Hawks sail by in the fall, most commonly accipiters and Red-taileds. Returning to FR-1500, you can take a left and go down FR-1500 to join SR-410, the Chinook Pass Highway, in about 16 miles (page 321). Otherwise, turn right and retrace your route up and over Bethel Ridge to US-12 in 11 miles.

AROUND RIMROCK LAKE

About three miles west of the FR-1500 intersection the Tieton River is dammed to form Rimrock Lake. US-12 follows the north shore of the reservoir closely. The deep, clear, cold waters are not inviting to birds, but you might see a few waterfowl, shorebirds, and gulls (and many swallows at the dam). Tieton Road goes around the south side of the lake through forest and wetland habitats, departing from US-12 about 2.5 miles below the dam and returning to it in 16 miles, near the west end of the lake. Although it is nine miles longer, this paved road is by far the better birding choice if you are not in a big hurry to get to the pass.

Three-tenths of a mile west of the FR-1500 intersection, turn left from US-12 onto Tieton Road (FR-1200). Cross the Tieton River to a junction with FR-1201, on the left (0.2 mile). The wetlands on both sides of the road near this junction host a nice variety of forest birds. Red-naped Sapsucker and Willow Flycatcher are common. Look for Gray Catbird and warblers around the small pond. FR-1201 climbs steadily to a turnoff for Jumpoff Meadows in about 3.5 miles. The mixed Ponderosa Pine and Douglas-fir forest alternating with alder-and-willow-lined meadows offers good birding possibilities, including Lincoln's Sparrow; Williamson's Sapsucker is reasonably common in areas with Western Larch. Back on Tieton Road, travel uphill past Goose Egg Mountain on your right (nesting White-throated Swifts) and Kloochman Rock on your left, and turn left onto FR-1202 (2.5 miles). Go 0.3 mile to a swamp by the road. In the numerous snags, watch for woodpeckers (including White-headed) and swallows. Many forest species occur in the surrounding pines, alders, and willows.

The turnoff for **Peninsula Campground**, on Rimrock Lake, is 0.2 miles farther along Tieton Road on the right. A marsh with Virginia Rail, Sora, and many blackbirds is on the right (north) side of the entrance road. Red-naped and Red-breasted (scarce) Sapsuckers nest in the Quaking Aspen and Black Cottonwood groves. Flammulated Owl occurs, if not in the campground, then along the steep, south-facing slopes of Goose Egg Mountain grown to Ponderosa Pines with an understory of Deerbrush, at the campground entrance.

Continue west on Tieton Road. At a fork in 1.6 miles, where FR-1000 goes left up the South Fork Tieton, stay right with FR-1200. A steady increase in precipitation is reflected in the changing habitats as you proceed westward to the entrance for Clear Lake South Campground (7.0 miles), including riparian areas with lush Mountain Alder and willow thickets, meadows, and tall, moist forests of Grand Fir and Engelmann Spruce. A stop at any of several pullouts or gravel lanes on your left may yield Ruffed Grouse, Willow and Hammond's Flycatchers, Calliope Hummingbird, Cassin's and Warbling Vireos, Chest-nut-backed Chickadee, and Orange-crowned, Nashville, Yellow, Yellow-rumped, Townsend's, and MacGillivray's Warblers. Open, south-facing slopes on your right have Douglas-firs and Ponderosa Pines. There, look for Blue Grouse, Clark's Nutcracker, Mountain Chickadee, Cassin's Finch, and Red Crossbill.

One mile past the Clear Lake South Campground turnoff, at the intersection with North Fork Tieton Road, keep right with FR-1200. In 0.6 mile, turn right into the **Clear Lake Day-Use Site** (USFS fee area). Take the paved nature walk through open forest of Douglas-fir and Grand Fir (Hammond's Flycatcher, Western Tanager, Cassin's Finch) to observation blinds at the edge of Clear Lake. During summer, look for nesting Ring-necked Duck, Barrow's Goldeneye, and Osprey. Loons, grebes, diving ducks (including Surf and White-winged Scoters), and Common Tern are regular, though uncommon, in fall migration.

Once again on Tieton Road, it is 0.7 mile to the bridge over **Clear Creek**. American Dippers often nest under the bridge. Snags and alder thickets have lots of Warbling Vireos and Yellow Warblers. American Redstarts, near the edge of their range, have been noted in the alders around the lake. **Clear Lake North Campground** (1.4 miles; USFS, primitive) is a fine spot to camp (one can scan Clear Lake from another vantage on the way there). Look for Northern Pygmy-Owl (uncommon) and Western Tanager in the surrounding forest. From the campground a short walk downstream along Clear Creek leads to the upper end of Rimrock Lake. Nesting birds here include Common Merganser, Osprey, Bald Eagle, Spotted Sandpiper, and American Dipper.

Tens of thousands of land-locked Kokanee Salmon spawn along the creek in October. Hundreds of gulls, mostly California but also a few Ring-billed, Herring, Thayer's, and Glaucous-winged, gather here for the fish feast. More Bald Eagles also arrive, usually in November, to partake of this buffet. Right from the campground, Tieton Road reaches US-12 in 0.4 mile.

WHITE PASS AND VICINITY

West and steadily uphill, US-12 traverses a hazardous rockslide area (stopping not advised, although Peregrine Falcons have nested on the cliffs right above the highway). At **Dog Lake Campground** (5.5 miles), check for Barrow's Goldeneye on the lake, Williamson's and Red-naped Sapsuckers (Red-breasted also possible), and Gray Jay in the Western Larches.

Another 1.5 miles on US-12 brings you to the turnoff to White Pass Campground (USFS, primitive), on the shores of **Leech Lake**. Mountain species noted here in summer include Ring-necked Duck, Barrow's Goldeneye, Osprey, Northern Pygmy- and Barred Owls, Williamson's (east of the lake around corrals) and Red-breasted (lakeshore snags) Sapsuckers, Pileated Woodpecker, Rock Wren (talus slides north of the highway), and Hermit and Varied Thrushes. Trails give access to extensive forests, subalpine meadows, and glacier-mantled peaks—for example, the Pacific Crest Trail south to the Goat Rocks Wilderness. The forest north up the Pacific Crest Trail may yield Three-toed Woodpecker, and a hike of at least several miles reaches subalpine openings—good habitat for Pine Grosbeak (perhaps irregular). Boreal Owl has been found here in late summer.

West again on US-12 brings you to the 4,500-foot summit of **White Pass** (0.4 mile). The willow scrub and conifers around the lodge, and particularly north of the highway by the shores of Leech Lake, have yielded Calliope and Rufous Hummingbirds, Tree and Violet-green Swallows, Gray Jay, Clark's Nutcracker, many quite tame Common Ravens, and Lincoln's and White-crowned (*pugetensis*) Sparrows.

About a mile west of the pass turn right (north) onto FR-1284. At 0.1 mile, keep right and uphill on the main gravel road. Spotted Owl was once reliable a few hundred yards along this road and may be still. In 2.8 miles, reach the **Sand Lake Trail**, which leads into the William O. Douglas Wilderness. One mile up this trail a large burn has been good for woodpeckers, including Three-toed, Black-backed, and Pileated. Don't be too surprised if all you see is Hairy Woodpecker, however. Remind yourself it's good exercise, whatever the bird list. Back on US-12, continue west. **Kuppenberg Lake** (0.8 mile) is worth a short stop; Barrow's Goldeneyes have nested here. Watch also for Gray Jays coming to beg for scraps.

In 8.4 miles note a pullout to the left (south) for **Palisades Viewpoint**, overlooking a basalt cliff across the canyon. The lazy, wheezy song of

Townsend's Warbler is easy to hear from this spot, but the birds often remain high in the tall Douglas-firs and can be difficult to spot. It is 2.3 miles to a major junction where you may turn north and ascend SR-123 along the Ohanapecosh River to Mount Rainier National Park (page 229), or continue southwestward with US-12, following the Cowlitz River to Packwood (page 237) and birding sites in Southwestern Washington.

EASTERN COLUMBIA GORGE AND KLICKITAT RIVER

by Bill LaFramboise, Nancy LaFramboise, Wilson Cady, and Andy Stepniewski

East of Mount Adams, the Klickitat River drains a large basin southward, reaching the Columbia River gorge at Lyle. With its rolling hills, dry Garry Oak and Ponderosa Pine forests, and patches of Buckbrush and other shrubs, this country has habitats similar to those of interior southern Oregon and northern California, and some of the same bird species. Acorn Woodpecker and Lesser Goldfinch reach their northern range limits here. Other breeding species with southern affinities are Anna's Hummingbird, Lewis's Woodpecker, Gray and Ash-throated Flycatchers, White-breasted Nuthatch, and Western Scrub-Jay, along with Southern Alligator Lizard and Western Gray Squirrel. Conboy Lake National Wildlife Refuge has birds of pine, riparian, marsh, and wet-meadow habitats, including a small breeding population of Sandhill Cranes. The Columbia Gorge and Columbia Hills are important raptor sites. Migrating and wintering waterfowl are numerous along the Columbia River. Be aware, however, that Poison Oak is especially abundant in the woodland understory. Western Rattlesnakes are common, too, particularly near rocky areas.

Our site descriptions begin with the eastern Columbia Gorge, picking up at Bingen where those for the western Gorge leave off (page 258) and proceeding upstream to the eastern terminus of the Columbia River Gorge National Scenic Area at Maryhill. Again, we use the mileposts along SR-14 as reference points.

BINGEN

Driving east on SR-14, cross the White Salmon River bridge (milepost 63.5). In a bit less than two miles is the turnoff for the toll bridge to Hood River, Oregon. Continue east on SR-14 into the town of Bingen. At milepost 66.5 (just east of the Shell station), turn right onto Maple Street at the sign for the Bingen Marina. Cross the railroad tracks and stay straight ahead through a small industrial district. In 0.1 mile you reach an intersection with Lakeview Boulevard. Keep straight onto Shore Drive; **Bingen Pond** will come into view on your left, surrounded by blackberry thickets and Reed Canary Grass. The pond may have grebes, ducks, and a few shorebirds, but the main attraction is winter sparrows. Song, Lincoln's, White-crowned, and Golden-crowned are common, White-throated and Harris's rare but regular. Rarer still are Sage and Swamp Sparrows. Lesser Goldfinch can sometimes be found (has nested nearby). The willows and cottonwoods can hold roosting owls or migrant passerines in season. The waters of the Columbia are easily scanned by going back and turning right onto Lakeview, then right again onto Harbor Way and following it to the small park at Bingen Point. Ring-necked Duck and Greater and Lesser Scaups are regular in the river in winter. A Tufted Duck also wintered here several years running. Local birders maintain a logbook of bird sightings at The Loafers Bakery, on SR-14 two blocks west of Maple Street.

Eastward on SR-14 at milepost 69.5, **Locke Lake** is divided in two by the highway. The southern half hosts flocks of ducks in winter. In migration, the oak forest here can be good for warblers and other passerines. Bullock's Oriole nests dangle from the oaks and Canyon Wrens call from the cliff face; an occasional Golden Eagle may be seen overhead. Courtney Road, at the west end of the lake, leads steeply up Burdoin Mountain through oak woodlands with Wild Turkey, Say's Phoebe, Western Bluebird, and Lesser Goldfinch. The views from this road are breathtaking and worth the two-mile drive.

LYLE

At milepost 70.9 the highway bisects **Rowland Lake**, used by wintering waterfowl. California Quail, Lewis's Woodpecker, and Ash-throated Flycatcher frequent the oaks along the shore. By turning left onto Old Highway 8 you may drive around the north side of the lake to a rocky grassland interspersed with pines where Mountain Quail were seen in the past; Wild Turkeys should be looked for today. In 1.5 miles is parking for the **Catherine Creek Preserve**, approximately 1,000 acres of oak/pine woods, cliffs, Poison Oak thickets, grasslands, and vernal ponds, owned by the U.S. Forest Service. A heavily-used trail goes uphill across slopes ablaze in spring with many colorful wildflowers to a massive basalt arch, providing a grand view of the eastern Columbia Gorge. Turkey Vultures, Bald Eagles, and Red-tailed Hawks are often noted soaring over the cliffs. Below, Columbia River waters have diving ducks in season.

Continue eastward on Old Highway 8, checking the oaks and fields for Lewis's Woodpecker, Western Scrub-Jay, and Lesser Goldfinch. In 1.8 miles, turn left onto **Balch Road**. Stop at the Lyle-Balch Cemetery in 0.3 mile; scruffy growth outside the cemetery is prime habitat for Lesser Goldfinch. After the cemetery, keep right at the fork in 0.2 mile. Visible from the road a short distance ahead on the right, Balch Lake can be good for Wood Duck and Hooded Merganser. Ash-throated Flycatcher and Lesser Goldfinch nest in the surrounding oak and pine forest. This area is closed to the public to protect a small population of the Western Pond Turtle, once fairly common in Washington but now nearly extirpated. Continue 0.6 mile to return to Old Highway 8.

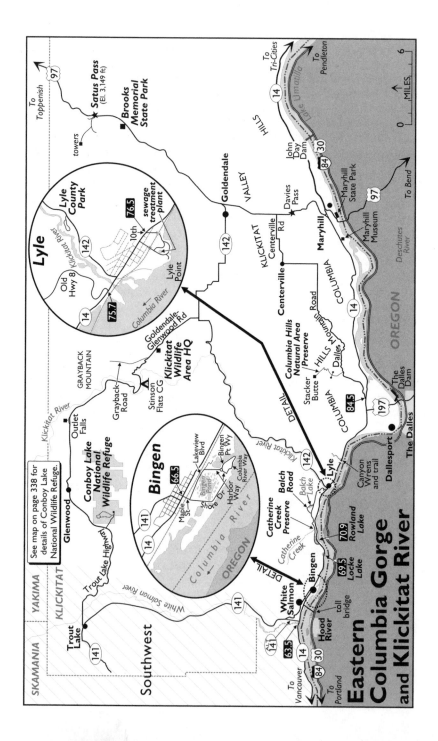

Eastern
Columbia Gorge
and Klickitat River

Turn left (east) and stop at the second power pole, about 100 yards from the Balch Road corner. Look several hundred yards south for a lone Ponderosa Pine snag riddled with holes, an **Acorn Woodpecker granary**. The woodpeckers are often seen on or near the snag—if you are lucky, even flying between it and the woods to the north of Old Highway 8. A scope and patience are requisites for success.

In 2.2 miles, Old Highway 8 rejoins SR-14 at milepost 75.7. Turn left, cross the Klickitat River, and in 0.1 mile turn left again onto SR-142. Drive 0.8 mile and turn left into **Lyle County Park** (unsigned). Take the dirt road that leads down to an overlook of the Klickitat River. Year-round residents of woods and stream include Wild Turkey (most easily seen at dawn), Lewis's Woodpecker, Anna's Hummingbird, Western Scrub-Jay, Bushtit, and White-breasted Nuthatch, joined in summer by Osprey, Spotted Sandpiper, Vaux's Swift, Ash-throated Flycatcher, Nashville, Black-throated Gray, and MacGillivray's Warblers, Western Tanager, Black-headed Grosbeak, and Lesser Goldfinch. Common Goldeneye may be on the river in winter. Bald Eagle is common then, patrolling for spawned salmon and other fish. Anna's Hummingbird can also be found by searching for feeders at residences in Lyle, if it is missed here.

From the intersection with SR-142, take SR-14 east 0.6 mile and turn right onto 10th Street (milepost 76.5). Drive through the railroad underpass to the tiny **Lyle sewage treatment plant**. In winter, Lesser Goldfinches sometimes forage in weeds near the sewage lagoon, while blackberry thickets on either side of the railway embankment swarm with Golden-crowned Sparrows. West a few hundred yards beyond the lagoon is **Lyle Point**. The Klickitat River delta may be scanned from here for Double-crested Cormorant, Bald Eagle, and a variety of gulls and terns.

COLUMBIA HILLS

SR-14 goes through a pair of tunnels on the eastern outskirts of Lyle. Stop at the small parking area just outside the east portal of the east tunnel to look for Canyon Wren on the steep cliffs (milepost 77.2). In winter, Gray-crowned Rosy-Finches can sometimes be found along the railway tracks, feeding on waste wheat blown from the numerous passing trains. Hikers will enjoy the **Lyle Cherry Orchard Trail**, which begins here and climbs steeply more than 1,000 vertical feet to the ridge above the river—the western extremity of the Columbia Hills. Lesser Goldfinches are fairly common along the trail in the breeding season; look also for Western Scrub-Jays. Views of the Gorge are incredible.

The Columbia Hills dominate the Washington side of the Gorge for nearly 50 miles, from the Klickitat River to Rock Creek. The river is less than 300 feet above sea level along this stretch, while the high point of the hills is above 3,000 feet. Goldendale and the Klickitat Valley, across the summit, are at an elevation of around 1,600 feet. Headed north on US-97, traction devices may be required in winter between the Gorge and Davies Pass.

Dalles Mountain Road—a marvelous, 22-mile birding route up and over the Columbia Hills—starts near Dallesport and connects to US-97 about a mile north of Davies Pass. Grasslands and fields all along this route host many raptors—particularly in winter, when Northern Harrier, Red-tailed and Rough-legged Hawks, Golden Eagle, and Prairie Falcon are common. The breeding season brings Horned Larks, and Vesper and a few Grasshopper Sparrows, to north flanks of the mountain. Turn north onto Dalles Mountain Road from SR-14 at milepost 84.5. In 3.4 miles, turn left onto a steep gravel road, drive 1.4 miles, and park at a gate. Watch for Lewis's Woodpecker and Western Scrub-Jay in the pine/oak woods on the way up, and for sparrows and Lesser Goldfinch in the bramble thickets in winter. You are in the **Columbia Hills Natural Area Preserve** (DNR), set aside in 1993 to protect a 3,593-acre remnant of a type of grassland ecosystem rare in Washington, along with thriving populations of three rare plants (Obscure Buttercup, Douglas's Draba, Hot-rock Penstemon). You may continue up the road on foot to the top of 3,220-foot Stacker Butte (2.3 miles, 1,200 feet elevation gain). Enjoy a panoramic view reaching from the Cascades on the west deep into Oregon. Keep an eye out for raptors. The spring wildflower show is fantastic.

Dalles Mountain Road continues northeastward, slowly climbing the south flank of the Columbia Hills, crossing the crest, and descending toward the Klickitat Valley. In 11.1 miles, keep left on Dalles Mountain Road as it makes a 90-degree turn to the north, reaching **Centerville** in another 3.0 miles. A right turn onto Centerville Road gets you to US-97 in 4.3 miles. Swales in the Centerville area can hold temporary lakes in spring, excellent for migrant Tundra Swans, Canada Geese, American Wigeons, Mallards, Northern Pintails, and Green-winged Teal. The farmlands here can also have numerous raptors.

The weedy fields around the **Maryhill Museum** are a good place to look for Lesser Goldfinch. The entrance is on the south side of SR-14 at milepost 98.8, two miles west of the intersection with US-97 to/from Goldendale. Still another possibility for this species is **Maryhill State Park**. From SR-14, take US-97 south toward Oregon (intersection half a mile east of the one for Goldendale). Turn left into the park in 1.6 miles, just before the Columbia River bridge. The goldfinches are often noted in the weedy growth and trees by the entrance kiosk or in surrounding fields. Look also for diving ducks on the river in winter, especially Barrow's Goldeneye.

KLICKITAT RIVER

West of Goldendale is the **Klickitat Wildlife Area**, 14,000 acres of rugged canyons, Garry Oak groves, and park-like grasslands interspersed with Ponderosa Pine, Douglas-fir, and Quaking Aspen thickets. These diverse habitats support good populations of gallinaceous birds (Chukar, Ruffed and Blue

Grouse, Wild Turkey, California Quail). Red-tailed Hawk, Golden Eagle, American Kestrel, Lewis's Woodpecker, American Dipper, Nashville Warbler, and Lark Sparrow are also common. Resident mammals include Mule Deer, Bighorn Sheep, Bobcat, Coyote, and California Ground Squirrel. Southern Alligator Lizard can be found in summer, along with Western Skink, Western Fence Lizard, Gopher Snake, and Western Rattlesnake.

To get there, turn north from SR-142 onto the Goldendale-Glenwood Road, marked by a sign *To Glenwood*. Coming up the winding canyon from Lyle, you will find this intersection on your left in about 24 miles; coming from US-97 in Goldendale, it will be on your right in 11.5 miles. Seven-tenths of a mile past the entrance to the wildlife-area headquarters, turn right onto poorly marked **Grayback Road** (5.6 miles from SR-142). This dirt road can be driven north through grasslands and pine/oak groves for slightly more than two miles, where it abruptly deteriorates (keep left at the fork in 0.5 mile). Watch for Gray Flycatcher, especially in the first mile. Western and Mountain Bluebirds nest in boxes along the road, and all three nuthatches can be found in the woodlands. Many other species are present in May and June, including Western Wood-Pewee, House Wren, and Vesper Sparrow. The views of nearby Mount Adams and of Mount Hood in Oregon are memorable, as is the spring wildflower display.

Proceeding westward, the Goldendale-Glenwood Road soon begins a dramatic descent into the **Klickitat River Gorge**. Lazuli Bunting is common along this stretch as are raptors such as Bald and Golden Eagles and Cooper's and Red-tailed Hawks. Near the bottom of the descent (4.3 miles), turn left onto a gravel road that drops down one mile through stately oaks to primitive **Stinson Flats Campground** (WDFW permit required), where lush growth and the Klickitat River attract many birds and other wildlife. The river, originating from melting glaciers and snowfields on Mount Adams, is famous for its Steelhead—an anadromous trout with a life cycle similar to that of most salmon.

Continuing toward Glenwood, the road soon crosses the Klickitat River (1.1 miles from the campground turnoff). Here begins the long ascent out of the gorge. An overlook of **Outlet Falls** is reached by driving right from the highway onto an unmarked dirt track (6.2 miles), then along this to another junction (0.2 mile) and right to a parking turnaround (0.1 mile). Walk several hundred feet down to a fenced observation point with spectacular views of the Klickitat River and Outlet Creek. Birds of cliffs and Douglas-fir forest can be found here, including Turkey Vulture, Vaux's Swift, Cassin's Vireo, Violet-green Swallow, Townsend's Warbler, and Western Tanager.

CONBOY LAKE NATIONAL WILDLIFE REFUGE

Conboy Lake National Wildlife Refuge, established in 1964, occupies 5,800 acres of meadows, marshes, and woodlands in a high basin south of Glenwood. It may be reached either via SR-142 and the Goldendale-Glenwood Road or via SR-141 and the Trout Lake Highway (page 259). The small community of Glenwood sits about six miles west of the Outlet Falls overlook, described above. Drive through town for about a mile and find Trout Lake Highway on the west side. Turn south here and drive 4.8 miles through Ponderosa Pine forest to the main refuge entrance, on the left. (If coming from the west, you will find this entrance on your right about ten miles from the town of Trout Lake.)

Drive in to the **Willard Springs Nature Trail** parking lot (0.8 mile), a short distance before refuge headquarters. A nice variety of bird species is present along this two-mile loop, especially in May and June. The Ponderosa Pine woodlands may have White-headed Woodpecker, Gray Flycatcher, Cassin's Vireo, Mountain Chickadee, all three nuthatches, Chipping Sparrow, and Purple Finch (surprisingly, Cassin's Finch is scarce or absent). Ruby-crowned Kinglet breeds in the Lodgepole Pine forest at the far northern end of the loop. Red-naped Sapsucker, Willow Flycatcher, and Eastern Kingbird are likely in riparian areas, while Sora, Marsh Wren, and Common Yellowthroat inhabit the marsh and wet-grass habitats.

The refuge can be spectacular in spring when large numbers of migrant Tundra Swans, Canada Geese, Mallards, Northern Pintails, and other waterfowl stop to rest and feed in the flooded fields and shallow lakes. Another attraction is several nesting pairs of Sandhill Cranes (17 in 2001). Essentially extirpated from Washington as a breeder, cranes first returned to Conboy Lake in 1979—a testimony to the effectiveness of habitat restoration efforts. Look for them from the observation platform on the trail, or with a scope as they feed far out in the open fields. A few Black Terns are also

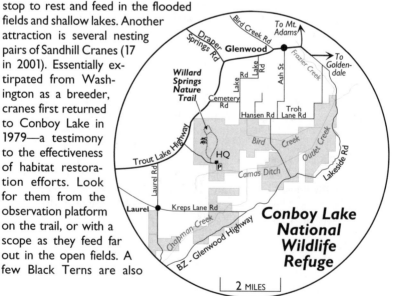

Bird Creek Rd
To Mt. Adams
Draper Springs Rd
Glenwood
To Goldendale
Frazier Creek
Willard Springs Nature Trail
Lake Rd
Lake Rd
Ash St
Cemetery Rd
Hansen Rd
Troh Lane Rd
Trout Lake Highway
Bird
Creek
Outlet Creek
HQ
P
Camas Ditch
Lakeside Rd
Laurel Rd
Laurel
Kreps Lane Rd
Chapman Creek
BZ - Glenwood Highway

Conboy Lake National Wildlife Refuge

2 MILES

usually present over the marshes and wet fields in the breeding season.

Fields and lakes can be viewed from an observation point at headquarters or by driving the roads that encircle the refuge. The most satisfying view may be from **Kreps Lane Road**. Leaving the headquarters road, turn left onto Trout Lake Highway. In one mile turn left on Laurel Road to Kreps Lane Road (1.4 miles). Turn left here and drive about two miles to where it crosses Chapman Creek. Close studies of Sandhill Cranes are often possible in this vicinity.

SATUS PASS

Birders connecting between the Klickitat country and sites around Yakima will likely travel on US-97 across Satus Pass, situated on the ridge dividing the Columbia and Yakima River watersheds at an elevation of 3,149 feet. From the summit it is 34 miles north to Toppenish, or 14 miles south to Goldendale. (See map on page 334.)

The combination of habitats on the drive up from Toppenish—from shrub-steppe to riparian to oaks, thence into Ponderosa Pine and finally mixed-conifer forests—boasts many birds. Most of the distance to the pass lies within the closed Yakama Indian Reservation. You must bird from the busy highway. Even so, a stop or two in strategically selected habitats should be productive. Lewis's Woodpecker, Ash-throated Flycatcher, Eastern Kingbird, Bushtit, and Bewick's Wren are among the many breeding species.

At the pass, an unimproved gravel road goes west and uphill. Take the second (larger) of two lefts at the fork in 0.1 mile, then keep right in 1.6 miles. In another 1.8 miles you reach communication towers at a ridgetop with spectacular views of the Cascade volcanoes. The north side of the ridge is forested, while the shallow-soiled south slopes are mostly open—great in spring and early summer for many wildflowers. Birds possible along the road in summer include Turkey Vulture, Northern Goshawk, Blue Grouse, Red-breasted and White-breasted Nuthatches, Rock Wren, Nashville, Yellow-rumped, and Townsend's Warblers, Fox Sparrow (especially in Deerbrush), Cassin's Finch, and Red Crossbill. Listen for Flammulated Owl at night. Williamson's Sapsucker is fairly common, especially in the mixed-conifer forests past the communication towers. The road becomes very rough, however.

Brooks Memorial State Park—2.5 miles south of Satus Pass on US-97—is excellent for breeding birds of Ponderosa Pine woods, riparian groves and thickets, and brushy patches. Look for Cooper's Hawk, Red-naped Sapsucker (Red-breasted is rare), Western Wood-Pewee, Hammond's and Dusky Flycatchers, Cassin's and Warbling Vireos, Brown Creeper, House Wren, Orange-crowned, Nashville, Yellow, Yellow-rumped, and MacGillivray's Warblers, Black-headed Grosbeak, Purple Finch, and Red Crossbill. Gray Flycatcher is reported from the open pines near the power lines. The park has a good campground (fee).

ROCK CREEK AND LAKE UMATILLA

by Bill LaFramboise and Nancy LaFramboise

Not far east of Maryhill, John Day Dam backs up the Columbia River for 70 miles to form Lake Umatilla (pronounced YOU-muh-TILL-uh). A long ridge known as the Horse Heaven Hills parallels the Columbia some 20 miles to the north, separating it from the Yakima River watershed. Draining the southwestern part of the Horse Heaven Hills, Rock Creek flows into Lake Umatilla about 15 miles upriver from the dam. A fine birding route runs up along Rock Creek and eastward to Bickleton, crosses the midsection of the Horse Heaven Hills, and descends to Mabton in the Yakima Valley. This route is especially good in spring and early summer for birds of streamsides, pine/oak woods, grasslands, wheat fields, and shrub-steppe. The Bickleton area is well known as Eastern Washington's bluebird trail. Nest boxes maintained for decades along 120 miles of roads are home to many Western and Mountain Bluebirds and a few other species—particularly Tree Swallows. Several excellent birding sites in the bottomlands along Lake Umatilla swarm with migrating and wintering waterfowl, attendant Bald Eagles, and other birds of marshes, fields, open water, and brushy tangles. Once again, we utilize the mileposts along SR-14 in our route descriptions.

ROCK CREEK AND HORSE HEAVEN HILLS

Turn north onto **Rock Creek Road** from SR-14 at milepost 121.1, about 20 miles east of the US-97 intersection. Be sure to have a full tank of gas: there are no services along the route before Mabton (60 miles), nor are there any along SR-14 for 20 miles in either direction. Check the mouth of the creek, now flooded by the impounded waters of Lake Umatilla, for waterfowl in winter. In 3.9 miles, stay straight where Old Highway 8 turns right. Then in 0.4 mile leave the main road, keeping right with Rock Creek Road (gravel). Most of the road is bordered by private property; please respect the numerous signs. Stop to check promising areas of streamside vegetation. Lewis's Woodpecker, Red-eyed Vireo, Yellow-breasted Chat, Lazuli Bunting, and Bullock's Oriole are common during the breeding season. This is a good location for Ash-throated Flycatcher and one of the few where Bushtit can be found east of the Cascades. Townsend's Solitaire is common during the winter. Bald Eagle may be found in winter and Golden Eagle year round. A side trip up Newell Road, on the right in 4.0 miles, provides similar habitats and birding opportunities. Continue north on Rock Creek Road. In 2.3 miles, find a ranch driveway on the left. Just beyond it, Rock Creek Road parallels a particularly inviting stretch of riparian woodland dominated by White Alder—best birded on foot from the roadway.

Turn right onto the **Goldendale-Bickleton Highway** (3.1 miles from the ranch driveway) and begin the ascent of the south face of the Horse Heaven Hills to Bickleton. Stop along the road at likely spots to inspect Garry

Oak, Ponderosa Pine, and grassland habitats for Vaux's Swift, Calliope and Rufous Hummingbirds, Lewis's Woodpecker, Red-naped Sapsucker and other woodpeckers, Western Wood-Pewee, Gray Flycatcher, Cassin's Vireo, White-breasted Nuthatch, warblers, Western Tanager, and Cassin's Finch. Open areas should have Western and Mountain Bluebirds and Vesper Sparrow. Explore side roads for more bluebird-viewing possibilities. Additional stops can be made at the Box Springs Road junction in 12.4 miles, and at a bridge in another 6.6 miles where the road crosses Pine Creek; check here for riparian species.

After passing through the small town of Bickleton the road makes a 90-degree left turn at the school (1.5 miles). Wheat country begins in 2.0 miles. Birds to be found in these fields in winter include Rough-legged Hawk, Prairie Falcon, Gray Partridge, Northern Shrike, gobs of Horned Larks, and sometimes a few Lapland Longspurs and Snow Buntings. The road (now known as **Glade Road**) descends the north side of the Horse Heaven Hills, reaching Alderdale Road in 17.6 miles. Keep on Glade Road, descending steeply through shrub-steppe and bunchgrass habitat. A fire during the summer of 2000 reduced shrub cover, impacting bird abundance for years to come. Patches of unburnt terrain remain, however, and you may still find Loggerhead Shrike, Say's Phoebe, Sage Thrasher, and Brewer's, Lark, and Sage Sparrows in smaller numbers. Be on the lookout for raptors such as Swainson's Hawk and Golden Eagle. Northern Shrikes winter along the route.

The floor of the lower Yakima Valley is reached at Mabton in 8.0 miles. To get to I-82, turn left onto SR-22, go 0.2 mile, then turn right onto SR-241, following it 6.3 miles to Alexander Road. Turn left here, then right in 1.0 mile onto Midvale Road. Find the I-82 interchange (Exit 67) in 0.2 mile.

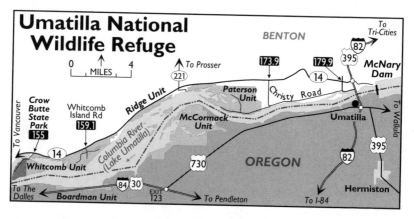

Umatilla National Wildlife Refuge

LAKE UMATILLA

The best birding along Lake Umatilla is in its eastern section—the 25 miles or so between Crow Butte State Park and McNary Dam. Two outstanding Washington rarities—Magnificent Frigatebird from the tropics and Ross's Gull from the Arctic—were recorded here. The three sites described below are easily accessible and offer a good mix of birds in all seasons.

The entrance road for **Crow Butte State Park** is on the south side of SR-14 at milepost 155, about 54 miles east of the US-97 intersection. Camping and other facilities are available in the warmer months; in winter you may park at the closed gate and walk in. As you drive toward the butte (now an island), stop along the causeway to bird the marsh on either side. Gulls and terns may be present. Virginia Rail and Marsh Wren are here year round and Swamp Sparrow has been found during the fall. Mudflats appear when the water is low, attracting migrating shorebirds. Raptors include Bald Eagle in winter and an occasional Peregrine Falcon. The lagoon can harbor many waterfowl. An oasis of trees and shrubs, the park (2.0 miles) is an effective passerine migrant trap. Trees regularly host Barn, Great Horned, Long-eared, and Northern

Saw-whet (especially migration) Owls. Long-eareds nest in locusts along the river; be careful not to disturb or attract attention to them.

Umatilla National Wildlife Refuge (23,555 acres) was established in 1969 as mitigation for habitat lost to flooding when John Day Dam was built. Areas of the refuge are intensively farmed to provide food and cover for wildlife, especially waterfowl. Late-fall Mallard counts reach 300,000, Canada Goose 30,000. Two of the refuge units are featured here. Neither has restrooms, and camping is not allowed.

Turn south from SR-14 at milepost 159.1 onto Whitcomb Island Road. Cross the channel (at times mud-lined) to a fork (0.3 mile). Explore the **Whitcomb Unit** by going either left or right. Thousands of geese winter here—mostly Canada, but also a few Greater White-fronted and Snow (100–300 of the latter in recent years). Ross's Goose is rare, though perhaps increasing. This is a great place to view Bald Eagles in winter. From late March through June the fields host many Long-billed Curlews; the refuge celebrates this phenomenon with a Curlew Day, with talks and tours. Burrowing Owls nest here, too. Fall can be good for shorebirds along the channel just south of SR-14.

The **Paterson Unit** is about 10 miles farther east. At milepost 173.9, turn south from SR-14 onto Christy Road (14.8 miles). In 3.7 miles, turn right just after the railroad tracks onto a road marked by a refuge sign. This bumpy gravel road goes west, paralleling the Columbia River. Watch for loons, grebes, American White Pelican, waterfowl, Osprey, Bald Eagle, and Caspian and Forster's Terns. In spring, Long-billed Curlews display in the fields to the north. At 3.8 miles, take the fork to the right. Birds in these fields include Northern Harrier and Western Meadowlark; Mule Deer are common in the Bitterbrush. Stop at a small parking area (1.0 mile) from which a short walk brings you to a slough lined with marsh and riparian vegetation. Two more access points to the slough may be reached by driving for less than another mile. Look for Eared Grebe (summer and migration), Greater White-fronted (especially fall) and Canada Geese, Blue-winged and Cinnamon Teals, Redhead, Ring-necked Duck, Lesser Scaup, Common Goldeneye, Ruddy Duck, Black-necked Stilt, American Avocet, Solitary and Stilt Sandpipers (fall), Wilson's and Red-necked Phalaropes, and Bonaparte's Gull. The brush is good for Bewick's Wren. Leaving the refuge, turn right onto Christy Road. In 5.8 miles turn left on Plymouth Road, reaching SR-14 in 0.7 mile at milepost 179.9. A right turn here points you to an interchange with I-82 (Exit 131) in 0.7 mile.

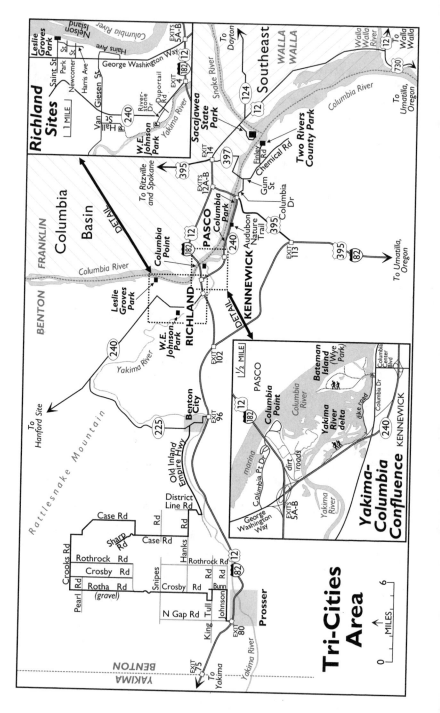

Richland Sites

Leslie Groves Park
Nelson Island
Columbia River
Hains Ave
George Washington Way
Saint St
Park
Newcomer St
Harris Ave
Giesen St
Van
Hall St
240
EXITS 5A-B
EXIT 4
182
Riverside Dr
Duportail
Yakima River
W.E. Johnson Park
1 MILE

Southeast

WALLA WALLA
To Dayton
Snake River
124
12
Walla Walla River
12
To Walla Walla
730
To Umatilla, Oregon
Columbia River
Sacajawea State Park
397
Finley Rd
Chemical Rd
Two Rivers County Park
Gum St
395
Columbia Dr
EXIT 14
395
87
To Umatilla, Oregon
EXIT 113

FRANKLIN
BENTON
Columbia Basin
To Ritzville and Spokane
DETAIL
Columbia Point
PASCO
Columbia Park
Audubon Nature Trail
KENNEWICK
EXITS 12A-B
182
12
240
Columbia River
Leslie Groves Park
W.E. Johnson Park
RICHLAND
Yakima River
240
DETAIL
EXIT 102
Benton City
EXIT 96
225
To Hanford Site
Rattlesnake Mountain
Old Inland Empire Hwy
District Line Rd

Yakima–Columbia Confluence

1/2 MILE
PASCO
Columbia Point
182
12
Columbia Pt Dr
marina
George Washington Way
EXITS 5A-B
Bateman Island (Wye Park)
Columbia River
Yakima River delta
dirt roads
dike road
Yakima River
240
KENNEWICK
Columbia Center Blvd
Columbia Dr

Case Rd
Rd
Rd
Sharp Rd
Case Rd
Hanks
Rothrock Rd
82
12
Crooks Rd
Rothrock Rd
Crosby Rd
Rd
Rd
Snipes
Crosby Rd
Bunn
Pearl Rd
Rotha Rd (gravel)
N Gap Rd
Tull
King
Johnson
Prosser
EXIT 80
EXIT 75
To Yakima
Yakima River

YAKIMA
BENTON

Tri-Cities Area

0 MILES 6

TRI-CITIES AND VICINITY

by Bill LaFramboise and Nancy LaFramboise

The Tri-Cities (Richland, Kennewick, Pasco) cluster along the Columbia River in the southern Columbia Basin. Originally sustained primarily by the railroad yards in Pasco, all three cities grew rapidly beginning in the 1940s, when war materials were produced at the nearby Hanford Site as part of the top-secret Manhattan Project. Though Department of Energy presence is still keenly felt, the region's economy has diversified somewhat over the past 50 years, led by the large-scale transformation of the native shrub-steppe landscape into irrigated agricultural production. West of Richland, shrub-steppe remnants on the south slope of Rattlesnake Mountain harbor species typical of that habitat. Birding opportunities within the cities focus on the many fine riverside preserves and parks. Taken together, these riparian sites have produced more records of songbird vagrants than any other area of comparable size in Washington.

RATTLESNAKE MOUNTAIN

Rattlesnake Mountain, a treeless, east-west ridge reaching 3,600 feet in elevation, is the dominant landform of the lower Columbia Basin. Its north slope is part of the newly created Hanford Reach National Monument, but public access is restricted at present. Much of the south slope has been converted to agriculture (orchards, vineyards, and hop fields lower down, dryland wheat farming higher up). However, pockets of native shrub-steppe habitat remain, where, in the breeding season (April through July), one may find Loggerhead Shrike, Sage Thrasher, and Brewer's and Sage Sparrows. Winter brings good hawkwatching and a chance to find northern birds such as Gyrfalcon (rare), Northern Shrike, Lapland Longspur, and Snow Bunting.

A tour of the south slope begins near Prosser and returns to Benton City. Be aware that there are no facilities in between. Take Exit 80 from I-82, about 25 miles west of Richland or 45 miles southeast of Yakima. Proceed north on N Gap Road to Johnson Road (0.4 mile), turn right, and go to Bunn Road (2.5 miles). Turn left here. Wetlands along the road (0.2 mile) are often good for migrant waterfowl and shorebirds from early to mid-spring. In late spring and early summer look for breeding Cinnamon Teal, Virginia Rail, Sora, Black-necked Stilt, American Avocet, Wilson's Snipe, Yellow-headed Blackbird, and other marshbirds.

Continue north along Bunn Road and turn left onto King Tull Road (0.7 mile). In 1.0 mile turn right onto **Crosby Road**, which begins the ascent of Rattlesnake Mountain. Be on the lookout for Prairie Falcon year round, Ferruginous and Swainson's Hawks in spring and summer, and Rough-legged Hawk and Northern Shrike in winter. Continue north on paved Crosby Road, following its turns for 6.7 miles. Here, the pavement turns right; continue straight on graveled **Rotha Road**, which will take you the rest of the way to the top. Beginning here, the road is flanked by a Big Sagebrush community—excellent for shrub-steppe residents such as Gray Partridge, Burrowing Owl, Loggerhead Shrike, Sage Thrasher, and Brewer's and Sage Sparrows. Short-eared Owl and Common Poorwill are possible at dusk. After passing Pearl Road (4.0 miles) the terrain has more grasses, attractive to Vesper Sparrow. Turn right onto **Crooks Road** (1.0 mile), one of the better locations in the lower Columbia Basin for Lapland Longspur and Snow Bunting in winter. Look for a few individuals among the swarms of Horned Larks that frequent the wheat fields. Side trips can be made south down Crosby or Rothrock Roads through similar habitat. From late April to early July, the Bluebunch Wheatgrass fields along Crosby Road can be good for Grasshopper Sparrow. Listen for its high-pitched song from the roadside.

After traveling east 4.1 miles from the junction of Rotha Road, Crooks Road bears to the right and becomes **Case Road**, descending the mountain and giving you another chance to see species you may have missed on the way up. In 6.5 miles turn right onto **Sharp Road**. Birding the riparian area along Snipes Creek and about the abandoned homestead at the end of Sharp Road (1.9 miles) can be productive during migration for Wilson's Snipe, *Empidonax* flycatchers, kinglets, warblers, and sparrows, and for American Kestrel, Great Horned Owl, Say's Phoebe, Western Kingbird, and Bullock's Oriole in the nesting season. The homestead is also a fairly reliable location for Gray Partridge. In winter, look for Golden Eagle and Merlin.

Return to Case Road, keeping straight ahead (south). At the intersection with Snipes Road (2.1 miles), scan the power poles for Ferruginous Hawks, which often nest in the nearby canyon. After another 2.1 miles, turn left onto Hanks Road. Travel this road to District Line Road (2.0 miles) and turn right. After 1.3 miles turn left onto **Old Inland Empire Highway**. Look for nesting Prairie Falcon, Barn and Great Horned Owls, and Rock and Canyon Wrens on the basalt cliffs. Traffic moves fast on this road. Be watchful, and be sure to pull completely off if you stop.

Old Inland Empire Highway intersects SR-225 in 7.1 miles. Turn right and make your way through Benton City for two miles to the I-82 interchange (Exit 96).

RIVERSIDE PARKS IN THE TRI-CITIES

The Columbia, Yakima, and Snake Rivers converge at the Tri-Cities, creating an inviting oasis of vegetation in an otherwise arid landscape. Parks and natural areas near the rivers provide opportunities to observe a great diversity (and often high numbers) of waterfowl, shorebirds, gulls, and passerines. Waterfowl uncommon inland turn up here with some regularity, including Surf and White-winged Scoters, Long-tailed Duck, and Red-breasted Merganser. The usual shorebirds are Killdeer, Black-necked Stilt, American Avocet, Greater and Lesser Yellowlegs, Spotted, Western, Least, and Pectoral Sandpipers, Dunlin, Long-billed Dowitcher, Wilson's Snipe, and Red-necked Phalarope. Less common but still quite regular are Black-bellied, American Golden-Plover, Semipalmated Plover, and Solitary, Semipalmated, Baird's, and Stilt Sandpipers. Larids are also seen in large numbers, with the possibility of Parasitic Jaeger and Common and Black Terns in migration. Several flycatchers, Cassin's and Warbling Vireos, six swallow species, most of the western warblers, and Western Tanager are typical of the many passerine migrants. Birds of special interest seen regularly include Clark's Grebe, Eurasian Wigeon, Barrow's Goldeneye, Peregrine Falcon, and Franklin's, Glaucous, and Sabine's Gulls. The list of Washington rarities recorded in the Tri-Cities over the years is staggering: Garganey, Hudsonian Godwit, Lesser Black-backed Gull, Northern Parula, Chestnut-sided, Black-throated Blue, Blackburnian, Blackpoll, Black-and-white, and Prothonotary Warblers, Ovenbird, Le Conte's Sparrow, Brambling. We describe below eight of the most consistently productive birding spots. The first five are in Richland, the next two are in Kennewick, and the final one is in Pasco.

Bateman Island lies at the confluence of the Columbia and Yakima Rivers, a well-traveled natural crossroads. Except during mid-summer, the island's riparian vegetation and planted Russian Olives support good numbers of birds. Spring and fall yield a great variety of passerine migrants. Wintering species include Winter Wren, Hermit and Varied Thrushes, American Tree, Fox, Song, Lincoln's, White-crowned, Golden-crowned, and Harris's Sparrows, and Dark-eyed Junco. American Robins gorge on the abundant Russian Olive fruits. Trails are well trod and walking is easy. *Note: a fire in 2001 burned much of the island's vegetation; habitats are now regenerating.* Take Exit 5A (SR-240 East) from I-182 and drive to Columbia Center Boulevard (2.6 miles). Turn left (north), drive 0.5 mile, and turn left (west) onto Columbia Drive. Park at the entrance to Wye Park, on the right in 0.1 mile, to access Bateman Island on foot.

The **Yakima River delta** is adjacent to Bateman Island. At least 30 species of waterfowl, and 32 of shorebirds, have been recorded here. Birding can be good at any time. Shorebirding is exceptional when low water levels (controlled by the Columbia River dams) coincide with spring (late March–May) or especially fall (end of July–early November) migration. Sightings have included Marbled Godwit, Red Knot, Sharp-tailed Sandpiper, Ruff, and Red Phalarope—all highly unusual for this part of Washington. From the parking lot at Wye Park, drive (or walk) right and downhill to the dike road on the south side of the delta. Look north across the water to Bateman Island, where Bank Swallow nests can be seen in a gravel bank. If Western Grebes are present there may be a Clark's or two among them. The best shorebird mudflats are midway along the road and at its west end, where the road is gated (0.8 mile). One can continue on foot along a path underneath noisy SR-240 for about half a mile.

Columbia Point forms the north shore of the Yakima River delta. If you are coming from the preceding site, return to SR-240, head west, and at the next interchange do not follow SR-240 but instead stay straight ahead beneath the freeway overpass onto George Washington Way. (From I-182, take Exit 5B north onto George Washington Way). At the first traffic light, turn right onto Columbia Point Drive (0.3 mile from SR-240). Travel past the golf course and the Richland Marina Park to the Columbia River (1.1 miles). Turn right onto the bumpy dirt road that goes under the I-182 bridge and proceed to an overlook of the river (0.4 mile) affording a panoramic view of the Yakima River delta and its many islands. Look for loons, grebes, American White Pelican, and waterfowl. Caspian and Forster's Terns can be found during spring and summer. Uncommon fall species include Red-necked and Eared Grebes, Surf Scoter, and Common and Black Terns. Continue on the gravel track to Russian Olive groves (0.4 mile). Walk into the trees and brush on unmarked trails to look for nesting Western Screech- and Long-eared Owls, and for passerines in migration. Be aware that off-road vehicles also use these trails on weekends.

Leslie Groves Park, along the Columbia River north of Columbia Point, can be an excellent location to study wintering grebes, American White Pelican, waterfowl, and gulls. Good riparian areas have birds similar to those on Bateman Island. In winter, Bohemian Waxwings are sometimes found in the Russian Olives as well as in nearby residential neighborhoods. From Columbia Point Drive, go north through Richland on George Washington Way to Saint Street (3.3 miles). Turn right and go 0.5 mile to a parking area by the river. From here one has a fine view of the north end of Nelson Island, which has attracted its share of uncommon species, including Ross's Goose, Long-tailed Jaeger, and Glaucous and Sabine's Gulls. Two more river access points are reached by going back one block on Saint Street and turning left (south) onto Harris Avenue, which parallels the park through a birdy residential area. Turn left at Park Street (0.2 mile) for one access; continue on Harris 0.2 mile to Newcomer Street for another. For a fourth access point, go back south on George Washington Way to Van Giesen Street (1.2 miles from Saint Street). Turn left (east), continuing past the stop sign (0.1 mile) as Van Giesen bends right and becomes Hains Avenue. Just beyond the bend (0.1 mile), turn left at an unmarked driveway to the parking lot of the park.

W.E. Johnson Park is a largely undeveloped natural space along the Yakima River, used primarily for horseback riding and archery. The park's extensive wetland and riparian habitats offer good birding in all seasons except in the heat of summer. To get to the north entrance from Leslie Groves Park, drive west on Van Giesen Street and turn left onto Hall Street (0.3 mile west of SR-240). Proceed 0.4 mile to a parking lot from which a trail goes south the entire length of the park. To go directly to the south end (the birdiest part of the park), turn south from Van Giesen onto SR-240, then right in 1.7 mile onto Duportail Road. (If you are coming from the south on SR-240, Duportail Road will be on your left 0.9 mile north of Exit 4 from I-182). Go 0.1 mile on Duportail and take a right onto Riverstone Drive. Turn left in 0.4 mile onto a dirt track and proceed 0.2 mile to a park gate. Walk either way on the trail inside the gate—right, along the base of a hillside, or left, toward the river. Dense riparian vegetation along this trail and in the rest of the park can host migrating flycatchers, vireos, kinglets, warblers, and Western Tanagers. Breeding species include Black-chinned Hummingbird (check the bare tops of trees and shrubs), Bewick's Wren, Black-headed Grosbeak, and Lazuli Bunting. In winter, the many fruit-laden Russian Olive trees attract Hermit and Varied Thrushes, Cedar Waxwing (Bohemian is rare), and Yellow-rumped Warbler; look also for Winter Wren. Pond and marsh often host Black-crowned Night-Heron, Wood Duck, Cinnamon Teal, Virginia Rail, Marsh Wren, Yellow-breasted Chat (in dense thickets with rose bushes), and Yellow-headed Blackbird. The park is good for owls: Barn, Western Screech-, Great Horned, and Long-eared have been found in the cottonwoods.

Columbia Park runs along the Columbia River for several miles between Columbia Center Boulevard and US-395, beginning just east of Bateman Island. To bird this park, drive east on Columbia Park Trail, stopping as often as you please. Many waterfowl and gull species can be found on the river in fall and winter, along with Common Loons (once in a while a Pacific). Bald Eagles roost in trees along the shoreline. Look carefully for a Eurasian Wigeon among the American Wigeons at the duck pond or the Family Fishing Pond. Large Canada Goose flocks sometimes contain a Greater White-fronted or Snow Goose. In 2.0 miles (0.4 mile east of Edison Avenue), walk the Lower Columbia Basin Audubon Nature Trail—actually a network of paved trails through woody habitat, attractive to migrating and wintering passerines including Winter Wren, Hermit and Varied Thrushes, and sparrows.

Two Rivers County Park has a large side lagoon off the Columbia River, offering easy waterfowl viewing. Possibilities include Greater White-fronted Goose, Eurasian Wigeon, and many species of diving ducks (Surf Scoter and Red-breasted Merganser rare but regular in late fall). The nature trail at the park's east end winds through nice riparian growth—excellent in migration. Lewis's Woodpecker, Winter Wren, Brown Creeper, and a variety of sparrows have been seen along this trail. From the junction of US-395 and SR-240, take Columbia Drive east 1.6 miles to Gum Street (SR-397). Turn right, following Gum Street (becomes Chemical Road) to Finley Road (2.1 miles). Turn left here and find Two Rivers Park on your left in 1.6 miles.

Sacajawea State Park is located across the Columbia River at the confluence of the Columbia and the Snake—directly opposite Two Rivers Park. Although busy in summer, the park offers great river viewing and has many riparian areas with species similar to those in the other riverine Tri-Cities parks. Wood Ducks are common in the marshes. Bald Eagles roost here in winter; although facilities are closed then, birders may walk in. In Pasco, take US-12 eastbound (toward Walla Walla). The turnoff to the park is 3.6 miles past the North US-395 interchange, and the park is two miles south of the highway. Make this your jumping-off point for a Columbia Basin birding route along the lower Snake River (page 372), or a tour of the Southeast (page 503).

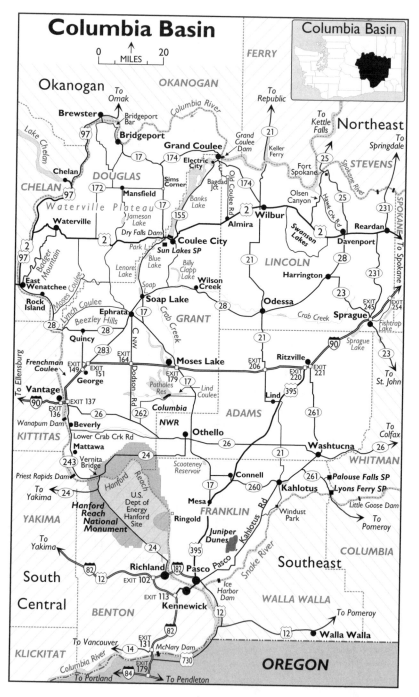

Columbia Basin

0 ——↑—— 20
MILES

Columbia Basin

Okanogan

OKANOGAN
FERRY

To Omak

Brewster

Bridgeport Bar

Columbia River

97

Bridgeport

Grand Coulee

Grand Coulee Dam

174

To Republic

21

To Kettle Falls

Northeast

To Springdale

Lake Chelan

Chelan

CHELAN

172

DOUGLAS

17

Electric City

Keller Ferry

25

Fort Spokane

STEVENS

Spokane River

25

Waterville Plateau

Mansfield

Sims Corner

17

Banks Lake

Olsen Canyon

Hawk Crk Rd

231

Jameson Lake

155

Bagdad Jct

174

Old Coulee Rd

2

Wilbur

Swanson Lakes

2

Reardan

231

Waterville

Dry Falls Dam

Almira

Davenport

28

2

97

Badger Mountain

Park Lk

Coulee City

Sun Lakes SP

Blue Lake

21

LINCOLN

Harrington

23

231

SPOKANE

To Spokane

East Wenatchee

Lenore Lake

Billy Clapp Lake

Wilson Creek

Odessa

EXIT 245

EXIT 254

Rock Island

Soap

Soap Lake

28

Crab Creek

Sprague

Fishtrap Lake

28

97

Moses Coulee

Lynch Coulee

Beezley Hills

Ephrata

17

Crab Creek

GRANT

21

90

Sprague Lake

23

Quincy

283

EXIT 164

Moses Lake

EXIT 206

Ritzville

EXIT 220

EXIT 221

To St. John

Frenchman Coulee

EXIT 149

EXIT 151

George

C NW

Dodson Rd

EXIT 179

17

Lind Coulee

Lind

395

261

Vantage

90

EXIT 137

EXIT 136

26

262

Potholes Res

Columbia

ADAMS

To Colfax

Beverly

Columbia NWR

Othello

26

21

Washtucna

26

Wanapum Dam

KITTITAS

Lower Crab Crk Rd

Mattawa

Scooteney Reservoir

WHITMAN

243

Vernita Bridge

24

Connell

260

Kahlotus

261

Palouse Falls SP

Lyons Ferry SP

Priest Rapids Dam

To Yakima

24

Hanford Reach

Mesa

17

Kahlotus Rd

Windust Park

Little Goose Dam

To Pomeroy

YAKIMA

U.S. Dept of Energy Hanford Site

Ringold

FRANKLIN

To Yakima

Hanford Reach National Monument

Juniper Dunes

Snake River

COLUMBIA

24

395

Pasco

Southeast

82

12

Richland

182

Pasco

South

EXIT 102

Ice Harbor Dam

WALLA WALLA

Central

EXIT 113

Kennewick

12

To Pomeroy

BENTON

82

12

Walla Walla

To Vancouver

EXIT 131

McNary Dam

14

730

KLICKITAT

Columbia River

EXIT 179

84

To Portland

To Pendleton

OREGON

COLUMBIA BASIN

The Columbia Basin of Eastern Washington, as viewed from space, can be likened to the hole in a doughnut, with mountains ringing a roughly circular, generally low-lying plateau. In no other part of Washington is geologic history more evident, largely because so much of it is recent. Sixteen to thirteen million years ago, during the Miocene period, outpourings of lava spread from what is now southeastern Washington and northeastern Oregon to bury the region under multiple layers of dense basalt—the most striking feature of this landscape still today. Beginning about 10 million years ago, volcanic activity shifted westward and built the arc of High Cascades volcanoes, sporadically active to the present. The uplift of the Cascades caused a change in climate as the source of moisture from the ocean very slowly was shut off, determining the Basin's arid shrub-steppe environment. Still more recently—a mere 13,000 or so years ago—dozens of calamitous, southwestward-trending ice-age floods stripped the soils and gouged deep coulees, shaping the unique topography of bare rock and potholes now known as the Channeled Scablands.

Another transformative event has taken place within the lifetime of many readers of this book. In a triumph of engineering on a geologic scale, dams converted the Columbia and the Snake from free-flowing rivers into a series of lakes, and hundreds of thousands of acres of shrub-steppe habitat into irrigated farmlands. Today the Basin is a major producer of grains, hay, potatoes, vegetables, apples, pears, cherries, wine grapes, and hops. Irrigation runoff has raised water tables, filling many formerly dry potholes and creating extensive wetlands. A patchwork of the original shrub-steppe flora and fauna survives, although greatly reduced in extent.

The Columbia Basin is an outlier of the Great Basin ecoregion. Here one may find breeding birds typical of northern Nevada or southeastern Oregon—American White Pelican, Greater Sage-Grouse, Black-necked Stilt, American Avocet, Long-billed Curlew, Burrowing Owl, and Brewer's, Lark, and Sage Sparrows. Wetlands and pothole lakes abound with marshbirds and waterfowl. Fall offers exciting shorebirding and the prospect of a few passerine vagrants at isolated riparian groves. Winter brings many raptors to bare agricultural fields, including Gyrfalcon and Snowy Owl.

The climate of the region is dry and continental. Temperatures climb to 90 degrees and above on 30–45 days in a typical summer and not uncommonly reach the low 100s. The southern Basin is the warmest and driest part. Pasco,

351

at an elevation of 340 feet above sea level, has a July average maximum temperature of 90 degrees and receives just eight inches of precipitation annually. By contrast, Davenport—in the northern Basin at an elevation of 2,400 feet—has a July average maximum temperature of 83 degrees and receives 15 inches of precipitation annually. The north is colder in winter (January average low temperature 14 degrees in Davenport compared to 27 in Pasco) and receives much more snow (average 40 inches in Davenport, eight in Pasco). Wind sometimes makes birding difficult in open terrain in spring, especially in the afternoons. Blowing dust can be annoying. Winter days often are marred by oppressive low clouds and fog. Drifting snow can impede travel in winter in northern areas; elsewhere the roads are occasionally glazed with ice. On the whole, however, Basin roads are well-maintained and travel is trouble-free in any season.

Lodging and services are available in Pasco, Moses Lake, Ephrata, Soap Lake, Coulee City, Electric City, Grand Coulee, Othello, Connell, Wilbur, Davenport, Odessa, and Ritzville.

THE POTHOLES AND MOSES LAKE

by Mike Denny and Andy Stepniewski

The western Columbia Basin has seen a wholesale conversion from dry shrub-steppe to irrigated cropland. *Increased runoff has caused water tables to rise, flooding innumerable potholes and other low-lying spots and creating a diverse, bird-rich mix of habitats. From the Columbia River to Moses Lake, I-90 provides access to cliffs, marshes, lakes, and remnant patches of shrub-steppe, large areas of which are managed by state and federal fish and wildlife agencies.*

FRENCHMAN COULEE AND QUINCY WILDLIFE AREA

Frenchman Coulee, an ice-age floodwater channel, is upriver from Vantage on the opposite bank of the Columbia. Take Exit 143 from I-90 and turn west onto Silica Road. Pause to check the marsh and small lake at the first bend in the road for Ruddy Duck, Virginia Rail, and Yellow-headed Blackbird, along with various diving ducks in spring. Proceed to the small oasis at Frenchman Spring—a few houses surrounded by trees. Concentrations of migrant passerines are often noted here during April–May and August–September. At the first intersection (0.7 mile), turn left and stop to check the trees around the ruins of a gas station; birds bathe and drink in the irrigation ditch. You are on the former US-10, the highway to Ellensburg and Seattle before the coming of the Columbia River dams and the interstate. Head west along the cracked asphalt pavement as it descends steeply through the chasm. Several overlooks allow you to observe White-throated Swifts slicing through the air at eye level—the smaller Violet-green Swallows that accompany them appear hardly to move by comparison. Look for nesting Red-tailed Hawk, American Kestrel, Rock Dove, Say's Phoebe, Common Raven, Rock and Canyon Wrens, and flocks of Gray-crowned Rosy-Finches (winter, especially late afternoon when they come in to roost on the cliffs). The basalt columns are also popular with rock climbers. Farther down, the road runs out onto flats and eventually disappears beneath Wanapum Lake (4.5 miles from Frenchman Spring). Sage Sparrows breed on the sparsely vegetated flats beyond the base of the cliffs. Scoping for waterbirds can be profitable except in summer.

Sage Sparrows also inhabit the upper plateau. Return to the oasis and make a left onto Silica Road, signed *Gorge Amphitheater*. Look for dirt tracks going off to the right (east) in 2.1 miles and again 0.5 mile farther on. From March through July you should find Sage Sparrows from the main road (do not trespass). The white diatomaceous earth here consists of minute shells of silica—sediment from the bottoms of lakes that formed during the intervals between basalt flows. The earth pits were mined during World War I to provide material for oil filters for battleships.

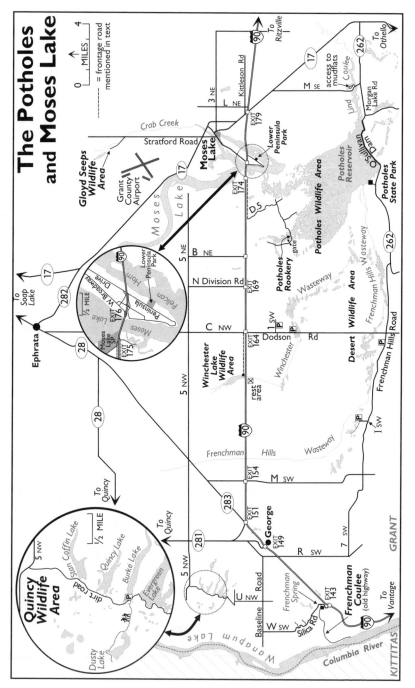

The Potholes and Moses Lake

0 MILES 4

------ = frontage road mentioned in text

From the last stop, continue north 2.6 miles on Silica Road (becomes Road W SW) to Baseline Road. Turn right (east) and go 2.0 miles to Road U NW, then left 2.0 miles to a T-intersection. Turn left (west) here and go 0.9 mile to the entrance sign for the **Quincy Wildlife Area**—15,266 acres of shrub-steppe-mantled uplands, ice-age flood channels, and high cliffs along Potholes Coulee and the Columbia River. Seepage and water from irrigation drainage have filled the numerous side coulees with cattail marshes and over 25 small lakes, connected by a network of gravel and sand trails. From the entrance (only walk-in traffic in hunting season), continue ahead past Evergreen Lake to a parking area and trailhead for **Dusty Lake**, on the left in 1.0 mile. The moderately strenuous trail is about three miles round-trip; even hiking the first portion provides a good sampling of the birding possibilities. After crossing a small creek, the trail descends steeply alongside cliffs to a series of small lakes—some with Beaver dams and lodges—down to larger Dusty Lake. Beyond the east end of this lake, the trail becomes much rougher and involves scrambling across talus slopes. Pied-billed Grebes and waterfowl can be numerous on the lakes, especially in migration. The marshes have Virginia Rail, Marsh Wren, and Yellow-headed Blackbird. Bullock's Oriole is conspicuous in the riparian areas. The cliffs host Red-tailed Hawk, American Kestrel, Chukar, White-throated Swift, Say's Phoebe, Common Raven, Violet-green and Cliff Swallows, and Rock and Canyon Wrens. Watch out for rattlesnakes in rocky areas—this is prime habitat.

From the parking area continue along the gravel road 1.6 miles—winding past Burke, Quincy, and finally Stan Coffin Lakes, with more opportunities to view waterbirds—to the north entrance of the wildlife area. In another 0.5 mile turn right onto Road 5 NW and drive east 3.1 miles to SR-281. Quincy is about five miles north on SR-281, and I-90 Exit 151 about four miles south.

WINCHESTER LAKE AND DESERT WILDLIFE AREAS

Eastbound on I-90, the ponds at milepost 161 (visible from the east end of the rest area about a dozen miles east of George) are worth a quick look. The next interchange is at Exit 164. Get off here and go west along the north frontage road of the interstate for 3.0 miles to the **Winchester Lake Wildlife Area** (1,950 acres). The lake is formed of irrigation runoff in a shallow depression amidst generally flat terrain, including rich, irrigated farmlands and rolling, sandy country. The lake itself is bordered by a narrow margin of cattails, willows, rushes, and some wetland grasses, while the remainder of the wildlife area supports typical Great Basin desert cover of Big Sagebrush, rabbitbrush, and various bunchgrasses. As many as 17 species of ducks may be found on the lake, with 11 known to nest. Gadwall, Mallard, and Cinnamon and Blue-winged Teals are common. Northern Pintail, American Wigeon, and Green-winged Teal are also present. Western Canada Geese nest here, and large numbers of Lesser Canada Geese stop off in migration. American White

Pelican, Northern Harrier, Sandhill Crane, Wilson's Snipe, and Mourning Dove are among the more than 100 species of birds known to the area.

Also reached from Exit 164 is the **Desert Wildlife Area** —35,100 acres of shrub-steppe, sand dunes, marsh, lakes, wasteways, and drainage canals south of I-90. Great numbers of waterfowl are found here, with species composition much the same as at Winchester Lake. From the exit, go south on **Dodson Road**. Watch for birds in the ponds, sloughs, and remnant shrub-steppe. When you spot something interesting, look for a place where you can pull completely off the road and walk back. Otherwise you may be ticketed (or—worse—cause an accident). Invasive Purple Loosestrife and Common Reed Grass have reduced the area's value to marshbirds, but many are still found here. From I-90 drive south two miles, turn left onto Road 1 SW, and take an immediate right to parking and trails to the first ponds of the **Audubon Dodson Road Nature Trail**. There should be many ducks, including courting Ruddies right next to the road in May and June. Look also for Redhead and numerous dabbling ducks, Black-necked Stilt, and Caspian and Forster's Terns. Drive another 1.4 miles farther south on Dodson Road to a WDFW pullout along Winchester Wasteway. Cattails here host large colonies of Red-winged and Yellow-headed Blackbirds. If water levels are low enough, you may encounter Caspian and Forster's Terns and a few shorebirds working the mudflats. Short walks to the north and east lead to shallow, open wetlands. Shrub-steppe habitat 2.5 miles farther south along Dodson Road, on the left, may have Sage Thrasher and Sage and Grasshopper Sparrows. Long-billed Curlews are occasionally seen along Dodson Road in spring, flying above the shrub-steppe or foraging in plowed fields.

Proceed to **Frenchman Hills Road** (3.8 miles). Birding opportunities are plentiful in both directions. To the right (west), pull off into a small parking lot beside some ponds on the north side of the road (0.5 mile). Cinnamon and Blue-winged Teals, Black-necked Stilt, American Avocet, and Wilson's Phalarope nest here, and other shorebirds occur in migration. Just west of these ponds look for Burrowing Owls (much scarcer in recent years) on fenceposts and farm equipment beside the road or at the entrances to their burrows. Continuing west 5.9 miles on Frenchman Hills Road, turn right onto Road 1 SW; drive north 1.2 miles and park in the WDFW access on the right. Cross the wire fence opposite (west of the parking area) and walk about half a mile directly west across the sand dunes to a superb marshy lake loaded with birds during spring and summer—American Bittern, Black-crowned Night-Heron, ducks, American Avocet, Black-necked Stilt, a number of smaller shorebird species, and Forster's and Black Terns. Be careful during the breeding season, as many of these birds nest on the marsh edge and may easily be disturbed if you linger in any one spot. Listen for a Grasshopper Sparrow singing between the road and the marsh. Lark, Sage, and Savannah Sparrows nest here, also.

Return to Frenchman Hills Road, drive back east, and continue 4.8 miles past Dodson Road to the intersection with SR-262. To the north, a good-sized lake (part of Frenchman Hills Wasteway) often has good numbers of ducks, gulls, terns, and even shorebirds roosting at its west end. In recent summers up to 50 American White Pelicans have divided their time among this lake and other nearby reservoirs. East from here on O'Sullivan Dam Road (SR-262) it is 5.6 miles to Potholes State Park and another 1.2 miles to the Mar Don Resort, both on the south side of Potholes Reservoir (camping, RV sites, stores). This area is popular with boaters and is often crowded on weekends.

POTHOLES WILDLIFE AREA

O'Sullivan Dam is at the south end of Potholes Reservoir, which serves the irrigation needs of the central Columbia Basin. The reservoir and surrounding land comprise the **Potholes Wildlife Area** —32,500 acres of sand dunes (now partially flooded), shrub-steppe, and riparian communites. Numerous islands at the north end are a paradise for waterbirds. In fall and spring this big lake draws Common Loons and Horned and Western Grebes. Many shorebirds are often near the boat launch at the southwest end of the reservoir in fall. Ring-billed and California Gulls, which nest on the islands, may be numerous about the dam. Caspian and Forster's Terns may be present.

The best birding occurs from March through October. Sandhill Cranes and large numbers of waterfowl begin to appear in late February. By April most ducks and cranes depart. Spring and fall passerine migration can be quite good. Reservoir levels decline in August, exposing large areas of mudflats that attract shorebirds. Expected species through late summer include Semipalmated Plover, Black-necked Stilt, American Avocet, a few Long-billed Curlews, Western, Least, Baird's, Pectoral, and Stilt Sandpipers, and Wilson's and Red-necked Phalaropes. Other shorebird species turn up occasionally. Several species of gulls and terns, and even a few jaegers, pass through during this season.

Fall marks the time when gulls begin drifting in from the north. Locally rare species such as Glaucous and Sabine's have been found here. Herring Gull is common in late fall and early winter. Winter brings ice—the lake is usually frozen and waterbird diversity is low at this time, except for scads of dabbling ducks.

Continue east atop O'Sullivan Dam, stopping (only at pullouts!) to check for waterbirds on the reservoir. Morgan Lake Road, on the right in 3.7 miles, is the turnoff for Columbia National Wildlife Refuge (page 363). Keep straight on O'Sullivan Dam Road (SR-262). In 2.4 miles turn left onto Road M SE and cross the lower end of **Lind Coulee**, flooded by the reservoir. Just after the guardrail ends on the north side of the inlet (0.4 mile), turn right and take the gravel track east around the bend about a half-mile to an area of mudflats—an arm of the coulee. These flats can be first-rate for shorebirds in late summer and fall. The common species include Greater and Lesser Yellowlegs, Spotted, Western, and Least Sandpipers, Long-billed Dowitcher, Wilson's Snipe, and Red-necked Phalarope. Regular in smaller numbers are Solitary,

Semipalmated, Baird's, and Pectoral Sandpipers. This has proven to be one of the better areas in Washington for Stilt Sandpiper, especially between 10 August and mid-September.

The **Potholes Rookery** at the north end of the reservoir is accessed from I-90 Exit 174, just west of the small city of Moses Lake. To get there from O'Sullivan Dam/Lind Coulee, go north on Road M SE about six miles to SR-17, then left (northwest) about two miles to I-90 Exit 179. Take the interstate westbound through Moses Lake to Exit 174. From here, get on the south frontage road and go west to Road D.5 (2.5 miles). Turn left (south) and wind through areas of sandy shrub-steppe with abundant rabbitbrush, Bitterbrush, and Needle-and-thread Grass, a bunchgrass adapted to sandy soils—look closely at the seed heads to see the needle and thread. This is prime habitat for Burrowing Owl, Sage Thrasher, Loggerhead Shrike, and Lark Sparrow.

At a major fork in 2.6 miles, turn right and go 1.1 miles to another fork. Make a right and traverse down a steep hill to the edge of the lake, which is lined with large willows (1.2 miles). You are now on a dike. Park where the dike road makes its first turn to the left. The state's largest wading-bird rookery occupies the groves of tall willows north of the dike, in the midst of what have been called Washington's Bayous. Recent population estimates include 50 pairs of Great Blue Herons, 60+ of Great Egrets, 300+ of Black-crowned Night-Herons, and 600+ of Double-crested Cormorants. Snowy Egrets—rare in Washington—have been noted here, but there are no breeding records. Look also for American White Pelicans, waterfowl, shorebirds (great for Solitary Sandpiper in August), gulls, terns, and passerines such as Eastern Kingbird, Tree Swallow, Bewick's Wren, and Bullock's Oriole. Keep ahead on the dike road to a gate in 0.3 mile. You can explore the maze of inlets and mudflats by walking north from here (rubber boots are a great help). Be careful not to approach nesting areas too closely. Up to 35 Bald Eagles roost here in winter, although birders rarely visit then.

MOSES LAKE AND GLOYD SEEPS WILDLIFE AREA

Clark's Grebes (usually with Westerns) may be seen during the nesting season on **Moses Lake** from waterfront locations in the city of the same name. One good place is Montlake Park. Take Exit 179 from I-90. Go north 0.5 mile to Yonezawa Boulevard, then left 1.3 miles to Division Street. Turn right and go 0.3 mile to Linden Avenue. The park is down the hill 0.2 mile. Tundra Swans and many other waterfowl can be here from fall through spring. Another possibility for Clark's Grebe is Lower Peninsula Park, south of I-90 on the east side of the peninsula between Moses Lake proper and Pelican Horn, at Peninsula Drive and Battery Road. The boat launch here provides a good vantage point. In fall migration passerines shelter and forage in the trees and brush of this 22-acre, largely undeveloped park.

In winter, open terrain around Moses Lake attracts northern species, including Rough-legged Hawk, Merlin, Gyrfalcon (rare), Short-eared Owl, Northern Shrike, and American Tree Sparrow. Snowy Owls are a highlight—a small number seem to appear each winter, even in years when there are none to be found in Western Washington. One of the two best areas for them is south of I-90 and SR-17 along Road M SE. The other is north of I-90. To reach it take Exit 179, then turn east immediately onto Kittleson Road just north of the interchange. Go 0.5 mile to Road L NE. Turn left (north) and look for the owls in the closely cropped fields for the next two miles. They often perch on irrigation equipment. Cloudy days are probably best.

The **Gloyd Seeps Wildlife Area** (9,600 acres) near the airfield just north of Moses Lake is also reached from I-90 Exit 179. Follow SR-17 north for 4.0 miles and turn right onto Stratford Road. Beginning in 3.5 miles shortgrass fields on the west side of the highway are attractive to Long-billed Curlews. Access to the wildlife area is on the left, 7.0 miles from SR-17. You will need to walk to bird this area effectively. Channeled Scablands slope from the irrigated farmlands on the east toward Crab Creek, which flows over bare rock in some places and through Salt Grass flats in others. In the early spring, American White Pelicans may frequent the lake adjacent to the WDFW farm one mile north of the Crab Creek bridge. Western Canada Geese nest in the area, and Black-necked Stilts and American Avocets sometimes nest, as well.

LOWER CRAB CREEK AND OTHELLO

by Bob Flores, Randy Hill, Andy Stepniewski,
Bill LaFramboise, and Nancy LaFramboise

Crab Creek originates near the Spokane-Lincoln County line between Cheney and Davenport and merges into Moses Lake and the Potholes Reservoir. Formerly an intermittent stream, it now flows yearlong thanks to summer runoff from the Columbia Basin Irrigation Project. Lower Crab Creek—the stretch below O'Sullivan Dam—supports fall Chinook Salmon and Steelhead. Bending westward from the dam, the stream reaches the Columbia at Beverly, about eight miles south of the Vantage bridge. Lower Crab Creek Road follows the creek through rocky coulees, seep lakes and marshes, steppe-sagebrush, and encroaching irrigated fields and orchards. To the north are the low Frenchman Hills and to the south the Saddle Mountains—a basalt ridge system that rises abruptly some 2,000 feet above the surrounding plateau. Sizable chunks of wetland and shrub-steppe habitats along Lower Crab Creek are protected in state wildlife areas and the Columbia National Wildlife Refuge. A good selection of the typical birds of the Columbia Basin may be found here and in the agricultural lands around Othello at the appropriate seasons. The spring migration of Sandhill Cranes is outstanding.

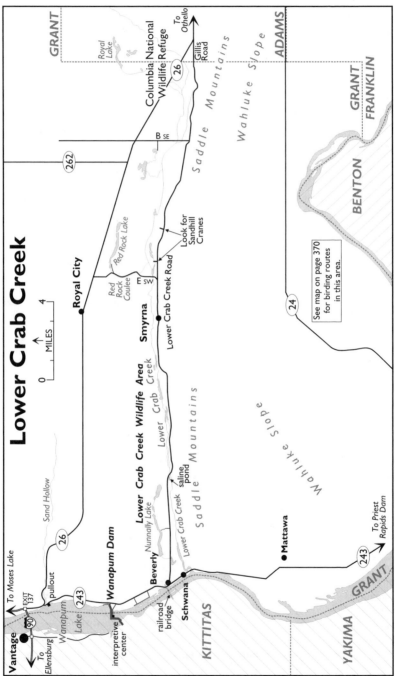

VANTAGE BRIDGE TO BEVERLY

SR-26 heads south along the Columbia River from the I-90 interchange at the east end of the Vantage bridge. At the junction in 0.9 mile, where SR-26 heads east toward Othello, turn right onto SR-243 (marked Beverly/ Mattawa/Vernita). Several good birding stops await you on the short drive down to Beverly, where Lower Crab Creek Road turns off. The first is in 0.2 mile at a pullout on the right above **Wanapum Lake**. Sea ducks such as Long-tailed Duck or scoters have been seen here in migration, while water-birds in fall and winter usually include many Greater Scaup. Winter flocks of Gray-crowned Rosy-Finches sometimes forage in weedy vegetation near the shoreline or across the highway to the east, below the cliffs. Continue south on SR-243 to a road on the right at **Wanapum Dam** (3.5 miles). This road immediately doubles back 0.3 mile to a cove that may have loons, grebes, and bay ducks. Return to SR-243, turn right, and in 0.3 mile turn off to the inter-pretive center below the dam. During July and August, Sockeye and Chinook Salmon pass through ladders and are visible at close range in the viewing room. Forster's Terns forage along the river.

Southbound once more on SR-243, turn right in 1.1 miles onto a gravel track (hard-packed and passable for ordinary vehicles). Park in 0.4 mile, where this track joins another that parallels the river. The strip of riparian growth in both directions is often filled with migrants. Loons, waterfowl, and Osprey frequent the river. Desert Buckwheat and various biscuitroots domi-nate the spring wildflower display on the cobbles and sandy terrain up from the riparian zone. Drive south (downstream) on the cobble track to rejoin SR-243 in 1.0 mile, a mile north of the old railroad bridge across the Columbia.

LOWER CRAB CREEK ROAD

Lower Crab Creek Road turns east from SR-243 about a quarter-mile south of the railroad-bridge underpass at Beverly. Opposite this intersection, along the river, Townsend's Solitaires are regular from fall through spring in a small grove of Rocky Mountain Junipers. A lake on the south side of Lower Crab Creek Road one mile east of the intersection often has diving ducks and waterbirds. Yellow-billed Loon—casual in eastern Washington—has been found here (and also on Wanapum Lake).

For the next 25 miles the road follows Crab Creek along a series of wide scabland channels at the base of the Saddle Mountains. This scenic route fea-tures wetlands, shrub-steppe, and cliff habitats, significant portions of which are set aside in the 17,000-acre **Lower Crab Creek Wildlife Area**. A short spur on the left (north) side of the road, 2.8 miles from SR-243, leads to a small parking area and trailhead for **Nunnally Lake**—a popular flyfishing and wa-terfowl hunting site within the wildlife area. The half-mile trail north to the lake passes through dense Russian Olive groves where Long-eared Owls roost in winter and nest in early spring. American Robins and Yellow-rumped Warblers can be abundant here in the same seasons. Look among them for a few individuals of less-common species (Townsend's Solitaire, Hermit and Varied Thrushes). Also check for wintering sparrows, especially at edges and openings where the grass is thick. The trail emerges from the thickets and crosses rocky ground with scant shrub-steppe vegetation, soon reaching an overlook of a chain of lakes set deep in an old coulee. Redheads and other diving ducks are common here, but skittish. Rails, orioles, and other marsh and riparian birds inhabit lake-edge vegetation in the nesting season. You may see a Prairie Falcon along the basalt cliffs or hunting over the open landscape.

Continue east on Lower Crab Creek Road, which quickly becomes gravel (0.2 mile). Power lines attract raptors all year long, including Golden Eagles. Migrant songbirds and breeding Eastern Kingbird, Lazuli Bunting, and Bullock's Oriole can be found at wet spots with willow growth. A saline pond on the south side of the road (2.5 miles) may have breeding American Avocet and Wilson's Phalarope. The road crosses Crab Creek (0.1 mile) and hugs the base of the Saddle Mountains. Check the cliffs for nesting Red-tailed Hawk, American Kestrel, Prairie Falcon, Great Horned Owl, White-throated Swift, and many Cliff Swallows. The bright green shrub along the valley floor is Greasewood, tolerant of alkaline soils. This is excellent habitat for Loggerhead Shrikes, which breed here rather commonly (uncommon in winter, when mostly replaced by Northern Shrikes). There are also a few records of Ash-throated Flycatcher in the nesting season.

At the community of Smyrna (7.8 miles), check the larger trees for migrants and wintering blackbirds. East of Smyrna look for shrub birds and for Barn and Great Horned Owls nesting in the low rock outcrops. In 1.5 miles, check the junipers and shrubs planted along the road by the WDFW. At the next junction (1.1 mile), keep left (north) onto Road E SW for a brief side trip. You soon cross Crab Creek and ascend through Red Rock Coulee, following a small stream, wet meadows, and a pocket marsh. In 2.5 miles, a right (east) turn takes you a short distance to **Red Rock Lake**, rimmed by shrubs and basalt cliffs, where you may find a variety of waterbirds, Say's Phoebe, and Rock Wren. Watch for rattlesnakes.

Headed east again on Lower Crab Creek Road, two likely spots to look for Sandhill Cranes in late March and April are at 1.0 and 2.3 miles from Road E SW. In another 1.2 miles (3.5 miles from Road E SW) the road starts a steep climb through rocks where Great Horned Owl and Rock Wren are found. From here to the next junction is a landscape of shrub-steppe (Loggerhead Shrike, Lark and Sage Sparrows) alternating with open grasslands (Long-billed Curlew, Horned Lark). At the fork in 3.8 miles, jog left on Road B SE to the Crab Creek crossing in 0.6 mile. Swales here can be profitable for waterfowl or shorebirds, depending on the season. The next 2.4 miles of this road, up to the intersection with SR-26, are reliable in winter for Prairie Falcon, Northern Shrike, and American Tree Sparrow, while Sandhill Cranes use the cropland in

March and April. A willow woodland several hundred yards south of the intersection, on the right, is excellent for migrant songbirds in May and for breeders such as House Wren, Lazuli Bunting, and Bullock's Oriole.

Continuing east on Lower Crab Creek Road, look for Chukar (upslope), Loggerhead Shrike, and Lark Sparrow in the first three miles of shrub-steppe habitats. Ferruginous Hawks nest some years. Prairie Falcons may be near a small colony of the seriously declining Washington Ground Squirrel that still survives in this vicinity. Irrigated pastures to the north have curlews and snipe in the nesting season, and sometimes other shorebirds during spring and fall migration. Lower Crab Creek Road becomes **Gillis Road** at the Adams County line (4.6 miles from Road B SE; cattle guard). Half a mile beyond, on the right, a driveway lined with pines leads to a home. Ask Mr. Kielien for permission to bird these pines as they often hold Barn and Long-eared Owls. East along Gillis Road, corn fields and pastures have Sandhill Cranes in spring, and the cattail marsh to the north has Virginia Rail, Wilson's Snipe, and blackbirds. Gillis Road ends in about half a mile at an intersection with SR-26, eight miles west of Othello (page 366).

COLUMBIA NATIONAL WILDLIFE REFUGE

Extending nearly ten miles south from Potholes Reservoir, the flood-carved **Drumheller Channels** offer some of the most rugged scablands terrain in the state. Seepage fills the lowest spots, creating innumerable lakes and small wetlands now mostly protected in a patchwork of public ownership—principally the 23,200-acre Columbia National Wildlife Refuge and the WDFW's Seep Lakes/Goose Lakes Wildlife Areas (8,163 acres). An excellent auto tour gives access to lake, shrub-steppe, cliff, and riparian habitats attractive to Columbia Basin birds. This route is especially good in spring when throngs of waterfowl are present. Certain areas are gated and closed during the winter months (October through February).

The north entrance to the refuge is at the east end of O'Sullivan Dam (page 357). Turn south from O'Sullivan Dam Road and drive down Morgan Lake Road, keeping an eye out for American Kestrel, Black-billed Magpie, Rock Wren, various sparrows, and Western Meadowlark. Check the large patch of willows on the left (1.5 miles) for Great Horned and Long-eared Owls. Northern Saw-whet Owl nested here in 1997. Continue to the **Soda Lake Dam** turnoff (0.7 mile), take a left, and drive onto the dam (0.2 mile). Look for Common Loon, grebes, American White Pelican, and Common Merganser. **Migraine Lake**, below the dam on the right, is part of the sanctuary area closed from October through February, but it is easily viewed from the road. It often holds large numbers of American Wigeons (good chance for Eurasian in March) and diving ducks. Shorebirds and Savannah Sparrows can often be found along the lake edge, and Rock and Canyon Wrens on the rocks. Bonaparte's and occasionally Franklin's Gulls are here during summer and fall.

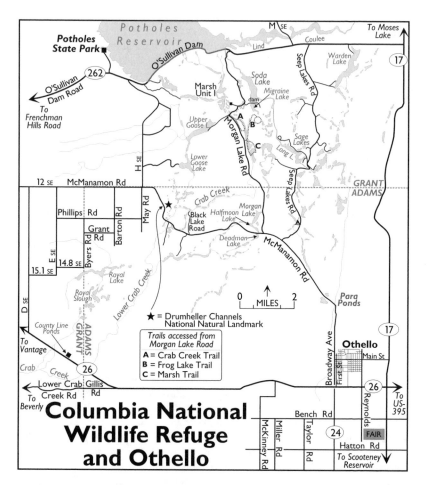

Potholes Reservoir

To Moses Lake

Potholes State Park

O'Sullivan Dam

Lind

Coulee

M SE

Warden Lake

17

262

O'Sullivan Dam Road

Soda Lake

Seep Lakes Rd

To Frenchman Hills Road

Marsh Unit I

dam

Migraine Lake

Upper Goose L.

A

B

Sage Lakes

C

Long L.

H SE

Lower Goose Lake

Morgan Lake Rd

Seep Lakes Rd

GRANT ADAMS

12 SE   McManamon Rd

Crab Creek

Phillips Rd

Barton Rd

May Rd

Black Lake Road

Morgan Lake

Halfmoon Lake

Grant Rd

Byers Rd

Deadman Lake

McManamon Rd

E SE 14.8 SE

Royal Lake

15.1 SE

Royal Slough

Para Ponds

0 MILES 2

17

D SE

★ = Drumheller Channels National Natural Landmark

County Line Ponds

ADAMS GRANT

Broadway Ave

First St

Othello

Main St

To Vantage

Lower Crab Creek

Trails accessed from Morgan Lake Road
A = Crab Creek Trail
B = Frog Lake Trail
C = Marsh Trail

Crab   Creek

26

To Beverly

Lower Crab Creek Rd

Gillis Rd

Reynolds

To US-395

26

Bench Rd

Columbia National Wildlife Refuge and Othello

McKinney Rd

Miller Rd

Taylor Rd

24

FAIR

Hatton Rd

To Scooteney Reservoir

Go back to Morgan Lake Road, turn left, then right at the next fork (0.2 mile). Stop at the parking area on the left just before the closed gate (0.2 mile). Scope **Marsh Unit I** from this overlook, or take a short walk down to the wetlands (may be closed in winter) for closer views of grebes, American Bittern, Great Blue Heron, Great Egret, Black-crowned Night-Heron, waterfowl, and shorebirds. Greater White-fronted Goose and Sandhill Crane are likely in early spring.

Return to Morgan Lake Road and turn right. Continue down the hill to the **Crab Creek Trail** (0.4 mile); turn left into the parking area. This mile-long trail (winter closure) follows the floodplain through willows and shrub sandwiched between shrub-steppe and cliffs; it loops back but an extension continues south to meet the two trails mentioned below. Birds expected include California Quail, Northern Flicker, Eastern Kingbird, five species of swallows, Rock and Marsh Wrens, migrant kinglets and warblers, Yellow-breasted Chat, Song Sparrow, Lazuli Bunting, and Bullock's Oriole. American Tree Sparrow is frequently found in winter in shrubs along the creek.

Continue on Morgan Lake Road (staying left just after crossing Crab Creek) to the parking area for the Frog Lake and Marsh Trails, on the right in 1.2 miles. While driving, look for Ferruginous Hawk and many Violet-green, Northern Rough-winged, Cliff, and Barn Swallows. The trailhead and kiosk with map are across the road from the parking lot. The **Frog Lake Trail**—two miles (round trip) of spectacular scenery, plus a one-mile loop extension beyond Frog Lake that is closed in winter—takes you through shrub-steppe, wetland, and riparian habitats, up to a plateau overlooking the Pillar and Wigeon chain of lakes. American Bittern might be heard along Crab Creek as you work your way to the top of the trail; look also for waterfowl, Common Nighthawk, various swallows, Rock and Canyon Wrens, Sage Thrasher, and Vesper and Savannah Sparrows. The 1.5-mile **Marsh Trail** (winter closure) turns right after crossing the creek and makes a loop through riparian and wetland habitats (the latter may dry up by late summer). Birds noted on this trail include Great Blue Heron, Great Egret, White-faced Ibis (rare), waterfowl, Black-necked Stilt, American Avocet, other shorebirds, Eastern Kingbird, Song Sparrow, and blackbirds.

Continue south on Morgan Lake Road, stopping at the north end of **Morgan Lake** in 2.8 miles. Listen for American Bittern (early and late in the day), Virginia Rail, and Rock and Canyon Wrens, and watch for Red-tailed Hawk, Prairie Falcon, Barn Owl, and Say's Phoebe. Wilson's Snipe often can be heard winnowing above the adjacent pasture in spring. Loggerhead Shrike may be seen between here and the corner of McManamon Road (0.8 mile).

At McManamon Road you may turn left to reach Othello (route described in reverse, pages 367–368). If you turn right instead, in 0.2 mile you reach two deep lakes straddling the road: **Halfmoon Lake** (north) and **Deadman Lake** (south). Park east of the guardrail. Ring-necked Duck, Bufflehead, Common Goldeneye, and Common Merganser are some of the expected ducks on these lakes; look closely for Barrow's Goldeneye. Look also for Virginia Rail and Marsh Wren around Halfmoon Lake, and scan the surrounding cliffs for Prairie Falcon.

Continue west on McManamon Road, scanning for American Kestrel, Long-billed Curlew, Rock Wren, and Loggerhead Shrike. In 2.7 miles look for unmarked **Black Lake Road** on the right (closed in winter). If the gate is open, drive through the coulees to the end of the road in one mile, admiring the spectacular columnar basalt. Take the footbridge across Crab Creek. Trails to the left (one mile long) and to the right (two miles long) through the narrow, rock-rimmed canyon offer a good variety of birds—some of them not found along McManamon Road. In the cliffs look for nesting Red-tailed Hawk, American Kestrel, Barn and Great Horned Owls, and Say's Phoebe, and listen for Rock and Canyon Wrens. Migrants such as Yellow, Yellow-rumped, MacGillivray's, and Wilson's Warblers can be found in riparian habitat along Crab Creek. Marsh Wren, Spotted Towhee, Song and White-crowned (especially April and September) Sparrows also occur. All of the Columbia Basin swallows can normally be found flying around the canyon. The wetland impoundments and creek will produce a variety of waterfowl, including Wood Duck, Virginia Rail, and Belted Kingfisher. Rare sightings include Common Poorwill in fall and Black and White-throated Swifts in spring.

Go back out to McManamon Road, turn right, cross over Crab Creek, and drive to the overlook at Drumheller Channels National Natural Landmark (1.7 miles). Interpretive signs explain the ice-age floods that stripped the soil and gouged these coulees. Look for Northern Harrier, various swallows, and Lazuli Bunting (Indigo once in July). Continue to Road H SE (1.1 miles). Turn right here to return to O'Sullivan Dam Road, at the west end of the dam, in about five miles. En route, watch for Say's Phoebe, Western and Eastern Kingbirds, Horned Lark, Sage Thrasher, Lark Sparrow, and Western Meadowlark in the shrub-steppe habitat. By continuing straight ahead on Road 12 SE you can reach Royal Lake and other birding sites, connecting to SR-26 west of Othello.

OTHELLO AND VICINITY

Within a short distance of Othello one can find deep, shallow, and saline lakes and wetlands, riparian habitats, grasslands, shrub-steppe, rock outcrops, and irrigated agricultural fields—all with a complement of characteristic birds. In migration, birds find the town's urban habitats a good stop-off. Sandhill Cranes can be abundant in March and April, when thousands of birds pause to feed on waste corn in the fields south and west of Othello. This spectacle has spawned the Sandhill Crane Festival, held annually at the end of March. Bus trips, other field trips, guest speakers, and exhibits draw thousands of visitors to this exciting weekend event organized by the Columbia National Wildlife Refuge and the Othello Chamber of Commerce. Lesser numbers of cranes occur during fall migration.

McKinney and Bench Roads, which intersect about a mile south and two miles west of Othello, are a good place to look for Sandhill Cranes. About eight miles west of town along SR-26, cranes sometimes roost in the open wetland directly north of the intersection with Gillis Road. Keep going west on SR-26, crossing Crab Creek in one mile, and pull off on the right side of the highway in another 0.9 mile before a guardrail. Saline **County Line Ponds** to the north have breeding shorebirds (Killdeer, Black-necked Stilt, American Avocet, Spotted Sandpiper, Wilson's Phalarope). Many migrant shorebirds can usually be found here from July into September, including Semipalmated and Baird's Sandpipers. The larger wetland south of the highway has fewer shorebirds but a greater variety of waterfowl, a crane roost some years, and

In April, migrating Sandhill Cranes drop from the sky to take a majestic and synchronized glide to their feeding grounds near Othello.

occasionally a flock of American White Pelicans. Sometimes Prairie and Peregrine Falcons zoom by, too. A short distance west of the ponds, at milepost 30, another, larger crane roost is south from the highway. It is quite far out—you will need a scope.

Continue west on SR-26 to Road D SE (1.6 miles from the ponds) and turn right. Go north for two miles, watching for curlews, then turn right onto Road 15.1 SE. Sandhill Cranes and curlews are often found south of this road. In one mile the road curves north and becomes Road E SE. Check the refuge field to the south, where cranes and large flocks of geese (occasional Greater White-fronted and Snow among them) feed from October to April. In 0.3 mile turn right (east) onto Road 14.8 SE. Stop at an overlook of **Royal Lake** (1.0 mile). Thousands of waterfowl winter on the lake, peaking at 40,000 to 50,000 birds in some years. To connect to the Columbia National Wildlife Refuge auto tour or to loop back to Othello from the northwest, go north on Byers Road 1.7 miles, then right on Phillips Road to Barton Road (1.0 mile). Both dark- and light-morph Harlan's Red-tailed Hawks have been seen here in winter. Continuing left for one mile, then right on Road 12 SE for one mile, brings you to the corner of Road H SE and McManamon Road.

Broadway heads north along the west edge of downtown Othello, becoming **McManamon Road** as it crosses the railroad tracks near a potato-processing plant. Spilled grain from transport trucks attracts hordes of blackbirds along the shoulder before the road starts down the hill. Just beyond a couple of potato sheds at the bottom of the descent are the **Para**

Ponds, one of the great birding spots in the Columbia Basin (2.5 miles from the corner of Broadway and Main in Othello). Traffic moves fast here. Play it safe. During winter and migration one can find large numbers of waterfowl, including Trumpeter and Tundra Swans, Eurasian Wigeon, Greater Scaup, and Barrow's and Common Goldeneyes along with the commoner species. Thousands of Canada Geese (Arctic-nesting subspecies) fatten up in the fields to the north of the ponds during their late-winter and spring migration; scanning these flocks may produce a few Greater White-fronted and Snow Geese. During spring, summer, and fall this wetland is a showy place, with Blue-winged and Cinnamon Teals, Ruddy Duck, Black-necked Stilt, American Avocet, Marsh Wren, and four species of blackbirds including Tricolored (rare, though apparently on the increase). This is one of the more reliable locations in Washington to see White-faced Ibis, usually in May. Past the ponds, keep an eye out for Long-billed Curlew, Burrowing Owl, Say's Phoebe, Common Raven, Lark Sparrow, and Western Meadowlark from spring through early summer in the surrounding shrub-steppe habitats. McManamon Road joins Morgan Lake Road and the Columbia National Wildlife Refuge auto tour in about three miles (page 365).

Northern Harrier, Swainson's and Red-tailed Hawks, American Kestrel, Long-billed Curlew, Black-billed Magpie, Horned Lark, Red-winged, Yellow-headed, and Brewer's Blackbirds, Western Meadowlark, Brown-headed Cowbird, House Finch, and American Goldfinch are common on the farmlands around Othello. Gyrfalcon is usually reported at least once each winter from the agricultural lands to the south and east of town, especially around the Adams County Fairgrounds. Burrowing Owls are traditionally found at the edges of flood-irrigated fields along Steele, Gillis, and Lemaster Roads, east of SR-17 and north of SR-26—more commonly in spring and summer, although a few overwinter. Short-eared Owls winter in this same area and are best found near dawn and dusk.

Scooteney Reservoir, southeast of Othello, can be a worthwhile stop. Take SR-17 to Coyan Road (about nine miles south of SR-26 or four miles north of SR-260). Turn west onto Coyan Road, parking on the left just after crossing the Potholes Canal (0.5 mile). Walk along the dike to view waterfowl and shorebirds on the reservoir to your left and the field and marsh on your right. To reach the main reservoir access, return to SR-17 and turn right, then right (west) again in 1.5 miles at the sign. Waterfowl can be abundant in winter. From March through early April, several hundred to over 2,000 Sandhill Cranes visit the reservoir and the surrounding farmland (and smaller numbers in fall). Shorebird migration (stronger in fall) brings Black-bellied Plover, both yellowlegs, Western, Least, and Pectoral Sandpipers, Dunlin, and Long-billed Dowitcher. Great Egret and American Pipit are sometimes present in fall migration. For another birding opportunity, try the small ponds 1.2 miles west of the SR-17/SR-260 intersection along Hendricks Road.

SOUTHERN COLUMBIA BASIN

by Bill LaFramboise, Nancy LaFramboise, Mike Denny,
MerryLynn Denny, and Bob Flores

A significant expanse of Columbia Basin landscape survives in a near-natural state, from the crest of the Saddle Mountains south to the Hanford Reach—the last free-flowing stretch of the Columbia River between the Bonneville Dam and Canada. In this magnificent setting birders may find species characteristic of arid grasslands, steppe-sagebrush, and streambanks. By contrast, dams along the lower Snake River have eradicated the original canyon-bottom habitats. Nonetheless, there are several important birding sites along the Snake and especially a few miles farther north. Lake Kahlotus, Washtucna, Palouse Falls State Park, and Lyons Ferry State Park are migration hotspots.

WAHLUKE SLOPE AND HANFORD REACH

In 2000 the **Hanford Reach National Monument** (195,000 acres) was created to protect permanently the former buffer zone around the top-secret Hanford Site, which had remained in a relatively undisturbed state. Parts of the monument along the north and east shores of the scenic Hanford Reach—incorporating the previously designated Wahluke Slope Wildlife Area and Saddle Mountain National Wildlife Refuge—are open to the public.

The **Wahluke Slope** (the south face of the Saddle Mountains) is accessed from SR-24 between Yakima and Othello. From the intersection with SR-243 at the north end of the Vernita Bridge, travel east on SR-24, watching for nesting Burrowing Owls and for the Sandhill Cranes that migrate overhead during spring and fall. Turn left (north) onto Road G SW (probably unsigned) just east of milepost 52 (8.2 miles). Cross the irrigation canal and turn right immediately. Unless this access is posted to keep out, continue to the grove of introduced Black Locusts on the canal embankment (0.2 mile). Search for Long-eared Owls during winter and spring. Wintering sparrow flocks may include American Tree Sparrows. Yellow-rumped Warblers are sometimes thick in fall migration, and Blackpoll Warbler has been noted here.

To explore the **Saddle Mountains**, turn north onto the unsigned gravel road east of milepost 60 in 8.3 miles. Shrub-steppe at lower elevations has Long-billed Curlew (grassy areas), Loggerhead Shrike, and Sage (common here in dense Big Sagebrush) and Lark Sparrows. Winding uphill, the road forks in 4.2 miles. Turn right and drive along the crest of the ridge to a viewpoint at the edge of a high cliff (1.2 miles). Red-tailed Hawk, American Kestrel, and Prairie Falcon (occasional) breed here, and a variety of other raptors such as Northern Harrier, Sharp-shinned, Cooper's, and Rough-legged Hawks, and Golden Eagle occur in modest numbers in migration. This is also a good place to look for Chukar (rocky south slopes with abundant Cheatgrass), Gray Par-

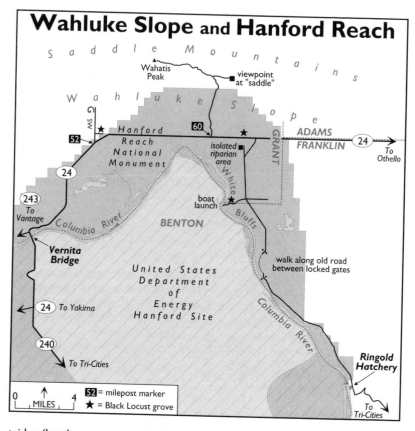

Wahluke Slope and Hanford Reach

S a d d l e   M o u n t a i n s

Wahatis
Peak

viewpoint
at "saddle"

W a h l u k e   S l o p e

G SW

Hanford
Reach
National
Monument

60

isolated
riparian
area

GRANT

ADAMS
FRANKLIN

24

To
Othello

52

24

White

Bluffs

243

To
Vantage

Columbia River

BENTON

boat
launch

Vernita
Bridge

United States
Department
of
Energy
Hanford Site

walk along old road
between locked gates

Columbia River

24 To Yakima

240

To Tri-Cities

Ringold
Hatchery

0   4
MILES

52 = milepost marker
★ = Black Locust grove

To
Tri-Cities

tridge (local on grassy north slopes), Say's Phoebe, Rock and Canyon Wrens, and Gray-crowned Rosy-Finch (late fall, winter, and spring). If you would like to explore this area further, return to the fork in the road and bear right. This gravel road winds west along the ridgeline toward communication-tower-studded Wahatis Peak. Sandhill Cranes migrate across the ridge in numbers, especially about one mile east of the peak.

Back on SR-24, another Black Locust grove is off to the left (north) side of the highway 2.2 miles farther east. In another 0.5 mile—just east of milepost 63—a partially paved road on the right gives access to the north portion of the Hanford Reach. Turn onto this road and stop south of the highway to hike to grassy areas to the left, where you may find Swainson's and Rough-legged Hawks, Burrowing Owl, Grasshopper Sparrow, and Western Meadowlark. Back in your vehicle, at 1.1 miles from the intersection make a hard right to bird an isolated riparian area. A Brown Thrasher was noted here recently in fall. Continue south on the original road and in 2.8 miles turn right at a four-way intersection. In 1.3 miles another Black Locust grove can be alive with Yellow-rumped Warblers and other passerines in migration. Search carefully—vagrant warblers and other rarities occur with some regularity in such places. Explore the marshy area and slough adjacent to the locust grove, as well.

The road ends in 0.5 mile at a boat launch on the **Hanford Reach** of the Columbia River. This is a great place to view loons, grebes, American White Pelican, waterfowl, gulls, and Caspian and Forster's Terns, in the appropriate seasons. Bank and Cliff Swallows nest in abundance on the **White Bluffs**. Winter brings Bufflehead, Common and Barrow's Goldeneyes, Bald Eagle, and Peregrine Falcon (rare). Gulls migrating to the Pacific stop here in fall for the incredible bounty offered by thousands of spawned-out Chinook Salmon. (In recent years, about 80,000 of these huge fish have made it up the Columbia past the gauntlet of dams and power turbines, back to their natal gravel bars on this 51-mile free-flowing section of the river.) Bonaparte's, Ring-billed, California, Herring, and Glaucous-winged Gulls are the usual species; Thayer's and Glaucous Gulls and Black-legged Kittiwake occur rarely. Large flocks of American Pipits are sometimes found along the river's edge in fall.

For another scenic overlook, return to the four-way intersection, turn right, and drive south through sandy shrub-steppe, stopping just before a gate (4.0 miles); foot traffic only is allowed beyond this point. Park here and enjoy the panoramic view of the Hanford Reach. American White Pelican, Double-crested Cormorant, migrant waterfowl, and Bald Eagle (winter) are often seen from this vantage. The steep slopes leading down to the river have a few Black-throated Sparrows in some years (late May through July). Sage Sparrows are common in the shrub-steppe to the east.

Ringold and southern parts of the Hanford Reach are most easily visited from the Tri-Cities. Take Exit 9 from I-182, between Pasco and Richland, and travel north on Road 68. Bear right with the arterial as it merges into Taylor Flats Road in 2.5 miles. Continue north to an intersection with Ringold Road (13.3 miles). Turn left and follow this road west, then north. In 3.0 miles turn left again following Ringold Road. At 0.8 mile at a T-intersection make a right onto Ringold River Road (gravel). In a few hundred feet turn left into the Ringold Springs/Meseberg Hatchery (a second entrance is 0.6 mile farther along Ringold River Road). Look here for Osprey, Belted Kingfisher, gulls, terns, and a variety of waterfowl. The surrounding trees—mostly introduced Russian Olives—may hold migrants such as flycatchers, vireos, thrushes, warblers, sparrows, and Bullock's Oriole. Return to Ringold River Road, turn left, and drive north. Several pullouts on the left side of the gravel road give access via short trails through good habitat to the Columbia River shores. The road is closed by a gate in about eight miles but you may continue on foot. Trees and cliffs provide perches for raptors and owls, with Great Blue Herons nesting in one of the groups of trees. Occasionally Great Egrets are found with the herons. Long-billed Curlews, Horned Larks, and Western Meadowlarks inhabit the surrounding grasslands. Inlets from the river provide rafting locations for waterfowl.

Another way to enjoy the Hanford Reach is by jet-boat tours offered by several companies. Call the Tri-Cities Visitor and Convention Bureau for information (509-735-8486).

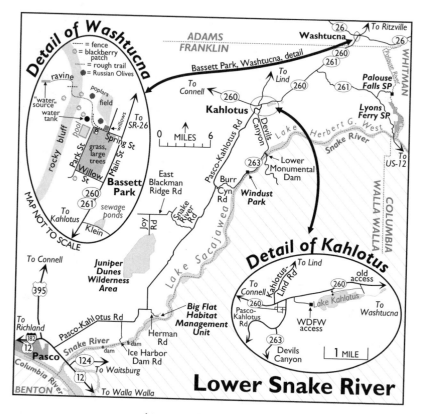

LOWER SNAKE RIVER

The lower Snake River—made famous in the annals of Lewis and Clark two centuries ago—has been tamed by four major dams, drowning the canyon bottoms beneath reservoirs over virtually its entire course. These dams have recently become the center of intense debate, as they have contributed to the near-total demise of a once fabulous salmon population. Although the canyon walls retain much of their natural character, most of the surrounding uplands are converted to agriculture—irrigated in the lower areas, dryland farther upstream. A number of birding sites are accessed by county roads and state highways paralleling the Snake River northeast from Pasco. Many other sites lie along the opposite bank of the river, in the Southeast (page 505).

The Pasco-Kahlotus Road turns east from US-12 just east of Pasco. Travel this road about nine miles to Ice Harbor Dam Road. Keep straight past this junction 3.9 miles to Herman Road. Turn right, and in 1.5 miles find **Big Flat Habitat Management Unit** (about 600 acres). Park and walk east across the causeway to an area of trees, brush, and fields that juts out like a fist into the Snake River. This site was developed by the U.S. Army Corps of Engineers in mitigation for habitat lost when Ice Harbor Dam drowned extensive riparian vegetation. Hunting is popular here in season, so use caution. Plantings of Western Juniper, Russian Olive, and other shrubby growth provide fine wildlife habitat. Corn is grown for waterfowl and upland gamebirds. Raptors such as Sharp-shinned, Cooper's, and Red-tailed Hawks and Merlin are seen frequently. In winter American Robin, Hermit and Varied Thrushes, European Starling, and other species are attracted to the abundant Russian Olive fruits. This is a great winter sparrow patch: Fox, Song, Lincoln's, and White-crowned Sparrows are common then, as are Dark-eyed Juncos. American Tree, White-throated, Harris's, and Golden-crowned Sparrows are much scarcer.

If you are visiting between March and May, you may wish to spend some time at the **Juniper Dunes Wilderness Area** (7,140 acres). Coming from the west, turn left from Pasco-Kahlotus Road onto Snake River Road (11.1 miles east of Herman Road) and travel 3.5 twisty miles to East Blackman Ridge Road. Take a left here to Joy Road (2.4 miles; Rybzinski Road on some maps). Make another left and drive south on Joy past Juniper Dunes Ranch to the road's end in two miles. From here one must cross private property to reach the wilderness area. The landowner limits public access to the period from March through May. Stay on the well-defined trail, and if you open any stock gates, take care to close them behind you. It is only a short walk to the edge of the wilderness area, but a full-day hike is required to get into the heart of the juniper groves. Wear hiking boots, protect yourself against wind and sun, and carry ample drinking water. Pay attention when crossing the dunes so as not to get lost.

This expanse of dunes and shrub-steppe has the largest Western Juniper groves in the state—northerly outposts of their wider distribution from eastern Oregon southward. It is also prime breeding habitat for Washington's remaining Ferruginous Hawks. To see these birds displaying, come in March or April when many colorful wildflowers also enliven the dunes. In addition to the hawks, look for Golden Eagle, Say's Phoebe, and Loggerhead Shrike. Ash-throated Flycatchers have been reported. Surprises are possible—the Juniper Dunes are little explored by birders.

Continuing northeast on Pasco-Kahlotus Road, the next intersection is with Burr Canyon Road (5.7 miles). Turn right here and descend five miles through wheat-farming country to Lake Sacajawea on the Snake River and **Windust Park**. In winter, spilled grain at the loading terminal draws diving ducks (mostly Canvasback, Redhead, Greater and Lesser Scaups, and Common and Barrow's Goldeneyes)—look for them downstream from the grain elevators. The ornamental plantings in the nearby park are often swarming in migration with flycatchers, vireos, warblers, and tanagers, making this a likely place for a vagrant search. The riverside road has now become SR-263. Keep on past the park 3.1 miles to Lower Monumental Dam, where you may see Double-crested Cormorant, Common Merganser, or a gull or two. The highway turns away from the river to enter **Devils Canyon**, a former ice-age flood channel. Look for hawks, Rock and Canyon Wrens, and Gray-crowned Rosy-Finch (winter, especially late afternoon) as you ascend this dry coulee, reaching the town of Kahlotus and an intersection with SR-260 in 5.9 miles.

Except in the driest years, **Lake Kahlotus** hosts most of the characteristic Columbia Basin waterbirds, including all three teal species, Redhead, and Ruddy Duck. Tundra Swans are often numerous in migration. White-faced Ibises appeared here in 2001; some attempted to nest, though none successfully. Fall brings a shorebird bonanza if water levels are just right, and passerine migrants can be abundant in the isolated clumps of trees. The WDFW maintains an access at the west end of the lake. This dirt road turns off right from SR-260 two or three hundred yards east of the intersection with SR-263 in Kahlotus and drops down to the lake in 0.4 mile.

An older WDFW access at the east end of the lake appears to have been decommissioned, but birders continue to go there hassle-free. Turn right from SR-260 down a dirt road 2.1 miles east of SR-263. Shorebirding can be excellent here when water levels cooperate. You can also drive (or walk) an old roadbed that contours westward from the access road across the hillside—a good vantage for scoping the lake. Ferruginous Hawks breed in the vicinity, so keep an eye out along the cliffs and in the sky (these regal birds often soar very high). Brush and scattered trees provide good cover for a variety of birds that like this rocky, hot, south-facing slope—especially in migration. Turn back when you reach a gate.

An island of greenery in the midst of an arid hillscape, **Washtucna** has proven to be one of the most consistent migrant traps in the Columbia Basin. The town is located at the intersection of three state highways about a dozen miles northeast of Lake Kahlotus. The best birding is in and immediately around **Bassett Park**, between Spring and Willow Streets one-half block west of Main Street (SR-260/261) and five blocks south of the intersection where SR-26 turns east. Habitats in this small park and its surroundings are amazingly varied—mini-wetland, dense willow grove, well-watered lawn, mature shade trees, Russian Olives, brush and blackberry thickets—all set against the steep slopes of a basalt cliff. The park teems with passerines on spring and fall passage; sparrows are abundant from fall through spring, lurking in patches of weeds and blackberries. By canvassing the habitats in this compact area, the following are commonly noted: Red-tailed Hawk, California Quail, Olive-sided Flycatcher, Western Wood-Pewee, Willow, Hammond's, Dusky, Gray, and Pacific-slope Flycatchers, Say's Phoebe, Warbling and

Red-eyed Vireo, Golden-crowned and Ruby-crowned Kinglets, Western and Mountain Bluebirds, Townsend's Solitaire, Swainson's, Hermit, and Varied Thrushes, Gray Catbird, Orange-crowned, Yellow, Yellow-rumped, Townsend's, MacGillivray's, and Wilson's Warblers, Western Tanager, many sparrows (including the odd Clay-colored, Lincoln's, and Harris's), blackbirds, Bullock's Oriole, and Evening Grosbeak. Least Flycatcher and American Redstart are seen less often, but regularly. The town **sewage ponds**—not far from the park—are worth a look. From Willow Street, go south one block on Main Street, turn left onto Klein Street, and continue 100 yards to the ponds, on the left. Here one can find a variety of waterfowl (including Wood and Ruddy Ducks), Virginia Rail, Sora, American Coot, Marsh Wren, and Red-winged and Yellow-headed Blackbirds.

Palouse Falls State Park deserves a stop at any season for birds and scenery. Here the Palouse River (made muddy by erosion of Palouse wheat-field soils) pours over a high basalt cliff, filling a narrow gorge with mist. From the junction of SR-260 and SR-261 (six miles west of Washtucna and eight miles east of Kahlotus), turn southeast onto SR-261. The highway winds through hill and dale to a well-signed intersection in 8.7 miles. Turn left here to reach the park in about two miles. In May and June and again from August through September, the small patch of trees near the parking lot is often full of migrants. A good fallout may bring an interesting mix, for example, Red-naped Sapsucker, four species of flycatchers, Clay-colored Sparrow, Bullock's Oriole, and a smattering of mountain species. A Blue-headed Vireo, only Washington's second, was seen here in late August 2000. Peregrine Falcons and White-throated Swifts probably breed nearby. The park is also good for Gray-crowned Rosy-Finches in the winter months, especially in late afternoon as they fly about the cliffs and ice-caked falls investigating their nighttime roosting sites.

Lyons Ferry State Park is a few miles downstream, at the union of the Palouse and Snake Rivers. The ferry is long gone, replaced by a bridge, and both rivers are now engulfed by Lake Herbert G. West, backed up behind Lower Monumental Dam. The park entrance is on SR-261, about five miles south of the Palouse Falls State Park turnoff. Passerine birding can be delightful in the ornamental plantings, especially in migration when mountain species such as Mountain Chickadee, Red-breasted Nuthatch, Winter Wren, and Golden-crowned Kinglet show up. Common Redpolls are irregular in winter. Search for owls in the planted conifers in fall and early winter. Be sure to walk the causeway to the two islands in the Palouse River. Washington's first Mourning Warbler was discovered on the near island in late May 2001. In fall a few American Tree, Lincoln's, White-throated, and Harris's Sparrows are often found there among large numbers of the common sparrow species.

The **Lyons Ferry Hatchery** is across from the state park entrance a few hundred yards back north along the highway. Gull species uncommon or rare for the interior—Mew, Thayer's, Glaucous—sometimes occur among the many gulls that haunt the rearing ponds. Barn and Long-eared Owls roost in the conifers. The heated restrooms are open through the winter, in contrast to those in the park.

SR-261 crosses the Snake River bridge and continues southeast for 21 miles to a junction with US-12 (page 517). From here one may reach birding sites south toward Walla Walla and east toward Clarkston.

BEEZLEY HILLS AND MOSES COULEE

by Andy Stepniewski and Dan Stephens

Across the Columbia River east of Wenatchee, a complex of ridges and coulees marks the transition between two broad, nearly level plateaus: the Potholes country on the south (elevation 1,100–1,300 feet) and the much higher Waterville Plateau to the north (elevation 2,300–2,600 feet). Moses Coulee, a deep gash incised by ice-age floods, skirts the edges of the higher plateau. The southern boundary of this area is defined by Lynch Coulee and the modest Beezley Hills. Rugged Badger Mountain lies to the west. The basalt cliffs and side canyons of Moses Coulee are populated by species such as Golden Eagle, Chukar, White-throated Swift, and Rock Wren. Some of the state's best shrub-steppe can be found on the coulee floor and in the Beezley Hills—home to Loggerhead Shrike, Mountain Bluebird, and Sage Sparrow. There is dry montane forest (Badger Mountain) and fine riparian habitat for residents and migrants (especially along Douglas Creek). All of this plus a few ponds, lakes, and the deepwater Columbia River reservoir behind Rock Island Dam adds up to a series of habitats where it is easy to find 100 species of birds in a day during the breeding season. The sites have been described in such a way that you can readily link a selection of them into a loop starting from and returning to Ephrata or Wenatchee. Overall, early May offers the best birding, although March is better for waterfowl along the Columbia.

BEEZLEY HILLS

The Nature Conservancy's **Beezley Hills Preserve** (about 5,000 acres) shows off some of Washington's most pristine shrub-steppe habitat. Coming from the south, the most convenient approach is by turning north from SR-28 onto Road P NW (also known as Columbia Way or Monument Hill Road), 0.8 mile east of the junction with SR-281 in Quincy. The road climbs steadily to a

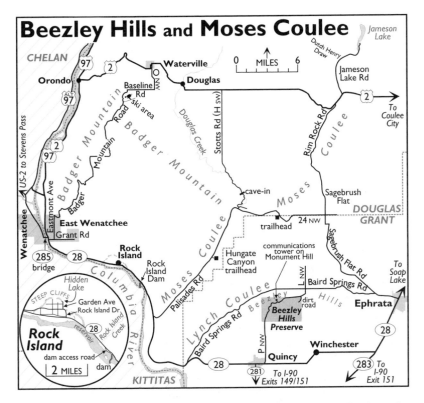

Beezley Hills and Moses Coulee

junction (7.2 miles). Turn left (west) onto a short spur and drive 0.1 mile to the communication towers atop **Monument Hill** at 2,882 feet elevation. There are no facilities. Be careful; the gravel road can be slick if muddy or snowy.

Ice-age winds, by shifting and redepositing fine soils, played an important role in the development of the mosaic of shrub-steppe plant communities found on these slopes and ravines. The many south slopes with thin or rocky soil (lithosol) have a dazzling wildflower display in April and May. Horned Lark (common) and Mountain Bluebird are present in this habitat. Look for Loggerhead Shrike and Sage Sparrow in deeper-soiled ravines below the summit where shrub cover is greater. In March and April and again from August through mid-October the top of Monument Hill makes a fine vantage to view migrating raptors.

To reach nearby north-facing habitats, with different birds, return to Monument Hill Road and drive left (east) along the ridgetop to a junction (2.1 miles); turn right and park off the dirt road in a couple of hundred yards. Relatively deep soils support a healthy growth of Big and Three-tip Sagebrush interspersed with Bluebunch Wheatgrass and a host of other interesting grasses and flowering plants. Common breeding birds here include Sage

Thrasher, Brewer's Sparrow (areas of sagebrush and grasslands), and Vesper Sparrow (tracts of denser grasslands). Grasshopper Sparrow is uncommon and Western Meadowlark ubiquitous. From late March through April keep a watch on the sky for migrating Sandhill Cranes—hundreds, even thousands exploit the thermals on these hills.

Back at Monument Hill Road, a right turn will take you down to Baird Springs Road via Road L NW in about 1.25 miles. Ephrata is ten miles east from this junction. Westbound, Baird Springs Road descends **Lynch Coulee** beside an intermittent stream to join SR-28 seven miles west of Quincy. Birding can be rewarding along this route in shrub-steppe habitats and in riparian growth at springs and other wet spots at the edges of the deeply eroded streambed—especially in migration.

MOSES COULEE

Moses Coulee—a giant, basalt-lined, ice-age flood channel—slices southwestward some forty miles from the high plateau near Mansfield down to the Columbia River. Cliffs provide excellent habitat for Golden Eagle, Chukar, Canyon Wren, and other rock-loving species. The broad coulee bottom—now mostly converted to hay farming—hosts many raptors, including the breeding species plus Rough-legged Hawk and Gyrfalcon (rare) in winter. Characteristic shrub-steppe birds can still be found in remnant parcels of habitat ranging in size from small pockets to large expanses.

Not far from the mouth of Moses Coulee, several waterbird sites in and near the small community of Rock Island are worth a visit. Rock Island Drive turns north from SR-28 about twelve miles east of the junction with US-2/US-97 in East Wenatchee. A large truck stop is on the left just after the turn. Follow the main road into downtown Rock Island and turn right onto Garden Avenue, across from the grocery store (0.3 mile). Drive to the end of this road (0.4 mile) and park at **Hidden Lake**—an excellent waterfowl spot from November to April, when up to 20 species can been seen at one time (including Eurasian Wigeon most winters). A good location for setting up a scope is a few feet to the right along the trail that goes around the lake. Check trees near the water's edge for roosting Northern Saw-whet Owls in winter. Return to SR-28 and turn left. Several more ponds beside the highway over the next mile are good for swans (early spring), other waterfowl, and gulls. Pull off to the right at the mouth of Rock Island Creek (2.1 miles from Rock Island Drive). Just across the railroad tracks are wetlands where the area's only Snowy Egret was found a few summers ago. **Rock Island Reservoir**, visible from here, has many waterfowl in winter, including Greater Scaup. Deeper waters of the reservoir can be seen from the road to the dam (0.3 mile farther along SR-28). A regularly used Golden Eagle nest about 150 yards southeast of the dam can be scoped from this spot.

Palisades Road turns off left from SR-28 and enters the lower end of Moses Coulee, 3.9 miles from the Rock Island Dam road. Cliffs over the next several miles are especially attractive to Golden Eagle and Prairie Falcon—there is a safe pullout for scanning on the left in 1.5 miles. Other birds common along the coulee are Chukar and Lark Sparrow. An obscure gravel lane on the right (9.2 miles from SR-28) leads to a trailhead parking lot for **Hungate Canyon** (BLM). A rough hike across sagebrush into a narrow side canyon with a tiny stream flanked by clumps of Water Birch and willow may reward you with Rock and Canyon Wrens and Lazuli Bunting.

Farther along Palisades Road, in 5.4 miles you come to the south access for **Douglas Creek**, especially known for its spring wildflowers but also for birds of the riparian zone and cliffs. At this writing, the road is blocked by a cave-in part way through the canyon, and may or may not be reopened in the near future. For now you can walk the rest of the way in or drive around to the north access (page 380). Birding possibilities are similar in both parts. Back on Palisades Road, another parking area and trail through shrub-steppe and along the base of cliffs is found on the right in 4.6 miles.

Proceed to an intersection in 5.0 miles. This road, which goes north to join US-2 in about 11 miles (or south and east to Ephrata in about 12 miles), is variously called Sagebrush Flat(s) Road, Road J NW, Rim Rock Road, Moses Coulee Road SE, and Coulee Meadows Road—depending on which signs or maps you happen to be consulting. Turn left (north). Off to your right is **Sagebrush Flat**, managed (WDFW) primarily for a few remaining Pygmy Rabbits. The disjunct Washington population of this Great Basin species appears to be virtually extirpated due to widespread conversion to agriculture of the deep, loose soils it requires for burrows, and the concomitant removal of sagebrush (the main component of its diet). Proceed north 1.8 miles to a dirt track going off to the right in Rimrock Estates. Walk this area of Big Sagebrush to find Sage Thrasher, Sage Sparrow, and Brewer's Sparrow. Mountain Bluebirds are also common here, thanks to numerous nest boxes. Continue north on the main road and descend into Moses Coulee. Cliffs in 6.1 miles are good for White-throated Swift and Canyon Wren. Reach US-2 in 3.2 miles.

Go right (east) 1.1 miles on US-2 to Jameson Lake Road and turn left. The road goes north on the floor of Moses Coulee, dead-ending in about seven miles at the south end of **Jameson Lake**. Significant (22,400 acres) parcels of the shrub-steppe ecosystem here and at nearby McCartney Creek are protected by The Nature Conservancy. Cliffs and talus line the route, home to Red-tailed Hawk, Golden Eagle, American Kestrel, Prairie Falcon, Chukar, White-throated Swift, and Rock and Canyon Wrens. Look for Mountain Bluebird (in boxes) and Sage Sparrow, particularly in the first two miles. At 3.9 miles from US-2, park at a trailhead on the left for **Dutch Henry Draw**. This interesting 15-minute walk brings you to the base of the cliffs and a dry waterfall, passing through brushy terrain that is good for Common Poorwill and Lazuli Bunting. As one continues toward Jameson Lake, the embankments by the road are actually giant ripple marks laid down by ice-age floods. Shrub-steppe habitat here has more native bunchgrasses than along the first part of the road, and hosts Sage Thrasher and Brewer's and Vesper Sparrows. The lake has been growing for the last few decades, making for some productive wetlands. Numerous waterfowl breed here, including all three teal species, Barrow's Goldeneye, and Ruddy Duck. Look also for Pied-billed and Eared Grebes and a colony of California Gulls. A small group of Franklin's Gulls was seen here in May 2001.

DOUGLAS CREEK

For the north approach to Douglas Creek, turn south from US-2 onto Road H SW (Stotts Road). The intersection is about 13 miles west of Jameson Lake Road and eight miles east of Waterville. Proceed south, watching for Short-eared Owl and Loggerhead Shrike along the way. This county road eventually descends Slack Canyon, reaching Douglas Creek in about eight miles. Turn right here, drive a short distance, and park by the binocular sign at a locked gate. You may walk up this unroaded part of the canyon for about eight miles for a true wilderness experience. More of Douglas Creek can be explored by returning to the main gravel road and going downstream for about a mile. Several primitive campsites are off to the side of the road. Park at the third campsite—the center of the Douglas Creek bird-banding station. Over 100 species of birds have been seen in this section of the canyon, with 68 species banded over the last 10 years. Common breeding species include Red-tailed Hawk, American Kestrel, Chukar, Common Poorwill, Western Wood-Pewee, Eastern Kingbird, Cliff Swallow, Rock and Canyon Wrens, Cedar Waxwing, Yellow-breasted Chat, Lazuli Bunting, Black-headed Grosbeak, and Lark Sparrow. During migration the canyon is jumping with most of the common transient flycatchers, vireos, warblers, and sparrows. Interesting passage species, among them a few rarities, are Least and Gray Flycatchers, Cassin's Vireo, Veery, Hermit Thrush, Nashville, Townsend's, and Black-and-white Warblers, American Redstart, Northern Waterthrush, Wilson's Warbler, and Lincoln's and Golden-crowned Sparrows. The county road is closed south of here due to a cave-in; if and when it reopens you will again be able to drive down the rest of the canyon to join Palisades Road in Moses Coulee (page 379). In the meantime you can walk.

BADGER MOUNTAIN

Badger Mountain lies between the Columbia River and Moses Coulee northeast of Wenatchee. Its upper elevations support the most extensive co-nifer forest in the western Columbia Basin. Badger Mountain Road goes up and over this large ridge system to Waterville in about 25 miles. In East Wenatchee, turn east from SR-28 onto Grant Road (the first intersection south of the SR-285 bridge), then left (north) in one long block onto Eastmont Avenue, which becomes Badger Mountain Road as it leaves town and begins climbing. Look for bluebirds (both species) at lower elevations and for Spotted Towhee, Chipping Sparrow, and Cassin's Finch higher up, in brushy terrain on south-facing slopes. The road crosses the crest in about six miles, then remains at an elevation of 3,000–3,500 feet as it contours along the southeast face of Badger Mountain until reaching a ski area about 20 miles from East Wenatchee. Along the way, stop in several places in the Ponderosa Pine and Douglas-fir forest to look and listen for Hairy Woodpecker, Dusky Flycatcher, Cassin's Vireo, White-breasted Nuthatch, Swainson's Thrush, and Western Tanager. Northern Goshawk has been seen here in May. Take the main road (now called Baseline Road) east from the ski area for two-plus miles, then turn north on Road O NW (also called Waterville Road) and drive another 2.5 miles to US-2 in Waterville. If you are driving this route in reverse from Waterville, go south from US-2 a block south of the Catholic church onto S Chelan Avenue, which becomes Road O NW/Waterville Road upon leaving town.

WATERVILLE PLATEAU AND BRIDGEPORT

by Andy Stepniewski

The northwest corner of the Columbia Basin is a high plateau bordered by the deep gorge of the Columbia River on the west and north, the Grand Coulee on the east and southeast, and Badger Mountain on the southwest. Technically, the name Waterville Plateau is reserved for a relatively small section north of Waterville, but by tradition birders employ this term to designate the whole 30-by-40-mile area described here. Ice-age floods gouged out Moses Coulee, a north-south gash that bisects the plateau for more than half its length. The Withrow Moraine, which marks the southern extent of glaciation in the last ice age, crosses the southern part of the plateau in a southeasterly direction, from near Chelan to Coulee City. Monotonous wheat fields extend for miles on the unglaciated land to the south, providing little habitat for birds other than the many Horned Larks. Northward, the plateau bears abundant evidence of glaciation—large "haystack" rocks and piles of glacial debris, kettle lakes, and generally uneven, stony ground. Because of this rough landscape, farming has proved marginal, despite near-heroic attempts over the past century. Significant areas of former farmland are now set aside in the USDA Conservation Reserve Program, and shrub-steppe habitats are slowly returning to some of these.

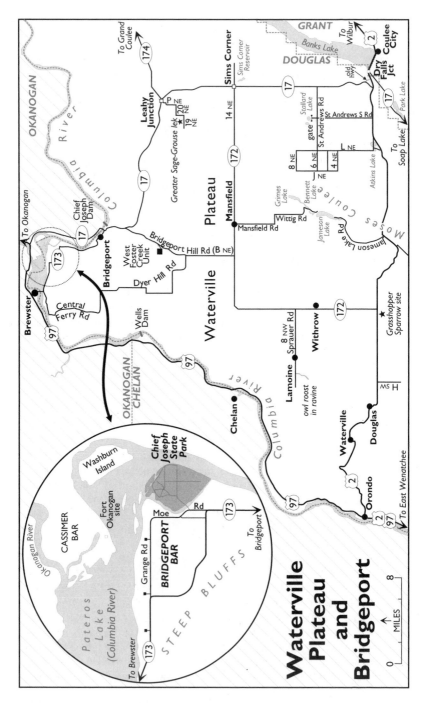

Waterville
Plateau
and
Bridgeport

Bird species such as Swainson's Hawk, American Kestrel, Gray Partridge, Greater Sage-Grouse, Short-eared Owl, and Vesper Sparrow benefit from the enhanced habitat.

The plateau is known for northern, open-country specialties in winter, including raptors such as Rough-legged Hawk and Gyrfalcon. Horned Lark (arcticola), Lapland Longspur, and Snow Bunting are usually findable among large flocks of the resident Horned Larks (merrilli). Raptors and shrub-steppe birds provide interest in the breeding season. Chukar, White-throated Swift (summer), and Gray-crowned Rosy-Finch (winter) can be found on cliffs and rockslides in upper Moses Coulee. Waterfowl, rails, and shorebirds are present seasonally at several lakes. A small population of Sharp-tailed Grouse inhabits brushy draws on the north slopes of the plateau, which descend toward the Columbia River. Orchards and ornamental plantings in and around Bridgeport support winter flocks of Bohemian Waxwings and finches. The Bridgeport Bar in the Columbia bottomlands is a great place in winter to sort through sparrow flocks and view waterbirds on the river.

Birding on the high plateau can be difficult in winter, even hazardous. Always check the weather first. Avoid storms. Blowing snow obscures vision and quickly buries roads, and it may be miles to the nearest human habitation. Even in fair weather you may find dense fog atop the plateau. Stick to the main, plowed roads. During thaws, beware of soft shoulders and ungraded secondary roads, or you may find your vehicle up to its axles in mud. It is advisable to bring tire chains, a shovel, extra clothing, emergency food and water, cell phone, and sleeping bags on any winter trip.

There is no single best way to bird the plateau. Much of it is served by a grid of gravel section-line roads, and the more you explore, the more birds you will see. Several consistently productive areas are described below, loosely grouped for convenience of presentation.

WATERVILLE PLATEAU (SOUTH)

Amidst the wheat fields 13 miles east of Waterville on US-2 is an intersection with SR-172. From May to July, pull off the highway about a quarter-mile west of this junction and walk to the south through grassland habitat with scattered Big Sagebrush, looking for Grasshopper Sparrow—a very local species on the plateau. In winter, an interesting roost for Great Horned and Long-eared Owls near **Lamoine** is reached by driving north on SR-172 past Withrow 8.0 miles to Road 8 NW (Sprauer Road), turning into town to check the Withrow grain elevators as you go for Gray Partridge and attendant Gyrfalcon or Prairie Falcon. Turn west onto Road 8 NW and travel 6.0 miles to a ravine, on the left, flanked by dense pines in the wheat fields. Walk along the pines to search for owls and Gray Partridge. Continuing north, then east, on SR-172 will bring you to Mansfield (page 385).

Eastward from the SR-172 junction, US-2 soon drops down to cross Moses Coulee, reaching the Jameson Lake turnoff (page 379) in about eight miles. After climbing back out of the coulee, look for the junction with Heritage

Road (aka Road L NE) in about nine more miles (coming from the east, this is about eight miles west of Dry Falls Junction). Turn north here and go 0.7 mile to an unmarked dirt road on the right leading to **Atkins Lake**. In periods of normal precipitation, this large swale in the wheat fields is a shallow lake that may have water for most of the year. During one of the irregular droughts, however, the lake may be entirely dry and not worth a stop. It can be a fabulous place for waterbirds, except in winter when frozen. Thousands of geese, dabbling and diving ducks, and Sandhill Cranes are present in spring if conditions are right. Raptors can also be conspicuous—look for Northern Harrier, Red-tailed Hawk, and Prairie Falcon year round. Swainson's Hawk is fairly common in summer. Winter possibilities include Northern Goshawk, Rough-legged Hawk, Golden Eagle, and Gyrfalcon. Bald Eagle and Peregrine Falcon occur mainly in migration. Late summer can prove attractive for shorebirds—many species uncommon or rare in the interior have been observed when suitable mud is exposed. Winter often brings Horned Larks, Lapland Longspurs, and Snow Buntings to the lake edges.

Greater Sage-Grouse can be found, with luck, at any season in patches of the original Big Sagebrush habitat about four to eight miles north of Atkins Lake. In the early morning, drive the grid of roads within the rectangle formed by Road 4 NE on the south, Road 8 NE on the north, Road L NE on the east, and Road J NE on the west.

Haynes Canyon is a good place for shrub-steppe birds, right off US-2. About six miles east of the Road L NE corner (1.6 miles west of Dry Falls Junction), go north on SR-17 toward Bridgeport; keep an eye out for Chukar in road cuts and for Gray Partridge in grassier stretches. A section of old highway projects south from SR-17 on the right, 1.1 miles north of US-2. Sage Sparrow is regular along this old road from April to July. Stop again 2.0 miles farther north on SR-17, where the shrub-steppe habitat has more native bunchgrasses and may produce Sage Thrasher and Brewer's Sparrow.

Continue north 2.8 miles on SR-17 to Saint Andrews E Road (Road 6 NE). Turn left here and go west three miles to the intersection with Road O NE (also reachable by driving east three miles from Road L NE). Turn north onto Road O NE and go half a mile to scope **Stallard Lake** from behind a closed gate. Waterfowl, Sandhill Crane (mainly April), Black-necked Stilt, American Avocet, and phalaropes are the attraction here. This is a good place for shrikes (Northern in winter and Loggerhead in the breeding season). In winter, look for American Tree Sparrows in brush near the gate.

WATERVILLE PLATEAU (NORTH)

Sims Corner marks the intersection of SR-17 and SR-172, eight miles north of Saint Andrews E Road (Road 6 NE). **Sims Corner Reservoir** lies just out of view to the southeast. In spring, large numbers of Sandhill Cranes may be seen from the road as they come in to or depart from this water body. The reservoir is on private property; do not enter without permission (ask at the only farmhouse at this corner).

The largest remaining population of Greater Sage-Grouse in the state—about 700 birds—persists on the northern part of the Waterville Plateau. A good site to view these birds lekking (peak season March–April) is near **Leahy Junction**. From Sims Corner, go north eight miles on SR-17 to the SR-174 intersection, then left on SR-17 to Road P NE (0.1 mile). Turn left and wind southward on a gravel road through hills covered with Big Sagebrush and Bluebunch Wheatgrass, watching for Loggerhead Shrike, Sage Thrasher, and Vesper and Brewer's Sparrows from April through August. In 1.6 miles turn right and drive west for 1.0 mile on Road 20 NE (aka Leahy Cutoff Road), then left (south) on Road O NE for 0.8 mile, and finally right onto Road 19 NE. Drive 0.3 mile to the overlook of the lek site—a five-foot-high berm on the right (north) side of the gravel road. Scan toward the northwest, looking for a shallow ravine several hundred yards distant. The grouse display on the slight rise above the ravine and can easily be heard from the road and seen with a scope. Activity is greatest before and at first light. *Do not cross the fence!* This is all private property. The landowner has shown little sympathy for birders or for the plight of the grouse, and trespassing may be interpreted as an act of provocation. Lek sites sometimes change. If the grouse are not present here, continue along the road, stopping occasionally, listening for their unique plopping sounds. Take time to admire the views of the Cascade Range, particularly beautiful in early morning light.

The 12.5 miles of SR-172 between Sims Corner and Mansfield can be good in winter for Rough-legged Hawk, Gyrfalcon, Gray Partridge, Lapland Longspur, and Snow Bunting. In summer these fields may have Northern Harrier, Swainson's and Red-tailed Hawks, and American Kestrel. You will also hear and see many Horned Larks—doubtless the commonest breeding bird on the Waterville Plateau.

Approaching Mansfield from the east, SR-172 veers left into town. In 0.4 mile, where SR-172 goes right, stay straight to visit **Bennett Lake** and **Grimes Lake** in upper Moses Coulee. Turn left onto Mansfield Road (0.3 mile). Follow this main road as it changes names several times, eventually becoming Wittig Road and reaching Bennett Lake in eight miles. A dirt road that turns off to the left here, open only July through October, leads in half a mile to Grimes Lake. These lakes have produced many Tundra Swans, a variety of dabbling and diving ducks, Virginia Rail and Sora, both yellowlegs, Semipalmated, Baird's, Pectoral, and Stilt Sandpipers, and other shorebird species. The cliffs and talus slopes have Chukar, Common Poorwill, White-throated Swift, Say's Phoebe, thousands of Cliff Swallows, Rock and Canyon Wrens, and in winter many roosting Gray-crowned Rosy-Finches that forage in the fields between these lakes and Jameson Lake (1.3 miles farther south on the main road). From the dilapidated resort at the road's end scan the waters of Jameson Lake for waterfowl—especially in migration.

WELLS WILDLIFE AREA AND BRIDGEPORT

Bridgeport Hill Road (Road B NE) goes north from SR-172 about three miles west of Mansfield. Note the intersection in 4.7 miles where Dyer Hill Road turns left; with a good map it is easy to find your way from here to Central Ferry Canyon. Continuing straight ahead, Bridgeport Hill Road descends along West Foster Creek. The poorly-signed entrance to the Wells Wildlife Area's **West Foster Creek Unit** (1,050 acres) is on the left in 2.4 miles. The access road (impassable if wet or snowy) doubles back sharply and descends steeply to a few parking spots (WDFW permit required). Small numbers of Sharp-tailed Grouse are sometimes found in Water Birches and brush near the stream, but California Quail are far more common. Take the rough trail downstream a couple of hundred yards to a feeder. In winter look for American Tree Sparrows here or in the nearby cattails. Another place for Sharp-tailed Grouse in winter is along Foster Creek on the right (east) side of Bridgeport Hill Road, beginning about three miles farther downhill. Look for them "budding" in the Water Birches by the roadside from here down to the SR-17 intersection in another mile or so, and on the east side of SR-17 after you turn left and drop down toward Bridgeport. The grouse will feed at any time of day but are sensitive to disturbance, so early morning is usually the best time to find them. Common Redpolls—irregular winter visitors—may feed in the Water Birches.

In 2.2 miles make a left from SR-17 onto SR-173 and keep on it through **Bridgeport**, on the Columbia River. In winter check residential streets for Merlins and flocks of Bohemian Waxwings and other winter songbirds. A Northern Hawk Owl wintered here once, too. Continuing west on SR-173, turn right onto Moe Road (5.6 miles), which runs north, then west, becoming Grange Road. In 1.5 miles, turn right into a parking area for the **Bridgeport Bar Unit** (502 acres) of the Wells Wildlife Area (WDFW permit required). A second parking area is 1.1 miles farther along Grange Road. The short walk from these access points down to the Columbia River can be productive for waterfowl, Bald Eagle, and scads of coots in winter. Rarities such as Yellow-billed Loon have shown up here. The scrubby growth can have loads of sparrows. Grange Road rejoins SR-173 in 0.1 mile. Turn right. Abundant brush and trees at a third WDFW access, on the right in 0.7 mile, attract passerines (Bohemian Waxwing in winter). This access also offers good waterbird viewing on the river, as do several pullouts on the right for the next two miles, where SR-173 turns right and crosses the Columbia to Brewster and close-by Okanogan birding sites (page 435).

Do not turn here with SR-173, but stay straight ahead onto Central Ferry (Canyon) Road. In 2.5 miles, where Crane Orchard Road turns right, stay left on Central Ferry Road, which turns to gravel, begins to climb through Central Ferry Canyon, and soon enters the **Central Ferry Unit** (1,538 acres) of the Wells Wildlife Area. Riparian vegetation all the way up can have good birding in winter. In 3.6 miles park on the right and walk the gravel road downhill on the left side of the road to a nice riparian area dominated by Water Birches and thickets of wild rose and Red-osier Dogwood, which attracts Townsend's Solitaire, Varied Thrush, Bohemian Waxwing, and Common Redpoll in winter. Sparrows can be numerous. Sharp-tailed Grouse, though present in modest numbers, are secretive and seldom seen. Continue up Central Ferry Road and turn left onto a dirt lane marked *Packwood Cemetery* (0.8 mile). Park and walk this quarter-mile spur through open Ponderosa Pine forest, watching for Northern Pygmy-Owl, Hairy Woodpecker, Steller's Jay, Clark's Nutcracker, Mountain Chickadee, White-breasted and Pygmy Nuthatches, Cassin's Finch, and Red Crossbill. Continuing uphill, the road soon breaks out onto the Waterville Plateau. With a good map and a bit of care you can bird your way in 15 miles or less to the Dyer Hill Road/Bridgeport Hill Road intersection.

GRAND COULEE

by Andy Stepniewski and Donald Haley

S ome 13,000 years ago, a lobe of the continental ice sheet dammed the Columbia River about where Grand Coulee Dam now stands. Diverted to flow south along a zone of weakness in the plateau basalts, the river gouged away rock and sediments, forming the ancestral Grand Coulee. This chasm was further enlarged by the numerous Spokane Floods that swept across the landscape in the waning years of the last ice age. When the ice sheets receded, the Columbia recaptured its prior course. The abandoned channel now has the form of a wide valley flanked by basalt cliffs. Its upper (northern) end is occupied by a large reservoir, Banks Lake. The floor of the lower (southern) part has lakes—some of them alkaline because there is little or no drainage—marshes, patches of shrub-steppe habitat, and riparian groves. This landscape supports a rich and interesting fauna, including some birds that are unusual away from the coast. Birding is best from spring through early winter. In a normal winter most of the lakes are frozen by January, and birds are few. Even then of interest are the winter roosts of Gray-crowned Rosy-Finch on the cliffs and northern visitors such as Gyrfalcon and Snow Bunting atop the adjacent plateaus. Our itinerary proceeds from south to north, starting from Soap Lake a few miles north of Ephrata (pronounced ee-FRAY-tuh). In spring and early summer, birders may also wish to visit the state's only nesting colony (so far) of Tricolored Blackbirds near Wilson Creek.

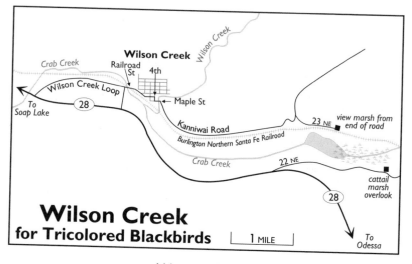

Wilson Creek
for Tricolored Blackbirds ⌐ 1 MILE ⌐

WILSON CREEK

The discovery in 1998 of a colony of Tricolored Blackbirds—the first state record for this species—put the town of Wilson Creek on the birding map. In the same vicinity, the seasonally inundated Crab Creek bottomlands attract many waterfowl, shorebirds, gulls, and terns. Cliffs, talus slopes, and brushy terrain provide nesting sites for raptors, including Ferruginous Hawk, and for a variety of shrub-steppe specialists.

There are two turnoffs for Wilson Creek on the north side of SR-28. The west turnoff is about 16 miles from the intersection with SR-17 at Soap Lake and the other is a mile and a half farther east (24 miles west of Odessa). Use whichever one is more convenient; either way you will be on Wilson Creek Loop. Continue to an intersection and take Railroad Street into town (straight ahead in 1.5 miles if coming from the west exit, or right at a stop sign in 0.3 mile if coming from the east exit). Follow Railroad Street through a couple of bends and turn right onto Fourth Street (0.5 mile). In 0.1 mile turn left onto Maple Street, which shortly crosses a bridge and reaches an intersection with Kanniwai Road. Turn right. For about two and a half miles the road runs through farmlands in a coulee with cliffs on the left where Ferruginous Hawks have nested, and marshes on the right in places (across the railway track). Tricolored Blackbirds are often noted in mixed-species blackbird flocks in fields along this road, away from their nesting sites in the Crab Creek marshes. Turn right onto Road 23 NE and drive to its end in 0.7 mile, again looking for blackbirds and waterbirds in the marshes. Respect private property signs.

To observe the nesting marsh, return to SR-28 at the east Wilson Creek Loop exit, turn left, and go 2.8 miles to Road 22 NE. Bear left here, stopping to scope the shallow seasonal lake on the left for swans (Tundra is abundant in spring), geese, ducks, shorebirds, gulls, and terns. In 1.9 miles pull off to the left and walk a few yards (watch out for rattlesnakes) to an overlook of the large cattail marshes where many Red-winged, Tricolored, and Yellow-headed Blackbirds nest.

Several sites along SR-28 between Wilson Creek and Soap Lake are worth a stop. (See map on page 390.) **Brooks Lake** (aka Stratford Lake) can be scoped from a gravel pullout on the right side of the highway 3.8 miles past the west Wilson Creek Loop turnoff. In fall this lake hosts upwards of 55,000 Canada Geese. Usually a few Greater White-fronted and Snow Geese are present in this huge throng. Rarities such as Ross's Goose and Brant have been seen here, too. Look also for Western Grebe and American White Pelican. Continuing west on SR-28, you come to an intersection with Pinto Ridge Road on the right (3.8 miles). If you are visiting during spring or fall migration, you might want to check the oasis at **Summer Falls**, reached by going 7.2 miles north on this road. Continuing west on SR-28, a dirt track turns off left in 4.2 miles. Go a short distance into a patch of Big Sagebrush and Bitterbrush, where Sage Thrasher and Lark Sparrow may be found. It is another 4.1 miles west on SR-28 to the junction with SR-17 at the south edge of Soap Lake.

LOWER GRAND COULEE

Go north 0.7 mile on SR-17 through the town of Soap Lake to the parking area at the south end of the lake. **Soap Lake** is slightly saltier than the ocean and distinctly alkaline—chemically akin to a salty solution of sodium bicarbonate. The reputed curative properties of these waters continue to draw vacationers, while Eared Grebe, Northern Shoveler, Ruddy Duck, and Ring-billed Gull are attracted by the copepods and other tiny invertebrates that swarm just below the lake's surface in the warmer months. Soap Lake is one of the better spots in Eastern Washington to look for scoters, Long-tailed Duck, and Franklin's and Sabine's Gulls (mainly fall). Shorebirds (Sanderling and Pectoral Sandpiper in fall) can be found on this beach as well as on the one at the north end of the lake. Pullouts along the way provide other opportunities for bird-viewing.

Much of the valley bottom to the north is occupied by four large lakes within the Sun Lakes Wildlife Area (9,140 acres; WDFW permit required). The southernmost, and largest, is **Lenore Lake**. Turn off left from SR-17 to a fishing access 6.0 miles north of the south parking area at Soap Lake. Many species of freshwater ducks use the lake except in mid-winter when it is frozen. Marine ducks such as scoters and Long-tailed Duck are regular. Look for Golden Eagles, which nest in the cliffs across the lake from here. A road-side pullout 1.8 miles farther north allows more views of the lake. Several Barrow's Goldeneyes nest here, an unusual location for this species. The cliffs close by are a reliable winter roost location for Gray-crowned Rosy-Finches.

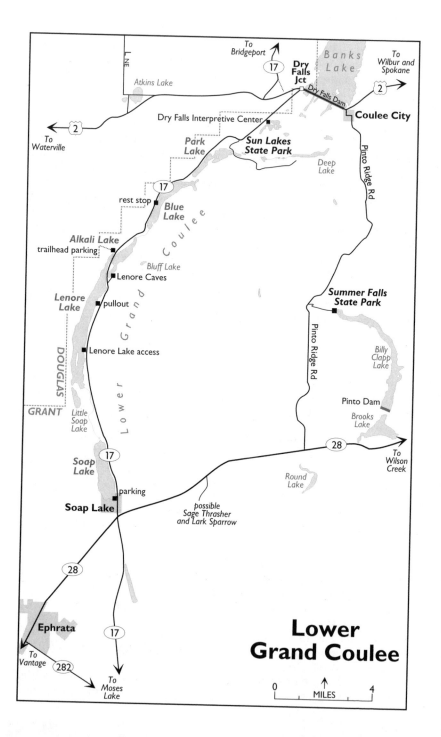

Lower Grand Coulee

Look for them beginning in late afternoon as they check out the crevices (and perhaps Cliff Swallow nests). Canyon Wren is fairly common here, though often difficult to spot.

Another 1.1 miles farther north on SR-17, at a sign marked *Lenore Caves*, turn left into a parking area. A short asphalt path leads north to a small spawning channel constructed for the Lahontan Cutthroat Trout that were stocked in Lenore Lake. Look for them in the channel from late March through June. Across the highway, take the Lenore Caves turnoff (parking lot in 0.4 mile); you will have a great overlook of **Alkali Lake**, the next lake in the chain. During spring and fall large numbers of ducks, coots, and other waterbirds can be observed here. A short hike (about one-quarter mile, in places a bit rough) leads to the **Lenore Caves**—which have been used by humans for at least 5,000 years—and another beautiful view. Some of the species you may observe are Golden Eagle, Say's Phoebe, and Canyon and Rock Wrens. Continue north on SR-17 to a parking lot on the north side of Lenore Lake (1.1 miles). Here a footpath passes through a fence opening and heads up through a rocky cleft to shrub-steppe habitat and the talus apron at the base of the tallest cliffs. In addition to shrub-steppe species such as Loggerhead Shrike and Brewer's Sparrow, check for Golden Eagle, Prairie Falcon, Chukar, and Canyon Wren. Rattlesnakes are abundant here.

Blue Lake (1.8 miles) is an excellent inland site for loons in migration. Commons are often present in large numbers, especially in fall, along with a few Pacifics in October. Yellow-billed has occurred. Red-necked Grebe has nested at the south end of the lake in recent years. Scope from the rest stop on the right in another 1.8 miles or from any of the pullouts along the highway.

Birds are abundant in the lakes, marshes, and riparian habitats of **Sun Lakes State Park** (3.1 miles). For a fine morning birdwalk from mid-May to mid-June, park in the lot (1.3 miles) beyond the campground entrance and walk the first mile or so of the 2.5-mile road to Deep Lake. The road follows a stream lined with Water Birch, Red-osier Dogwood, and wild rose. Look for waterfowl, Red-tailed Hawk, Black-billed Magpie, Common Raven, swallows, Rock Wren, Yellow-breasted Chat, Lazuli Bunting, Yellow-headed Blackbird, Bullock's Oriole, and Lark Sparrow.

Dry Falls is one of the geologic marvels of the state. Stop at the overlook and interpretive display 1.9 miles farther north on SR-17, on the right. In summer you can often go eyeball to eyeball with White-throated Swifts as they slice the sky right before you. Look for Chukar here, too. In winter rosy-finches roost in the cliffs below the overlook. The lakes far below often have waterfowl.

The Lower Grand Coulee ends at Dry Falls Junction, where SR-17 meets US-2 (2.0 miles; page 384). Turn left for birding sites on the Waterville Plateau or right to continue to the Upper Grand Coulee.

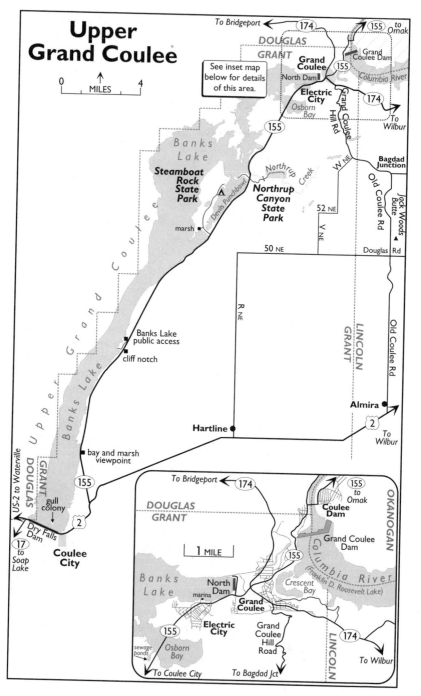

Upper Grand Coulee

0 — MILES — 4

See inset map below for details of this area.

To Bridgeport

174

155 to Omak

DOUGLAS
GRANT

Grand Coulee
North Dam

Grand Coulee Dam

155

Columbia River

Electric City

Osborn Bay

Grand Coulee Hill Rd

174

To Wilbur

155

Banks Lake

Steamboat Rock State Park

Northrup Creek

Devils Punchbowl

Northrup Canyon State Park

W NE

Bagdad Junction

52 NE

V NE

Old Coulee Rd

Jack Woods Butte

marsh

50 NE

Douglas Rd

R NE

LINCOLN
GRANT

Old Coulee Rd

Upper Grand Coulee

Banks Lake

Banks Lake public access

cliff notch

Almira

2

To Wilbur

Hartline

bay and marsh viewpoint

155

GRANT
DOUGLAS

gull colony

US-2 to Waterville

Dry Falls Dam

2

17 to Soap Lake

Coulee City

To Bridgeport

174

155 to Omak

Coulee Dam

DOUGLAS
GRANT

OKANOGAN

Grand Coulee Dam

1 MILE

155

Columbia River
(Franklin D. Roosevelt Lake)

Banks Lake

North Dam

marina

Grand Coulee

Crescent Bay

Electric City

Grand Coulee Hill Road

Osborn Bay

155

sewage ponds

LINCOLN

174

To Wilbur

To Coulee City

To Bagdad Jct

UPPER GRAND COULEE

North from the Dry Falls Dam at Coulee City lies the huge Upper Grand Coulee, now mostly flooded by artificial Banks Lake. Filled with water pumped up from Franklin D. Roosevelt Lake with 12 of the world's largest pumps, Banks Lake constitutes the headworks of the Columbia Basin Irrigation Project. About 2,360 miles of canals and laterals thread their way downslope from Dry Falls Dam to irrigate 640,000 acres of productive farmland throughout the southern Columbia Basin. The lake and most of the shoreline are included in the Banks Lake Wildlife Area.

Banks Lake may host birds more often seen along the coast, especially during fall migration. Sea ducks are regular, including inland Washington's largest congregation of Red-breasted Mergansers (late fall; a few winter). Jaegers are possible. Large numbers of Herring Gulls winter on the lake if areas of open water persist, and Glaucous Gulls are sometimes seen with them.

From Dry Falls Junction, drive east across **Dry Falls Dam** on US-2, checking the waters north of the dam for loons, grebes, and diving ducks. A pullout midway across (1.2 miles) provides a vantage for an extensive area of lake and mudflat on the south side of the dam. Blue-winged and Cinnamon Teals, Black-necked Stilt, American Avocet, and Wilson's Phalarope can often be scoped from here. Swivel your scope 180 degrees across the dam to a rocky island in Banks Lake that supports a large colony of Ring-billed and California Gulls and a few Double-crested Cormorants and Caspian Terns, along with some Great Blue Herons and Black-crowned Night-Herons nesting in dwarf Hackberry trees.

Proceed east on US-2 through Coulee City to a junction with SR-155, where US-2 goes right (3.0 miles). Keep straight here and head north on SR-155 along the east shore of **Banks Lake**. At an area of bays and marshes (2.3 miles) look for Western and Clark's Grebes. American White Pelican is frequently noted here, as are Tundra Swan, Canada Goose, Redhead, many other waterfowl, and Bald Eagle in winter. A pullout and overlook at a large notch in the cliff (5.5 miles) is a great place to see nesting White-throated Swift, Violet-green Swallow, Canyon Wren, and occasionally Peregrine Falcon. In fall, check for Common Loon and flotillas of Red-breasted Mergansers on the waters far below. Banks Lake Public Access (1.0 mile) goes to the lake, passing a dense patch of Big Sagebrush filled with Brewer's Sparrows (April through July).

SR-155 parallels the lakeshore to the turnoff to **Steamboat Rock State Park** (6.7 miles). On the way, stop at as many pullouts as time permits. Common Loon, Horned Grebe, Greater Scaup, and mergansers may be found in fall and spring. Note the large Cliff Swallow colonies on cliffs beside the highway. After turning into the park, a dirt road goes off to the left in 0.4 mile. Walk this road to a grove of Russian Olives beside a cattail marsh. Check the trees for Long-eared Owl, American Robin, Varied Thrush, and American Tree Sparrow (winter). The park has a developed campground with ornamental plantings that attract migrants in season. Chukar and Gray Partridge occur here. Berry-consuming birds such as California Quail, American Robin, Varied Thrush, and Townsend's Solitaire are especially common. The ready prey attracts accipiters. Northern Goshawk is regular in winter. For the hardy, a steep trail ascends to the top of mesa-like Steamboat Rock. Although not particularly good for birds, the rock is famous for its display of Bitterroot (May and June). Bald and Golden Eagles and Prairie Falcon nest here. Bats roost in the cliffs, including the rare Spotted Bat. North from the park entrance on SR-155, a bay known as Devils Punchbowl hosts Western Grebe families in summer and hundreds of mergansers in fall, including many Hooded and Red-breasted. Scan for these from one of the many pullouts.

The gravel road into **Northrup Canyon State Park** turns off right in 3.4 miles and ends at a gate (0.6 mile). The park is in a natural state, with no facilities other than a wide trail along a canyon lined by towering granitic rocks. These witnesses of the older rocks that underlie much of the Columbia Basin protrude up into the otherwise widespread, and recent, Columbia Plateau basalts. The canyon has scattered forests of Ponderosa Pine and Douglas-fir and a riparian corridor lined with Water Birch and dense brush. Resident bird species include Golden Eagle, Chukar, Great Horned Owl, Downy Woodpecker, Northern Flicker, Black-capped and Mountain Chickadees, Red-breasted and White-breasted Nuthatches, Canyon Wren, Song Sparrow, and Red Crossbill (irregular). Spring brings many migrants and summer visitors, including Long-eared and Northern Saw-whet Owls, Common Poorwill, White-throated Swift, Lewis's Woodpecker, Red-naped Sapsucker, Western Wood-Pewee, Say's Phoebe, Lazuli Bunting, Bullock's Oriole, and Cassin's Finch. During the warm months the parking lot by the gate is a good place to find Spotted Bats—identifiable at night by their clearly audible clicking. In late fall and early winter dozens of Bald Eagles fly into the tall conifers in late afternoon to roost. Their cacklings and wild aerobatics against the backdrop of the cliffs are an exciting spectacle. This is one of the largest roosts in interior Washington, with over 100 birds in some years. Numbers decline when arctic air masses arrive in late December or January, and Banks Lake freezes.

Returning to SR-155, turn right, passing a small bay at 1.7 miles, then crossing larger **Osborn Bay** (2.4 miles). On both, look for Western and Clark's Grebes, which nest. Fall and early winter see the arrival of thousands of waterfowl of many species. In **Electric City** the small boat launch and marina (1.6 miles) often has many diving ducks, and the booms in the bay attract gulls in late fall and early winter. Ring-billed, California, Herring, and Glaucous-winged are the regular species. Rarer species include Bonaparte's, Thayer's, Iceland (once, November), Glaucous, and Sabine's. In 0.5 mile turn left from SR-155, park, and walk onto **North Dam**. Scan this end of the lake for loons, grebes, waterfowl (especially Common Goldeneye in the colder months), and gulls (especially Herring). Cruising the residential streets in Electric City and the nearby towns of Grand Coulee and Coulee Dam can yield Bohemian Waxwing and Common Redpoll in winter.

The plateau above Grand Coulee is known in winter for Rough-legged Hawk, Gyrfalcon, Prairie Falcon, Snowy and Short-eared Owls, Gray Partridge, Northern Shrike, Horned Lark (abundant), Bohemian Waxwing (junipers around the isolated farmhouses), Lapland Longspur, Snow Bunting, and Gray-crowned Rosy-Finch. However, it is best avoided when conditions of fog or drifting snow prevail. From the North Dam approach road, continue east on SR-155 to its junction with SR-174 (0.4 mile). Turn right (south) onto SR-174 and go 0.5 mile to Grand Coulee Hill Road. Turn right and climb steeply to a junction (4.7 miles). Bear left (east) here (road name changes to Old Coulee Road at the Lincoln County line) to **Bagdad Junction** (2.2 miles). This expansive plateau country is grown to wheat. The best strategy is to drive the main, plowed section roads, looking for birds. The highest part of the plateau, and possibly the best for birds, is reached by continuing south on Old Coulee Road from Bagdad Junction to **Jack Woods Butte** (elevation 2,818 feet), just northeast of the junction with Douglas Road (4.0 miles). From here you can bird graveled Douglas Road westward for the next eight miles (road changes name to Road 50 NE at the Grant County line) to the intersection with Road R NE.

Mile-wide **Grand Coulee Dam**, completed in 1941, backs up the Columbia River more than 150 miles. Tours are offered into the innards of this gigantic structure, where a cavernous room is lined with 24 enormous turbines that generate enough power to supply the needs of two cities the size of Seattle (take SR-155 two miles north from Grand Coulee). The dam is also a salmon exterminator; no fish ladders were constructed to surmount this monumental barrier. Check the roiling waters below the dam from fall through spring for Common Merganser, gulls, and dippers. In winter protected waters behind the dam may have loons, grebes, diving ducks, Bald Eagle, and loafing gulls.

NORTHEASTERN COLUMBIA BASIN

by Jim Acton, Mark Houston, and Andy Stepniewski

Endless wheat fields flank US-2 as it crosses the northern Columbia Basin east from Coulee City, interrupted only when the highway dips into scablands where soils scoured away by ice-age floods have been slow to redevelop. Shrub-steppe, scattered Ponderosa Pine forests, riparian vegetation, marshes, and pothole lakes are found in these unfarmable places. Because of elevation and proximity to the Selkirk Mountains, precipitation is higher than in most other parts of the Columbia Basin. The increased moisture sustains verdant grasslands with much Idaho Fescue—a snow- and cold-tolerant bunchgrass—and Quaking Aspen copses. Similar scablands habitats are found near Sprague, 25 miles farther south.

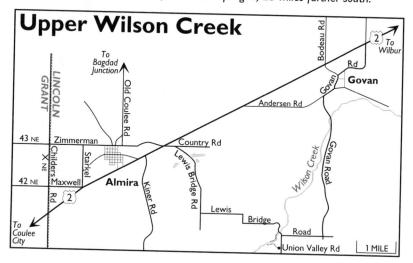

UPPER WILSON CREEK

Southeast of Almira, Wilson Creek flows down a coulee famous for wild-flowers from late March through May. Part of the coulee is BLM land and open for public enjoyment. Turn east from US-2 onto Country Road less than a mile east of Almira (18 miles east of the US-2/SR-155 junction near Coulee City). Make another right onto Lewis Bridge Road (0.3 mile) and follow this main gravel road as it winds across wheat fields and down into an impressive Channeled Scablands landscape. Stop just before crossing Wilson Creek (4.2 miles). A ribbon of riparian vegetation meanders along the valley floor and nearby benches are mantled in a diverse shrub-steppe flora. Red-tailed Hawk, American Kestrel, and Rock Wren can be found in rocky places, and Lazuli Bunting and Yellow-breasted Chat in the Water Birches and shrubs along the creek (take the trail downstream, on the right). Swarms of Cliff Swallows nest on the cliffs. Drive across the bridge and in 0.1 mile turn right onto Union Valley Road. From a tiny parking lot on the right (0.5 mile) a half-mile trail leads through excellent shrub-steppe communities (Sage Thrasher, Brewer's Sparrow) to a view of the basalt cliffs and lush growth along Wilson Creek. If your next destination is east along US-2, return to Lewis Bridge Road and turn right. At Govan Road (1.1 miles), turn left and follow it through many turns to reach US-2 in 5.4 miles. From here it is about five miles east to Wilbur.

SWANSON LAKES

Nine miles east of Wilbur on US-2 (20 miles west of Davenport), Creston is the gateway to the **Swanson Lakes Wildlife Area**—20,000 acres of shrub-steppe, lake, marsh, riparian, and scattered Ponderosa Pine habitats. Taken together with close to 20,000 acres of adjacent BLM lands, this constitutes one of the most significant Channeled Scablands tracts in public ownership in Washington. Lakes host high numbers of swans, geese, and ducks in spring and again in fall. Shorebirding can be exciting, particularly in late summer. Shrub-steppe denizens include Loggerhead Shrike, Sage Thrasher, and Brewer's Sparrow in Big Sagebrush, and Vesper and Grasshopper Sparrows in bunchgrass with less shrub cover. A primary habitat-management focus for these lands is a remnant population of about 100–150 Sharp-tailed Grouse. Concerted efforts to maintain this species are underway, particularly by the state personnel at Swanson Lakes. Unfortunately, cattle-grazing on the federal portion stymies grouse-preservation efforts. The grouse are few and spread over a large area, so there is no sure-fire way of finding them. The more walking you do, the more apt you are to chance upon one. The best solution is to take a lek tour, customarily offered in April each year (contact the wildlife area manager at 509-636-2344 or *swanlake@bossig.com*).

The following circuit visits the major habitats, returning to US-2 east of Creston. Swanson Lakes Road turns south from US-2 just east of the grain elevators in Creston. Drive south through wheat farms and in 8.0 miles stop to scan steppe habitats on both sides of the road—excellent for Burrowing and Short-eared Owls, Horned Lark, and Vesper, Savannah, and Grasshopper Sparrows. Continue two miles to Swanson School Road. The old one-room schoolhouse on the left is plastered with Cliff Swallow nests. Just south of the schoolhouse the road crosses a narrow neck separating the two **Swanson Lakes**. When water levels are favorable, scoping the lakes from this vantage can yield most of the expected Columbia Basin waterbirds in spring and early summer, including Blue-winged and Cinnamon Teals, Northern Shoveler, Canvasback (a few), Redhead, Lesser Scaup, Ruddy Duck, Black-necked Stilt, American Avocet, and Wilson's Phalarope. Interesting shorebirds observed here from July through September include Black-bellied Plover, American Golden-Plover, Willet, Marbled Godwit, Red Knot, and Semipalmated, Baird's, Pectoral, and Stilt Sandpipers, in addition to the common species.

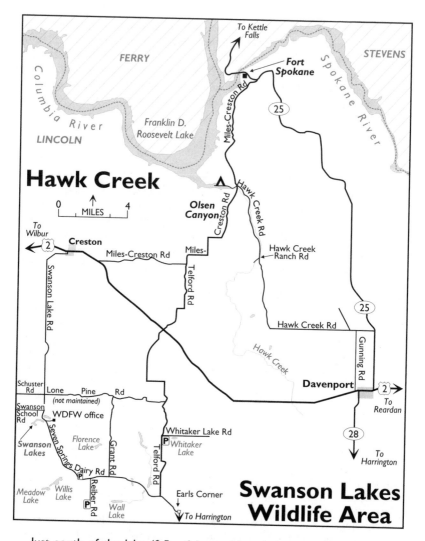

Hawk Creek

0 ↑ 4
MILES

**Swanson Lakes
Wildlife Area**

Just south of the lake (0.5 mile) note the road going left (east) to the WDFW office (information, restrooms). Continue south from this intersection; you are now on Seven Springs Dairy Road. In 4.4 miles search for Sage Thrasher and Brewer's Sparrow in shrub-steppe habitat accessible from a parking area on the left. Turn right onto Reiber Road (0.3 mile) and go south 1.3 miles to a BLM parking area. By walking the grasslands here you might encounter Sharp-tailed Grouse. Return to Seven Springs Dairy Road, turn right, and drive to an intersection (4.3 miles). Turn left and go north on Telford Road to Whitaker Lake Road (3.7 miles). If you are interested in searching for Sharp-tailed Grouse, park in the lot at this corner and explore the shrub-steppe terrain. **Whitaker Lake** lies 0.7 mile east, with possibilities for waterfowl, shorebirds, and Black Tern. Starting about two miles farther north on Telford Road, an area of lake and marsh followed by an aspen copse may be worth some stops. Continue north on Telford Road to reach US-2 in a bit less than six miles (11.3 miles from Seven Springs Road).

HAWK CREEK

For a quick change of scenery and birdlife, go straight across US-2 on Telford Road to visit Hawk Creek—rich in breeding birds, particularly in May and June. This 45-mile circuit takes you down Olsen Canyon to Lake Roosevelt and Fort Spokane, returning via Hawk Creek to US-2 in Davenport. Go north on Telford Road 4.6 miles and turn right onto Miles-Creston Road. Follow this road 3.6 miles across rolling uplands interspersed with Ponderosa Pine stands to the top of **Olsen Canyon**. Stop in the open pine woods anywhere along Telford or Miles-Creston Roads to listen for the harsh, two-part song of Gray Flycatcher—the only breeding *Empidonax* in this habitat. You should also expect Lewis's Woodpecker, Mountain Chickadee, Pygmy Nuthatch, and Red Crossbill. It is about three miles down Olsen Canyon to Hawk Creek Road. Logged Douglas-fir stands along this stretch have a species-diverse cover of deciduous growth. The breeding empid of this quite different habitat is Dusky Flycatcher, which has a more spirited song than Gray. Several old logging tracks lead off to the left, allowing you to search for this species and many other birds.

At the intersection with Hawk Creek Road you may turn left and drive half a mile to Hawk Creek Campground (hookups, fee) in the Franklin Roosevelt National Recreation Area. Or continue straight ahead on Miles-Creston Road for 7.2 miles, then left on SR-25 for half a mile to historic **Fort Spokane** (campground, hookups, fee). The Ponderosa Pine forest here has all three nuthatches, Cassin's Finch, and possibly White-headed Woodpecker.

Hawk Creek Road follows **Hawk Creek** uphill from the intersection with Miles-Creston Road. In 4.6 miles turn right onto Hawk Creek Ranch Road and park. A small parcel of state land with riparian vegetation along the creek offers a nice assortment of birds. Common breeding species include Ruffed Grouse, Calliope Hummingbird, Red-naped Sapsucker, Belted Kingfisher, Veery, MacGillivray's Warbler, Yellow-breasted Chat, Black-headed Grosbeak, and Lazuli Bunting. There are several reports of Least Flycatcher from this area. Once again winding up Hawk Creek Road to the upper reaches of the canyon, check the stands of mixed Douglas-fir and Ponderosa Pine for Blue Grouse, Wild Turkey, Long-eared and Northern Saw-whet Owls, Lewis's Woodpecker, Steller's Jay, Clark's Nutcracker, and Townsend's Solitaire. On the plateau be alert for Mountain Bluebird and Lark Sparrow. Hawk Creek Road turns left in 4.1 miles and goes east to an intersection with Gunning Road in five more miles. Turn right here to reach US-2 on the western outskirts of Davenport in 3.3 miles.

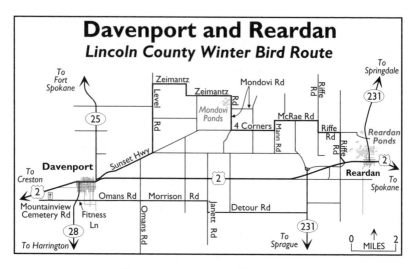

DAVENPORT AND REARDAN

In birding circles the **Davenport cemetery** is well known as a migrant trap. Near the west edge of town turn south from US-2 onto SR-28, drive 0.9 mile, and turn right onto Mountainview Cemetery Road, reaching the cemetery in 0.7 mile. In spring and fall this isolated patch of tall spruces, firs, and pines can be full of migrant flycatchers, vireos, Ruby-crowned Kinglets, thrushes, warblers, Western Tanagers, sparrows, Bullock's Orioles, and finches. Vagrants seen here over the years include Palm, Blackpoll, and Black-and-white Warblers, and Ovenbird. Fall and winter bring an influx of Red and White-winged (irregular) Crossbills, Common Redpolls (irregular), and Pine Siskins.

Reardan is the next town east of Davenport, 13 wheat-field-lined miles on US-2. Turn north with SR-231 in the middle of town and drive 0.4 mile to the **Reardan Ponds**, a series of marshy ponds on both sides of the road. The shoulder on the east side is fairly wide but there is virtually none on the west side; be careful if you stop. It is best to park north of the ponds and walk back along the road to bird. You may walk out to the sides of the ponds in some places but not everywhere. Obey private property signs. The ponds are good for many species of ducks and marshbirds, including Black Terns from April to August. This is one of the best spots in Eastern Washington for shorebirds, especially in late summer after the water level has fallen off to expose mud. Less-common species such as Solitary, Semipalmated, and Baird's Sandpipers, occur regularly. Rarities such as Piping Plover (only Washington record), Ruff, and White-rumped Sandpiper (two of the three state records) have turned up here.

From December to February, try the 32-mile **Lincoln County Winter Bird Route** that loops around the high wheat fields north and south of US-2 between Reardan and Davenport. Rough-legged Hawks can be common along this route. Snowy and Short-eared Owls are seen regularly, as are Northern Harrier, Prairie Falcon, Gray Partridge, large numbers of Horned Larks (including side-by-side studies of the pale *arcticola* race and much yellower, resident *merrilli* race), American Tree Sparrow, Lapland Longspur, Snow Bunting, and Gray-crowned Rosy-Finch. Gyrfalcon is rare but annual. Most years, early spring finds some of the deeper swales in the wheat fields filled with snowmelt water. These temporary lakes can attract migrating Tundra Swans and clouds of dabbling ducks such as American Wigeon, Mallard, Northern Pintail, and Green-winged Teal, tempting Gyrfalcons to linger well into March.

Use these directions and the accompanying map to find your way along the loop. Begin in Reardan at the junction where SR-231 turns off north to the ponds. Go west on US-2 to Riffe Road (1.1 miles). Turn right and follow Riffe Road as it winds north and west. In 2.8 miles turn left onto McRae Road. Wind west and south for 2.4 miles, then turn right onto Four Corners Road. Keep straight west for two miles and turn right onto Mondovi Road. In one mile keep straight as paved Mondovi Road swings to the right. You are now on Zeimantz Road (gravel). Go a half-mile, then swing left with Zeimantz Road. Waterfowl may be present in the shallow Mondovi Ponds on the left. Continue west and north 3.9 miles to Level Road. By going left here, you reach Sunset Highway in three miles. Go right 2.8 miles to SR-25. Here, go left for 0.1 mile to US-2. Turn right and go through Davenport (mind the speed limits); in 0.8 mile turn left onto SR-28. In another 0.9 mile turn left onto Fitness Lane, which becomes Omans Road. In 2.9 miles keep straight as Omans Road turns right. You are now on Morrison Road. In 2.9 miles turn right onto Janett Road. Turn left in 0.5 mile onto Detour Road. The knolls along this road are a good bet for Snowy Owl. Turn left onto SR-231 in 4.5 miles, rejoining US-2 in 1.7 miles. Reardan is about three miles east of this intersection and Davenport about ten miles west.

SPRAGUE AND VICINITY

Road-weary birders traveling I-90 will welcome a break to visit several sites in the Channeled Scablands topography near Sprague. A variety of habitats here includes deep-water **Sprague Lake**, several shallow lakes and ponds (some with marshy edges and mudflats), sewage lagoons, deciduous and riparian habitats, productive grasslands, and Ponderosa Pine groves. Leave I-90 at Exit 245 and go south on SR-23 to Poplar Street (0.2 mile). Turn right and go 0.2 mile to B Street. Turn left (south) and go 0.2 mile. Turn right onto First Street (becomes Max Harder Road) and drive west out of Sprague 2.7 miles to a fishing access to Sprague Lake, on the right. Scoping the small bay from here should reveal a variety of waterbirds. Continue west on Max

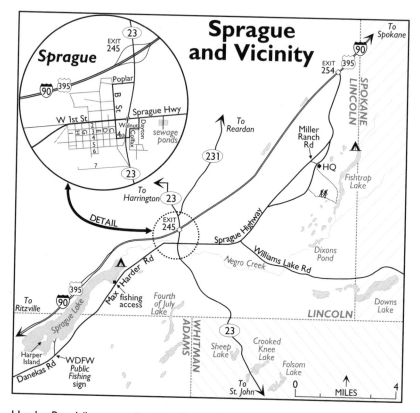

Harder Road (becomes Danekas Road in Adams County) to a WDFW *Public Fishing* sign (3.8 miles). Turn right and drive north 0.3 mile to a fork, then left to an overlook of Harper Island, where Ring-billed and California Gulls nest in large numbers. American White Pelicans began nesting here recently—one of only two breeding colonies in Washington. Double-crested Cormorants are frequently seen and may also nest. With a scope, you should find other interesting waterbirds, including loons, grebes, and ducks (Franklin's and Bonaparte's Gulls possible in spring, Long-tailed Duck and Sabine's Gull in fall).

Return to B Street in Sprague. Turn right and go south 0.1 mile to Fourth Street. Turn left and drive 0.1 mile to SR-23. Turn right and drive south out of town through grasslands with many Western Meadowlarks (and a chance for Grasshopper Sparrow), passing a number of often birdy ponds and small lakes. The best of these for birding is **Crooked Knee Lake** (5.5 miles from Fourth Street, 6.0 miles from I-90). Look for Ruddy Duck, Black-necked Stilt, Wilson's Phalarope, Black Tern, and Yellow-headed Blackbird in the nesting season, and migrant shorebirds in fall.

Return to Fourth Street in Sprague and turn right one short block. In quick succession jog left onto Colfax Street, right onto Walnut, left onto Dayton, and in 0.2 mile you are again at First Street (Sprague Highway). Turn right and go 0.3 mile to the **Sprague sewage ponds**, on the right. Scoping from the road should yield a variety of ducks and gulls (including Bonaparte's on occasion). If water levels are not too high, the eastern pond can have shorebirds, especially in August and September. Look for Black-necked Stilt, American Avocet, both yellowlegs, Semipalmated, Western, Least, Baird's, Pectoral, and Stilt Sandpipers, Long-billed Dowitcher, and Wilson's and Red-necked Phalaropes.

Continuing east on Sprague Highway another 3.6 miles brings you to the southern access to 8,000 acres of federal land at **Fishtrap Lake**. Habitat diversity is high for such a relatively small area—Palouse steppe, shrub-steppe, Ponderosa Pine forests, riparian thickets, and marsh-lined lakes. Turn right at the BLM entrance sign. Birding can be excellent in spring and early summer along this gravel road for the next three miles to BLM headquarters. En route you will find the trailhead for Fishtrap Lake, on the right. A 3.5-mile trail starts here and visits all the major habitats including deeper waters of the lake, looping back to end at headquarters. You can also bird quite effectively by making frequent stops along the road to sample the different habitats, most of which can be found close by. Shallow ponds and wetlands attract marsh species, including scads of waterfowl (Blue-winged and Cinnamon Teals, Northern Shoveler, Redhead, Ruddy Duck), Virginia Rail, Sora, Wilson's Phalarope, Black Tern, Marsh Wren, and Yellow-headed Blackbird. Grasslands and shrub-steppe have Northern Harrier, Swainson's Hawk, American Kestrel, Gray Partridge, Sharp-tailed Grouse (a remnant population), Long-billed Curlew, Common Nighthawk, Loggerhead Shrike, Horned Lark, and Vesper, Savannah, and Grasshopper Sparrows. Red-tailed Hawk, Ruffed Grouse, Great Horned Owl, Downy Woodpecker, Black-capped Chickadee, House Wren, Western Bluebird, and Lazuli Bunting nest in aspen and riparian habitats. Look for Pygmy Nuthatch and Red Crossbill in the pines.

The road forks at headquarters. Take the right branch, reaching Sprague Highway in 1.3 miles. Turn right here to reach I-90 (Exit 254) in 2.3 miles.

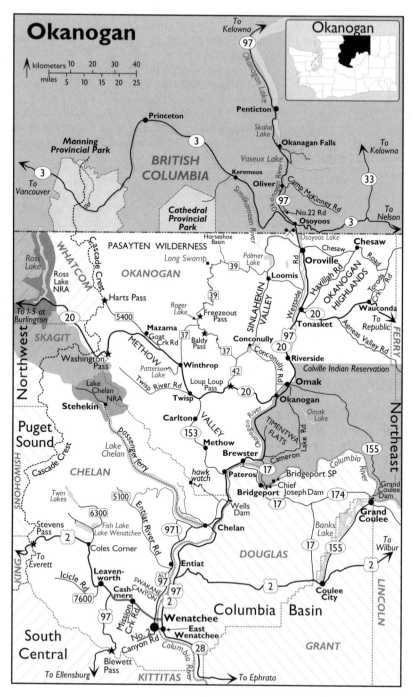

Okanogan

kilometers 10 20 30 40
miles 5 10 15 20 25

To Kelowna
97

Okanogan

Princeton

Penticton

Skaha Lake

Okanagan Falls

Manning Provincial Park

3

BRITISH COLUMBIA

Vaseux Lake

To Kelowna

Keremeos

3

To Vancouver

Cathedral Provincial Park

Oliver

97

Camp McKinney Rd

33

To Nelson

No.22 Rd

Osoyoos

3

To Republic

Osoyoos Lake

PASAYTEN WILDERNESS

Horseshoe Basin

Chesaw

Chesaw

Ross Lake

WHATCOM

Cascade Crest

OKANOGAN

Long Swamp

Palmer Lake

Oroville

Ross Lake NRA

Harts Pass

39

Loomis

Havillah Rd

OKANOGAN HIGHLANDS

Toroda Crk Rd

Wauconda

To I-5 at Burlington

20

5400

39

Roger Lake

Freezeout Pass

SINLAHEKIN VALLEY

Westside Rd

20

Tonasket

Aeneas Valley Rd

To Republic

FERRY

SKAGIT

Mazama

Goat Crk Rd

37

Baldy Pass

Conconully

97

20

Riverside

Colville Indian Reservation

Northwest

Washington Pass

METHOW

Patterson Lake

Winthrop

37

42

Conconully Rd

Omak

Lake Chelan NRA

Twisp River Rd

Loup Loup Pass

20

Okanogan

Stehekin

Twisp

Okanogan River

Omak Lake

Northeast

Puget Sound

Carlton

VALLEY

153

Methow

TIMENTWA FLATS

155

Columbia River

Cascade Crest

CHELAN

Lake Chelan

passenger ferry

Brewster

Cameron

Grand Coulee Dam

Twin Lakes

5100

hawk watch

Pateros

17

Bridgeport SP

Grand Coulee

Stevens Pass

6300

Fish Lake Lake Wenatchee

Entiat River Rd

971

Wells Dam

Chelan

Bridgeport

Chief Joseph Dam

17

174

Banks Lake

2

To Wilbur

KING

2

To Everett

Coles Corner

Entiat

DOUGLAS

17

155

LINCOLN

Icicle Rd

Leaven-worth

SWAKANE CANYON

ALT

97

Coulee City

2

South Central

Cash-mere

Mission Crk Rd

2

Columbia Basin

97

7600

No.2 Canyon Rd

Wenatchee

East Wenatchee

GRANT

Blewett Pass

28

To Ellensburg

KITTITAS

Columbia River

To Ephrata

OKANOGAN

If you like birding in wide open spaces, give north central Washington a try. This vast area stretches more than half the distance from the Cascade crest to the Idaho line, and more than half that from British Columbia to Oregon. Composed of just two counties, Okanogan and Chelan—largest and third-largest in Washington, respectively—the region accounts for less than two percent of the state's population. Of people, that is. When it comes to birds, few other places in North America have as many breeding species (about 200). Migration and winter bring yet more birds; in all, more than 300 species occur in the region.

The geography is simple enough: mountains to the east (Okanogan Highlands) and to the west (northeastern Cascades), separated by the broad valley of the Okanogan River that gives the region its name. All three of these zones continue north, oblivious of the U.S.-Canada border. The Okanogan River flows south to join the Columbia River, which forms the southern boundary of the region. The Columbia channel marks the point where the recent basalt flows that inundated the Columbia Basin stopped abruptly upon contact with the much older rocks of the Okanogan country. West and south from the Okanogan River mouth, high ridges of the Cascades come right to the Columbia, side by side with the Methow, Stehekin/Chelan, Entiat, and Wenatchee River valleys.

Elevational differences produce a great variety of habitats. At 6,000–7,000 feet, the subalpine and alpine zones at Harts Pass and in the Okanogan Cascades offer superb opportunities to search for species such as White-tailed Ptarmigan and Boreal Chickadee. At the lower extreme (700–2,500 feet elevation), shrub-steppe habitats on the drier slopes of the river valleys and on the Timentwa Flats support Great Basin species such as Sage Thrasher and Brewer's Sparrow. Well-watered sites in river bottoms—e.g., the Sinlahekin, the Similkameen, and the Okanogan near Oroville—sustain a bonanza of bird species of riparian, marsh, wet-meadow, and lacustrine habitats. Extensive Ponderosa Pine and mixed-conifer forests mantle the middle elevations between these extremes. The Okanogan Highlands offer a quite special landscape of grasslands, Ponderosa Pine, Douglas-fir and mixed-conifer forests, and extensive riparian areas, interspersed with lakes and marshes. A small population of Great Gray Owls appears to be established in this mid-elevation mosaic of habitats, which is also excellent for Flammulated, Northern Pygmy-, and Northern Saw-whet Owls.

Summers are generally warm in the valleys (July average high temperature 87 degrees in Omak, 86 degrees in Winthrop) but cooler in the mountains (July average high 76 degrees in Chesaw, 66 degrees at Stevens Pass). If camping, be aware that nights are cold (even freezing) at 6,000 feet. Winters are cold in the lowlands (January average low temperature 22 degrees in Wenatchee, 17 degrees in Omak) and colder still in the mountains (January average low 11 degrees in Chesaw and Winthrop). Storms along the Cascade crest are frequent and often prolonged, bringing heavy precipitation (494 inches annual snowfall and 81 inches total precipitation at Stevens Pass). To the east, precipitation is uniformly low, ranging from 9 inches annually at Wenatchee to 14 in Winthrop and Chesaw. The amount that comes as snowfall is much more variable, however—annual average 26 inches at Omak, 28 at Wenatchee, 50 at Chesaw, and a perfect 72 inches at Winthrop, making for famed cross-country skiing. Except for SR-20 (closed for the winter above Mazama) all of the state and federal highways are plowed and sanded, as are many secondary roads. With reasonable precautions, and allowance made for occasional severe conditions, winter driving in the Okanogan poses few or no difficulties.

Wenatchee—with 30,000 inhabitants, the largest city in Eastern Washington north of the Columbia Basin—offers a full range of accommodations and all essential services. Leavenworth, Cashmere, Chelan, Stehekin, Twisp, Winthrop, and Mazama cater to travelers and vacationers in the Cascades. Along the Okanogan Valley on US-97, motels, restaurants, provisions, and gas stations can be found at Brewster, Okanogan, Omak, Tonasket, and Oroville. The region has many USFS and other campgrounds.

STEVENS PASS TO WENATCHEE

by Dave Beaudette, Lee Cain, Dan Stephens, and Andy Stepniewski

From Puget Sound at Everett, US-2 follows the Snohomish and Skykomish River valleys to the Cascade crest at Stevens Pass, then descends along the Wenatchee River drainage to the Columbia River at Wenatchee. The highway is open all year, except for temporary winter closures for avalanche control. Eastward from the summit it is only a one-hour drive from moist lower-subalpine forests to dry Eastside woodlands and semi-arid shrub-steppe habitats. To the south, hundreds of glacial lakes nestle beneath serrated granite ridges in the rugged, sparsely timbered Alpine Lakes Wilderness.

STEVENS PASS

The **Old Cascade Highway**—closed to through traffic—offers about the same mix of species as the far busier Stevens Pass. This road turns north from US-2 about a quarter-mile west of the summit. The habitat at the top end is a thick forest of Silver Fir, Mountain Hemlock, and some Alaska Yellowcedar. A good birding spot is at the first switchback (1.5 miles). The forest is more open here, with Noble Fir, Douglas-fir, and heavy brush. Blue Grouse hoot along the road in spring and early summer, and Golden Eagles sometimes fly along the ridge to the north. Forest and openings should have Gray Jay, Clark's Nutcracker, Hermit and Varied Thrushes, Yellow-rumped, MacGillivray's, and Wilson's Warblers, Red Crossbill, Pine Siskin, and Evening Grosbeak, along with Townsend's Chipmunk and Snowshoe Hare. Dusky Flycatcher and Nashville Warbler sometimes can be found in brushy places. Look for American Dipper from the footbridge over the Tye River at the road's end (3.4 miles).

The Silver Fir forest at Stevens Pass (elevation 4,061 feet) has been opened to make the **Stevens Pass Ski Area**, creating an abundance of brushy habitats easily accessible from US-2. Walk along any of the roads around the ski slopes. Breeding birds include Rufous Hummingbird, Olive-sided and Willow Flycatchers, Violet-green and Barn Swallows, Hermit and Varied Thrushes, Yellow, Yellow-rumped, Townsend's, MacGillivray's, and Wilson's Warblers, Slate-colored Fox, Lincoln's, and White-crowned (*pugetensis* and possibly *gambelii*) Sparrows, Dark-eyed Junco, and Pine Siskin. Purple and Cassin's Finches occur in fall; later, a few Common Redpolls may appear among the more numerous siskins. White-winged Crossbills are regular here in irruption years. Mammals include Hoary Marmot and the occasional Black Bear. The Pacific Crest Trail crosses Stevens Pass, providing access to the Alpine Lakes Wilderness to the south and the Henry M. Jackson Wilderness to the north.

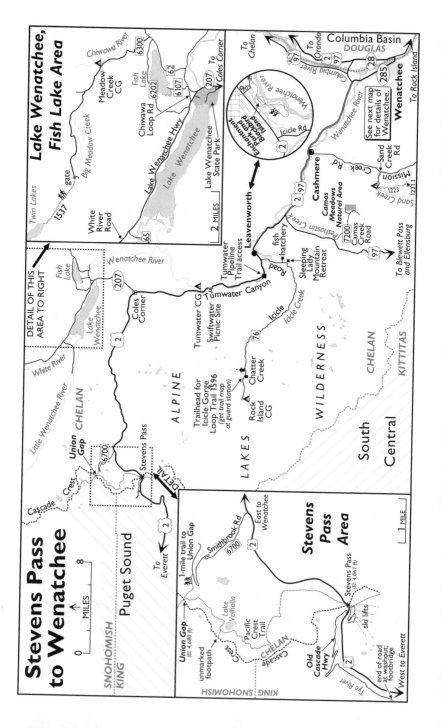

Stevens Pass to Wenatchee

SNOHOMISH
KING

Puget Sound

To Everett

0 — MILES — 8

White River

Little Wenatchee River

CHELAN

Union Gap

6700

Stevens Pass

Cascade Crest

DETAIL

To Everett

2

Lake Wenatchee, Fish Lake Area

Chiwawa River

6300

Meadow Creek CG

Fish Lake

6202

62

6107

Chiwawa Loop Rd

207

To Coles Corner

Big Meadow Creek

Lake Wenatchee Hwy

Lake Wenatchee

Lake Wenatchee State Park

Twin Lakes

gate 1537

White River Road

65

2 MILES

DETAIL OF THIS AREA TO RIGHT

Fish Lake

Wenatchee River

207

Coles Corner

2

Tumwater CG

Tumwater Canyon

Tumwater Pipeline Trail access

Swiftwater Picnic Site

Trailhead for Icicle Gorge Loop Trail 1596 (get trail map at guard station)

Chatter Creek

76

Icicle

Icicle Creek

Rock Island CG

ALPINE LAKES WILDERNESS

CHELAN

KITTITAS

South Central

Columbia Basin

DOUGLAS

To Chelan

To Orondo

ALT 97

97

2

28

285

Columbia River

Wenatchee

To Rock Island

See next map for details of Wenatchee.

Wenatchee River

9th

Enchantment Park and Blackbird Island

Icicle Rd

2

Leavenworth

fish hatchery

Cashmere

2 97

Peshastin Creek

Camas Meadows Natural Area

7200

Camas Creek Road

Sleeping Lady Mountain Retreat

Road

Sand Creek Rd

Mission

1223

1221.1

Sand Creek

To Blewett Pass and Ellensburg

97

Stevens Pass Area

Smithbrook Rd

6700

2

East to Wenatchee

1-mile trail to Union Gap

Union Gap (El. 4,680 ft)

Lake Valhalla

Pacific Crest Trail

unmarked footpath

CHELAN

Cascade Crest

KING SNOHOMISH

Stevens Pass (El. 4,061 ft)

ski lifts

Old Cascade Hwy

2

Tye River

end of road washout; footbridge

West to Everett

1 MILE

Perhaps the easiest way to reach upper-subalpine parkland habitats is on the trail above **Union Gap**. From Stevens Pass, drive 4.1 miles east and downhill on US-2, turning left onto Smithbrook Road (FR-6700). In 3.2 miles, park (Northwest Forest Pass required) and walk the one-mile trail to Union Gap. The trail passes through brushy slopes, old-growth forest (where Northern Pygmy-Owl and other birds typical of moist forest can be expected), and a small sedge meadow (check for Lincoln's Sparrow). At the crest (elevation 4,680 feet), turn left and take the Pacific Crest Trail to Lake Valhalla (1.5 miles). Mature Silver Fir and Mountain Hemlock forest is encountered first, then parkland with lots of Mountain Ash and huckleberries. From the ridge above the lake, climb right (west) on an unmarked footpath up a small peak, reaching open slopes with huckleberry pastures (good picking in late summer) and views south to Mount Rainier and north to Glacier Peak. This habitat is especially good for migrants in late summer and fall: Sharp-shinned, Cooper's, and Red-tailed Hawks, American Kestrel, Prairie Falcon, Bohemian Waxwing (after mid-October), and a variety of warblers and sparrows.

LAKE WENATCHEE

Five miles long and a mile wide, Lake Wenatchee enjoys a spectacular setting in a glacial trench between two high mountain ridges. The state park at the outlet (east) end of the lake is often crowded and noisy, and much of the shoreline is private. Better birding can usually be had at the inlet end. Turn north from US-2 onto SR-207 at Coles Corner, about 20 miles below Stevens Pass and 14 miles north of Leavenworth. At a fork in 4.3 miles, 0.8 mile past the entrance to Lake Wenatchee State Park South (camping, picnicking), bear left onto Lake Wenatchee Highway, passing the north park entrance in 0.3 mile. Continue 5.8 miles on the highway to a junction with White River Road. Keep left here onto FR-65. Another half-mile brings you to a bridge over the **White River**. Bird the riparian groves and conifer forest for the next half-mile, from the road and on a couple of dirt tracks that lead off into the forest. Birds to look for include Common Merganser, Osprey, Ruffed Grouse, Black and Vaux's Swifts, Calliope Hummingbird, Red-naped Sapsucker, Western Wood-Pewee, Willow, Hammond's, and Pacific-slope Flycatchers, Warbling and Red-eyed Vireos, Steller's Jay, Common Raven, many Tree and Violet-green Swallows, Mountain and Chestnut-backed Chickadees, Red-breasted Nuthatch, American Dipper, Veery, Swainson's and Hermit Thrushes, Nashville, Yellow, Townsend's and MacGillivray's Warblers, Western Tanager, Lazuli Bunting, Purple and Cassin's Finches, and Red Crossbill.

Smaller, quieter **Fish Lake**—just northeast of Lake Wenatchee—is worth a look. If coming from the preceding site, drive east on Lake Wenatchee Highway 5.6 miles from the White River Road intersection, then make a left on Chiwawa Loop Road (this turn is 0.2 mile west of the Lake Wenatchee State Park North entrance). Stay left at the next intersection in 0.5 mile, and turn left onto FR-6107 in another 0.1 mile. If coming from the south, turn right at the fork 0.8 mile after the Lake Wenatchee State Park South entrance (just after crossing the Wenatchee River). Keep right in 0.4 mile at the next intersection. You are now on Chiwawa Loop Road, from which FR-6107 turns left in 0.1 mile. Drive north 0.8 mile on the latter road, park on the left just before a crowded resort area, and take the forest trail that winds along the southwest edge of Fish Lake . Red-necked Grebe, geese and ducks, Osprey, and a variety of swallows, including Bank, should be looked for as this short trail nears the marshy west end of the lake.

FR-62 goes northwestward from Fish Lake deep into the Cascades, offering many USFS campgrounds along the Chiwawa River and trailheads for wilderness hiking and backpacking. For a quick sample of the lower part of these forest habitats, continue east on Chiwawa Loop Road from the FR-6107 turn-off, and in 0.7 mile turn left onto FR-62. At an intersection in 2.2 miles, where FR-62 goes straight, turn left onto FR-6300. In 2.5 miles, note Meadow Creek Campground (fee) on the right. At a fork in another 0.4 mile, keep left on FR-6300, which traverses moist forest for the most part. In 3.5 miles, a small stretch of Deerbrush hugs the steep south-facing slopes. Breeding birds in this habitat are Calliope Hummingbird, Dusky Flycatcher, Orange-crowned and Nashville Warblers, and Fox Sparrow. Continue driving up the road another 1.2 miles and park near a locked gate (Northwest Forest Pass required). Just before the gate, walk left along FR-6309 for a hundred yards over a creek to explore riparian habitat dominated by alders. From the gate, Trail 1537 heads into the Glacier Peak Wilderness, reaching the **Twin Lakes** (elevation 2,822 feet) in two miles. Barrow's Goldeneye and Spotted Sandpiper nest here. Birding riparian and conifer habitats near the gate and along the trail might yield Vaux's Swift, Rufous Hummingbird, Red-naped and Red-breasted Sapsuckers (and hybrids), Olive-sided Flycatcher, Warbling Vireo, Chestnut-backed Chickadee, Winter Wren, Swainson's and Varied Thrushes, Nashville, Yellow, Townsend's, and MacGillivray's Warblers, Western Tanager, and Black-headed Grosbeak.

LEAVENWORTH AND ICICLE CREEK

US-2 follows the Wenatchee River as it tumbles down the **Tumwater Canyon**, flanked by towering granitic peaks. Tumwater Campground (USFS, fee) is on the left side of the highway at the head of the canyon, 5.6 miles south of the SR-207 junction. Stop at the Swiftwater Picnic Site, on the right in another 1.9 miles, to scan across the river for an Osprey nest. Continue down the highway toward Leavenworth. In 5.0 miles, turn right into a parking area (not marked and easy to miss). Take the Tumwater Pipeline Trail across the steel bridge that once supported water pipes leading to generators that powered Great Northern electric locomotives through the eight-mile Cascade Tunnel, where coal-burning engines could not operate. The power plant was abandoned decades ago when diesel replaced steam. Walk upstream on the smooth path. Look among the giant boulders in the torrent below for Harlequin Duck, Common Merganser, and American Dipper. Trailside thickets of Bigleaf Maple and Ocean Spray, interspersed with Douglas-fir and Ponderosa Pine, have breeding Cassin's Vireo, Nashville Warbler, and Western Tanager. In one mile you come opposite Castle Rock. Scan for Peregrine Falcon, which may nest in the vicinity.

Continue down US-2 and turn right in 1.6 miles onto Icicle Road, on the western outskirts of Leavenworth. In 2.2 miles turn left on Hatchery Road to reach **Leavenworth National Fish Hatchery**. If the gate is closed, park outside and walk in. Cross the dam to the east side of the hatchery to find a natural area that features a one-mile loop trail where over 120 bird species have been recorded. Breeding season and migration are the best times for birding. The habitat is primarily deciduous forest and brush, with a few conifers. Wood and Harlequin Ducks nest nearby, as do Osprey, Western Screech-Owl, Black-chinned and Rufous Hummingbirds, Red-naped and Red-breasted Sapsuckers (and hybrids), White-headed (pines) and Pileated Woodpeckers, Pacific-slope Flycatcher, Red-eyed Vireo, all three nuthatches, American Dipper (dam), Veery, Swainson's Thrush, Gray Catbird, and ten species of warblers. Black Swift is often seen overhead and evidently breeds somewhere in these mountains. In migration, check for Fox and Golden-crowned Sparrows. Winter brings a few Pine Grosbeaks.

The turnoff to **Sleeping Lady Mountain Retreat** is 0.3 mile farther along Icicle Road. Many environmental conferences are held here, along with music festivals and other events open to the public. For an activities calendar and more information, visit *www.sleepinglady.com* or call 800-574-2123. Birders are free to wander the grounds: look for White-headed Woodpecker, Lazuli Bunting, and Cassin's Finch, among many others, and for Harlequin Duck and American Dipper in the creek.

Icicle Road (becomes FR-76/FR-7600) goes up Icicle Creek for more than 15 miles, serving a number of campgrounds (USFS). The blacktop ends in 10 miles; continue on the gravel road for another 2.3 miles to the USFS Chatter Creek Guard Station (maps, information). Half a mile farther on is parking (Northwest Forest Pass required) for the **Icicle Gorge Loop Trail 1596**, a four-mile loop on a smooth, gentle trail that follows alongside boulder-strewn Icicle Creek. Walk left to cross the creek on a bridge. The trail goes upstream, then veers away from the noisy creek into moist forest followed by a dry forest of Ponderosa Pine and Douglas-fir, reaching the Jack Creek trailhead. From there follow FR-615 to FR-7600 (0.2 mile). Turn right and cross Icicle Creek into Rock Island Campground (0.1 mile), picking up the trail again on the opposite bank. Walk downstream on this trail to return to the parking lot. Species to look for at various places along the loop include Harlequin Duck, Common Merganser, Calliope and Rufous Hummingbirds, Belted Kingfisher, Red-naped Sapsucker, Hairy Woodpecker, Olive-sided, Hammond's, and Pacific-slope Flycatchers, Chestnut-backed Chickadee, Hermit Thrush, Townsend's Warbler, Red Crossbill, and Pine Siskin. To reach drier habitats and vistas of Icicle Canyon, consider taking View Trail 1596.1. From the same parking lot, walk 50 yards back toward the guard station and head uphill on a moderately steep trail about three-quarters of a mile to a prominence over-looking the valley, passing through Douglas-fir and Deerbrush forest—good habitat for Cassin's Vireo and Western Tanager.

Trailheads along FR-76/FR-7600 give access to the **Alpine Lakes Wilderness Area** (393,000 acres), renowned for its picturesque lakes set in glacially polished basins and framed by Alpine Larches that turn blazing yellow in fall. White-tailed Ptarmigan, American Pipit, and other alpine species occur above treeline, but getting into their habitat demands lengthy hiking or back-packing on steep, rocky trails, which few birders undertake.

Just past the Icicle Road intersection, US-2 enters **Leavenworth**. Made up as a Bavarian village, this friendly community offers many shops, restaurants, and motels, as well as prime riparian birding practically in the middle of town. Turn right onto Ninth Street (0.9 mile from Icicle Road) and go downhill three blocks to an intersection. Turn left here onto a gravel lane to parking for Enchantment Park (0.1 mile). A short trail goes upstream along the Wenatchee River to a bridge over a slough to **Blackbird Island**. This luxuriant riparian community, created a century ago by a logging mill pond

The stream surface of Icicle Creek is momentarily alive with bold patterns of blue-gray and white as a male Harlequin Duck leads his mate around a bend and out of sight.

(breached in 1932), is home to many birds. In May and June, look for Common Merganser, Osprey, Vaux's Swift, Western Wood-Pewee, Warbling and Red-eyed Vireos, a variety of swallows, House Wren, Veery, Gray Catbird, Yellow and MacGillivray's Warblers, and Black-headed and Evening Grosbeaks. Downy Woodpecker, Northern Flicker, and Black-capped Chickadee are here year round, joined by Bald Eagle in winter. This place can be hopping in migration, too.

PESHASTIN CREEK AND MISSION CREEK

About four and a half miles east of Leavenworth, US-97 turns south from US-2 and ascends the Peshastin Creek drainage for 21 miles to Blewett Pass (page 282). Take this highway, and in 5.2 miles from US-2 turn left (east) onto Camas Creek Road (FR-7200). Go uphill 3.1 miles to an intersection with a minor road on the left. This large, tree-rimmed meadow is the 1,300-acre **Camas Meadows Natural Area** (DNR), dedicated to preserving a number of rare plants. It is also a great place for birds and butterflies. Take the road to the left for a half-mile through partly burned Ponderosa Pine forest with occasional aspen thickets and meadows. Hairy, White-headed, and Black-backed Woodpeckers have all been noted in the vicinity. Good birding continues along FR-7200 to the next junction (0.7 mile) in similar habitat, including a large Camas meadow. (Camas is a type of lily with a carbohydrate-rich bulb, once a prized food of resident Native Americans.) FR-7200 runs through riparian habitat for another half-mile after that, followed by moist forest. Look here for Northern Goshawk, Northern Pygmy-Owl, Williamson's and Red-naped Sapsuckers, Hairy and White-headed Woodpeckers, Dusky Flycatcher, all three nuthatches, Western Bluebird, Veery, Swainson's Thrush, Nashville Warbler, Vesper Sparrow, Cassin's Finch, and Red Crossbill. Black Bears are seen regularly in the area, and Mountain Lions occasionally.

Drive east on the combined US-2/US-97, and in 6.4 miles turn right onto Aplets Way in the town of Cashmere, noted for a fruit confection called "Aplets and Cotlets" that can be purchased in any of the innumerable shops. The road soon changes name to Division Street. Stay right at a sharp bend in 0.6 mile and in about 0.1 mile turn left onto **Mission Creek Road**. In 0.5 mile the road jogs right, then left, and runs south along Mission Creek—initially through orchards, then through a mosaic of riparian and coniferous habitats. Birding is especially productive in May and June along lower parts of the road where you can expect Cooper's Hawk, Ruffed Grouse, Red-naped Sapsucker, Hammond's and Pacific-slope Flycatchers, Cassin's and Warbling Vireos, Black-capped and Mountain Chickadees, Veery, Hermit Thrush, Gray Catbird, Yellow-rumped, Black-throated Gray, MacGillivray's, and Wilson's Warblers, Black-headed Grosbeak, Lazuli Bunting, Bullock's Oriole, and Purple Finch.

In 6.2 miles, turn right onto Sand Creek Road, which ends in one mile at a primitive campground (USFS, fee) and trailhead for Red Hill Mountain. Calliope Hummingbird, Hammond's Flycatcher, and Nashville Warbler can be found near the parking lot. The surrounding slopes are part of the **Devil's Gulch Roadless Area** (25,000 acres), known for its old-growth Ponderosa Pine, an increasingly rare habitat type in Washington. Surveys have been conducted here for several years; the list of breeding species includes Sharp-shinned Hawk, Northern Goshawk, Flammulated, Northern Pygmy-, Spotted, and five other species of owls, Common Poorwill, Vaux's Swift, Rufous Hummingbird, Williamson's Sapsucker, Hairy, White-headed, Black-backed, and Pileated Woodpeckers, Gray, Dusky, and Pacific-slope Flycatchers, Cassin's Vireo, White-breasted and Pygmy Nuthatches, Swainson's and Hermit Thrushes, and Purple and Cassin's Finches. Trail 1223 provides an excellent birding route. You will share it with dirt- and mountain-bikers, but they are generally not abroad in the early morning when birding is at its best. The trail begins at the restroom, crosses Sand Creek, and gently switchbacks up through open Douglas-fir on a moist, north-facing slope to meet a ridgeline where Ponderosa Pines dominate. A small logged-over area is met, now in a brushy state (Dusky Flycatcher). In 3.8 miles you reach a saddle among still more imposing pines. Go left about a quarter-mile on Trail 1221.1 for great views of the Stuart Range.

WENATCHEE

From the Aplets Way junction in Cashmere, continue east toward Wenatchee for 7.7 miles and take the exit signed *North US-97/East US-2*. In another 0.6 mile, take the exit for **Wenatchee Confluence State Park**. At the end of the long exit ramp (0.3 mile), go right on Penny Road 0.4 mile to Euclid Avenue. Turn left here, go 0.4 mile, turn left into the park then right into the first parking lot. This popular park (camping, picnicking) at the confluence of the Wenatchee and Columbia Rivers has the best riparian birding in Wenatchee. It is also a proven site for local and even state rarities, with records for Great Egret, Green Heron, Yellow-crowned Night-Heron, Brant, Eurasian Wigeon (regular), Long-tailed Duck, Red-breasted Merganser, Gyrfalcon, Laughing, Little, Thayer's, Mew, and Western Gulls, Arctic Tern, Eurasian Collared-Dove, Purple Martin, Magnolia Warbler, and other interesting species.

A paved path leads from the parking lot to a footbridge over the Wenatchee River. From the bridge, search for Great Blue Heron, Black-crowned Night-Heron, Common Merganser, Spotted Sandpiper, Vaux's Swift, and Northern Rough-winged Swallow, among many others. Ospreys nest on the neighboring railway span. Just south of the footbridge, leave the paved path at the entrance to the **Horan Natural Area** (interpretive signage and trail map, on the left), a 97-acre, undeveloped part of the park. Birding in the open, weedy spaces and riparian habitat with a dense grove of Black Cottonwoods can be good at any season but is especially fine in spring and early summer. Birds seen regularly include Ring-necked Pheasant, California

Quail, Mourning Dove, Western Screech-Owl, Eastern Kingbird, Gray Catbird, Spotted Towhee, and Purple and House Finches. Sparrows are often abundant in migration and winter. Among the many White-crowneds, look for Lincoln's, White-throated, Harris's, and Golden-crowned. Wood Duck, Mallard, and Red-winged Blackbird frequent the ponds along with Bullfrog and Western Painted Turtle. Black-tailed Deer and Striped Skunk are frequently seen along the trails. Overhead, look for Black Swifts in summer (occasional). Bald Eagles are common in winter.

Trails through the natural area eventually rejoin the paved path. From here, you can continue along the Columbia River to **Walla Walla Point Park**. Stop at the first bench inside this park to scope the river edge for waterfowl, gulls, and terns and to admire the fine views of the river and surrounding hills. Birds often seen here include Great Blue Heron, Canada Goose, Caspian Tern, Spotted Sandpiper, and, in migration, small numbers of Western, Least, and Baird's Sandpipers. Forster's and Black Terns occur uncommonly. Water levels fluctuate frequently due to dam operations. When water levels are high, inspect the lawns in both parks for gulls and shorebirds.

A very different spot on the outskirts of Wenatchee is **No. Two Canyon**.

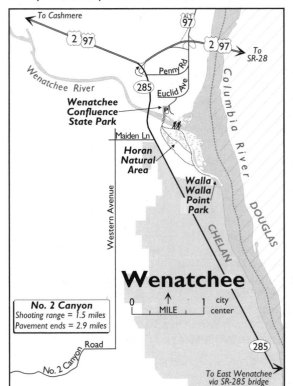

Leaving Confluence State Park, turn left onto Penny Road, travel 0.6 mile, and turn left onto SR-285. Go 0.8 mile, turn right onto Maiden Lane, and continue uphill 0.5 mile to Western Avenue. Make a left here and go 2.8 miles to No. 2 Canyon Road. Turn right onto this road. In 1.5 miles, note a shooting range on your right. Scattered tall serviceberry bushes, on the left at the base of a steep, rocky slope, are attractive to Ash-throated Flycatcher—here at the northern extreme of its breeding range. From this point forward the road hugs a verdant strip of riparian vegetation, inviting many stops (private property: please bird from the road). An early-morning walk through the steep-walled canyon in spring or early summer may yield Red-tailed Hawk, Golden Eagle, American Kestrel, Chukar, Common Poorwill, Western Wood-Pewee, Dusky Flycatcher, Warbling Vireo, Violet-green Swallow, Black-billed Magpie, Common Raven, Townsend's Solitaire (especially migration), Veery, Yellow-breasted Chat, Black-headed Grosbeak, Lazuli Bunting, and Bullock's Oriole. The pavement ends in 2.9 miles, but you can go farther on a primitive road (summer only) into Douglas-fir and Ponderosa Pine habitat to look for Northern Pygmy- and Northern Saw-whet Owls, Calliope Hummingbird, Dusky Flycatcher, Nashville and MacGillivray's Warblers, Chipping Sparrow, Red Crossbill, and Cassin's Finch.

ENTIAT MOUNTAINS TO LAKE CHELAN

by Jim Alt, Bob Kuntz, Kraig Kemper, and Andy Stepniewski

North of Wenatchee several rugged, southeastward-trending ridges and valleys dissect the eastern slopes of the Cascade Range, from the crest down to the Columbia River. In succession from the Wenatchee River, these are the Entiat Mountains, the Entiat River, the Chelan Mountains, Lake Chelan, and finally Sawtooth Ridge, whose northeast face drains to the Methow River (page 426). Alternate US-97 and US-97 follow the Columbia from Wenatchee to Pateros. For almost the whole 50-mile distance the river is actually Lake Entiat, created by Rocky Reach Dam—a reservoir with impoverished habitat and limited birding access. Birding can be excellent, however, along the deep canyons that penetrate into the Cascades, accessible from the highway on a number of side roads. Typically, these canyons are grown to semi-arid shrub-steppe habitats at lower elevations, transitioning to dry Ponderosa Pine and Douglas-fir and then to moist forests at upper elevations.

SWAKANE CANYON

Swakane Creek drains the south end of the Entiat Mountains to the Columbia. The rough and rocky track that follows this minor stream is worth enduring not only for birds but also for scenery, wildflowers, and butterflies. From the combined US-2/US-97 just north of Wenatchee, go north on Alt US-97 to a primitive road (FR-7415) marked *Swakane Canyon* (5.3 miles). Turn left to enter this spectacular canyon, known for its diversity of migrants and breeding birds, and even for its winter birding possibilities. Much of the lower canyon is within the **Swakane Wildlife Area** (19,200 acres).

In 0.1 mile, stop below a cliff (Chukar, Black-billed Magpie, Rock and Canyon Wrens). Check Water Birch and other riparian growth for Yellow-breasted

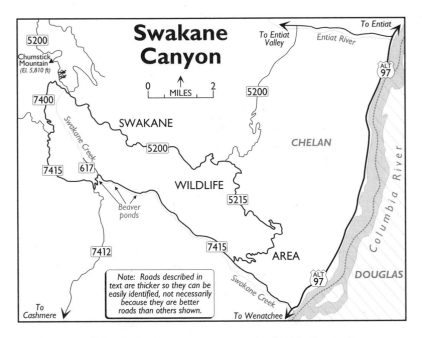

Swakane Canyon

To Entiat
To Entiat Valley
Entiat River
ALT 97
5200
Chumstick Mountain (El. 5,810 ft)
7400
Swakane Creek
SWAKANE
5200
CHELAN
Columbia River
7415
617
WILDLIFE
Beaver ponds
5215
7412
7415
AREA
ALT 97
DOUGLAS
5200
0 MILES 2
Swakane Creek
To Cashmere
To Wenatchee

Note: Roads described in text are thicker so they can be easily identified, not necessarily because they are better roads than others shown.

Chat, Black-headed Grosbeak, Lazuli Bunting, and Bullock's Oriole. Continue up for four more miles to the lower limit of Ponderosa Pine forest and patches of serviceberry shrubs. Watch for Red-tailed Hawk, Golden Eagle, California Quail, Mourning Dove, Calliope Hummingbird, Lewis's Woodpecker, Dusky Flycatcher, Western Kingbird, Violet-green Swallow, Mountain Chickadee, all three nuthatches, House Wren, Nashville Warbler, and American Goldfinch. The first of several Beaver ponds is reached in another three miles, then excellent riparian habitat and a series of larger ponds by the road—great habitat for Black-chinned Hummingbird, Red-naped Sapsucker, Downy and Hairy Woodpeckers, Western Wood-Pewee, Willow and Pacific-slope Flycatchers, Cassin's and Warbling Vireos, Tree and Violet-green Swallows, Black-capped Chickadee, Veery, Cedar Waxwing, Nashville, Orange-crowned, Yellow, and MacGillivray's Warblers, and Black-headed Grosbeak. In winter, the alders in these swamps attract Pine Siskins (and perhaps redpolls). In 1.5 miles, the road turns left and crosses Swakane Creek to a lush aspen grove and meadow where you may expect Calliope Hummingbird, Willow and Dusky Flycatchers, Cassin's Vireo, Nashville and MacGillivray's Warblers, and Chipping Sparrow. Or walk upstream on the opposite bank for half a mile on FR-617 through forest, riparian, and meadow habitats. It is possible to see all three *Carpodacus* finches (Purple, Cassin's, House) in this part of the canyon.

From here the adventurous can embark on a summer-only high-country loop, returning to the lower Swakane 2.8 miles upstream from Alt US-97. Continue up FR-7415 for 3.6 miles to an intersection with FR-7400. Turn right onto this road, and in 3.0 miles stop at the intersection with FR-5200. To the left, a one-mile hike up FR-5200 brings you to the top of **Chumstick Mountain** (elevation 5,810 feet)—a fine hawkwatching vantage in fall. Turning right from the FR-7400 intersection, FR-5200 follows mostly along the ridgetop for 7.6 miles to FR-5215. Turn right here and continue 8.5 miles, the last four miles being very steep, down to Swakane Canyon. Mixed-conifer forests with Western Larch (Williamson's Sapsucker, Hammond's Flycatcher), burns (woodpeckers, Dusky Flycatcher), Ponderosa Pine forests (nuthatches, crossbills), and finally open bunchgrass slopes (Common Poorwill at dusk, Vesper Sparrow) are featured along this route.

ENTIAT RIVER

The Entiat River basin reaches far into the heart of the Cascades, giving access to the Glacier Peak Wilderness (576,865 acres), one of Washington's largest expanses of wild country. The Entiat River Road turns left from Alt US-97 about 10 miles north of the mouth of Swakane Canyon. The road proceeds first through open farmland with orchards and some riparian habitats. Check the thickets near the Entiat River mouth on the left in a half-mile (the old highway that follows the edge of the riparian zone downstream makes a good birding trail). Hooded Merganser, Bald Eagle, Western Wood-Pewee, and Bullock's Oriole are some possibilities here. Flycatchers, warblers, Western Tanager, and sparrows can be thick in migration, particularly during inclement weather.

Upriver, in another 5.5 miles, find the **Entiat National Fish Hatchery**. Tall Black Cottonwoods here have Red-eyed Vireo. Look for Veery, Gray Catbird, and many other species in the lush understory. Continuing along Entiat River Road, habitats in the lower reaches of the basin are always in transition due to recurring fires. Characteristic species of brushy lower elevations include Golden Eagle, Chukar, Calliope Hummingbird, and White-headed and Black-backed (in recently burned timber) Woodpeckers. Riparian areas have Red-naped Sapsucker, Yellow and MacGillivray's Warblers, and Yellow-breasted Chat.

Turn right in 4.9 miles from the hatchery onto FR-5300. Driving this road for twelve miles to its junction with SR-971 at Navarre Coulee, just south of Lake Chelan State Park, gives good exposure to Ponderosa Pine forest including areas of burned timber. Brushy slopes with some snags attract Common Poorwill, Western Wood-Pewee, Dusky Flycatcher, and Orange-crowned and Nashville Warblers. Vegetation along **Mud Creek**, on the way up to the ridgeline, has Calliope Hummingbird, Black-headed Grosbeak, Lazuli Bunting, Bullock's Oriole, and other typical riparian species. The downslope segment along **Johnson Creek** is good for woodpeckers (Lewis's, White-headed, Black-backed, Pileated).

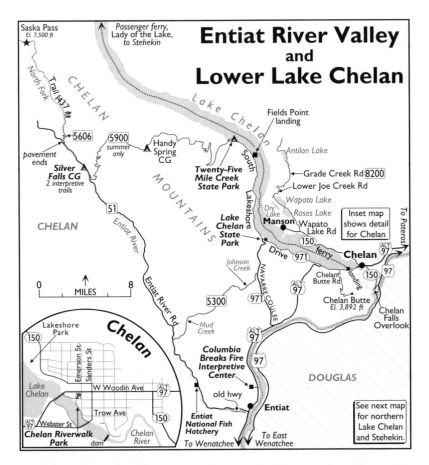

Entiat River Valley
and
Lower Lake Chelan

Saska Pass
El. 7,500 ft

Passenger ferry,
Lady of the Lake,
to Stehekin

North Fork

Trail 1437

CHELAN

pavement
ends

Silver
Falls CG
2 interpretive
trails

5606

5900
summer
only

Handy
Spring
CG

Twenty-Five
Mile Creek
State Park

Fields Point
landing

Antilon Lake

Grade Creek Rd 8200

Lower Joe Creek Rd

Wapato Lake

51

CHELAN

Entiat River

MOUNTAINS

Lake
Chelan
State
Park

South Lakeshore

Dry
Lake

Roses Lake

Manson

Wapato
Lake Rd

Inset map
shows detail
for Chelan

To Pateros

0   MILES   8

Entiat River Rd

Johnson
Creek

5300

971

Drive   971

ferry

150

Chelan

ALT
97

150   97

Chelan
Butte Rd

ALT
97

NAVARRE COULEE

Chelan
Butte
El. 3,892 ft

landing

Chelan
Falls
Overlook

Lakeshore
Park

150

Chelan

Emerson St

Sanders St

Lake
Chelan

W Woodin Ave

ALT
97

Trow Ave

150

ALT
97   Webster St

Chelan Riverwalk
Park   dam

Chelan
River

Mud
Creek

Columbia
Breaks Fire
Interpretive
Center

old hwy

Entiat
National Fish
Hatchery

To Wenatchee

97

Entiat

To East
Wenatchee

DOUGLAS

See next map
for northern
Lake Chelan
and Stehekin.

Continue up Entiat River Road (becomes FR-51) to an intersection with FR-5900 in 17.8 miles. Here you may turn right and begin a summer-only, 28-mile tour up and over the Chelan Mountains (high point 6,600 feet) to Twenty-Five Mile Creek State Park on Lake Chelan. Boreal Owl and Pine Grosbeak have been noted at Handy Spring Campground 13 miles along this road. Vast areas of old burns characterize the descent from here to the lake.

Silver Falls Campground—a bit less than a mile farther up FR-51 from the FR-5900 intersection—has two easy interpretive trails exploring different habitats; both are perfect for a bird walk. Beginning in the campground, the 1.2-mile Riverside Trail features tall, moist forest where you can expect Hammond's Flycatcher, Winter Wren, and Townsend's Warbler. Areas of alder have Yellow and MacGillivray's Warblers, and American Dippers should be easy to find from the several river overlooks. The 1.4-mile trail to Silver Falls leaves FR-51 a hundred yards past the campground. Birds of moist and dry forests can be found here, including Cassin's Vireo, Western Tanager, and Evening Grosbeak.

The paved road ends about three miles above Silver Falls Campground, at an intersection with FR-5606. Moist forests in this vicinity have Gray Jay, Clark's Nutcracker, Mountain Bluebird, Veery, and Hermit Thrush. Northern Goshawk and Spotted Owl are regular along the **North Fork** of the Entiat River, in some of Washington's largest stands of ancient forest outside designated wilderness areas. Take FR-5606 about four miles to a trailhead. From here Trail 1437 follows the North Fork for some nine miles, reaching the boundary of the Glacier Peak Wilderness at Saska Pass (elevation 7,500 feet).

As you head north on Alt US-97 toward Chelan, turn left into the **Columbia Breaks Fire Interpretive Center** (2.7 miles from Entiat River Road). A half-mile trail winds through Ponderosa Pine, Bitterbrush, and Big Sagebrush, abutting tall granite cliffs. Look for Bald and Golden Eagles, Lewis's Woodpecker, Say's Phoebe, Clark's Nutcracker, Canyon Wren, and Bullock's Oriole. Migration brings many other birds; Golden-crowned and other sparrows may be found in winter.

CHELAN AND VICINITY

A popular destination for vacationers and outdoor recreationists, the community of Chelan (year-round population 3,500) sits at the southeast tip of Lake Chelan, two miles inland from the Columbia River and about 40 road miles north of Wenatchee. Numerous nearby sites offer dry-forest habitats as well as opportunities to scope the lake for waterbirds.

The ornamental plantings and forest of Ponderosa Pine, Douglas-fir, and Bigleaf Maple at **Lake Chelan State Park** can be rewarding in migration and the early part of the nesting season. Look for forest species such as White-headed Woodpecker, White-breasted and Red-breasted Nuthatches, and Brown Creeper. American Dipper can often be found by walking upstream along a well-beaten trail from the far end of the boat launch. Loons, grebes, and diving ducks are seen on the lake from fall through spring. Birding is frustrating in summer, however, when the park is crowded with campers and powerboaters. The park is located about nine miles west of Chelan on South Lakeshore Drive (Alt US-97 for the first three miles, then right onto SR-971). If coming from the south on Alt US-97, turn left onto SR-971 about nine miles north of the Entiat River Road intersection and drive north for about nine more miles through Navarre Coulee to the park entrance.

Views of Lake Chelan, the Columbia River, and the wheat fields on the Waterville Plateau to the east are well worth the nerve-wracking drive to the top of **Chelan Butte**. About a mile and a half west of Chelan, turn left from South Lakeshore Drive (Alt US-97) onto Millard Street (also signed Chelan Butte Road), which soon changes to dirt. Dusty in spring and summer, super-steep in places, slick and often impassable after a rain, the 4.7-mile road to the summit is usually closed by snow in winter. Varied habitats along the way—deciduous thickets, Ponderosa Pines, steep slopes with bunchgrass and some sagebrush—all attract interesting birds. Park where you can and walk over the hillsides, particularly near the summit (watch out for rattlesnakes in rocky areas). In spring and summer look for Swainson's Hawk, Golden Eagle, California Quail, White-throated Swift, Lewis's and White-headed Woodpeckers, Say's Phoebe, Western and Eastern Kingbirds, Clark's Nutcracker, all three nuthatches, Gray Catbird, and many others. Fall and winter possibilities include accipiters, Red-tailed and Rough-legged Hawks, Northern Pygmy-Owl, Gray-crowned Rosy-Finch, and Pine Grosbeak.

If you are stopping in Chelan, paved **Chelan Riverwalk Park** makes a fine diversion right in the center of downtown. Park on Emerson Street about 200 yards south of West Woodin Avenue. Walk southeast along the water, cross the narrow neck of the lake on the bridge, then continue northwest to the West Woodin Avenue bridge to return to the starting point. In winter, check for Common Loon, Pied-billed and Western Grebes, a sprinkling of waterfowl, and Belted Kingfisher. In migration, Yellow-rumped Warblers flit in the trees. Four species of swallows are common in summer.

Scanning the cliffs at the **Chelan Falls Overlook** may reveal Golden Eagle, White-throated Swift, and Canyon Wren: take SR-150 south 2.4 miles from Alt US-97 in Chelan.

In the opposite direction, SR-150 leaves Alt US-97 in Chelan and winds along the north shore of Lake Chelan. Stop at any of the pullouts to watch for Common Loon, Horned, Red-necked, and Western Grebes, Redhead, Greater Scaup, Bufflehead, and Common Goldeneye. In 6.7 miles, turn right on Wapato Lake Road and climb through apple and pear orchards alternating with new development, passing Roses and Wapato Lakes (waterbirds, especially in fall and spring). After a peek at the marsh just beyond Wapato Lake, proceed to Lower Joe Creek Road (4.1 miles from SR-150). Turn right here, then left in 1.9 miles onto Grade Creek Road (becomes FR-8200), which passes through mixed pine and riparian habitat to **Antilon Lake** (2.0 miles), nestled in a rocky gorge with Ponderosa Pines (Pygmy Nuthatch, Cassin's Finch, Red Crossbill). Beyond the lake the landscape is one of scattered pines with thick patches of shrubby Deerbrush—the result of past fires. This habitat has many Common Poorwills, easily seen on an evening drive.

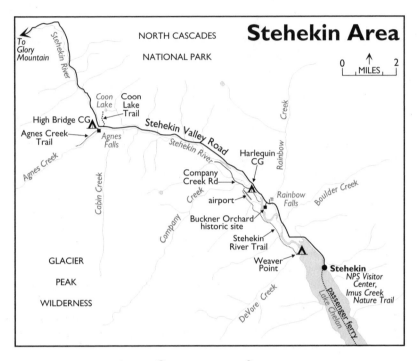

LAKE CHELAN AND STEHEKIN

A narrow, glacier-forged trench, **Lake Chelan** probes 50 miles into the North Cascades. While the eastern end is developed, the rest is wild and scenic. To experience the lake, it is well worth taking the boat trip to Stehekin, a resort village at the upper end in the heart of the Lake Chelan National Recreation Area. Beyond is the vast North Cascades National Park and trail access to various USFS wilderness areas, making this the largest contiguous expanse of wild country in Washington.

The parking lot and docks for the **Lady of the Lake** are on Alt US-97 (South Lakeshore Drive) a half-mile west of downtown Chelan; a second boarding point is at Fields Point, 16 miles northwest of Chelan on South Lakeshore Drive. Frequency of service, duration of the trip, and fare vary according to the season and/or which of three boats you take. The most leisurely one-way cruise requires four hours, while the fastest boat makes the same run in an hour and a quarter. Contact the Lake Chelan Boat Company for full information (509-682-4584, www.ladyofthelake.com).

Lake Chelan is the third-deepest lake in the United States (1,528 feet). At one place its bottom is over 400 feet below sea level. Fed by 27 glaciers and 59 streams, the lake is cold and relatively unproductive for birds. Nonetheless you might see a few Common Loons, Red-necked or Western Grebes, diving ducks, Ospreys, and Bald and Golden Eagles, especially around the small shallows and marsh on the approach to Stehekin. The bordering vegetation changes from semi-arid shrub-steppe and Ponderosa Pine to moist conifer forests as the boat travels deeper into the mountains, bringing a good possibility of seeing Mountain Goats or Black Bears on the cliffs and steep slopes. In winter, when snow forces many Mule Deer down to lower elevations, there is even a slim chance of spotting a Mountain Lion.

Stehekin is a wonderful place to relax in an unhurried atmosphere. Plan on staying one or two days to extract the most from the birding possibilities. There are several primitive campgrounds in the area plus a number of homes or cabins available to rent. Three lodges provide more complete services. For information, contact the Lake Chelan Chamber of Commerce (800-424-3526, *www.visitlakechelan.com*) or stop by the National Park Service visitor center.

Even if you are pressed for time, try to allow at least a few hours before re-boarding the boat. Calliope and Rufous Hummingbirds, Olive-sided and Hammond's Flycatchers, swallows (including Violet-green), Nashville Warbler, Western Tanager, and Cassin's Finch are among the species commonly observed near the boat landing. Just behind the visitor center is the three-quarter-mile **Imus Creek Nature Trail**, which climbs a hill with views. In spring, Veeries often sing beside the creek and American Dippers forage along the lakeshore at the creek mouth. You can also take the narrated bus tour to 312-foot Rainbow Falls, 3.5 miles up Stehekin Valley Road. Black Swifts may nest behind these falls. Train your eyes skyward on occasion to look for them anywhere in the Stehekin area.

Most visitors travel up-valley by the National Park Service shuttle bus, which goes to the end of Stehekin Valley Road at Glory Mountain (20 miles), or by the privately operated Stehekin Valley Shuttle, which goes only as far as High Bridge (11 miles). Alternatives to the bus include renting bicycles and riding up the road to the birding spots or renting a canoe and paddling around the head of the lake.

For the first 1.5 miles the Stehekin Valley Road parallels the east shore of Lake Chelan. In recent years, Horned Grebes have attempted to nest at the head of the lake. Trumpeter Swan, Harlequin Duck, and Osprey are occasionally observed near the mouth of the Stehekin River. Check the marsh, willows, and cottonwoods for owls (Great Horned and Barred), woodpeckers (particularly Red-naped Sapsucker), and breeding passerines such as Veery, Gray Catbird, Nashville and Yellow Warblers, and American Redstart.

A few hundred yards after passing the turnoff to Rainbow Falls (3.5 miles), take a dirt road left into **Buckner Orchard**, a pioneer homestead site. Look here in spring and summer for hummingbirds (Calliope and Rufous), flycatchers, warblers, Western Tanager, Bullock's Oriole, and Cassin's Finch. Harlequin Bridge and Campground are another three-quarters of a mile up

Stehekin Valley Road (yes, Harlequin Ducks are sometimes seen here from mid-April through August). A couple of hundred yards past the campground, take Company Creek Road left to the National Park Service maintenance yard and check the pond area for Wood Duck and passerines. Birding is excellent along the **Stehekin River Trail**, which starts at the maintenance yard and meanders southward four miles through marsh (Beaver ponds) and riparian forest to Weaver Point at the northwest edge of the lake. Western Screech-Owls have nested near the south end of the Stehekin Airport and a pair of Bald Eagles has nested near Weaver Point.

From Harlequin Bridge continue up Stehekin Valley Road another six miles to **High Bridge**, a major trailhead for North Cascades National Park. Of interest to birders is the 1.2-mile trail to Coon Lake, a swampy lake with waterfowl (Barrow's Goldeneyes nest here) and excellent also for passerines. Northern Goshawk and Spotted Owl have been observed on the Old Wagon Trail from near Coon Lake and also along the first two miles of Agnes Creek Trail (trailhead 0.3 mile past High Bridge). Stehekin makes a great base camp for hiking or backpacking into the wilderness. Free permits are required for overnight trips and may be obtained at the visitor center.

COOPER RIDGE

Cooper Ridge forms the eastern end of the Sawtooth Ridge system that divides the Chelan and Methow watersheds. The high point, Cooper Mountain (5,867 feet), is ten straight-line miles north and a bit west of Chelan. The driving distance is 25 miles, however—much of it over steep, twisting roads. Allow at least an hour for the trip. The main attraction for birders is the fall hawk migration (late August–late October). Typical bird species of farms, streams, cliffs, Ponderosa Pine forest, and shrub-steppe may be found at several places on the way up.

In Chelan, from the junction where SR-150 turns south to the Chelan Falls overlook, head east on Alt US-97. Travel 2.9 miles and turn left (north) onto **Apple Acres Road**. In 3.5 miles, stop by the roadside below impressive cliffs of gneiss to scan for Golden Eagle and other raptors and to listen for Canyon Wren. Peer downward from the west side of the highway to a kettle lake, an erosional feature remaining from the withdrawal of the Okanogan Ice Lobe at the close of the Pleistocene. Check the Ponderosa Pine forest for Pygmy Nuthatch.

Continue another 1.2 miles, turn left (west) onto **Antoine Creek Road**, and drive through farmlands. In late fall, Pine Grosbeaks have been found in the last orchard (2.6 miles) and at scattered sites in the dense riparian vegetation along Antoine Creek for the next three miles. The pavement ends in another 1.2 miles. Continue steeply uphill (west) on the main gravel road. Antoine Creek Road becomes FR-8140 (1.9 miles); the Okanogan National Forest boundary is in another 1.9 miles. From here to the intersection at the

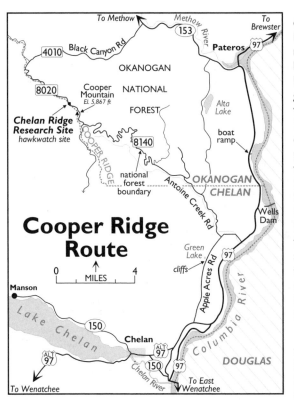

To Methow
Methow River
153
To Brewster
Pateros 97
4010 Black Canyon Rd
OKANOGAN
8020 Cooper Mountain El. 5,867 ft
NATIONAL
Alta Lake
Chelan Ridge Research Site hawkwatch site
FOREST
COOPER RIDGE
8140
boat ramp
national forest boundary
Antoine Creek Rd
OKANOGAN
CHELAN
Wells Dam

Cooper Ridge Route

Green Lake
cliffs
Apple Acres Rd
97

0 — MILES — 4

Columbia River

Manson

Lake Chelan
150
Chelan
ALT 97
ALT 97
150 97
Chelan River
DOUGLAS
To East Wenatchee

To Wenatchee

crest of Cooper Ridge (8.0 miles) nearly the entire landscape is of young Ponderosa Pines, grown back in the wake of a huge fire in 1970. Bitterbrush covers many slopes, providing critical winter forage for a large Mule Deer herd. A small area of Lodgepole Pine and Engelmann Spruce forest at the crest apparently survived the recent fires and may provide suitable habitat for Spruce Grouse.

Under proper weather conditions, hawkwatching can be memorable at the **Chelan Ridge Research Site**. A cooperative project begun in 1997 by the Okanogan and Wenatchee National Forests and HawkWatch International has documented this as the best fall hawkwatching site so far discovered in Eastern Washington. Even though tens of thousands of raptors pass through the Cascades in migration, there are so many ridges that movement is widely dispersed across a broad front. Defying the general pattern, the Chelan Ridge site may see more than 100 individuals on a good day; 2000–3000 are tallied annually. The station is active from the last days of August to the end of October unless closed earlier by snow. Visitors are welcome.

From the T-intersection with FR-8140 at the crest of Cooper Ridge turn right onto FR-8020, which contours around the east side of Cooper Mountain. After 1.5 miles, park just beyond a cattle guard; the Forest Service has placed two portable toilets here. Find the rough, steep trail marked by ribbons on the west side of the road and hike about three-quarters of a mile across a sagebrush-covered, south-facing sidehill to the hawkwatching station, located on a promontory at an elevation of 5,100 feet. The ridge crest here is narrow; level sites for spotting scopes are limited. The view in all directions is fabulous—west to the high peaks of the North Cascades, north across the Methow Valley to the Tiffany Mountain area, east to the wheatlands of the northern Columbia Basin, and south to a sliver of Lake Chelan about 4,000 feet below. Bring all provisions; there is no water anywhere in the area. Sun protection may be important. Be prepared for wind and cold. Please pack out all garbage.

Favored hawk flight paths change with wind direction and during the course of the day; you will need to determine which quadrants of the landscape and the sky are most productive at the time of your visit. Sharp-shinned Hawk is the species most frequently spotted, followed (in descending order) by Red-tailed Hawk, Cooper's Hawk, Golden Eagle, Northern Harrier, American Kestrel, Osprey, Northern Goshawk, and Merlin. Seven other species occur in lesser numbers, including five or six Broad-winged Hawks each year—the great majority of the Washington records. In October 2000, a passing Northern Hawk Owl caused a stir.

For the shortest route to the Methow Valley, continue north on FR-8020 for 3.5 miles, turn right, and descend on FR-4010 (Black Canyon Road) for nine miles to join SR-153 above Pateros. If you are instead going back the way you came along Antoine Creek Road, keep left at Apple Acres Road and go 1.9 miles to US-97 above the Columbia River. Turn left and travel 4.4 miles to a boat ramp on the right. Ospreys nest nearby and are usually easy to spot. From fall through spring, scope the waters of the Columbia anywhere in this area for diving birds. Pacific Loons, though scarce, are seen regularly—particularly in stretches where the river is flowing (above reservoir levels). The junction with SR-153 in Pateros, gateway to the Methow Valley, is another 4.6 miles north.

METHOW VALLEY

by Andy Stepniewski

The Methow River drains a broad slice of the North Cascades, much of it wild and remote. Near the crest, dense, somber conifer forests mantle the glacially overdeepened valleys, cut through by alder-choked avalance chutes. The maritime climate dumps immense, wet winter snowfalls. A few miles east from the crest, however, a rainshadow effect sets in, allowing a steady transition to drier, more open forests. Just 30 miles downslope rangelands occupy the valley bottoms, and Bitterbrush and other shrub-steppe flora cover the south-facing hillsides—prime winter range for a Mule Deer herd numbering over 20,000 animals.

About 75 species of birds breed in the varied habitats of the lower parts of the valley. Killdeer, Black-billed Magpie, American Crow, Western Kingbird, swallows, Western Meadowlark, and Brewer's Blackbird can be abundant in farm fields. Several species of "eastern" affinity—Eastern Kingbird, Red-eyed Vireo, Veery, Gray Catbird, American Redstart (uncommon)—occur in cottonwoods. Typical dry-forest species such as Lewis's Woodpecker, Western Wood-Pewee, Yellow-rumped Warbler, and Cassin's Finch can be found in the pines. White-tailed Ptarmigan, American Pipit, Gray-crowned Rosy-Finch, and Pine Grosbeak may repay a summer foray to the Cascade crest at Harts Pass and Slate Peak. Winter brings Bohemian Waxwings and Common Redpolls to the valley; Bald and a few Golden Eagles are drawn to spawned salmon in the Methow River.

After a brief gold-mining boom in the late 1800s the Methow went the way of many another Eastside mountain economy, getting by on logging, grazing, and limited tourism (much of it tied to the fall deer-hunting season). A swelling Washington population, and the opening of the North Cascades Highway (SR-20) in 1972, have stimulated residential and tourism development. The Methow is now a year-round destination with many resorts in all price ranges offering fishing, hiking, whitewater rafting, horseback riding, and golf in summer, and cross-country skiing, snowshoeing, and snowmobiling in winter. Snowfall forces the winter closure of SR-20 west from Mazama (typically November or December to April); during those months the sole approach to the Methow country is from the east. Winthrop is the main town and a fine base of operations for birders, summer or winter.

PATEROS TO TWISP

Year-round access to the Methow Valley begins at the junction of US-97 and SR-153 in Pateros on the Columbia River. Heading west on SR-153, one drives along impounded Columbia River waters for the first mile, full of waterfowl in spring and fall—Redhead, American Wigeon, and many other species. At 1.7 miles from US-97, turn left onto Alta Lake Road. From here it is 1.6 miles to **Alta Lake State Park**. The park is crowded at times; nonetheless an early-morning exploration of the pine forest and other habitats should yield a good representative bird list. Species to look for in the campground and on the trail uphill toward the steep, rocky bluffs include Chukar, Rock Dove (nesting on the cliffs), Common Poorwill, White-throated Swift, Calliope Hummingbird, Olive-sided Flycatcher, Western Wood-Pewee, Clark's Nutcracker, Mountain Chickadee, Red-breasted Nuthatch, Western Bluebird, Gray Catbird (in riparian growth near the end of the lake), Nashville Warbler, Western Tanager, Black-headed Grosbeak, and Cassin's Finch.

As you continue up SR-153 beside the Methow River keep an eye out for American Dipper and for Bald and Golden Eagles in winter. In 5.0 miles, Black Canyon Road (FR-4010) provides access to the Chelan Ridge hawkwatching site (page 425). In another 15.8 miles, just before Carlton, turn left from SR-153 onto the **Twisp-Carlton Road**. This quiet alternative to SR-153 passes orchards, hay fields, pine woods, and excellent riparian habitat. A particularly good one-mile stretch with a tall Black Cottonwood overstory and a lush shrub layer begins in 6.7 miles. Park at Sungate Road (0.4 mile) and bird on foot along the main road for the next 0.6 mile to Beaver Pond Road, looking and listening for Least Flycatcher (uncommon), Red-eyed Vireo, Veery (com-

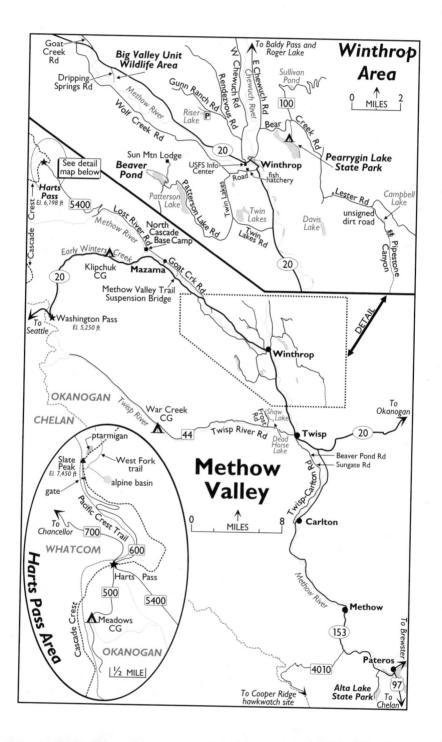

Winthrop Area

Goat Creek Rd

Big Valley Unit Wildlife Area

Dripping Springs Rd

To Baldy Pass and Roger Lake

Sullivan Pond

Gunn Ranch Rd

W Chewuch Rd

E Chewuch Rd

E Chewuch River

Rendezvous Rd

Methow River

Riser Lake

100

Bear Creek Rd

0 MILES 2

20

Sun Mtn Lodge

Beaver Pond

USFS Info Center

Road

Winthrop

fish hatchery

Pearrygin Lake State Park

See detail map below

Wolf Creek Rd

Cascade Crest

Harts Pass El. 6,198 ft

5400

Lost River Rd

Methow River

Patterson Lake

Patterson Lake Rd

North Cascade Base Camp

Twin Lakes Rd

Twin Lakes

Twin Lakes Rd

Davis Lake

Lester Rd

unsigned dirt road

Campbell Lake

Pipestone Canyon

20

Early Winters Creek

Klipchuk CG

Mazama

Goat Crk Rd

Methow Valley Trail Suspension Bridge

20

To Seattle

Washington Pass El. 5,250 ft

DETAIL

Winthrop

OKANOGAN

CHELAN

Twisp River

War Creek CG

44

Frost Rd

Shaw Lake

Twisp River Rd

Dead Horse Lake

Twisp

20

To Okanogan

ptarmigan

Slate Peak El. 7,450 ft

West Fork trail

alpine basin

gate

Pacific Crest Trail

Methow Valley

0 MILES 8

Twisp-Carlton Rd

Beaver Pond Rd

Sungate Rd

To Chancellor

700

WHATCOM

600

Harts Pass

500

5400

Carlton

Harts Pass Area

Cascade Crest

Meadows CG

OKANOGAN

½ MILE

Methow River

Methow

153

To Brewster

4010

Pateros

Alta Lake State Park

97

To Cooper Ridge hawkwatch site

To Chelan

mon), Gray Catbird, and Black-headed Grosbeak, among others. Black Swifts often join the many swallows overhead, especially in periods of cool or stormy weather. In 2.6 miles, the road meets SR-20. Turn left into Twisp.

Twisp River Road reaches deep into the Cascades, with fine birding of dry and wet habitats. In 0.2 mile, turn left onto this road (Second Avenue in Twisp), drive 2.8 miles, and turn right onto Frost Road. In 1.4 miles, reach **Shaw Lake** in the Big Buck Unit (5,600 acres) of the Methow Wildlife Area. Habitats here include several shallow lakes, dense riparian thickets, and Bitterbrush-dominated shrub-steppe. Waterfowl, shorebirds, and Yellow-headed Blackbird are possibilities from this overlook. From Shaw Lake, return 0.2 mile on Frost Road. Park and walk the dirt track going off to the left (east) toward **Dead Horse Lake**. Groves of Quaking Aspen and Black Cottonwood with shrubby thickets, alternating with bunchgrass-covered hillsides, provide habitat for many breeding birds including Red-naped Sapsucker, Gray Catbird, and Bullock's Oriole. The lake should have waterfowl or shorebirds, depending on the water level. Dry forests and brushy hillsides as one proceeds along Twisp River Road have Flammulated Owl, White-headed Woodpecker, Pygmy Nuthatch, Red Crossbill, and Cassin's Finch. Farther upriver the road becomes FR-44 upon entering the Okanogan National Forest. In 12 miles, wetter forest in and around **War Creek Campground** has Spotted Owl (a few), Hammond's Flycatcher, Red-breasted Nuthatch, Hermit Thrush, and Townsend's and MacGillivray's Warblers.

WINTHROP AND VICINITY

Winthrop, on SR-20 nine miles north of Twisp at the confluence of the Methow and Chewuch Rivers, is an agreeable community with a made-over Western theme and fine year-round birding. Summer has the greatest diversity of birds, especially in riparian habitats. Harlequin Duck can be found then along the Methow River right in town. American Dipper is common in the colder months. Winter also brings roving flocks of Bohemian Waxwings and Common Redpolls (irregular) along with a few Pine Grosbeaks. The best strategy for winter songbirding is to drive the streets of Winthrop, checking feeders and yard plantings. Five sites offering good spring and early-summer birding close to Winthrop are outlined below. Directions are given from the main intersection in the heart of the Winthrop business district, where SR-20 westbound makes a 90-degree left turn to cross the Chewuch River. Zero your trip-odometer here.

Beaver Pond is a few miles southwest of Winthrop. Drive south on SR-20 for 3.1 miles to an intersection with Twin Lakes Road, signed to Sun Mountain. (Coming from Twisp, this intersection is 5.6 miles north of the Second Avenue/Twisp River Road junction.) Turn west onto Twin Lakes Road, go 1.9 miles, and turn left onto Patterson Lake Road. Continue 5.3 miles to a public parking area and trailhead on the left. Take the trail around Beaver

Pond, a prime birding spot with open water, marsh, riparian vegetation, and coniferous forest. Look for Barrow's Goldeneye, Ruffed Grouse, Virginia Rail, Sora, Spotted Sandpiper, Rufous Hummingbird, Belted Kingfisher, Red-naped Sapsucker, Downy and Pileated Woodpeckers, Willow Flycatcher, Eastern Kingbird, Veery, Cassin's (parking-lot pines) and Warbling Vireos, Tree Swallow, Orange-crowned, Yellow, and Townsend's Warblers, Western Tanager, Song Sparrow, Black-headed Grosbeak, and Red-winged Blackbird.

To reach **Pearrygin Lake State Park** from downtown Winthrop, take the continuation of the main street north from SR-20 through the end of the business district. Curving to the right, this street becomes Bluff Street, then East Chewuch Road as it heads north out of town, reaching an intersection with Bear Creek Road in 1.6 miles. (Continuing straight with East Chewuch Road will take you to Baldy Pass and Roger Lake, page 449.) Turn right; the park entrance is on the right in 1.7 miles. Park in the main parking area, walk past the restrooms to the far southeast corner of the tent-camping loop, and continue south along a gravel lane signed No Unauthorized Vehicles, quickly leaving the commotion of the campground behind. Vesper Sparrows nest on the bunchgrass- and Bitterbrush-grown slopes on the left, while the lakeshore on the right offers marsh and riparian habitats where you may find Pied-billed Grebe, Red-naped Sapsucker, Lewis's and Downy Woodpeckers, Willow Flycatcher, Eastern Kingbird, Gray Catbird, Mourning Dove, Black-capped Chickadee, House Wren, Veery, Yellow Warbler, American Redstart (occasional), Spotted Towhee, Black-headed Grosbeak, Lazuli Bunting, Red-winged Blackbird, Western Meadowlark, Brewer's Blackbird, Brown-headed Cowbird, and Bullock's Oriole. Ospreys are often seen around the lake, and Common Nighthawks over the surrounding hills. Persistent seeds and fruits on lakeside trees and brush attract waxwings, finches, and other birds in winter.

Bear Creek Road (now gravel) continues 0.2 mile past the park entrance to an intersection with FR-100. **Sullivan Pond** is reached by turning left onto FR-100, which climbs steeply to the pond in 2.0 miles (check boxes along the way for Western and Mountain Bluebirds). Nestled on a broad ledge, this small lake has wonderful views of the Methow Valley below. Enjoy the cacophany of nesting Pied-billed Grebes and Yellow-headed Blackbirds; Ring-necked and Ruddy Ducks are also here in summer. Open, mixed forest and riparian growth have Red-naped Sapsucker, Dusky Flycatcher, Warbling Vireo, and Vesper Sparrow. All three nuthatches may be found in Ponderosa Pines throughout the area (White-headed Woodpecker is scarce).

Backtrack along FR-100 and take Bear Creek Road in the other direction (left if coming from Sullivan Pond, straight ahead if coming from the state park). Stay right at the T-intersection in 2.0 miles, and in another 1.6 miles turn left and follow Lester Road for 2.4 miles to an unsigned dirt road. Turn right and drive past Campbell Lake, ending in 1.3 miles at the trailhead for **Pipestone Canyon** in the Methow Unit (16,775 acres) of the Methow Wildlife Area (WDFW permit required). Walk a half-mile on the wide trail along the canyon floor through habitats of cliffs, talus slopes, Bitterbrush, fruiting shrubs, and Douglas-fir forest with a Douglas Maple understory. A great diversity of birds can be found here including Golden Eagle, American Kestrel, Blue Grouse, White-throated Swift, Northern Flicker, Western Wood-Pewee, Dusky Flycatcher, Say's Phoebe, Cassin's and Warbling Vireos, Violet-green Swallow, Red-breasted and White-breasted Nuthatches, Rock and Canyon Wrens, Gray Catbird, Cedar Waxwing, Nashville Warbler, Spotted Towhee, Lazuli Bunting, and Red Crossbill.

From the main intersection in downtown Winthrop take SR-20 westbound across the Chewuch River bridge. In 0.2 mile, on the opposite side of the highway from the USFS Methow Valley Information Center, turn right onto West Chewuch Road. Drive north 0.9 mile to Rendezvous Road. Turn left, proceed 1.1 miles, and make another left onto Gunn Ranch Road. In 0.8 mile, stop at a parking area off to the left for the Rendezvous Lake Unit (3,180 acres) of the Methow Wildlife Area (WDFW permit required). Except in the fall hunting season, the riparian thickets and open fields around **Riser Lake**, a short walk ahead, make an excellent birding site. Look for Pied-billed Grebe, Cinnamon Teal, Barrow's Goldeneye, Spotted Sandpiper, Eastern Kingbird, Tree Swallow, House Wren, Western Bluebird, and Bullock's Oriole.

UPPER METHOW VALLEY

Wolf Creek Road offers an easygoing route upvalley on the opposite bank of the Methow River from the highway. Headed southeast from the main intersection in the Winthrop business district, SR-20 bends right and crosses the Methow River (0.5 mile). Take a right 0.1 mile after the bridge onto Twin Lakes Road, passing the Winthrop National Fish Hatchery (short trail with good riparian birding) and reaching the intersection with Wolf Creek Road in 1.3 miles. Turn right onto this gravel road, which runs beside riparian areas (Purple Finch) and pine and Douglas-fir forest. Look for Black Swifts overhead (easier to spot when foraging low in cool and cloudy weather). Reach SR-20 in nine miles.

An access to **Big Valley Unit** (847 acres) of the Methow Wildlife Area is not far downstream from this intersection. Turn right onto SR-20, travel 1.6 miles, and turn right onto Dripping Springs Road. Park in 0.3 mile. Choose the trail that takes off directly behind the restrooms. It is about a quarter-mile walk to the Methow River. Pines and Douglas-firs en route should have Western Wood-Pewee, Hammond's Flycatcher, Red-breasted Nuthatch, and Yellow-rumped Warbler. Riparian growth nearer the river may produce Red-naped Sapsucker, Northern Flicker, Red-eyed Vireo, Veery, American Robin, Cedar Waxwing, and Nashville, Yellow, and MacGillivray's Warblers. Bald Eagle and American Dipper are found along the river, especially in winter. Irrigated and dryland pastures in other parts of the wildlife area are managed for Mule and White-tailed Deer. Golden Eagles hunt over these fields in winter.

Turn left from Dripping Springs Road and backtrack northwestward on SR-20, then go right in 1.1 miles onto Goat Creek Road. In 3.5 miles an obscure, unmarked gravel spur on the left leads to parking for the **Methow Valley Trail Suspension Bridge**. Follow the old roadbed for one mile to an impressive bridge over the Methow River, passing coniferous and riparian habitats. Look for Harlequin Duck, Common Merganser, Calliope and Rufous Hummingbirds, Red-naped Sapsucker, Mountain Chickadee, Red-breasted and White-breasted Nuthatches, American Dipper, Veery, Yellow Warbler, American Redstart, Black-headed Grosbeak, Cassin's Finch, and Red Crossbill.

Mazama (limited services) is 1.7 miles ahead on Goat Creek Road. A short connector on the left leads to SR-20 (0.4 mile). From here SR-20 (closed in winter) begins its ascent of the North Cascades along Early Winters Creek, reaching Western Washington via Washington Pass (17.5 miles; page 130). On the way up, **Klipchuk Campground** (4.3 miles) is a fine place to study birds of the upper forest, including Blue Grouse, Williamson's Sapsucker (uncommon), Hammond's Flycatcher, and Varied Thrush.

In Mazama, Goat Creek Road changes name to Lost River Road and continues straight ahead up the Methow Valley. In 2.1 miles, find **North Cascade Base Camp** (866-996-2334, *www.ncbasecamp.com*), a rustic lodge set in forest. Birders are welcome to walk the grounds, but be quiet in the early morning to avoid disturbing guests. The Tractor and Beaver Trails can be walked as a loop (about a mile) past a number of Beaver ponds lined with riparian vegetation, and areas of wet coniferous forest with giant Western Redcedars. Typical birds in summer include Ruffed Grouse, Barred Owl, Red-naped Sapsucker, Downy, Hairy, and Pileated Woodpeckers, Hammond's Flycatcher, Warbling and Red-eyed Vireos, Veery, Swainson's Thrush, Townsend's and MacGillivray's Warblers, and Red Crossbill. Calliope and Rufous Hummingbirds visit the feeders outside the dining-room windows. Winter birders on cross-country skis might encounter Northern Pygmy-Owl, Brown Creeper, and Pine Grosbeak.

HARTS PASS

Famous for mountain scenery, backcountry trails, and subalpine meadows with an extravagant summer wildflower display (160 species), the Cascade crest around Harts Pass is an exceptional site for high-country and boreal bird species. The first rocky wagon track to the gold mines west of the crest at Chancellor and Barron was engineered by Colonel W. Thomas Hart in 1900. The road was widened (to 36 inches!) in 1903 and a second time in 1936. Although well maintained and easily travelable by any passenger auto, it is too narrow in some places for two cars to pass. One half-mile section subject to rockslides and washouts must be negotiated carefully. The main complication is not there, however, but on the rest of the road where the smooth surface may give drivers a false sense of security and tempt them to go too fast, leading to hair-raising close encounters at the many blind curves and dips. Nor is this a place for long, wide vehicles; trailers are expressly forbidden.

Continue west on Lost River Road (becomes FR-5400), staying right at a fork seven miles past North Cascade Base Camp. The steep gravel road cut into the side of the mountain continues steadily uphill through a variety of forested habitats harboring bird species such as Blue Grouse, Rufous Hummingbird, Western Wood-Pewee, Hammond's Flycatcher, Cassin's and Warbling Vireos, Swainson's and Hermit Thrushes, Nashville, Yellow, Yellow-rumped, Townsend's, and MacGillivray's Warblers, Western Tanager, Chipping Sparrow, Dark-eyed Junco, Lazuli Bunting, and Pine Siskin. Silver snags in the upper basin remain from a Spruce Beetle infestation years ago—a natural thinning process that killed half the forest. Today these snags support a great variety of wildlife, including woodpeckers.

At a junction in 9.8 miles, just before Harts Pass, turn left onto FR-500 to reach **Meadows Campground** (primitive) in one mile and the road's end at the Pacific Crest Trail a mile beyond that. These meadows and lichen-festooned forests of Engelmann Spruce, Subalpine Fir, and Subalpine Larch can be excellent for boreal specialties such as Spruce Grouse, Boreal Owl, Three-toed Woodpecker, Boreal Chickadee, Pine Grosbeak, and White-winged Crossbill (irregular). Other inhabitants include Rufous Hummingbird, Gray Jay, Clark's Nutcracker, Common Raven, Mountain Chickadee, Red-breasted Nuthatch, Winter Wren, Golden-crowned and Ruby-crowned Kinglets, Mountain Bluebird, Hermit Thrush, American Robin, Varied Thrush, Yellow-rumped and Townsend's Warblers, Chipping and Fox Sparrows, Cassin's Finch, and Red Crossbill.

Return to the junction with FR-5400 and turn left for 0.1 mile to reach Harts Pass (elevation 6,198 feet) and another small USFS campground. The road forks again; go right onto FR-600 and continue past a trailhead parking area for the Pacific Crest Trail to another parking lot where the road is gated (2.4 miles). You are at the highest point reached by road in Washington (elevation 7,200 feet). Walk up the road for a few hundred yards beyond the gate to a trailhead for the **West Fork Pasayten River Trail**. Often closed by lingering snow until well into July, the trail switchbacks down through the meadowsn onto a cirque. At the first fork, go left with the main trail a few hundred yards onto the rocky north slopes of Slate Peak, or right into a compact basin that contains examples of most of the upper subalpine and alpine plant communities found in the North Cascades. Fox Sparrows are numerous in trees at timberline, joined by a few White-crowned Sparrows (*gambelii* race); the adjacent forb meadows have Savannah Sparrows. Above treeline American Pipits perform their flight song and aerial display. Search the snowbank edges and mats of alpine vegetation for Gray-crowned Rosy-Finch. White-tailed Ptarmigan are here, but luck and hard work are usually needed to find one. Males seem tied to boulder-strewn slopes with scattered heather patches: you might even spy one by looking down from the parking lot. Females with broods are most often noted in seep habitats with high insect availability, just below the snowbanks.

The summit of **Slate Peak** is another few minutes' walk up the road. In good weather beginning in August and continuing through mid-October the summit can be a decent hawkwatching platform. Expect Sharp-shinned and Red-tailed Hawks in modest numbers, with a sprinkling of other species. The peak's north ridge is another possibility for ptarmigan.

OKANOGAN VALLEY

by Andy Stepniewski and Richard Cannings

The Okanogan River winds along the broad trench of the Okanogan Valley through irrigated orchards and hay fields, open rangeland, and areas of riparian habitat. Bold, rounded domes of granitic and metamorphic rocks (gneiss) provide a dramatic backdrop in many places. Glacial terraces, formed when a large trunk glacier partially filled the valley, are conspicuous along the sides. Common species throughout the valley in May and June, when birding possibilities peak, include Red-tailed Hawk, American Kestrel, Ring-necked Pheasant, California Quail, Killdeer, Mourning Dove, Common Nighthawk, Downy Woodpecker, Northern Flicker, Western Kingbird, Black-billed Magpie, American Crow, Violet-green, Northern Rough-winged, Bank, Cliff, and Barn Swallows, Black-capped Chickadee, House Wren, American Robin, Cedar Waxwing, Black-headed Grosbeak, Brewer's Blackbird, Bullock's Oriole, and House Finch. In winter, flocks of Bohemian Waxwings rove about the orchards and brushy draws. Some years there are also flocks of Common Redpolls—look for these in areas of Water Birch and alders, or in ornamental birches in the towns, where a few Pine Grosbeaks may also turn up. Agriculture, grazing, and urbanization have diminished the natural qualities of the landscape close to US-97. However, towns along the highway serve as good jump-off points for birding sites away from the valley bottom.

BREWSTER AND VICINITY

The small community of Brewster—gateway to the Okanogan Valley—is located on the north shore of the Columbia River (actually Lake Pateros, the reservoir behind Wells Dam) about seven miles above Pateros and three miles below the mouth of the Okanogan River. In winter, drive the town's residential streets: ornamental plantings and feeders often attract Bohemian Waxwings and various finches. Before heading off to explore the several birding routes that converge in Brewster, take the time to visit some of the excellent birding sites close by. In this section, mile zero in Brewster is the intersection of US-97 and SR-173. Going south here on SR-173 across the Columbia River bridge will bring you to birding sites near Bridgeport (page 386).

Drive southwest on US-97 from Brewster to Indian Dan Canyon Road (2.5 miles). Turn right onto this gravel road and go 1.4 miles to the **Indian Dan Canyon Unit** of the Wells Wildlife Area (5,036 acres). Slopes are covered with Bitterbrush and Big Sagebrush, while ravines have riparian habitats with clumps of aspen. Birding these habitats in spring and summer should yield many of the usual Eastside breeding birds, including Lark Sparrow. Northern Goshawk occurs fairly regularly in winter. In another mile, turn left and pass a small, marshy lake in the valley bottom; look for Ruddy Duck and Marsh Wren. Sharp-tailed Grouse is a remote possibility.

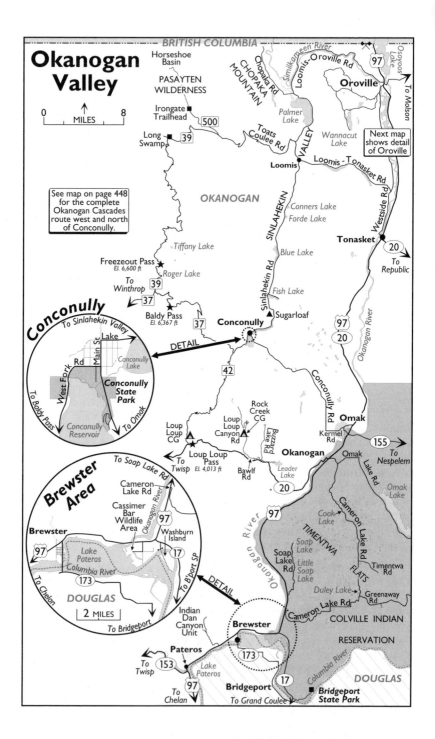

Okanogan Valley

0 —↑— 8
MILES

See map on page 448 for the complete Okanogan Cascades route west and north of Conconully.

BRITISH COLUMBIA

Horseshoe Basin
PASAYTEN WILDERNESS

CHOPAKA MOUNTAIN

Chopaka Rd

Similkameen River

Loomis-Oroville Rd

Osoyoos Lake

97

To Molson

Oroville

Next map shows detail of Oroville

Palmer Lake

Irongate Trailhead
500

Long Swamp
39

Toats Coulee Rd

VALLEY

Wannacut Lake

Loomis

Loomis - Tonasket Rd

OKANOGAN

SINLAHEKIN

Conners Lake
Forde Lake

Tonasket

20

To Republic

Westside Rd

Tiffany Lake

Blue Lake

Freezeout Pass
El. 6,600 ft
Roger Lake
To Winthrop
39
37

Sinlahekin Rd

Fish Lake

97
20

Okanogan River

Baldy Pass
El. 6,367 ft
37

Conconully

Sugarloaf

Conconully

To Sinlahekin Valley

Lake

Main St

West Fork Rd

Conconully Lake

DETAIL

Conconully State Park

To Baldy Pass

Conconully Reservoir

To Omak

42

Loup Loup CG

Rock Creek CG

Loup Loup Canyon Rd

Conconully Rd

Omak

Kermel Rd

155

To Nespelem

Buzzard Lake Rd

Okanogan

Omak

Lake Rd

Omak Lake

Brewster Area

To Soap Lake Rd

Cameron Lake Rd

Cassimer Bar Wildlife Area

Okanogan River

97

Brewster

97

Washburn Island

17

Lake Pateros

Columbia River

173

DOUGLAS

2 MILES

To Chelan

To B'port SP

To Bridgeport

Loup Loup Pass
El. 4,013 ft
To Twisp
Bawlf Rd
Leader Lake
20

River

Okanogan

TIMENTWA

Cook Lake

Soap Lake Rd

Soap Lake
Little Soap Lake

Cameron Lake Rd

Timentwa Rd

FLATS

Duley Lake
Greenaway Rd

Indian Dan Canyon Unit

DETAIL

Brewster

COLVILLE INDIAN

RESERVATION

Cameron Lake Rd

Pateros

To Twisp
153

Lake Pateros

97

To Chelan

173

17

Bridgeport

To Grand Coulee

Bridgeport State Park

Columbia River

DOUGLAS

East from Brewster on US-97, stop in 3.4 miles at a wide pullout on the right side of the highway to survey **Cassimer Bar** and the mouth of the Okanogan River. Scope for loons, grebes, American White Pelican, Double-crested Cormorant, and waterfowl. For a closer look at this rich birding area, continue another 0.7 mile across the Okanogan River bridge and turn right onto a gravel road marked *Cassimer Bar Access*. Follow this for a half-mile, then go right onto a dirt track that ends in another half-mile in the Cassimer Bar Wildlife Area, where groves of introduced Russian Olives and other trees alternate with ponds and marshes. Spring and fall can be excellent for migrant passerines. Summer residents include Osprey, Virginia Rail, Forster's Tern, Western Wood-Pewee, Willow Flycatcher, numerous swallows, Marsh Wren, and Yellow-headed Blackbird.

The intersection of US-97 and SR-17 is 0.5 mile farther east. Turn right here and go south on SR-17 for 0.2 mile. Turn right onto an unmarked road that ends in half a mile at a causeway to **Washburn Island**. Park and scan the water and marshlands from here or walk across to the island. Depending on the season, this embayment may be filled with waterbirds. Osprey, Marsh Wren, and Yellow-headed Blackbird are a few of the many species that nest here. In winter, check brushy areas for sparrows.

Go south another 7.9 miles on SR-17 and turn left for 2.7 miles to **Bridgeport State Park**. Rock Wrens inhabit rocky ravines uphill from the campground. Adjacent deeper-soiled slopes have a well-developed shrub-steppe habitat (Sage Thrasher, Lark Sparrow). In winter, look for Great Horned, Long-eared, and Northern Saw-whet Owls, and Bohemian Waxwings in the park's ornamental plantings.

TIMENTWA FLATS

East of the southern Okanogan Valley, on the Colville Indian Reservation, is a high plateau sometimes called the Timentwa Flats, although you will not find the name on all maps. This wide-open, rolling upland dotted with monstrous glacial erratics has the same terrain as the adjacent Waterville Plateau across the Columbia River to the south, but is wilder, with no towns and far fewer signs of habitation. Shrub-steppe, Ponderosa Pine forests, small lakes, riparian-zone groves with Quaking Aspen and Water Birch, and dryland wheat farms are the principal habitats. One main gravel road and a few offshoots permit easy, safe exploration of this remote region, but be especially careful during winter and the spring thaw when side roads can become difficult or impossible to negotiate.

From the junction with SR-17 east of Brewster, go north 2.6 miles on US-97 to **Cameron Lake Road** (called Wakefield-Cameron Lake Road on some maps), an excellent year-round birding route that crosses the heart of the Timentwa Flats to end in Okanogan. Sharp-tailed Grouse (becoming rare), Downy Woodpecker, Black-billed Magpie, and Black-capped Chickadee are resident in copses along wetland edges. Breeding species include Calliope Hummingbird, Red-naped Sapsucker, House Wren, Western Bluebird, and Bullock's Oriole. The many small lakes attract waterfowl and migrant shorebirds. Northern specialties such as Rough-legged Hawk and Snow Bunting await those properly equipped for winter birding.

Cameron Lake Road ascends 6.3 miles to the edge of the plateau. On the way up, look in areas of shrub-steppe vegetation for Burrowing Owl (perhaps extirpated), Loggerhead Shrike, and Brewer's, Vesper, and Grasshopper Sparrows. Continue east, then north to an intersection with Greenaway Road (5.7 miles). This is raptor country; Red-tailed and Rough-legged Hawks, Golden Eagle, Gyrfalcon (rare), and Prairie Falcon occur seasonally. Check ponds and lakes for shorebirds. Semipalmated, Baird's, and Pectoral Sandpipers are regular in fall migration along with the commoner species (and some less-common ones). Sandhill Cranes can be common in wheat-field stubble and wet swales from late March to mid-April. If road conditions permit, head east on **Greenaway Road** to a grassy area (3.0 miles). Park here and walk south about a half-mile to a grassy and brushy coulee bottom where Sharp-tailed Grouse still survive in small numbers.

Continue north on Cameron Lake Road for 0.7 mile to **Duley Lake**. Except when frozen in winter, this lake attracts numerous waterfowl. Unusual records include Thayer's Gull and Forster's Tern. Depending on water levels, shorebird diversity and numbers can be good beginning in late July and continuing through August. Red-tailed Hawks have nested on the cliffs at the north end of the lake, site of an impressive Cliff Swallow colony.

Turn right onto **Timentwa Road** (3.2 miles) and drive 1.5 miles through wheat fields and weedy swales. This higher-elevation portion of the plateau (above 2,700 feet) has proven excellent in winter and early spring for Lapland Longspur and Snow Bunting. Fantastic numbers of Snow Buntings (>2,500) have been observed in late February and early March. Gyrfalcon, though rare, is seen regularly in winter.

Once more headed north on Cameron Lake Road, stop in 0.6 mile to check an area of dense riparian habitat for Sharp-tailed Grouse, especially in winter. In another 2.1 miles a dirt lane gives access to three small lakes in an area of wheat fields west of the road that sometimes have waterfowl and shorebirds. The main road winds north for 2.4 miles through shrub-steppe (Common Raven and Horned Lark year round, Sage Thrasher and Brewer's Sparrow in summer). Here begins the descent, gradual at first, through pines alternating with riparian groves. **Cook Lake** (0.9 mile) seems particularly good for Greater Scaup and other diving ducks in spring. For the next 2.3 miles, up to where the Ponderosa Pine forest abruptly ends, make a number of stops to look for Northern Pygmy-Owl, Gray Flycatcher (May–July), White-headed Woodpecker, Mountain Chickadee, White-breasted and Pygmy Nuthatches, and Red Crossbill.

An area of denser brushland by the road (1.1 mile from the last pines) attracts Brewer's, Vesper, and Grasshopper Sparrows and Lazuli Bunting. Singing Clay-colored Sparrows have been noted on a number of occasions in June and might breed in the densest thickets of wild rose. At the intersection with Cameron Lake–Omak Lake Road (2.6 mile) stay left on Cameron Lake Road and proceed west, inspecting the shrub-steppe habitats with Bitterbrush and Big Sagebrush for Loggerhead Shrike (uncommon) and Lark Sparrow from April through July. In 1.4 miles, reach the combined US-97/SR-20 a mile north of Okanogan.

The **Soap Lake** area, on the western slope of the Timentwa Flats, is good for waterbirds from spring through fall. From the junction of US-97 and SR-17 east of Brewster, go north 4.1 miles on US-97 (1.5 miles north of the Cameron Lake Road turnoff) and turn right onto Soap Lake Road, which climbs the flanks of a glacial terrace into rangelands with scattered alkaline lakes. Bunchgrass at the top of the hill, 1.0 mile from the highway, is Grasshopper Sparrow habitat, although excessive grazing has diminished sparrow numbers here. About 1.5 miles farther, in open areas, look for Red-tailed Hawk, Golden Eagle, Long-billed Curlew, Burrowing Owl (rare), and Lark Sparrow. For the next three miles you pass three alkaline lakes: Little Soap Lake, an even smaller unnamed lake, and finally mile-long Soap Lake. Look here in the nesting season for Eared Grebe, teals (all three species) and other puddle ducks, Barrow's Goldeneye, Wilson's Phalarope, and Yellow-headed Blackbird. Shorebirds occur in migration, especially yellowlegs, Baird's Sandpiper, and other peeps.

CONCONULLY

US-97 offers little in the way of birding between Omak and Oroville. A more interesting route follows a fold in the mountains at the west edge of the Okanogan Valley from Conconully north to Loomis and Palmer Lake via the Sinlahekin Valley, then back east to Oroville along the Similkameen River. The starting point is the junction of US-97 and Riverside Drive at the north end of Omak. Proceed west 1.0 mile and turn right onto Cherry Avenue (becomes Kermel Road), following signs for Conconully Lake. Go 2.1 miles to a stop sign, then right (north) onto Conconully Road. For about half the 15-mile distance from here to Conconully the road passes through orchards and grazing country (Red-tailed Hawk, American Kestrel, Western Kingbird, Black-billed Magpie, Western Meadowlark, Brewer's Blackbird, House Finch, American Goldfinch). For the remainder, rangelands alternate with shrub-steppe habitats where Chukar, Vesper and Lark Sparrows, and Western Meadowlark are common. A tiny number of Sharp-tailed Grouse still hang on in the Scotch Creek Wildlife Area but the chance of spotting one is remote.

On the left in 15.0 miles is the first entrance for **Conconully State Park** (not well signed), which affords a good view of Conconully Reservoir. Scan for nesting Red-necked Grebe, various waterfowl, and gulls. Return to Conconully Road and turn left. Go 0.5 mile to turn left on West Fork Road, then left in one block into the main park entrance. The trees here are worth checking in migration, as is the open area west of the campground at the head of the reservoir. Farther along on West Fork Road, forest birds typical of the Ponderosa Pine forests are fairly common between the road and the reservoir, including Northern Pygmy-Owl, Calliope Hummingbird (feeders at cabins), all three nuthatches, Cassin's Finch, and Evening Grosbeak. After leaving Conconully Reservoir, the road enters a riparian area and then begins ascending West Fork Salmon Creek through forests of Douglas-fir, Western Larch, and Ponderosa Pine. Baldy Pass and Roger Lake lie ahead (page 449).

SINLAHEKIN VALLEY

Sinlahekin Creek threads its way along a glaciated valley for 17 miles, from Blue Lake (elevation 1,686 feet) north to Palmer Lake (elevation 1,145 feet). This broad trench probably holds a greater diversity of breeding birds than any other area of comparable size in Washington. On both sides, steep slopes with rock outcrops and cliffs ascend abruptly to an elevation of more than 5,000 feet. Ponderosa Pine forest and various bunchgrasses alternate with large areas of Bitterbrush, serviceberry, chokecherry, and Snowberry. The valley floor has tangled, dense stands of Water Birch, willow, and aspen, with numerous Beaver ponds and several other impoundments.

The south approach is from Omak via Conconully (see preceding section). At the intersection in Conconully where West Fork Road goes left, stay straight ahead on Main Street. In 0.2 mile turn right onto Lake Street, which becomes **Sinlahekin Road**, running east, then north along the shore of Conconully Lake before contouring around Sugarloaf and descending toward Fish Lake. In 5.3 miles, stop in the Douglas-fir forest to look and listen for Hairy Woodpecker, Hammond's Flycatcher, Cassin's Vireo, and Nashville Warbler, among many other breeding species.

From here most of the way north to Loomis the route passes through the **Sinlahekin Wildlife Area** (13,814 acres)—Washington's oldest state wildlife area. When purchased, these lands were intended primarily to provide habitat for the large Mule Deer herd. Today they are managed for a diversity of wildlife species. White-tailed Deer have increased substantially in recent decades. Bighorn Sheep were first reintroduced in 1949 from a herd in British Columbia. Waterfowl, raptors, and passerines are also present in impressive diversity and numbers.

At an intersection with Fish Lake Road (1.4 miles), stay left with Sinlahekin Road to a view of Blue Lake (3.4 miles), where Common Loon and Hooded Merganser are regular. Shallower Forde Lake, 5.1 miles farther north, has Pied-billed Grebe, a variety of waterfowl, and many Willow Flycatchers and Common Yellowthroats. Marsh-fringed **Conners Lake** is an exceptional birding site. Turn off right from Sinlahekin Road in 1.5 miles, go a few yards, then turn right again to find the lake and primitive campground in 0.4 mile. The many nesting waterbirds include Red-necked Grebe, Canada Goose, Wood Duck, Gadwall, Mallard, Blue-winged and Cinnamon Teals, Redhead, Lesser Scaup, Barrow's Goldeneye, Ruddy Duck, Spotted Sandpiper, and Black Tern. Surrounding riparian and marsh habitats are great for Black-chinned Hummingbird, Red-naped Sapsucker, Willow Flycatcher, Eastern Kingbird, Warbling Vireo, Tree, Northern Rough-winged, Bank, Cliff, and Barn Swallows, Marsh Wren, Veery, Gray Catbird, Cedar Waxwing, Yellow Warbler, Common Yellowthroat, Yellow-breasted Chat, Yellow-headed Blackbird, and Bullock's Oriole. On forested and brushy slopes away from water, look for Cooper's and Red-tailed Hawks, Golden Eagle, Chukar, Wild Turkey, Common Nighthawk, Common Poorwill, Lewis's and Hairy Woodpeckers, Western Wood-Pewee, Dusky Flycatcher, Western Kingbird, Clark's Nutcracker, Mountain Chickadee, White-breasted Nuthatch, Rock, Canyon, and House Wrens, Western Bluebird, Townsend's Solitaire, Nashville Warbler, Western Tanager, Spotted Towhee, Chipping Sparrow, Lazuli Bunting, Cassin's Finch, and Red Crossbill.

About five miles farther north Sinlahekin Road enters Loomis and becomes Palmer Avenue. At the fork, turn left onto Loomis–Oroville Road. (If you wish to connect to US-97 or SR-20 in Tonasket, the other branch— Loomis-Tonasket Road—will take you east 11.6 miles to an intersection with Westside Road; turn right here to reach the Okanogan River bridge in Tonasket in another 5.2 miles.) Northward from Loomis in 2.1 miles, the Loomis-Oroville Road intersects with Toats Coulee Road (access to Horseshoe Basin and Long Swamp, page 452). Another 2.1 miles north lies **Palmer Lake**, nestled in a trough. American Bittern, Virginia Rail, Sora, Wilson's Snipe, Willow Flycatcher, several swallow species, and Common Yellowthroat should be looked for in the marshes at the southern end of the lake. A few Common Loons, Western Grebes, and Common Mergansers can sometimes be scoped from here on the deep waters of the lake; White-winged Scoter and other sea ducks occur rarely. Continuing around the lake 4.4 miles to its north end is usually a better bet for waterbirds, however. Sandbars may have resting gulls or Caspian Terns.

SIMILKAMEEN RIVER

The outlet creek of Palmer Lake meanders north for a couple of miles to reach the Similkameen River and outstanding birding. Eight-tenths of a mile north of the previous stop at Palmer Lake, turn left from the Loomis-Oroville Road onto **Chopaka Road**, which goes up the Similkameen Valley for 6.5 miles to a closed gate a short distance before the U.S.-Canada border (no port of entry). Virtually all land is private here. This is not a hardship, however, as interesting habitats come to the road. In the first mile are meadows, fields, and areas of brush, featuring Eastern Kingbird, Savannah Sparrow, and a variety of blackbirds; Bobolink is also possible. A few Long-billed Curlews can usually be found along this stretch. Sloughs lined with riparian vegetation lie ahead—great for Black-chinned Hummingbird, Red-naped Sapsucker, Willow Flycatcher, Warbling Vireo, Veery, Gray Catbird, and Yellow and MacGillivray's Warblers. To the west, Chopaka Mountain sweeps precipitously down from its summit for more than 6,000 feet in one unbroken slope. The cliffs have White-throated Swift, Violet-green Swallow, and Rock and Canyon Wrens. Farther along, look for Pileated Woodpecker, Calliope Hummingbird, Dusky Flycatcher, Cassin's Vireo, House Wren, and Nashville Warbler on the open, brushy slopes and in Douglas-fir forest at the base of the mountain. A few areas of open water expand the possibilities.

Return to the Loomis-Oroville Road and turn left. In 0.5 mile, pull out to the left at an overlook of **Champney Slough**, in the heart of an area of exceptional diversity of breeding birds. More than 100 species have been documented here, including Osprey, Bald Eagle, Cooper's Hawk, Chukar, Western Screech-Owl, Common Poorwill, Lewis's Woodpecker, Red-naped Sapsucker, Least Flycatcher (regular, calling from riparian vegetation on the island), Warbling and Red-eyed Vireos, Northern Rough-winged Swallow, Rock and Canyon Wrens, Veery, Gray Catbird, Yellow Warbler, American Redstart (uncommon), Yellow-breasted Chat, Black-headed Grosbeak, and Bullock's Oriole. Continuing north, then east, the Loomis-Oroville Road follows the Similkameen River downstream to Oroville (15.7 miles). Various unmarked accesses to the stream allow you to see Lewis's Woodpecker, Eastern and Western Kingbirds, and Bullock's Oriole. Farther, the steep slopes and cliffs have Golden Eagle, Chukar, Common Poorwill, White-throated Swift, and Rock and Canyon Wrens.

OROVILLE AND VICINITY

The small farming and ranching community of Oroville, just below the U.S.-Canada border, is a crossroads of excellent birding routes. From the corner of Main Street (US-97) and Central Avenue (Loomis-Oroville Road) you can go west on the Similkameen Valley route (preceding section); jog south one block and east on Central (Chesaw Road) toward Molson and the Okanogan Highlands (page 457); or go north on US-97 to the Okanagan Valley of British Columbia (page 444). But first, zero your trip-odometer at this corner and check out several sites close to town.

Driscoll Island Wildlife Area (220 acres) is south of Oroville near the confluence of the Okanogan and Similkameen Rivers. Currently, access to the island is by boat, except when extremely low water levels permit wading. However, observing the island from a concrete platform on the shore offers good birding, especially early on a May or June morning. Drive south 2.9 miles from Oroville on US-97 to milepost 329.1 and turn right onto Gavin Road (also signed *Public Fishing Access*). The lush streambank habitats host Spotted

Sandpiper, Belted Kingfisher, Willow Flycatcher, Eastern Kingbird, Gray Catbird, Yellow Warbler, American Redstart, Northern Waterthrush, Blackheaded Grosbeak, and Bullock's Oriole. Another access 0.8 mile farther north on US-97 (closer to Oroville) has similar birding possibilities.

Three-tenths of a mile south of Central Avenue, 12th Avenue turns west from US-97 (Main Street), crosses the Similkameen River, and becomes Westside Road. In 1.0 mile, turn right at a sign for **Ellemeham Mountain** to begin a 20-mile loop through the old mining district southwest of Oroville. The many bird-rich habitats include steep, barren slopes and rocky outcrops, shrub-steppe, aspen-lined watercourses, grasslands, and a few areas of marsh and lakes. This route is especially good during the breeding season.

At the fork in 0.1 mile, keep right on Ellemeham Road, which climbs steeply out of the Okanogan Valley. In 2.0 miles, look for ducks and shorebirds at **Mud Lake**. Horned Grebe (rare as a breeding species in Washington), American Wigeon, Ring-necked Duck, Hooded Merganser, and Ruddy Duck all nested here in 2001. The next ten miles, as the road leaves the lake, drops down into **Ellemeham Draw**, and climbs again to the top of Hicks Canyon, is one of the better places in Washington to search for Clay-colored Sparrows—especially in early June. Their preferred habitat is the bright-green patches of Snowberry and wild rose that contrast strongly with the silver-hued Big Sagebrush. Also look for Sage Thrasher (uncommon) and Brewer's, Vesper, and Grasshopper Sparrows in areas of shrub-steppe.

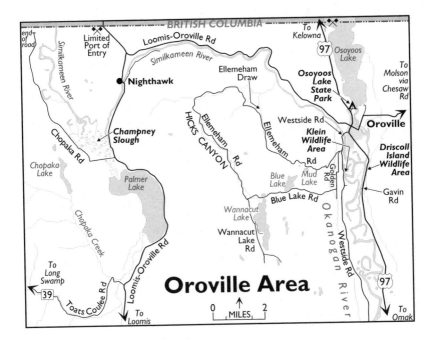

Heading down **Hicks Canyon**, riparian vegetation has Red-naped Sapsucker, Dusky Flycatcher, Warbling Vireo, House Wren, Veery, Orange-crowned and Yellow Warblers, and Black-headed Grosbeak. At a fork in 3.5 miles, a right turn onto Wannacut Lake Road takes you to a fishing access at the south end of **Wannacut Lake** (2.4 miles) where you can look for waterbirds and for Cassin's Finches in the Ponderosa Pines. Backtrack on Wannacut Lake Road, turn right on Blue Lake Road, stopping at a couple of other lake viewpoints. In 4.1 miles turn left onto Golden Road, then right in 1.6 miles to reach the starting place on Westside Road in another 0.1 mile. Turn left here to return to Oroville.

Klein Wildlife Area is 0.7 mile south of the Ellemeham Mountain intersection on Westside Road. Park at a pullout on the left and take the trail across a slough (Wood Duck, Gray Catbird) and through weedy fields to tall riparian habitat flanking the Okanogan River. Expect the same assortment of birds as at Driscoll Island a mile to the north, including Yellow-breasted Chat. Here, however, you can immerse yourself in their habitat.

The entrance to **Osoyoos Lake State Park** is 0.6 mile north of the Main Street-Central Avenue corner in Oroville, on the east side of US-97. The park is a busy place in summer but worth a stop at other seasons. Osoyoos Lake is a good bet for Osprey, and the marsh near the lake's outlet has Marsh Wren and Yellow-headed Blackbird (common). Ornamental plantings and riparian vegetation can be productive for passerines in migration, especially during inclement weather. Migration and winter also attract a sprinkling of loons (mostly Common, but Yellow-billed has occurred), grebes, and diving ducks. Greater Scaup and Red-breasted Merganser often winter in small numbers.

OKANAGAN VALLEY (BRITISH COLUMBIA)

US-97 becomes provincial Highway 97 at Canada Customs, about four miles north of Oroville and two miles south of Osoyoos, British Columbia. Birders visiting Washington may want to consider spending a day or two in the grasslands, riparian woodlands, and pine forests of the southern part of the Okanagan Valley (note the spelling difference). The 25-mile stretch from Osoyoos to Okanagan Falls boasts some of the country's best-known birding sites. Owling, in particular, can be outstanding.

No. 22 Road is one of British Columbia's top birding spots, reached by driving north five miles on Highway 97 from the intersection with Highway 3 in Osoyoos. Turn east onto No. 22 Road and bird the fields along the way to the bridge over the Okanagan River. Park in the pullout just before the bridge (0.6 mile). The dikes along the river channel provide access to public lands adjacent to the old river oxbows amid lush pastures and arid benches. Regular spring and summer species in the grassy fields are Long-billed Curlew, Wilson's Phalarope, and Bobolink; in the birch woodlands, Veery, Gray Catbird, American Redstart, and Yellow-breasted Chat; and in the marshes, Virginia

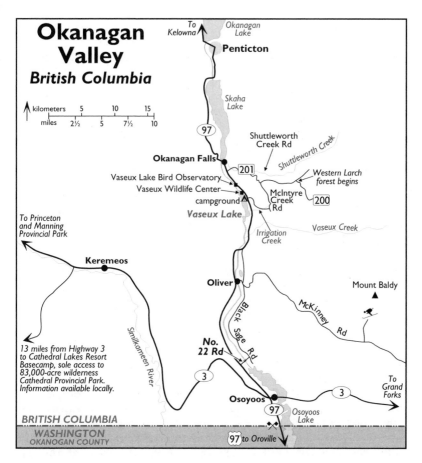

Okanagan Valley
British Columbia

kilometers 5   10   15

miles 2½   5   7½   10

To Kelowna

Okanagan Lake

Penticton

Skaha Lake

97

Shuttleworth Creek Rd

Shuttleworth Creek

Okanagan Falls

201

Western Larch forest begins

Vaseux Lake Bird Observatory

Vaseux Wildlife Center

McIntyre Creek Rd

200

campground

Vaseux Lake

Irrigation Creek

Vaseux Creek

To Princeton and Manning Provincial Park

Keremeos

Oliver

Mount Baldy

McKinney Rd

Black Sage Rd

Similkameen River

No. 22 Rd

3

13 miles from Highway 3 to Cathedral Lakes Resort Basecamp, sole access to 83,000-acre wilderness Cathedral Provincial Park. Information available locally.

Osoyoos

97

Osoyoos Lake

3

To Grand Forks

BRITISH COLUMBIA

WASHINGTON
OKANOGAN COUNTY

97 to Oroville

Rail, Sora, and Yellow-headed Blackbird. A walk through the woodlands along the river oxbows could yield Great Horned, Long-eared, or Northern Saw-whet Owls at any time of year, but especially in winter and early spring (mosquitoes are intense in June). If you continue east beyond the river you soon come to a T-junction at some old outbuildings from the historic Haynes ranch—once the largest landholding in the Okanagan valley, stretching from Penticton to the U.S. border. Turning left (north) puts you on Black Sage Road to Oliver; Lark Sparrows are common in the Bitterbrush along this road.

McKinney Road is reached in 7.8 miles at the north end of Black Sage Road; turn right (east) for good birding in a variety of habitats. For the first six miles you are in the Osoyoos Indian Reserve, so do not leave the road. There is a large Bank Swallow colony on the north side of the road about 0.5 mile east of Oliver; Long-billed Curlews are commonly seen on the large flat about a mile farther on. The road climbs gradually through open Ponderosa Pine forests; the next five miles are good for Lewis's Woodpecker and Lazuli Bunting.

Kilometer (km) signs mark the distance from Oliver along this road; just past km 10 park at the cattle guard across the road. This is public land again, and one of the best places in Canada to see Gray Flycatcher. Dusky Flycatcher, White-breasted and Pygmy Nuthatches, Townsend's Solitaire, and Cassin's Finch are also common here.

The pine forests around km 13 are good for Flammulated Owl in late May and June, while the logged-over Western Larch forests around km 20 can yield Blue Grouse and Williamson's Sapsucker. The sedge marsh on the south side of the road just past km 22 usually has Green-winged Teal, Ring-necked Duck, Virginia Rail, Sora, Northern Waterthrush, Common Yellowthroat, and Lincoln's Sparrow. Rusty Blackbirds occasionally summer here as well, and Moose are seen commonly. Barred Owl, Williamson's and Red-naped Sapsuckers, Hairy, Three-toed, and Pileated Woodpeckers, Hammond's Flycatcher, Gray Jay, and Townsend's Warbler are found in the Western Larch-Engelmann Spruce-Lodgepole Pine forest. The road continues through logged-over, high-elevation forests; about 21 miles from Oliver you reach a junction where you can turn left to go to the Mount Baldy ski area. The patchy forests along this stretch of the road have Boreal Chickadee, Winter Wren, Fox Sparrow, and Pine Grosbeak.

Vaseux Lake—a federal bird sanctuary located along Highway 97 about eight miles north of Oliver—is another Okanagan hotspot. As you reach the lake, keep an eye out for Bighorn Sheep on the steep slopes above the highway. Note the Vaseux Lake Provincial Park Campground toward the north end of the lake. Three-tenths of a mile past the north campground entrance, turn left into the parking lot for **Vaseux Wildlife Center**, from which a boardwalk provides access to an observation tower overlooking Vaseux Lake at the mouth of the Okanagan River. The lake hosts Trumpeter and Tundra Swans and substantial numbers of other waterfowl in spring, fall, and early winter (best from October through early December, or whenever freezeup takes place, and again from late February through April). The most abundant waterbirds are Canada Goose, American Wigeon, Mallard, Common Merganser, and American Coot, with occasional concentrations of Ring-necked Duck and Hooded Merganser. Watch for Wood Ducks in the oxbows in spring and summer. The birch woodlands are good for Downy Woodpecker, Black-capped Chickadee, Yellow Warbler, Black-headed Grosbeak, and occasionally Yellow-breasted Chat. The **Vaseux Lake Bird Observatory** conducts mist-netting and bird censuses in August and September (and sometimes April–May). Stop at the white gate 0.6 mile north of the wildlife center on the west side of Highway 97. Visitors and volunteers are welcome.

Directly opposite the north campground entrance, McIntyre Creek Road (which actually follows **Irrigation Creek** for much of its length) goes east off Highway 97, providing access to rocky cliffs, grasslands, and Ponderosa Pine woodland. The cliffs and talus are home to Golden Eagle, Chukar, White-throated Swift, Violet-green Swallow, and Rock and Canyon Wrens, while the trees and shrubs at their base have Lewis's Woodpecker, Lazuli Bunting, and Bullock's Oriole. Lark Sparrows are common in the grasslands, and the pine forests have Northern Pygmy-Owl, Calliope Hummingbird, White-breasted and Pygmy Nuthatches, and occasionally White-headed Woodpecker. Stay left at the fork in 2.3 miles; from here the bumpy road (usually negotiable with care by most cars) passes through some excellent habitat for a variety of forest birds. Listen after dark for Western Screech-Owl and Northern Saw-whet Owl in spring and Flammulated Owl and Common Poorwill in summer. The road ends in 2.2 miles at a junction with Shuttleworth Creek Road. (See next paragraph for directions to this corner directly from Highway 97.)

Okanagan Falls Forest Service Road 201—a decent gravel road popularly known as **Shuttleworth Creek Road**—meets Highway 97 at the south edge of Okanagan Falls. Look for the sign for the Weyerhaeuser Mill. This is your road; turn east and follow signs for Allendale Lake. The bumpy road from Irrigation Creek comes in from the right in 4.8 miles (see preceding paragraph). In about four more miles (just past the km 12 sign) Shuttleworth Creek Road reaches good Western Larch forest with Williamson's Sapsucker, Three-toed and Black-backed Woodpeckers, Hammond's Flycatcher, MacGillivray's Warbler, and occasionally Great Gray Owl.

OKANOGAN CASCADES

by Andy Stepniewski and Richard Cannings

Some 20–25 miles west of Omak and Oroville a high divide separates the Methow and Okanogan drainage basins. Loup Loup Pass, on the crest of the divide at 4,020 feet elevation, is in the mixed-conifer belt with interesting forest species. Farther north, the peaks, valleys, ridges, and meadows of the Cascade Range along and east of the divide are justly famous for their boreal habitats and avian specialties such as Spruce Grouse, Boreal Owl, Three-toed Woodpecker, Boreal Chickadee, Pine Grosbeak, and White-winged Crossbill. FR-39 provides ready summer access to this country; a map of the Okanogan National Forest, obtainable at headquarters in Okanogan or at most USFS ranger stations, is a useful aid. Superb subalpine and alpine birding can also be had just across the international boundary in the British Columbia Cascades.

LOUP LOUP PASS

Loup Loup Pass, on SR-20 toward the south end of the Methow-Okanogan divide, is an especially good place to observe species of the mid-elevation forests. (See map on page 436.) From the intersection of US-97 and SR-20, turn west with SR-20, cross the river to Okanogan, and turn left with SR-20 to climb out of the Okanogan Valley. In 9.0 miles from US-97, turn right to check the Ponderosa Pines around **Leader Lake**, a popular camping

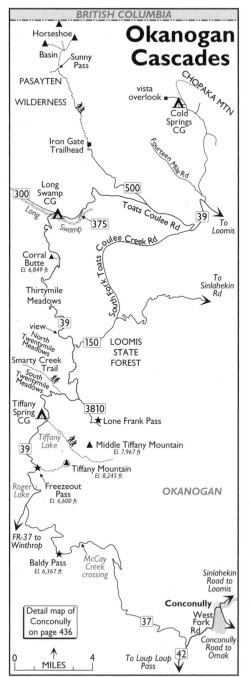

Okanogan Cascades

BRITISH COLUMBIA

Horseshoe
Basin
Sunny Pass
PASAYTEN
WILDERNESS

vista overlook
Cold Springs CG
CHOPAKA MTN

Iron Gate Trailhead
Fourteen Mile Rd

Long Swamp CG
300
500
Long Swamp
375
Toats Coulee Rd
39
To Loomis
Coulee Creek Rd

Corral Butte
El. 6,849 ft

Thirtymile Meadows

To Sinlahekin Rd

South Fork Toats Coulee Creek Rd

view
39
North Twentymile Meadows
150
LOOMIS STATE FOREST
Smarty Creek Trail
South Twentymile Meadows

Tiffany Spring CG
3810
Lone Frank Pass
Tiffany Lake
39
Middle Tiffany Mountain
El. 7,967 ft
Tiffany Mountain
El. 8,245 ft

Roger Lake
Freezeout Pass
El. 6,600 ft
OKANOGAN

FR-37 to Winthrop

Baldy Pass
El. 6,367 ft
McCay Creek crossing
Sinlahekin Road to Loomis

Conconully
West Fork Rd
Conconully Road to Omak

Detail map of Conconully on page 436

37

0   MILES   4

To Loup Loup Pass
42

spot. Pygmy Nuthatch and Cassin's Finch are common here. Four-tenths of a mile farther along SR-20, turn right onto Buzzard Lake Road. Look and listen for Common Poorwill at dusk during the warmer months. Bear left in 0.4 mile onto Bawlf Road, keeping straight where a connector from SR-20 comes in from the left. The road from here to **Rock Creek Campground** is good for Flammulated Owl, especially along the mountainside about 3.5 miles from SR-20.

Take the connector back to SR-20 and travel west 8.3 miles to the turnoff for **Loup Loup Campground** (USFS, fee). Go right on FR-42 for 0.5 mile, then right another 0.5 mile to the campground. Birding at Loup Loup is especially good in May and June. The camping area is usually uncrowded then, but nights can be cold at 4,000 feet elevation. Great Horned, Northern Pygmy-, and Barred Owls, Williamson's Sapsucker, Olive-sided Flycatcher, Western Wood-Pewee, Hammond's Flycatcher, Mountain Chickadee, Brown Creeper, Ruby-crowned Kinglet, Swainson's and Hermit Thrushes, Yellow-rumped and Townsend's Warblers, Western Tanager, Cassin's Finch, and Red Crossbill are some of the species found in this forest of Douglas-fir, Grand Fir, and

Western Larch. A small wet meadow adds many other species. Snowshoe Hare, Northern Flying Squirrel, and Black Bear are among the mammals observed here.

Descending west from Loup Loup Pass, SR-20 reaches the Methow Valley and a junction with SR-153 in about 11 miles (page 429). Going north 16 miles on FR-42 from the Loup Loup Campground takes you to a junction with FR-37 between Conconully and Baldy Pass—a shortcut to the route described in the following section.

BALDY PASS TO TIFFANY SPRING

Taken consecutively, this and the two following sections form an extraordinary 75-mile loop through more high-elevation habitats than any other birding route in the state, beginning in the Okanogan Valley at Conconully and returning to it near Loomis (no services available between these two points). The road is usually snow-free from June through early November. This route traverses miles and miles of mixed-conifer and boreal forests with several trailheads to the alpine, and is especially good for sought-after boreal bird species. The vast, high-altitude, rolling terrain is the remaining stronghold of Lynx (and the Snowshoe Hares they prey on) south of Canada. Nearby are riparian habitats, lakes, and marshes. Moose are increasing and becoming regular in the willow-studded meadows and bogs.

From Conconully Road (Main Street) in Conconully, go west on West Fork Road, continuing past the entrance to the state park (page 440). After you leave Conconully Reservoir, bird the riparian area and begin ascending the South Fork of Salmon Creek through forests of Douglas-fir, Western Larch, and Ponderosa Pine. At the next junction (3.1 miles), keep right on FR-37 (marked *Winthrop*) and continue uphill. (Going left here on FR-42 brings you to Loup Loup, described in the preceding section, in 16 miles.) Look for Williamson's Sapsucker, especially as you enter the Okanogan National Forest where Western Larches are numerous (2.4 miles). The road continues steadily up to **McCay Creek** (10.5 miles), where Engelmann Spruce and Subalpine Fir furnish the first suitable habitat on the route for Spruce Grouse and Boreal Owl.

Views of the many granite peaks become spectacular as you approach **Baldy Pass** (1.8 miles, elevation 6,367 feet). Stop here and walk around to look for Spruce Grouse, Boreal Owl (better bet at a pullout a half-mile farther ahead), Three-toed Woodpecker, Gray Jay, Clark's Nutcracker, Boreal Chickadee, Winter Wren, Ruby-crowned Kinglet, Hermit and Varied Thrushes, and Slate-colored Fox Sparrow. From the pass, the road winds west down the mountain for 5.6 miles to a junction with FR-39. Continuing straight ahead on FR-37 from this junction for 12 miles, then turning left onto East Chewuch Road, will bring you down the Chewuch River drainage to Winthrop (page 430) in 20 miles total.

Go right (north) on FR-39 for 1.5 miles to the **Roger Lake** spur, on the right (may not be well marked). The wet fen surrounding the lake, rimmed by a dense Engelmann Spruce forest, is recognized as an area of many unusual boreal plants. A walk around the lake, though not easy (littered with fallen logs and boggy in places; wear rubber boots), is an excellent way to observe boreal species in a superb setting. Spruce Grouse, Boreal Owl, Three-toed Woodpecker, Gray Jay, Clark's Nutcracker, Boreal Chickadee, and Lincoln's Sparrow all breed in the area. White-winged Crossbills irrupt from Canada at unpredictable intervals; invasion years see an influx beginning in July and lasting through the following winter. Although ongoing logging changes the birding possibilities in these forests, Roger Lake has been set aside as a Natural Area, as has nearby Tiffany Mountain. Beginning in 2000, an outbreak of Spruce Bark Beetle has killed many mature spruces, creating a short-term bonanza for Three-toed Woodpeckers.

Continuing north on FR-39 from Roger Lake, the road climbs steeply to **Freezeout Pass** (1.8 miles, elevation 6,600 feet). A worthwhile two-mile hike to the 8,245-foot summit of **Tiffany Mountain** begins here. Species to look for include Spruce Grouse (near parking area), White-tailed Ptarmigan (scarce, above treeline), Blue Grouse (especially openings on south aspects), Clark's Nutcracker (often near Whitebark Pines), Common Raven, Horned Lark, Boreal Chickadee (near pass), Townsend's Solitaire, American Pipit (wet swales), Bohemian Waxwing (feeds on Common Juniper berries above treeline, especially late October), Lapland Longspur (fall), Snow Bunting (mainly November), and Gray-crowned Rosy-Finch. The fall raptor migration (August through October) can often be exciting from these slopes. In October a magnificent display of color from the scattered Subalpine Larches is an added treat.

From the pass, descend 4.0 miles to **Tiffany Spring Campground** (USFS, primitive). From here a trail climbs past Tiffany Lake to Middle Tiffany Mountain (elevation 7,967 feet), another good fall raptor lookout. The initial mile is through towering Engelmann Spruce (Three-toed Woodpecker, Boreal Chickadee). White-tailed Ptarmigan are perhaps easier to find on Middle Tiffany than on Tiffany Mountain. In late fall, look for flocks of Gray-crowned Rosy-Finches in the cirque basin north of the peak.

TWENTYMILE AND THIRTYMILE MEADOWS

North from Tiffany Spring, FR-39 traverses a band of high-elevation Lodgepole Pine, Engelmann Spruce, and Subalpine Fir forest with meadows and boggy areas in valley bottoms. Northern Goshawk, Olive-sided Flycatcher, Ruby-crowned Kinglet, Hermit Thrush, Yellow-rumped Warbler, and Savannah and Lincoln's Sparrows are some of the many species that make use of these habitats. At 3.3 miles, Smarty Creek Trail leads downstream, reaching the first of the **South Twentymile Meadows** in a short distance.

Spruce Grouse hens and their broods frequent bottomlands along the trail, beginning in July. Keep left on FR-39 at the junction with FR-3810 to Lone Frank Pass (1.3 miles). The forest floor near this junction is another good place to look for Spruce Grouse munching the minute leaves of the Grouseberry (a type of huckleberry).

In 4.4 miles, go right onto FR-150 (becomes South Fork Toats Coulee Creek Road) into the Loomis State Forest. Bottomlands along this primitive road are excellent Spruce Grouse habitat, and there are several enticing meadows along the way; unfortunately, the area has been impacted by poor logging practices. Return to FR-39 and continue north, stopping in 1.4 miles to enjoy the view of Twentymile Meadows and the rugged crest of the Cascades off to the west. In another 3.2 miles **Thirtymile Meadows** are reached. Forests in this area were burned in the 1996 Thunder Mountain burn. Although the initial boom in woodpecker numbers has ended, Three-toeds remain fairly common; you may still find a few Black-backeds. The Dwarf Willow patches attract Mule Deer and the occasional Moose. In 4.0 miles, park at a pass and take the half-mile hike up **Corral Butte** (400 feet elevation gain) for another outstanding view of the entire region. Open slopes may have Blue Grouse and Townsend's Solitaire.

LONG SWAMP TO CHOPAKA MOUNTAIN

Ever northward, look for Spruce Grouse, Boreal Owl, and Boreal Chickadee as FR-39 descends steadily. Townsend's Warblers are common in ravines with tall spruces. Continue to **Long Swamp** (4.2 miles), an extensive area of bog and willow-grown marsh hemmed in by Engelmann Spruce and Subalpine Fir. Boreal Owl, Boreal Chickadee, Ruby-crowned Kinglet, Wilson's Warbler, and Lincoln's Sparrow are regular here, as are Moose and Lynx; the latter may occasionally be seen when driving the road at night. A few hundred yards after the tiny campground, a spur road on the left (FR-300) parallels the north side of the wetland for two miles. The main road (FR-39) goes right from this intersection, following the swamp toward the east. A dirt spur (FR-375) on the right in 1.9 miles gives access to lower reaches of Long Swamp (Willow Flycatcher, Northern Waterthrush).

Keep east on FR-39 (becomes Toats Coulee Road), descending until reaching a junction marked *Iron Gate Trailhead* (5.0 miles). This spur (FR-500) leads north to a trailhead offering a fabulous 4.5-mile hike to Sunny Pass, gateway to the **Horseshoe Basin** region of the eastern Pasayten Wilderness Area (530,000 acres). This trip is best done as a backpack. Outfitters are available in any of the surrounding towns to facilitate travel to this remarkable region, considered by many naturalists the crown jewel of Washington's alpine. Once at the pass, it is another mile into the heart of the meadows and two or three miles farther still to various alpine summits—all straightforward rambles on tundra and sketchy trails. These high, rounded summits—markedly different from the jagged peaks of the North Cascades some 35 miles to the west—were enveloped in ice and smoothed over during the Pleistocene. Alpine-zone vegetation is better developed in the Horseshoe Basin than anywhere else in Washington, bringing to mind that of many Colorado alpine areas; a number of unusual plants have been documented here. Spruce Grouse, White-tailed Ptarmigan, Boreal Owl, Three-toed Woodpecker, Boreal Chickadee, American Pipit, Gray-crowned Rosy-Finch, Pine Grosbeak, and White-winged Crossbill (irregular) are all expected. Other interesting species include Northern Harrier (may breed), Golden Eagle, Prairie Falcon, Wilson's Snipe, Olive-sided Flycatcher, Gray Jay, Clark's Nutcracker, Common Raven, Horned Lark, Mountain Chickadee, Red-breasted Nuthatch, Rock and Winter Wrens, Golden-crowned and Ruby-crowned Kinglets, Mountain Bluebird, Townsend's Solitaire, Hermit and Varied Thrushes, Yellow-rumped and Townsend's Warblers, Vesper (uncommon), Savannah, Fox, Lincoln's, and White-crowned Sparrows, Cassin's Finch, and Red Crossbill.

Farther down Toats Coulee Road is an intersection with Fourteen Mile Road (5.8 miles from FR-500). Turn left (north). Keep right at 0.4 mile, left in another 3.8 miles and again left at 1.2 miles. In another 1.1 miles is the Cold Springs Campground. Beyond, in 0.2 mile, turn right into the parking at the trailhead for **Chopaka Mountain Natural Area Preserve** (2,764 acres), which protects 14 state-sensitive plant species, including Few-flowered Shooting Star and a number of rare sedges, gentians, moonworts, and cinquefoils. A four-mile hike on an old mining track leads to the summit (7,800 feet). Palmer Lake lies nearly 6,600 feet below, straight down the escarpment. White-tailed Ptarmigan are found with some regularity on alpine meadows on the north side of the summit, and Horned Lark is reliable. If you are not in a hiking mood, drive past the trail turnoff for 0.4 mile to **Vista Overlook**. Expansive views of the Pasayten country to the west are your reward after a short stroll on this wheelchair-accessible trail. In the forest nearby, look for Spruce and Blue Grouse and Boreal Chickadee.

From Fourteen Mile Road, Toats Coulee Road descends in 7.4 miles to irrigated hay fields on the Sinlahekin Valley floor, where a large colony of Bobolinks can be seen (best late May through mid-July). In another half-mile reach the Loomis-Oroville Road, two miles north of Loomis (page 441).

BRITISH COLUMBIA CASCADES

In summer and early autumn, birders heading north into British Columbia to seek boreal species will want to consider two excellent parks in the Cascade Range along the Canada-U.S. border between Vancouver and Osoyoos.

Manning Provincial Park (175,000 acres) straddles the Cascade crest at the headwaters of the Skagit River (west slope) and the Similkameen River (draining to the Okanogan). Highway 3 bisects the park, providing easy year-round access. Coming from Hope it is 16 miles to the West Gate, an-

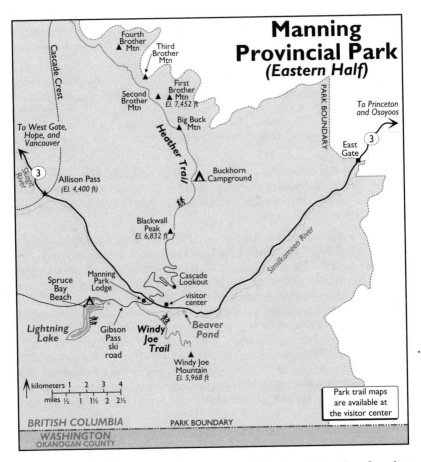

Manning
Provincial Park
(Eastern Half)

Cascade Crest

Fourth
Brother
Mtn

Third
Brother
Mtn

First
Brother
▲ Mtn
El. 7,452 ft

Second
Brother
Mtn

Big Buck
▲ Mtn

PARK BOUNDARY

To Princeton
and Osoyoos

To West Gate,
Hope, and
Vancouver

Heather Trail

East
Gate

3

Skagit River

3

Allison Pass
(El. 4,400 ft)

Buckhorn
Campground

Blackwall
Peak
El. 6,832 ft

Similkameen River

Spruce
Bay
Beach

Manning
Park
Lodge

Cascade
Lookout

visitor
center

Lightning
Lake

Gibson
Pass
ski
road

Windy
Joe
Trail

Beaver
Pond

Windy Joe
Mountain
El. 5,968 ft

kilometers 1   2   3   4
miles ½   1 1½ 2 2½

Park trail maps
are available at
the visitor center

BRITISH COLUMBIA   PARK BOUNDARY
WASHINGTON
OKANOGAN COUNTY

other 20 miles to Allison Pass (elevation 4,400 feet), and six miles after that down the east slope to the visitor center, where you may obtain maps and trail information. Coming from Princeton it is 32 miles to the East Gate and another 10 miles to the visitor center. This popular park has campgrounds (fee) as well as a lodge and other commercial facilities. Gas pumps and a convenience mart are located just outside East Gate.

Several good areas for boreal and mountain birds are reached from Manning Park Lodge (0.5 mile west of the visitor center) by following signs along the Gibson Pass ski road. Spruce Grouse, Clark's Nutcracker, and Boreal Chickadee are regularly seen on the good, four-mile trail up **Windy Joe Mountain**. The trailhead—marked *Windy Joe/Pacific Crest Parking*—is a short distance south of the lodge. **Lightning Lake** is three miles west of the lodge on the Gibson Pass ski road. From Lightning Lake Campground and Spruce Bay Beach a graded trail encircles the lake in boreal habitats with Engelmann

Spruce, Subalpine Fir, and Lodgepole Pine. Look for Barrow's Goldeneye, Osprey, Three-toed Woodpecker, Boreal Chickadee, and Pine Grosbeak.

North from the lodge a 10-mile road with many switchbacks leads past Cascade Lookout to a parking area and trailhead amidst subalpine meadows at Blackwall Peak (elevation 6,832 feet). The **Heather Trail** goes north seven miles from here—a very long day trip (better as a backpack) to the Three Brothers where White-tailed Ptarmigan and American Pipit breed. Northern Hawk Owl has nested at Buckhorn Campground about 2.5 miles along the trail.

Beaver Pond, excellent in early morning, is 0.3 mile east of the visitor center on the south side of Highway 3. Look for Olive-sided Flycatcher, Tree Swallow, Yellow Warbler, Common Yellowthroat, Lincoln's Sparrow, and Pine Grosbeak.

Forty miles east of Princeton (two miles west of Keremeos), the access road to **Cathedral Provincial Park** turns off south from Highway 3. (See map on page 445.) The 83,000-acre park is a wilderness area, without supplies of any kind; motor vehicles, mountain bikes, and pets are not permitted. Drive the access road along the Ashnola River and leave your vehicle at the Cathedral Lakes Resort Basecamp (13.0 miles). Veteran hikers might entertain taking one of the trails from here to the high country (minimum of 10 miles and 4,000 feet up!), but most visitors take the jeep transportation ($75 Cdn round-trip in 2002) to Cathedral Lakes Lodge in the heart of the park at 6,800 feet elevation. In this region of boreal forests, glacial lakes, extensive alpine meadows, and granite peaks, day-trippers can find subalpine birds with relative ease. But you will need to stay at least one night to work the alpine habitats effectively.

The resort—lodge, cabins, and amenities (*www.cathedral-lakes-lodge.com*, toll-free 888-255-4453)—offers a superb getaway. The first of several wilderness campsites (first-come, first-served) is a five-minute walk from the lodge, set in dense forests of Engelmann Spruce, Subalpine Fir, Lodgepole and Whitebark Pines, and Subalpine Larch (golden-yellow in September). In these woods, Spruce Grouse, Three-toed Woodpecker, Boreal Chickadee, and Hermit and Varied Thrushes are common. Boreal Owl has also been found nearby.

A well-developed trail system leads farther afield to good areas for alpine specialties—not just birds but also butterflies at or near the southern limits of their distribution (such as the sought-after Labrador Sulphur). Recommended is the **Cathedral Rim Trail** via Red Mountain. Just before the final push to the summit, where the trail becomes very rocky at about 7,500 feet elevation, veer off to the right (northeast) and amble about the alpine tundra. Look for White-tailed Ptarmigan, Horned Lark, American Pipit, and Gray-crowned Rosy-Finch along the edge of the meadows near lingering snowbanks, and for Savannah Sparrow in nearby willows. Fox and White-crowned Sparrows occur in the willow thickets as one descends on the Diamond Trail. Another fine trail for alpine birds climbs to Lakeview Mountain (elevation 8,628 feet). White-tailed Ptarmigan, Prairie Falcon, and Mountain Goat are seen regularly along the popular loop trail that leads to Ladyslipper and Glacier Lakes and the southern limb of the Rim Trail. Beginning in late August, watch for migrating raptors anywhere in the high, open country.

OKANOGAN HIGHLANDS

by Andy Stepniewski

East of the Okanogan River lies a terrain of ancient gneiss, schist, and granitic bedrock smoothed over by glaciation. Once a large island—the Okanogan subcontinent—this territory became embedded in the North American continent that moved westward and collided with it some 100 million years ago. Kettle Falls is about on the east coast of the former island; the Columbia River flows through a trench where the two plates engaged. Tonasket is on the island's other coast—the west coast of the North American landmass until 70–50 million years ago when another subcontinent, the North Cascades, collided and docked. The Okanogan Valley is the remnant of the trench on the ocean floor where these two plates met. Coincident with the latter event, a massive magma flow pushed up the older continental crust of gneiss many miles east of the trench. The resultant Okanogan Dome—a granite intrusion some 20 miles across—forms the core of the Okanogan Highlands.

Habitats are varied in this scenic region: shrub-steppe and Ponderosa Pine forests at valley-bottom elevations; open grasslands and Douglas-fir/Western Larch forests at higher and moister elevations, interrupted by marshes and glacial lakes; and higher still, stands of Engelmann Spruce and alder and willow thickets in cold swales. Of the many breeding birds, some have boreal affinities (e.g., Common Loon, Great Gray Owl); non-breeding visitors of interest to birders include Snow Bunting, White-winged Crossbill (irregular), and Common Redpoll.

The most productive birding areas extend north from SR-20 to the U.S.-Canada border. This is a remote region; once you leave US-97 in the Okanogan Valley, services are few. The main roads are kept open in winter and are usually well sanded. Nonetheless, make sure you are properly equipped if contemplating a winter visit. Carry chains, a shovel, and cold-weather survival supplies (extra clothing, extra food, sleeping bags). Four-wheel drive, though not absolutely necessary, may be reassuring.

TONASKET TO MOLSON

At the north end of Tonasket on US-97, bear east onto Whitcomb Avenue, which merges into Jonathan Street, then becomes **Havillah Road** (Tonasket-Havillah Road on some maps) as it leaves town and begins climbing out of the Okanogan Valley. In early summer check for Bobolinks in the irrigated fields on the left side of the road (3.6 miles). Ahead, while ascending a long slope, begin looking for Western Bluebirds as you enter a scattered forest of Ponderosa Pine (3.5 miles). Still farther, a denser stand of pines on the right side of road at 5.9 miles can be good for White-breasted and Pygmy Nuthatches and Red Crossbill. Open fields from here up—and throughout the region—are excellent for raptors. In summer check for Northern Harrier, Swainson's and Red-tailed Hawks, Golden Eagle, and American Kestrel, and in winter for Rough-legged Hawk and the occasional Gyrfalcon.

At the **Highland Sno-Park** sign (2.2 miles), turn right onto FR-3230, a gravel road that winds south through a mosaic of fields and forests—excellent Great Gray Owl habitat. Begin looking at the end of the meadow beyond the third cattle guard (0.5 mile), especially at dawn and dusk. A particularly good area for this rare, highly local breeding species has been the selectively logged Douglas-fir and Western Larch forest south of the fourth cattle guard (0.4 mile). Walk south from here on the old logging roads (cross-country ski trails in winter). Watch also for Williamson's Sapsucker (early April through September), Hairy, Three-toed, Black-backed (uncommon), and Pileated Woodpeckers, and Northern Flicker. Continue driving uphill on FR-3230. Turn right onto FR-260, signed *Highland Sno-Park* (0.4 mile), and park at the gate (0.1 mile). Great Gray Owls have been seen here regularly. Listen for Barred and Northern Saw-whet Owls after dark (Boreal Owl was heard here one cold March night).

Return to Havillah Road and turn right, passing the village of Havillah (0.6 mile) with its imposing Lutheran church, testimony to the hardy settlers who farmed this area in the late 1800s. Beyond Havillah is another area of grasslands, excellent in winter for Rough-legged Hawk and Gray-crowned Rosy-Finch. At the next junction (2.7 miles), turn left (north) toward Chesaw on Havillah Road (Kipling Road on some maps). Beyond the **Sitzmark Ski Area** (1.1 miles), turn right (east) onto Hungry Hollow Road and go 0.2 mile to a dense grove of Engelmann Spruce and Quaking Aspen, a fine place to find White-winged Crossbills in invasion years (typically late July through winter). Listen for their loud, staccato *chif...chif...chif* call with an inflective quality quite different from the strident, harder notes of most Red Crossbills. Search also for Northern Pygmy-Owl and Pine Grosbeak, especially in winter. Great Gray Owls have nested nearby on fenced, private land (no access, but birds are sometimes seen from the road). Willow Flycatcher and Northern Waterthrush nest in an alder swamp on the downhill side of the road.

Return to Havillah Road and turn right, stopping at an overlook above **Muskrat Lake** (0.6 mile) with a beautiful view of the Okanogan Highlands. Scope the lake and margins for nesting waterfowl, Red-necked and Eared Grebes, Tree Swallow, Mountain Bluebird, and Vesper Sparrow. In winter, the snowy fields attract Rough-legged Hawks and Snow Buntings. Continuing north on Havillah Road, in winter check the vicinity of several cattle feedlots beginning in 1.4 miles for Northern Goshawk, Rough-legged Hawk, Golden Eagle, American Tree Sparrow (roadside weeds), Snow Bunting, Gray-crowned Rosy-Finch, and Snow Bunting.

In 1.6 miles Havillah Road meets Chesaw Road (aka Oroville-Toroda Creek Road; turning left here will bring you to Oroville and US-97 in a dozen miles, page 442). Continue ahead on Davies Road to reach **Teal Lake** (2.0 miles). Red-necked Grebe, Ring-necked Duck, Ruby-crowned Kinglet, and Gray Jay are representative of the many species found on and around the lake. North of Teal Lake, turn left (west) onto Fletcher Road (0.7 mile) and go steeply down to Molson Road (2.0 miles), passing another area of grasslands. Turn right to the all-but-abandoned mining town of Molson (1.5 miles). During its brief heyday in the early 1900s Molson was the terminus for a railway, at that time the highest in the state. The open fields around town are excellent in summer for Swainson's Hawk, Say's Phoebe, and Mountain Bluebird, and in winter for Snow Bunting and Common Redpoll (weedy areas).

Continuing northwest out of town, Molson Road becomes Ninemile Road (the former railroad grade). For the next two miles, a string of shallow lakes known as the **Molson Lakes** hosts Common Loon (apparently non-breeders), Red-necked Grebe, many waterfowl (including Canvasback), and Yellow-headed Blackbird in the warmer months. The lakes are usually frozen in winter except for a small patch of open water at the west end of the westernmost lake that sometimes attracts Bufflehead and Common Goldeneye. Within the following two miles the road turns west and follows a fenceline on the U.S.-Canada border where you may find Northern Pygmy-Owl and Pygmy Nuthatch in the pines.

CHESAW TO BONAPARTE LAKE

On the southern outskirts of Molson, turn east toward Chesaw on Mary Ann Creek Road (aka Molson Summit Road). Keep left with this road at a fork in 2.9 miles, passing through a region of Engelmann Spruce and Quaking Aspen on north slopes and valley bottoms, and Douglas-fir on south-facing slopes. The spruces have breeding Ruby-crowned Kinglet, the deciduous bottom-lands Ruffed Grouse. Beginning in 3.0 miles and continuing for the next 2.0 miles to the intersection with Chesaw Road (aka Oroville-Toroda Creek Road), the 2,480-acre **Chesaw Wildlife Area** protects habitat for a remnant population of Sharp-tailed Grouse (but Gray Partridge and Ruffed Grouse are more common here). Grasslands on the left (east) side of the road are nesting habitat; wintering habitat is in the riparian growth on the right. Sharp-taileds are especially fond of the buds of Water Birch, identifiable from its distinctive copper-colored bark; seed cones of this tall shrub also attract Common Redpolls some winters.

Turn left at the intersection; it is 2.1 miles east to the center of the village of Chesaw. Keep straight ahead onto Bolster Road. For the next three miles the road parallels alder- and willow-lined **Myers Creek**, an excellent place in late spring and early summer for American Redstart, Northern Waterthrush, Common Yellowthroat, and Lincoln's Sparrow. Ruby-crowned Kinglets are common in patches of Engelmann Spruce. This is all private land, so you must bird from the road; creek noise is an added challenge. In winter, check the Mountain Alder and Water Birch thickets around Chesaw for Common Redpoll (erratic).

Return to Chesaw, turn left onto Chesaw Road, and travel 2.3 miles to an intersection on the right with Myers Creek Road (aka Lost Lake Road). This road (closed by snow in winter) follows Myers Creek upstream, becoming FR-34 as it enters the Okanogan National Forest (3.1 miles). At a four-way intersection (1.7 miles) take FR-050, following signs to Lost Lake. In 0.4 mile, just before the Lost Lake Campground entrance, turn left (south) with FR-050, proceed 0.5 mile, and park at a slight rise overlooking **Lost Lake** and adjacent marsh, where Common Loon and Black Tern usually nest. Williamson's Sapsucker can be found in the campground; watch also for Three-toed Woodpecker.

Return to Chesaw Road and turn right. For the next 7.2 miles to Beaver Lake Campground the road passes through a succession of interesting habitats. First comes a forest-rimmed meadow (Great Gray Owl has been seen here), followed by a mature forest of Douglas-fir and Engelmann Spruce in a deep gorge (Northern Goshawk, Northern Pygmy-Owl, Barred Owl). Finally **Beth Lake** and **Beaver Lake** have nesting Red-necked Grebe, Barrow's Goldeneye, Black Tern, and many other wetland birds. From Beaver Lake Campground at night, listen for Flammulated Owl "booting" from the steep, south-facing slopes north of the campground and Barred Owl hooting from the dense, old-growth forests on the steep ridges to the south.

FR-32 turns right at a fork next to the campground. In summer you may drive this road south from Beaver Lake to Bonaparte Lake (following paragraph). When winter snow closes the gravel forest roads, continue instead on Chesaw Road to its end in about four miles at a T-intersection with Toroda Creek Road. Go right here and ascend the Toroda Creek valley to reach SR-20 at Wauconda in about 14 miles. Great Gray and Northern Pygmy-Owls have been seen in fields and forest edges at various places along this route. Northern Saw-whet Owls call from the hillsides in late winter, and flocks of Common Redpolls sometimes feed along the weedy roadsides. From Wauconda it is 3.5 miles west on SR-20 to the intersection with Bonaparte Lake Road.

Except in winter, you may turn right (southwest) onto FR-32 at Beaver Lake Campground and drive south to Bonaparte Lake. Stay left with FR-32 at the fork with FR-33 in 3.2 miles. In another 1.4 miles, turn left (east) onto FR-3240, marked **Virginia Lilly Nature Trail**. Drive this road slowly at dawn or dusk, watching for Great Gray Owl. Park at the nature trail parking lot (spur on the left in 6.6 miles). The loop trail (may be overgrown in places) goes through Douglas-fir and Engelmann Spruce forests, with marsh and pond habitats. Black-backed Woodpeckers have been seen here.

Bonaparte Lake Campground, another 1.3 miles down FR-32, is a good base for exploring this part of the Okanogan country. Bonaparte Lake itself is usually not too productive, but the surrounding forests have Flammulated Owl. South from the campground, FR-32 becomes Bonaparte Lake Road (open year round) and continues past peat bogs with Virginia Rail, Sora, and Wilson's Snipe, reaching SR-20 in five-plus miles. From this corner it is 20 miles west to Tonasket or 20 miles east to Republic (page 463).

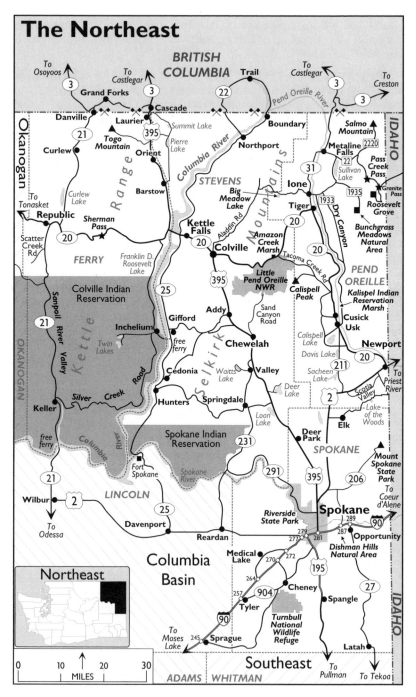

The Northeast

BRITISH COLUMBIA

To Osoyoos
3

To Castlegar
3

Trail
22

To Castlegar
3

Pend Oreille River

To Creston
3

Grand Forks

Danville

Cascade

Laurier

395

Summit Lake

Pierre Lake

Togo Mountain

Orient

Curlew

Barstow

Columbia River

Northport

Boundary

Salmo Mountain

Metaline Falls
2220

22
Sullivan Lake

Pass Creek Pass

STEVENS

Big Meadow Lake

31

Ione

1935

Granite Pass

Roosevelt Grove

Curlew Lake

Republic
20

Sherman Pass

Aladdin Rd

Tiger
1933

Dry Canyon

Bunchgrass Meadows Natural Area

Scatter Creek Rd

FERRY

Franklin D. Roosevelt Lake

Kettle Falls
20

Colville

Amazon Creek Marsh
20

Tacoma Creek Rd
20

PEND OREILLE

Colville Indian Reservation

Kettle

25

395

Little Pend Oreille NWR

Sand Canyon Road

Calispell Peak

Kalispel Indian Reservation Marsh

Sampoil River Valley

21

Gifford

Inchelium

free ferry

Addy

Chewelah

Cusick

Usk

Calispell Lake

Twin Lakes

Selkirk

Valley

Davis Lake

Newport
20

Keller

Cedonia

Silver Creek

Hunters

Road

Waitts Lake

Springdale

Deer Lake

Sacheen Lake

211

2

Scotia Valley

To Priest River

Lake of the Woods

Columbia River

Spokane Indian Reservation

231

Loon Lake

Deer Park

Elk

SPOKANE

Mount Spokane State Park

free ferry

Fort Spokane

Spokane River

291

395

206

To Coeur d'Alene

21

Wilbur
2

LINCOLN

25

Davenport

Reardan

Riverside State Park

279
277

281

289

287

Spokane

90

Opportunity

Dishman Hills Natural Area

Medical Lake

270
272

264

257

904

Tyler

90

Cheney

195

Spangle

27

IDAHO

Columbia Basin

Turnbull National Wildlife Refuge

Latah

To Moses Lake

245

Sprague

To Pullman

To Tekoa

Southeast

ADAMS   WHITMAN

Northeast

0   10   20   30
MILES

OKANOGAN

THE NORTHEAST

Northeast of the Columbia Basin lies a dramatically different landscape. The arid Basin, with its geologically young plateau basalts overlain by a mantle of undulating shrub-steppe, pothole lakes, and Ponderosa Pine forests, ends abruptly at the Columbia and Spokane Rivers, at an elevation of about 1,500 feet. North from these rivers, three main north-south-trending ridge systems composed of much older metamorphic and granitic rocks rise to a little over 7,000 feet. These mountains—from west to east, the Kettle Range and two ridges of the Selkirk Mountains—are divided by the broad, glacier-carved valleys of the Sanpoil, Kettle, Columbia (now mostly flooded by Franklin D. Roosevelt Lake), and Pend Oreille Rivers.

Precipitation in the region increases with gain in elevation from the Columbia Basin, and also on a southwest-to-northeast gradient. Spokane, for example, gets about 18 inches annually, Ione in the northeast corner about twice as much. The higher peaks get upwards of 60 inches, much of it in the form of snow that lingers into July in an average year. Parts of the Selkirks in the extreme northeast corner are moist enough that forest communities resemble those of the west slopes of the Cascades. A critical difference from coastal climes is a higher frequency of summer thunderstorms that results in many fires. A past history of fire is revealed on virtually every mountainside in this part of the state, except on the higher, north-facing slopes.

The lower foothills, and the scablands around Spokane, have open stands of Ponderosa Pine. Forests of Douglas-fir, Grand Fir, Western Larch, and Engelmann Spruce are common at mid-elevations. Dense, even-aged Lodgepole Pine stands now typify many forests—a result of past fires. Lush riparian corridors line the major north-south rivers. Elsewhere in the valley bottoms, hay farming and cattle ranching are the dominant land use.

A large part of northeastern Washington's forests has been logged. Recognition of the aesthetic and non-timber value of these forests heightened in the 1980s, too late to assure protection for significant parcels. There is, however, lots of interesting habitat remaining, particularly in riparian corridors, where a number of "eastern" passerines occur. Logged-over areas show a diverse deciduous component, also rich in breeding birds. Lakes and marshes have many breeding waterfowl, and the subalpine forests hold a number of sought-after boreal bird species.

Compared to the rest of the state, the Northeast has a long, cold winter, less moderated by mild Pacific weather systems. Outbreaks of arctic air from north and east of the Rocky Mountains spill into the region with greater frequency and intensity, bringing sub-zero temperatures. January average low temperatures are 22 degrees at Republic and 29 degrees at Spokane. The mostly dry snow comes in moderate quantities. Main highways are well plowed and sanded; indeed, winter driving is quite often easier here than in milder parts of the state. If traveling in winter, it is always advisable to have emergency food, extra clothing, and a sleeping bag stashed in your vehicle.

Summer is characterized by more rainfall than elsewhere in Eastern Washington; violent thunderstorms do occur. July and August see a good number of bothersome insects anywhere near standing water or in forests. Summer days are hot (average July high temperatures 81 degrees in Republic, 86 in Spokane) but nights are cooler, especially in the mountains.

Services and accommodations are available in the Spokane metropolitan area, and also in the smaller communities of Cheney, Chewelah, Colville, Ione, Kettle Falls, Metaline Falls, Newport, Republic, and Usk.

Its throat pouch full of Whitebark Pine seeds, a Clark's Nutcracker will cache its harvest in the ground. What isn't retrieved will often germinate, propagating new stands of this favorite food source.

KETTLE RANGE

by Andy Stepniewski

Republic, an old mining town, provides the jumpoff for several birding routes. South along SR-21 through the Sanpoil River valley one encounters exceptional riparian habitats that support several "eastern" bird species. Near the south end of this route one can go east for 50 miles on the Silver Creek Road, a superb birding trail through a mosaic of habitats. East from Republic, SR-20 crosses the Kettle Range at Sherman Pass, with opportunities for boreal species. The descent of the east slope is also good for birds of riparian habitats. From the Columbia River other options abound, including the Kettle River valley and Togo Mountain to the north, or east across the Columbia to Colville and the Little Pend Oreille (page 473).

SANPOIL RIVER VALLEY

SR-21 runs down the Sanpoil River valley some 50 miles from Republic to Keller Ferry. This relatively lightly-traveled route offers outstanding birding during the breeding season (May–July), when a morning's effort should net 85 or 90 species. Extensive riparian habitats alternate with dry, open Ponderosa Pine forests and wetter forests of Douglas-fir; short side trips lead to mountain lakes. Some of the northern part of the route lies within the Colville National Forest. The southern four-fifths is in the Colville Indian Reservation, 1.4 million acres of forested mountains, rangeland, and lakes. This reservation is home to 12 different tribes, all shoehorned together in 1872 by President Grant in an executive order. Birders may visit the reservation freely. Camping, fishing, or hunting require permits.

The Sanpoil River winds through a dramatic valley known in geologic parlance as a graben—an elongate, depressed block between the raised Okanogan Highlands mountain block on the west and the Kettle Dome on the east. In places, tall cliffs loom over the highway. Everywhere, the landscape reveals the recent action of ice-age glaciers that overrode the mountaintops and molded the valleys into broad, U-shaped troughs. This is gold- and silver-mining country. Since the late 1800s, various mines have yielded over 2.5 million ounces of gold and 14 million ounces of silver. A few mines are still producing, and others are proposed.

Begin at the junction of SR-20 and SR-21 on the southern outskirts of Republic. (Alert: the gas stations and convenience marts at this junction are the last dependable services until Wilbur, nearly 70 miles south.) Go south on SR-21 for 0.4 mile and make a sharp left, then take the first right in a few hundred feet to the **Republic sewage ponds**, which lie 0.2 mile along this gravel road. You must scope the ponds from the road. Expect dabbling and diving ducks, and sometimes phalaropes.

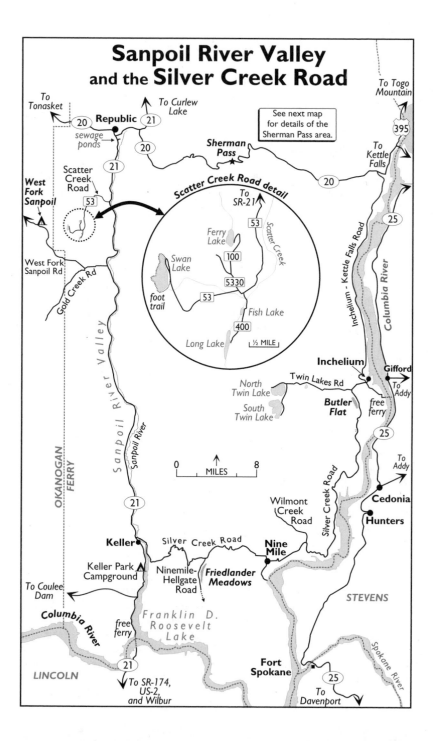

Sanpoil River Valley
and the Silver Creek Road

To Togo
Mountain

To
Tonasket

To Curlew
Lake

Republic

See next map
for details of the
Sherman Pass area.

sewage
ponds

Sherman
Pass

To
Kettle
Falls

Scatter
Creek
Road

Scatter Creek Road detail

West
Fork
Sanpoil

To
SR-21

Ferry
Lake

Scatter Creek

West Fork
Sanpoil Rd

Swan
Lake

foot
trail

Gold Creek Rd

Fish Lake

½ MILE

Long Lake

Inchelium

Gifford

North
Twin Lake

Twin Lakes Rd

To
Addy

Butler
Flat

South
Twin Lake

free
ferry

OKANOGAN
FERRY

Sanpoil River Valley

Sanpoil River

0   8
MILES

To
Addy

Wilmont
Creek
Road

Cedonia

Hunters

Keller

Silver Creek Road

Nine
Mile

Keller Park
Campground

Ninemile-
Hellgate
Road

Friedlander
Meadows

STEVENS

To Coulee
Dam

Columbia River

free
ferry

Franklin D.
Roosevelt
Lake

LINCOLN

Fort
Spokane

Spokane River

To SR-174,
US-2,
and Wilbur

To
Davenport

Inchelium - Kettle Falls Road

Columbia River

Silver Creek Road

Return to SR-21, turn left, and go 6.5 miles to **Scatter Creek Road** (FR-53). Turn right here for a series of small mountain lakes with primitive campgrounds in a forested setting. The rich riparian zone along Scatter Creek is worth checking en route if traffic is not too heavy, especially early in the morning. Swainson's Thrush is common, and many other birds of the moist coniferous forest should be found. Turn left in 5.6 miles onto FR-400 to reach Fish and Long Lakes. From where the road ends in about a mile, take the hiking trail to look for nesting Barrow's Goldeneyes on **Long Lake**. Return to FR-53 and turn left. Turn right in 0.1 mile onto FR-5330. In another 0.3 mile, bear right onto FR-100 to the access to **Ferry Lake** (1.2 miles), which has hosted nesting Common Loons. These birds are sensitive to human encroachment; please avoid disturbing them. Return again to FR-53 and turn right to **Swan Lake** (1.6 miles). Here, waterfowl and Osprey can be found, as well as birds of the moist forest. Take time to walk the mile-and-a-half trail that encircles this pretty mountain lake, birding marshy edges, alder thickets, and moist conifer forest. The trail begins a few hundred yards before the boat launch and ends at the far end of the campground.

Return to SR-21, turn right, and go 7.6 miles to Gold Creek Road, on the right. Park here and scan the high cliffs on the east side of the highway for Golden Eagle, White-throated Swift, and Clark's Nutcracker. A detour along forest roads leads to an old campground known locally as **West Fork Sanpoil**. Take Gold Creek Road 2.5 miles to a fork just before a bridge, then go right onto unmarked West Fork Sanpoil Road. In another 6.6 miles FR-205, on the right, goes into the campground. Look for American Redstart, Northern Waterthrush, and other birds of wet-forest habitats in the alder-dominated, boggy terrain along the creek. If you want to head across into the Okanogan country, the West Fork Sanpoil Road connects northwest from here via the Aeneas Valley Road to SR-20 in about 23 miles. The hayfield just before the SR-20 intersection is excellent for Bobolinks (June and July). The Bonaparte Lake Road turnoff (page 459) is 7.6 miles east on SR-20 and Tonasket (page 456) about 12 miles west.

The riparian habitat along the **Sanpoil River valley** for the next 20 miles or so south from the Gold Creek Road intersection is probably unmatched in Eastern Washington for both extent and quality. Birding beside the road is a sound strategy to experience this habitat. Make stops as often as you have time for. There are a number of obvious access points on abandoned gravel lanes and on side roads with bridges that cross the river. Traffic is usually light, but do take care to find a safe pullout. Dominated by Black Cottonwood, various willows, and Quaking Aspen as overstory trees, the riparian zone boasts a species-rich shrub-and-herb layer. There is probably more habitat here for "eastern" passerines than anywhere else in the state. Indeed, Eastern Kingbird, Red-eyed Vireo, Veery, Gray Catbird, and Northern Waterthrush are all common breeding species. Least Flycatcher and American Redstart, though far less common, can often be found as well. Other interesting species include Red-naped Sapsucker, Pileated Woodpecker, Willow, Hammond's, and Dusky Flycatchers, Warbling Vireo, Clark's Nutcracker (pines near cliffs), Violet-green Swallow, Pygmy Nuthatch (pines), Cedar Waxwing, Orange-crowned, Nashville, Yellow, and MacGillivray's Warblers, Common Yellowthroat, Yellow-breasted Chat, Black-headed Grosbeak, Lazuli Bunting, and Bullock's Oriole. The forested slopes away from the river have Calliope Hummingbird (easiest at feeders scattered about the residential areas of Republic), Hairy Woodpecker, Western Wood-Pewee, Steller's Jay, Mountain Chickadee, Nashville, Yellow-rumped, and Townsend's Warblers, and Western Tanager. Fields of hay along the road have many Savannah Sparrows and Red-winged and Brewer's Blackbirds. In 19 miles, one area of wet, grassy fields on the left (east) side of the highway may have a few Bobolinks.

From Gold Creek Road, it is about 29 miles to the intersection with Silver Creek Road at the north edge of Keller; birding possibilities along this road are described in the following section. Keeping south on SR-21 will bring you in 3.4 miles to **Keller Park Campground**, in the national recreation area along what used to be the lower reach of the Sanpoil River but is now an arm of Franklin D. Roosevelt Lake. Ospreys nest south of here and can often be seen cruising the shoreline. It is about seven more miles to **Keller Ferry** (free; operates 6AM to 11:45PM). Bald and Golden Eagles are often noted from the ferry, and a loon or two might be about. Once across the lake, it is about 14 miles on SR-21 to a junction with SR-174. Turn left here to reach Wilbur and US-2 in less than a mile.

SILVER CREEK ROAD

This splendid gradient winds for about 50 miles across the Colville Indian Reservation to Inchelium, passing through a variety of habitats: Ponderosa Pine, Douglas-fir, riparian, and mountain meadows. The road surface is good—gravel for the first 30 miles and pavement for the remainder. There are *no* services, and you will encounter few if any other vehicles. The starting point is from SR-21 at Keller. For about nine miles, the road climbs out of the Sanpoil River Valley, eventually reaching a burned area near the top of a series of switchbacks. Woodpeckers, including Hairy and White-headed, should be looked for here. Turn right down Ninemile-Hellgate Road (13.7 miles from SR-21). **Friedlander Meadows** stretch along the east side for more than two miles. Northern Goshawk, Great Gray Owl (two records, May–June), Williamson's Sapsucker, and Gray Jay are just a few of the tantalizing prospects in and around these beautiful, wet mountain meadows. Back at Silver Creek Road, turn right and continue the descent into the drainage basin of South Fork Ninemile Creek. Riparian habitats here attract species such as Red-naped Sapsucker, Olive-sided, Hammond's, and Pacific-slope Flycatchers, Brown Creeper, Veery, Swainson's Thrush, American Redstart, and Yellow-breasted Chat. In 13.2 miles, stop at the **Wilmont Creek Road** junction. Ponderosa Pine forest and grasslands around this corner and for a mile or so south have many birds, including American Kestrel, Mourning Dove, White-headed Woodpecker, Western Wood-Pewee, Dusky Flycatcher, Western Kingbird, Cassin's Vireo, Black-capped Chickadee, Red-breasted and Pygmy Nuthatches, House Wren, Western Bluebird, Western Tanager, Spotted Towhee, Chipping Sparrow, Lazuli Bunting, Western Meadowlark, and Cassin's Finch. Black Swifts have sometimes been seen in June in this general vicinity, suggesting the possibility of nearby nesting.

Continuing along Silver Creek Road, through yet more open Ponderosa Pine forest where Wild Turkeys should be looked for, you soon come into view of Franklin D. Roosevelt Lake. **Butler Flat**, a large sedge-and-cattail wetland (open water in wet seasons) is visible on the west at about 22 miles from the Wilmont Creek Road corner. Depending on water levels and the season, look for Tundra Swan, geese, scads of dabbling ducks, Northern Harrier, Bald Eagle, other raptors, Virginia Rail, Sora, Savannah Sparrow, and blackbirds. The intersection with Twin Lakes Road is about two miles ahead. By going left (west), you will reach the turnoff to North and South Twin Lakes in about eight miles. Common Loons nest on these lakes. Turning right onto Twin Lakes Road brings you in 1.6 miles to Inchelium. South from Inchelium, it is 2.7 miles to the free ferry to Gifford and SR-25 on the east shore of Franklin D. Roosevelt Lake (page 473). Alternatively, one can go north on the Inchelium-Kettle Falls Road to join SR-20 a few miles west of the US-395 junction and the Kettle Falls bridge (page 470).

SHERMAN PASS AND SHERMAN CREEK

The next route picks up once more in Republic. East from here, SR-20 ascends to Sherman Pass at the crest of the granitic Kettle Range, en route passing an impressive old burn, then winds its way down Sherman Creek toward the Columbia River and Colville. Sherman Pass reaches subalpine elevations and some boreal birding possibilities. Typical species of riparian and coniferous forest are definite attractions of this route. Where SR-20/SR-21 divide, three miles east of Republic, turn right with SR-20 and begin the long climb to Sherman Pass. Somewhat more than halfway to the summit the road enters the 20,000-acre, lightning-caused **White Mountain Burn**. An interpretive display (11 miles) explains the 1988 fire and its aftermath. The habitat here is in early stages of succession (brush). Willow Flycatcher, Orange-crowned and MacGillivray's Warblers, and Fox Sparrow are common. Pine Grosbeak might be looked for in winter.

The road surmounts **Sherman Pass** (elevation 5,575 feet) in another 3.3 miles amidst a forest of Lodgepole Pine, Subalpine Fir, and Engelmann Spruce. To explore boreal habits around the pass, continue east downhill one mile to **Sherman Pass Campground**, on the left. Drive to the west end of the campground loop and park. Trail 96 contours west from here, reaching a junction with Trail 82 in about one-half mile. Turn right to explore more of this

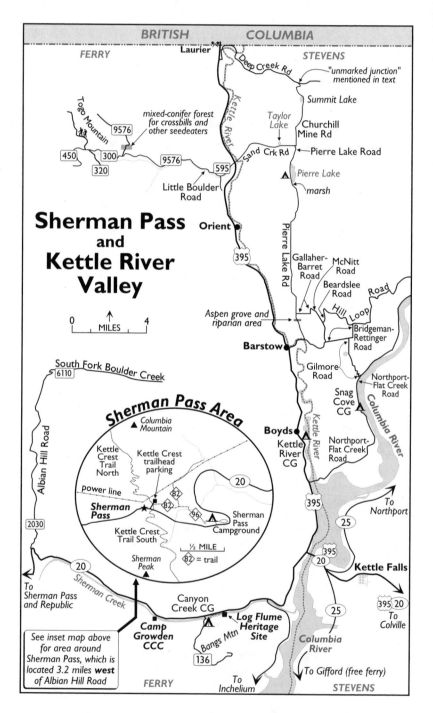

BRITISH COLUMBIA

FERRY

Laurier

STEVENS

Deep Creek Rd

"unmarked junction" mentioned in text

Togo Mountain

mixed-conifer forest for crossbills and other seedeaters

9576

450 300

320

9576

595

Little Boulder Road

Kettle River

Taylor Lake

Summit Lake

Churchill Mine Rd

Sand Crk Rd

Pierre Lake Road

Pierre Lake

marsh

Sherman Pass
and
Kettle River Valley

Orient

395

Pierre Lake Rd

Gallaher-Barret Road

McNitt Road

Beardslee Road

Hill Loop Road

Aspen grove and riparian area

Bridgeman-Rettinger Road

0 MILES 4

Barstow

Gilmore Road

Northport-Flat Creek Road

South Fork Boulder Creek

6110

Snag Cove CG

Columbia River

Sherman Pass Area

Columbia Mountain

Kettle Crest Trail North

Kettle Crest trailhead parking

power line

Sherman Pass

82 82

99

Sherman Pass Campground

Boyds

Kettle River CG

Northport-Flat Creek Road

Kettle River

Albian Hill Road

2030

Kettle Crest Trail South

½ MILE

82 = trail

Sherman Peak

395

To Northport

25

20

Sherman Creek

To Sherman Pass and Republic

Canyon Creek CG

Camp Growden CCC

Log Flume Heritage Site

Bangs Mtn

136

395 20

20

Kettle Falls

25

395 20

To Colville

See inset map above for area around Sherman Pass, which is located 3.2 miles **west** of Albian Hill Road

FERRY

To Inchelium

Columbia River

To Gifford (free ferry)

STEVENS

forest, or left to reach the Kettle Crest Trail and Sherman Pass in about another half-mile. These trails, especially Trail 96 near and in the campground, pass through typical boreal plant communities with abundant huckleberries and other members of the heath family and a rich assemblage of forbs. This is prime habitat for Spruce Grouse. However, this species can be maddeningly difficult to find. An early morning or evening walk might be the best strategy to stumble upon one. This habitat is also excellent for Boreal Owl. Sherman Pass provides the only all-year road access to this species' habitat in Washington, but your best bet for finding one is probably September–October. Other common species here include Hairy Woodpecker, Gray Jay, Mountain Chickadee, Winter Wren, Golden-crowned and Ruby-crowned Kinglets, Townsend's Solitaire, Hermit and Varied Thrushes, Yellow-rumped and Townsend's Warblers, Red and White-winged (erratic) Crossbills, and Pine Siskin. Look for Three-toed Woodpecker, too. Boreal Chickadee has been noted on Sherman Pass, but is not common.

Headed downhill again on SR-20, in 3.2 miles one reaches **Albian Hill Road** (FR-2030), on the left. If you've just struck out on Spruce Grouse at the pass trails, and really want to see one, try exploring this high route north along North Fork Sherman Creek, then east onto FR-6110 along South Fork Boulder Creek (a Colville National Forest map is helpful). Hens with chicks are often noted at wet areas in July and August. The nearby drier, huckleberry-grown slopes harbor most males.

Back on SR-20, continue down another 7.7 miles to **Camp Growden CCC** on the right, a fine, birdy place with Beaver ponds, wet meadow, riparian vegetation, and nearby conifer stands. Species noted here include Common Merganser, Willow and Hammond's Flycatchers, Cassin's Vireo, Northern Rough-winged Swallow, American Dipper, Swainson's Thrush, Yellow and MacGillivray's Warblers, and Song Sparrow.

From **Canyon Creek Campground**, on the right in 2.8 miles, an easy, one-mile trail follows Sherman Creek downstream. Cross the creek and look for the trail on the left, emanating from the alders not far from the south bank. Hammond's Flycatcher (common), Veery, Swainson's Thrush, and Orange-crowned and Yellow Warblers are to be expected. The other end of the trail is at the parking area for the Log Flume Heritage Site along Sherman Creek (one mile farther east on SR-20). **Bangs Mountain Road** (FR-136) goes right at a fork at the entrance to Canyon Creek Campground, a short distance past the creek crossing. This road climbs 5.0 miles through moist, mixed-conifer forest with abundant deciduous growth—excellent owl habitat. Great Horned, Northern Pygmy-, Great Gray, Barred, and Northern Saw-whet Owls are recorded here. At a pond at 3.0 miles, look for nesting Hooded Mergansers. Ruffed Grouse are common, from the bottom of the road to the top. The open, brushy terrain where the road ends is reputed to be good for Blue Grouse.

The road to Inchelium turns off to the right 2.9 miles past the Log Flume Heritage Site, giving access to the Silver Creek Road (page 467). It is a further 4.1 miles on SR-20 to US-395. Follow the combined highways across the Columbia to Kettle Falls (USFS district ranger station) and Colville (page 473).

KETTLE RIVER AND TOGO MOUNTAIN

Before crossing the Columbia, you might want to explore birding possibilities to the north, along the Kettle River. A tour through this area offers impressive breeding-bird diversity and opportunities for mountain species such as Spruce Grouse and crossbills. From the SR-20 intersection, go north on US-395 for 6.2 miles to the **Kettle River Campground**, on the right along the flooded lower end of the river (now part of Roosevelt Lake). A surprising mix of habitats is found in or adjacent to this campground, including brushy fields, lake and river shore, and Ponderosa Pine woodland. Birds to look for include Spotted Sandpiper, Western Wood-Pewee, Eastern Kingbird, Cassin's Vireo, Red-breasted and Pygmy Nuthatches, Western Bluebird, Chipping Sparrow, and Red Crossbill.

To visit **Togo Mountain**, long known for Spruce and Blue Grouse, continue north 16.0 miles on US-395 and turn left onto Little Boulder Road (3.6 miles north of the village of Orient). At 1.1 miles, stay right at a fork, then left at another fork in 2.7 miles. You are on FR-9576. The next main fork is at 3.5 miles, where FR-300 goes straight ahead. Go right here on FR-9576, and make a stop (0.4 mile) in the towering, mixed-conifer forest of Western Larch, Lodgepole Pine, and Engelmann Spruce. This forest provides ample seed for crossbills and other seedeaters. Both Red and White-winged Crossbills have been noted here. Return to the last fork and turn right onto FR-300. In 2.0 miles, FR-320 turns off left, marked by a battered wooden sign indicating *Verdant Ridge Road* and *End of Road 1.5 Miles*. Continue straight here on FR-300 across a cattle guard. In 0.2 mile is another fork. The branch straight ahead is signed FR-450; take the one on the right, which may have a shot-up, illegible sign. This badly rutted old mining track goes north three miles toward the summit of Togo Mountain (elevation 6,043 feet), and is best walked. In the ravines, dense Engelmann Spruce and Subalpine Fir offer good habitat for Spruce Grouse, Three-toed Woodpecker, Winter Wren, Hermit and Varied Thrushes, and Yellow-rumped and Townsend's Warblers. Boreal Owl might be looked for here. Farther, the track swings out onto exposed, south-facing slopes and a more open forest where Douglas-firs host Townsend's Solitaires.

Return to US-395. Armed with a Colville National Forest map or DeLorme Washington Atlas (and forewarned that road names and numbers on these maps don't always match reality), you can explore many roads east of here, across the Kettle River, searching a variety of habitats. For one interesting extension, turn left onto US-395 and travel north 5.7 miles to the Deep

Creek-Summit Lake Road. Turn right here and wind down and east virtually on the international border, crossing the Kettle River and then winding uphill, still eastward, another 6.9 miles to an unmarked junction. Keep right, and go another 1.4 miles to **Summit Lake**. This small lake is set in moist forest of Western Redcedar, Western Larch, and other conifers, with areas of shrubby alder and willows. This is truly a remote area, ripe for the adventuresome. Riparian alders and surrounding spruce forest would seem to be attractive to American Redstart, Northern Waterthrush, and who knows what else? Continue another 2.5 miles down the gravel road (becomes Churchill Mine Road), turn right on Sand Creek Road, then immediately left onto Pierre Lake Road.

A shorter option after coming back out from Togo Mountain is to cross directly over US-395 onto Sand Creek Road. After passing Taylor Lake, with views from the road of lake and marsh, bend right; the road is now Pierre Lake Road (4.1 miles). Whichever way you got here, in 0.9 mile is the first view of **Pierre Lake**. This is a picture-perfect scene, with buttressed cliffs, forested slopes, and a marsh-fringed lake. Habitats are diverse, as a sampling of the bird species attests: Barrow's Goldeneye, Common Merganser, Pileated Woodpecker, Willow Flycatcher, Swainson's Thrush, and Common Yellowthroat. Farther down the road, you pass the USFS campground, then the marsh at the south end of the lake.

In 9.0 miles from the Sand Creek Road intersection, note the intersection where Gallaher-Barret Road comes in from the left. Keep straight here, then stop to check the aspen grove and riparian habitat on both sides of the road one-half mile ahead. Least Flycatcher is just one possibility, among many other riparian species. Turn around, drive back north, and turn right onto Gallaher-Barret Road (which becomes McNitt Road). In 2.2 miles, turn left onto graveled **Beardslee Road**. Check brush patches along this stretch for Clay-colored Sparrow, especially after the hairpin turn where the road changes names to Hill Loop Road. In three miles, turn right at an aspen grove and follow it around a 90-degree bend; here the road is named Bridgeman-Rettinger Road. Turn left in one mile onto **Gilmore Road**. You can only glimpse a lake on the right, but roadside birding is good, with dry scrub on the hillsides alternating with riparian habitats. Check for Black-chinned Hummingbird, Red-naped Sapsucker, Hairy and Pileated Woodpeckers, Western Wood-Pewee, Least and Dusky Flycatchers, Eastern Kingbird, Warbling and Red-eyed Vireos, Veery, Swainson's Thrush, Gray Catbird, Orange-crowned, Yellow, and Wilson's Warblers, Common Yellowthroat, Western Tanager, Spotted Towhee, Chipping and Clay-colored Sparrows, Black-headed Grosbeak, and Lazuli Bunting. From this delightful spot the road descends to the Columbia River. Turn right in 2.7 miles onto Northport-Flat Creek Road. In 1.8 miles is **Snag Cove Campground**. To reach interesting brushy and pine habitats, walk about 1,000 feet north of the camp and hike uphill on a faint track just before (south of) an old fence. Continue along Northport-Flat Creek Road 6.8 miles from the campground, across the Kettle River, to reach US-395. Turn left 3.5 miles to the junction with SR-20.

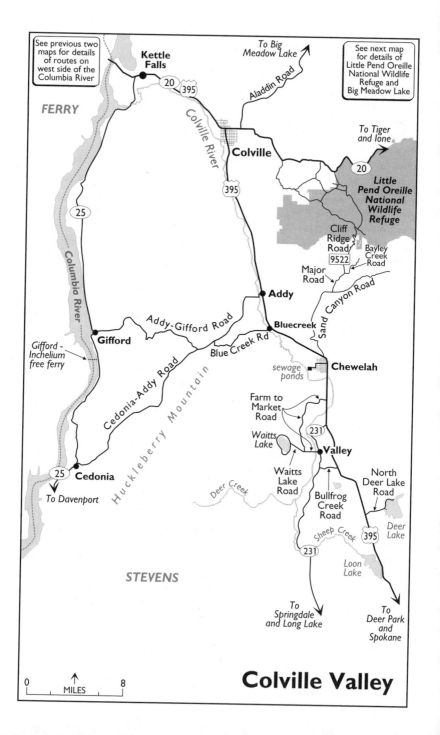

See previous two maps for details of routes on west side of the Columbia River

See next map for details of Little Pend Oreille National Wildlife Refuge and Big Meadow Lake

To Big Meadow Lake

Kettle Falls

Aladdin Road

20
395

FERRY

Colville River

Colville

395

To Tiger and Ione

20

Little Pend Oreille National Wildlife Refuge

Columbia River

25

Cliff Ridge Road

9522

Bayley Creek Road

Major Road

Sand Canyon Road

Addy

Addy-Gifford Road

Bluecreek

Gifford

Blue Creek Rd

Gifford - Inchelium free ferry

Cedonia-Addy Road

sewage ponds

Chewelah

Huckleberry Mountain

Farm to Market Road

Waitts Lake

231

25

Cedonia

To Davenport

Deer Creek

Waitts Lake Road

Valley

Bullfrog Creek Road

North Deer Lake Road

Deer Lake

395

STEVENS

Sheep Creek

231

Loon Lake

To Springdale and Long Lake

To Deer Park and Spokane

0 MILES 8

Colville Valley

FROM THE COLUMBIA TO THE PEND OREILLE

by Hal Opperman and Andy Stepniewski

This part of Northeastern Washington, centered on Colville, is characterized by rolling, forested mountain ridges interrupted by broad valleys. The entire region was glaciated, leaving hummocky terrain and many boggy and riparian sites; glacial lakes provide more wetland habitat. The northern reaches are moist forest with Engelmann Spruce, Western Larch, Douglas-fir, and abundant deciduous understories. The southern portion is much drier, with open Ponderosa Pine woodlands. Several sites representative of these habitats are here grouped along three routes leading out from Colville: south, up the Colville Valley to Chewelah and Deer Park; east, up the Little Pend Oreille drainage to Tiger; and northeast, up the Mill and Deep Creek drainages to Big Meadow Lake. The last two routes connect to Ione, the gateway to the Northeast Corner.

COLVILLE VALLEY

The broad Colville Valley is a region of hay farms, scattered conifer forest, streams, and glacial lakes. Mountains flank the valley on both sides. Riparian areas are numerous and have many birds, including Veery, American Redstart, and Northern Waterthrush from May to July. Lands in this region are mostly private, so birding is confined to roadsides and a few water overlooks.

A system of mountain ridges, with peaks above 5,800 feet, separates the Colville River from the Columbia River to the west. The **Addy-Gifford Road** is the most scenic route through these mountains. It also provides a direct connection between the Colville Valley and the Silver Creek Road (page 467) via the free Gifford-Inchelium Ferry. Although access is limited, there are enough places to pull off the road that you will be able to find birds typical of the several habitats it crosses. From the US-395/SR-20 intersection in Colville, go south on US-395 about 14 miles and turn right onto Addy-Gifford Road at the south edge of Addy. The road passes first through hay fields, then moves up the picturesque valley of Stensgar Creek with small farms, riparian vegetation, mixed forest, and Ponderosa Pines on the sunny hillsides. Blue Creek Road—an alternate route back to US-395—comes in from the left at 6.6 miles. Stay right at the junction with Cedonia-Addy Road in another 1.7 miles. The road continues to climb through mixed woods, with dry grasslands on exposed slopes (check the pond below the road on the left at about three miles), then goes over the summit amidst mountain peaks with cliffs and patches of forest. At 10.7 miles, just as Roosevelt Lake comes into view, the road enters a gorge along Stranger Creek with several pullouts where you can stop to bird the mixed forest. The Gifford post office, at the corner of SR-25, is reached in 12.4 miles from the Cedonia-Addy Road intersection. The ferry landing is two miles south.

The **Cedonia-Addy Road** runs southwest for about 16 miles from the intersection with Addy-Gifford Road to SR-25 at the north edge of Cedonia. This road folllows the Harvey Creek drainage along Huckleberry Mountain—reputedly great owling country, especially for Northern Pygmy-, Barred, and Northern Saw-whet Owls. Owl habitat is continuous in the mixed-conifer forests on the northwest-facing slope on the left, beginning where the road starts to descend (about eight miles from the intersection) and continuing for most of the way down to open rangeland. From the road's end it is ten miles north on SR-25 to the Gifford-Inchelium Ferry.

The traffic light at Main Avenue in **Chewelah** is about 8.5 miles south of Addy on US-395. Turn right (west) and follow Main 0.8 mile to Hunt. Jog left, then right to the **Chewelah sewage ponds** for breeding waterfowl, Wilson's Phalarope, and Black Tern. Hay fields nearby may have Bobolinks, as may other fields north and northwest of town. One possibility is **Sand Canyon Road**, which turns north from US-395 0.6 mile north of Main Avenue. There are some hay fields in the first two miles, and more uphill past the airport and golf course. In seven miles, graveled Major Road turns off left (north), leading in 2.0 miles to the start of FR-9522 (at the junction with Bayley Creek Road, stay straight ahead). This primitive road crosses **Cliff Ridge** and reaches Bear Creek Road in 5.8 miles, providing an interesting shortcut to the Little Pend Oreille National Wildlife Refuge. Birding is good in cut-over forest habitats at different stages of succession and along exposed, dry, brushy ridges. Though rough in places, the road should be passable with care for all but low-clearance vehicles.

Lakes in the upper part of the Colville Valley are ringed by summer homes; birding will be more tranquil outside the vacation period. From Main Avenue in Chewelah, go south 4.7 miles on US-395 to SR-231. Turn right here and go 3.4 miles to Farm to Market Road in Valley. Turn right and go 1.3 miles to where Farm to Market turns right. Stay straight on Waitts Lake Road for 1.3 miles, reaching other roads that encircle **Waitts Lake**, affording good views (especially along the west side) of a variety of waterfowl including scoters in fall. Decent riparian habitat, along the road in places, is worth checking for Willow Flycatcher, Warbling Vireo, Gray Catbird, and Yellow Warbler.

Return to SR-231 in Valley and turn right. In 1.3 miles, you reach Bullfrog Creek Road. Turn left and drive 1.6 miles to US-395. Turn right, go 4.9 miles, and turn left onto North Deer Lake Road. In about 1.5 miles **Deer Lake** comes into view. At the fork just ahead, stay left on North Deer Lake Road to a public fishing access on the right in 0.1 mile. Especially in migration, the lake can be good for Common Loon (has nested), grebes, and diving ducks. Return to US-395. Left (south) from here, it is about 29 miles to US-2 on the north edge of Spokane.

LITTLE PEND OREILLE

East of Colville lies an extensive forested plateau and mountain complex, crisscrossed by old logging roads, with many lakes, marshes, and streams. The forests on drier uplands are mainly composed of Ponderosa Pine and Douglas-fir. Poorly drained wetter sites have Engelmann Spruce, Lodgepole Pine, and Western Larch.

To reach this area, go east on SR-20 from the intersection with US-395 in Colville. In 0.3 mile, you might want to check the woods and brush around the Colville Hatchery (WDFW), on the left—a patch of habitat with Pacific-slope Flycatcher, Red-eyed Vireo, and Gray Catbird. About five miles east of the hatchery is **White Mud Lake**, on the south side of SR-20. Look here for a variety of waterfowl, including nesting Common Goldeneyes. In another half-mile, turn right onto Artman-Gibson Road (brown sign for *Little Pend Oreille NWR*). On the left in 0.8 mile is **Hatch Lake**. Depending on season and water level, you may find waterfowl (nesting Barrow's Goldeneyes) and shorebirds. Look for Mountain Bluebirds at the intersection with Kitt-Narcisse Road in 0.8 mile, then turn left onto this road, which meanders southeastward. In 2.2 miles, turn right (south) onto Bear Creek Road. Check **Horse Thief Lake** and marsh on the left in 1.0 mile for Pied-billed Grebe, Ring-necked Duck, Osprey, Bald Eagle, rails, American Coot, and Yellow-headed Blackbird.

The 40,200-acre **Little Pend Oreille National Wildlife Refuge**, established in 1939, is one of the largest in the state. Curiously, it also seems to be one of the least birded. Given the diversity, extent, and quality of its habitats, this site has the potential to become a first-class birding destination. Large areas of unfragmented forest are interspersed with streams, lakes, wetlands, and meadows. Forest composition ranges from Ponderosa Pine at 1,800 feet elevation up to Subalpine Fir at 5,600 feet. Birding is most productive from the nesting season through fall migration (late May–early September). Hunting season runs from September through December. The road to headquarters is open year round. The rest of the refuge is closed off by gates from 1 January to 14 April, but you may walk or ski in.

Refuge headquarters is on the right, 2.2 miles from the Horse Thief Lake stop. Wild Turkey, Wilson's Snipe, Black-chinned Hummingbird, White-headed Woodpecker, and five species of swallows are regular in this vicinity. In winter you may see Cassin's Finch (uncommon), Red Crossbill, Pine Siskin, and Pine and Evening Grosbeaks; Common Redpoll occurs erratically.

Continue east 0.8 mile along Bear Creek Road to **Cottonwood Campground**, on the right. Excellent riparian, marsh, and wet-meadow habitats make this one of the birdiest spots on the refuge. Breeding species include Western Wood-Pewee, Willow Flycatcher, Eastern Kingbird, Cassin's and Red-eyed Vireos, House Wren, American Dipper, Veery, Cedar Waxwing,

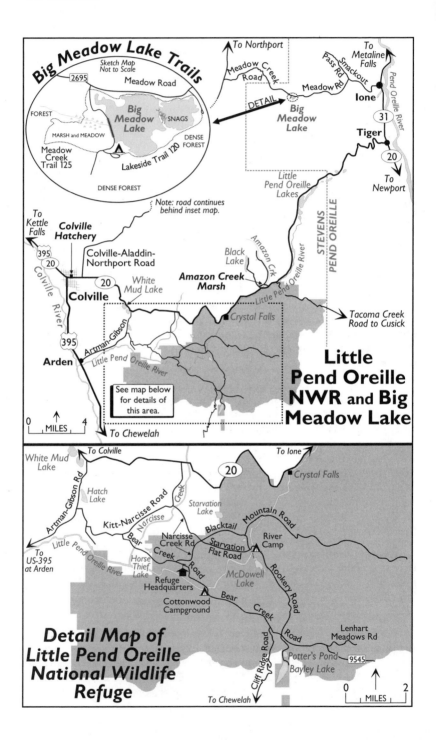

Big Meadow Lake Trails

Sketch Map
Not to Scale

2695

Meadow Road

FOREST

Big Meadow Lake

SNAGS

MARSH and MEADOW

DENSE FOREST

Meadow Creek Trail 125

Lakeside Trail 120

DENSE FOREST

To Northport

Meadow Creek Road

Pass Rd

Smackout

To Metaline Falls

Meadow Rd

Ione

DETAIL

Big Meadow Lake

Tiger

31

20

To Newport

Pend Oreille River

Note: road continues behind inset map.

Little Pend Oreille Lakes

To Kettle Falls

Colville Hatchery

395

20

Colville-Aladdin-Northport Road

White Mud Lake

20

Colville

Black Lake

Amazon Creek Marsh

Amazon Crk

Little Pend Oreille River

STEVENS
PEND OREILLE

Crystal Falls

Tacoma Creek Road to Cusick

395

Arden

Colville River

Artman-Gibson

Little Pend Oreille River

See map below for details of this area.

0   MILES   4

To Chewelah

Little Pend Oreille NWR and Big Meadow Lake

White Mud Lake

To Colville

To Ione

20

Crystal Falls

Artman-Gibson Rd

Hatch Lake

Kitt-Narcisse Road

Narcisse

Creek

Starvation Lake

Blacktail

Mountain Road

River Camp

To US-395 at Arden

Little Pend Oreille River

Bear

Creek

Horse Thief Lake

Narcisse Creek Rd

Starvation Flat Road

McDowell Lake

Rookery Road

Refuge Headquarters

Road

Cottonwood Campground

Bear

Creek

Road

Lenhart Meadows Rd

Detail Map of Little Pend Oreille National Wildlife Refuge

Cliff Ridge Road

Potter's Pond

Bayley Lake

9545

To Chewelah

0   MILES   2

Yellow and MacGillivray's Warblers, American Redstart, Common Yellowthroat, Song Sparrow, Black-headed Grosbeak, Lazuli Bunting, and Bullock's Oriole. Look also for Olive-sided and Dusky Flycatchers, Varied Thrush, and Yellow-rumped and Townsend's Warblers on the forested hillside.

Turn off right in 2.7 miles onto **Cliff Ridge Road** (FR-9522). White-headed Woodpeckers are sometimes found among the many large Ponderosa Pines near this corner. The somewhat rough road climbs a forested hillside and soon crests out along a ridgeline overlooking Bayley Lake. Northern Goshawks nest in these forests. Look for Ruffed Grouse and Orange-crowned and MacGillivray's Warblers on brushy slopes or in the open understory. The road continues down the south slope of the ridge to Sand Canyon Road and Chewelah (page 474).

Back on Bear Creek Road, go 0.3 mile, then veer off to the right onto a dirt road that leads in 0.9 mile to an observation platform and interpretive display at **Potter's Pond**. Marsh and pond are home to many birds, among them Ring-necked Duck, Common Goldeneye, Ruddy Duck, Willow Flycatcher, Warbling Vireo, Tree Swallow, Marsh Wren, Yellow Warbler, Common Yellowthroat, and Yellow-headed Blackbird. A few shorebirds sometimes appear here in fall migration. Moose also like this spot. The road continues another 0.2 mile to the north end of a large wetland and **Bayley Lake**, a good place for Common Goldeneye and other waterfowl. Ospreys and Bald Eagles nest at the south end of the lake.

Bear Creek Road continues east from the Potter's Pond turnoff, becoming FR-9545. In 2.5–3 miles, south of Lenhart Meadows and Bear Creek, listen for Flammulated Owl at night.

Look for **Rookery Road** directly across Bear Creek Road from the Potter's Pond turnoff. This narrow dirt track is gated from 1 January to 14 July to protect nesting birds, but you may walk or bicycle in. Good-looking forest habitat with Beaver ponds and other wet areas is inhabited by many species, including Wood Duck, Hammond's and Pacific-slope Flycatchers, Warbling Vireo, Black-capped Chickadee, Winter Wren, Swainson's Thrush, Orange-crowned and Yellow-rumped Warblers, Northern Waterthrush, Western Tanager, Chipping Sparrow, Red Crossbill, and Evening Grosbeak. The gate at the other end is in 2.7 miles, just before a pullout on the left overlooking **McDowell Lake** from a bluff. It is a steep but easy walk down to the shoreline. Red-necked Grebes and Hooded and Common Mergansers nest here, and paired Buffleheads have been observed in the breeding season. The road leads to River Camp in another 1.2 miles. Park here and walk back through a gate on the left along a short trail (less than a mile) through marshy habitat to the north end of McDowell Lake. Return to your car and continue driving ahead, crossing a bridge over the Little Pend Oreille River to a fork in about a hundred yards. The right branch joins Blacktail Mountain Road in 0.5 mile, while the left branch, Starvation Flat Road, leads across pine flats for two miles to Narcisse Creek Road.

Even when Rookery Road is closed you may reach McDowell Lake by auto from the west. From refuge headquarters, turn back west along Bear Creek Road, then go right in 0.6 mile onto Narcisse Creek Road. Travel 1.1 miles and turn right through a green gate. The road forks immediately ahead. Take Starvation Flat Road (the right branch) to River Camp and the lake. The left branch is **Blacktail Mountain Road**. This dirt road should be passable to most vehicles, but watch out for soft sand and for wet and muddy spots. The road starts in dry Ponderosa Pine woodland, then proceeds eastward through areas that have been logged at various times, providing an interesting succession of habitats. At 7.6 miles one reaches moist, uncut forest of Engelmann Spruce, Western Redcedar, Western Larch, and Lodgepole Pine at about 3,600 feet elevation. Breeding species along this route include Spruce Grouse, Three-toed Woodpecker, Hammond's Flycatcher, Cassin's and Warbling Vireos, Mountain and Chestnut-backed Chickadees, Red-breasted Nuthatch, Brown Creeper, Winter Wren, Golden-crowned Kinglet, Swainson's and Varied Thrushes, Nashville (in brushy clearcuts), Yellow-rumped, and Townsend's Warblers, Western Tanager, Chipping Sparrow, Dark-eyed Junco, and Red Crossbill. You may drive this road eastward for several more miles, eventually reaching a divide at 4,900 feet elevation.

Back at Narcisse Creek Road, a right turn brings you to Kitt-Narcisse Road in 1.7 miles. Turn right again to reach SR-20 in 1.4 miles. From this intersection you may turn left to reach Colville in about nine miles. If you wish to go east toward Tiger, turn right from Kitt-Narcisse Road onto SR-20. Travel 8.9 miles and turn left onto Black Lake Road. Then make an immediate right onto Amazon Creek Road, which follows the north side of **Amazon Creek Marsh**, at the confluence of Amazon Creek and the Little Pend Oreille River. At the fork in 0.3 mile, bear right onto Spruce Canyon Road, which loops back to SR-20 in 0.4 mile. The extensive alder-and-willow marsh is excellent for American Bittern, Wilson's Snipe, Vaux's Swift, Willow Flycatcher, Red-eyed Vireo, Ruby-crowned Kinglet (spruces at the marsh edge), Gray Catbird, American Redstart, Northern Waterthrush, MacGillivray's Warbler, Common Yellowthroat, and Fox Sparrow.

Continuing east and north, SR-20 follows the Little Pend Oreille River, eventually joining SR-31 at Tiger (17.5 miles); turn left here to reach Ione in about three miles. For much of this distance SR-20 runs past the **Little Pend Oreille Lakes**, a chain of lakes given over to resorts and recreational activities. The large surrounding area, served by numerous roads and trails, is managed by the state Department of Natural Resources and the U.S. Forest Service for off-road-vehicle use. Depending on your (and their) tolerance for noise, dust, and hurtling ATVs, you may find Spruce Grouse, Flammulated and Barred Owls, and Three-toed and Black-backed Woodpeckers nearly anywhere. Ospreys nest near some of the many small lakes, and Red-necked Grebes and a few waterfowl may nest on quieter waters.

One good road, outside the ORV zone, is **Tacoma Creek Road**. Look for the intersection on the right not quite a mile east of Amazon Creek Marsh. Stay right in about 600 yards, where Flodell Creek Road continues straight. The reasonably well-maintained gravel road ascends for five miles along Olson Creek—mostly within the Little Pend Oreille National Wildlife Refuge—to a divide at about 4,200 feet elevation, then descends eastward along the Tacoma Creek drainage, through excellent habitat on both slopes. Spruce Grouse are sometimes seen on the road, and Three-toed Woodpeckers in the spruces. The many passerine possibilities include Olive-sided Flycatcher and Cassin's Vireo. You may drive the whole 20-mile length of this road to its intersection with SR-20 north of Cusick (page 489).

BIG MEADOW LAKE

One of the birding jewels of the Northeast, **Big Meadow Lake** is also a popular weekend destination for local residents, so you may find it quieter on weekdays. Coming from Colville, turn north from SR-20 onto Colville-Aladdin-Northport Road (signed Aladdin Road) on the east edge of town, across from the airport. Look for Wild Turkeys in the fields as you drive up the picturesque valley for about 20 miles to the intersection with Meadow Creek Road (brown sign for *Meadow Lake*). Turn right and follow this gravel road to the entrance to Big Meadow Lake Campground, on the right in 6.2 miles. Coming from Ione, go west from SR-31 in the middle of town on Houghton Street. In 0.4 mile, turn left onto Greenhouse Road and go 0.1 mile to Smackout Pass Road. Turn right and head west out of town. In 2.7 miles is an intersection with Meadow Road, on the left. Follow this road south and west 5.0 miles to your first view of Big Meadow Lake, a trailhead pullout on the left. A variety of waterbirds should be present. The entrance to Big Meadow Lake campground is 0.4 mile farther, also on the left.

Big Meadow Lake enjoys a beautiful setting with a variety of habitats and a high diversity of breeding birds. In the low and boggy terrain are Engelmann Spruce-dominated forests with a diverse shrub-and-moss understory, very boreal in character. Uplands have Lodgepole Pine and Douglas-fir, Mountain Alder, and willow thickets. Nearby are extensive grass-and-sedge meadows. An island toward the east end of the lake is studded with snags, ideal for nesting ducks, woodpeckers, and swallows. This is one of the few sites in Washington where Common Goldeneyes and Buffleheads regularly breed; Barrow's Goldeneyes also breed here. The wails, grunts, and cries of Red-necked Grebes break the peaceful atmosphere in summer. Common Loons are also frequently seen, though breeding here is rare, probably on account of human disturbance. At the alder-dominated swampy lake edges, especially near the campground, the staccato song of Northern Waterthrush is frequently heard. American Redstart is a less-common summer visitor.

The campground at the south end of the lake makes a fine base camp. A Barred Owl often hoots here at night. By walking two trails from the campground on a June morning one can easily find 45–50 species of birds. From near the end of the campground loop, **Lakeside Trail 120** (about 2.5 miles total) heads east and encircles the lake, passing through alders and willows in swampy sections, and dense Engelmann Spruce and other conifers on higher ground. Three-toed Woodpecker, Olive-sided and Hammond's Flycatchers, Warbling Vireo, Chestnut-backed Chickadee, Brown Creeper, Winter Wren, Golden-crowned and Ruby-crowned Kinglets, Swainson's and Hermit Thrushes, and Orange-crowned, Yellow, Yellow-rumped, Townsend's, and MacGillivray's Warblers are all present along this trail. Viewpoints of the lake afford opportunities to study loons, grebes, waterfowl, Osprey, and Tree Swallow.

Meadow Creek Trail 125 goes west from the middle of the campground and ends at the road at the campground entrance in about two miles. Swampy and marshy terrain along this trail is excellent for American Redstart and Common Yellowthroat, plus a wide variety of other forest birds. In the marshes, listen for Virginia Rail, Sora, and Lincoln's Sparrow. Dense deciduous understory in the coniferous forest, particularly at the west end, is excellent for a variety of warblers. Watch for Northern Goshawk, an uncommon and secretive raptor in the breeding season, closely tied to mature forests such as found here.

NORTHEAST CORNER

by Andy Stepniewski

This is the most remote and the least populated part of the Northeast, and also the wettest. Opportunities for birding are many and varied in broadleaf and conifer forests and in meadow, riparian, marsh, and lacustrine habitats, at a range of elevations. Reflecting the diversity of habitats, four species of chickadees can be found in this region in a single day: Black-capped, generally in lowland deciduous growth; Chestnut-backed in conifer forests, especially those with Engelmann Spruce and Western Redcedar; Mountain in the montane forest stands; and Boreal in the higher spruce and Subalpine Fir stands. Good roads into the subalpine zone make the Northeast Corner one of the best places in the state to look for boreal bird species.

SULLIVAN LAKE

Access to the Northeast Corner is either from Ione or from Metaline Falls, ten miles farther north on SR-31. A good way to begin your visit is by following Sullivan Lake Road, which loops between these towns along the west shore of Sullivan Lake (elevation 2,600 feet). Here you will find four Colville National Forest campgrounds and good forest and lake birding possibilities. Other birding routes branch off from this road into the backcountry to the northeast, east, southeast, and south.

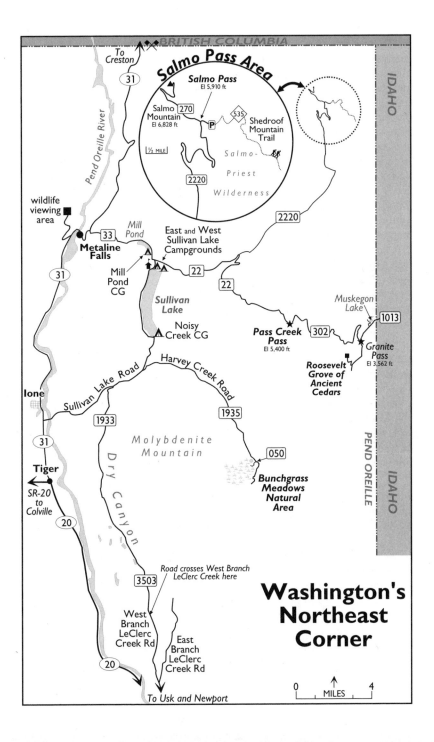

To Creston

31

Salmo Pass Area

BRITISH COLUMBIA

Salmo Pass
El 5,910 ft

Salmo
Mountain
El 6,828 ft

270

P

535

Shedroof
Mountain
Trail

½ MILE

2220

*Salmo-
Priest
Wilderness*

IDAHO

wildlife
viewing
area

2220

*Mill
Pond*

33

**Metaline
Falls**

31

Mill
Pond
CG

East and West
Sullivan Lake
Campgrounds

22

22

*Sullivan
Lake*

Noisy
Creek CG

*Muskegon
Lake*

1013

**Pass Creek
Pass**
El 5,400 ft

302

*Granite
Pass*
El 3,562 ft

Harvey Creek Road

**Roosevelt
Grove of
Ancient
Cedars**

Ione

Sullivan Lake Road

1933

1935

*Molybdenite
Mountain*

050

Dry Canyon

**Bunchgrass
Meadows
Natural
Area**

PEND OREILLE

IDAHO

Tiger

SR-20
to
Colville

20

Road crosses West Branch
LeClerc Creek here

3503

West
Branch
LeClerc
Creek Rd

East
Branch
LeClerc
Creek Rd

Washington's
Northeast
Corner

20

To Usk and Newport

0   MILES   4

Coming from Ione, find the intersection with Sullivan Lake Road, on the east side of SR-31 at the south edge of town (about a mile from the downtown business district). Turn east here and cross the Pend Oreille River. Note the intersection with FR-1933 on the right in 4.6 miles; this is the turnoff for Dry Canyon, described below (page 484). In another 1.9 miles FR-1935 turns off on the right toward Bunchgrass Meadows (page 484). It is an additional 1.8 miles to the south end of Sullivan Lake and **Noisy Creek Campground**, an excellent place for Red-eyed Vireos and other riparian woodland birds. American Dippers nest at the bridge where Noisy Creek enters Sullivan Lake. Check the lake for nesting Red-necked Grebes. The road follows the shore-line 4.1 miles to the small dam at the north end of the lake (more dippers). One-tenth mile ahead is the entrance to **West Sullivan Lake Campground**, on the right, opposite the Sullivan Lake Ranger District office (information, maps, books). The combination of coniferous and deciduous habitats in the campground and nearby is attractive to a wide array of breeding species, including a number of woodpeckers, flycatchers, vireos, thrushes, and warblers (Nashville, Yellow, Wilson's, American Redstart, and Northern Waterthrush). Black-chinned Hummingbirds have been seen here, too. Rarities have occurred at Sullivan Lake, among them Broad-winged Hawk, Magnolia Warbler, and Nelson's Sharp-tailed Sparrow.

Four-tenths of a mile farther north, FR-22 turns off to the right, providing access to high-mountain birding at Salmo Pass and Pass Creek Pass. Continuing ahead on Sullivan Lake Road, one reaches Mill Pond Campground in one mile, and the Mill Pond Historic Site half a mile beyond that. Both are linked into a system of trails around **Mill Pond**. Recommended are Trails 520 and 550 from the Historic Site. Red-necked Grebe, Harlequin Duck (especially near the inlet of the pond), Osprey, and Bald Eagle should be looked for here. Other species include Spotted Sandpiper, Cassin's, Warbling, and Red-eyed Vireos, chickadees, Swainson's Thrush, and warblers.

Sullivan Lake Road ends in 3.3 miles at a junction with SR-31. Turn left; the foot of the bridge over the Pend Oreille River at Metaline Falls is 2.2 miles ahead. Follow SR-31 across the bridge to return up the Pend Oreille Canyon to Ione. (For a chance to see imported Mountain Goats, turn right from SR-31 in 1.1 miles onto a county road, signed for Boundary Dam. In 2.3 miles, on the right, is a turnoff to the parking lot of a wildlife viewing area. Look for the goats on the cliffs to the west of the road. The season starts in spring after the snow melts, but the goats are mostly absent in summer.)

SALMO PASS

Doubtless, the main attraction of the Northeast Corner is the boreal birding possibilities. Ready access to some fine high-country sites bordering the roadless, 39,937-acre Salmo-Priest Wilderness Area, is via FR-22. Turn east from Sullivan Lake Road about 700 yards north of the ranger station. **East Sullivan Lake**

Campground is on the right one-half mile or so ahead. Check Sullivan Creek in the campground and farther up the road for Harlequin Duck and American Dipper. In six miles from Sullivan Lake Road, where FR-22 turns right toward Pass Creek Pass, bear left onto FR-2220. After 12.6 miles of steady climbing through mostly old-growth Western Hemlock, Engelmann Spruce, Western White Pine, and Western Redcedar (Interior Wet Belt species), one reaches a fork at **Salmo Pass** (elevation 5,910 feet). Park here to bird the immediate area; then walk or drive along the right branch to a parking lot in 0.2 mile, where the road ends. Continue walking another mile along a closed portion of the road. The surrounding subalpine forest of Engelmann Spruce, Subalpine Fir, and Whitebark Pine has a diverse layer of boreal shrubs, including Sitka Mountain Ash, several types of huckleberries, and a dense cover of False Azalea and White Rhododendron — prime habitat for Northern Goshawk, Spruce Grouse, Three-toed Woodpecker, Boreal Chickadee, Slate-colored Fox Sparrow, Pine Grosbeak, and White-winged Crossbill. The steep slopes on your left are probably the best easily accessible site in the Northeast to search for Boreal Owl. Common mammals include Hoary Marmot, Pika, and Red-tailed Chipmunk. Grizzly Bears are very rare, but apparently some still survive in this area. A few (about 30 in 2001) Caribou also roam these high mountains, the only ones south of Canada. Shedroof Mountain Trail 535 follows a ridge at 6,200–6,400 feet elevation for another two miles from where the roadbed ends—a good day-hike through similar habitat.

Return to the fork at the pass. The other branch, FR-270, is a spur climbing 2.2 miles to the summit of **Salmo Mountain** (elevation 6,828 feet). The views extend far into British Columbia—the Selkirks to the north, the Purcells to the northeast—and east to the Idaho Selkirks. The scrubby vegetation here has had a small breeding population of White-crowned Sparrows of the *oriantha* subspecies. Other species to look and listen for on the mountain and at the pass include Golden Eagle, Merlin, Blue Grouse (late summer), Northern Pygmy-Owl, Gray Jay, Clark's Nutcracker, Mountain Bluebird, Townsend's Solitaire, Bohemian Waxwing (post-breeding), Fox Sparrow, and crossbills flying over.

PASS CREEK PASS

From the intersection with FR-2220 (the road to Salmo Pass), FR-22 turns south and in 7.8 miles reaches Pass Creek Pass (elevation 5,400 feet). This vicinity has proven particularly good for Boreal Owl, especially in fall. Across the pass the road number changes to FR-302 upon entering the Kaniksu National Forest. Granite Pass (elevation 3,562 feet) is reached in 7.4 miles. Stay right at an intersection; it is another 1.8 miles along FR-302 to the parking lot for the **Roosevelt Grove of Ancient Cedars**, on the right (trails to cedars and waterfalls). This area shows off what is perhaps Washington's finest remaining Interior Wet Belt forest, with magnificent stands of Western Hemlock, Western Redcedar, and Engelmann Spruce. The list of birds to look for resembles one for the coastal habitats of Western Washington: Vaux's Swift,

Pileated Woodpecker, Hammond's Flycatcher, Chestnut-backed Chickadee, Winter Wren, and Hermit and Varied Thrushes. Return to Granite Pass. At the intersection where FR-302 goes left, stay straight onto FR-1013. Just ahead, a small Beaver pond and alder and boggy habitats lie next to the road—worth checking for Ruffed Grouse, vireos, and warblers. Nine-tenths of a mile from Granite Pass, walk north on closed FR-656. There is an intriguing June sight record of a Great Gray Owl along this road. Continue 0.3 mile on FR-1013 and look on your left for a small pullout, barely inside the Idaho line. A trail leads from here to **Muskegon Lake** (elevation 3,441 feet) in a few hundred yards. Barrow's Goldeneyes and many Swainson's Thrushes nest here.

BUNCHGRASS MEADOWS

Another excellent boreal birding spot lies southeast of Sullivan Lake. Turn east from Sullivan Lake Road onto Harvey Creek Road (FR-1935) and begin winding up along the creek through a steep-sided chasm, densely grown to Interior Wet Belt forests. The road is rugged but should be passable to ordinary vehicles. After about eight miles one enters a recently logged section. FR-050 branches off to the right in 9.2 miles from Sullivan Lake Road. This dirt track (best walked if muddy) ends in 0.3 mile at an access to **Bunchgrass Meadows Natural Area**, a 795-acre boreal sedge meadow and sphagnum bog (elevation 4,961 feet) set in a subalpine basin rimmed by Engelmann Spruce, Subalpine Fir, and Lodgepole Pine. Put on rubber boots to explore the wet-meadow habitat, home to Wilson's Snipe and Savannah, Fox, and Lincoln's Sparrows. This is a good spot for Moose. Rare mammals here include Masked Shrew and Northern Bog Lemming.

To bird the forested edge of Bunchgrass Meadows, return to FR-1935, turn right, and continue about one mile to a divide where the meadow is below you to the right, draining westward to the Pend Oreille River. To the left the Granite Creek drainage slopes east toward Idaho. Here is an open spruce-and-fir forest, with a tall shrub layer of White Rhododendron, False Azalea, Big-leaf Huckleberry, and Beargrass. Birds of this habitat include Three-toed Woodpecker (watch for scaled-off bark on spruce trees), Chestnut-backed and Boreal Chickadees, Red-breasted Nuthatch, Winter Wren, Golden-crowned and Ruby-crowned Kinglets, Swainson's, Hermit, and Varied Thrushes, Townsend's and Wilson's Warblers, and Pine Grosbeak. White-winged Crossbills are irregularly common, and Great Gray and Boreal Owls have been noted in the past.

DRY CANYON

A quiet route south toward Usk, Dry Canyon offers lower-elevation woodland and riparian birding even when the high country of the Salmo-Priest

Wilderness is inaccessible or unproductive due to inclement weather or the earliness of the season. This is also a fine choice as an entrance or exit route between the Northeast Corner and points south. Turn south from Sullivan Lake Road onto FR-1933. In 0.5 mile, at a junction with FR-4536, stay right on FR-1933. Soon you enter Dry Canyon, with Dry Canyon Ridge on the right and an area of boggy terrain on the left. There is excellent birding along this good gravel road for about the next six miles, up to a fair-sized lake on the left (look for Barrow's Goldeneyes). The songbird mix along this narrow canyon is interesting, with Red-eyed Vireo, Swainson's Thrush, and Northern Waterthrush in the valley bottom forest, and Nashville Warbler in brush along the exposed talus slopes to the west. Upon leaving the national forest about a mile past the lake (sign and cattle guard), the road surface is poor for about another half-mile, then improves. You are now on CR-3503. Clearcuts start to appear. In 5.6 miles from the cattle guard, the road crosses the West Branch of LeClerc Creek. Extensive willow-and-alder riparian habitat here has Willow Flycatcher (numerous), Warbling Vireo, Gray Catbird, Yellow Warbler, American Redstart, Northern Waterthrush, Fox Sparrow, and Evening Grosbeak. In another 2.1 miles is a large meadow with Vesper Sparrows. Pavement starts in two miles as you reach a T-intersection with LeClerc Creek Road. Turn right and travel another mile to a T-intersection with LeClerc Road (CR-9325). You may turn left here toward Usk, Newport, and birding sites of the Pend Oreille Valley described in the following section.

PEND OREILLE VALLEY

by Andy Stepniewski and Jim Acton

The Pend Oreille River flows west from Idaho into Washington at Newport, then bends north toward British Columbia, where it empties into the Columbia River. The southern Pend Oreille Valley sits in a depression known as the Newport Fault, which also marks the southern edge of the last glaciation. As the glaciers began to recede at the end of the ice age, ice dammed the streams, flooding the valleys to the south and leaving behind a landscape of glacial debris and lakes. Today, this area and the glaciated land along the Pend Oreille just north of it have a number of notable birding sites in riparian and wetland habitats.

LAKE OF THE WOODS TO CALISPELL LAKE

Coming from the junction of US-2 and US-395 at the north edge of Spokane, take US-2 north toward Newport. For some good owling and other birding possibilities, turn right in about 21 miles onto Elk-to-Highway Road and travel eastward to Elk. In 3.4 miles, just after the Elk post office, turn left onto Elk-Camden Road, which follows the Little Spokane River northeastward. Turn right in 2.3 miles onto Frideger Road, cross the river, and climb out of the valley. The road soon becomes gravel; look for Wild Turkeys

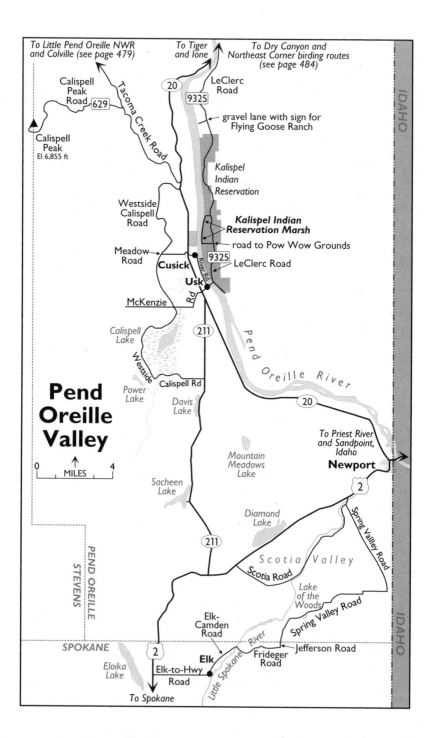

To Little Pend Oreille NWR
and Colville (see page 479)

To Tiger
and Ione

To Dry Canyon and
Northeast Corner birding routes
(see page 484)

Calispell
Peak
Road 629

Tacoma Creek Road

20

9325

LeClerc
Road

gravel lane with sign for
Flying Goose Ranch

Calispell
Peak
El 6,855 ft

Westside
Calispell
Road

Kalispel
Indian
Reservation

Meadow
Road

**Kalispel Indian
Reservation Marsh**

road to Pow Wow Grounds

Cusick

River Rd

9325

Usk

LeClerc Road

McKenzie

Rd

211

Calispell
Lake

Westside

Pend Oreille River

Power
Lake

Calispell Rd

Davis
Lake

20

**Pend
Oreille
Valley**

To Priest River
and Sandpoint,
Idaho
Newport

2

0   4
MILES

Mountain
Meadows
Lake

Sacheen
Lake

Spring Valley Road

Diamond
Lake

211

PEND OREILLE

STEVENS

Scotia Valley

Scotia Road

Lake
of the
Woods

Spring Valley Road

Elk-
Camden
Road

Little Spokane River

Spring Valley Road

Jefferson Road

SPOKANE

2

Elk

Frideger
Road

Eloika
Lake

Elk-to-Hwy
Road

To Spokane

IDAHO

IDAHO

where it crosses Ponderosa Pines with brushy understory. In 3.1 miles, turn left onto Jefferson Road. Drive 0.5 mile, bear left at a junction onto paved Spring Valley Road, and continue to **Lake of the Woods**, set in a deep, forested valley. Stop at a pullout bordered by large rocks, on the right (2.3 miles). Summer finds Willow Flycatchers, Gray Catbirds, and Common Yellowthroats conspicuous about the large marsh at the east end of the lake, below the pullout. Douglas-fir forest by the road should yield Olive-sided Flycatcher, Cassin's Vireo, and Western Tanager. Searching for Barred and Northern Saw-whet Owls can be profitable in late winter and spring. The best spot is about one-half to one mile east of the lake, up the hill along Spring Valley Road. This is timber company land, and some logging is taking place; bird from the road. Barred Owls are in dense, swampy forest to the south (uncut as of this writing), along with Warbling and Red-eyed Vireos, Black-capped, Mountain, and Chestnut-backed Chickadees, Swainson's Thrush, American Redstart, Northern Waterthrush, and MacGillivray's Warbler.

Continue east, then north, on Spring Valley Road for about nine miles to the intersection with Scotia Road. (Continuing straight, then turning right onto US-2—just ahead—brings you to Newport in about three miles). Turn left onto Scotia Road, which follows the Little Spokane River down the **Scotia Valley** (all private property—bird from the road). Alder and Water Birch thickets along the river may have Common Redpoll and Pine Siskin in winter. In ten miles, turn left onto US-2, drive west 1.7 miles, then turn right onto SR-211.

Follow SR-211 for 4.1 miles to **Sacheen Lake**. Turn left onto Sacheen Terrace Drive, which immediately curves to the right and passes a fire station. Stop clear of the station and view the moist grasslands across the road to the south. Red-necked Grebe, American Bittern, Spotted Sandpiper, various swallow species, Common Yellowthroat, and Savannah Sparrow occur here. Three-tenths of a mile from the highway, turn left at a *Public Fishing Access* sign (WDFW permit required). Park near the boat ramp. Willow Flycatchers abound, along with Gray Catbirds and Cedar Waxwings; some warblers are always around. Look for Ospreys and Vaux's Swifts. You might see a Hooded Merganser or other waterbirds on the lake.

Return to SR-211 and turn left. In 4.3 miles is a turnout on the right (east) side, about half a mile south of **Davis Lake**. Opposite, a paved road crosses private land to Camp Spaulding. Although traffic noise can be bothersome, birds that may be found on either side of the highway include Virginia Rail, Willow Flycatcher, Warbling and Red-eyed Vireos, Gray Catbird, Swainson's Thrush, Cedar Waxwing, Yellow Warbler, American Redstart, MacGillivray's Warbler, and Common Yellowthroat. The most recent of Washington's four records of Black-billed Cuckoo was found in this area in June 1988. A public boat ramp (1.4 miles) provides access to the shoreline at the other end of the lake. You may see a few Red-necked Grebes in the breeding season and a small number of ducks in migration.

Continuing north on SR-211, in 1.1 miles go left onto Westside Calispell Road. Here begins a loop around bird-rich **Calispell Lake**. Birding the moist woodlands, forested hillsides, wet meadows, marshes, and open waters along this road should prove rewarding. However, all bordering land is private property, and you must bird from the road. Stop to investigate marshy areas for American Bitterns and rails. Check the tall riparian woodlands and fields. Red-eyed Vireo should be found, along with an array of breeding birds such as Eastern Kingbird, Warbling Vireo, Yellow and MacGillivray's Warblers, Black-headed Grosbeak, Lazuli Bunting, and Bobolink (likely at 6.6 miles). For the first part of the loop one is distant from Calispell Lake; the road draws nearer between seven and eight miles, allowing reasonable scope views. In migration, this is a well-known stopover for large numbers of Tundra Swans and many other waterfowl. Breeding waterfowl are also numerous. Birders fantasize that Yellow Rails might be present on the vast sedge meadows around this lake, but the fantasy remains unfulfilled. Beginning in July, look for shorebirds in the shallows, especially yellowlegs. In 9.1 miles from SR-211, turn right onto McKenzie Road. Go east across a slough, the outlet of Calispell Lake, checking fields to the north for Bobolinks. Turn left at a junction in 1.1 miles, keeping on McKenzie Road until reaching the stop sign at SR-20 (1.2 miles). Fifth Street, the entrance to Usk, is directly across the highway.

USK AND VICINITY

Take Fifth east from SR-20 into the tiny mill town of **Usk**, home of the Ponderay Newsprint plant. Continue ahead over the railroad track to the Pend Oreille River bridge (0.5 mile). The numerous pilings in the river here were used to corral logs as they floated downstream to local sawmills. Today they provide nesting platforms for a growing colony of Double-crested Cormorants and numerous Ospreys. There are many places for close-up views along River Road (turn north one block before the bridge). Gray Catbirds frequent the bushes near the shore.

Several excellent birding sites along the opposite bank of the Pend Oreille River are easily reached from Usk. Cross the bridge, turn left onto LeClerc Road (CR-9325) on the other side, and drive north to the Kalispel Indian Reservation (access to some areas may be restricted; check at the tribal headquarters). In 2.1 miles, turn left onto a road marked by a sign for the Qualispe Pow Wow Grounds. Continue 0.7 mile and turn right onto a dike road at the edge of the river. This gravel lane goes north along the river through the **Kalispel Indian Reservation Marsh**, returning to LeClerc Road in 1.8 miles. Take time to bird the many habitats: hay meadows (Northern Harrier, Bobolink), riparian woodlands (Red-eyed Vireo), rich sedge-and-cattail marshes, oxbow lakes, and the open river with pilings on the opposite shore (Double-crested Cormorant, Wood Duck, Osprey).

Continue north on LeClerc Road. In 5.6 miles, turn left onto a gravel lane marked by a sign for the **Flying Goose Ranch**. The Kalispel Tribe now manages this extensive area of bottomland (formerly a farm) for wetland wildlife habitat, in mitigation for a dam built elsewhere by the Bonneville Power Administration. The gravel lane goes west from here about one-half mile to the Pend Oreille River. Along the way are broadleaf trees, grasslands, and marsh and river habitats, a combination offering excellent birding potential. Look for American Bittern, many ducks, Virginia Rail, Sora, and Black Tern. About eight miles farther north, LeClerc Creek Road turns off from LeClerc Road. This is the jumpoff point for the Northeast Corner via the Dry Canyon route (pages 484–485).

Back across the river, the community of **Cusick** is situated a couple of miles north of Usk on SR-20. (If you take River Road to see the nesting cormorants and Ospreys, stay on this road until it turns left, then go one block to First Avenue in Cusick and turn right. Swing left in another block onto Monumental Drive, cross the railroad track, and continue ahead to an intersection with SR-20.) Hay meadows on both sides of SR-20 north and south of Cusick have large colonies of Bobolinks; Savannah Sparrows and Red-winged and Brewer's Blackbirds are also abundant. The shoulders are narrow here, so be careful. For safer viewing, turn west from SR-20 onto **Meadow Road** at the north edge of Cusick (across a bridge 0.1 mile north of the intersection with Monumental Drive). Deep hay meadows, patrolled by Turkey Vultures and Ospreys, have Bobolinks and other wet-meadow birds. Deciduous shrubs at each end of this 1.7-mile road often harbor Black-chinned Hummingbird, both kingbirds, Veery, Gray Catbird, and Lazuli Bunting. At the intersection where Meadow Road ends, turn right (north) onto Westside Calispell Road, which loops back to SR-20 in 6.1 miles, just south of the Tacoma Creek bridge. Hay fields, wetlands, marshy sloughs, and riparian habitats along this route have produced Lewis's Woodpecker (rare), Red-eyed Vireo, Mountain Bluebird, Yellow Warbler, and American Redstart.

TACOMA CREEK AND CALISPELL PEAK

About 3.5 miles north of Cusick, just after the intersection with Westside Calispell Road, SR-20 crosses the Tacoma Creek bridge (Cliff Swallow colony). In another 0.3 mile, turn left from SR-20 onto **Tacoma Creek Road**. For the next few miles the gravel road follows the creek through marshy riparian habitat with Red-eyed Vireo, American Dipper, American Redstart, Northern Waterthrush, and many other species. **Sportsman Pond**, on the right in 4.2 miles (just after the USAF Survival School), can be good for Ring-necked Duck, Common Goldeneye, Hooded Merganser, and Tree and Northern Rough-winged Swallows. Vaux's Swifts skim the water when the weather is overcast, allowing you to look down on them to observe their brown rumps and tails.

The turnoff for **Calispell Peak Road** (FR-629) is on the left in another 2.1 miles. In years past, this road had a great reputation for boreal bird specialties. However, a once-productive Beaver swamp has been drained, and the roadbed has been allowed to deteriorate. The birds are apparently still here, but it is probably easier to look for them someplace else. Exercise judgment if you decide to proceed. You may encounter deep mudholes or water over the road, especially early in the season. The road climbs through a number of cut-over areas where the forest has been opened. The remnant Western Larch and invading brush are fine habitat for Red-naped Sapsucker, Cassin's and Warbling Vireos, Gray Jay, Mountain and Chestnut-backed Chickadees, Red-breasted Nuthatch, Swainson's and Varied Thrushes, Orange-crowned, Yellow-rumped, Townsend's, MacGillivray's, and Wilson's Warblers, and Red Crossbill. Look for a cattle guard 4.6 miles in. Continue to a clearing on the left side of the road a few hundred yards past the cattle guard, at about 4,100 feet elevation. Spruce Grouse, Northern Pygmy-Owl, Barred Owl, Three-toed and Black-backed Woodpeckers, Black-capped, Mountain, and Chestnut-backed Chickadees, Townsend's Solitaire, Northern Waterthrush, and Moose have all been found in this vicinity. If you have time on your hands and an adventuresome spirit, you may be able to keep driving the remaining six miles to enjoy the view and good fall hawkwatching from the 6,855-foot summit of Calispell Peak (high-clearance, four-wheel-drive vehicle advised). It is a rough go, especially the final mile and a half, where the road is decorated with large rocks.

Continuing west, Tacoma Creek Road climbs for 8.8 miles to a 4,200-foot crest, then descends the Olson Creek drainage along one edge of the Little Pend Oreille National Wildlife Refuge, reaching SR-20 in another 4.9 miles (page 479). This road is far better maintained than Calispell Peak Road, and passes through similar habitats where you can expect to find most of the same birds.

SPOKANE AND VICINITY

by Andy Stepniewski and Jim Acton

The southern end of Washington's Northeast belongs to the Columbia Basin. Rolling plateaus—originally grown to steppe and scattered shrub-steppe, and groves of Ponderosa Pine—are interrupted by Channeled Scablands topography of lakes and marshes. Much of the deeper-soiled terrain is now given over to dryland wheat farming. This is, on average, the warmest and driest part of the Northeast and holds the bulk of the human population, mainly in the Spokane Valley. The Spokane metropolitan area has numerous sites for finding birds of dry forest, grassland, and riparian habitats, especially in late spring and early summer when breeding activity is at a peak. These same sites can also be excellent in spring and fall migration. Notable Spokane vagrant records include Broad-winged Hawk (September), Tennessee Warbler (August), Black-throated Green Warbler (July; the only state record), Blackpoll Warbler (May), Ovenbird (November), Indigo Bunting (September), and Rose-breasted Grosbeak (June, October). Less than an hour from the city, Mount Spokane State Park offers mountain birding with a flavor of the Selkirks, while Turnbull National Wildlife Refuge is a fine Channeled Scablands birding site.

SPOKANE CANYONS

If you find yourself in Spokane with a half-day or less at your disposal, your best bet for seeing both typical birds and possible vagrants is the canyons of the Spokane River and tributaries, in the western part of the city. The following itinerary visits several of the most productive sites.

To reach the **Little Spokane River Natural Area**, leave I-90 at Exit 281 and go north on US-2/US-395 (Division Street) 4.4 miles to the intersection with Francis Avenue. Turn left (west) here onto SR-291. In 2.2 miles swing right onto Indian Trail Road, which ends in 4.8 miles at Rutter Parkway. Bear right onto Rutter and continue 0.9 mile to a parking lot on the left, just across the Little Spokane River bridge. A two-mile trail goes west from here, ending at a parking lot on SR-291 not far from the Spokane House Interpretive Center in Riverside State Park. By walking the first half-mile you will encounter a variety of habitats, including river, marsh, a fine riparian zone (Black Cottonwood, Quaking Aspen, willows, Red-osier Dogwood), brushy slopes, Ponderosa Pine woodland, and granitic cliffs. Species expected on this trail include Great Blue Heron (rookery about one mile along the trail), Hooded Merganser, Osprey, Bald Eagle (winter), Northern Pygmy-Owl, Red-naped Sapsucker, Downy, Hairy, and Pileated Woodpeckers, Western Wood-Pewee, Willow Flycatcher, Eastern Kingbird, Cassin's, Warbling, and Red-eyed Vireos, Clark's Nutcracker, a variety of swallows, Black-capped and Mountain Chickadees, all three nuthatches, Rock, Canyon, Bewick's, House, and Winter (moist bottomlands, November–February) Wrens, Veery, Yellow Warbler, American Redstart, Yellow-breasted Chat, Black-headed Grosbeak, Red-winged Blackbird, Bullock's Oriole, Cassin's Finch, and Red Crossbill. Back at the parking lot and across the bridge, another trail runs upstream (eastward) on the opposite bank, through Douglas-fir habitats on shady, north-facing slopes.

Turn right (south) out of the parking lot, recross the Little Spokane River, and keep right on Rutter Parkway to SR-291 (3.1 miles from the parking lot). Turn left here, travel 3.9 miles, and turn right onto Seven Mile Road, which soon crosses the Spokane River. Look for a sign for the **Riverside Park ORV Area** in 2.2 miles. Turn left (south) here onto Inland Road and drive through dry Ponderosa Pine woodlands, continuing past the parking lot

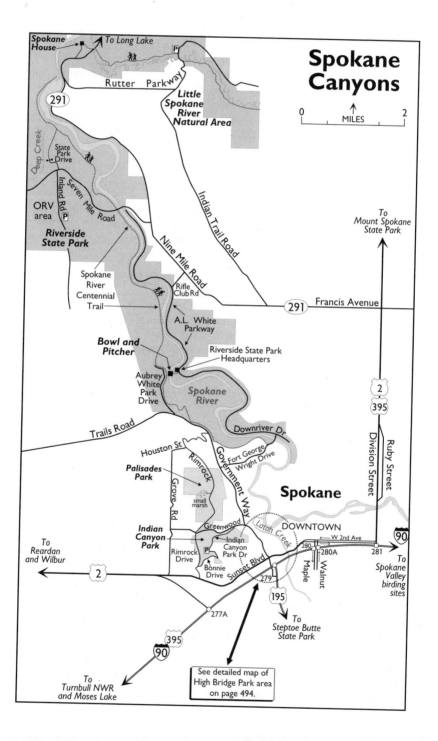

Spokane Canyons

Spokane House

To Long Lake

P

Rutter Parkway

291

Little Spokane River Natural Area

0 — MILES — 2

Deep Creek

State Park Drive

Inland Rd

ORV area

P

Riverside State Park

Seven Mile Road

Spokane River Centennial Trail

Nine Mile Road

Indian Trail Road

Rifle Club Rd

291 Francis Avenue

To Mount Spokane State Park

A.L. White Parkway

Bowl and Pitcher

Riverside State Park Headquarters

Aubrey White Park Drive

Spokane River

2
395

Trails Road

Downriver Dr.

Government Way

Houston St

Fort George Wright Drive

Division Street

Ruby Street

Rimrock

Palisades Park

Grove Rd

small marsh

Spokane

DOWNTOWN

Latah Creek

90

Indian Canyon Park

Greenwood

Indian Canyon Park Dr

W 2nd Ave

280

281

To Spokane Valley birding sites

Rimrock Drive

P

Bonnie Drive

Sunset Blvd

280A

Maple

Walnut

2 To Reardan and Wilbur

279

195

277A

To Steptoe Butte State Park

395

90

To Turnbull NWR and Moses Lake

See detailed map of High Bridge Park area on page 494.

where ORVs load and unload. In about 1.1 miles you reach the beginning of an area of open grasslands where you may encounter a few hikers, bicyclists, or horseback riders, but no ORVs. For the next half-mile, grasslands and bordering pines are home to White-headed Woodpecker (uncommon), Gray Flycatcher, Red-breasted and Pygmy Nuthatches, Western Bluebird, and Chipping, Vesper, and Lark Sparrows. Turkey Vultures fly around the dry basalt cliffs to the west.

Return to Seven Mile Road and cross over the pavement onto State Park Drive, about 75 feet to the right. The road is gated in 0.3 mile, but you may walk in past the gate and look down into the forested basalt canyons along **Deep Creek**, on the left. Listen for Rock and Canyon Wrens. Northern Goshawks have been seen on snags here.

Retrace your route along Seven Mile Road back across the Spokane River to SR-291 (Nine Mile Road), and turn right. In 1.4 miles, turn right onto Rifle Club Road (brown sign for Riverside State Park), then left in 0.4 mile onto A.L. White Parkway. Turn into the parking lot on the right for the **Riverside State Park Headquarters** (1.6 miles). A short trail affords great views of the Spokane River in a gorge with the **Bowl and Pitcher** and other dramatic rock formations as a backdrop. Check for Osprey and, in winter, Bald Eagle. White-throated Swifts nest on the high basalt cliffs to the west, and an impressive Cliff Swallow colony resides just below the viewpoint. Pygmy Nuthatch, Western Bluebird, and Red Crossbill are also common in this part of the park and in the old burn in the Ponderosa Pine woodland to the north. A newer burn on the other side of the river may have various woodpeckers (Black-backed nested here recently); drive or walk down to the picnic area, cross the suspension footbridge, and hike the trail to the right to reach it.

Continuing along the parkway (becomes Downriver Drive), exit left in 3.4 miles, before the underpass, and circle right, crossing a bridge over the Spokane River onto Fort George Wright Drive. In 1.4 miles, turn right onto Government Way and in another 1.4 miles reach Aubrey White Park Drive (might be signed slightly differently), an access to Riverside Park and the **Spokane River Centennial Trail**. At this junction, extensive areas of brush mantle the hillside to the south, very attractive to Nashville Warbler, Spotted Towhee, Lazuli Bunting, and many other species. Drive in one mile to a parking area that overlooks the Bowl and Pitcher from the other side of the river. If you continue on foot past the gate and down toward the river, you will reach the previously mentioned recent burn with woodpecker potential. Pacific-slope Flycatchers and Cassin's Vireos also reside in this area.

Turn around and follow Government Way back the way you came. At the traffic light where Fort George Wright Drive goes left, stay straight on Government Way for 1.2 miles, then turn right onto Greenwood Road. Bear right where the roadway splits (0.3 mile) and go uphill into **Indian Canyon Park**. The dense riparian growth along the creek on your left is filled with vireos and warblers, including a few Yellow-breasted Chats. There are a few places to park and walk trails. As you reach the top of the hill along Greenwood, the roadway splits again (0.7 mile). Take Rimrock Drive to the right (north) through **Palisades Park**. This overlooks the city and has large-rock borders to prevent off-road activities. The length of the road all the way to Houston Street (2.0 miles) can be especially good for passerines in fall migration (late August–September), when you might see Olive-sided Flycatcher, Western Wood-Pewee, and Chipping, Lark, and White-crowned Sparrows, among other species. Accipiters are to be looked for here, also, including Northern Goshawk during the winter period. Midway along this route a sketchy path follows a small creek westward for 150 yards along the forest edge to a marsh (may dry up in summer); look here for Downy and Hairy Woodpeckers, all three nuthatches, and Red Crossbill.

Double back along Rimrock Drive, continuing past the Greenwood Road intersection 0.6 mile to the junction with **Bonnie Drive**. Turn left onto Bonnie, drive 200 yards or so, and stop anyplace suitable. Walk left to the canyon edge. You are at the narrow upper end of a forested funnel through which a small creek flows down to Latah Creek. In fall migration, birds work their way up the canyon to this spot and can often be seen at or below eye level as you look out onto the Douglas-firs. Eastern Kingbirds stay for days; small numbers of Hammond's, Gray, Dusky, and Pacific-slope Flycatchers may be seen. Cassin's, Warbling, and Red-eyed (scarce) Vireos pass through. Cedar Waxwings and Western Tanagers are interested in the many berry-producing shrubs. Fall warblers found here include Orange-crowned, Nashville, Yellow, Yellow-rumped, Townsend's, Palm (rare), MacGillivray's, Wilson's, Yellow-breasted Chat, and sometimes even a Common Yellowthroat. Sparrows are everywhere in September, with White-crowned most numerous, Chipping and Lincoln's in moder-

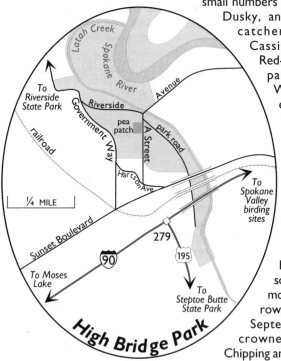

To Riverside State Park

Latah Creek

Spokane River

Avenue

Riverside

Government Way

pea patch

A Street

park road

railroad

Hartson Ave

¼ MILE

Sunset Boulevard

279

90

195

To Moses Lake

To Spokane Valley birding sites

To Steptoe Butte State Park

High Bridge Park

ate numbers, Golden-crowned uncommon, and White-throated, Harris's, and Clay-colored appearing once in a while. Cooper's Hawks breed in the canyon, and Sharp-shinneds and Northern Goshawks are possibilities during the later dates of fall and in winter.

Continue east on Bonnie Drive, turn left at **Indian Canyon Park Drive** (0.4 mile), and go downhill to a small parking place on a hairpin curve (0.2 mile), another good fall migration spot for vireos, warblers, and some sparrows. Below the cliff is a small waterfall. This middle part of the canyon is breeding territory for Pacific-slope Flycatcher, Cassin's Vireo, Western Tanager, and Dark-eyed Junco. Calliope Hummingbirds breed throughout the canyon—Black-chinneds too, although they are not as numerous. Other possibilities are Vaux's Swift, Black-capped and Mountain Chickadees, Rock, Canyon, Bewick's, House, and Winter (creek bottoms in winter) Wrens, Golden-crowned (winter) and Ruby-crowned (migration) Kinglets, Gray Catbird, and Black-headed and Evening (fall and winter) Grosbeaks.

To have a look at Spokane's urban Peregrine Falcons, take Indian Canyon Park Drive ahead to rejoin Greenwood Road (0.6 mile), continue to Government Way (0.3 mile), and turn right, reaching Riverside Avenue in about 0.1 mile. Turn left, go 0.3 mile, turn right onto A Street, and then immediately left into **High Bridge Park**. Latah Creek is on the left, with three bridges towering ahead. The Peregrines nest under the Sunset Boulevard bridge (the closest of the three) and use the piers of the railroad bridge just behind it as observation posts. They often target the White-throated Swifts that zoom in and out of the openings on the underside of the I-90 bridge (the farthest one back), where the swifts nest. Otherwise, birdlife in the park is slim, but the community gardens (pea patch) one block up A Street, on the right, can be alive with seed-eating birds in late summer and fall.

To reach I-90, go back to Government Way and turn left. In 0.5 mile, turn left onto Sunset Boulevard, continue 1.1 miles to Maple Street, then turn right and follow the signs a few blocks to the onramps.

SPOKANE VALLEY

The Spokane Valley, stretching east from the city to the Idaho line, is rapidly being gobbled up by suburban development. The small population of Upland Sandpipers that once nested here was extirpated a decade ago, but remnant patches of habitat still support a few Grasshopper Sparrows, Western Meadowlarks, and other grassland birds. Also of interest to birders are some forested preserves in the hills at the valley's south edge.

The **Dishman Hills Natural Area** consists of 530 rugged acres of dry forest, brushland, small seasonal springs and ponds, and rocky cliffs. Over 100 species of birds, nearly 400 of plants, and more than 50 of butterflies have been found here. The best time to visit is May or June; bird activity is much diminished in the hot summer months. Birds to expect include Western Wood-Pewee, Pacific-slope Flycatcher, Cassin's and Warbling Vireos, Violet-green Swallow, Black-capped and Mountain Chickadees, all three nuthatches, Rock Wren, Yellow-rumped Warbler, Chipping Sparrow, and Red Crossbill. To reach this natural island in the midst of urban development, go east from downtown Spokane on I-90 to Exit 285 (Sprague Avenue), which dumps you directly onto Appleway Boulevard, the eastbound lanes of Sprague. In 1.4 miles, turn right onto Sargent Road and go two blocks to the north parking lot and entrance at Camp Caro. The preserve has an extensive network of trails. The Pinecliff Discovery Trail visits the main habitats in a one-mile loop, starting just behind the environmental education center. Walk south through Ponderosa Pine woodland and patches of brushland. In about 500 yards, note granitic Caro Cliff to your left. Just beyond the cliff, take the right branch of the trail to Enchanted Ravine. Dense vegetation has developed in the shade of the gorge, dominated by Douglas-firs. From the ravine, the trail ascends to a high, forested plateau. Here and there, openings afford good views of the Spokane Valley. A spur trail leads to East and West Ponds— potholes that fill with water from winter and spring rains. Although they dry out in summer, the depressions are moist enough year round to maintain wetland vegetation, a magnet to many birds. The trail returns to the parking lot in about one-quarter mile.

Iller Creek Conservation Area is a 796-acre tract at the core of a much larger proposed nature area in the hills south of the Spokane Valley. Iller Creek has a number of different habitat types, including riparian and brushy and forested slopes. A walk up the trail offers some of the best passerine birding in the Spokane area. Of the regularly occurring Eastern Washington vireos, thrushes, and warblers, all but Northern Waterthrush and Common Yellowthroat can be found here, and even these two have been recorded. Although best from mid-May through June, birding holds up quite well through the heat of summer.

From Camp Caro, return to Appleway, turn right, and go 0.4 mile to Dishman-Mica Road. Turn right, go 2.3 miles, and turn right onto Schafer Road. In 0.9 mile, turn right onto 44th Avenue; left in 0.2 mile onto Farr Road; and right in 0.3 mile onto Holman Road, which ends in 0.8 mile at a turnaround where the trail starts. Park out of the way. Look for Calliope Hummingbird, Orange-crowned Warbler, and Yellow-breasted Chat in the Buckbrush on the west side of the road, and Lazuli Bunting and perhaps Black-headed Grosbeak along the slopes of the creek below. The lower part of the trail follows Iller Creek closely in a riparian zone of Mountain Alder, Douglas Maple, willows, and Black Cottonwood. Ponderosa Pines grow on the exposed sunny slopes of the gorge. Look for Red-naped Sapsucker, Willow and Dusky Flycatchers, Warbling and Red-eyed (uncommon) Vireos, Black-capped Chickadee, House Wren, Veery, Swainson's Thrush, Gray Catbird, Nashville, Yellow, MacGillivray's, and Wilson's Warblers, American Redstart, Spotted

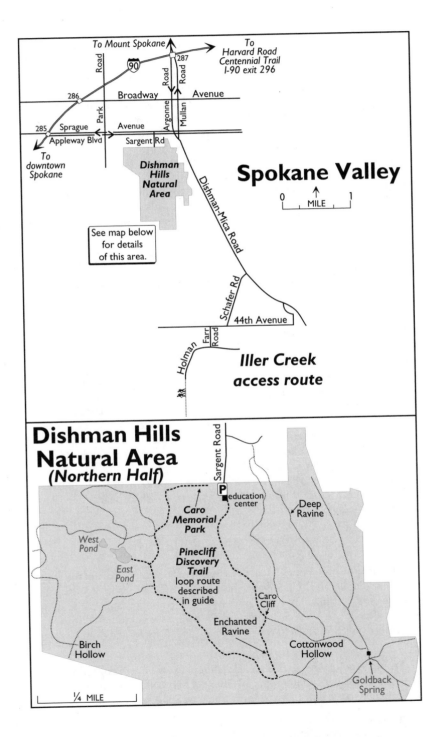

Towhee, Chipping, Fox, and Song Sparrows, Dark-eyed Junco, and Brown-headed Cowbird. As one works upstream, Ponderosa Pine and Black Cottonwood are replaced by Western Hemlock, Douglas-fir, Grand Fir, and Western Larch. Birds common along this portion include Ruffed Grouse, Olive-sided (along the ridge) and Hammond's Flycatchers, Mountain Chickadee, Red-breasted Nuthatch, Winter Wren, Golden-crowned Kinglet, Nashville, Yellow-rumped, and Townsend's Warblers, Western Tanager, and Red Crossbill. Ruby-crowned Kinglet and Hermit Thrush are conspicuous in migration. The trail tops out in about two miles at an old burn cradled between Krell Hill and Big Rock. American Kestrel, Lewis's and Pileated Woodpeckers, and Brown Creeper have nested in the burn area, and Rock Wrens are regularly found in the rocky outcrop to the east. The usual raptors along the drainage are Northern Harrier, Sharp-shinned and Red-tailed Hawks, and sometimes Barred Owl.

Returning from Iller Creek, go back on Dishman-Mica to Sprague. Here, two one-way streets face you across Sprague: Mullan Road (northbound) and Argonne Road (southbound), connecting to and from I-90 at Exit 287 in 1.2 miles.

The paved **Harvard Road Centennial Trail** is reached by taking Exit 296 from I-90. Go north 0.8 mile on Harvard Road to the parking area, on the left. The trail flanks the Spokane River through riparian growth and brushy patches. The main attraction is a tiny number of nesting Clay-colored Sparrows (may not be present every year). Walk west, noting the numbers on AT&T cable-markers that begin at Harvard Road with 6W146. From the middle of May until early August, listen for the song of the Clay-colored Sparrow between markers 6W148 and 6W154 (about a mile). A cautionary note: Brewer's Sparrows sometimes utter truncated, buzzy notes reminiscent of the mechanical buzzes of the Clay-colored. Other possibilities at this location include Osprey, Spotted Sandpiper, Eastern Kingbird, Gray Catbird, Cedar Waxwing, Yellow Warbler, Brewer's, Vesper, and Grasshopper (better in fields along both sides of Harvard Road) Sparrows, Black-headed Grosbeak, and Bullock's Oriole.

MOUNT SPOKANE STATE PARK

Mount Spokane, about 25 miles northeast of Spokane, is part of the southern Selkirk Mountains. Upper-elevation forests offer a chance of finding Blue Grouse and Hermit Thrush. Gray Jays are common and conspicuous. Sought-after boreal species such as Pine Grosbeak and White-winged Crossbill occur erratically in winter. Moose are possible, and even Mountain Lions.

From the point where US-2 and US-395 split at the north edge of Spokane, go east on US-2 until it intercepts SR-206 (4.4 miles). Turn right onto SR-206 and proceed to the entrance to Mount Spokane State Park (15.4 miles). Alternatively, from I-90 take Exit 287, go north on Argonne Road (later Bruce Road) 8.5 miles to SR-206, and turn right. It is 13.3 miles to the park.

Dense forest on the initial stretch of park road has resident Barred Owls. On reaching the pass (3.2 miles), turn right and park by **Selkirk Lodge** (0.3 mile). Enjoy the views extending to the mountains of the Northeast Corner and east into Idaho. Wet-forest habitats with abundant Douglas Maple, alder thickets, and Western Hemlock make this probably the best area for birds in the park. Walk (or ski) the trails south and east of the lodge during the winter period for Northern Pygmy-Owl, Gray and Steller's Jays, Common Raven, Chestnut-backed Chickadee, Pine Grosbeak, Cassin's Finch, Red and White-winged (irregular) Crossbills, and Common Redpoll (irregular). During the breeding season, look for Ruffed and Blue Grouse, Vaux's Swift (inclement weather), Black-backed Woodpecker, Cassin's and Warbling Vireos, Winter Wren, Swainson's, Hermit (more common higher up), and Varied Thrushes, Orange-crowned, Townsend's, MacGillivray's, and Wilson's Warblers, Fox Sparrow, Lazuli Bunting, and Pine Siskin. During migration, large numbers of Ruby-crowned Kinglets, Yellow-rumped Warblers, and White-crowned and Golden-crowned Sparrows can be present. Always be on the watch for Northern Goshawk and Golden Eagle.

The road from Selkirk Lodge north to the **downhill ski area** passes through more stands of mature Interior Wet Belt forest—especially good for Chestnut-backed Chickadee and crossbills—although this stretch can be a human zoo, especially on weekends. The four-mile **road to the summit** offers a different set of habitats (road closed to vehicles during the winter, but open to foot or ski traffic). Montane forests of Subalpine Fir, Douglas-fir, Lodgepole and Western White Pines, and Western Larch, encountered first, are home to Blue Grouse, Mountain Chickadee, and Hermit Thrush. High south slopes with grasslands and lichen-covered rocks have Horned Larks and Mountain Bluebirds. Check this area in fall for migrating raptors. Bohemian Waxwings, Lapland Longspurs, and Snow Buntings may be around at times in fall and early spring. Gray-crowned Rosy-Finches have been seen along the road.

TURNBULL NATIONAL WILDLIFE REFUGE

The 16,000-acre refuge, situated about 20 miles southwest of Spokane, is one of the area's prime birding sites, with over 200 species recorded. Coming from Spokane, go west on I-90 to Exit 270, then south on SR-904 to Cheney-Plaza Road in Cheney (6.4 miles). Coming from the west, take I-90 Exit 257 and follow SR-904 to Cheney and the intersection with Cheney-Plaza Road on the right, marked with a brown refuge sign (10.4 miles). Go south 4.3 miles on Cheney-Plaza Road to the main visitors' entrance (Smith Road), on the left. Roads inside the refuge are well signed. Drive to an interpretive display at the entrance station (fee) where you may pick up a refuge brochure

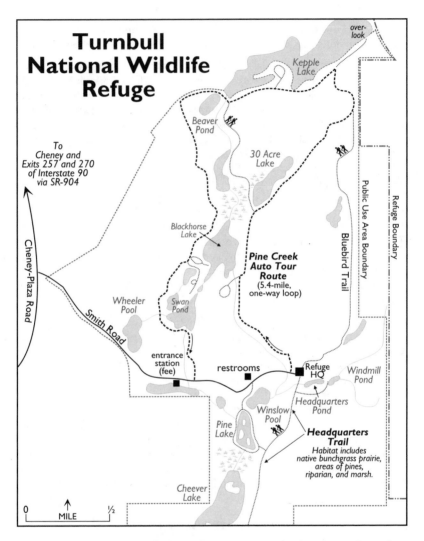

Turnbull
National Wildlife
Refuge

overlook

Kepple Lake

Beaver Pond

To
Cheney and
Exits 257 and 270
of Interstate 90
via SR-904

30 Acre Lake

Public Use Area Boundary

Refuge Boundary

Cheney-Plaza Road

Blackhorse Lake

Pine Creek
Auto Tour
Route
(5.4-mile,
one-way loop)

Bluebird Trail

Wheeler Pool

Smith Road

Swan Pond

entrance
station
(fee)

restrooms

Refuge HQ

Windmill Pond

Headquarters Pond

Winslow Pool

Pine Lake

Headquarters
Trail
Habitat includes
native bunchgrass prairie,
areas of pines,
riparian, and marsh.

Cheever Lake

0   ½
MILE

with a map. Maps and birdfinding information may also be obtained at refuge headquarters during weekday business hours. June is the best month overall, when nesting is at its peak, but May and September are good for landbird migrants, and April, October, and November for waterfowl migration. Rare vagrants recorded on the refuge include Mountain Plover (May), Golden-winged Warbler (August), Rose-breasted Grosbeak, and Rusty Blackbird (October).

Most of the refuge is closed to the public, but a large visitor-use area permits sampling of all of the habitats. The 5.4-mile **Pine Creek Auto Tour Route** is the most convenient way to do this. The tour starts just before refuge headquarters, on the left, and runs one way counterclockwise, ending near the entrance station. Three main habitats are encountered on this drive.

In the open Ponderosa Pine parkland, look for many bird species characteristic of the dry coniferous forest, including Hairy Woodpecker, Western Wood-Pewee, Mountain Chickadee, Red-breasted and Pygmy (common) Nuthatches, Western Bluebird, Chipping Sparrow, Cassin's Finch (rare), and Red Crossbill.

In the scattered groves of Quaking Aspen, Water Birch, Douglas Hawthorn, and alder, with understory thickets of wild rose, Red-osier Dogwood, serviceberry, and other shrubs, expect Ruffed Grouse, Northern Saw-whet Owl, Red-naped Sapsucker, Downy Woodpecker, Willow Flycatcher, Warbling and Red-eyed (uncommon) Vireos, Black-capped Chickadee, White-breasted Nuthatch, House Wren, Gray Catbird, Veery, Yellow Warbler, American Redstart, and more. With the substitution of a Yellow-bellied Sapsucker for its western cousin, note that this would be a typical list from an "eastern" deciduous forest. In addition, Black-chinned Hummingbird is recorded from Turnbull, and Least Flycatcher is possible in the aspens.

Most of the common waterfowl species of the West nest in Turnbull's marshes and lakes, including Canada Goose, Mallard, Blue-winged, Cinnamon, and Green-winged Teals, Redhead, and Ruddy Duck. Small flocks of Tundra Swans, and many other species of waterfowl, come through the refuge during migration. Other marshbirds include Pied-billed Grebe, American Bittern, Virginia Rail, Sora, American Coot, Spotted Sandpiper, Wilson's Snipe, Black Tern, Marsh Wren, Common Yellowthroat, and Yellow-headed and Red-winged Blackbirds.

To reach areas of native bunchgrass prairie, another habitat on the refuge, take the hike south along **Headquarters Trail**, which runs east of Winslow Pool and Pine Lake about 1.5 miles to the far end of Cheever Lake. Areas of pines, and riparian and marsh habitats, are also met with on this trail, making this probably the most species-rich area open to the public on the refuge. In the grasslands, look for Red-tailed Hawk and American Kestrel, Gray Partridge, Say's Phoebe, Vesper and Grasshopper Sparrows, and Western Meadowlark.

The refuge is also good habitat for mammals, including Columbian Ground Squirrel, Red Squirrel, Yellow-pine Chipmunk, White-tailed Deer, Coyote, Badger, River Otter, and Long-tailed Weasel. In May and June, the open spaces among the pines are carpeted with an astonishing collection of wildflowers. Take precautions against Wood Ticks, which are especially plentiful from March through May.

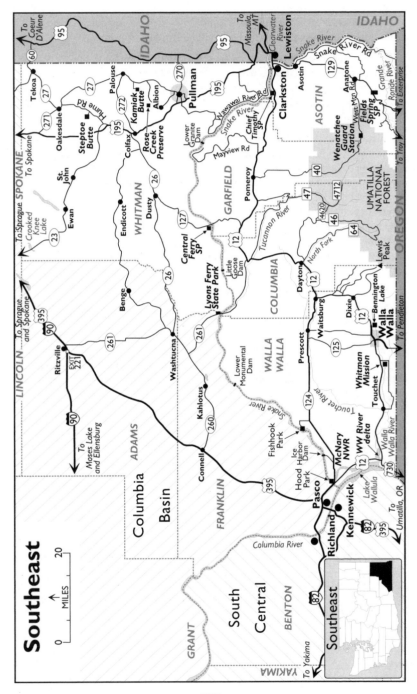

Southeast

MILES
0   20

SOUTHEAST

If the Selkirk Mountains of the Northeast put one in mind of the Canadian Rockies, with species such as Spruce Grouse, Boreal Chickadee, and White-winged Crossbill, then birders visiting the Blue Mountains of the Southeast might think they were in Utah. Here the ranges of species of the Middle Rockies—Broad-tailed Hummingbird, Cordilleran Flycatcher, Green-tailed Towhee—flirt with the corner of the state.

Remote and uninhabited, the rugged Blues rise as a forested rampart above a sea of former steppe habitats, now virtually all converted to cropland. The Columbia River borders the region on the west; the Snake River forms its eastern and part of its northern boundary. Many who live here are dependent on a resource-based economy, with wheat farming, cattle grazing, and logging as primary industries. Tamed by four large dams, the Snake has become the region's economic lifeline. Each year tugs push countless barges laden with millions of tons of grain, lumber, and other goods through the Snake River locks and along the Columbia River waterway. The once-legendary Snake River runs of salmon and Steelhead are now approaching extinction, an enormous environmental cost of the dams.

The Southeast is divided into four subregions, each with its own distinctive topography, habitats, and birdlife.

The *western lowlands* provide typical Columbia Basin birding in the irrigated agricultural lands of the Walla Walla River drainage and along the shoreline of Lake Wallula, the reservoir at the region's western edge. In particular, the Walla Walla delta is renowned as one of Eastern Washington's consistently best sites for shorebirds, gulls, and waterfowl, with numerous records of rarities.

The deeply eroded *Blue Mountains* of Washington's southeast corner and adjacent Oregon are home to owls, woodpeckers, and other forest birds in good variety and numbers. Forest types are transitional to those of the Rockies to the east, while brush associations have affinities with the Great Basin to the south. Far too seldom visited, the surprising Blues are one of the birding frontiers of the state.

The Grande Ronde volcano—source of the basalt flows that engulfed the Columbia Basin—forms the backside of the Blues, above a high plateau. Arid steppe habitats extend along the *Snake and Grande Ronde River gorges*. Very lightly birded, this remote and scenic region at the eastern edge of the state is

503

great for birds of bare rock, high cliffs, open fields, and riparian vegetation in canyon bottoms.

North of the Snake River, the *Palouse* is an arresting landscape of great mounds of windblown silt from prehistoric floods, now given over to dryland wheat farming. Birds still thrive in the few remaining pockets of original grassland habitats. The highest spots are pre-Cambrian rocks of the ancient North American continent. Islands of trees and brush in the surrounding wheat barrens, these eminences offer good vagrant potential.

The climate of the Southeast varies considerably but predictably. Lake Wallula—in the lowest part of the Columbia Basin, just 340 feet above sea level—is hot in summer (temperatures exceeding 90 degrees on about 40 days during a typical year), fairly mild in winter (January average low 28 degrees), and dry (eight inches average annual precipitation). Thirty miles east and 1,000 feet above sea level, Walla Walla experiences similar temperatures but receives twice as much precipitation (18 inches). Although winter temperatures remain about the same as one moves toward the Idaho line, summers are cooler. Pullman (2,400 feet above sea level) sees 15 days above 90 degrees, while at Anatone, in the shadow of the eastern Blues at 3,570 feet, the thermometer climbs above 90 degrees only eight days per year. Precipitation increases slightly (22 inches at Pullman, 20 at Anatone).

The highlands are another story. Data are meager, but the Blues are much cooler and wetter than the rest of the region. Average annual precipitation in the highest parts (above 5,500 feet) is 8–10 times greater than at the Columbia River. Summer thunderstorms, though infrequent, may be severe; be alert for washouts. Most gravel roads in the high Blues are closed throughout the winter and may not be entirely snow-free until mid-June or even later.

Snowfall is generally light in the lowlands (19 inches annually at Walla Walla, 29 at Pullman, but 66 at Anatone). Highways and most secondary roads are kept plowed; nonetheless, watch for blowing and drifting snow. Be cautious if traveling off the main roads at this season.

Services including accommodations may be found in Walla Walla, Waitsburg, Dayton, Pomeroy, Clarkston, Asotin, Pullman, and Colfax.

WESTERN LOWLANDS

by Mike Denny and MerryLynn Denny

The western part of the region, extending to the base of the Blue Mountains, occupies the lowest and some of the driest parts of the Columbia Basin. Notable topographic features include the confluence of the Snake and Columbia Rivers, Wallula Gap, and the Walla Walla River valley. Bedrock is basalt from the Miocene lava flows, covered over in many places by deep layers of silt deposited on the bed of a succession of temporary lakes as the Columbia backed up behind the constriction of Wallula Gap. Irrigation has dramatically changed the landscape. Shrub-steppe habitats are now mostly only a memory, replaced with productive farmland grown to wheat, potatoes, orchards, vineyards, alfalfa and hay, onions (the famous Walla Walla Sweets), and other crops. Open country is devoted mainly to cattle grazing. The following sites are accessed from US-12, the main highway across southeastern Washington.

LOWER SNAKE RIVER

Heading southeast from Pasco, US-12 crosses the Snake River to Burbank. Immediately after crossing the bridge, turn left onto SR-124. In 0.1 mile, make another left into **Hood Park**. Ornamental plantings predominate. Birds are plentiful in the extensive Russian Olive thickets and in the marshy area near the entrance. In fall and winter the many berry-producing trees attract American Robin, Hermit and Varied Thrushes, Cedar Waxwing, and Yellow-rumped Warbler; careful searching may reveal a rarity. The sloughs have Wood Duck and other waterfowl.

Continue east on SR-124, turning left in 5.2 miles onto Ice Harbor Dam Road toward **Ice Harbor Dam**. Bear left in 3.0 miles before reaching the dam and take a gravel road downstream a half-mile to a point opposite a mid-river island—a good place to scope gulls (Glaucous has been noted in winter).

Back on SR-124, Fishhook Park Road is 10.9 miles farther east. Turn left here and go 4.3 miles through one of the world's largest orchards (about 4,000 acres) to the entrance of **Fishhook Park**, along the Snake River. The clumps of ornamental plantings, including conifers, in this mostly manicured park attract many birds. The park is gated and closed to camping and picnicking from October through March, so there is little disturbance during those months. Park to the side of the gate and walk in. Barn, Great Horned, Long-eared, and Northern Saw-whet Owls may be present then. Look also for Northern Harrier and for Sharp-shinned, Cooper's, and Rough-legged Hawks. Check trees and brushy areas for Hermit and Varied Thrushes, Rusty Blackbird (rare), large flocks of sparrows, and mountain species uncommon in the lower Columbia Basin such as Red-breasted Nuthatch, Golden-crowned

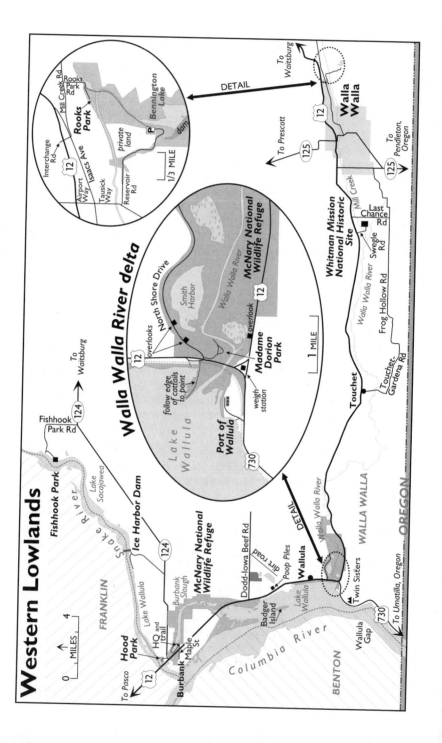

Western Lowlands

Walla Walla River delta

DETAIL

To Waitsburg

Walla Walla

12

To Prescott

125

To Pendleton, Oregon

125

Mill Creek

Rooks Park Rd
Mill Creek Rd
Bennington Lake
Rooks Park
P
dam
private land
Interchange Rd
12
Airport Way
Isaacs Ave
Tausick Way
Reservoir Rd
1/3 MILE

North Shore Drive
Walla Walla River
McNary National Wildlife Refuge
Smith Harbor
overlooks
12
overlook
12
Madame Dorion Park
follow edge of cattails to point
weigh station
Lake Wallula
Port of Wallula
730
1 MILE

Whitman Mission National Historic Site
Last Chance Rd
Swegle Rd
Walla Walla River
Frog Hollow Rd
Touchet
Touchet-Gardena Rd

To Waitsburg
124
Fishhook Park Rd
Fishhook Park
Lake Sacajawea
Snake River
Ice Harbor Dam
124
FRANKLIN
Lake Wallula
Hood Park
HQ and trail
Burbank
Maple St
12
To Pasco

McNary National Wildlife Refuge
Burbank Slough
Dodd-Iowa Beef Rd
dirt road
Poop Piles
Badger Island
Lake Wallula
Wallula
Twin Sisters
Wallula Gap
730
To Umatilla, Oregon

DETAIL
Walla Walla River
WALLA WALLA
OREGON
BENTON
Columbia River

MILES
0   4

Kinglet, and Townsend's Solitaire. Huge numbers of waterfowl seek sanctuary on the river during hunting season; in November, up to 100,000 ducks (mostly Mallards) may raft off the park in the evening. Spring migration can also be good—watch for Cassin's Vireo, Nashville, Townsend's, and Wilson's Warblers, and Fox Sparrow.

Birding sites on the opposite bank of the Snake are described in the Columbia Basin chapter, page 372.

LAKE WALLULA

Lake Wallula is the name given to the huge impoundment of Columbia River waters behind McNary Dam. The east bank of the reservoir from the mouth of the Snake River to the Oregon line is one of the most productive areas in Washington for birds associated with water and shorelines; the shallows are an important nursery for fall Chinook Salmon. Most of the best birding spots are in the **McNary National Wildlife Refuge**—15,894 acres of river islands, backwater sloughs, seasonal wetlands, delta mudflats, riparian areas, and shrub-steppe uplands set aside for wildlife in 1954 in mitigation for bottomlands drowned by the dam.

From the intersection of US-12 and SR-124 in Burbank, go southeast on US-12 to Maple Street (0.9 mile). Turn left and go 0.3 mile to McNary National Wildlife Refuge headquarters. Pamphlets and other refuge information are available here. Except in the summer doldrums or when occasionally frozen in mid-winter, **Burbank Slough**—an abandoned oxbow of the Columbia River—is filled with waterfowl. A trail, about one mile in length, encircles one end of the slough, beginning just below the parking area. The best viewing is from a blind and other vantage points near the beginning. From fall through spring 15 or more species of dabbling and diving ducks are often in this pool, along with Tundra Swans and geese; there may be no better place in Eastern Washington to view such a diverse array of waterfowl closely. Sparrows, including White-throated and Harris's (both regular though rare), may be found in brush and Russian Olives on the trail. Cattail stands near brush are one of the better Eastside places for Swamp Sparrow, especially in late fall.

There are several spots along US-12 to park and bird other units of the refuge as one continues southeast. In summer and fall a pond on the right just past **milepost 300** often attracts shorebirds, including rarities such as Ruff (pullout 3.9 miles from Maple Street, but access may change due to widening of the highway).

Dodd-Iowa Beef Road is another 1.6 miles along US-12. Turn left here and proceed past the large slaughterhouse to feedlots where blackbirds may be seen by the thousands. Rusty is rare but regular, especially in fall and early winter. Cattle Egrets are sometimes found along this road in late fall. Several large ponds along a dirt road (second right east of the livestock yards) attract waterfowl, raptors, and shorebirds. Back on US-12, turn left. Another 1.5 miles brings you to a pullout at the "Poop Piles," where entrails from the slaughterhouse are spewed out and mixed with waste from a nearby paper mill. If not promptly covered, these piles of questionable material provide a smorgasbord for thousands of gulls. Ring-billed, California, Herring, and Glaucous-winged are the usual cast. Starlings and blackbirds abound, with lesser numbers of other opportunists such as magpies, crows, and House Sparrows. Look west to Badger Island in Lake Wallula, one of only two known places in the state where American White Pelicans breed.

It is another 4.5 miles to the junction of US-12 and US-730 at the **Walla Walla River delta**, southeastern Washington's premier birding site. About 200 species have been recorded here; birds rare or unusual for the interior of the state turn up regularly. Administered as part of the McNary National Wildlife Refuge, this area includes the lower four miles of the Walla Walla River, bordering hills with shrub-steppe vegetation, several large ponds, a substantial riparian zone, the delta where the Walla Walla empties into Lake Wallula, a strip of shoreline, and Crescent Island out in the lake. Water levels on Lake Wallula fluctuate as reservoir control officials respond to competing demands for power generation, barge traffic, irrigation, recreation, movement of salmon, and various other wildlife considerations. Occasionally water levels are so high that the area is attractive to birds favoring deeper waters. Lower levels expose mud; shorebirds then find great habitat.

Birding at this outstanding site can cause the adrenaline to rise. Interesting species in fall migration (the most rewarding period) include Merlin, Peregrine Falcon, Black-bellied Plover, American Golden-Plover, Solitary Sandpiper, Whimbrel, Marbled Godwit, Sanderling, Semipalmated (best late July through mid-August), Baird's, Sharp-tailed, and Stilt Sandpipers, Ruff, Short-billed Dowitcher (best late July through August), Red Phalarope, Parasitic Jaeger, Franklin's and Sabine's Gulls (especially early September), and Common Tern. Shorebird movements peak in August and September, with lesser numbers arriving through mid-October. Rarities include Brant, Garganey, Steller's Eider, Hudsonian Godwit, Ruddy Turnstone, Red Knot, Long-tailed Jaeger, Black-legged Kittiwake, and Arctic Tern. Fall migration of small landbirds begins in mid-July and runs through late September. In addition to great numbers of Vaux's Swifts, swallows, pipits, and warblers, rare birds to watch for include Northern Waterthrush and American Tree and White-throated Sparrows.

Waterfowl hunting starts in mid-October and can greatly impact the quality of birding at this site. Check with refuge staff to determine hunter-free days during the long hunting season.

In late fall and winter tens of thousands of waterfowl (mostly Canada Geese and Mallards) and many gulls arrive. This may be one of the best sites in Eastern Washington for gulls, including Mew, Ring-billed, California, Herring, Thayer's, Iceland (one November record), Western, Glaucous-winged, and

Glaucous. Late winter 2000 brought the state's first Lesser Black-backed Gull (returning the next two winters). Thousands of gulls may arrive each winter afternoon. Other species to watch for in this season include Snow Goose (with a few blue-morph), Tufted and Long-tailed Ducks, Dunlin, and Northern Shrike.

Spring migration brings Greater White-fronted Goose, Eurasian and American Wigeons, Northern Pintail, and thousands of Green-winged Teal to the delta and to other refuge ponds and sloughs. Summer breeders on the delta include Virginia Rail and Caspian Tern.

Access to the delta proper is from a one-lane dirt track on the west side of US-12 across from the entrance to Madame Dorion Park (0.4 mile north of the truck weigh station at the US-730 intersection). Drive in to the railroad, then bear right paralleling the tracks to a dirt parking area (0.1 mile). The delta lies to the west across the tracks (watch out for trains) and is reached by a trail that winds down through the brush to an overlook. Scope the delta from here, or if you have rubber boots, bring your scope and wade the narrow channel at the water's edge to wander westward along the Cattail beds out to the end of the delta. Beware the few areas of soft and sticky mud. White-tailed Deer inhabit the dense thickets; Mule Deer is the usual species on the surrounding hills. Raccoons leave their tracks in the delta mud. *Be forewarned that access to the delta may change with future construction of a trail along the Walla Walla River from Madame Dorion Park.*

Madame Dorion Park (restrooms, primitive campground, picnic site) is on the east side of US-12 opposite the delta access. Turn onto North Shore Drive, then immediately right into the park, which lies along the Walla Walla River. Willows and brush are excellent for Western Screech-Owl, Downy Woodpecker, Black-capped Chickadee, and Bewick's Wren. White-throated and Harris's Sparrows are sometimes found in brushy patches across (west) from the restrooms in winter. Turn right from the park and continue on North Shore Drive to a lake overlook (0.4 mile). In winter, thousands of waterfowl (mostly Mallards) can be scoped from here. Shorebirds can be numerous in fall. Another marshy lake, just east of the park, can be scoped from a pullout on the north side of US-12 (0.2 mile east of the truck weigh station). This site can be teeming with shorebirds if water levels are low. Look for Black-crowned Night-Herons in summer and fall.

In winter and early spring, spilled grain attracts hundreds of diving ducks to the **Port of Wallula** grain-loading facility. From US-12, go west 0.5 mile to the turnoff on the north side of US-730. Drive to but not through the entrance gate, then left on a rough dirt track to an overlook of Lake Wallula (0.1 mile) and scope for Canvasback, Redhead, Greater and Lesser Scaups, and Common Goldeneye. Return to the gate and enter the port on foot. Walk past the grain elevators (the *No Trespassing* signs do not seem to be an issue at present) to brushy thickets where sparrows, including Harris's, sometimes feed on waste grain. The wetland just below holds species such as Virginia Rail and Marsh Wren.

US-730 bends south toward Oregon through **Wallula Gap**, the mile-wide channel slowly eroded by the Columbia River through the layered basalts of the Horse Heaven Hills. Here the river exits the Columbia Basin. Pull off into the parking area on the east side of the busy highway 1.4 miles from the port facility entrance, cross through the fence onto BLM land, and take the dirt path east for a few hundred yards to the base of the **Twin Sisters**. These picturesque basalt peaks (erosional remnants of the Spokane Floods) have also been called the Two Captains in honor of Lewis and Clark, who passed by here, but the old Indian name is the one that has stuck. Listen and look for Prairie Falcon, Chukar, Say's Phoebe, and Rock and Canyon Wrens on these and other cliffs in the area, but stay inside the boundary fence. The land to the south is private.

WALLA WALLA VALLEY

Look for raptors in the Walla Walla Valley wherever there are alfalfa and hay fields. Northern Harrier and Red-tailed and Rough-legged Hawks are common in winter; Prairie Falcon is also present. Swainson's Hawk replaces Rough-legged in summer. In the late-summer harvest season, raptors concentrate to feed in fields where rodents are dislodged by the cutting process. A good raptor loop through farming country begins at **Touchet** (pronounced *TOO-chee*), 12.5 miles east on US-12 from the weigh station at the US-730 intersection. Turn right (south) on Walnut Street to McKay Road (0.3 mile), right on McKay to Gardena Road (0.2 mile), and left here to Touchet-Gardena Road (1.2 miles). Turn left, go 3.5 miles on Touchet-Gardena, and turn left again onto Frog Hollow Road. Stay on this road in a mostly eastward direction to Last Chance Road (8.2 miles), where you may turn left to rejoin US-12 in 2.4 miles.

The **Whitman Mission National Historic Site** is located just off US-12 between Touchet and Walla Walla. Turn south onto Swegle Road 10 miles east of Walnut Street in Touchet (1.1 miles west of Last Chance Road if coming from the other direction); in 0.5 mile take the first turn to the east, following the signs. The mission founded here in 1836 by Dr. Marcus Whitman and his wife, Narcissa, figures prominently in the early history of Euro-American immigration and the often tragic interactions with the local Indians, the Cayuse. The deciduous trees, shrubs, farm fields, and wetlands on the grounds of the small museum can be good in spring and fall migration for species such as Black-crowned Night-Heron, Orange-crowned and Nashville Warblers, Lincoln's and White-crowned Sparrows, and Black-headed Grosbeak, while Sharp-shinned Hawk, Merlin, Varied Thrush, Harris's Sparrow (uncommon), Pine Siskin, and American Goldfinch may be present from November to February.

US-12 skirts the north edge of Walla Walla, established in 1856 as Fort Walla Walla and now a tidy farming, college, and service community where large shade trees and 19th-century mansions mix with younger neighborhoods.

East of town, **Bennington Lake** on the U.S. Army Corps of Engineers Mill Creek site is productive for a wide array of birds. Turn south from US-12 onto Airport Way (10 miles from the Whitman Mission turnoff). The road soon changes name to Tausick Way. In 0.5 mile, turn left onto Reservoir Road and wind along for 1.7 miles to the far end of the parking lot. A network of trails begins here, including a spur that ends at Rooks Park at the north end of the site. Bewick's Wrens are resident, and brush and trees attract many sparrows in winter—mostly White-crowned, but White-throated and Harris's have been recorded. The introduced junipers are excellent for Townsend's Solitaire. Check the lake for an assortment of waterfowl.

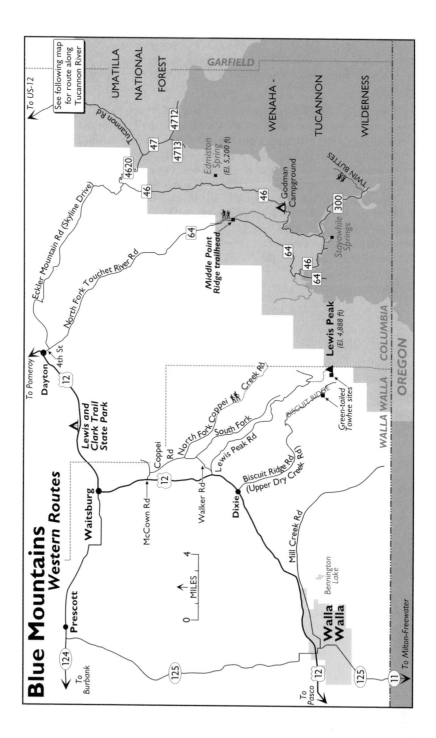

Blue Mountains
Western Routes

BLUE MOUNTAINS

by Mike Denny, MerryLynn Denny, and Andy Stepniewski

Encompassed by the Umatilla National Forest, the Blue Mountains rise abruptly to the east of Walla Walla, peaking above 6,000 feet. The exposed rock of these mountains is an upfolding of Columbia Plateau basalts from the recent (Miocene) lava flows, but geologists hypothesize that these layers mask an ancient coastal range of the original North American continent. Precipitation increases dramatically as one ascends the western slopes; mountain streams cascade down to the Walla Walla and Tucannon River basins. Erosional forces have produced steep-sided canyons and rocky escarpments, home to raptors and other birds of the cliffs. At lower elevations, wheat- and rangelands reach up to the lower forest zone. Lush riparian growth along the drainages is filled with birds in spring and early summer. At middle elevations, brushy patches clinging to steep valley sides host Washington's only breeding Green-tailed Towhees. A mosaic of forest communities (low, high, wet, dry) ranges from Ponderosa Pine, Douglas-fir, and Grand Fir up to Subalpine Fir, Engelmann Spruce, and Western Larch, with bird species appropriate to these habitat types. Some call the Blue Mountains Washington's Woodpecker Heaven; as more and more birders are discovering, the same might be said for owls. Elk, Mule Deer, Bighorn Sheep, and Black Bear are also common.

A good strategy to bird the Blues is to begin at low elevations in the morning and work to higher, forested habitats toward mid-day. Or, during periods of inclement weather (which can be frequent in the high mountains), one might be advised to take refuge low down all day. Birding is best from mid-June to early October, after which the higher roads begin to drift over with snow.

US-12 traces the western and northern base of the Blue Mountains on its way from Walla Walla to Clarkston, passing through Dixie, Waitsburg, Dayton, and Pomeroy—well-preserved towns established in the 1870s on lumbering, wheat farming, and supplying Idaho-bound miners. The core of the high Washington Blues is set aside in the roadless Wenaha-Tucannon Wilderness Area (177,469 acres, partly in Oregon). Access by road is thus mostly an in-and-out affair from US-12 along various ridgelines and drainages. An exception is the up-and-over route via the Wenatchee Guard Station, providing an excellent connection between Pomeroy and the canyonlands east of the mountains.

BISCUIT RIDGE AND LEWIS PEAK

Two of the best spots for Green-tailed Towhee are a dozen miles due east of Walla Walla in the mid-elevation Blues. These ridgeline sites are only a mile apart, separated by the valley of North Fork Dry Creek—but there is no direct connecting road between them.

On the eastern outskirts of the village of Dixie, about eight miles northeast of Walla Walla on US-12, turn south onto Biscuit Ridge Road (also known as Upper Dry Creek Road). After 6.5 miles this road becomes gravel and steep, but is well-maintained and passable for ordinary vehicles. In another 3.7 miles, stop on the crest of **Biscuit Ridge**. Walk downhill (west) from the right side of the road to the edge of a steep escarpment. From mid-May to at least mid-August Green-tailed Towhees may be in Mountain Snowberry and wild rose near the top of the hillside or (more likely) in shrub patches about halfway down the precipice (be careful if you trek downslope). Spotted Towhees also occur here. If you fail to find the Green-taileds, head back toward Dixie and look for them downslope on this same side of the road, down to about 0.5 mile before the blacktop begins. Great Gray Owls have also been found nesting recently along this stretch of Biscuit Ridge Road.

The junction with Lewis Peak Road is 2.0 miles farther north on US-12 from the Biscuit Ridge turnoff. Turn right here and stay right at the fork a few hundred feet ahead. As the road ascends, watch for Gray Partridge, Western and Mountain Bluebirds, Vesper Sparrow, Elk, and Black Bear. By about mile six the road has entered conifers. Most of the land here is privately owned and liberally posted; please do not trespass. The road forks at 8.6 miles from US-12. Park, lock your vehicle, and walk along the right branch for about a mile and a half to **Lewis Peak** (elevation 4,888 feet). Most of this land is private, though presently open to the public. Look for Green-tailed Towhee on the southwest side of the peak in brushy situations. Also watch and listen for White-throated Swift, Three-toed Woodpecker, Cassin's Vireo, Gray Jay, Pine Grosbeak (winter; irregular), and Red Crossbill.

COPPEI CREEK

Coppei (pronounced COP-eye) Creek flows north from the vicinity of Lewis Peak to join the Touchet River at Waitsburg. The lower portion of the South Fork is lined with superb riparian habitats, while the upper reaches of South and North Forks offer good mid-elevation forest birding. During winter, both drainages may have hardy bark- and twig-gleaning species such as chickadees, nuthatches, and Brown Creeper, as well as flocks of American Robins and Bohemian Waxwings.

Take the Lewis Peak turnoff from US-12 as described in the preceding section. At the fork in a few hundred feet go left onto Walker Road, which ends in 1.4 miles at **South Fork Coppei Creek Road**. In either direction, the lush riparian corridor of the South Fork is passerine heaven from late April through mid-July; fall migration can also be good. A few of the many interesting species to look for from the road are Ruffed Grouse, Vaux's Swift, Calliope Hummingbird, Eastern Kingbird, Red-eyed Vireo, Veery, Gray Catbird, American Redstart, Yellow-breasted Chat, and Black-headed Grosbeak. There have also been a number of unusual sightings. One can continue right (upstream) for nearly six miles, reaching forests of Douglas-fir and Grand Fir.

Here, look for Northern Goshawk, Northern Pygmy-Owl, Pileated Wood-pecker, Winter Wren, Townsend's Solitaire, and Townsend's Warbler.

To reach another excellent area, go left (downstream) to **North Fork Coppei Creek Road** (0.8 mile from the Walker Road corner). Turn right onto this gravel road and continue 3.2 miles to just past a bridge at the base of a steep hill. Park here and continue walking uphill on the road, watching for owls, woodpeckers, and other forest birds. This branch of the creek tumbles down out of the Blue Mountains through alders, conifers, and willows. It lies within the Waitsburg city watershed and is closed to entry, except for the road. Birds seen here include Wild Turkey, Northern Pygmy- and Northern Saw-whet Owls, Red-naped Sapsucker, Pacific-slope/Cordilleran-type fly-catchers, Cassin's Vireo, and Chestnut-backed Chickadee. Upper reaches of the North Fork road are not plowed in winter.

From the intersection of the North Fork and South Fork roads, continue north (downstream) on Coppei Road to McCown Road (2.5 miles). Turn left here, then right in 0.5 mile onto US-12 and continue into Waitsburg, where US-12 makes a right-angle turn to the east (3.3 miles). **Lewis and Clark Trail State Park** (campground) is 4.5 miles farther east on the north side of US-12. Many birds inhabit the dense riparian woodland along the Touchet River here, including Mourning Dove, Western Screech-Owl, Eastern Kingbird, Warbling and Red-eyed (uncommon) Vireos, Black-billed Magpie, Veery, Gray Catbird, Yellow Warbler, Yellow-breasted Chat, Black-headed Grosbeak, and Bullock's Oriole.

NORTH FORK TOUCHET RIVER

An excellent loop into the high Blue Mountains follows a ridgeline south from Dayton above the North Fork Touchet River, returning via the river val-ley. Turn right onto Fourth Street in Dayton (5.5 miles from Lewis and Clark Trail State Park), then left in 0.5 mile onto Eckler Mountain Road (Skyline Drive). Follow this road (summer only) for about 16 miles to an intersection on the left with FR-4620 (connects in about four miles to Tucannon Road, page 517). Keep straight ahead on Eckler Mountain Road, which becomes FR-46 upon entering the Umatilla National Forest in another 0.8 mile. **Edmiston Spring** (6.0 miles, elevation 5,200 feet) offers a fine sample of the higher-elevation birdlife (Wild Turkey, Williamson's Sapsucker, Ruby-crowned Kinglet). Another 5.1 miles uphill is **Godman Campground**, on the high Blue Mountain divide (north slope draining to the Touchet River, south slope to the Wenaha River in Oregon). These forests of Subalpine Fir and Western Larch are inhabited by Northern Goshawk and by Williamson's Sapsucker and other woodpeckers, including Three-toed (uncommon). Five miles farther, FR-300 turns off left from FR-46, leading in about six miles to the trailhead for the short hike to Twin Buttes. These high-altitude forests should be checked in September and October for Boreal Owl. At that season, birds respond to a tape recording of their primary call with a piercing *skiew*. Great Gray Owl has also been reported recently in the nesting season.

Return to FR-46 and turn left. The road snakes along the ridgetop, mostly in subalpine forest (good for Boreal Owl). In about two-thirds of a mile park at the trailhead on the left and make the short hike to **Stayawhile Springs**. Flammulated Owls have been noted in the dense stringer to the west and south of this spot; forests to the east and north are prime habitat for Boreal Owl. At the junction with FR-64 (5.1 miles from FR-300), turn right and head down the North Fork Touchet River. In 6.9 miles, park at the **Middle Point Ridge Trailhead**. Cross the rushing stream on a footbridge. As you walk downstream on the trail through old-growth forest of Grand Fir, Engelmann Spruce, and Western Larch, with abundant Western Yew in the understory, look for Hammond's and Pacific-slope Flycatchers, Chestnut-backed Chickadee, Winter Wren, and Townsend's Warbler. From the trailhead it is about 17 miles downhill via FR-64 (becomes North Fork Touchet River Road, then Fourth Street) to US-12 in Dayton.

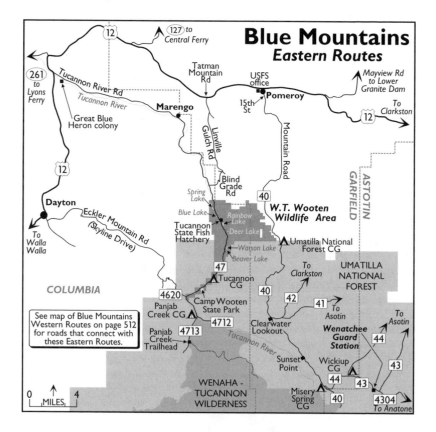

TUCANNON RIVER

The Tucannon River drains the large midsection of the Washington Blues northward to the Snake River. US-12 crosses the Tucannon 13 miles north of Dayton (1.6 miles south of the junction with SR-261 to Lyons Ferry State Park, page 376). Turn east (right if coming from Dayton) at the north end of the bridge onto Tucannon River Road and follow the beautiful **Tucannon Valley**, a mosaic of farms and riparian vegetation rimmed with basalt cliffs. In 1.1 miles look toward the river for the large Great Blue Heron colony in the Black Cottonwoods. Also watch for Spotted Sandpiper, Belted Kingfisher, and Eastern Kingbird in summer. In the fields, watch for Wild Turkey and White-tailed Deer early in the morning or in the evening. Good bets on the way to tiny Marengo (10 miles from the heronry viewpoint) include many Red-tailed Hawks (nesting on the cliffs north of the road, especially along the first few miles), Chukar, Great Horned and Short-eared Owls, Common Nighthawk, and Rock Wren. Ferruginous Hawk is also possible.

Beyond Marengo the road bends to run more or less south. One enters the **William T. Wooten Wildlife Area** (11,778 acres), reaching the first of five artificial impoundments at Spring Lake (10.1 miles). This is a rugged area of valleys and ridges with conifers and brush on the high, steep slopes. Look for Red-naped Sapsucker, Red-eyed Vireo, and Gray Catbird in streamside vegetation on the valley floor. Park at the **Tucannon State Fish Hatchery** (1.0 mile) and walk south to Rainbow Lake, watching for Pacific-slope/Cordilleran-type flycatchers, Cassin's and Red-eyed Vireos, Gray Catbirds, and huge numbers of butterflies in spring. In August and early September, Solitary Sandpipers (as many as eight at once) occur at the hatchery ponds and Rainbow Lake.

Continuing south, the road soon enters the Umatilla National Forest and becomes FR-47. **Camp Wooten State Park** (6.1 miles from the hatchery) is good for most of the middle-elevation birds of the Blue Mountains. Reservations are needed to stay here (phone 360-902-8600). Northern Pygmy-, Barred, and Northern Saw-whet Owls are present in March and April; in summer, Flammulated Owl can be found another 1.3 miles south on FR-47. Watch for woodpeckers and American Dipper along this portion of the river. In another 0.7 mile (2.0 miles from Camp Wooten) you will come to FR-4620, on the right, which connects to the North Fork Touchet River loop (page 515). Continuing south on FR-47, Panjab Creek Campground is reached in 1.8 miles (USFS, primitive, fee). The road divides here; take the right fork (FR-4713) to the **Panjab Creek Trailhead** (3.0 miles). This trail traverses a superb example of a moist Eastside forest (elevation about 4,000 feet). Look for Northern Goshawk, Pileated Woodpecker, Chestnut-backed Chickadee, Hermit and Varied Thrushes, and Western Tanager.

If you will next be heading east on US-12 toward Pomeroy, a shortcut (weather permitting) can be made by turning right from Tucannon Road onto

A male Williamson's Sapsucker, his stunning plumage set off against the subtle hues of the Ponderosa Pine forest, pauses for a moment to take the morning sunlight in Fields Spring State Park.

Blind Grade Road, 2.0 miles downstream from Spring Lake. This aptly-named gravel road switchbacks steeply up to a four-way junction (2.4 miles). From here, take the paved Linville Gulch Road (becomes Tatman Mountain Road) for 6.5 miles down to US-12. Turn right to reach Pomeroy in about five miles.

WENATCHEE GUARD STATION

Wenatchee Guard Station, on the crest of the Washington Blues at an elevation of about 5,200 feet, may be approached either from the north (US-12 at Pomeroy) or from the east (SR-129 at Anatone). Time and other considerations allowing, the 40-mile drive between these two towns—over the top and down again, in either direction—is a perfect way to experience the birds of this remote corner of Washington. Breathtaking vistas of deep gorges and into three states are an added inducement.

On the east side of Pomeroy, turn south from US-12 onto 15th Street. (You can obtain maps, road and trail information, and a Northwest Forest Pass at the USFS ranger district office on US-12 a mile west of this corner.) Upon leaving town 15th Street changes name to Mountain Road and eventually becomes FR-40. In about 15 miles you reach **Umatilla National Forest Campground**, just within the national forest boundary. Ponderosa Pine dominates; look for White-headed Woodpecker, Pygmy Nuthatch, Yellow-rumped Warbler, and Cassin's Finch. In another 7.9 miles, at Clearwater Lookout, you enter the eastern Blue Mountains. From this point forward the slopes to the left of the road drain to Asotin Creek, which reaches the Snake River at Asotin. **Sunset Point** (5.0 miles) affords spectacular views of the upper Tucannon Basin on the south side of the road. Although this is not officially designated wilderness, no sign of humankind is visible below—a rare experience nowadays.

In another 3.7 miles is **Misery Spring Campground**. Here, at 6,200 feet, the trees are Subalpine Fir, Engelmann Spruce, and Western Larch. Ruby-crowned Kinglets are abundant. Look also for Three-toed Woodpecker, Gray Jay, Winter Wren, Townsend's Warbler, and Fox and White-crowned (*oriantha*) Sparrows. The road forks; go left on FR-44 to **Wickiup Campground** (3.2 miles). These high forests have been good for Northern Goshawk, Blue Grouse, and Williamson's Sapsucker.

The road forks again by the campground; stay right with FR-43 and enjoy the dramatic vistas on your way to **Wenatchee Guard Station** (3.2 miles). You are at the crest of the Blue Mountains, a broad anticlinal arch (inverted U) of Columbia Plateau basalts. South from this vantage the terrain has been deeply incised by stream erosion, to the point that virtually none of the original plateau remains. Some of the northernmost Mountain Mahogany, a gnarled and grayish-hued small tree, clings to these rocky, south-facing ridges. Cool, moist forests blanket the north slopes, which have yet to be chewed away by erosion. Green-tailed Towhee was first documented as a breeder in

Washington in a canyon near the guard station in 1923. Since then, however, records from this area have been few. If you're in an exploratory mood, try hiking about the south-facing slopes, checking dwarfish shrub patches.

To join the Grande Ronde country, continue east on FR-43 along the ridgeline, then stay right onto FR-4304 at a fork in 0.6 mile. In another 6.9 miles the road changes name to West Mountain Road as you leave the Umatilla National Forest. In 5.6 miles, merge right onto Mill Road, reaching SR-129 in Anatone in 1.8 miles. Turn right here for Fields Spring State Park (page 524).

SNAKE AND GRANDE RONDE RIVER CANYONS

by Mike Denny, MerryLynn Denny, and Andy Stepniewski

The extreme southeast corner of Washington is a paradise for those who love arid, hot slopes and grandiose scenery. This may be the Golden Eagle capital of the state. Other birds of cliffs and rocky slopes are well represented as are birds of prey, including wintering Bald Eagles. In the breeding season, riparian corridors host many neotropical visitors, especially along tributary streams of the main rivers. Geologists and rockhounds will find much of interest, too. A swarm of feeder dikes (fissures formed as the earth's crust stretched) here and in nearby Oregon was the source of the succession of intermittent lava flows that covered the entire Columbia Basin with layers of basalt, ending around 13 million years ago. More recent uplift of the Blue and Wallowa Mountains resulted in Hells Canyon—one of the deepest gorges in North America (8,000 feet), carved by the Snake River a few miles south in Oregon. The depth of the Snake and Grande Ronde canyons in Washington is only modestly less. Both rivers retained their courses, downcutting through the thousands of feet of Columbia Plateau basalts as the mountains gradually rose. The incised meanders of the lower Grande Ronde River are a particularly striking testimony to its origins as a slow-moving stream on a level plain.

LOWER GRANITE LAKE

Lower Granite Dam—the uppermost of the four Snake River dams—has backed up the river past Clarkston (population 7,500), at the confluence of the Snake and Clearwater Rivers across from Lewiston, Idaho. The system of dams downriver has enabled barge traffic to reach these two communities, prompting the creation of major facilities for the transshipment of grain to lower Columbia River ports.

Though off the beaten track, **Lower Granite Dam** is worth a visit. Turn north from US-12 onto Mayview Road 5.4 miles east of the corner of 15th Street in Pomeroy (about 17 miles west of Chief Timothy State Park). At an intersection in 15 miles, keep right with Kirby-Mayview Road, reaching the canyon bottom in 10 miles. Here the road (called Almota Ferry Road on some maps) follows the shoreline upstream 5.4 miles to the dam, ending in another mile. Keep an eye to the steep slopes for raptors. Bald Eagle (except summer), Northern Harrier, Cooper's and Red-tailed Hawks, Golden Eagle, and American Kestrel are common. Chukars and Canyon Wrens reside on the basalt cliffs and talus. In spring and summer, look for Say's Phoebe, Rock and Bewick's Wrens, Lazuli Bunting, and Bullock's Oriole in brush and stunted Hackberry trees anywhere along the way. Gray-crowned Rosy-Finches arrive in late afternoon in winter to roost in rocky clefts. Also in winter, scope the waters around the grain terminal across the lake for rafts of diving ducks, especially scaups and goldeneyes.

Chief Timothy State Park, on US-12 and Lower Granite Lake 22 miles east of Pomeroy, is a great place for loons, grebes, waterfowl, and Bald Eagles in winter. In migration, a number of species rare for the region have been noted here, including an individual of the interior form of Western Scrub-Jay in March 2002.

Grain spilled while loading barges at the **Port of Clarkston** (5.8 miles east on US-12 from the entrance to Chief Timothy State Park) results in a buffet for a flotilla of wintering waterfowl, including Wood Duck, Canvasback, Redhead, Ring-necked Duck, Greater and Lesser Scaups, Common and Barrow's Goldeneyes, and Hooded, Common, and Red-breasted (rare) Mergansers; late fall sees a few Surf and White-winged Scoters. Scope the rafts of ducks from a pullout here. Watch also for Bald Eagle, Peregrine Falcon, and the occasional gathering of various gulls.

SR-129 turns south from US-12 in the center of Clarkston, 2.0 miles east of the port. **Swallows Park** is a mostly manicured community park on SR-129 and the Snake River at the south edge of town (2.0 miles from the US-12 intersection). A paved shoreside path extending south more than five miles to near Asotin is at its best in migration and winter, when waterfowl, Bald Eagles, and gulls are usually present. Many regionally rare species have been recorded here, including Brant and Bonaparte's, Mew, Lesser Black-backed, Thayer's, Iceland, Glaucous-winged, and Glaucous Gulls. The winter waterfowl concentrations attract Cooper's Hawk and Prairie Falcon. Eurasian Wigeon is uncommon, and the relatively mild winters sometimes allow a few Say's Phoebes to linger. A short distance beyond the park is the information center for the Hells Canyon National Recreation Area, which begins at the Oregon line about 33 miles upriver (not accessible by road from Washington).

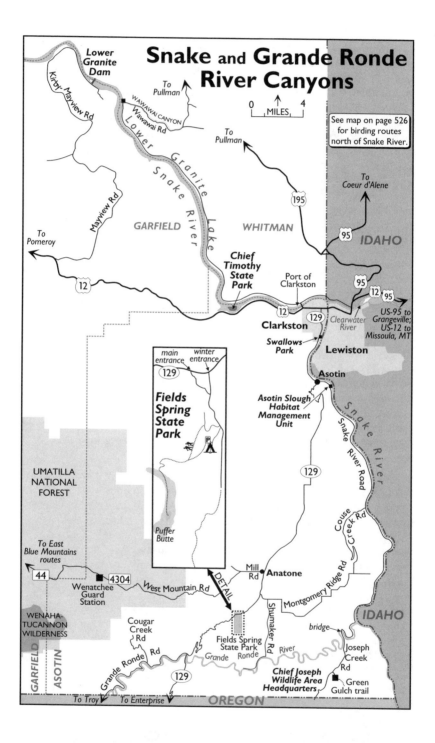

Snake and Grande Ronde River Canyons

Lower Granite Dam

Kirby-Mayview Rd

WAWAWAI CANYON
Wawawai Rd

To Pullman

0 4 MILES

To Pullman

See map on page 526 for birding routes north of Snake River.

Lower Granite Lake

Mayview Rd

GARFIELD

Lower Granite Snake River

WHITMAN

To Coeur d'Alene

195

95 IDAHO

To Pomeroy

12

Chief Timothy State Park

Port of Clarkston

12

95

12 95

US-95 to Grangeville; US-12 to Missoula, MT

Clearwater River

12

129

Clarkston

Swallows Park

Lewiston

main entrance   winter entrance

129

Fields Spring State Park

Asotin

Asotin Slough Habitat Management Unit

Snake River

P

129

Snake River Road

Puffer Butte

UMATILLA NATIONAL FOREST

Couse Creek Rd

To East Blue Mountains routes

Montgomery Ridge Rd

44

4304

Wenatchee Guard Station

West Mountain Rd

DETAIL

Mill Rd

Anatone

IDAHO

WENAHA-TUCANNON WILDERNESS

Cougar Creek Rd

Shumaker Rd

bridge

Fields Spring State Park

Joseph Creek Rd

GARFIELD   ASOTIN

Grande Ronde Rd

Grande Ronde River

Chief Joseph Wildlife Area Headquarters

Green Gulch trail

129

To Troy   To Enterprise

OREGON

SNAKE RIVER ROAD

Snake River Road turns left from SR-129 at Asotin, 4.2 miles south of the entrance to Swallows Park. The road winds alongside the Snake to the mouth of the Grande Ronde River and on to Chief Joseph Wildlife Area at the Oregon border. It is a long drive. SR-129, on the other hand, climbs to the plateau from Asotin and parallels the eastern base of the Blues to Fields Spring State Park before dropping down to the Grande Ronde a dozen straight-line miles upstream from its mouth. One may also connect between Snake River Road and SR-129 via secondary roads without returning to Asotin.

A postage-stamp-sized patch of riparian woodland along Snake River Road 0.9 mile south of the SR-129 junction, **Asotin Slough Habitat Management Unit** is attractive mainly in migration. The river has had unusual sightings such as Pacific Loon, White-winged Scoter, and Long-tailed Duck.

Continuing south, the gorge becomes ever more impressive (keep an eye out for Peregrine Falcon). In 10.9 miles, note the junction with Couse Creek Road, the cutoff to SR-129 and Fields Spring State Park (page 524). It is another 13.7 miles south along Snake River Road to the bridge over the Grande Ronde River. Here, go left, crossing to Joseph Creek Road on the other bank of the winding Grande Ronde. In 3.1 miles, turn left into 9,735-acre **Chief Joseph Wildlife Area** (WDFW permit required). Park at headquarters in 0.4 mile. This vicinity is sure to have Wild Turkeys, particularly in morning or late afternoon. Say's Phoebes and Western Bluebirds nest here. Watch the surrounding cliffs for Bald Eagle (winter), Red-tailed Hawk, Golden Eagle, and Prairie Falcon. Bighorn Sheep and Mule Deer are seen regularly. An interesting hike begins at the gate 100 yards east of the residence and climbs a jeep track mercilessly up Green Gulch to an overlook of the Grande Ronde River with stupendous views (elevation gain 2,000 feet). Look for Mountain Quail in brushy draws on north-facing ravines along the way—remnant coveys are still reported occasionally in this region.

Spring and summer are particularly good in riparian areas along **Chief Joseph Creek**, birdable from the road as one continues a couple of miles upstream from the wildlife-area entrance to the Oregon state line. Warbling and Red-eyed Vireos, Yellow and MacGillivray's Warblers, Black-headed Grosbeak, Lazuli Bunting, and Bullock's Oriole are common. Winter brings Common Redpolls (irregular) and Pine Siskins, attracted to the abundant alder cones. In fall and winter many Townsend's Solitaires, Hermit Thrushes, American Robins, Varied Thrushes, and Evening Grosbeaks come to feed on the fruits of the gnarled Hackberry trees that characterize the rocky slopes and dry drainages throughout this region.

For the shortest connection to birding sites along SR-129, return about 17 miles on Snake River Road to Couse Creek Road (marked Shelly Gulch Road at the top but known by locals as the Shelly Grade) and turn left. This gravel road climbs steadily to the wheat fields on the plateau 2,000 feet above. In 7.7 miles, turn right onto **Montgomery Ridge Road**. For many miles the landscape along this road is great for Rough-legged Hawk and Prairie Falcon from fall through spring. Look for Short-eared Owl over terrain not recently tilled, where grass cover is deeper. In winter, be on the lookout also for Gyrfalcon, Bohemian Waxwing, and Snow Bunting. Spring and summer bring Western and Mountain Bluebirds, which nest in boxes along the road—particularly as Ponderosa Pines are approached.

In 10.7 miles, turn left onto **Shumaker Road**. This graded, gravel road switchbacks straight down to the Grande Ronde River—not for the faint of heart! Tremendous variation in habitat is displayed as one plunges almost 3,000 feet into the canyon, from moist understory and Douglas-fir-filled ravines to a nearly barren rockscape at river level. The road ends in 8.4 miles at a tunnel blasted into the basalts. Check for Common Poorwill, Warbling Vireo, Nashville, Yellow, Yellow-rumped, and MacGillivray's Warblers, and Western Tanager on the upper canyon sides, and for Golden Eagle, Chukar, swarms of Cliff Swallows, and Yellow-breasted Chat lower down.

Return to Montgomery Ridge Road; turn left to reach SR-129 in another mile (see following paragraph).

STATE ROUTE 129

From the junction with Snake River Road in Asotin, SR-129 climbs onto a 3,000-foot-high plateau and heads south through wheat fields and rangelands to Anatone (19 miles; jumpoff for Wenatchee Guard Station, page 520). Farther south on SR-129 is the junction with Montgomery Ridge Road, the cutoff to Snake River Road (1.7 miles; see preceding paragraph). The main entrance for Fields Spring State Park is on the left side of SR-129 2.3 miles after that.

Perched near the rim of the Grande Ronde Canyon at the base of the Blue Mountains, 445-acre **Fields Spring State Park** is a great place to relax and study a long list of birds in the relatively open forests of Douglas-fir, Grand Fir, Ponderosa Pine, and Western Larch. Look for Blue Grouse, Great Horned Owl, Northern Pygmy-Owl, Rufous Hummingbird, Williamson's Sapsucker, Hairy, White-headed (uncommon), Three-toed, and Pileated Woodpeckers, Northern Flicker, Western Wood-Pewee, Hammond's, Dusky, and Pacific-slope Flycatchers, Cassin's Vireo, Mountain and Chestnut-backed Chickadees, all three nuthatches, Brown Creeper, Golden-crowned Kinglet, Swainson's and Hermit Thrushes, Orange-crowned, Yellow, Yellow-rumped, Townsend's, and MacGillivray's Warblers, Western Tanager, Lazuli Bunting, and Cassin's Finch. Western Bluebirds are conspicuous in the surrounding fields. A spectacular view into Oregon and Idaho and of the Grande Ronde River far below is reached by a mile-long trail to **Puffer Butte** (elevation 4,500 feet), one of the few cinder-cone volcanoes on the Columbia Plateau not buried by the outpourings of basalt. The trailhead is a few yards west of the main bathrooms in the campground. The trail climbs through a moist forest with an understory of shrubs and wildflowers to the broad, forested summit. Hike south on a rocky trail into the steppe vegetation below, where the birdlife includes Gray Partridge and Vesper and Lark Sparrows. Overhead, check for raptors such as Red-tailed Hawk, American Kestrel, and Prairie Falcon.

Beyond Fields Spring State Park, SR-129 twists its way down to the **Grande Ronde River** in about nine miles. Here is more scenery on a grand scale. The river has cut classic entrenched meanders into the many successive layers of basalt. As one reaches lower elevations, Warbling and Red-eyed Vireos and Yellow Warbler are common in the dense, narrow riparian woodland of White Alder along Rattlesnake Creek. Everywhere in this region, the strident song of Lazuli Bunting can be heard in brush patches on the dry, rocky slopes, even in mid-day heat. Where SR-129 reaches the river, turn right (west) onto Grande Ronde Road. In 4.6 miles, take Cougar Creek Road to the right. Red-eyed Vireo is present in the streamside woodland along the lower stretches for the next 1.7 miles, to the creek crossing. The road then climbs steeply into conifer forests atop a plateau.

South from the Cougar Creek turnoff, Grande Ronde Road hugs the riverbank, crossing the Oregon state line in 6.4 miles and reaching civilization at Troy. From the state line south to its confluence with the Wallowa River the Grande Ronde is part of the National Wild and Scenic River System.

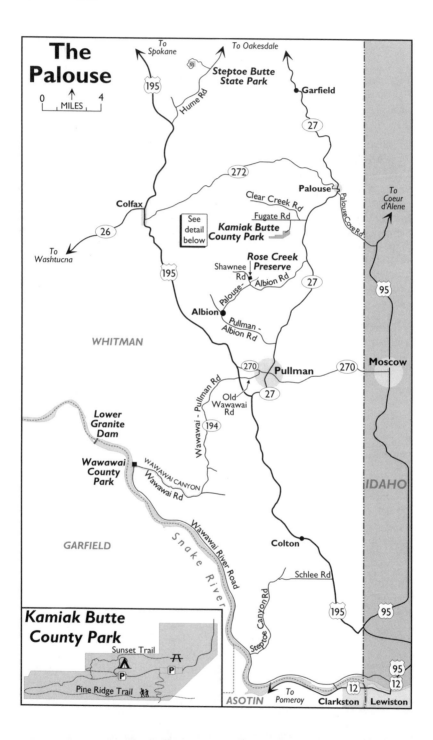

The Palouse

0 — MILES — 4

To Spokane
To Oakesdale

195

Steptoe Butte State Park

Hume Rd

●Garfield

27

272

Clear Creek Rd

●Palouse

Palouse Cove Rd

To Coeur d'Alene

Colfax

See detail below

Fugate Rd

Kamiak Butte County Park

26

To Washtucna

195

Shawnee Rd

Rose Creek Preserve

Albion Rd

27

95

Palouse-

Albion●

Pullman - Albion Rd

WHITMAN

270

Pullman

270

Moscow

Old Wawawai Rd

27

Wawawai - Pullman Rd

194

Lower Granite Dam

Wawawai County Park

WAWAWAI CANYON

Wawawai Rd

GARFIELD

Snake River

Colton●

IDAHO

Wawawai River Road

Schlee Rd

195

95

Steptoe Canyon Rd

95

12

Kamiak Butte County Park

Sunset Trail

P   P

Pine Ridge Trail

ASOTIN

To Pomeroy

Clarkston **Lewiston**

12   12

THE PALOUSE

by Joe Lipar and John Roberson

The Palouse (pronounced puh-LOOSE) is a 3,000-square-mile district covered by piles of windblown, yellowish-brown silt called loess (rhymes with muss). Each successive ice-age flood deposited thick layers of sediment in the lowest parts of the Columbia Basin to the southwest. Later, as the waters retreated, silt was carried by the prevailing southwest winds and dropped here, forming the Palouse Hills. In some places the underlying basalt is covered by as much as 200 feet of loess. The rolling hills that the French-Canadian explorers and fur traders called la pelouse (grassland) were once a realm of bunchgrass with a high forb component. Ravines had dense stringers of Douglas Hawthorn and scattered Ponderosa Pine. North slopes were clothed in Snowberry, serviceberry, and Wood's Rose. This landscape has virtually all been converted to one of Washington's most bountiful agricultural regions. Wheat is king. Indeed, some of the highest per-acre yields anywhere are consistently harvested in the Palouse, all without irrigation. With such productive soil, it is not surprising that only a few remnant tracts of native vegetation survive. Gone, too, are the huge numbers of Sharp-tailed Grouse, replaced by introduced Gray Partridge and Ring-necked Pheasant.

Pullman, some 70 miles south of Spokane on US-195, is the major city in the region and the site of Washington State University. Exploring the extensive mature plantings of conifers and deciduous trees in the older residential districts can be worthwhile during migration. Winter brings flocks of Bohemian Waxwings, sometimes in large numbers. Away from Pullman, the following sites, though relatively small, have some of the best remaining patches of natural Palouse brush and grassland habitat. You will encounter fine birding here, especially in the breeding season.

An outstanding site close to Pullman is the **Rose Creek Preserve**, a 22-acre property of The Nature Conservancy. Take SR-27 (Grand Avenue) 2.2 miles north from SR-270 to Pullman-Albion Road. Turn left and go five miles to Albion, turning right on Main Street. Go 2.8 miles on the Palouse-Albion Road (Old Albion Road on some maps) to Shawnee Road (aka Four Mile Road). Turn left, make another left in 0.1 mile to stay on Shawnee Road, and continue 0.3 mile to the tiny parking area on the right at the entrance of the preserve. Walk up the private driveway and find the trailhead just before the wooden bridge over Rose Creek. The trail winds through a fine remnant of Palouse riparian vegetation, featuring thickets of hawthorn, Bitter Cherry, and Cow Parsnip. More than 250 species of plants are recorded here, attracting mammals such as White-tailed Deer, Porcupine, and Coyote. Birds are abundant and varied. Permanent residents include Northern Harrier, Red-tailed Hawk, American Kestrel, Gray Partridge, California Quail, Great Horned Owl, Downy Woodpecker, Black-capped Chickadee, and Bewick's Wren. The riparian area comes alive in spring and summer; look then for Calliope Hummingbird, Western Wood-Pewee, Willow Flycatcher,

Eastern Kingbird, Warbling and Red-eyed Vireos (migrant only), House Wren, Ruby-crowned Kinglet (migrant), Veery (scarce), Gray Catbird, Yellow and MacGillivray's Warblers, and Bullock's Oriole.

After birding the streamside woodland and scrub of Rose Creek, walk along Shawnee Road for birds of the open country and pine forests. The 750-acre tract west for the next mile is the **Smoot Hill Research Facility** of Washington State University. A mosaic of Ponderosa Pine forests, riparian areas, and steppe makes this a very birdy place, especially in spring and summer. In addition to the list for Rose Creek, look for Swainson's (summer) and Rough-legged (winter) Hawks, Hairy Woodpecker, Pygmy Nuthatch, Western Bluebird, and Townsend's Solitaire (winter, in junipers). Taken together, Smoot Hill and Rose Creek make up one of the largest contiguous parcels of the Palouse ecosystem still in a natural or near-natural state.

Kamiak Butte is just northeast of Rose Creek. To reach this site, go back to Palouse-Albion Road, turn left, and go 5.1 miles to SR-27. Turn left and go 2.9 miles to Clear Creek Road. (If you are coming from Pullman, this is 11.8 miles north on SR-27 from its intersection with SR-270.) Turn left, keeping left again at the first junction (0.3 mile). You are now on Fugate Road. Go another 0.7 mile to the Kamiak Butte County Park entrance. Turn left; parking is a mile up the hill. This elevated, forest-covered extension of the Rocky Mountains is a great place to hike. A three-mile loop trail goes uphill from the parking area to the top of the butte, then along the crest and down to the upper parking area. At the top are magnificent views of the surrounding Palouse. Shorter hikes on a network of trails near the parking area are also possible. Interesting resident species in the Ponderosa Pine and Douglas-fir forests and extensive brushy understory include Mountain Chickadee, three nuthatches, Brown Creeper, Bewick's Wren, and Red and White-winged (during irruptions) Crossbills. Summer visitors of note are Red-naped Sapsucker, Olive-sided and Cordilleran-type (not as yet incontrovertibly documented in Washington, but this site is a good bet) Flycatchers, Cassin's Vireo, House Wren, Western Bluebird, Swainson's and Hermit Thrushes, MacGillivray's Warbler, and Western Tanager. Owling can be very good (best in March and April), mainly for Great Horned, Northern Pygmy-, Barred, and Northern Saw-whet Owls. As an isolated stand of trees in an otherwise mostly unforested landscape, Kamiak Butte offers the possibility of rare strays in migration. Black-billed Cuckoo and Hooded Warbler are two examples of vagrants that have been noted here.

A similar eminence is **Steptoe Butte**, an isolated, 3,612-foot hill of 400-million-year-old quartzite. Like Kamiak Butte, this is a rare visible example of the North American basement in the Columbia Basin—a region where almost all such older rocks are completely buried by thick sequences of much younger basalts. From the junction with SR-270 (two miles west of Pullman), go north 14.2 miles on US-195 to the junction with SR-26 in Colfax. Continue north on US-195 and in 6.6 miles turn right onto Hume Road. Stay right with

Hume where it meets Sholz Road (1.2 miles); another 3.9 miles brings you to the Steptoe Butte State Park entrance road, on the left. The terrain is mostly open, lacking the forest cover of Kamiak Butte. However, deciduous trees and brush around the picnic area at the base of the butte provide habitat for a number of species including Northern Flicker, Western Wood-Pewee, Bewick's and House Wrens, and Bullock's Oriole. As you wind your way to the top and a spectacular overlook of the Palouse (4.2 miles), look for Gray Partridge, Western and Eastern Kingbirds, sparrows, Black-headed Grosbeak, and Lazuli Bunting. A pair of out-of-place Black-throated Sparrows was enjoyed by birders atop the butte in June 2000. Raptors are conspicuous, especially in March–April and again in September–October.

South of Pullman is **Wawawai Canyon**, which descends 2,000 feet to the Snake River. It is reached by taking Davis Way (SR-270) west from Grand Avenue (SR-27) in Pullman 0.6 mile, turning left on Old Wawawai Road and continuing 1.7 miles to US-195. Go straight across the highway (the road is now called Pullman-Wawawai Road) and continue to a T-intersection in 10 miles. Turn right into Wawawai Canyon on Wawawai Road. Birding the riparian habitat along the creek and on brushy hillsides to the south can be profitable in spring and early summer. Near brushy terrain in particular, pull safely off the road and look for Willow Flycatcher, Say's Phoebe, Eastern Kingbird, Black-capped Chickadee, House Wren, Gray Catbird, Yellow Warbler, Yellow-breasted Chat, Spotted Towhee, Black-headed Grosbeak, Lazuli Bunting, and Bullock's Oriole. In about 2.5 miles, before crossing to the north side of canyon, check the Mount Mazama ash deposit (from the violent explosion 6,600 years ago that led to the formation of Oregon's Crater Lake) on the north side of the creek for nesting Bank Swallows. Toward the Snake River is **Wawawai County Park** (another 2.5 miles). Here you may find Bewick's Wren in the brush, Yellow-breasted Chat and Bullock's Oriole nesting in the campground, or migrants in the ornamental plantings. Scope for waterbirds on the Snake River reservoir behind Lower Granite Dam (0.4 mile).

South from here, Wawawai River Road follows the reservoir along a gorge; various pullouts allow safe stops. Red-tailed Hawk, Chukar, Say's Phoebe, and Rock and Canyon Wrens are common on the high cliffs. Bald (winter) and Golden Eagles might also be seen. In 16.8 miles, turn left onto **Steptoe Canyon Road**. As you ascend to an intersection with Schlee Road (6.4 miles), stop in about three miles at an area of sparse brush and grasslands to look for Lark Sparrow (rare in this region), along with Say's Phoebe and Eastern Kingbird. Turn right onto **Schlee Road**. Riparian vegetation along the ravine and dense brush on the hillside for the next mile attracts birds similar to those of the upper reaches of Wawawai Canyon but with little or no competing traffic. In another mile you break into wheat fields of the Palouse. Western Kingbirds have been seen near the farms here. Continue east to US-195 (3.7 miles). Turn left to Pullman or right to Lewiston, Idaho.

BIRDS OF WASHINGTON BAR GRAPHS

by Tom Aversa

Included here are all the species of annual occurrence in Washington—i.e., rare or better as determined by the abundance definitions on the facing page. Westside (W) and Eastside (E) have separate graphs if status differs; otherwise they are combined (WE). The Cascade crest is the division. Species graphed on one side of the state but not on the other are no more than Accidental in occurrence on the side where they are not graphed—i.e., a species must attain the frequency of Casual or better on a second side of the state in order to be graphed there. The status of *all* species recorded in the state, graphed or not, is discussed in the Annotated Checklist (pages 548–592).

Most species have pronounced habitat associations; some occur quite locally. For example, Black Oystercatcher is shown as Uncommon in Western Washington but in fact can be found only along rocky saltwater shorelines. For a fuller picture, the bar graphs should be used in conjunction with the Annotated Checklist. These two sections were reviewed and revised conjointly, and complement one another. A primary source of information in the preparation of both has been the database of records maintained since 1993 by the Washington Field Notes compilers (Russell Rogers, succeeded in 2001 by Tom Aversa), derived from reports submitted to them by field observers.

Abundance definitions strike a balance between the probability of finding (seeing or hearing) the bird and its actual abundance. Certain retiring species or those in hard-to-cover habitats may be numerically more abundant yet more difficult to detect than certain other, numerically scarcer ones with exhibitionist tendencies, or that frequent exposed habitats.

In 2000, ABA's Checklist Committee drafted a set of standard definitions for the bar graphs used in the ABA Birdfinding Guide series. Their aim was to create a set of sensible, easily understandable definitions for the terminology used to denote the abundance and findability of birds, which would be useful not only within ABA, but also for the birding community continent-wide. It is ABA's hope that, over time, those persons or groups publishing field checklists, annotated checklists, and other compilations dealing with abundance of bird species will adopt these definitions. When standardized terms gain widespread acceptance, disparities between the various meanings of terms such as *fairly common* and *casual* will disappear, giving birders a realistic understanding of a species' actual abundance as well as a good idea of how likely finding it might be. ABA encourages widespread adoption of these abundance definitions; no specific permission is necessary.

COMMON: Found in moderate to large numbers, and easily found in appropriate habitat at the right time of year.

FAIRLY COMMON: Found in small to moderate numbers, and usually easy to find in appropriate habitat at the right time of year.

UNCOMMON: Found in small numbers, and usually—but not always—found with some effort in appropriate habitat at the right time of year.

RARE: Occurs annually in very small numbers. Not to be expected on any given day, but may be found with extended effort over the course of the appropriate season(s).

CASUAL: Occurs less than annually, but there tends to be a pattern over time at the right time of year in appropriate habitat.

ACCIDENTAL: Represents an exceptional occurrence that might not be repeated again for decades; there are usually fewer than 5 records.

IRREGULAR: Represents an irruptive species whose numbers are highly variable from year to year. There may be small to even large numbers present in one year, while in another year it may be absent altogether.

		January	February	March	April	May	June	July	August	September	October	November	December
Red-throated Loon	W												
	E												
Pacific Loon	W												
	E												
Common Loon	W												
	E												
Yellow-billed Loon	W												
	E												
Pied-billed Grebe	W												
	E												
Horned Grebe	W												
	E												
Red-necked Grebe	W												
	E												
Eared Grebe	W												
	E												
Western Grebe	W												
	E												
Clark's Grebe	W												
	E												
Laysan Albatross	W												
Black-footed Albatross	W												
Northern Fulmar	W												

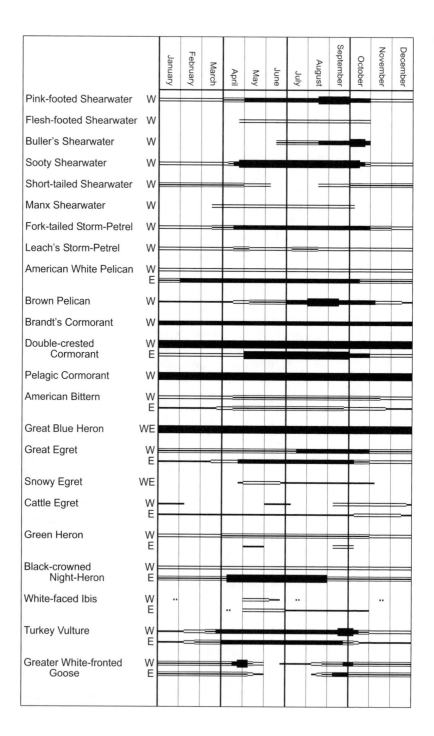

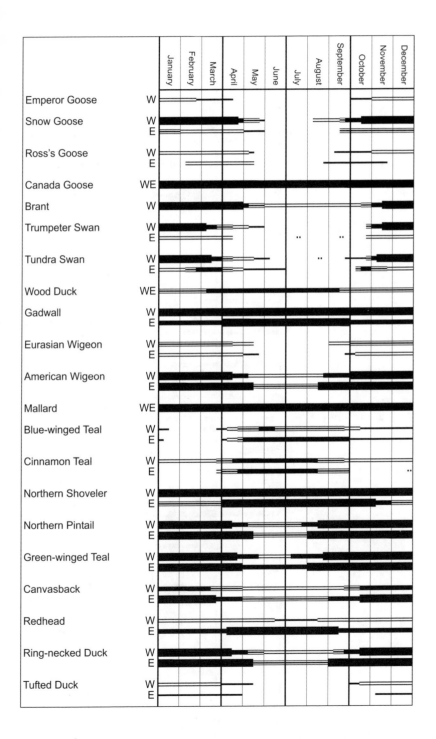

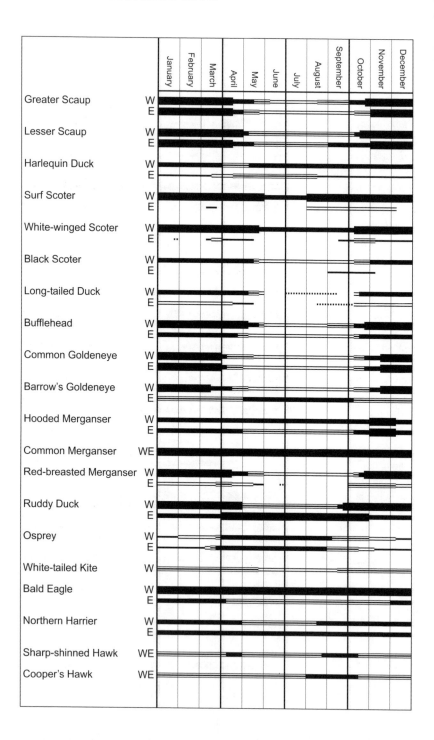

		January	February	March	April	May	June	July	August	September	October	November	December
Northern Goshawk	W												
	E												
Red-shouldered Hawk	W												
	E												
Broad-winged Hawk	E												
Swainson's Hawk	W												
	E												
Red-tailed Hawk	W												
	E												
Ferruginous Hawk	E												
Rough-legged Hawk	W												
	E												
Golden Eagle	W												
	E												
American Kestrel	W												
	E												
Merlin	W												
	E												
Gyrfalcon	WE												
Peregrine Falcon	W												
	E												
Prairie Falcon	W												
	E												
Chukar	E												
Gray Partridge	E												
Ring-necked Pheasant	WE												
Ruffed Grouse	WE												
Greater Sage-Grouse	E												
Spruce Grouse	E												
White-tailed Ptarmigan	WE												
Blue Grouse	WE												
Sharp-tailed Grouse	E												
Wild Turkey	WE												

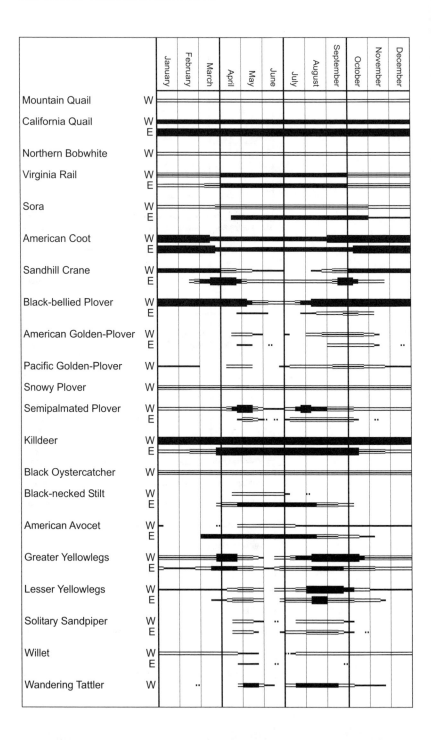

Species	W/E	January	February	March	April	May	June	July	August	September	October	November	December
Spotted Sandpiper	W												
	E												
Whimbrel	W												
	E												
Long-billed Curlew	W												
	E												
Bar-tailed Godwit	W												
Marbled Godwit	W												
	E												
Ruddy Turnstone	W												
	E												
Black Turnstone	W												
Surfbird	W												
Red Knot	W												
	E												
Sanderling	W												
	E												
Semipalmated Sandpiper	W												
	E												
Western Sandpiper	W												
	E												
Least Sandpiper	W												
	E												
Baird's Sandpiper	W												
	E												
Pectoral Sandpiper	W												
	E												
Sharp-tailed Sandpiper	W												
	E												
Rock Sandpiper	W												
Dunlin	W												
	E												
Stilt Sandpiper	W												
	E												
Buff-breasted Sandpiper	W												
	E												

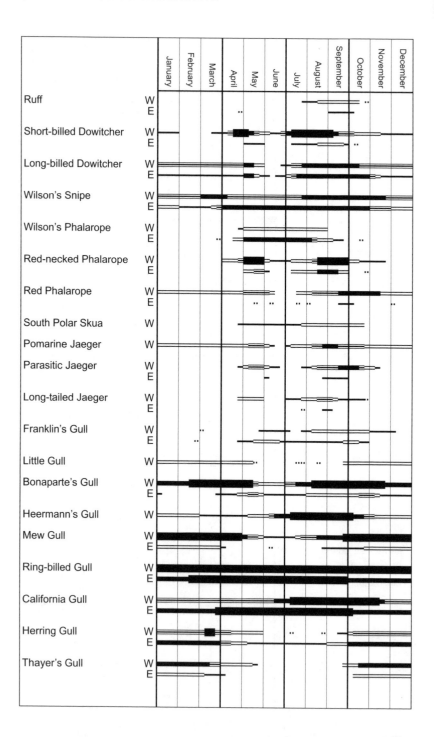

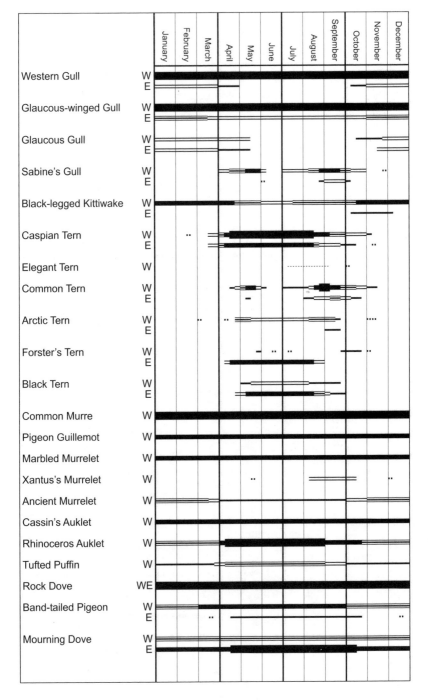

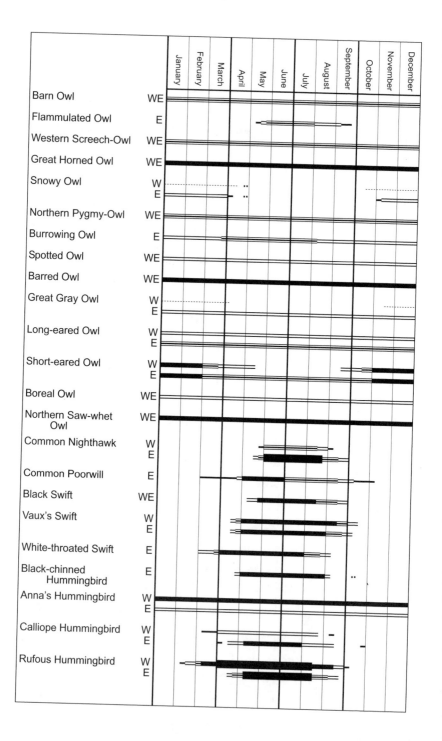

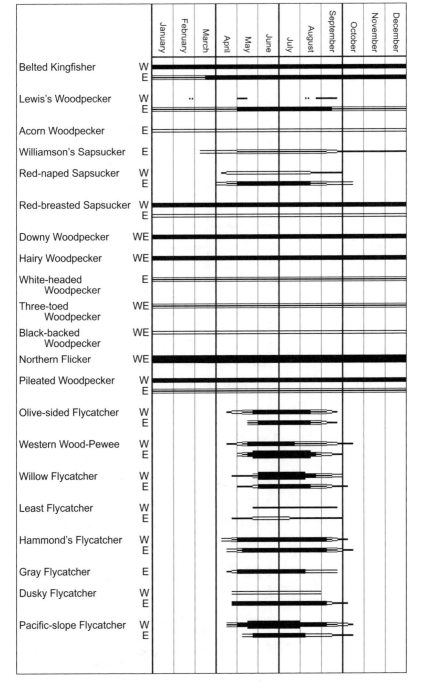

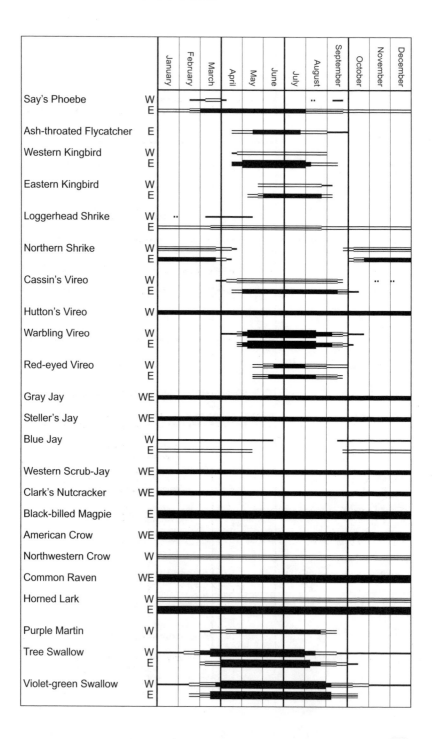

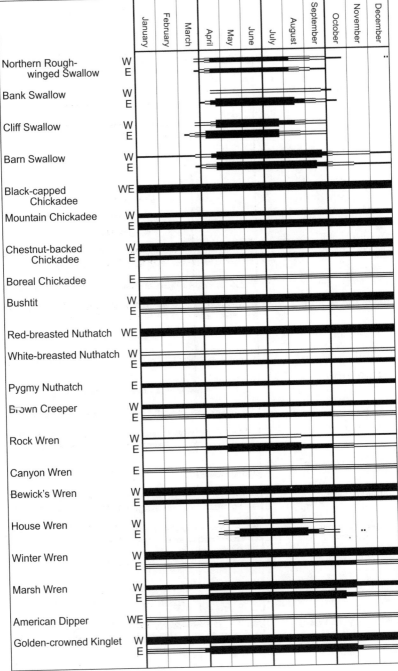

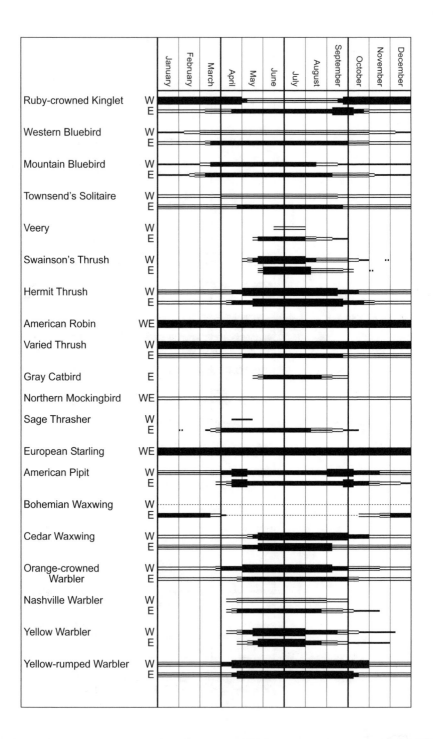

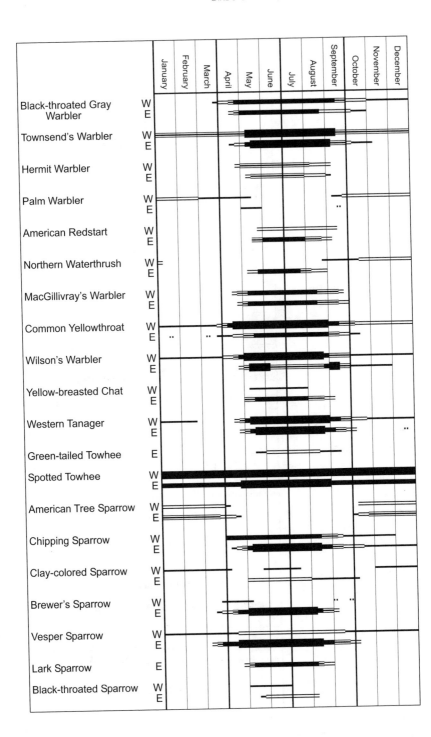

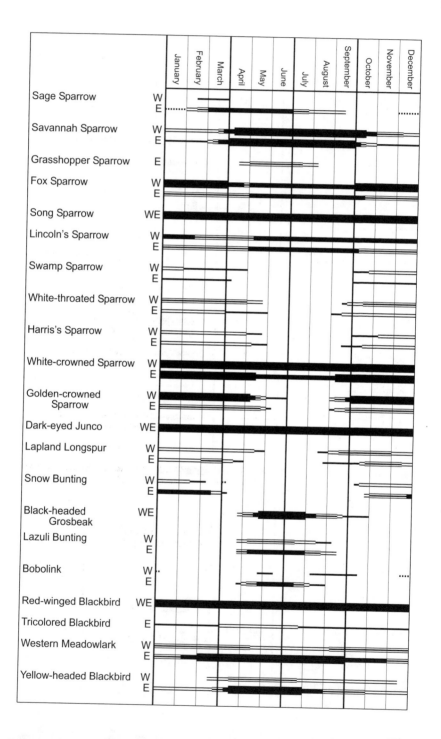

		January	February	March	April	May	June	July	August	September	October	November	December
Rusty Blackbird	WE												
Brewer's Blackbird	WE												
Brown-headed Cowbird	W E												
Bullock's Oriole	W E												
Gray-crowned Rosy-Finch	W E												
Pine Grosbeak	W E												
Purple Finch	W E												
Cassin's Finch	W E												
House Finch	WE												
Red Crossbill	WE												
White-winged Crossbill	WE												
Common Redpoll	WE												
Pine Siskin	W E												
Lesser Goldfinch	E												
American Goldfinch	W E												
Evening Grosbeak	WE												
House Sparrow	WE												

ANNOTATED CHECKLIST

by Andy Stepniewski and Hal Opperman

The 478 species listed here have been recorded at least once in Washington. Italicized common names indicate species on the Review List of the Washington Bird Records Committee (WBRC). Observations of any of these species, or of species not on this list, should be reported to the WBRC with written details and any supporting evidence such as photographs and sound recordings (see page 613 for addresses and an outline report form). Reports of the WBRC in *Washington Birds* (1994 ff.) are the authority for records of rarities used in the compilation of this list, with the addition of several credible reports too recent to have been reviewed yet. Abundance terms (common, fairly common, etc.) are employed here in a manner consistent with those for the bar graphs of seasonal occurrence—see page 531 for definitions.

Red-throated Loon *Gavia stellata* — Common migrant, winter resident on protected marine waters, sometimes close to shore in shallow water. High numbers winter at Bowman Bay/Deception Pass. Tokeland, Grays Harbor (especially Ocean Shores), Hood Canal Bridge area, Sequim Bay, Dungeness NWR, Padilla Bay also excellent sites. Rare migrant, winter resident on Westside lowland lakes, lower Columbia River. Casual on Eastside reservoirs in winter.

Arctic Loon *Gavia arctica* — Two records, one from each side of Cascades: Priest Rapids Lake, January–March 2000; Puget Sound, December 2000–January 2001 (probably 2–3 birds).

Pacific Loon *Gavia pacifica* — Common spring, fall migrant along outer coast, often in impressive numbers—especially May, late September–October. Common winter resident on deeper inland marine waters; attracted in large numbers to tidal rips, e.g., at Deception Pass, Rosario Strait, Spieden Channel, Cattle Pass, Obstruction Pass, Admiralty Inlet, Point No Point. Uncommon migrant, rare winter resident in Eastern Washington, mainly on Columbia River reservoirs.

Common Loon *Gavia immer* — Common migrant, winter resident on sheltered coastal waters; fairly common migrant, winter resident on Columbia River reservoirs. Uncommon, local summer resident of secluded lakes in northern half of state on both sides of Cascades. A few breeding pairs on Chester Morse Lake in Cedar River Watershed (closed to visitors except on special tours) produced half of Washington's fledgling loons over last several years.

Yellow-billed Loon *Gavia adamsii* — Rare migrant, winter resident in Western Washington, usually on sheltered coastal waters, frequently in fairly shallow bays. Elusive, often not staying in any one location for extended periods. Semi-regular at Westport, Ocean Shores, Neah Bay, John Wayne Marina on Sequim Bay, various spots in north Puget Trough. Casual winter resident in Eastern Washington—recorded

Lake Chelan, Priest Rapids Lake, Park Lake in Lower Grand Coulee, near Bridgeport. Casual west in summer.

Pied-billed Grebe *Podilymbus podiceps* — Common (west) to fairly common (east) summer resident in marshes, wetlands, shallow lakes with emergent vegetation; absent from mountains, heavily forested zones. Migrant statewide, including mountain lakes. In winter, common resident in western lowlands, less common, local east. Strong preference for freshwater habitats, rarely in saltwater bays.

Horned Grebe *Podiceps auritus* — Common winter resident west of Cascades on protected marine waters, occurring singly or in small groups; small numbers on large freshwater lakes. Uncommon to locally fairly common on Columbia River reservoirs in winter. Uncommon summer resident on Eastside, nests rarely in Okanogan, Northeast.

Red-necked Grebe *Podiceps grisegena* — Common winter resident west of Cascades on protected marine waters, highest abundance in Port Townsend area; a few also on large freshwater lakes. Fairly common breeder on forested lakes in Okanogan, Northeast (e.g., Sinlahekin Valley, Molson Lake, Big Meadow Lake, Sullivan Lake).

Eared Grebe *Podiceps nigricollis* — Fairly common summer resident in shallow Eastern Washington alkaline ponds, pothole lakes with emergent vegetation. Known sites include Turnbull NWR, Molson Lake, Muskrat Lake, Big Goose Lake, Fishtrap Lake. Large numbers congregate in fall, a few birds winter, on Soap Lake (Grant County). Uncommon, local winter resident on Westside, mostly on sheltered marine waters.

Western Grebe *Aechmophorus occidentalis* — Fairly common but local summer resident on large lakes in Eastern Washington. Nests on Moses Lake, Potholes Reservoir, Banks Lake (Steamboat Rock State Park). Spectacular courtship display peaks late April–early May. Uncommon winter resident on Columbia River reservoirs. Common winter resident on marine waters, occupying variety of habitats from sheltered bays to rough waters just beyond breakers. Local winter resident on large Western Washington lowland lakes (e.g., Lake Washington). Wintering numbers declining.

Clark's Grebe *Aechmophorus clarkii* — Uncommon, local summer resident in Columbia Basin, invariably with Westerns. Nests on Moses Lake, Potholes Reservoir, Banks Lake (Steamboat Rock State Park). Rare migrant, winter resident on lakes, protected marine waters elsewhere in state.

Shy Albatross *Thalassarche cauta* — First North American record collected 35 miles off Quillayute River mouth in September 1951, apparently New Zealand-breeding subspecies *steadi*. Second Washington record, on pelagic trip off Westport in January 2000, said to represent subspecies *cauta* that breeds in Australia.

Laysan Albatross *Phoebastria immutabilis* — Rare pelagic visitor, best October–April. Numbers steadily increasing in Northeastern Pacific since 1990s, including recent establishment of breeding colony off northwestern Mexico.

Black-footed Albatross *Phoebastria nigripes* — Year-round pelagic visitor, uncommon only in winter when most nesting in mid-subtropical Pacific. Hundreds often recorded on summer–fall trips off Westport—best way to see this species in Lower 48.

Short-tailed Albatross *Phoebastria albatrus* — Once common off Pacific Coast, disappeared from Washington waters before 1900. With partial recovery of breeding population in Western Pacific in recent years, sighted twice on Westport pelagic trips (January 1993, January 2001), once on Puget Sound (April 1997).

Northern Fulmar *Fulmarus glacialis* — Fairly common to common pelagic visitor, usually well offshore, with definite peak in fall (beginning August). Numbers vary year to year. Both color morphs occur, with lightest birds representing about 10 percent of total. In winter, recorded in inland marine waters (Straits of Juan de Fuca, Georgia), also often as beached birds on outer coast.

Murphy's Petrel *Pterodroma ultima* — First Washington record at least 24 birds on deepwater pelagic trip from Westport in April 1992. Several records of dark *Pterodroma* petrels in subsequent years in May, June, August, September—some Murphy's, others with insufficient detail to exclude Solander's Petrel (not recorded in Washington).

Mottled Petrel *Pterodroma inexpectata* — Seldom-seen but probably regular migrant, post-breeding visitor off outer coast. Three birds reported from research vessel during fierce storm off Westport in December 1995, but incompletely documented. Four recorded on Westport pelagic trip in February 1997. Numerous individuals seen from Ocean Shores jetty during storm in late November 2000. Several records of birds found dead on Pacific beaches, February–July.

Cook's Petrel *Pterodroma cookii* — One bird found dead on Pacific beach in December 1995.

Pink-footed Shearwater *Puffinus creatopus* — Fairly common to common pelagic visitor May–October, rare winter.

Flesh-footed Shearwater *Puffinus carneipes* — Rare pelagic visitor, most likely late September–October but scattered records in other warm months. Almost always seen near shrimp trawlers. Less frequent in recent years.

Greater Shearwater *Puffinus gravis* — One record, 45 miles off Westport in August 2002.

Wedge-tailed Shearwater *Puffinus pacificus* — One bird found dead on Pacific beach in September 1999.

Buller's Shearwater *Puffinus bulleri* — Fairly common to common pelagic visitor August–October.

Sooty Shearwater *Puffinus griseus* — Common offshore visitor in warmer months, from just beyond breakers to pelagic waters. Rare winter. Most commonly seen shearwater from shore. Immense numbers pass by August–September, sometimes thousands entering Grays Harbor, Willapa Bay. Uncommon in Strait of Juan de Fuca, rare in Puget Sound, particularly during, after fall storms.

Short-tailed Shearwater *Puffinus tenuirostris* — Uncommon late summer–winter pelagic visitor, numbers variable year to year. Probably uncommon to rare in Strait of Juan de Fuca during, after fall storms (particularly late October–November), but true status obscured by difficulty in separating from Sooty Shearwater.

Manx Shearwater *Puffinus puffinus* — First securely documented records in North Pacific Ocean from Westport, Ocean Shores in September–October of 1990, 1992. Since then, records have multiplied rapidly along North American Pacific Coast, Manx Shearwater now annual in small numbers in Washington. Most records from well offshore in Pacific Ocean, a few from outer coastline, Strait of Juan de Fuca, Puget Sound. Dates range March–October with peak in June–July.

Wilson's Storm-Petrel *Oceanites oceanicus* — Two records, both off Westport: July 1984, September 2001.

Fork-tailed Storm-Petrel *Oceanodroma furcata* — Southern subspecies *plumbea* nests on islets off Outer Olympic Coast but rarely seen from shore. Fairly common spring through early fall on pelagic trips, seldom missed when chumming over Grays Canyon. Seen almost annually on inland marine waters east to Admiralty Inlet, most likely after storms. Larger, paler, Aleutian-breeding subspecies *furcata* known from a few birds collected offshore or found dead on beaches.

Leach's Storm-Petrel *Oceanodroma leucorhoa* — Common breeder on islets off Outer Olympic Coast but virtually never noted from shore. Leaves breeding sites under cover of darkness, heads out to deeper, warmer waters than those reached by most pelagic boats. On Westport trip found fairly regularly late July–early August, hit-or-miss late April–early May. Occasionally seen on inland marine waters, usually after storms.

Red-billed Tropicbird *Phaethon aethereus* — One bird collected off Westport in June 1941.

Blue-footed Booby *Sula nebouxii* — One bird collected in Puget Sound off Everett in September 1935.

Brown Booby *Sula leucogaster* — One bird seen at Protection Island for several days in October 1997; second seen in Seattle, Tacoma for two days in May 2002; third found on Westport pelagic trip in October 2002.

American White Pelican *Pelecanus erythrorhynchos* — Fairly common year-round resident along Columbia River, nearby reservoirs, lakes in South Central Washington—most numerous late summer–early fall, least numerous winter. Increasing, spreading; noted regularly north to Bridgeport, Banks Lake. In 1994, resumed breeding near Wallula after 60-year hiatus in state. Still more recently began breeding at Sprague Lake. Strays to Western Washington regularly, in small numbers, at any season.

Brown Pelican *Pelecanus occidentalis* — Common, apparently increasing post-breeding summer–fall visitor along outer coast, particularly conspicuous at Westport, Ocean Shores. Has made remarkable recovery since 1970s when populations crashed. In fall, uncommon in Strait of Juan de Fuca, casual in Puget Sound—a very few have persisted well into winter. Recorded east.

Brandt's Cormorant *Phalacrocorax penicillatus* — Large numbers of non-breeders in summer along North Olympic Coast, in San Juans, northern Puget Trough. Breeding records from small number of rocks and promontories on Outer Olympic Coast, also at Cape Disappointment. Fairly common to locally common winter resident on marine waters (uncommon in southern Puget Trough). Good winter sites include Point No Point, Possession Bar, Port Susan, Hale Passage, deeper channels in San Juans. Frequents deeper water, more tidal rips than Double-crested or Pelagic.

Double-crested Cormorant *Phalacrocorax auritus* — Common summer resident along saltwater coastlines including inland marine waters, locally in Columbia Basin, Pend Oreille River valley. Large numbers winter in Western Washington, much smaller numbers east. Only cormorant seen in freshwater habitats.

Red-faced Cormorant *Phalacrocorax urile* — One bird seen at mouth of Elwha River in May 1999.

Pelagic Cormorant *Phalacrocorax pelagicus* — Common year-round resident on marine waters. Prefers deep, clear waters to shallow bays.

Magnificent Frigatebird *Fregata magnificens* — One Eastside record, from Umatilla NWR in July 1975. One Westside record, bird seen at several locations on Puget Sound, South Coast, mouth of Columbia River for much of October 1988.

American Bittern *Botaurus lentiginosus* — Uncommon, local, possibly declining summer resident in extensive marshes statewide. Rare winter. Good bet at

Nisqually NWR, Dungeness Recreation Area in Western Washington, Toppenish NWR east of Cascades.

Great Blue Heron *Ardea herodias* — Common year-round resident statewide. Nesting colonies declining in some areas due to habitat loss, nest predation by burgeoning Bald Eagle population.

Great Egret *Ardea alba* — Fairly common, increasing summer resident at Potholes Reservoir. Uncommon elsewhere in Columbia Basin, but breeding colonies appearing recently at new sites such as Hanford Reach. Fairly common late-summer–fall visitor, uncommon winter resident in Southwest, also along outer coast north to about Grays Harbor. Two pairs nesting recently at Ridgefield NWR.

Snowy Egret *Egretta thula* — Rare but regular visitor to Eastern, Western Washington, average 1–2 birds annually since 1993. All records of single birds, ranging late April–early November. Most in spring (peak May).

Little Blue Heron *Egretta caerulea* — Two records of immatures from Puget Lowlands: October 1974–January 1975, October 1989. One record of adult near Ellensburg in June 2002.

Cattle Egret *Bubulcus ibis* — Rare (irregularly uncommon) late-fall post-breeding visitor to lowlands on both sides of Cascades, mainly in fields. Most disappear in cold winter weather. Casual spring–summer. Decreasing in recent years.

Green Heron *Butorides virescens* — Once casual (first nested 1939), now uncommon summer resident of sloughs, swamps in lowland Western Washington; rare winter. Rare in Eastern Washington.

Black-crowned Night-Heron *Nycticorax nycticorax* — Common but local breeding resident of Columbia Basin; winters in small numbers. Rare on Westside, except winter roost sites at Fir Island (Skagit County), Warm Beach (Snohomish County).

Yellow-crowned Night-Heron *Nyctanassa violacea* — Two records: Walla Walla May–June 1993, Wenatchee September 2001.

White Ibis *Eudocimus albus* — One record, from Pacific County in late December 2000–January 2001.

White-faced Ibis *Plegadis chihi* — Rare but increasing visitor on both sides of Cascades, mostly May–June. Sometimes appears in large flocks. Several pairs attempted nesting at Lake Kahlotus in 2001. Many reports have insufficient detail to exclude Glossy Ibis (not recorded in Washington).

Turkey Vulture *Cathartes aura* — Fairly common summer resident of open country in Westside lowlands, along lower east slopes of Cascades. Uncommon, local in Northeast; inexplicably absent from much of Columbia Basin. Common migrant across Strait of Juan de Fuca in fall, many arriving in vicinity of Salt Creek County Park after passage south from Vancouver Island.

California Condor *Gymnogyps californianus* — Noted along Columbia River by Lewis-Clark Expedition in 1805, from Wind River to ocean. Many other records from various parts of state across 19th century, last from September 1897 at Coulee City. Large numbers of condors once came to Columbia to feast on salmon carcasses in fall spawning season. Nesting, though hypothesized, not demonstrated north of California.

Fulvous Whistling-Duck *Dendrocygna bicolor* — One bird shot from flock of 10 at Grays Harbor in October 1905.

Bean Goose *Anser fabalis* — One bird of large, taiga-breeding Siberian subspecies *middendorffii* observed at Hoquiam over 12-day period in December 2002.

Greater White-fronted Goose *Anser albifrons* — Uncommon winter resident, usually with Canada Geese. Fairly common (fall) to common (spring) in migration. Impressive migration along outer coast in late April. Large flocks of migrants occasionally noted August–September, taking direct overwater route from breeding grounds in southwestern Alaska to coastal Washington, thence across Cascades to staging area in Klamath Basin en route to central California for winter. Many stop briefly at McNary NWR.

Emperor Goose *Chen canagica* — Rare visitor along tidewater shorelines in Western Washington. Most records from sheltered waters along Pacific, North Olympic Coasts, smaller number from Puget Sound, Vancouver Lowlands.

Snow Goose *Chen caerulescens* — Common winter resident on Skagit, Stillaguamish River deltas, nearby farmlands. These birds comprise genetically distinct portion of Wrangel Island breeding population that migrates south along Pacific Flyway, winters mainly from Fraser River delta south to Port Susan. Birds noted in small numbers in Eastern Washington (principally fall, but hundreds now winter at Umatilla NWR) belong to breeding populations in northeast Siberia, Alaska, western Canadian Arctic that utilize Central Flyway to winter mostly in southern Oregon, Central Valley of California. Blue-morph birds rare in Washington (do not occur in Wrangel Island population).

Ross's Goose *Chen rossii* — Rare (almost uncommon), probably increasing migrant in Eastern Washington, predominantly spring. Most frequent, numerous in Southeast where sometimes seen in small flocks. Rarer on Westside in winter or spring (usually singles). Most migrants take direct route from Klamath Basin northeast into Saskatchewan in April, back again in fall, passing east of Washington; off-course birds expected April, occasionally other seasons. Blue form accidental in Washington.

Canada Goose *Branta canadensis* — Common year round as migrant, breeder, wintering resident. Seven subspecies present—three light-breasted (abundant), four dark (Vancouver common, others vulnerable). **Western Canada Goose** (subspecies *moffitti*): largest, palest of light-breasted forms. Year-round resident statewide; numbers greatly augmented in winter with British Columbia breeders. Canada Geese did not breed in Western Washington until transplanted birds of this race established sedentary populations beginning in 1950s. Now widespread, common, reaching nuisance levels in some city parks. **Lesser Canada Goose** (subspecies *parvipes*): medium-sized (about two-thirds size of Western), light-breasted. Nests from eastern Alaska across Yukon, Northwest Territories; common migrant in Washington on way to wintering sites in Willamette Valley, California. Most common wintering form on Eastside, less common Westside. **Taverner's Canada Goose** (subspecies *taverneri*): on average, smallest (slightly smaller than Lesser), darkest of light-breasted races occurring in Washington, but variable. Breeds northern, western Alaska, winters in Central Valley of California. Growing numbers wintering recently in southwestern Washington (e.g., Ridgefield NWR). **Dusky Canada Goose** (subspecies *occidentalis*): large, dark-breasted form (close to Western in size), usually lacks neck-ring. Breeds in relatively small numbers on Copper River delta in Alaska, winters primarily in southwestern Washington (e.g., Julia Butler Hansen, Ridgefield, Steigerwald NWRs), Willamette Valley of Oregon. **Vancouver Canada Goose** (subspecies *fulva*): often considered inseparable from Dusky, but slightly larger. Breeds in coastal rainforest zone from southeast Alaska to northern Vancouver Island; some southward movement in winter through western Washington to Willamette Valley. **Aleutian Canada Goose** (subspecies *leucopareia*): small, darkish, with fairly prominent white neck-ring. Between Dusky, Cackling in size but slightly paler than either. Breeds on a few Aleutian Islands, winters mostly in Central Valley of California. Once near extinction; protection has aided recovery in recent years—now uncommon at Willapa NWR in fall migration, may winter. **Cackling Canada Goose** (subspecies *minima*): tiny (half again larger than Mallard), dark-breasted, short-necked, with characteristic yelping call. Most have indistinct neck-ring. Migrates from breeding grounds in western Alaska across northeastern Pacific to wintering sites in Central Valley of California, Willamette Valley, southwestern Washington (e.g., Ridgefield NWR). Population small, protected; appears stable.

Brant *Branta bernicla* — Alaska-breeding **Black Brant** (subspecies *nigricans*) common migrant, local winter resident on saltwater bays, closely tied to beds of Eelgrass. Large numbers at Dungeness, Willapa NWRs, usually a few at Alki Beach, West Point in Seattle. Accidental fall–winter in Eastern Washington. **Gray-bellied Brant** (thought to be distinct taxon but not yet described), from Melville Island in Canadian High Arctic, winters on Padilla Bay.

Mute Swan *Cygnus olor* — Introduced to North America from Europe. Unwelcome invader in Washington; has bred. Numbers held in check by WDFW removal program.

Trumpeter Swan *Cygnus buccinator* — Once close to extinction, essentially disappeared from Washington. Began to winter again locally in Mount Vernon area in early 1970s, spread as numbers increased. Now common winter in northwestern Washington lowlands. Readily found on farm fields on Skagit/Samish Flats, also Snohomish River valley, Chehalis River floodplain. Regular in smaller numbers on lakes elsewhere in Western Washington, especially on outer coast. Still rare east of Cascades; attempted reintroduction at Turnbull NWR failed, but 1–2 birds might still be present. Small numbers sometimes winter on ponds near Ellensburg.

Tundra Swan *Cygnus columbianus* — Common migrant, winter resident on Westside. Many winter on Skagit/Samish Flats (with Trumpeters), also Ridgefield, Franz Lake NWRs in Southwest. East of Cascades in spring, impressive flocks often noted high in sky flying northeastward over broad front: Blue Mountains, Palouse, Northeast. Fairly common spring at stopover sites (e.g., McNary NWR, Atkins Lake, Turnbull NWR, Calispell Lake), less numerous fall.

Wood Duck *Aix sponsa* — Fairly common resident statewide. Numbers dwindle in winter, especially east.

Gadwall *Anas strepera* — Common resident statewide, especially numerous around Puget Sound. Much less common on Eastside in winter.

Falcated Duck *Anas falcata* — Three records, all from near coasts: January 1979 from Naselle River, July 1993 at Sequim, February–March 2002 at Samish Island.

Eurasian Wigeon *Anas penelope* — Uncommon to locally fairly common winter resident west of Cascades—more winter in Western Washington than anyplace else in Lower 48. Especially numerous near Samish, Dungeness River estuaries. Can often be picked out in American Wigeon flocks in city parks. Rare but regular winter resident east of Cascades (usually not difficult to find in Tri-Cities), more often noted in spring. Eurasian x American hybrids occur regularly, at rate of about five percent of Eurasians.

American Wigeon *Anas americana* — Common winter resident, migrant statewide. Uncommon breeder east of Cascades; rare, local west.

American Black Duck *Anas rubripes* — Tiny introduced population formerly at Everett sewage ponds, now probably extirpated. Small number of records of true vagrants from various parts of state. Observers encouraged to report sightings, with details.

Mallard *Anas platyrhynchos* — Common resident statewide, winter numbers higher east than west until waters freeze. Astronomical numbers on Columbia River during hunting season.

Blue-winged Teal *Anas discors* — Fairly common summer resident in Eastern Washington, uncommon in Puget Trough. Fairly common in migration. Casual early-winter resident, mostly east of Cascades.

Cinnamon Teal *Anas cyanoptera* — Fairly common summer resident of ponds, marshes, sloughs in Eastern Washington, less common in Western Washington. Rare winter on Westside.

Northern Shoveler *Anas clypeata* — Common summer resident, principally in Columbia Basin, Puget Trough. Common migrant. Common winter resident west, uncommon east (locally fairly common in warmer parts of Columbia Basin).

Northern Pintail *Anas acuta* — Uncommon summer resident, much more local west of Cascade crest. Common migrant statewide. Common winter resident in Western Washington lowlands, especially Puget Trough; common to uncommon on Eastside, with numbers, wintering localities varying greatly year to year.

Garganey *Anas querquedula* — Two records: Chehalis River floodplain near Satsop (April–May 1991), Richland (December 1994).

Green-winged Teal *Anas crecca* — Continental North American subspecies *carolinensis* fairly common but local summer resident east; rare, local west. Common migrant, winter resident on both sides of Cascades. **Common Teal** (Eurasian-breeding subspecies *crecca*) rare winter visitor (mainly Western Washington), usually with flocks of *carolinensis*.

Canvasback *Aythya valisineria* — Uncommon summer resident on lakes in Eastern Washington; rare west. Fairly common (west) to common (east), but local, winter resident. Can be abundant in vicinity of grain terminals on Columbia, Snake River reservoirs. East of Cascades many gather in early spring migration on temporary lakes (especially Atkins Lake).

Redhead *Aythya americana* — East of Cascades, common summer, fairly common winter resident. Rare on Westside, largely restricted to fresh water.

Ring-necked Duck *Aythya collaris* — Uncommon summer resident on Eastside (most numerous in Northeast), uncommon to rare on Westside. Common migrant, winter visitor statewide. Largely restricted to fresh water.

Tufted Duck *Aythya fuligula* — Rare winter resident (mostly November–April) in lowlands, usually with flocks of scaups or Ring-necked Ducks. Dependable stakeout occasionally found, sometimes returning for successive winters. Several interior records (Walla Walla River delta, Columbia NWR, Wenatchee, Turtle Rock, Pateros, Omak) but great majority from west of Cascades. Most reliable places probably around Grays Harbor, Everett, Columbia River from gorge to mouth—but records widely scattered. Several records of hybrids, presumably with undetermined scaup species.

Greater Scaup *Aythya marila* — Common migrant, winter resident in Western Washington, especially on sheltered marine waters. In Eastern Washington, locally common migrant, winter resident on Columbia, Snake River reservoirs, especially near grain terminals.

Lesser Scaup *Aythya affinis* — Uncommon, local summer resident east (especially Northeast), west (especially Ridgefield NWR). Common migrant, winter resident on low-elevation fresh-, saltwater bodies statewide.

Steller's Eider *Polysticta stelleri* — One bird stayed at Port Townsend for nearly four months (October 1986–February 1987). Another seen for several days at Walla Walla River delta in September 1995.

King Eider *Somateria spectabilis* — Eleven records extend from late October to mid-May, all but one on inland marine waters; exception was at Westport. Only one bird stayed for more than a few days.

Harlequin Duck *Histrionicus histrionicus* — Fairly common winter resident of coastal waters with rocky substrates. Good sites include Salt Creek County Park, Ediz Hook, Sequim Bay, Fort Worden, Fort Flagler, west side of Whidbey Island, Alki Beach in West Seattle. Scarce on coast for only short period in spring, as many males return to salt water soon after breeding. Uncommon summer resident on rivers at low to middle elevations in Olympic, Cascade, Selkirk Mountains. Good sites include Stehekin River upstream from Stehekin, Methow River near Winthrop, Tieton River below Rimrock Lake, Naches River above Cliffdell, Sullivan Creek above Sullivan Lake.

Surf Scoter *Melanitta perspicillata* — Common winter resident of coastal waters, in sheltered bays as well as rougher waters just off breakers. Non-breeding flocks local in summer, especially Penn Cove, Drayton Harbor. Rare in Eastern Washington—mostly fall on Columbia, Snake River reservoirs, Grand Coulee lakes.

White-winged Scoter *Melanitta fusca* — Similar to Surf Scoter in status, distribution, except uncommon in Eastern Washington in fall.

Black Scoter *Melanitta nigra* — Fairly common but local winter resident on marine waters with rocky bottom, rare in summer. Good sites include Ocean Shores, Ediz Hook, Fort Worden, Fort Flagler, Lummi Bay, Alki Beach in West Seattle. Casual in Eastern Washington fall.

Long-tailed Duck *Clangula hyemalis* — Fairly common but local winter resident on sheltered marine waters. Good sites include Ediz Hook, Dungeness Spit, Sequim Bay, Protection Island, Fort Worden, Fort Flagler, Point Roberts, Birch Bay, west side of Whidbey Island, deepwater sounds on Orcas Island. Rare in Eastern Washington—mostly fall on Columbia, Snake River reservoirs, Grand Coulee lakes.

Bufflehead *Bucephala albeola* — Common winter resident, migrant west, fairly common east; found on fresh, salt water. Breeds on a few lakes in Northeast, most reliable site Big Meadow Lake.

Common Goldeneye *Bucephala clangula* — Common winter resident on fresh, salt water statewide. Rare breeder east of Cascades in northern part of state, e.g., lakes in Sinlahekin Valley, Soap, Beth Lakes in Okanogan, Big Meadow Lake in Northeast (probably most reliable site). Rare summer on Westside, mainly at sewage ponds. Identification confusion with female Barrow's Goldeneye clouds true status as breeding species.

Barrow's Goldeneye *Bucephala islandica* — In Western Washington, common but local winter resident on sheltered saltwater bays, to much lesser extent freshwater lakes (usually with rocky bottoms, shores). Highly associated with pilings—e.g., on parts of Hood Canal. Uncommon winter resident in Eastern Washington, most at grain ports on Columbia, Snake Rivers, a few on flowing rivers (especially Columbia within Hanford Reach). Fairly common summer resident at mid-elevations on forested lakes (nesting in tree cavities near lakeshore) in Cascades, Okanogan Highlands, Selkirks. Colonies nest in cliff cavities in treeless areas at Lenore Lake in Grand Coulee, Jameson Lake in Moses Coulee, thus akin to Iceland, Labrador breeders.

Smew *Mergellus albellus* — Two records of adult males near Columbia River in Skamania County in successive winters (December 1989, January–February 1991), considered to be same individual. Another at McKenna (Pierce County) in March 1993.

Hooded Merganser *Lophodytes cucullatus* — Fairly common summer resident in Western Washington lowlands, mainly around Puget Trough. On Eastside, uncommon summer resident, mostly in Northeast. Fairly common (briefly common fall) in migration, winter across state, although numbers fall off on Eastside when freezing reduces available habitat.

Common Merganser *Mergus merganser* — Common resident year round, nesting in tree cavities along lowland rivers, lakes. In winter, also found on deep, clear saltwater bodies, larger lakes, lower Columbia River.

Red-breasted Merganser *Mergus serrator* — Common winter resident on inland marine waters, protected coastal bays. Uncommon fall migrant along Columbia River, rare fall in central Columbia Basin except regular on Banks Lake (a few winter).

Ruddy Duck *Oxyura jamaicensis* — Fairly common to locally common summer resident in Eastern Washington, highest concentration around Potholes; also breeds uncommonly in southern Puget Trough. Common winter resident of freshwater habitats in Western Washington lowlands, especially around Puget Sound; local on salt water, mostly in mud-bottomed bays. Fairly common winter resident in Eastern Washington.

Osprey *Pandion haliaetus* — Fairly common, increasing migrant, summer resident statewide. Large numbers nest semi-colonially at mouth of Snohomish River in Everett, along Pend Oreille River at Usk. Casual winter.

White-tailed Kite *Elanus leucurus* — Uncommon, local, probably increasing winter resident in Southwest, occupying bottomlands, open fields, rank grasslands of Chehalis River drainage in Lewis, Thurston, Grays Harbor counties. Also along Willapa River, lower Columbia River floodplain, tributaries (especially Wahkiakum, Pacific counties). Rare in summer (first nesting record Raymond 1988). Good sites include Chinook Valley Road east of Ilwaco, Julia Butler Hansen NWR, Curtis/Boisfort area of Lewis County, Lincoln Creek Valley west of Centralia, prairies south, west of Littlerock. Casual wanderer northward in western lowlands, especially late winter–spring.

Bald Eagle *Haliaeetus leucocephalus* — Common year-round resident in Western Washington lowlands, mostly along coasts. Breeding numbers increased dramatically in last decade. Densest breeding population on San Juan Islands, fewer on Olympic Peninsula, outer coast but still common. Nests around Lake Washington in Seattle, suburbs. Famous early-winter concentration on Skagit River near Marblemount, attracted to spawning salmon. High numbers also winter on Samish, Skagit, Stillaguamish River deltas. In Eastern Washington, uncommon breeder in Okanogan, Northeast (mostly along Okanogan, Sanpoil, Kettle, Columbia, Colville, Pend Oreille Rivers). Numbers east of Cascades highest in winter as Canadian lakes freeze, forcing many birds south. Large numbers gather on Banks Lake in Grand Coulee (roosting in Northrup Canyon near Electric City). Also found locally in open fields coincident with calving, discarded afterbirth.

Northern Harrier *Circus cyaneus* — Fairly common (east), uncommon, local (west) summer resident in grassland habitats; fairly common to locally common winter resident in similar habitats statewide when free of deep snow.

Sharp-shinned Hawk *Accipiter striatus* — Uncommon year-round resident in conifer-forest landscapes statewide. Most nest in relatively remote localities where can be secretive, difficult to find. In winter, descend from higher elevations (or farther north), concentrate near sources of songbird prey such as feeders in towns. Fairly common migrant, especially fall.

Cooper's Hawk *Accipiter cooperii* — Uncommon, probably increasing year-round resident in open forests (conifer, mixed, deciduous) throughout state, especially in riparian settings. In nesting season, outnumbers Sharp-shinned in lowlands, around towns; reverse true in winter. Fairly common migrant, especially fall.

Northern Goshawk *Accipiter gentilis* — Rare summer resident in mountains wherever mature forests occur. Declining due to loss of habitat. Probably rarest in Olympic Mountains, Southwest; most common at mid-elevations along east slopes of Cascades, in Okanogan Highlands, Selkirk, Blue Mountains. Difficult to locate in breeding season—occasionally chanced upon soaring over nesting territory, particularly mid-morning. Uncommon fall migrant along high mountain ridges. Rare to locally uncommon winter resident in lowlands, mainly east of Cascades—especially wooded areas close to waterfowl or pheasant concentrations.

Red-shouldered Hawk *Buteo lineatus* — Rare winter resident of lowland riparian forests in Southwest; expanding northward from Oregon. Regular (1–2 birds) each winter in recent years at Ridgefield NWR, probably increasing elsewhere along lower Columbia River. Recent records northward to Nisqually NWR, Skagit Game Range, Dungeness, eastward to riparian bottomlands in South Central.

Broad-winged Hawk *Buteo platypterus* — Rare migrant east, accidental west; much more frequent fall (annual in recent years). Most fall sightings from hawk observatory at Chelan Ridge. A few seen regularly each fall from observatory at Rocky Point on southern tip of Vancouver Island, headed south across Strait of Juan de Fuca—indicating largely undetected southbound migration through Western Washington.

Swainson's Hawk *Buteo swainsoni* — Fairly common summer resident in Eastern Washington, occupying agricultural fields, moister shrub-steppe grasslands; uncommon in lowermost, driest portions of southern Columbia Basin. Formerly widespread in prairies with scattered trees for nesting. Has adapted to irrigated alfalfa, hay farming, dryland wheat fields, nesting wherever windbreaks or clumps of trees available nearby. Several hundred pairs nest in Columbia Basin, future seems reasonably secure. Casual in spring migration west.

Red-tailed Hawk *Buteo jamaicensis* — Common year-round resident in most habitats statewide, except dense forest. Can be harder to find when nesting. Numbers augmented in migration, winter with visitors from north, interior of continent, including uncommon **Harlan's Hawk** (*B.j. harlani*), rare **Krider's Hawk** (*B.j. krideri*).

Ferruginous Hawk *Buteo regalis* — Uncommon, local summer resident in Columbia Basin, typically nesting on coulee walls in most arid portions. Winters casually in Walla Walla region. Declining due to loss of habitat, about 30–40 pairs remain in state. Some may be adapting to forage on irrigated fields with high rodent populations, if disturbance-free nest sites available nearby. Hanford Site best, but much of it off-limits to birders. Other known sites: Juniper Dunes Wilderness Area, Webber Canyon south of Benton City, Eureka Flats, Esquatzel Coulee (both northeast of Pasco), Washtucna Coulee east of Connell, Crab Creek east of town of Wilson Creek. Recorded west.

Rough-legged Hawk *Buteo lagopus* — Fairly common winter resident. Local west of Cascades, most likely on Samish/Skagit Flats. In Eastern Washington, especially in dryland wheat fields, Kittitas Valley.

Golden Eagle *Aquila chrysaetos* — Uncommon, declining, year-round resident of cliffs, rugged terrain from low to mid-elevations on Cascades east slopes, Okanogan Highlands, Selkirks, Snake River Canyon, Blues. Rare resident in San Juan Islands,

Olympics, locally on west slopes of Cascades. Fairly common migrant along alpine ridges fall. In winter, some descend to open country in lowlands.

Eurasian Kestrel *Falco tinnunculus* — One bird discovered late October 1999 on Samish Flats, seen irregularly into December.

American Kestrel *Falco sparverius* — Common summer resident in Eastern Washington open habitats—farmlands, meadows, shrub-steppe, clearcuts, alpine parklands. In winter, withdraws from higher elevations, shrub-steppe; numbers increase in farmlands. Uncommon (summer) to fairly common (winter) resident locally in similar habitats in Southwest, uncommon elsewhere on Westside except rare to absent along outer coast.

Merlin *Falco columbarius* — Fairly common migrant, uncommon winter resident along outer coast, margins of inland marine waters, especially where swarms of Dunlins occur. Usually fairly easy to find at Nisqually, Dungeness NWRs, Ocean Shores, Leadbetter Point, Skagit/Samish Flats. Uncommon to rare winter resident statewide around towns, cities, farms. A few pairs of coastal **Black Merlin** (subspecies *suckleyi*) breed in forests of Olympic Peninsula, Puget Trough (also in cities). **Taiga Merlin** (subspecies *columbarius*) suspected to breed (rarely) in Eastern Washington forests. **Prairie Merlin** (subspecies *richardsoni*) rare in migration, winter.

Eurasian Hobby *Falco subbuteo* — One record, from Discovery Park, Seattle, in October 2001.

Gyrfalcon *Falco rusticolus* — West of Cascades, rare winter resident on Skagit/Samish Flats, coastal marshes, beaches (e.g., Dungeness Spit), other open lowland landscapes frequented by large flocks of dabbling ducks. East of Cascades, rare winter resident on higher plateaus—most reports from Waterville Plateau, Davenport-Reardan region, Moxee Valley east of Moxee, farm country between Moses Lake, Quincy. Drawn to waterfowl concentrations, also wheat fields bordered by brushy or grassy terrain where Gray Partridge, Ring-necked Pheasant likely targets.

Peregrine Falcon *Falco peregrinus* — Three races. **Peale's Peregrine** (subspecies *pealei*) increasing but still uncommon summer resident along cliffs of Outer Olympic Coast, San Juan Islands—particularly in vicinity of seabird colonies. Fairly common fall migrant, uncommon winter resident of marshes, open country, coastlines. **Continental Peregrine** (subspecies *anatum*) formerly widely distributed in Eastern Washington, mostly extirpated as breeder in decades after World War II. Now found statewide as migrant, winter resident (much less common east), especially near waterfowl, shorebird concentrations. **Tundra Peregrine** (subspecies *tundrius*) found in migration, mostly along outer coast. Reintroduced birds (subspecies uncertain) successfully established, increasing locally in Cascades, along Columbia River; a few pairs now nest on tall buildings, bridges in Seattle, Tacoma, Spokane.

Prairie Falcon *Falco mexicanus* — Uncommon year-round resident in Eastern Washington lowlands, breeding mostly on basalt cliffs in southern half of Columbia Basin, rare north to Okanogan County. In winter, often in open agricultural country. Widespread wanderer late summer, fall over subalpine meadows, ridges east of Cascade crest, locally west (especially Mount Rainier). Rare winter on Westside, most reliable site Samish Flats.

Chukar *Alectoris chukar* — Introduced from Near East. Fairly common year-round resident on rocky slopes of Eastern Washington lowlands, especially near cliffs. Often difficult to find. Best looked for near dawn, dusk when calling most intense, comes to roadsides for grit. Good sites include Huntzinger Road south of Vantage, Lower Crab Creek Road, Lower Grand Coulee (especially slopes north of Sun Lakes State Park), Conconully Road northwest of Omak.

Gray Partridge *Perdix perdix* — Introduced from Europe. Fairly common year-round resident of Eastern Washington, mostly in wheat fields, nearby brushy areas but also on native steppe on higher plateaus, ridges. Elusive. One good strategy: cruise wheat-field roads near dawn, dusk for birds gathering roadside grit, listen for peculiar, scratchy call. Also check around grain elevators.

Ring-necked Pheasant *Phasianus colchicus* — Introduced from Old World. Fairly common year-round resident of wheat fields, brushy edges, shrub-steppe, parks, similar open landscapes at lower elevations on both sides of Cascades. Presumably securely established in many parts of state but continuing releases make true status difficult to determine.

Ruffed Grouse *Bonasa umbellus* — Fairly common year-round resident of deciduous woodlands statewide, mostly at lower elevations. Absent from Columbia Basin below Ponderosa Pine zone. Best looked for in spring when drumming.

Greater Sage-Grouse *Centrocercus urophasianus* — Rare, local, year-round resident of Big Sagebrush habitats with good cover of native grass, difficult to find except at lek sites. Two populations survive—about 700 birds in central Douglas County (especially south, west of Leahy Junction, around Jameson Lake), estimated 300 birds on Yakima Training Center.

Spruce Grouse *Falcipennis canadensis* — Uncommon year-round resident of subalpine forests in Northeast, Okanogan, barely west across Cascade crest in Mountain Hemlock in Whatcom County. Small, disjunct population on mid- to upper Cascades slopes in northwestern Yakima County. Often difficult to find due to elusive behavior—definitely an asset for survival of this tame-as-a-barnyard-chicken species. Best looked for along gravel roads in September–October as birds gather grit, especially early or late in day, or in late July–August along streams as hens lead broods to insect-rich foraging areas. Harts Pass good bet, also Salmo Pass, FR-39 from Roger Lake to Long Swamp.

White-tailed Ptarmigan *Lagopus leucurus* — Uncommon, local summer resident in alpine areas of Cascades. Highly cryptic, sits tight, hence usually missed. Best odds: mossy, herb-rich seeps above treeline in late July–August where hens lead chicks to forage for insects. Good sites include Mount Rainier (Panorama Point, Burroughs Mountain, Fremont Peak), Slate Peak, Chopaka Mountain. Wintering sites unknown, but probably wanders downslope in fall, especially to thickets of Sitka Alder.

Blue Grouse *Dendragapus obscurus* — Fairly common year-round resident statewide in coniferous forests with openings, though scarce in dense coastal forests as well as those dominated by Lodgepole Pine, Engelmann Spruce. Best looked for in spring when males hoot, summer when broods out and about. Never a sure thing, but Hurricane Ridge, Deer Park come close.

Sharp-tailed Grouse *Tympanuchus phasianellus* — Rare year-round resident in grassy shrub-steppe habitats in northern Columbia Basin, Okanogan (Douglas, Lincoln, Okanogan Counties). Once widely distributed throughout Eastern Washington grasslands, now close to extirpation. Remaining sites largely on private property; information on whereabouts difficult to obtain. Colville Indian Reservation has most remaining birds. Seen occasionally in winter at Swanson Lakes Wildlife Area, West Foster Creek Unit of Wells Wildlife Area, along Bridgeport Hill Road.

Wild Turkey *Meleagris gallopavo* — Introduced from eastern North America. Uncommon to locally fairly common year-round resident of open forests, farmlands east of Cascades—usually near streams, never far from woods. Populations fluctuate with fresh releases. Appears well established in Klickitat County, Southeast, Northeast. In Western Washington, reliable only on San Juan Island where protected from hunting, quite tame.

Mountain Quail *Oreortyx pictus* — Rare, local year-round resident. Native population in Skamania, Klickitat Counties apparently extirpated. Possibly native population in Snake River drainage close to extirpation—a few coveys still reported occasionally along Grande Ronde River. Widely introduced in Western Washington late 19th–early 20th centuries, thrived on logged-over land in early successional stages as forests left to regenerate unaided. Modern industrial forests inhospitable, quail now reduced to scattered populations from Kitsap Peninsula southwest to Mason, northwestern Thurston, southeastern Grays Harbor Counties. Secretive, unpredictable; feeder stakeout best bet if one can be located.

California Quail *Callipepla californica* — Introduced from California. Common, conspicuous (east), fairly common, local (west) at lower elevations except in dense forests—especially farmlands, brushy places, parks, lightly developed residential areas. Absent from dryland wheat fields, where replaced by Gray Partridge. Present populations firmly established, descend from long history of releases.

Northern Bobwhite *Colinus virginianus* — Introduced from eastern U.S. Rare year-round resident of South Sound Prairies, where populations generally considered self-sustaining, countable. Frequently released in small numbers in other parts of state but rarely survives for more than one or two seasons.

Yellow Rail *Coturnicops noveboracensis* — Two old records: Columbia Basin (Adams County) in April 1969, Skagit River delta in November 1935.

Virginia Rail *Rallus limicola* — Year-round resident of freshwater, brackish marshes. Fairly common summer; numbers lower in winter, especially east of Cascades.

Sora *Porzana carolina* — Uncommon (west) to fairly common (east) summer resident of freshwater (rarely saltwater) marshes, wet fields, ranging up to mid-elevation sedge meadows on Eastside. Rare west in winter.

American Coot *Fulica americana* — Winter resident in huge numbers on lowland lakes, ponds, reservoirs; much smaller numbers on protected marine waters. Fairly common but local summer resident of lakes, ponds statewide.

Sandhill Crane *Grus canadensis* — In March–April, again September, **Lesser Sandhill Crane** (subspecies *canadensis*) passes through Eastern Washington by thousands—especially conspicuous west of Othello in corn stubble, on Waterville Plateau. In Western Washington, fairly common migrant in Woodland Bottoms, Vancouver Lowlands; hundreds winter. Also sometimes seen in spring passage along outer coast. **Greater Sandhill Crane** (subspecies *tabida*) formerly widespread summer resident on both sides of Cascades, now virtually extirpated. A few still nest at Conboy Lake NWR, also near Signal Peak on Yakama Indian Reservation (closed to public). Rare migrant, mixed in with Lessers.

Black-bellied Plover *Pluvialis squatarola* — Common migrant, winter resident in or near marine habitats; casual spring, uncommon fall migrant east of Cascades. Often seen in plowed, wet fields.

American Golden-Plover *Pluvialis dominica* — Rare spring, uncommon fall migrant on coasts—Damon Point at Ocean Shores reliable site. Rare fall migrant in Eastern Washington, casual spring.

Pacific Golden-Plover *Pluvialis fulva* — Rare spring, uncommon fall migrant along outer coast; recorded east. Casual in winter west. Best sites Damon Point at Ocean Shores, Leadbetter Point, Dungeness NWR. Often occurs side-by-side with American Golden-Plover; separation challenging but brightest golden juvenile Pacifics readily identifiable.

Snowy Plover *Charadrius alexandrinus* — Uncommon, local year-round resident along South Coast beaches north to Ocean Shores (Damon Point); most on Leadbetter Point, Midway Beach (Grayland). Recorded east.

Semipalmated Plover *Charadrius semipalmatus* — Common migrant, rare winter resident on saltwater beaches, tideflats. Uncommon migrant in interior. Has nested at Ocean Shores.

Piping Plover *Charadrius melodus* — One record, at Reardan Ponds for four days in July 1990.

Killdeer *Charadrius vociferus* — Common year-round resident, except uncommon to rare in winter east of Cascades. Open-country bird, most often seen on lawns, fields, gravel roads/parking lots, beaches, tideflats, bare ground.

Mountain Plover *Charadrius montanus* — Two records from outer coast (Pacific County) in November 1964, December 2000; one from Turnbull NWR, May 1968.

Eurasian Dotterel *Charadrius morinellus* — Three fall records (3 September–4 November), all from Ocean Shores, in 1934, 1979, 1999. One bird remained for over two weeks.

Black Oystercatcher *Haematopus bachmani* — Uncommon year-round resident on rocky coastlines. Paired in nesting season, often concentrates into localized flocks (up to 40 birds) in winter. Most numerous in Northwest—especially San Juans, Fidalgo Island, northern Whidbey Island. Virtually absent from Puget Sound proper, very local along South Coast. A few often noted on log booms at Ediz Hook. Recorded east.

Black-necked Stilt *Himantopus mexicanus* — Locally fairly common summer resident in Columbia Basin, lower Yakima River valley—especially Potholes, Toppenish NWR, Satus Wildlife Area. Recent arrival in Washington, first nested 1973. Rare migrant, summer resident in Western Washington; nested 2001 at Ridgefield NWR.

American Avocet *Recurvirostra americana* — Locally fairly common summer resident in Columbia Basin, nesting around pond edges, other wet habitats (especially alkaline). Migrants may be seen as early as March, as late as November. Rare migrant, summer resident in Western Washington. Has nested recently at Crockett Lake (successfully 2000, attempted 2002).

Greater Yellowlegs *Tringa melanoleuca* — Common (west) to fairly common (east) in migration, uncommon (west) to rare (east) winter resident, in both freshwater, saltwater habitats.

Lesser Yellowlegs *Tringa flavipes* — Uncommon spring, common fall migrant statewide; casual in winter west. Favors same habitats as Greater Yellowlegs (mudflats, shorelines, shallow marshes).

Solitary Sandpiper *Tringa solitaria* — Uncommon fall, rare spring migrant, generally more numerous east. Almost always seen at ponds, other freshwater sites from lowlands up to forested mountain lakes.

Willet *Catoptrophorus semipalmatus* — Rare to locally uncommon winter resident of coastal estuaries, salt marshes, north to Drayton Harbor; most often noted at Tokeland, nearby New River mouth, Ediz Hook, Dungeness NWR. Casual spring migrant through interior.

Wandering Tattler *Heteroscelus incanus* — Fairly common migrant on rocky shores, jetties on outer coast; local in appropriate saltwater habitats elsewhere. Best sites include Westport, Ocean Shores jetties. Accidental in winter. Recorded east.

Gray-tailed Tattler *Heteroscelus brevipes* — One record, in October 1975 at Leadbetter Point.

Spotted Sandpiper *Actitis macularia* — Fairly common, widespread summer resident; nests close to water on both sides of Cascades, from sea level to alpine lakes. A few winter in western lowlands.

Upland Sandpiper *Bartramia longicauda* — Formerly uncommon summer resident in Spokane Valley between Spokane, Idaho line; no records there since 1993. Probably extirpated as breeder in state, although one recent summer record from western Spokane County. Casual fall, accidental spring migrant east, west.

Little Curlew *Numenius minutus* — One record, at Leadbetter Point in May 2001.

Whimbrel *Numenius phaeopus* — American subspecies *hudsonicus* fairly common migrant, rare, local winter resident in various wet habitats west of Cascades. Casual migrant (mostly fall) in Eastern Washington. Two May records of white-rumped Siberian subspecies *variegatus*, both from Ocean Shores.

Bristle-thighed Curlew *Numenius tahitiensis* — A dozen or more individuals observed length of outer coast, from Leadbetter Point to Tatoosh Island, in May 1998. One prior record from Leadbetter Point in May 1982.

Long-billed Curlew *Numenius americanus* — Uncommon spring, early-summer resident in Columbia Basin grasslands, agricultural fields. Winters at Tokeland, rare elsewhere; most migrate to California, Mexico. Migrants occasionally noted on outer coast, along Columbia River, even in mountain meadows.

Hudsonian Godwit *Limosa haemastica* — Casual fall migrant. Most records juveniles from Pacific Coast, Semiahmoo Bay, Columbia Basin, late August to mid-October. One July adult in alternate plumage at Crockett Lake. Accidental in spring.

Bar-tailed Godwit *Limosa lapponica* — Rare fall, casual spring migrant, mostly on outer coast; one bird stayed into winter. Best places Willapa Bay (especially Tokeland), Grays Harbor (especially Ocean Shores). Scattered records from other saltwater bays, shorelines such as Dungeness area, southern Puget Sound.

Marbled Godwit *Limosa fedoa* — Common winter resident at Tokeland, uncommon migrant, winter resident elsewhere on coastal mudflats. Rare migrant in Columbia Basin (e.g., Columbia River, Potholes Reservoir).

Ruddy Turnstone *Arenaria interpres* — In Western Washington, fairly common migrant, rare winter resident on saltwater shorelines; also on plowed fields in spring (e.g., Chehalis River floodplain). Casual fall migrant east of Cascades.

Black Turnstone *Arenaria melanocephala* — Common migrant, winter resident on rocky coasts. Best sites include Penn Cove, Fort Flagler, jetties at Ocean Shores, Westport, mouth of Columbia River. Roosts on log booms (e.g., Ediz Hook), piers, boats, rafts. Accidental in Columbia Basin in migration.

Surfbird *Aphriza virgata* — Fairly common but local migrant, winter resident on rocky saltwater shorelines. Some favored sites include Penn Cove, Fort Flagler, Ediz Hook, Neah Bay, jetties at Ocean Shores, Westport.

Great Knot *Calidris tenuirostris* — One record, from early September 1979 at La Push.

Red Knot *Calidris canutus* — Uncommon to rare migrant on outer coast, except briefly fairly common in Grays Harbor (Bottle Beach, Bowerman Basin) late April–early May. Casual migrant in Puget Sound region (mostly spring). Winters rarely on coast. Casual fall migrant in Eastern Washington.

Sanderling *Calidris alba* — Common migrant, winter resident along sandy beaches of outer coast; fairly common but local in similar situations around Puget Trough. Casual spring, uncommon fall migrant east of Cascades.

Semipalmated Sandpiper *Calidris pusilla* — Uncommon fall migrant, rare in spring. Most Western Washington reports come from Northwest (especially Crockett Lake).

Western Sandpiper *Calidris mauri* — Common spring, fall migrant west, uncommon winter resident on saltwater shorelines. Greatest numbers along outer coast in spring, especially Bowerman Basin, where upwards of 500,000 birds may stop in a single day. Rare spring, fairly common fall migrant east.

Least Sandpiper *Calidris minutilla* — On Westside, common spring, fall migrant; on Eastside, uncommon (spring) to fairly common (fall). Uncommon (west) to rare (east) winter resident. Forages on muddy borders of ponds, estuaries, saltwater mudflats, also in shallow freshwater, saltwater marshes. Typically seen in small groups rather than large flocks.

White-rumped Sandpiper *Calidris fuscicollis* — Two May records from Reardan, 1962, 1964. One from Dungeness in early July 1992, presumably returning fall migrant.

Baird's Sandpiper *Calidris bairdii* — Uncommon to locally fairly common fall migrant east of Cascades, including at high-mountain lakes August–early September; uncommon, local on coasts (especially Damon Point at Ocean Shores, Crockett Lake). Casual west, rare east in spring.

Pectoral Sandpiper *Calidris melanotos* — Fairly common fall migrant statewide; rare (west) to casual (east) in spring.

Sharp-tailed Sandpiper *Calidris acuminata* — Rare, irregular fall migrant, often in company of Pectoral Sandpiper, mostly on outer coast. Favored sites include Ocean Shores, Leadbetter Point, Dungeness. Casual in Eastern Washington (Potholes, Walla Walla River delta). Records almost all of juveniles. Two records of adults: Leadbetter Point in April (only spring record for state), Crockett Lake in July.

Rock Sandpiper *Calidris ptilocnemis* — Uncommon, declining migrant, winter resident on Pacific, North Olympic Coasts, rare along marine waters farther inland. Favored sites jetties at Ocean Shores, Westport, mouth of Columbia River; other possibilities include Penn Cove, Ediz Hook. One record of distinctive Pribilofs subspecies *ptilocnemis*. Question of which other subspecies reach Washington not fully resolved, although most birds surely *tschuktschorum*.

Dunlin *Calidris alpina* — Commonest wintering shorebird at this latitude. Common migrant, winter resident on coastal bays, flocks numbering in tens of thousands at favored sites such as Samish/Skagit Flats, Grays Harbor, Willapa Bay. Uncommon migrant, rare winter resident in Columbia Basin.

Curlew Sandpiper *Calidris ferruginea* — Accidental spring (one record each from Potholes, Leadbetter Point), casual fall migrant. Fall records all from coasts (mid-July–early October), all but one an adult.

Stilt Sandpiper *Calidris himantopus* — Rare fall migrant in Western Washington (Crockett Lake appears best); uncommon fall, accidental spring east of Cascades.

Buff-breasted Sandpiper *Tryngites subruficollis* — Rare, possibly declining fall migrant. Juveniles occur most years along coast from mid-August to mid-September; Damon Point at Ocean Shores most reliable place. A few fall records from Puget Trough, Eastern Washington; one late-May record from Leadbetter Point.

Ruff *Philomachus pugnax* — Rare fall migrant in Western Washington, peak August–September. Most records juveniles along outer coast—Grays Harbor (especially Ocean Shores), Willapa Bay best. Casual fall in Columbia Basin.

Short-billed Dowitcher *Limnodromus griseus* — Common migrant on outer coast—mostly in bays but occasionally on beaches. Impressive spring concentrations in Grays Harbor (Bowerman Basin, Bottle Beach). Much more frequent than Long-billed on saltwater, estuarine habitats. Rare fall, casual spring migrant in Eastern Washington. Most adults migrating through Washington belong to subspecies *caurinus*, less extensively red beneath in alternate plumage, hence fairly readily separable from Long-billed, especially in spring. Subspecies *hendersoni* casual migrant east.

Long-billed Dowitcher *Limnodromus scolopaceus* — Fairly common migrant statewide, usually on fresh water; uncommon winter on coastal bays.

Jack Snipe *Lymnocryptes minimus* — One record, from Skagit Game Range in September 1993.

Wilson's Snipe *Gallinago delicata* — Fairly common migrant statewide. Fairly common summer resident east; uncommon, local west. Fairly common west, uncommon to rare east in winter. Found in many types of wet habitats, from lowland fields to mountain meadows.

Wilson's Phalarope *Phalaropus tricolor* — Locally fairly common migrant, summer resident of marshes, wet meadows, pond edges in Eastern Washington. Rare migrant in similar freshwater habitats on Westside (mostly spring); a few breeding records. Rare migrant on salt water.

Red-necked Phalarope *Phalaropus lobatus* — Common spring, fall migrant west, often abundant in pelagic waters. In Eastern Washington, uncommon spring migrant, fairly common fall (sometimes locally abundant at sewage ponds).

Red Phalarope *Phalaropus fulicarius* — Mainly noted on Westport pelagic trips where uncommon spring, fairly common fall. Occasionally wrecks along outer coast after severe October–November storms. Casual migrant east of Cascades.

South Polar Skua *Stercorarius maccormicki* — Rare late-summer, fall pelagic visitor. Usually seen as quick flyby or with concentrations of shearwaters, gulls at fishing trawlers, well off Westport.

Pomarine Jaeger *Stercorarius pomarinus* — Fairly common pelagic visitor, numbers higher during migration than mid-winter, mid-summer. Rarely seen from shore, then usually distant, making identification difficult. Casual on inland marine waters; recorded east.

Parasitic Jaeger *Stercorarius parasiticus* — Uncommon (spring) to fairly common (fall) pelagic migrant; substantial numbers also on inland marine waters, coastal bays in fall, apparently tracking Common Tern migration. Casual fall migrant along Columbia River east of Cascades.

Long-tailed Jaeger *Stercorarius longicaudus* — Uncommon fall (peak August), rare spring pelagic visitor well offshore, quite scarce some years. Casual on inland marine waters. Casual fall in Eastern Washington, mainly along Columbia River.

Laughing Gull *Larus atricilla* — Two records from South Coast—September 1975, August 1982; one from Wenatchee, September 2001.

Franklin's Gull *Larus pipixcan* — Rare fall migrant east, west—mostly juveniles. Rare (east) to casual (west) spring migrant. Best sites include Everett sewage lagoons (fall), Grand Coulee lakes, Sprague Lake, Walla Walla River delta.

Little Gull *Larus minutus* — Rare migrant, winter resident west of Cascades, most often with Bonaparte's Gulls. Annual at Point No Point in migration. Recorded east.

Black-headed Gull *Larus ridibundus* — Casual fall migrant, winter resident on marine waters. Records (more than dozen) range from mid-August to early April. One from outer coast (Ocean Shores); others extend from Dungeness Spit, Orcas Island to Seattle, Nisqually NWR.

Bonaparte's Gull *Larus philadelphia* — Common spring, fall migrant in Western Washington lowlands, fairly common but local winter resident; sometimes impressive concentrations at sewage lagoons, tidal rips. Uncommon migrant in Eastern Washington.

Heermann's Gull *Larus heermanni* — Common post-breeding visitor to outer coastal waters, Strait of Juan de Fuca; rare into winter. Progressively less frequent on marine waters farther inland. Easy to see August–October at Grays Harbor, Tokeland. Recorded along Columbia River east.

Mew Gull *Larus canus* — Common winter resident of coastal waters, near-coastal freshwater lakes, lowland agricultural fields west of Cascades; rare late-fall migrant, winter resident in Eastern Washington, mainly along Columbia, Snake Rivers. Impressive late-winter concentrations along lower Columbia, where attracted to smelt runs.

Ring-billed Gull *Larus delawarensis* — Locally common summer resident in Eastern Washington, nesting colonially on sand, gravel islands in lakes, rivers; has also nested on dredge-spoil islands in Grays Harbor, Willapa Bay. Non-breeders abundant, widespread in Western Washington in summer. Common migrant west. Locally uncommon to variably common winter resident on both sides of Cascades, with good numbers most years around Tri-Cities, Walla Walla, Skagit River deltas. Often roosts, forages in agricultural fields.

California Gull *Larus californicus* — Common but local spring, summer resident in Eastern Washington. Breeding sites include Potholes Reservoir, Banks Lake, Columbia River north of Richland. Common summer, fall along coasts, even well offshore to pelagic waters. In winter, common only in Tri-Cities region along Columbia River, uncommon in coastal Western Washington.

Herring Gull *Larus argentatus* — Winter resident. Locally fairly common in Eastern Washington along Columbia, Snake Rivers, Grand Coulee lakes. In Western Washington, uncommon except locally common at late-winter smelt runs on Columbia River. Higher numbers on outer coast than on inland marine waters; more common in fresh water than salt water around Puget Trough. Casual at Columbia River dams in summer.

Thayer's Gull *Larus thayeri* — Uncommon to locally common winter resident of coastal waters; most abundant along North Olympic Coast (Elwha River mouth, Ediz Hook), south Puget Sound (City of Tukwila Shops, Gog-Le-Hi-Te Wetland), least common on outer coast where outnumbered by Herring Gull. Rare in winter on Grand Coulee lakes, along Columbia, Snake Rivers in Eastern Washington. Use caution in separating from Western X Glaucous-winged hybrids.

Iceland Gull *Larus glaucoides* — **Kumlien's Gull** (subspecies *kumlieni*) casual winter visitor (November–April) around marine waters (pelagic, Strait of Juan de Fuca, Puget Sound), Columbia, Snake Rivers. Separation from Thayer's Gull tricky, controversial.

Lesser Black-backed Gull *Larus fuscus* — Records in three successive winters (2000–2002) at Walla Walla River delta, other nearby sites likely refer to a single individual. Another was at Clarkston in March 2002. One Westside record, from Port Angeles in September 2002.

Slaty-backed Gull *Larus schistisagus* — Accidental winter visitor (early November–mid-March) to inland marine waters. Majority of records come from lower Puget Sound.

Western Gull *Larus occidentalis* — Common resident on South Coast, where breeds; fairly common on northern coasts, uncommon on inland marine waters. Washington birds represent lighter-mantled northern (nominate) subspecies. Intergrades readily with Glaucous-winged Gull, complicating identification. Rare but increasing winter resident in Eastern Washington, most likely just below Columbia, Snake River dams.

Glaucous-winged Gull *Larus glaucescens* — Common year-round resident on all coastal waters, wandering short distance inland to forage, loaf, roost on agricultural fields, freshwater lakes. Many Washington birds (in some areas, most) intergrades with Western Gull, generally exhibiting shade or two darker mantle than pure Glaucous-wingeds, primary tips darker than mantle. In Eastern Washington, uncommon winter resident along Columbia, Snake Rivers, Grand Coulee lakes. A few breed.

Glaucous Gull *Larus hyperboreus* — Rare winter resident. Immature birds predominate near coasts, adults more frequent in Eastern Washington. Favored Westside sites include Elwha River mouth, Ediz Hook, Port of Tacoma (Gog-Le-Hi-Te Wetland, mouth of Puyallup River). East of Cascades, mainly along Columbia River (especially Tri-Cities, Walla Walla River delta), semi-regular on Grand Coulee lakes.

Sabine's Gull *Xema sabini* — Fairly common to sometimes common spring, fall pelagic migrant; rare in Puget Sound, other protected marine waters. In Eastern Washington, rare fall migrant along Columbia River, Grand Coulee lakes, mainly September.

Black-legged Kittiwake *Rissa tridactyla* — Fairly common on pelagic waters, except uncommon summer. Often seen from shore at Westport jetty, north jetty of Columbia River, less often at Neah Bay, Cape Flattery. Occurs eastward in small numbers along Strait of Juan de Fuca in late fall, particularly just after major storms; casual at same time on marine waters farther inland, as well as along Columbia River in Eastern Washington.

Red-legged Kittiwake *Rissa brevirostris* — Casual along/off Pacific Coast. Most records in winter (December–March). One bird stayed week at Tatoosh Island late June–early July. Another found on Westport pelagic trip in mid-August.

Ross's Gull *Rhodostethia rosea* — One record, at McNary Dam for five days at end of November 1994.

Ivory Gull *Pagophila eburnea* — One record, from Ocean Shores in December 1975.

Caspian Tern *Sterna caspia* — Non-breeders abundant summer residents in coastal bays, inland marine waters; breeding colonies local, erratic, partly due to human persecution. Fairly common summer resident in Eastern Washington on a few major lakes, Columbia River.

Elegant Tern *Sterna elegans* — Irregular post-breeding visitor to outer-coastal beaches, bays in El Niño years, rarely to Puget Sound. Typically arrives in July or August.

Common Tern *Sterna hirundo* — Fairly common spring, fall migrant on outer coast, smaller numbers on pelagic waters. Virtually absent spring, common fall on inland marine waters. Uncommon fall migrant along Columbia River to coast.

Arctic Tern *Sterna paradisaea* — Uncommon pelagic migrant, easiest to see in August–September. Tiny breeding colony, southernmost on Pacific coast of North America, on Jetty Island in Everett. Casual east in fall.

Forster's Tern *Sterna forsteri* — Fairly common but local summer resident from Potholes south along Columbia River to Tri-Cities; uncommon north to mouth of Okanogan River, west to Columbia Gorge. Nests on gravel islands, also in marshes. Casual west, mostly fall.

Least Tern *Sterna antillarum* — One record, at Ocean Shores for a few days in late August 1978.

Black Tern *Chlidonias niger* — Fairly common but local summer resident of Eastern Washington marshes, shallow lakes. Good sites include Muskrat, Beth Lakes in Okanogan County, Turnbull NWR, Sprague Lake. Rare migrant in Western Washington. Nested at Ridgefield NWR in 2001, 2002.

Common Murre *Uria aalge* — Fairly common to common year round on pelagic waters, Pacific Coast. Breeds in summer on islets along Outer Olympic Coast; numbers, nesting success vary greatly, depending on water temperature, food availability. Numbers increase in summer, early autumn from individuals moving north for winter. On inland marine waters, fairly common to common in winter (especially northern parts), uncommon to absent in summer.

Thick-billed Murre *Uria lomvia* — Casual fall–winter visitor on outer coast, pelagic waters; accidental in Straits of Juan de Fuca, Georgia. Dates range from late September to mid-February with strong peak in December.

Pigeon Guillemot *Cepphus columba* — Fairly common year-round resident of deep coastal waters, nesting in rocky bluffs, jetties, sandbank burrows, locally on pilings. Largest numbers around Protection Island. Not pelagic. Withdraws from outer coast in winter. Numbers increase on protected waters in winter, from California breeding populations that move north.

Long-billed Murrelet *Brachyramphus perdix* — Five accepted records, all since 1993: August from outer coast; August (2), November from inland marine waters; August from Garfield County in Southeast. Recent split from Marbled Murrelet has increased birders' awareness of this species, which may be more frequent visitor than supposed.

Marbled Murrelet *Brachyramphus marmoratus* — Declining but still fairly common year-round resident of deep, protected coastal waters. Nests in old-growth coastal forests, especially on Olympic Peninsula, fewer on west slopes of Cascades. Usually easy to see at Salt Creek County Park, also tidal rips such as at Point No Point, Fort Flagler, off southern ends of Orcas, San Juan Islands. Decline due primarily to loss of nesting habitat, but other factors may contribute.

Kittlitz's Murrelet *Brachyramphus brevirostris* — Single record, from Friday Harbor (January 1974).

Xantus's Murrelet *Synthliboramphus hypoleucus* — Average one record/year of northern-breeding subspecies *scrippsi* on Westport pelagic trips, almost all in fall (August–October). Observers on research vessels report small numbers of southern-breeding subspecies *hypoleucus* during these same months in Washington waters farther offshore (50 nautical miles or more). Many reports from pelagic birding trips—especially older ones—have insufficient detail to exclude Craveri's Murrelet (not recorded in Washington).

Ancient Murrelet *Synthliboramphus antiquus* — Uncommon to locally fairly common late-fall–early-winter resident of marine waters—mostly in deeper waters of eastern Strait of Juan de Fuca, northern Puget Sound. Usually arrives after strong November storms, becomes decidedly uncommon by January. Most easily found at tidal rips at Point No Point, Forts Flagler, Worden, or from Keystone Ferry. Sometimes seen on pelagic trips from Westport, mostly in winter as distant flyby. Possibly breeds intermittently in tiny numbers in seabird colonies along Outer Olympic Coast. Recorded east.

Cassin's Auklet *Ptychoramphus aleuticus* — Once most abundant breeding non-gull seabird in Washington, now fairly common, seriously declining. Nests on islets off Outer Olympic Coast but infrequently seen from shore. Regular on Westport pelagic trips. Rare on inland marine waters.

Parakeet Auklet Aethia psittacula — About 12 records (February–April) of birds found dead on beach or seen from one of rare pelagic boats that venture out in those months. Probably regular in winter in small numbers well offshore.

Whiskered Auklet Aethia pygmaea — One record, at Penn Cove for two days in May 1999.

Rhinoceros Auklet *Cerorhinca monocerata* — Common summer resident in deeper coastal waters, though scarcer in southern Puget Sound. Thousands nest on Protection Island. Large numbers often seen at entrance to Grays Harbor on pelagic boat trips. Uncommon in winter.

Horned Puffin Fratercula corniculata — Casual visitor to inland marine waters, along outer coast. Seventeen records, including seven birds found dead on beach, fall into three groups—seven in winter (December–February), four in spring (April–June), six in fall (August–October).

Tufted Puffin *Fratercula cirrhata* — Locally uncommon summer resident on islands along Outer Olympic, North Olympic coasts. Infrequent on Westport pelagic trips. Easiest to see at Cape Flattery, La Push; also Diamond Point, Protection Island boat trip.

Rock Dove *Columba livia* — Native to Old World; domesticated birds introduced to North America by early European settlers. Common year-round resident around farms, towns, cites. Naturalized Rock Doves breed on basalt cliffs in Eastern Washington.

Band-tailed Pigeon *Columba fasciata* — Fairly common (summer) to uncommon (winter) resident of forests, well-treed residential areas in lowland Western Washington. Requires large conifers for nesting; core populations may be declining. Nests in smaller numbers upward to subalpine, spilling across Cascade crest at Snoqualmie Pass; casual reports east to Walla Walla (April–October). Noted to gather at mineral springs.

Eurasian Collared-Dove Streptopelia decaocto — Introduced to New World from Eurasia. Two Washington records so far: Spokane January 2000, Wenatchee July–September 2002. Records expected to increase as northwestward range expansion continues. Recently discovered feral population just north of Washington border at Keremeos, British Columbia, another potential source.

White-winged Dove Zenaida asiatica — One old record, collected in Puyallup (Pierce County) in November 1907. Four more Western Washington records since 1997, spanning May–October (Tokeland, Tatoosh Island, Anacortes, Redmond), one in Kittitas Valley (June).

Mourning Dove *Zenaida macroura* — Common summer resident east of Cascades, from Columbia Basin up into lower forest zones. Winters locally in much smaller numbers, mainly near feedlots. Uncommon to locally fairly common year-round resident in Western Washington lowlands, mostly in open forests, agricultural areas, towns.

Black-billed Cuckoo *Coccyzus erythropthalmus* — Accidental. Four records in narrow window 19 June–1 July—three from eastern edge of state, one from Puget Sound.

Yellow-billed Cuckoo *Coccyzus americanus* — Formerly rare, local summer resident in lowland hardwood, riparian forests in Western Washington, extirpated by 1940. Now casual, with seven spring–summer records (five west, two east), one fall record (from Omak), all since 1974.

Barn Owl *Tyto alba* — Uncommon to locally fairly common year-round resident of open agricultural areas in lowlands on both sides of Cascades. Often nests in haystacks. Probably declining in Western Washington due to urban encroachment, retirement of pasturelands. Populations east of Cascades suffer in severe winters.

Flammulated Owl *Otus flammeolus* — Uncommon, local summer resident in Ponderosa Pine, mixed pine/Douglas-fir forests in Eastern Washington. Some good sites include Old Blewett Pass, Bonaparte Lake, Rock Creek west of Okanogan, Bethel Ridge, Satus Pass. Often near brushy terrain (especially Deerbrush), where an abundance of moths is possibly an attraction. Recorded west.

Western Screech-Owl *Otus kennicottii* — Uncommon to locally fairly common year-round resident in lowland deciduous groves on both sides of state, but absent from many parts of central Columbia Basin.

Great Horned Owl *Bubo virginianus* — Fairly common year-round resident at all elevations up to treeline in wide array of habitats, but usually absent from intact, moist conifer forests.

Snowy Owl *Nyctea scandiaca* — Irruptive winter resident. In invasion years, easily found at coastal sites such as Skagit/Samish Flats (salt marshes, nearby fields), Ocean Shores (Damon Point), Dungeness NWR. Also in croplands across northern Columbia Basin. In non-flight years when absent on Westside, a few usually present near Moses Lake, Davenport, Reardan.

Northern Hawk Owl *Surnia ulula* — Casual winter visitor, far more frequent east of Cascades than west. Records for five winters of last eleven (1992–2002), usually just 1–2 birds but sometimes up to 4–5 per season. One record from Chelan County in breeding season (has nested not far from Washington state line in British Columbia, Idaho Panhandle).

Northern Pygmy-Owl *Glaucidium gnoma* — Uncommon year-round resident of conifer, mixed forests at low to mid-elevations; some upslope movement to treeline in fall. Perhaps most numerous at mid-elevations on east slopes of Cascades. At least some move downslope in winter in Eastern Washington, where they can reach valley bottoms, though usually not far from mountains. Most active at dawn, dusk.

Burrowing Owl *Athene cunicularia* — Uncommon, local, declining summer resident of steppe habitats in Columbia Basin, rare north to Okanogan County. A few winter. Most readily found in Tri-Cities area. Accidental migrant west, formerly bred at Grays Harbor.

Spotted Owl *Strix occidentalis* — Rare year-round resident of extensive mature forests of Cascades, Olympics; a few pairs in Willapa Hills. Good numbers east of Cascade crest in forests much different in structure than colossal old growth they inhabit on Westside. Information on whereabouts difficult to obtain due to sensitive nature of national debate concerning ancient forests, inescapable fact these owls indeed declining.

Barred Owl *Strix varia* — Fairly common resident in moist, mixed forests statewide. Recent arrival in state, first noted 1965 in Pend Oreille County. Has spread, increased phenomenally, now found even in well-treed large cities, for example in Seattle's Discovery Park. Some evidence that it is replacing Spotted Owl (with which it occasionally hybridizes).

Great Gray Owl *Strix nebulosa* — Rare, local, perhaps irregular year-round resident of mid-elevation mixed-conifer forests adjacent to openings, meadows in eastern Okanogan County, with perhaps 1–2 pairs west of Okanogan River. Recent nesting documented from near Havillah, Bonaparte Lake, Colville Indian Reservation. Nested 2002 on Biscuit Ridge in Blue Mountains. Rare winter resident, possible breeder in Northeast. On Westside, rare, irregular winter resident in lowlands of northern Puget Trough, presumably birds coming coastward from east of Coast Mountains in British Columbia via Fraser River.

Long-eared Owl *Asio otus* — Uncommon summer resident in copses in shrub-steppe, lower-conifer habitats east of Cascade crest. In winter, gathers at roosts, often in densely treed parks. Rare west of Cascades in any season; has nested.

Short-eared Owl *Asio flammeus* — Uncommon, local summer resident in Eastern Washington, declining due to loss of suitable grassland habitat. Most numerous in wetter, northern portions of Columbia Basin. Formerly nested locally in Western Washington grasslands but now apparently extirpated. Fairly common but local winter resident, often seen on Samish, Skagit, Stillaguamish Flats, Vancouver Lowlands, at Nisqually NWR, in open country east of Cascades (e.g., Kittitas Valley).

Boreal Owl *Aegolius funereus* — Rare year-round resident of Engelmann Spruce–Subalpine Fir forests at/east of Cascade crest, also Mount Rainier. Distribution poorly understood. Some known sites include Harts Pass, Roger Lake, Tiffany Campground, Long Swamp, Salmo Pass, Upper Ahtanum drainage west of Yakima, Sunrise (Mount Rainier), higher Blue Mountains. Most easily detected in fall when birds answer taped calls with piercing *skiew*. Primary call given in spring, rarely heard in Washington due to deep snow making owls' habitat inaccessible at that season.

Northern Saw-whet Owl *Aegolius acadicus* — Fairly common resident of mature conifer, mixed forests at low to middle elevations statewide, withdrawing from snowy parts of range in winter. Winter roost sites often frequented for long periods, marked by pellets, whitewash on ground. Active calling begins in winter but declines greatly by May, making detection much more difficult later in spring.

Common Nighthawk *Chordeiles minor* — Common summer resident of open country, lower forest zones east of Cascade crest. Once common west of Cascades, now uncommon, local, declining in open lowland habitats. Still fairly common in San Juans, also seen regularly on upper west slopes of Cascades along rocky, logged-off ridges. Arrives late in spring (late May).

Common Poorwill *Phalaenoptilus nuttallii* — Fairly common summer resident in rocky portions of shrub-steppe habitats, brushy terrain of Ponderosa Pine zone in Eastern Washington. Sits on gravel roads at dusk, fluttering up to hawk for moths; most easily found by red eyeshine. Accidental west, usually in fall.

Black Swift *Cypseloides niger* — Fairly common but local summer resident of cliffs in Cascades, mostly from Snoqualmie Pass north; smaller numbers in Olympics. Inclement weather pushes birds into lowland foraging sites where they may be seen low to ground—often over water. Sometimes observed along Outer Olympic Coast. Probable nesting sites include North Cascades near Newhalem; vicinity of Darrington, Index (Snohomish County); gorges just north of Snoqualmie Pass where often seen over ski runs morning, evening; Cle Elum River valley north of Cle Elum Lake; Stehekin at north end of Lake Chelan.

Vaux's Swift *Chaetura vauxi* — Fairly common summer resident in moist forests statewide, also cities in forest zones (e.g., Seattle, Walla Walla). Probably declining due to loss of large trees with cavities for nesting; has not made wholesale adaptation to chimneys, although occasionally nests in them. Away from moist forests, noted in breeding season in areas of mature Garry Oaks. In fall migration, gathers in large numbers at favorite roosts such as smokestacks, abandoned icehouses.

White-throated Swift *Aeronautes saxatalis* — Fairly common summer resident on cliffs in Columbia Basin, Okanogan Valley. Easily seen in Grand Coulee, Frenchman Coulee. Recorded west.

Ruby-throated Hummingbird *Archilochus colubris* — One record, on east slope of Cascades in June 1992.

Black-chinned Hummingbird *Archilochus alexandri* — Uncommon to locally fairly common summer resident in lowland, lower-elevation mountain riparian habitats bordering Columbia Basin, Okanogan Valley. Often visits wells drilled by Red-naped Sapsucker. Recorded west.

Anna's Hummingbird *Calypte anna* — Recent arrival from south. First Washington record Seattle 1964, first nesting record Tacoma 1972. Now fairly common to locally common year-round resident in lowland residential areas, parks in Western Washington, east along Columbia River to about Lyle. Easily seen at visitor center in Seattle's Discovery Park. Humans undoubtedly aiding spread (year-round feeding, winter-blooming ornamental plantings). East of Cascades, rare but increasing post-breeding visitor; nested at Ephrata in March 2002.

Costa's Hummingbird *Calypte costae* — One fall, two spring records since 1998 of birds frequenting feeders in Puget Lowlands.

Calliope Hummingbird *Stellula calliope* — Fairly common summer resident in brushlands of lower forests of Eastern Washington mountains; majority in Ponderosa Pine zone. Regular in western Columbia Gorge, locally in small numbers in upper Skagit Valley (may breed). Rare migrant elsewhere in Western Washington.

Broad-tailed Hummingbird *Selasphorus platycercus* — Two records, August 2000 in Asotin County, June 2002 in Walla Walla County.

Rufous Hummingbird *Selasphorus rufus* — Common summer resident in forest zones statewide, including brushy clearcuts. Arrives early spring, coincident with first flowering Salmonberries and currrants. Especially conspicuous, widespread in summer when postbreeders take to mountain meadows. Sometimes noted zooming southward along barren alpine ridges in fall migration.

Allen's Hummingbird *Selasphorus sasin* — Only state record collected in Seattle in May 1894.

Belted Kingfisher *Ceryle alcyon* — Fairly common year-round resident of streambanks, shorelines (freshwater, saltwater) statewide. Numbers much lower east of Cascades after winter freezeup.

Lewis's Woodpecker *Melanerpes lewis* — Fairly common but local summer resident in Eastern Washington, most depart in winter. Favors Garry Oak groves, large Ponderosa Pine snags, cottonwood-lined river valleys. Declining due to loss of cavities for nesting (including competition with European Starlings), human encroachment, degradation of understory in otherwise good nesting areas. Largest numbers at Fort Simcoe; winters there some years. Lyle also good bet year round. Formerly fairly common resident locally west of Cascades—extirpated as consequence of management practices that changed forest structure, suppressed nesting snags. Now casual migrant on Westside.

Acorn Woodpecker *Melanerpes formicivorus* — Resident in tiny numbers around Lyle—most consistent site near Balch Lake. Also recorded at other sites along Columbia as far west as Clark County. One record from Fort Simcoe.

Williamson's Sapsucker *Sphyrapicus thyroideus* — Uncommon summer resident in mixed-conifer forests at middle elevations of east slopes of Cascades, Okanogan Highlands, Blue Mountains. Birds in Washington strongly associated with Western Larch. Good sites include Havillah, Loup Loup Campground, Lodgepole Campground (on SR-410 east of Chinook Pass), many sites above 5,000 feet in Blue Mountains. Also Swauk Basin, Table Mountain, Manastash highlands.

Yellow-bellied Sapsucker *Sphyrapicus varius* — Accidental in winter east, west. Reports increasing.

Red-naped Sapsucker *Sphyrapicus nuchalis* — Fairly common summer resident in Eastern Washington in relatively open forests (except oaks)—especially riparian corridors. Usually easy to find at Wenas Campground. Intergades with Red-breasted Sapsucker near Cascade crest, mostly along east slope. Highly migratory; winter reports more likely involve hybrids. Rare in spring in western lowlands.

Red-breasted Sapsucker *Sphyrapicus ruber* — Fairly common year-round resident in conifer, mixed forests west of Cascade crest, including less-developed parts of Puget Lowlands with sufficient remaining trees. Becomes more conspicuous in city parks, other marginal habitats when severe winter weather forces birds downslope. Spills over onto east slopes of Cascades (dominant sapsucker species in moist forests for many miles eastward from Snoqualmie Pass). Intergrades with Red-naped in broad zone at upper edge of drier Eastside forest habitats.

Downy Woodpecker *Picoides pubescens* — Fairly common year-round resident in lower-elevation deciduous, mixed forests (especially riparian), windbreaks, woodlots, ornamental plantings around farms, towns, parks. Local in conifer forests east of Cascade crest. Underparts, center of back dusky in Westside populations, white in birds from Eastern Washington.

Hairy Woodpecker *Picoides villosus* — Fairly common year-round resident of conifer forests statewide, at all elevations. Interior breeding populations brightly contrasting black-and-white; Westside breeding race dingier.

White-headed Woodpecker *Picoides albolarvatus* — Uncommon, local year-round resident east of Cascades in Ponderosa Pine zone. Seldom easy to find. Declining due to loss of mature pines, now nearly extirpated in Spokane region, Blue Mountains. Fairly dependable at Wenas Campground, nearby Maloy Road, along lower White Pass Highway, at Little Pend Oreille NWR, along Silver Creek Road in Colville Indian Reservation. Recorded west.

Three-toed Woodpecker *Picoides tridactylus* — Uncommon year-round resident in higher forests from Cascade crest east, locally on upper west slopes of Cascades. Favors Engelmann Spruce, to lesser extent Lodgepole Pine. Attracted to recent burns; locations thus vary. Wanders down to mid-elevation burns but core range higher than that of Black-backed. Perhaps most easily found along FR-39 between Roger Lake, Long Swamp.

Black-backed Woodpecker *Picoides arcticus* — Rare, nomadic year-round resident of mid- to high-elevation conifer forests east of Cascade crest (barely west). Frequents lower elevations, drier forests than Three-toed. To find one, look for recent burns, as post-burn explosion of insects concentrates populations for several years. Absent productive burns, birds spread out thinly over large areas.

Northern Flicker *Colaptes auratus* — Commonest woodpecker statewide, year-round resident from sea level to subalpine. Breeding form **Red-shafted**

Flicker (subspecies *cafer*); populations augmented in winter by large influx from north. **Yellow-Shafted Flicker** (subspecies *auratus*) rare winter resident. Red-shafted x Yellow-shafted intergrades numerous in winter; a few also noted in breeding population.

Pileated Woodpecker *Dryocopus pileatus* — Fairly common year-round resident in mature conifer forests, woodlots in Western Washington; much less common on Eastside in similar habitats. Requires large territories with ample decaying snags, downed logs for nesting, foraging. Declines in forests where development, forest-management practices suppress these, but otherwise tolerant of human encroachment, breeding successfully in wooded city parks, suburbs, semi-rural residential areas.

Olive-sided Flycatcher *Contopus cooperi* — Fairly common summer resident in conifer forests, especially with openings, tall snags. Vocalizes, hawks insects from high, exposed perches.

Western Wood-Pewee *Contopus sordidulus* — Common summer resident in riparian woodlands, dry conifer forests east of Cascade crest. Avoids wet, closed conifer forests, hence much less common, local in Western Washington, where confined mostly to lowland riparian situations.

Alder Flycatcher *Empidonax alnorum* — One well-documented record from Okanogan County, June 2002. More may appear in Washington as southward range expansion in British Columbia continues.

Willow Flycatcher *Empidonax traillii* — Common summer resident of Western Washington wetland habitats, shrubby areas, including clearcuts. Less common, local east of Cascades, except widespread, common in Northeast. Absent as breeder from Columbia Basin. Arrives late in spring, becoming conspicuous only late May when calling begins.

Least Flycatcher *Empidonax minimus* — Rare, possibly increasing migrant, summer resident. Most likely in aspen copses, cottonwood stands in Okanogan, Northeast, but has occurred widely in hardwood groves on both sides of Cascades. Has nested in Puget Lowlands, perhaps elsewhere.

Hammond's Flycatcher *Empidonax hammondii* — Fairly common summer resident of denser conifer forests—sometimes with deciduous component—statewide. Although favors upper portions of taller trees, may also perch, forage low, in open, especially on migration.

Gray Flycatcher *Empidonax wrightii* — Recent arrival in Washington (first nested 1972), now fairly common but local summer resident of open, brush-free understories of Ponderosa Pine forests, especially along driest, easternmost slopes of Cascades, northern Columbia Basin. Repeated selective logging may be responsible for creating microhabitat structurally similar to its customary Great Basin habitats. Easy to find in upper Wenas Creek region. Accidental west, mostly spring.

Dusky Flycatcher *Empidonax oberholseri* — Fairly common migrant, summer resident of brushy openings of forests east of Cascade crest. Also in higher-elevation aspen clumps, recent lava flows (Mount Adams). Generally favors drier, sunnier, more open habitats than Hammond's. Rare in clearcuts in early successional stages on upper west slopes of Cascades. Rare migrant west.

Pacific-slope Flycatcher *Empidonax difficilis* — Common summer resident of moist forest understories in Western Washington; fairly common east of Cascades, mostly in riparian habitat. **Cordilleran Flycatcher** *Empidonax occidentalis* may occur in Southeast, but evidence contradictory, incomplete. Best to call all Washington birds Pacific-slope until status of this recently-split species pair can be resolved.

Black Phoebe *Sayornis nigricans* — Five fall–winter records on lower Columbia River, outer coast; may stay for weeks or months in same location. One spring record near White Pass.

Eastern Phoebe *Sayornis phoebe* — Casual spring visitor (late May–June)—four records east, one west. One December record from outer coast.

Say's Phoebe *Sayornis saya* — Fairly common summer resident in open terrain of lowland Eastern Washington, particularly in shrub-steppe zone; uncommon in openings in Garry Oak, Ponderosa Pine zones. For nesting, favors ranch-building eaves, rocky outcroppings. Hardy; some may attempt wintering in warmest parts of Columbia Basin. Rare but regular in spring migration west of Cascades.

Vermilion Flycatcher *Pyrocephalus rubinus* — Four fall–winter records, all from Western Washington lowlands.

Ash-throated Flycatcher *Myiarchus cinerascens* — Fairly common summer resident in Garry Oak zone along Columbia River from White Salmon east to about Rock Creek. Easy to find in oaks near Lyle or along Rock Creek. Less frequent northward, e.g., Satus Creek, Fort Simcoe. Rare, local breeder east base of Cascades north to Wenatchee. Not as conspicuous as many flycatchers, often perching within tree canopy. Easiest to detect in early morning when calling most intense. Recorded west.

Tropical Kingbird *Tyrannus melancholicus* — Casual fall visitor (October–December) to Western Washington lowlands, usually near salt water, almost always along outer coast. Grays Harbor, Willapa Bay best bets for finding one. Silent birds cannot be separated from Couch's Kingbird (not recorded in Washington).

Western Kingbird *Tyrannus verticalis* — Common summer resident in open habitats in Eastern Washington. Characteristic, easily found species along roadsides in farming, ranch country, often building nest on utility-pole insulators. In Western Washington, breeds in small numbers in Fort Lewis area, Skagit River valley; rare in migration.

Eastern Kingbird *Tyrannus tyrannus* — Fairly common summer resident in lowland Eastern Washington in riparian habitats, particularly with dense, tall shrub layer. Rare, local breeder in Western Washington.

Scissor-tailed Flycatcher *Tyrannus forficatus* — Two records from Potholes: September 1983, May 1985.

Fork-tailed Flycatcher *Tyrannus savana* — One record, from Chinook River valley in September 1995.

Loggerhead Shrike *Lanius ludovicianus* — Uncommon summer, rare winter resident in shrub-steppe landscapes, declining due to habitat loss. Good sites include Crab Creek in Grant County, Pumphouse Road west of Toppenish NWR, Yakima Training Center. Also Greasewood thickets at Lenore Lake. Casual in Western Washington lowlands in spring migration.

Northern Shrike *Lanius excubitor* — Fairly common (east) to uncommon, local (west) winter resident in open habitats with some brushy terrain. Many good sites on Eastside—e.g., Waterville Plateau. Skagit/Samish Flats typical of Westside sites.

White-eyed Vireo *Vireo griseus* — One record, from Vashon Island (King County) in July 1981.

Yellow-throated Vireo *Vireo flavifrons* — One record, from Spencer Island in October 1995.

Cassin's Vireo *Vireo cassinii* — Fairly common (east) to uncommon (west) summer resident in drier forests at low to middle elevations. Commonest in open Eastside forests with tall shrub or alder component—especially Douglas-fir, less often Ponderosa Pine. Also fairly easy to find in drier, open Douglas-fir forests in Western Washington, especially in rainshadowed northeastern Olympics, San Juan Islands.

Blue-headed Vireo *Vireo solitarius* — Two records—September 1995 in Seattle, August 2000 in Franklin County.

Hutton's Vireo *Vireo huttoni* — Fairly common year-round resident of lowland hardwood or mixed forests, woodlands in Western Washington. Generally frustrating to locate except when singing (begins February, frequency tapers off into spring). Not usually found in small patches of woods such as gardens or small city parks, but occurs in large parks (e.g., Discovery Park in Seattle, Watershed Park in Olympia). In winter, often joins roving, mixed-species flocks of chickadees, nuthatches, creepers, kinglets, other small passerines. Recorded east slopes of Cascades.

Warbling Vireo *Vireo gilvus* — Common migrant, summer resident in deciduous woodlands statewide. Washington's commonest vireo, often breeding in tiny patches of willows, aspens, alders in otherwise conifer-dominated landscapes.

Philadelphia Vireo *Vireo philadelphicus* — Two records: Grant County in September 1991, Lincoln County in June 2002.

Red-eyed Vireo *Vireo olivaceus* — Fairly common but local summer resident in tall Black Cottonwood stands along major river valleys. Good sites include Skagit, Nooksack Valleys, Snoqualmie Valley from North Bend to Fall City, floodplain forests along Columbia River (Clark, Skamania, western Klickitat Counties). Probably most numerous, widespread in Northeast—especially valleys of Pend Oreille (easy to find at Sullivan Lake), Sanpoil, Kettle, Colville Rivers. Rarely noted in migration.

Gray Jay *Perisoreus canadensis* — Fairly common year-round resident in mature conifer forests of higher mountains throughout state. Uncommon, local at lower elevations in southwestern Washington. Usually easy to find at Paradise on Mount Rainier, Hurricane Ridge, picnic areas/campgrounds along upper portions of North Cascades Highway. Populations inhabiting Okanogan Highlands, mountains of Northeast, Southeast characterized by dark-gray underparts, contrasting, nearly all-white head. Birds from Cascades west have smaller white forehead area, extensive, dusky crown, auricular patch, nape; light-gray underparts appear almost white.

Steller's Jay *Cyanocitta stelleri* — Fairly common year-round resident of coniferous forests virtually statewide, mostly at low to middle elevations; post-breeding wandering up to subalpine habitats, down to Garry Oak zone. Coastal movements in fall may be striking.

Blue Jay *Cyanocitta cristata* — Rare but regular winter resident in Eastern Washington towns/cities, especially along eastern edge of state (e.g., Spokane, Pullman, Walla Walla). Casual winter resident in western lowlands, mostly in residential areas.

Western Scrub-Jay *Aphelocoma californica* — Fairly common year-round resident in lowlands of Southwest. Species on the move, with recent breeding records north to Seattle, west to Raymond, east to Goldendale. Most common in habitats dominated by Garry Oak, as well as in towns/cities. Resident Washington birds belong to coastal form of species (dark upperparts contrast vividly with white underparts). Individual of distinctive interior population (more muted in coloration) observed at Chief Timothy State Park (Asotin County) in February 2002.

Pinyon Jay *Gymnorhinus cyanocephalus* — Captain Charles Bendire found this species "quite numerous" in oak openings at Fort Simcoe in June 1881. Only other state record small flock near Goldendale in April 1967 (one bird collected).

Clark's Nutcracker *Nucifraga columbiana* — Fairly common year-round resident in drier subalpine forests in Cascades, Selkirks. Small numbers in Olympics (northeastern rainshadow), Blues. Whitebark Pine major food source. Also found in Ponderosa Pine forests, especially if rugged terrain nearby for seed caching. Easily seen at Mount Rainier (Paradise, Sunrise), Chinook Pass, where seeks handouts. Occasionally wanders to lowlands.

Black-billed Magpie *Pica hudsonia* — Common, conspicuous year-round resident throughout unforested Eastern Washington, about ranches, farms, riparian edges, shrub-steppe habitats up to lower Ponderosa Pine zone. Generally shuns highly built-up cities. Post-breeding wanderers reach subalpine habitats, especially in Okanogan Highlands, Blue Mountains. Recorded west in winter.

American Crow *Corvus brachyrhynchos* — Common, prodigiously increasing year-round resident of Western Washington, from lowlands up into middle elevations of mountains, especially about farms, cities, suburbs, recently logged areas. In Eastern Washington, common summer resident, uncommon to locally fairly common winter resident in Okanogan, Columbia, Yakima, Walla Walla River valleys. Still scarce or absent in eastern parts of Columbia Basin. Wherever irrigation, development spread into formerly unirrigated tracts of dryland wheat farming, American Crows soon follow. Not found in dense, contiguous conifer forests. Probably still absent from San Juan Islands, Outer Olympic Coast (see Northwestern Crow).

Northwestern Crow *Corvus caurinus* — "After lengthy discussion it is pretty well settled that the Crow of the northwestern sea-coasts is merely a dwarfed race of [American Crow], and that it shades perfectly into the prevailing western type whenever that species occupies adjacent regions" (William Leon Dawson, *The Birds of Washington*, 1909). True a hundred years ago, still true today. Northwestern Crow originally inhabited Puget Trough shoreline, outer coast from Grays Harbor north, isolated by uncut, deep forests from American Crow populations along streams in Eastern, southwestern Washington. Deforestation by settlers, commercial loggers fostered interbreeding along south Puget Sound by late 1800s, with result that Dawson found it "impossible to pronounce with certainty upon the subspecific identity of Crows seen near shore in Mason, Thurston, Pierce, or even King County." With continuing development American Crow invaded whole Puget Trough, swamping indigenous Northwestern population. Phenotypically pure Northwestern Crows still recognizable along Outer Olympic Coast (e.g., La Push), in San Juan Islands.

Common Raven *Corvus corax* — Widespread, conspicuous, year-round resident in most terrestrial habitats except cities, towns. Lacking from main urban corridor Everett–Tacoma. Amazingly adaptable, found from sea level to alpine elevations, even in winter. May form sizable winter flocks in lowlands.

Sky Lark *Alauda arvensis* — Casual visitor at American Camp on southern San Juan Island; formerly bred in tiny numbers. Strayed there from introduced, non-migratory population established on southeastern Vancouver Island since early 1900s (subspecies *arvensis* from western Europe). First recorded on San Juan Island 1960, first documented nesting 1970, apparently extirpated as breeder by mid-1990s. Subspecific identity of two birds seen across Strait of Juan de Fuca near Sequim, in winter 1998–1999, not determined. Perhaps wanderers from introduced population, perhaps migrants from Asia (Kamchatkan-breeding subspecies *pekinensis*).

Horned Lark *Eremophila alpestris* — Common, widespread, year-round resident, especially in open areas of Eastern Washington. Three breeding races, at least one more as winter resident. Subspecies *strigata* uncommon year-round resident in lowlands west of Cascades. Seriously declining on account of habitat loss, now confined as breeder to prairies on Fort Lewis, beach dunes at Ocean Shores, sandbars in Columbia River (Wahkiakum, Pacific Counties). Subspecies *alpina* fairly common but local during nesting season in alpine communities—Olympics, high volcanoes, elsewhere in Cascades (especially east side of crest). Burroughs Mountain on Mount Rainier one fairly accessible site. Subspecies *merrilli* common year round in most open, low-elevation habitats in Eastern Washington—especially wheat fields, shallow-soiled portions of shrub-steppe zone. Characteristic, conspicuous bird of Columbia Basin, beginning breeding cycle early in spring (February some years), raising as many as three broods. Forms large, roving flocks in winter, especially over wheat fields. Pale subspecies—including *arcticola* from interior British Columbia as well as *alpina*—common winter residents, especially in northern parts of Columbia Basin. Good numbers on Waterville Plateau, Timentwa Flats mixed in with *merrilli* flocks.

Purple Martin *Progne subis* — Fairly common, increasing, but still local summer resident of Western Washington lowlands, mainly around Puget Sound, lower Columbia River. Historically rare in Washington, increased with Euro-American development until late 1950s when European Starlings began appropriating nesting cavities. Martin numbers crashed to point of near-extirpation by early 1990s; numerous nest-box schemes have greatly aided recovery. Currently, most nest on pilings over water, shunned by starlings. Recorded east.

Tree Swallow *Tachycineta bicolor* — Common summer resident near open country (where forages, often over water), cavities (where nests, usually in stubs, snags), at low to mid-elevations; absent from dense forests, central Columbia Basin. Casual winter west. Earliest swallow to return in spring (first birds usually February).

Violet-green Swallow *Tachycineta thalassina* — Common summer resident throughout Washington, including cities, agricultural areas, open forests of all ages, around open water. In Columbia Basin, local in towns, around farm buildings; uncommon on high cliffs (Yakima Canyon, Hanford Reach, Columbia River south of Vantage). Nests in cavities in trees, cliffs, buildings, also in nest boxes. Casual winter west. Early migrant, appearing in March (even February in south).

Northern Rough-winged Swallow *Stelgidopteryx serripennis* — Fairly common summer resident along streams, other water bodies with sandy banks, where nests.

Bank Swallow *Riparia riparia* — Locally common summer resident in Eastern Washington, mostly near rivers, irrigation canals. Nests colonially, absent from some areas, abundant in others. Especially numerous along Hanford Reach (one colony may contain 10,000 nests some years), parts of lower Yakima River valley. Sometimes forms large roosting or staging flocks during fall migration. Nests locally in Western Washington, perhaps increasing; colonies discovered recently along Toutle River (Cowlitz County), Green River (King County). Also noted regularly along Skagit River near Marblemount (Skagit County). Rare migrant elsewhere on Westside.

Cliff Swallow *Petrochelidon pyrrhonota* — Common summer resident in lowlands throughout state, often nesting in large colonies under bridges. Abundant locally in Eastern Washington—e.g., on cliffs of Grand Coulee, Yakima Canyon, Hanford Reach, Snake River.

Barn Swallow *Hirundo rustica* — Common summer resident statewide at all but highest elevations—wherever open habitat for foraging exists in proximity to suitable nest-building sites (almost always man-made structures such as buildings, bridges). Casual winter west.

Black-capped Chickadee *Poecile atricapilla* — Common year-round resident nearly statewide in habitats with deciduous vegetation, mostly at lower elevations. Distinctly less common with westward progression on Olympic Peninsula. Absent from main San Juan Islands, also from some areas in central Columbia Basin that appear to contain suitable habitat.

Mountain Chickadee *Poecile gambeli* — Common year-round resident of coniferous forests throughout Eastern Washington. Spills west over Cascade crest into higher subalpine forests in a few places—fairly common around Mount Rainier. Also fairly common in drier forests southwest of Mount Adams. Casual in lowlands outside nesting season.

Chestnut-backed Chickadee *Poecile rufescens* — Common year-round resident of coniferous forests in Western Washington. Only chickadee on most of San Juan Islands, where found in all forested habitats. In Eastern Washington, fairly common in wetter forest habitats along east slopes of Cascades (above Ponderosa Pine zone), in Northeast (Mount Spokane north), Blue Mountains.

Boreal Chickadee *Poecile hudsonica* — Uncommon year-round resident of dense, high-elevation forests along northern tier of counties in Eastern Washington, reaching west across Cascade crest barely into Whatcom County. Favors Engelmann Spruce, Subalpine Fir forests, occasionally nearby Lodgepole Pines. Harts Pass, Tiffany Mountain area, Salmo Pass good bets. Hardest to find in June, when nesting. Inhabits some of most remote parts of Washington; one of last of state's regular resident species to be discovered (1920).

Bushtit *Psaltriparus minimus* — Brown-crowned Pacific form (subspecies *minimus*, *saturatus*) common year-round resident in shrubby growth in mixed-forest openings, parks, gardens throughout Puget Lowlands. Scarce on outer coast. East through Columbia Gorge at least to Rock Creek, also locally along base of east slopes of Cascades in south central Washington (Satus Creek south of Toppenish, Yakima River near Cle Elum). Old record of gray-crowned interior form (subspecies *plumbeus*) from Mabton (Yakima County), November 1953; recent record of flock at Potholes Reservoir, October 2002.

Red-breasted Nuthatch *Sitta canadensis* — Common year-round resident in all forested zones, from city parks, suburban gardens to treeline. Winter populations in lowlands—particularly east—include migrants from higher latitudes or elevations.

White-breasted Nuthatch *Sitta carolinensis* — In Eastern Washington, subspecies *tenuissima* uncommon to locally fairly common year-round resident in Ponderosa Pine/Garry Oak woodlands ringing Columbia Basin. Coastal subspecies *aculeata* once locally fairly common in Garry Oak/Douglas-fir woodlands of Western Washington but now virtually extirpated; Ridgefield NWR most important remaining site.

Pygmy Nuthatch *Sitta pygmaea* — Fairly common but local year-round resident of Eastern Washington Ponderosa Pine forests. Easy to find at Kamiak Butte, Turnbull NWR, forests around Spokane. Usually not difficult in upper Wenas Creek drainage, many parts of Okanogan. Recorded west.

Brown Creeper *Certhia americana* — Fairly common summer resident of moist forest habitats statewide. In winter, fairly common resident of Western Washington lowlands, foothills. In Eastern Washington, fairly common in migration, uncommon to rare winter resident at lower elevations.

Rock Wren *Salpinctes obsoletus* — Common summer resident of rocky canyons, coulees, talus slopes in Eastern Washington. Uncommon to rare in winter in southern parts of Columbia Basin. A few on west slopes of Cascades—e.g., has colonized blast area of Mount Saint Helens. Otherwise, casual in Western Washington lowlands in migration, winter.

Canyon Wren *Catherpes mexicanus* — Uncommon year-round resident of cliffs in Eastern Washington, usually best detected by vocalizations. Recorded west near Cascade crest.

Bewick's Wren *Thryomanes bewickii* — Common year-round resident in Western Washington lowlands, including urban environments. In Eastern Washington, until recently confined to Columbia River from Gorge east to about Tri-Cities, lower Yakima River (especially around Satus Creek south of Toppenish). Recent dramatic range expansion; now fairly common to locally common length of Snake River into Idaho, north through Palouse to Spokane area. May die back in severe winters.

House Wren *Troglodytes aedon* — Common summer resident of relatively open, brushy habitats at low elevations in Eastern Washington, especially around edges of lower forest zones, in towns. Fairly common to common but highly local summer resident of similar habitats in Western Washington, notably dry prairies, forests of South Sound, Whidbey Island, San Juans, Dungeness, Vancouver Lowlands.

Winter Wren *Troglodytes troglodytes* — Common year-round resident of coniferous forest west of Cascade crest, mostly withdrawing downslope to escape heavy snows in winter. In Eastern Washington, summer resident of wetter habitats at higher elevations, fairly common migrant at lower elevations; winters sparingly in well-vegetated lowland stream bottoms.

Marsh Wren *Cistothorus palustris* — Common summer resident of low-elevation marshes with cattails or other emergent vegetation suitable for nest sites. In winter, fairly common resident in variety of wetland habitats, but Eastside populations thin out or disappear when subfreezing temperatures settle in. In all seasons, widely distributed west, much more local east (Potholes, Toppenish NWR, Turnbull NWR major Eastside population centers).

American Dipper *Cinclus mexicanus* — Uncommon year-round resident on rushing streams throughout state. As higher-elevation streams freeze either partially or wholly in winter, many descend to lower elevations. Also gather in fall, early winter in streams where salmon spawn, to dip for eggs.

Golden-crowned Kinglet *Regulus satrapa* — Common, widespread summer resident of coniferous forests, nesting even in well-treed city neighborhoods. Common outside nesting season in lowland Western Washington, important component of mixed-species foraging flocks. Common migrant, uncommon local winterer in lowlands of Eastern Washington.

Ruby-crowned Kinglet *Regulus calendula* — Common migrant, winter resident in Westside lowland habitats. Uncommon spring, common fall migrant east. Fairly common summer resident in drier, higher Eastern Washington subalpine forests, also west on rainshadowed northeastern slopes of Olympics, possibly Mount Rainier. Stays late in lowlands in spring until breeding grounds open up, often heard singing then.

Blue-gray Gnatcatcher *Polioptila caerulea* — Casual in fall–winter (October–February) at low elevations in Western Washington. One September record from Walla Walla. One territorial male stayed in Hardy Canyon (Yakima County) for five weeks, late May–June 2002.

Western Bluebird *Sialia mexicana* — Fairly common summer resident in Eastern Washington, primarily in lower portions of Ponderosa Pine, upper shrub-steppe zones. Favors openings in drier forests. Easy to find in suitable habitat in Okanogan Valley, also on bluebird nest-box trails (e.g., Bickleton area, Umtanum/Wenas Road). In Western Washington, uncommon in Fort Lewis area; rare, local in forest clearings, around farmlands elsewhere in Puget Trough. Usually findable somewhere in state in any month. Returns early in spring (first birds back by February). Strong numbers winter most years at Lyle in Columbia Gorge, a few others in Columbia Basin, Puget Trough.

Mountain Bluebird *Sialia currucoides* — Fairly common summer resident, mostly in Eastern Washington in open terrain from upper shrub-steppe habitats upslope to alpine. Easy to find on bluebird trails (Umtanum/Wenas Road, Bickleton area). On Westside, fairly common on Mount Rainier (easy to see at Sunrise), Mount Saint Helens. Uncommon on upper west slopes of Cascades, especially in wind-blasted, open forest near crest, descending lower very locally in clearcuts. Casual winter resident east, west.

Townsend's Solitaire *Myadestes townsendi* — Fairly common (east) to uncommon (west) summer resident of forest openings in mountains, except apparently absent from wet west side of Olympics. Usually near steep, rugged terrain, occupying wide range of elevations from lower forest line (Eastside), middle elevations (Westside) up to alpine. Often nests under overhanging roots or near rock crevices on steep roadcuts. Uncommon (east) to rare (west) in winter in berry-rich habitats (riparian areas, ornamental plantings, groves of junipers).

Veery *Catharus fuscescens* — Fairly common summer resident of dense riparian habitats in lower forest zones (especially Ponderosa Pine) of Eastern Washington, with small, disjunct populations around Trout Lake in western Klickitat County, Skagit River drainage in Whatcom County. Easy to find along Wenas Creek. Arrives relatively late in spring (singing after about 25 May).

Gray-cheeked Thrush *Catharus minimus* — One record, from McNary NWR in October 1990.

Swainson's Thrush *Catharus ustulatus* — Common summer resident in moist, leafy understory of mixed or hardwood forests at low to middle (occasionally higher) elevations virtually statewide. Especially widespread, conspicuous in lowlands west of Cascades—even in parks, small woodlots. Two well-marked races breed in state—**Russet-backed Thrush** (subspecies *ustulatus*) of Western Washington, southeastern Cascades, **Olive-backed Thrush** (subspecies *swainsoni*) of northeastern Cascades, Northeast, Southeast.

Hermit Thrush *Catharus guttatus* — Fairly common to common summer resident in most mid-, upper-elevation mountain forests. Favors habitats with sparser shrub understory than Swainson's Thrush, at higher elevations, although elevational overlap substantial. Uncommon or absent in moistest forests. Washington's hardiest *Catharus* thrush, only one in winter when occurs in small numbers in western lowlands, milder parts east.

Dusky Thrush *Turdus naumanni* — One record, from Mount Vernon (Skagit County) in June 2002.

American Robin *Turdus migratorius* — Most common, widely distributed Washington thrush in all seasons. Nests wherever there are trees or heavy brush (but not in dense, wet forests), forages in nearly every conceivable habitat. Large post-breeding flocks congregate in mountains in summer. Wintering numbers in lowlands apparently swelled by birds arriving from mountains or farther north. Spring, fall movements often impressive, but migration patterns, various populations involved not worked out.

Varied Thrush *Ixoreus naevius* — Common summer resident in mature, moist, relatively intact Westside forests, from sea level to lower subalpine. Generally descends below zone of heavy snow in winter. Now largely absent as breeding bird from Puget Lowlands due to forest fragmentation, urbanization, but fairly common there as winter resident, attracted to native, exotic food sources. Common in winter in forests along outer coast. East of Cascade crest, fairly common to locally common summer resident in lower, closed subalpine, upper mixed-conifer forests—lower along stream courses—but mostly absent in drier Douglas-fir, Ponderosa Pine forests.

Descends to low elevations where uncommon in winter. Like other retiring woodland thrushes, stays close to cover, can be difficult to see; haunting song, given especially in early morning, betrays its presence.

Gray Catbird *Dumetella carolinensis* — Fairly common but skulking summer resident along streams in Eastern Washington in dense, shrubby vegetation (willows, Red-osier Dogwood, wild rose, Blue Elderberry). Most common in major river valleys of Okanogan, Northeast (e.g., Pend Oreille, Colville, Kettle, Sanpoil, Okanogan). Less common, local south to Yakima area along east base of Cascades; disjunct population near Trout Lake. Recorded west.

Northern Mockingbird *Mimus polyglottos* — Rare wanderer from south to lowlands on both sides of state, mostly fall–winter. Sometimes appears in urban settings. Three recent breeding records, from most arid portions of shrub-steppe zone in southern Columbia Basin.

Sage Thrasher *Oreoscoptes montanus* — Fairly common summer resident in Eastern Washington in areas of extensive Big Sagebrush with associated vigorous cover of perennial grasses. Mostly absent where ground cover is introduced Cheatgrass, hence from southern Columbia Basin except on a few high-elevation or north-facing ridges (Rattlesnake Mountain, Horse Heaven Hills east of Bickleton). Easy sites include Quilomene Wildlife Area, Umtanum Road. Equally good on northern Timentwa Flats, Swanson Lakes Wildlife Area, Yakima Training Center. Casual spring migrant in western lowlands.

Brown Thrasher *Toxostoma rufum* — Accidental spring, fall migrant on both sides of Cascades; one winter record from Spokane County.

European Starling *Sturnus vulgaris* — Common statewide in lowland habitats. Absent from relatively intact forest, also higher elevations except around developed sites. Introduced to North America from Europe. Reached Washington from east by early 1950s, abundant statewide only 20 years later. Implicated in significant declines of cavity-dependent species in Washington such as Lewis's Woodpecker, Purple Martin, Western Bluebird. Forms huge flocks in winter.

Siberian Accentor *Prunella montanella* — One record—first for Western Hemisphere outside Alaska—at Indian Island (Jefferson County) in October 1983.

Yellow Wagtail *Motacilla flava* — Two records from Ocean Shores: late July 1992, mid-September 2000.

White Wagtail *Motacilla alba* — One record from Puget Sound (January–May 1984), one from outer coast (April 1984). Two other Puget Sound records (November 1981, April 1990) either this species or Black-backed.

Black-backed Wagtail *Motacilla lugens* — Four records, from range of sites: outer coast (May 1986), Puget Sound shoreline (May 1993), Puget Lowlands freshwater shoreline (November 2000), hatchery pond on east slope of Cascades (May 1985). See also White Wagtail.

Red-throated Pipit *Anthus cervinus* — One record, from San Juan Island in September 1979.

American Pipit *Anthus rubescens* — Common migrant (April–May, September–October) in open areas of lowlands virtually statewide, especially along coast (shores, dunes), agricultural fields; often detected calling overhead. Fairly common but local summer resident at high elevations of Cascades, Olympics, occupying moist seeps where alpine vegetation well developed. Easy to find on trails above Paradise at Mount Rainier (especially from Panorama Point up), Hurricane Ridge, Deer Park, high passes in North Cascades. Uncommon winter on shorelines, open farmlands in lowland Western Washington.

Bohemian Waxwing *Bombycilla garrulus* — Fairly common to irregularly common winter resident in orchards, vineyards, residential areas of Eastern Washington, usually in large flocks. Rare, irregular west of Cascades. Probably easiest to find from Lake Chelan north to Methow, Okanogan River valleys, also Spokane, urban areas in Southeast (Pullman, Walla Walla). Once regular south to Yakima but scarcer last 20 years. Handful of confirmed breeding records from North Cascades. Sometimes found in fall in upper subalpine (Cascades, Northeast), feeding on Common Juniper berries.

Cedar Waxwing *Bombycilla cedrorum* — Common summer resident of open forests, orchards, residential areas with mature ornamental plantings, usually at low to mid-elevations. Irregular winter resident in lowlands; numbers, locations vary year to year. Most consistent in winter in Columbia Basin; lesser numbers around Puget Sound.

Phainopepla *Phainopepla nitens* — One record, from Seattle in September 1994.

Blue-winged Warbler *Vermivora pinus* — One record, from Anacortes in September 1990.

Golden-winged Warbler *Vermivora chrysoptera* — One record, banded at Turnbull NWR in August 1998.

Tennessee Warbler *Vermivora peregrina* — Casual fall, accidental spring migrant east, west. One long-staying winter record from Satsop (Grays Harbor County).

Orange-crowned Warbler *Vermivora celata* — Common (west) to fairly common (east) migrant, rare winter resident in lowlands. Two subspecies breed. Relatively bright *lutescens* common summer resident of deciduous forests, brushy places in Western Washington lowlands, becoming less common, local at higher elevations; decidedly uncommon, spottily distributed in forest zones on east slope of Cascades. Duller *orestera* fairly common summer resident in mountains of Northeast, Southeast.

Nashville Warbler *Vermivora ruficapilla* — Fairly common summer resident in forested zones of Eastern Washington, extending west in Columbia Gorge to around Mount Adams. Inhabits brushy, open habitats, often along streams, at forest edges, in regenerating clearcuts, near rock slides, road cuts. Small numbers drift down upper west slope of Cascades to nest in similar habitats. Uncommon spring, fall migrant through lowlands on both sides of Cascades.

Northern Parula *Parula americana* — Casual (west) to accidental (east) spring, fall migrant.

Yellow Warbler *Dendroica petechia* — Common summer resident statewide. Nests in riparian areas, similar places where willows, other deciduous trees grow near water (ponds, ditches, mountain streamlets).

Chestnut-sided Warbler *Dendroica pensylvanica* — Casual migrant, more frequent spring than fall. Fall records about equally balanced east-west, whereas Eastside records outnumber Westside records by about 2 : 1 in spring.

Magnolia Warbler *Dendroica magnolia* — Casual fall migrant on both sides of Cascades; two spring records on Eastside (Ione, Twisp).

Cape May Warbler *Dendroica tigrina* — One record, at Bellingham in September 1974.

Black-throated Blue Warbler *Dendroica caerulescens* — Accidental fall migrant east, west; accidental winter visitor west.

Yellow-rumped Warbler *Dendroica coronata* — Breeding form **Audubon's Warbler** (subspecies *auduboni*)—common summer resident in open coniferous forests of Eastern Washington, somewhat less numerous but still widespread, common in open forests of Western Washington (northeastern Olympics, subalpine parkland, old-growth Douglas-fir on upper west-slope Cascades), though mostly shunning tree farms, moist forests of outer coast, dense Silver Fir forests of Cascades. Common migrant statewide. **Myrtle Warbler** (subspecies *coronata*) common (west) to uncommon (east) migrant in lowlands. Both subspecies uncommon in western lowlands in winter, mostly around Puget Trough (Myrtle fairly common on South Coast). In Eastern Washington, Audubon's uncommon winter resident in Columbia Basin (fairly common in southern portion), especially attracted to Russian Olive; Myrtle, though scarcer, also occurs, especially in willows.

Black-throated Gray Warbler *Dendroica nigrescens* — Fairly common summer resident in mixed deciduous/conifer woodlands at low elevations west of Cascade crest. On Eastside, fairly common summer resident locally in similar habitats along Yakima, lower Cle Elum Rivers in western Kittitas County, also a few in mixed woodlands in western Klickitat County; rare migrant elsewhere.

Black-throated Green Warbler *Dendroica virens* — One record, from Dishman (Spokane County) in July 1975.

Townsend's Warbler *Dendroica townsendi* — Common summer resident of conifer forests (especially fir-dominated) almost statewide; now local in Puget Lowlands due to fragmentation of habitat. In Eastern Washington, absent from Ponderosa Pine zone, uncommon in subalpine parkland. Many individuals in southwestern Cascades, eastern Olympics show signs of hybridization with Hermit Warbler (see discussion on page 237). Uncommon winter resident of Westside lowlands.

Hermit Warbler *Dendroica occidentalis* — Uncommon, local summer resident of conifer forests on south, east slopes of Olympic Mountains, in Southwest. Local on upper east slopes of Cascades from White Pass south. Not on outer coast. Recent research reveals two narrow zones of hybridization with Townsend's Warbler: one in eastern Olympics, other along west slope of Cascades from about Mount Adams north to White Pass (see discussion on page 237). Many individuals in/near these zones not safely separable.

Blackburnian Warbler *Dendroica fusca* — Two spring records (late May, June) from Eastern Washington, two fall records (September, December) from Western Washington.

Yellow-throated Warbler *Dendroica dominica* — One bird visited feeders in Twisp for several weeks in winter 2001–2002.

Prairie Warbler *Dendroica discolor* — One record, from Wallula (Walla Walla County) in December 1989.

Palm Warbler *Dendroica palmarum* — In Western Washington, rare fall migrant, winter resident. Easiest to find on outer coast (especially in Scot's Broom thickets at Ocean Shores). Casual spring migrant east, west; accidental east in fall.

Bay-breasted Warbler *Dendroica castanea* — Two state records, both recent: near Granite Falls (Snohomish County), June 2002; near Moses Lake, September 2002.

Blackpoll Warbler *Dendroica striata* — Casual fall migrant (late August–September) in Eastern Washington. One May record from Spokane, one June record from outer coast (Tatoosh Island).

Black-and-white Warbler *Mniotilta varia* — Casual migrant, occurs almost annually. Records scattered across calendar, map; largest concentration in Eastern Washington in spring (May–June).

American Redstart *Setophaga ruticilla* — Uncommon to locally fairly common summer resident of dense alder/willow-dominated wetlands in Okanogan, Northeast. Good sites include Myers Creek north of Chesaw, Sullivan Lake, West Fork Sanpoil Campground, Big Meadow Lake; nested recently near Trout Lake (south of Mount Adams). Rare to locally uncommon west of Cascade crest, most dependable site County Line Ponds in Skagit River valley. Rare migrant anywhere away from breeding grounds.

Prothonotary Warbler *Protonotaria citrea* — One record, from Richland in September 1970.

Ovenbird *Seiurus aurocapillus* — Casual migrant. Westside records all from June—Cascade slopes, Puget Trough, lower Columbia River (none from Pacific Coast counties). Eastside records from east slopes of Cascades, Columbia Basin, most mid-May to mid-July (one September, one November). Seasonal imbalance may be artifact of easier detection when birds singing.

Northern Waterthrush *Seiurus noveboracensis* — Fairly common summer resident of alder/willow-lined wetlands, swamps of Okanogan, Northeast. Good sites include Amazon Creek Marsh, Little Pend Oreille Lakes, Myers Creek north of Chesaw, Big Meadow Lake. Rare fall migrant, early-winter visitor to sloughs in lowland Western Washington.

Kentucky Warbler *Oporornis formosus* — One record, near Darrington (Snohomish County) in June 1992.

Mourning Warbler *Oporornis philadelphia* — One record, at Lyons Ferry State Park in May 2001.

MacGillivray's Warbler *Oporornis tolmiei* — Fairly common summer resident of shrubby tangles almost statewide, easiest to find in regenerating clearcuts, rank vegetation along roadsides, avalanche chutes, from middle elevations to subalpine. Typical of riparian vegetation through much of Eastern Washington conifer zone. Quite uncommon in Puget Lowlands except locally (e.g., South Sound Prairies). Absent from dense, wet forests, Columbia Basin. Uncommon to fairly common migrant in lowlands virtually statewide.

Common Yellowthroat *Geothlypis trichas* — Common summer resident of wetlands, brushy fields at mostly lower elevations in Western Washington; a few winter. Fairly common but local summer resident east of Cascades, where more characteristic of cattail marshes.

Hooded Warbler *Wilsonia citrina* — Two records from easternmost Washington (June 1986, December 1989), each of several days duration. One Westside record, wintering at Discovery Park in Seattle (December 1975–April 1976).

Wilson's Warbler *Wilsonia pusilla* — Bright-golden subspecies *chryseola* common summer resident west of Cascade crest in variety of moist, wooded habitats with well-developed understory vegetation; arrives on breeding territory late April–early May. Casual in winter. East of crest, duller *pileolata* subspecies common spring, fall migrant, most passing through late in spring (late May–early June); uncommon, local summer resident of moist, shrubby places in open mountain forests, particularly in Northeast.

Yellow-breasted Chat *Icteria virens* — Fairly common to locally common summer resident of lower-elevation, open, brushy streamside habitats in Eastern Washington, mostly at Ponderosa Pine/shrub-steppe margin around edges of Columbia Basin. Scattered records from Western Washington in migration, nesting season.

Summer Tanager *Piranga rubra* — One bird visited Skagit County feeder, December 1997–January 1998.

Western Tanager *Piranga ludoviciana* — Common summer resident statewide in conifer forests (except coastal rain forests). Now largely absent as breeder from developed areas of Puget Trough. Most common in Eastern Washington; Douglas-fir forests favored breeding habitat there. Fairly common migrant nearly statewide. Casual in winter west.

Green-tailed Towhee *Pipilo chlorurus* — Rare, local summer resident of brushy habitats on steep hillsides in Blue Mountains, often requiring time, physical commitment to reach. Good sites include Lewis Peak, Biscuit Ridge, Wenatchee Guard Station. Accidental in Puget Lowlands in winter.

Spotted Towhee *Pipilo maculatus* — Common summer resident statewide, except in high mountains, dense forest, Columbia Basin. Mostly in low to mid-elevation shrubby habitats, including urban areas, open forests, clearcuts, margins of wetlands, brush-filled ravines. Common west, fairly common east in winter; withdraws from snowy areas.

American Tree Sparrow *Spizella arborea* — Uncommon (east) to rare (west) winter resident of cattail-marsh edges, brushy habitats. Most frequent November–December around Molson, West Foster Creek, Potholes, Big Flat Habitat Management Unit. West of Cascades, most reports from mixed-species sparrow flocks at Skagit Game Range, Snoqualmie Valley.

Chipping Sparrow *Spizella passerina* — Common summer resident of open conifer forests in Eastern Washington, especially Ponderosa Pine zone, subalpine. Fairly common but local in dry-forest habitats of Western Washington—e.g., northeastern Olympics (Hurricane Ridge to Sequim), Mount Constitution on Orcas Island, Fort Lewis prairies, Mount Rainier (especially rainshadow side).

Clay-colored Sparrow *Spizella pallida* — Rare, local summer resident in Okanogan, Northeast. Has nested several years running along Harvard Centennial Trail east of Spokane; reported almost annually on benches, hillsides with dense brush in Okanogan, Stevens Counties. Scattered summer records elsewhere in Eastern Washington. Casual in Western Washington in any season, perhaps increasing.

Brewer's Sparrow *Spizella breweri* — Nominate subspecies common summer resident of Big Sagebrush communities with healthy understory of native bunchgrasses (not Cheatgrass). Good sites include Ryegrass Summit on I-90 east of Ellensburg, Quilomene Wildlife Area, Beezley Hills, Harvard Centennial Trail east of Spokane, northern Timentwa Flats. Casual (spring) to accidental (fall) on Westside in migration. Slightly larger, darker, longer-tailed **Timberline Sparrow** (subspecies *taverneri*) recorded a few times in migration, mostly April–early May. Best chance brushy ravines east of Cascades away from sagebrush; field identification perilous.

Vesper Sparrow *Pooecetes gramineus* — Coastal subspecies *affinis* rare, local, declining summer resident of lowland prairies in Western Washington—remnant populations at Fort Lewis, McChord Air Force Base, Yelm, Shelton, Scatter Creek, Mima Mounds, American Camp on San Juan Island. Casual in winter. Widespread interior subspecies *confinis* common summer resident east of Cascades in flourishing stands of native grasses, often with scattered sagebrush—particularly in wetter, higher elevations of northern Columbia Basin. In South Central, mainly on north aspects of higher east-west trending ridges (Rattlesnake Mountain, Horse Heaven Hills). Also found near small trees, brush around edges of agricultural lands.

all elevations statewide, though spottily distributed through heavily populated portions of Puget Trough in summer. In winter, numbers increase on both sides of Cascades—particularly at lower elevations, including Columbia Basin where absent in breeding season. **Slate-colored Junco** uncommon winter resident, usually noted among flocks of Oregons. Some winter birds intermediate (females often impossible to separate).

Lapland Longspur *Calcarius lapponicus* — In Western Washington, uncommon fall migrant, rare winter resident, rare spring migrant in open terrain along outer coast, locally in Puget Trough. Uncommon fall migrant along alpine ridges in Cascades. Most easily found late September–November in open habitats at Ocean Shores Game Range, Damon Point, outer portions of Dungeness Spit. In Eastern Washington, uncommon migrant, rare winter resident in northern parts of Columbia Basin, over higher ridges southward. Flocks on Waterville Plateau, Timentwa Flats late March–April may contain birds in breeding plumage. Statewide, fewer reports in recent years.

Chestnut-collared Longspur *Calcarius ornatus* — In spring (late May–early July), one record from Okanogan County, two from outer coast. In fall (early November–mid-December), one record from Seattle, two from outer coast.

Rustic Bunting *Emberiza rustica* — Immature stayed at former Kent sewage ponds (King County) for winter of 1986–1987. Adult male wintered two years later at same spot—possibly same bird. Another individual visited feeders at Leavenworth, November 1998–January 1999.

Snow Bunting *Plectrophenax nivalis* — Local, somewhat irregular fall migrant, winter resident on open terrain. Rare at best in Western Washington, most often found late fall along Pacific, North Olympic Coasts (Ocean Shores, Dungeness Spit), occasionally on beaches elsewhere. Numbers much higher in Eastern Washington. Often fairly common on high Columbia Plateau (Waterville Plateau, Timentwa Flats, Davenport/Reardan area). Highest numbers there in February, perhaps bottled up awaiting snowmelt farther north.

McKay's Bunting *Plectrophenax hyperboreus* — Two records of birds wintering with Snow Buntings at Ocean Shores (December 1978–March 1979, January–February 1988). Another bird seen for two days in November 1993 on Lummi Flats.

Rose-breasted Grosbeak *Pheucticus ludovicianus* — Casual statewide in spring, summer (May–July)—occurs almost annually. Accidental fall, winter (September–January).

Black-headed Grosbeak *Pheucticus melanocephalus* — Common summer resident of mature lowland broadleaf forests (especially riparian) statewide. Can occur with scattered conifers, but absent where conifers dominate.

Lazuli Bunting *Passerina amoena* — Fairly common summer resident of brushy habitats in Eastern Washington, mostly at lower elevations but extending higher in recently logged sites; uncommon, local on subalpine ridges. In lowlands west of Cascades, uncommon spring migrant, local summer resident at Fort Lewis, Skagit River valley, along Columbia River in Clark, Skamania Counties, scattered other sites.

Indigo Bunting *Passerina cyanea* — Casual in spring, summer on both sides of state. Accidental in fall (September–October): one record from Seattle, one from Spokane.

Painted Bunting *Passerina ciris* — Well-photographed male visited Seattle feeders in February–March 2002.

Dickcissel *Spiza americana* — One June record from Grant County, four fall–winter records from Western Washington.

Bobolink *Dolichonyx oryzivorus* — Fairly common but local summer resident of irrigated hay fields in Okanogan, Northeast; outpost colony near Toppenish in Yakima County. Casual in migration in other parts of state when most often detected calling in flight. First noted in Washington in hay fields at Valley (Stevens County) in 1907, about same time invaded similar irrigated habitats in neighboring parts of Idaho, British Columbia.

Red-winged Blackbird *Agelaius phoeniceus* — Common summer resident statewide in wetland habitats of all types, sizes. Also common in winter, when birds move away from frozen-over sites to forage in fields, feedlots in large flocks, frequently with other blackbirds, starlings. Males establish, advertise territories early. Females frequently remain in segregated flocks prior to pair formation.

Tricolored Blackbird *Agelaius tricolor* — Rare, extremely local summer resident in Eastern Washington, known from small breeding colony discovered 1998 in wetlands along Crab Creek east of town of Wilson Creek. Casual in winter in Columbia Basin—usually one or a few birds among larger flocks of other blackbird species. Also a few recent fall, winter reports from Vancouver Lowlands.

Western Meadowlark *Sturnella neglecta* — Common summer resident in open, low-elevation landscapes of Eastern Washington—shrub-steppe, agricultural fields, ranchland. Once locally common breeder on Western Washington prairies but now rare, seriously declining due to habitat loss; can still be found on South Sound Prairies (Weir Prairie, Mima Mounds), has colonized blast zone on northwest side of Mount Saint Helens. Uncommon to locally fairly common winter resident west of Cascades, mostly in agricultural fields or near coasts. Uncommon, quite local in winter east, mostly on bare, snow-free fields (rarely in shrub-steppe).

Yellow-headed Blackbird *Xanthocephalus xanthocephalus* — Common summer resident of cattail, tule marshes in Eastern Washington, mostly in lowlands but locally up into forest zones (as at Molson). Uncommon to rare in winter in Columbia Basin, mostly at feedlots or in corn stubble. In Western Washington nests regularly at a few places including Fort Lewis, Ridgefield NWR; rare elsewhere or in other seasons.

Rusty Blackbird *Euphagus carolinus* — Rare statewide at lower elevations in fall–winter, usually among flocks of Brewer's, Red-wingeds.

Brewer's Blackbird *Euphagus cyanocephalus* — Widespread, common resident summer (east), year round (west) at low- to mid-elevations. Mostly found around agricultural lands but also in shrub-steppe, open forest, cities. Forms large foraging flocks in winter, often with other blackbird species. Very locally common east in winter, mostly in feedlots, but absent from vast majority of summer range.

Common Grackle *Quiscalus quiscula* — Casual but increasing, annual since 1995. Eastside records outnumber Westside records by 3 : 1. About half of records concentrated mid-May–early July, rest scattered August–April. First breeding record Ephrata 2002.

Great-tailed Grackle *Quiscalus mexicanus* — First record Yakima County May 1987, second Stanwood September 2000–February 2001, third Othello July 2002.

Brown-headed Cowbird *Molothrus ater* — Common migrant, summer resident statewide, except in closed forests or at high elevations; small flocks winter at feedlots on both sides of Cascades. Originally local in Eastern Washington grasslands, increased with Euro-American settlement. On Westside, occurred only casually until first breeding record (Seattle 1955), spread explosively after that. Strongly implicated in decline of many vireos, warblers, other passerines, although specific data for Washington are meager.

Orchard Oriole *Icterus spurius* — One record, on Samish Island for two weeks in December 1991.

Hooded Oriole *Icterus cucullatus* — Casual spring–summer visitor to Western Washington lowlands; records span from late April to mid-July.

Bullock's Oriole *Icterus bullockii* — Common summer resident of lowland riparian habitats, farmlands, orchards in Eastern Washington. Once rare in Western Washington, expanded into lowlands there after about 1970—now uncommon to locally fairly common in farmlands, parks, suburbs, riparian areas of lower Puget Trough, where often associated with cottonwoods.

Baltimore Oriole *Icterus galbula* — One fall record from Seattle, November 1975; two spring records from lower east slopes of Cascades, June 1987, May 1999.

Scott's Oriole *Icterus parisorum* — One bird visited feeder in Chehalis, February–April 1980.

Brambling *Fringilla montifringilla* — Casual (west) to accidental (east) winter visitor. Dates range from November to mid-April. Prolonged stays typical—over four months, in one case. Records tend to bunch up. Two–three records each in winters of 1990–1991, 1991–1992, 1992–1993 but only two records since then.

Gray-crowned Rosy-Finch *Leucosticte tephrocotis* — Uncommon summer resident in alpine zone of Cascades, small population in Olympics. Often seen above Paradise (Panorama Point), Sunrise (Burroughs Mountain) on Mount Rainier. Nests in rocky areas, forages among rocks or on snow or icefields. In fall, gradually descends through mountains to winter in open country in Eastern Washington, especially northern parts (locally in Southeast). Usually easier to find than in summer, but still uncommon; frequented sites include Lenore Lake, Lower Monumental Dam, Lower Granite Dam, among many others. Often roosts at night in abandoned nests of Cliff Swallows or crevices in cliffs, dispersing by day to weedy areas in open fields or along roads where feeds on grain spilled from passing trucks. Casual in winter west of Cascade crest. Washington breeders, most winterers belong to gray-cheeked subspecies *littoralis*, **Hepburn's Rosy-Finch**. Small numbers of brown-cheeked subspecies *tephrocotis* (nominate form, breeding in Rocky Mountains) occur among winter flocks of *littoralis*, particularly in Southeast.

Pine Grosbeak *Pinicola enucleator* — Rare summer resident of subalpine in high Olympics, Cascades (around Mount Rainier, from Snoqualmie Pass north), Selkirks, historically in Blues (no recent records). Most suitable breeding habitat accessible only by hiking or backpacking. By auto, seems most reliable at Harts Pass, Rainy Pass in North Cascades. Descends to lower levels in winter when locally uncommon in Eastern Washington, particularly in drainages with abundance of berry-producing shrubs or seed-laden conifers, towns with Mountain Ash trees, apple orchards with persistent fruit. Check especially northern Okanogan, Methow River valleys. Rare wanderer in western lowlands in winter.

Purple Finch *Carpodacus purpureus* — In Western Washington lowlands, foothills, fairly common but apparently declining year-round resident of mixed forests, particularly near openings. Uncommon to locally fairly common summer resident of forest zones along lower east slopes of Cascades (especially drainages of Methow River in Okanogan County, Wenatchee River in Chelan County, Yakima River in Kittitas County, Wenas Creek in Yakima County). Rare in winter in Eastern Washington.

Cassin's Finch *Carpodacus cassinii* — In Eastern Washington, common summer, uncommon winter resident in Ponderosa Pine zone. Summer resident in open subalpine forests along both slopes of Cascade crest (uncommon), on Mount Rainier (fairly common). Otherwise, accidental west in any season.

House Finch *Carpodacus mexicanus* — Common year-round resident in variety of relatively open lowland habitats throughout state, especially cities, towns, agricultural areas, wandering in non-breeding season to weedy fields in shrub-steppe zone. First reported in Eastern Washington in 1885, apparently self-introduced from Idaho or Oregon. By 1920s spread through non-forested eastern parts of state. Casual in Western Washington until first nesting, Christmas Bird Count records (both in 1952), expanded rapidly after that.

Red Crossbill *Loxia curvirostra* — Fairly common but often irregular year-round resident of most conifer-forest zones in state. Of nine types of Red Crossbill described in North America (potential species splits), six occur in Washington (Types I, II, III, IV, V, VII). Although call-notes distinctive, types difficult to separate in field (may intermingle). Understanding of Washington status a work in progress.

White-winged Crossbill *Loxia leucoptera* — Erratic visitor at any season, mainly to higher mountains in Okanogan, Northeast, especially in forests of Engelmann Spruce. Often absent for extended periods (even years). Invades from north in major flight years, typically in July or August, spreading through mountains, sometimes lowlands. Singing conspicuous in these years; breeding suspected but never confirmed. Harts Pass, Tiffany Mountain, Salmo Pass good bets even in non-invasion years.

Common Redpoll *Carduelis flammea* — Irregular winter visitor, extremely rare some years to irruptively uncommon others. Most often noted in Okanogan, Northeast in alders, birches at mid-elevations of major river valleys, ornamental birches in towns—Winthrop, Chesaw good sites. Winter 2001–2002 saw irruption of historic dimensions, with redpolls in large, pure flocks or mixed with other foraging finch species observed all over state.

Hoary Redpoll *Carduelis hornemanni* — Irruptive winter visitor, casual at best; not reported every year. Experience of invasion of 2001–2002 suggests minute but fixed proportion of redpolls reaching Washington will be Hoary Redpolls (subspecies *exilipes*).

Pine Siskin *Carduelis pinus* — Washington's most abundant, ubiquitous finch. Common summer resident of conifer forest, mixed forest with important conifer component, statewide; found at all elevations, even in small conifer stands in cities. Presumably most descend from higher elevations in winter, when fairly common to irregularly common in western lowlands—numbers vary from year to year. Uncommon (irregularly fairly common), local winter resident in Columbia Basin.

Lesser Goldfinch *Carduelis psaltria* — Uncommon year-round resident in agricultural or weedy habitats along Columbia River in southern Klickitat County. Usually in open areas not far from Garry Oaks. Around Lyle good place to look, also entrance to Maryhill State Park. Strays east, west along Columbia; accidental elsewhere in state.

American Goldfinch *Carduelis tristis* — Fairly common to common statewide in variety of lowland habitats in all seasons. Numbers drop in winter, especially west. Often commences nesting in June or July, well after most other birds.

Evening Grosbeak *Coccothraustes vespertinus* — Fairly common summer resident in low- to mid-elevation conifer forests statewide (except wettest forests on coast), somewhat irregular in winter but usually uncommon. On the move in spring, when common visitor to deciduous trees (for buds), bird feeders. Seeks areas of insect concentrations such as Spruce Budworm outbreaks, thus numbers at any given locality can vary from year to year. Perhaps most readily detected calling high overhead.

House Sparrow *Passer domesticus* — Locally common at lower elevations, mostly around cities, farms; more confined to urban areas west. Introduced to North America from Europe. Moved west with railroads, reaching Spokane in 1895, Seattle by 1897.

MAMMALS OF WASHINGTON

by Dennis Paulson
Richard Johnson graciously reviewed this section.

Distribution information is from: R.E. Johnson and K.M. Cassidy. 1997. *Terrestrial Mammals of Washington State: Location Data and Predicted Distributions.* Volume 3 *in* Washington State Gap Analysis—Final Report (K.M. Cassidy, C.E. Grue, M.R. Smith, and K.M. Dvornich, eds.). Washington Cooperative Fish and Wildlife Research Unit, University of Washington, Seattle.

* - species most likely to be seen

Marsupials
Family Didelphidae: Opossums

Virginia Opossum. *Didelphis virginiana.* Farmland, mixed woodlands. Local west of Cascades, where introduced. Local east of Cascades. Frequently seen as road kill.

Insectivores
Family Soricidae: Shrews

Masked Shrew. *Sorex cinereus.* Moist forest, thickets in mountains. Mostly northern third of state.

Montane Shrew. *Sorex monticolus.* Widespread in moist coniferous forests statewide.

*Vagrant Shrew. *Sorex vagrans.* Most widely distributed shrew in state. Moist meadows, brushy areas. Throughout except Columbia Basin, Southeast.

Preble's Shrew. *Sorex preblei.* High, moist areas in Blue Mountains. Evidently rare.

Water Shrew. *Sorex palustris.* Streams, ponds in mountains.

Bendire's Shrew. *Sorex bendirii.* Marshes, bogs, swamps west of Cascades.

Trowbridge's Shrew. *Sorex trowbridgii.* Coniferous forest, Cascades westward.

Merriam's Shrew. *Sorex merriami.* Shrub-steppe in Columbia Basin. Only from Vantage south on west side of Columbia River.

Pygmy Shrew. *Sorex hoyi.* Variety of habitats in extreme northeast corner.

Family Talpidae: Moles

Shrew-mole. *Neurotrichus gibbsii.* Moist forest west of Cascades. Often found dead.

Townsend's Mole. *Scapanus townsendii.* Moist forest, meadows west of Cascades. Mounds conspicuous.

Coast Mole. *Scapanus orarius.* All habitats in western lowlands, Cascades, Yakima Valley, Walla Walla region. Mounds conspicuous in moist areas.

Bats
Family Vespertilionidae: Vespertilionid Bats

*Myotis. Eight species of similar habits, some of them difficult to distinguish. Most *Myotis* species roost in caves or old buildings, less often under tree bark.

California Myotis. *Myotis californicus.* Common in forested areas. Status in Columbia Basin uncertain, probably only along major watercourses.

Small-footed Myotis. *Myotis ciliolabrum.* East of Cascades, where it roosts in crevices in basalt cliffs.

Long-eared Myotis. *Myotis evotis.* Generally distributed, probably most common in Eastside forests, often at high elevations.

Keen's Myotis. *Myotis keenii.* Coastal, especially on Olympic Peninsula, possibly tied to old-growth forests.

Little Brown Myotis. *Myotis lucifugus.* Widespread in forested parts of state.

Fringed Myotis. *Myotis thysanodes.* Found in shrub-steppe, arid grasslands, forest east of Cascades; probably rare.

Long-legged Myotis. *Myotis volans.* Mainly mountain forests throughout state, even cool, wet ones at high elevations. Also western lowlands.

Yuma Myotis. *Myotis yumanensis.* Virtually throughout state, more closely associated with water than any other bat in Washington.

Hoary Bat. *Lasiurus cinereus.* Wooded areas statewide. Roosts in trees. Tends to fly in straight line, rather than fluttery flight typical of most bats.

Silver-haired Bat. *Lasionycteris noctivagans.* Statewide in forested areas. Roosts in trees.

Big Brown Bat. *Eptesicus fuscus.* Widespread, most abundant in wooded areas, but also in shrub-steppe. Roosts in caves, crevices, buildings.

Western Pipistrelle. *Pipistrellus hesperus*. Near water in Southeast along Snake, Columbia Rivers in deep river canyons. Roosts in crevices.

Spotted Bat. *Euderma maculatum*. Rare. High cliffs. Known from Grant, Okanogan, Douglas (especially Moses Coulee) Counties. Call audible to humans, high-pitched metallic clicks.

Townsend's Big-eared Bat. *Plecotus townsendii*. Variety of habitats; local. Roosts in caves, crevices, old buildings. Roosts, maternity sites especially sensitive to human disturbance.

Pallid Bat. *Antrozous pallidus*. Open areas of Columbia Basin. Roosts in caves, cliff crevices. Beetles form much of prey, obtained by gleaning from ground, only occasionally catching insects in flight.

Lagomorphs
Family Ochotonidae: Pikas

*****Pika**. *Ochotona princeps*. Talus slopes in Cascades, northeastern mountains, mostly at higher elevations.

Family Leporidae: Rabbits and Hares

*****Snowshoe Hare**. *Lepus americanus*. Forests, thickets in mountains, western lowlands, but apparently rare in Garry Oak habitats. Most common in northeastern mountains.

Black-tailed Jack Rabbit. *Lepus californicus*. Sagebrush of Columbia Basin. Formerly common; now becoming rare.

White-tailed Jack Rabbit. *Lepus townsendii*. Grasslands on periphery of Columbia Basin, higher ridges west of Columbia River. Has seriously declined.

Pygmy Rabbit. *Brachylagus idahoensis*. Remnant population in Big Sagebrush, mainly central Douglas County. Virtually extirpated.

*****Eastern Cottontail**. *Sylvilagus floridanus*. Thickets locally west of Cascades, around Pullman, Walla Walla, Yakima, elsewhere. Introduced from eastern North America.

*****Nuttall's Cottontail**. *Sylvilagus nuttalli*. Widespread in brushy habitats of Columbia Basin.

*****European Rabbit**. *Oryctolagus cuniculus*. Thickets, meadows on San Juan Islands, Gedney Island, Destruction Island. Introduced from Europe. Formerly abundant, much reduced as of this writing.

Rodents
Family Aplodontiidae: Mountain Beavers

Mountain Beaver. *Aplodontia rufa*. Moist thickets, forest in Cascades, Western Washington. Burrow openings often seen.

Family Sciuridae: Squirrels

*****Hoary Marmot**. *Marmota caligata*. Talus slopes, meadows, mainly high in Cascades.

*****Yellow-bellied Marmot**. *Marmota flaviventris*. Arid, open rocky areas east of Cascades, from pines down into shrub-steppe.

*****Olympic Marmot**. *Marmota olympus*. Talus slopes, meadows, high elevations of Olympics.

*****California Ground Squirrel**. *Spermophilus beecheyi*. Grassy fields, oak groves, valleys from Ellensburg southward on lower east side of Cascades, also locally along Columbia, Cowlitz Rivers west of Cascades. Usually near rocky areas. Entered state in about 1912 from south.

*****Columbian Ground Squirrel**. *Spermophilus columbianus*. Meadows, grasslands from Harts Pass north in Cascades, eastward around Columbia Basin in eastern third of state, peripheral to shrub-steppe region.

*****Golden-mantled Ground Squirrel**. *Spermophilus lateralis*. Wooded, open rocky areas in Northeast, Blue Mountains.

*****Cascade Golden-mantled Ground Squirrel**. *Spermophilus saturatus*. Wooded, open rocky areas in Cascades. Often seeks handouts along roads, trails.

Townsend's Ground Squirrel. *Spermophilus townsendii*. Grasslands, shrub-steppe. Lower Columbia Basin west of Columbia River, south of Yakima River. Active for a few months in early spring. Becoming rare, local, due to conversion of habitat to agriculture.

Piute Ground Squirrel. *Spermophilus mollis*. Grasslands, shrub-steppe west of Columbia River, north of Yakima River, not overlapping with preceding species. Active for a few months in early spring. Now rare, local, due to conversion of habitat to agriculture.

Washington Ground Squirrel. *Spermophilus washingtoni*. Shrub-steppe. Lower Columbia Basin east of Columbia River; now very rare, local.

*****Yellow-pine Chipmunk**. *Tamias amoenus*. Ponderosa Pine zone east of Cascades, open habitats in subalpine zone in all mountains. In more open areas than Townsend's.

*****Least Chipmunk**. *Tamias minimus*. Shrub-steppe of Columbia Basin from Douglas County southward.

Red-tailed Chipmunk. *Tamias ruficaudus*. Coniferous forest, talus slopes of mountains in extreme Northeast. Difficult to distinguish from Yellow-pine, usually occurs at higher elevations.

*Townsend's Chipmunk. *Tamias townsendii.* Coniferous forest, brush from Cascades west. On east slopes, apparently only above Ponderosa Pine zone.

*Eastern Gray Squirrel. *Sciurus carolinensis.* Parks, residential areas, mainly from Seattle to Tacoma but scattered in cities elsewhere. Introduced from eastern North America.

Western Gray Squirrel. *Sciurus griseus.* Local in oak woodlands on lower east side of southern Cascades, also from Tacoma southward. Now rare.

*Eastern Fox Squirrel. *Sciurus niger.* Asotin, Clarkston, Pullman, Walla Walla, Orcas Island, along Okanogan River near Okanogan. Introduced from eastern North America.

*Douglas's Squirrel. *Tamiasciurus douglasii.* Coniferous forest from Cascades west. Contacts Red Squirrel locally in North Cascades, with some hybridization.

*Red Squirrel. *Tamiasciurus hudsonicus.* Forested areas north, east of Lake Chelan, also in Blue Mountains.

Northern Flying Squirrel. *Glaucomys sabrinus.* Coniferous, mixed forest almost statewide. Nocturnal, unlike other members of family.

Family Castoridae: Beaver

Beaver. *Castor canadensis.* Ponds, lakes, slow streams, rivers almost statewide. Most ponds along stream courses were formed by Beavers. Dams, lodges easily seen.

Family Geomyidae: Pocket Gophers

Mazama Pocket Gopher. *Thomomys mazama.* Open prairies from Tacoma south; now rare because of habitat loss. Also in meadows in high Olympics.

Northern Pocket Gopher. *Thomomys talpoides.* Most open habitats, Cascades eastward. Pattern of winter tunnels obvious after snow melts.

Family Heteromyidae: Kangaroo Mice and Kangaroo Rats

Ord's Kangaroo Rat. *Dipodomys ordii.* Sandy shrub-steppe in Benton, Franklin, Walla Walla Counties.

Great Basin Pocket Mouse. *Perognathus parvus.* Shrub-steppe of Columbia Basin. Tracks, burrow openings conspicuous in sandy areas.

Family Cricetidae: Mice, Lemmings, and Voles

Bushy-tailed Woodrat. *Neotoma cinerea.* Local in rock piles, cliffs almost statewide; most common in Columbia Basin. Characteristic white urine stains on cliffs, sometimes mistakenly attributed to raptors (which also leave white lumpy deposits, but texturally distinct).

Northern Grasshopper Mouse. *Onychomys leucogaster.* Sandy grasslands, shrub-steppe of Columbia Basin.

Forest Deer Mouse. *Peromyscus keeni.* Dense, coniferous forests Cascades west. Formerly included with following species.

Deer Mouse. *Peromyscus maniculatus.* All habitats, open to forested, shrub-steppe to subalpine. Less frequent in old-growth coniferous forests, where outnumbered by preceding species.

Western Harvest Mouse. *Reithrodontomys megalotis.* Grasslands, shrub-steppe, usually near water, east of Cascades. Often lives in old blackbird nests.

Gapper's Red-backed Vole. *Clethrionomys gapperi.* Moist coniferous forest nearly statewide, most abundant at higher elevations.

Sagebrush Vole. *Lemmiscus curtatus.* Shrub-steppe of Columbia Basin. Not in Okanogan Valley.

Gray-tailed Vole. *Microtus canicaudus.* Vicinity of Vancouver.

Long-tailed Vole. *Microtus longicaudus.* Wet areas throughout, mostly in mountains.

*Montane Vole. *Microtus montanus.* Grasslands at base of Cascades; also from Spokane south in Palouse country. Populations cyclic, highly variable in numbers.

Creeping Vole. *Microtus oregoni.* All habitats, especially grassy meadows, Cascades west.

Meadow Vole. *Microtus pennsylvanicus.* Wet meadows in mountains of Northeast, locally in central Columbia Basin along waterways.

Richardson's Vole. *Microtus richardsoni.* Marshes, streams, wet meadows in Cascades, Blue Mountains, extreme Northeast. Seldom more than a few feet from water.

*Townsend's Vole. *Microtus townsendii.* Wet meadows west of Cascades. Populations cyclic, highly variable in numbers. Runway systems often obvious.

*Muskrat. *Ondatra zibethicus.* Marshes, ponds, slow streams throughout.

Heather Vole. *Phenacomys intermedius.* Meadows, forests in high mountains.

Northern Bog Lemming. *Synaptomys borealis.* Cold, wet bogs in subalpine meadows in North Cascades, extreme Northeast.

Family Zapodidae: Jumping Mice

Western Jumping Mouse. *Zapus princeps.* Meadows, thickets near streams in mountains of northeast, southeast corners.

Pacific Jumping Mouse. *Zapus trinotatus.* Meadows in coniferous forests in Cascades, Western Washington.

Family Erethizontidae: Porcupine

*Porcupine. *Erethizon dorsatum.* Forested areas, but wanders far into open habitats.

Family Capromyidae: Nutria

Nutria. *Myocastor coypus.* Marshes. Escaped from fur farms in Puget Sound lowlands, Nespelem area. Well established in southwestern Washington, along Yakima River.

Family Muridae: Old World Rats and Mice

*House Mouse. *Mus musculus.* Probably in every town, city in state. Near human habitations but may be away from them in agricultural areas. Introduced from Old World.

*Norway Rat. *Rattus norvegicus.* Urban areas, especially around water, sometimes penetrating into countryside. Introduced from Old World.

Black Rat. *Rattus rattus.* Vicinity of human habitations, also nearby forest, brush. Introduced from Old World.

Carnivores

Family Canidae: Dogs and Foxes

*Coyote. *Canis latrans.* Virtually statewide. Most common in open habitats, also woodlands, forest. From lowlands (including urban areas) to high in mountains. Absent from most of San Juan Islands.

Gray Wolf. *Canis lupus.* Rare visitor along Canadian border. Recently found in North Cascades National Park, also possible outside park, in Okanogan Highlands.

Red Fox. *Vulpes vulpes.* Native populations in mountains. Also introduced into western lowlands from eastern U.S.

Family Ursidae: Bears

Black Bear. *Ursus americanus.* Wooded areas throughout state, except absent on most of San Juans.

Grizzly Bear. *Ursus arctos.* Rare wanderer to northernmost North Cascades, also in remote parts of Selkirks in Northeast.

Family Procyonidae: Raccoons and Coatis

*Raccoon. *Procyon lotor.* Nearly statewide in many habitats, including urban. Especially near water.

Family Mustelidae: Weasels

Marten. *Martes americana.* In mature coniferous forest of mountains, most common in Engelmann Spruce, Subalpine Fir east of Cascade crest.

Fisher. *Martes pennanti.* Old-growth, mixed forests of Cascades, Olympics. Severely reduced due to overtrapping, cutting of forests. Recently reintroduced after local extirpation.

Ermine. *Mustela erminea.* Widespread, but mostly in coniferous forests.

*Long-tailed Weasel. *Mustela frenata.* All habitats; near water in dry regions. Road-killed males common in spring.

Mink. *Mustela vison.* At or near fresh water statewide.

Wolverine. *Gulo gulo.* Rare in high Cascades, mountains of Northeast.

Badger. *Taxidea taxus.* Shrub-steppe, grasslands, open pinelands east of Cascades. Burrow openings conspicuous.

Striped Skunk. *Mephitis mephitis.* Widespread, common, inhabiting brushy, agricultural, open country. Frequent as road kill.

Western Spotted Skunk. *Spilogale gracilis.* Wide variety of habitats west of Cascades, in southeast corner. Much less common than Striped Skunk.

*River Otter. *Lutra canadensis.* Freshwater lakes, rivers, also many in saltwater bays, inlets.

Sea Otter. *Enhydra lutris.* Recently reintroduced on North Olympic Coast, where found near offshore kelp beds. Most otters seen along outer coast, and all seen along shorelines east of Sekiu River, are River Otters.

Family Felidae: Cats

Mountain Lion. *Felis concolor.* Forested areas, widespread but extremely unlikely to be seen.

Lynx. *Lynx canadensis.* Forested areas, eastern mountains. Now mostly east of Cascade crest near Canadian border, mountains of Northeast.

Bobcat. *Lynx rufus.* Most habitats, though rare at high elevations.

Sea Lions and Seals

Family Otariidae: Sea Lions and Fur Seals

Northern Fur Seal. *Callorhinus ursinus.* Usually well offshore, especially during spring migration. Only females, young recorded as far south as Washington.

*Northern Sea Lion. *Eumetopias jubatus.* Coast, inland marine waters, especially rocky areas, including jetties, where may haul out. No breeding sites. Numbers decreasing. Also known as Steller's Sea Lion.

*California Sea Lion. *Zalophus californianus.* Outer coast, inland marine waters. Conspicuous, especially hauled out on rocks, islets, docks, buoys. Non-breeding visitor from farther south; increasing recently, often regarded as pest.

Family Phocidae: Hair Seals

*Harbor Seal. *Phoca vitulina*. Common along outer coast, in protected marine waters, even up lower Columbia River. Hauls out on sand beaches, rocks, docks, log rafts.

Northern Elephant Seal. *Mirounga angustirostris*. Occasional offshore in oceanic, deeper protected waters; increasing.

Ungulates (Hoofed Animals)
Family Cervidae: Deer

*Elk. *Cervus elaphus*. Forest, meadows of all mountainous regions, migrating from lowlands to subalpine zone. Locally in shrub-steppe of Columbia Basin (Arid Lands Ecology Reserve of Hanford Reach National Monument). Extirpated, reintroduced in many areas, with only native form in Olympics ("Roosevelt Elk") having persisted. Increasing in Cascades.

*Mule Deer. *Odocoileus hemionus*. Most habitats from shrub-steppe to subalpine zone, in open to forested landscapes. From Cascades west tail black ("Black-tailed Deer"), from east slopes eastward tail white at base ("Mule Deer"); intermediates seen near Cascade passes.

*White-tailed Deer. *Odocoileus virginianus*. Riparian areas, mixed woodlands, farms, forests, fields in Northeast; isolated population ("Columbian White-tailed Deer") in floodplain forests near mouth of Columbia River in Wahkiakum County. Also introduced in Blue Mountains.

Moose. *Alces alces*. Rapidly expanding in state, probably result of logging. Forested areas near water in Northeast from Spokane north. Also in Cascades of Okanogan County; a few have turned up in Whatcom, Skagit Counties.

Caribou. *Rangifer tarandus*. Small, vanishing population in Interior Wet Belt forests of Selkirks of extreme Northeast, perhaps mostly wanderers from British Columbia or northern Idaho.

Family Bovidae: Bison, Goats, Muskox, and Sheep

*Mountain Goat. *Oreamnos americanus*. Rocky alpine, subalpine slopes of Cascades south to Mount Saint Helens (at least before 1980), Mount Adams; migrates downward in winter. Also introduced into Olympics. Few in mountains of Northeast.

Bighorn Sheep. *Ovis canadensis*. Rocky slopes with scattered trees. Once virtually extirpated in Eastern Washington, then reintroduced on east slope of Cascades, Blue Mountains, mountains of northeast.

Cetaceans

The following list includes all species recorded to date. Killer Whale, Harbor Porpoise, and Dall's Porpoise are relatively widespread in protected waters, and Minke Whale is seen with some frequency in San Juan Islands waters and the eastern Strait of Juan de Fuca. Killer Whale, Harbor Porpoise, and Gray Whale are regularly seen from shore along either the outer coast or inland waters. Other asterisked species have been seen with some regularity well offshore.

Family Balaenidae: Baleen Whales
Northern Right Whale. *Eubalaena glacialis*.

Family Balaenopteridae
Minke Whale. *Balaenoptera acutorostrata*.
Sei Whale. *Balaenoptera borealis*.
Blue Whale. *Balaenoptera musculus*.
Fin Whale. *Balaenoptera physalus*.
Humpback Whale. *Megaptera novaeangliae*.

Family Eschrichtiidae
*Gray Whale. *Eschrichtius robustus*.

Family Delphinidae: Dolphins
Striped Dolphin. *Stenella coeruleoalba*.
Common Dolphin. *Delphinus delphis*.
Short-finned Pilot Whale. *Globicephala macrorhynchus*.
*Risso's Dolphin. *Grampus griseus*.
*Pacific White-sided Dolphin. *Lagenorhynchus obliquidens*.
Northern Right Whale Dolphin. *Lissodelphis borealis*.
*Killer Whale. *Orcinus orca*.
False Killer Whale. *Pseudorca crassidens*.

Family Phocoenidae: Porpoises
*Harbor Porpoise. *Phocoena phocoena*.
*Dall's Porpoise. *Phocoenoides dalli*.

Family Physeteridae: Sperm Whales
Pygmy Sperm Whale. *Kogia breviceps*.
Sperm Whale. *Physeter catodon*.

Family Ziphiidae: Beaked Whales
Baird's Beaked Whale. *Berardius bairdii*.
Hubbs' Beaked Whale. *Mesoplodon carlhubbsi*.
Stejneger's Beaked Whale. *Mesoplodon stejnegeri*.
Cuvier's Beaked Whale. *Ziphius cavirostris*.

AMPHIBIANS AND REPTILES OF WASHINGTON

by Dennis Paulson
Kelly McAllister graciously reviewed this section.

Distributional data from: K.M. Dvornich, K.R. McAllister, and K.B. Aubry. 1997. *Amphibians and Reptiles of Washington State: Location Data and Predicted Distributions*, Volume 2 *in* Washington State Gap Analysis—Final Report. (K.M. Cassidy, C.E. Grue, M.R. Smith, and K.M. Dvornic, eds.). Washington Cooperative Fish and Wildlife Research Unit, University of Washington, Seattle.

Amphibians appear to be decreasing in many areas. Reports of rare species should be sent to Non-game Section, Washington Department of Fish and Wildlife, 600 N Capitol Way, Olympia WA 98501-1091.

* - species most likely to be seen

Salamanders

Family Ambystomidae: Mole Salamanders

Tiger Salamander. *Ambystoma tigrinum*. Occurs widely in eastern Washington lowlands. Larvae in ponds and lakes; adults may be far from permanent water in shrub-steppe.

Northwestern Salamander. *Ambystoma gracile*. In or near ponds in forest, most easily found in spring. East slope of Cascades to coast.

***Long-toed Salamander**. *Ambystoma macrodactylum*. Usually near water, most easily found in spring. Throughout except lowest parts of Columbia Basin. Probably scarce on outer coast.

Family Dicamptodontidae: Giant Salamanders

Cope's Giant Salamander. *Dicamptodon copei*. Small streams, primarily in coniferous forest, Olympic Peninsula, southwestern part of state. Metamorphosed adults very rare.

Pacific Giant Salamander. *Dicamptodon tenebrosus*. In or near streams, mountain lakes in moist coniferous forest, adults usually underground. Cascades to coast but lacking on Olympic Peninsula.

Family Rhyacotritonidae: Torrent Salamanders

Olympic Torrent Salamander. *Rhyacotriton olympicus*. Cold streams, seeps in mature forest of Olympic Peninsula.

Columbia Torrent Salamander. *Rhyacotriton kezeri*. Cold streams, seeps south of Chehalis River in Southwest.

Cascades Torrent Salamander. *Rhyacotriton cascadae*. Cold streams, seeps in Cascades south of Mount Rainier.

Family Salamandridae: Newts

***Roughskin Newt**. *Taricha granulosa*. In or near ponds, lakes where often visible; adults often cross roads. East slope of Cascades to coast.

Family Plethodontidae: Lungless Salamanders

Dunn's Salamander. *Plethodon dunni*. Southwestern corner of Washington in forest, near water, usually associated with rocks.

Larch Mountain Salamander. *Plethodon larselli*. Moist talus slopes, usually near waterfalls, most easily found in spring. South Cascades, mostly in Skamania County.

Van Dyke's Salamander. *Plethodon vandykei*. Small streams in moist areas, under logs, talus. Local in mountains, lowlands of Olympic Peninsula, Southwest, Pierce County south in Cascades.

***Western Red-backed Salamander**. *Plethodon vehiculum*. In dense forest, under or in logs. West of Cascade crest.

***Ensatina**. *Ensatina eschscholtzii*. In forest, under or in logs, woody debris west of Cascade crest.

Frogs

Family Ascaphidae: Tailed Frogs

Tailed Frog. *Ascaphus truei*. In or near mountain streams, most easily found at night. East slope of Cascades west to coast, also in Blue Mountains.

Family Pelobatidae: Spadefoots

Great Basin Spadefoot. *Scaphiopus intermontanus*. Over much of Columbia Basin. Shrub-steppe, grasslands, most easily found in spring when breeding in ponds. Spends much of its life underground.

Family Bufonidae: Toads

*****Western Toad**. *Bufo boreas*. All habitats central Columbia Basin except shrub-steppe, usually near water. Black tadpoles form aggregations in mountain lakes.

Woodhouse's Toad. *Bufo woodhousei*. Little known in state. Drier areas, breeding in quiet water bodies. Southern border of state from eastern Klickitat to Whitman County along Columbia, Snake Rivers.

Family Hylidae: Treefrogs

*****Pacific Treefrog**. *Hyla regilla*. Most common, widespread frog in state. Almost ubiquitous (but not in trees!), usually near water.

Family Ranidae: True Frogs

*****Red-legged Frog**. *Rana aurora*. Near or in ponds, mostly in forest. Mostly west of Cascade crest.

*****Cascades Frog**. *Rana cascadae*. In ponds, slow streams, mostly above 3,000 feet in subalpine zone. Cascades, Olympics.

*****Columbia Spotted Frog**. *Rana luteiventris*. In ponds, slow streams, mostly northeastern Cascades east, Blue Mountains. Not in shrub-steppe of Columbia Basin.

Oregon Spotted Frog. *Rana pretiosa*. Formerly much of Puget Trough, now extirpated from much of historic range. Small populations survive in Thurston, Klickitat Counties.

Northern Leopard Frog. *Rana pipiens*. Formerly much of Columbia Basin, now only near Crab Creek in Moses Lake area. Ponds, slow streams. Introduced in Pend Oreille, Spokane, Okanogan Counties.

*****Bullfrog**. *Rana catesbeiana*. Ponds, lakes, sloughs. Introduced widely in lowlands, probably still expanding range.

Green Frog. *Rana clamitans*. Ponds, lakes. Introduced to Toad Lake (Whatcom County), Lake Gillette (Stevens County).

Turtles

Family Chelydridae:
Snapping, Musk, and Mud Turtles

Snapping Turtle. *Chelydra serpentina*. Present in King, Pierce Counties, presumably released captives.

Family Emydidae: Terrapins

*****Painted Turtle**. *Chrysemys picta*. Ponds, lakes; may be seen basking. Throughout east of Cascades. Local, probably introduced, from Puget Sound southward.

Western Pond Turtle. *Clemmys marmorata*. Endangered in Washington. Extirpated from virtually all of Puget Trough. Ponds, slow streams; may be seen basking. Very local in Klickitat, Skamania Counties, reintroduction efforts elsewhere.

Slider. *Trachemys scripta*. Escapes from captivity may be encountered in quiet waters almost anywhere, especially in Puget Trough. No evidence as yet of successful breeding in wild in Washington.

Family Cheloniidae: Sea Turtles

Green Turtle. *Chelonia mydas*. Rarely found beached on outer coast.

Loggerhead Turtle. *Caretta caretta*. Rarely found beached on outer coast.

Family Dermochelyidae:
Leatherback Turtle

Leatherback Turtle. *Dermochelys coriacea*. Uncommon off outer coast, very rarely near shore or in Strait of Juan de Fuca.

Lizards

Family Iguanidae: Iguanids

*****Sagebrush Lizard**. *Sceloporus graciosus*. Warmest portions of shrub-steppe of Columbia Basin.

*****Western Fence Lizard**. *Sceloporus occidentalis*. On or near rocks, logs, usually in open woodlands. East slope of Cascades; Blue Mountains; also local around Puget Sound.

*****Side-blotched Lizard**. *Uta stansburiana*. Shrub-steppe, talus, cliffs of lower, warmest parts of Columbia Basin.

*****Pygmy Short-horned Lizard**. *Phrynosoma douglassii*. Shrub-steppe, high grasslands in Columbia Basin. Usually near loose soil, where it burrows. Restricted to Northwest; now considered separate species from Rocky Mountain populations.

Family Scinidae: Skinks

Western Skink. *Eumeces skiltonianus*. Shrub-steppe, grasslands, dry woodlands, often near water; secretive. East of Cascades.

Family Anguidae: Alligator Lizards

*****Northern Alligator Lizard**. *Elgaria coerulea*. Forest, edge, often around logs. East slope of Cascades to southwestern coast; also locally in Northeast.

Southern Alligator Lizard. *Elgaria multicarinata*. Pine, oak woodlands of lower east slopes of Cascades from Ellensburg south, barely overlapping with above species.

Snakes

Family Boidae: Boas

Rubber Boa. *Charina bottae*. Forest, pine/oak woodlands. Throughout except Columbia Basin; rare, local west.

Family Colubridae: Colubrid Snakes

Ringneck Snake. *Diadophis punctatus*. Oak/pine, riparian woodlands, open rocky or brushy areas, hidden during day. Southern border from Cowlitz to Whitman Counties, north almost to Ellensburg.

Sharptail Snake. *Contia tenuis*. Forest, woodlands, usually in moist areas, hidden during day. Very local: most recent records from Cle Elum (Kittitas County), Lyle (Klickitat County).

*Racer. *Coluber constrictor*. Shrub-steppe, grasslands, open woodlands. East of Cascades.

Striped Whipsnake. *Masticophis taeniatus*. Shrub-steppe, especially dry rocky canyons in south part of Columbia Basin.

*Gopher Snake. *Pituophis melanoleucus*. Shrub-steppe, grasslands, open woodlands. East of Cascades.

California Mountain Kingsnake. *Lampropeltis zonata*. Oak woodlands. Records from Klickitat, Skamania Counties along Columbia River.

*Common Garter Snake. *Thamnophis sirtalis*. Most habitats except shrub-steppe, often near water (always, in dry areas). Throughout.

*Western Terrestrial Garter Snake. *Thamnophis elegans*. Most habitats except shrub-steppe. Usually near water, including salt water. Occurs throughout but less common west of Cascades.

*Northwestern Garter Snake. *Thamnophis ordinoides*. Most habitats except driest ones. Western lowlands, also local on east side of Cascades.

Night Snake. *Hypsiglena torquata*. Sagebrush, under rocks during day. Columbia Basin.

Family Viperidae: Vipers

*Western Rattlesnake. *Crotalus viridis*. Sagebrush, grasslands, lower edge of Ponderosa Pine woodlands, usually near extensive rocky areas (for winter denning). East of Cascades, usually below 2,500 feet elevation.

BUTTERFLIES OF WASHINGTON

This list is an editorial compilation based on a draft by Jim Christensen. Taxonomy, nomenclature, and much habitat and life-history information are drawn from: R.M. Pyle. 2002. *The Butterflies of Cascadia*. Seattle Audubon Society, Seattle. Robert Michael Pyle graciously reviewed the final product.

Family Hesperidae: Skippers
Subfamily Pyrginae:
Dicot Skippers or Spread-wing Skippers

Silver-spotted Skipper. *Epargyreus clarus*. Local in Western Washington at low to mid-elevations around forest heaths, clearings. Along riparian habitats of southern, Eastern Washington rivers. May–July.

Northern Cloudywing. *Thorbyes pylades*. Along small creeks in canyons of Ponderosa Pine, Douglas-fir zones of Cascades. Isolated populations in Spokane, Stevens, Mason Counties. May–early July.

Dreamy Duskywing. *Erynnis icelus*. Low to mid-elevation pine woodlands, forests throughout much of Washington, apparently absent from outer coast, Columbia Basin. May–July.

Propertius Duskywing. *Erynnis propertius*. Garry Oak woodlands. Puget Trough, both slopes of Cascades. April–June.

Pacuvius Duskywing. *Erynnis pacuvius*. Pine woodlands, forest clearings, high mountain meadows across northern Washington, also along east slopes of Cascades. Late May–July.

Persius Duskywing. *Erynnis persius*. Montane meadows, forest clearings throughout much of state, except coast. Late April–July.

Alpine Checkered Skipper. *Pyrgus centaureae*. Alpine tundra of windswept ridges in Okanogan County. Late June–early August.

Two-banded Checkered Skipper. *Pyrgus ruralis*. Moist forest clearings, high mountain meadows throughout state. April–August.

Common Checkered Skipper. *Pyrgus communis*. Variety of open spaces in Eastern Washington, especially at low elevations in residential, agriculturally disturbed areas. Late April–early October.

Northern White Skipper. *Heliopetes ericetorum*. Along small streams in narrow canyons in Ponderosa Pine, shrub-steppe zones of Eastern Washington, local in Northeast. June–mid-September.

Common Sootywing. *Pholisora catullus*. Weedy waste areas along roadsides, in residential, agriculturally disturbed areas east of Cascade crest. Late April–August.

Subfamily Hesperiinae: Monocot Skippers or Folded-wing Skippers

Arctic Skipper. *Carterocephalus palaemon*. Small streams in forested areas, high mountain meadows of Western, northern Washington. Mid-May–mid-July.

Garita Skipperling. *Oarisma garita*. Grasslands along eastern border of Washington, mountain meadows of Northeast; apparently spreading. June–July.

European Skipperling. *Thymelicus lineola*. Disturbed areas, pastures in Whatcom County. July.

Juba Skipper. *Hesperia juba*. Almost anywhere, especially in shrub-steppe, pine woodlands east of Cascades, drier open areas west of Cascades. Scarcer in Western Washington. Late April–September.

Common Branded Skipper. *Hesperia comma*. Two subspecies: one in forest clearings, high mountain meadows across northern Washington. Another in alpine zone in Olympics. Both late June–August.

Western Banded Skipper. *Hesperia colorado*. Two subspecies: one in shrub-steppe summits, Ponderosa Pine woodlands east of Cascades, up to alpine. June–September. Another in South Sound Prairies, meadows of western Cascades. Late June–August.

Nevada Skipper. *Hesperia nevada*. Isolated colonies in high shrub-steppe on dry lithosols along east slope of Cascades. Mid-May–June.

Sachem. *Atalopedes campestris*. Columbia Gorge, Tri-Cities. June, October.

Peck's Skipper. *Polites peckius*. Sparse in Okanogan Highlands, Northeast. July–August.

Yellowpatch Skipper. *Polites coras*. Mountain meadows in northeastern Washington. July.

Sandhill Skipper. *Polites sabuleti*. Disturbed weedy areas, shorelines, along roadsides, especially over lawns in residential areas east of Cascades. Mid-May–August.

Mardon Skipper. *Polites mardon*. Idaho Fescue grasslands in South Sound Prairies (Thurston County), local in openings in Ponderosa Pine forests (Yakima, Klickitat Counties). Mid-July–August.

Tawny-edged Skipper. *Polites themistocles*. Wet meadows, forest glades in Northeast. Late May–August.

Long Dash. *Polites mystic*. Forest clearings, streamsides, large mountain meadows in Northeast. Early June–July.

Sonora Skipper. *Polites sonora*. Openings in coniferous forests, drier grasslands of southwestern Washington. Mountain meadows in northern Cascades. Mid-June–August.

Woodland Skipper. *Ochlodes sylvanoides*. Virtually all moist, montane, or grassy habitats, including residential areas throughout state. Also Columbia Basin. July–September.

Yuma Skipper. *Ochlodes yuma*. In vicinity of Great Reed Grass at Sun Lakes State Park (Grant County). Also Maryhill Museum (Klickitat County). July–early September.

Dun Skipper. *Euphyes vestris*. Mountain, valley damp grassy habitats in Western Washington, local along lower east slopes of Cascades. Rare in Northeast. Mid-June–July.

Common Roadside Skipper. *Amblyscirtes vialis*. Grassy roadsides in pine woodlands, forest clearings, east of Cascade crest, also Clark County. Mid-May–July.

Family Papilionidae: Swallowtails and Parnassians

Subfamily Parnassiinae: Parnassians.

Clodius Parnassian. *Parnassius clodius*. Four subspecies with different ranges. One in mountain meadows of Eastern Washington. June–August. Second in woodlands, coniferous forests of Western Washington. June–August. Third in subalpine meadows of Olympics, Cascades. July–August. Fourth in canyon draws along Snake River. May.

Mountain Parnassian. *Parnassius smintheus*. Two subspecies. One in pine woodlands, meadows of Cascades, Blue Mountains. June–August. Second occupies subalpine meadows of Olympics. July–August.

Subfamily Papilioninae: Swallowtails

Oregon Swallowtail. *Papilio oregonius*. Attracted to thistles in shrub-steppe adjacent to Columbia, Snake canyons. April–September, 2 broods.

Anise Swallowtail. *Papilio zelicaon*. Woodlands, shrub-steppe, summits, subalpine meadows throughout state, except deepest woodlands. April at lower elevations to August at high elevations. Fall brood near coast.

Indra Swallowtail. *Papilio indra*. Canyons, shrub-steppe through alpine tundra, mostly along east slope of Cascades, in Blue Mountains. April at low elevations to mid-August in alpine tundra.

Canadian Tiger Swallowtail. *Papilio canadensis*. Rare in riparian habitat along streams in Okanogan, Ferry Counties, perhaps hybrids with *P. rutulus*. June.

Western Tiger Swallowtail. *Papilio rutulus*. Residential areas, woodlands, riparian habitat throughout state. May–early September.

Two-tailed Tiger Swallowtail. *Papilio multicaudatus*. Pine woodlands, riparian canyons east of Cascades. May–early August.

Pale Tiger Swallowtail. *Papilio eurymedon*. Frequents streams in woodlands, Buckbrush chaparral, open forests throughout state. May–mid-August.

Family Pieridae:
Whites, Marbles, and Sulphurs
Subfamily Pierinae: Whites and Marbles

Pine White. *Neophasia menapia*. Frequents Ponderosa Pine woodlands, coniferous forest throughout state. Mid-July–September.

Becker's White. *Pontia beckerii*. Disturbed weedy areas, shrub-steppe, pine woodlands of Eastern Washington. May–August.

Spring White. *Pontia sisymbrii*. Widespread in Eastern Washington shrub-steppe, subalpine ridges. Also high Olympics. March–August.

Checkered White. *Pontia protodice*. Accidental. Disturbed weedy areas of Garfield, Pend Oreille Counties. July–mid-September. Only four records.

Western White. *Pontia occidentalis*. Disturbed weedy areas, shrub-steppe, pine woodlands, high mountain meadows, summits. Early June–August.

Margined White. *Pieris marginalis*. Two subspecies occupying different areas. First in moist forest margin from east slope of Cascades through Western Washington. Second in pine woodlands east, north of Columbia Basin. Both May–July.

Cabbage White. *Pieris rapae*. Introduced. Most open, disturbed habitats throughout Washington. April–September.

Large Marble. *Euchloe ausonides*. Shrub-steppe, pine woodlands, high mountain meadows east of Cascade crest. Mid-April at low elevations to mid-July at high elevations. Rare subspecies occurs at American Camp on San Juan Island.

Desert Marble. *Euchloe lotta*. Shrub-steppe. Mid-March–mid-June.

Sara Orangetip. *Anthocharis sara*. Shrub-steppe, pine woodlands, mountain meadows east of Cascade crest. Meadows, open woodlands west of Cascades. Mid-March–July.

Subfamily Coliadinae:
Sulphurs, Yellows, and Oranges

Clouded Sulphur. *Colias philodice*. Agricultural, wild habitats throughout Eastern Washington, expanding upslope and to Western Washington in late summer. April–September.

Orange Sulphur. *Colias eurytheme*. Common over alfalfa fields, also in open areas of all habitats throughout state, Eastside in spring, expanding into Western Washington in late summer. Late April–September.

Western Sulphur. *Colias occidentalis*. Pine woodlands, forest openings, mountain meadows in Cascades (south of Lake Chelan), Olympics. Late May–early August.

Queen Alexandra's Sulphur. *Colias alexandra*. Two forms. One in pine woodlands, forest openings across northern Washington. June–August. Another in shrub-steppe of Eastern Washington. Late April–September.

Labrador Sulphur. *Colias nastes*. Alpine tundra in northern Okanogan County. Mid-July–August.

Pink-edged Sulphur. *Colias interior*. Pine woodlands, forest openings along east slope of Cascades, across northeastern Washington. Early June–mid-August.

Dainty Sulphur. *Nathalis iole*. Immigrant. Only recorded once in Washington, at junction of Grand Ronde, Snake Rivers in Asotin County.

Family Lycaenidae: Gossamer Wings
Subfamily Lycaeninae:
Coppers, Hairstreaks, and Blues
Tribe Lycaenini: Coppers

Lustrous Copper. *Lycaena cuprea*. Rocky alpine ridges, slopes near Slate Peak in Okanogan, Whatcom Counties. July–August.

Edith's Copper. *Lycaena editha*. Forest clearings, high meadows in Blue Mountains. Mid-June–August.

Ruddy Copper. *Lycaena rubida*. Shrub-steppe habitats of Eastern Washington. Late May–August.

Blue Copper. *Lycaena heteronea*. Prefers shrub-steppe, pine woodlands east of Cascades, but can also be found in buckwheat flats. Late May–August.

Purplish Copper. *Lycaena helloides*. Occurs in many damp, weedy habitats from sea level to high elevations throughout state. May–September.

Lilac-bordered Copper. *Lycaena nivalis*. Pine woodlands, coniferous forest glades, high mountain meadows, east of Cascade crest. Also Olympics. Mid-May at low elevations through August at high elevations.

Mariposa Copper. *Lycaena mariposa*. Two subspecies with different ranges. "Makah Copper" in coastal bogs. Another at 3,000–7,000 feet in forest clearings in Cascades, Olympics, mountains of Eastern Washington. Both mid-July–early September.

Tribe Theclini: Hairstreaks

Chinquapin (Golden) Hairstreak. *Habrodais grunus*. In vicinity of larval food plant, Chinquapin, in Skamania County. Late July–mid-September.

Coral Hairstreak. *Satyrium titus*. Near cherry-lined streams in shrub-steppe in foothills of Cascades, mountains of Eastern Washington. Late June–mid-August.

Behr's Hairstreak. *Satyrium behrii*. Near Bitterbrush in shrub-steppe, pine woodlands along east slope of Cascades. Late May–mid-August.

Sooty Hairstreak. *Satyrium fuliginosum*. Shrub-steppe, high mountain meadows on east slope of Cascades, in Blue Mountains. June–July.

California Hairsteak. *Satyrium californicum*. Shrub-steppe, oak/pine woodlands in foothills along east slope of Cascades. Also Dishman Hills (Spokane County), Blue Mountains. Late June–August.

Sylvan Hairstreak. *Satyrium sylvinum*. Near willow-lined streams on both sides of Cascades, Olympics. July–mid-August.

Hedgerow Hairstreak. *Satyrium saepium*. Near Buckbrush in pine woodlands, Douglas-fir forests of Cascades, Blue Mountains. Mid-June–early September.

Bramble Green Hairstreak. *Callophrys perplexa*. Heaths, forest openings of Western Washington. Sparse in southern Yakima, Klickitat Counties. April–May.

Western Green Hairstreak. *Callophrys affinis*. Shrub-steppe of Eastern Washington. Also Blue Mountains. April–mid-July.

Sheridan's Green Hairstreak. *Callophrys sheridanii*. Two forms with different ranges. One flies along washes, ridge tops in shrub-steppe, canyon roads in pine woodlands on east slope of Cascades, in Blue Mountains. Another occupies shrub-steppe of Columbia Basin, pine woodlands north, east of basin. Both late March–May.

Johnson's Hairstreak. *Mitoura johnsoni*. Mostly tops of lowland old-growth Douglas-fir, hemlock forests of Western Washington. Late May–July.

Thicket Hairstreak. *Mitoura spinetorum*. Pine woodlands, forest clearings of Eastern Washington. Late May–July.

Cedar Hairstreak. *Mitoura grynea*. Occurs near Western Redcedar or junipers on both sides of Cascades. Mid-April–July.

Brown Elfin. *Incisalia augustinus*. Coniferous woodlands, heaths, forest openings, shrub-steppe throughout state, though not wettest or driest parts. April–May at low elevations through July at high elevations.

Moss's Elfin. *Incisalia mossii*. Flies in narrow canyons in Ponderosa Pine, Douglas-fir zones east of Cascade crest, mossy balds in coniferous forest of Western Washington. Mid-March–early June.

Hoary Elfin. *Incisalia polia*. Openings in coniferous forests, flying over Kinnikinnick in Puget Trough, northeastern Washington. Mid-May–June.

Western Pine Elfin. *Incisalia eryphon*. Two forms. One in pine woodlands of Eastern Washington. Another in Lodgepole Pine woodlands of southern Puget Sound. Both late March–early July.

Gray Hairstreak. *Strymon melinus*. Agricultural land, disturbed areas, forest clearings, residential areas west of Cascades; shrub-steppe habitats east of Cascades. April–early September.

Tribe Polomatini: Blues

Reakirt's Blue. *Echinargus isola*. One record, near Ellensburg (1993).

Western Tailed Blue. *Everes amyntula*. Riparian areas, meadows, legume-bearing habitats on both sides of Cascades. April–mid-May at lower elevation to July–mid-August at higher elevation.

Eastern Tailed Blue. *Everes comyntas*. Occurs in pastures, meadows with clover in Kittitas, Spokane, Stevens Counties. April–mid-August.

Spring Azure. *Celastrina argiolus*. Near water in shrub-steppe, pine woodlands, forest clearings, high mountain meadows throughout most of state. Mid-March–April at low elevation to August at high elevation.

Pacific Dotted Blue. *Euphilotes enoptes*. Shrub-steppe, pine woodlands along east slope of Cascades in southern Washington. Mid-May–July.

Rocky Mountain Dotted Blue. *Euphilotes ancilla*. Buckwheat stands. East slopes Cascades, Blue Mountains. Distribution, flight dates uncertain due to confusion with *E. enoptes*.

Square-spotted Blue. *Euphilotes battoides.* Shrub-steppe, pine woodlands with buckwheats in foothills throughout Eastern Washington. Mid-May–July.

Silvery Blue. *Glaucopsyche lygdamus.* Occurs in various lupine, legume habitats throughout state. April at low elevations through early August at high elevations.

Arrowhead Blue. *Glaucopsyche piasus.* Local populations in shrub-steppe, pine woodlands along east slope of Cascades, throughout Eastern Washington. Mid-May–mid-July.

Northern Blue. *Lycaeides idas.* High mountain meadows in northeastern, southeastern Washington. Late June–early September.

Anna's Blue. *Lycaeides anna.* High mountain meadows of Cascades, Olympics. Late June–early September.

Melissa's Blue. *Lycaeides melissa.* Shrub-steppe, alfalfa fields, roadsides, pine woodlands east of Cascade crest. Late May–September.

Greenish Blue. *Plebejus saepiolus.* Frequents bogs in shrub-steppe, pine woodlands, coniferous forests, wet meadows east of Cascades. Sparse in Western Washington. Mid-May–mid-August.

Boisduval's Blue. *Icaricia icarioides.* At least three subspecies. One in shrub-steppe, pine woodlands east of Cascade crest. Mid-May–June. Another in high mountain meadows of Cascades, Olympics. Mid-July–early August. Third in South Sound Prairies. Mid-May–mid-July.

Acmon Blue. *Icaricia acmon.* Shrub-steppe, pine woodlands, forest openings east of Cascade crest, Puget Sound lowlands, plus isolated population in Olympics. Late April–mid-September.

Arctic Blue. *Agriades glandon.* Alpine tundra on leeward side of windswept ridges in Cascades, Olympics. Mid-July–mid-August.

Subfamily Riodininae: Metalmarks

Mormon Metalmark. *Apodemia mormo.* Scattered colonies in shrub-steppe, buckwheat flats, canyons east of Cascade crest. Especially Bear Canyon west of Naches, Sun Lakes State Park. August–early October.

Family Nymphalidae: Anglewings, Tortoiseshells, Painted Ladies, Admirals, Fritillaries, Crescents, and Checkerspots

Subfamily Nymphalinae: Spiny Brushfoots

Tribe Heliconini: Longwings and Fritillaries

Great Spangled Fritillary. *Speyeria cybele.* Two subspecies. One around thistles, violets in forest openings, post-glacial prairies west of Cascades. Another on thistles in pine woodlands, Douglas-fir forests, canyons east of Cascade crest. Both late June–early September.

Coronis Fritillary. *Speyeria coronis.* Pine woodlands, shrub-steppe, forest glades, high mountain meadows from Cascade crest eastward, few in Blue Mountains, not in Northeast. Mid-May–early October.

Zerene Fritillary. *Speyeria zerene.* Three subspecies. One on Long Beach Peninsula; Federally Threatened, considered extinct in Washington, though reintroduction efforts being considered. August–September. Another in Puget Trough prairies, islands. Late June–July. Third in mountain meadows, pine woodlands of Cascades. Mid-July–August.

Callippe Fritillary. *Speyeria callippe.* Two subspecies. First occupies montane canyons, shrub-steppe, pine/oak woodlands of Cascades, Northeast; also in Blue Mountains. Other penetrates south into northern Okanogan County. Both mid-June–July.

Great Basin Fritillary. *Speyeria egleis.* Two subspecies. One uncommon in pine woodlands of Yakima County. Another sporadic elsewhere in montane forests, woodlands of far Eastern Washington. Both late June–early-August.

Atlantis Fritillary. *Speyeria atlantis.* Three subspecies. First in pine woodlands, forest openings east of Cascade crest. Absent from northern counties. Second has similar habitat, but restricted to northern counties east of Cascades. Third restricted to Northeast such as at Tiger Meadows (Pend Oreille County). All three late June–August.

Hydaspe Fritillary. *Speyeria hydaspe.* Two subspecies. One in woodlands, mountain meadows in Okanogan, Selkirk, Blue Mountains. Second in mountain meadows, roads, forest openings west of Cascade crest. Both late June–September.

Mormon Fritillary. *Speyeria mormonia.* Two forms. First occupies subalpine meadows in Cascades. Another in Okanogan, Selkirk, Blue Mountains. Both July–early September.

Silver-bordered Fritillary. *Boloria selene.* Isolated bogs in shrub-steppe in Kittitas, Yakima (Moxee Bog), Grant Counties. Wet meadows in forests, pine woodlands of Northeast. Early June–September.

Meadow Fritillary. *Boloria bellona.* Meadows, clearings among pine or aspen in Okanogan County, Blue Mountains. Late June–early August.

Western Meadow Fritillary. *Boloria epithore.* Wet meadows, grassy glades, woodlands, sea level to treeline, mostly Western

Washington. Spreads across to Northeast, also Blue Mountains. Late May–August.

Freija Fritillary. *Boloria freija.* Alpine bogs, meadows in northern Okanogan County. June–August.

Astarte Fritillary. *Boloria astarte.* Occurs on talus on windswept barren ridges of North Cascades. Late July–early August of even-numbered years.

Arctic Fritillary. *Boloria chariclea.* Subalpine meadows of Cascades, Olympics. Mid-July–September.

Tribe Melitaeini: Checkers and Crescents

Hoffmann's Checkerspot. *Chlosyne hoffmanni.* Pine woodlands, forests, mountain meadows of Cascades. Late May–mid-June at low elevation to mid-July–August at high elevation.

Northern Checkerspot. *Chlosyne palla.* Two subspecies. One in eastern mountains, Blues to Okanogan Highlands. May–early August. Other on lower east slope of Cascades at streams, roadside seeps in pine woodlands. May–July.

Northern Crescent. *Phyciodes cocyta.* Two subspecies. One in wetlands, grasslands around edge of Columbia Basin. Another from North Cascades eastward across northern Washington. Both June–August.

Field Crescent. *Phyciodes pulchellus.* Seeps, bogs in pine woodlands, forests, subalpine meadows, rare west of Cascade crest except in Olympics. Mid-May–early September.

Pale Crescent. *Phyciodes pallida.* Streambeds, dry gullies on hillsides of dry plateaus above Columbia, Snake Rivers. April–June.

Mylitta Crescent. *Phyciodes mylitta.* Disturbed weedy roadsides, canyons, agricultural, residential areas throughout state. March–September.

Anicia Checkerspot. *Euphydryas anicia.* Three subspecies. One in dry rocky alpine areas of North Cascades, mountains of northeastern Washington. Late July–mid-August. Another from shrub-steppe lithosols in Chelan, Okanogan, Douglas Counties. Mid-June–mid-July. Third on lithosols in shrub-steppe of Kittitas, Yakima, Lincoln Counties. Mid-May–mid-July.

Chalcedona Checkerspot. *Euphydryas chalcedona.* Three subspecies plus unnamed endemic form in Olympic Mountains. One along forest roads, clearings in Clark, Cowlitz, Skamania Counties. Second from pine woodlands, forest clearings, mountain meadows of central, southern Cascades. Third from woodlands, forest openings in foothills of Blue, Selkirk Mountains, also Palouse Hills. All May–June.

Edith's Checkerspot. *Euphydryas editha.* Four subspecies. First from Puget Trough prairies. April–May. Second from high, dry rock outcrops, meadows of Cascades south of Stevens Pass, also Olympics. Mid-June–mid-July. Third on lithosols in shrub-steppe east of Cascades. Mid-May–mid-July. Fourth from dry lithosols in North Cascades. July–early August.

Tribe Nymphalini: True Nymphs

Satyr Anglewing. *Polygonia satyrus.* Moist woodlands, forests, edges, parks, nettlebeds (especially) throughout state. Mid-March–mid-September.

Green Comma. *Polygonia faunus.* Low-to-middle-elevation forests, mountain meadows throughout state. March–September.

Hoary Comma (Zephyr). *Polygonia gracilis.* Mid-to-high-elevation forests, mountain meadows throughout state. Late April–early September.

Oreas Anglewing. *Polygonia oreas.* Two subspecies. First in mature forests, streams of Western Washington, North Cascades. April–September. Second from Okanogan Valley east in northern Washington. Also Blue Mountains. Mid-March–early September.

California Tortoiseshell. *Nymphalis californica.* Woodlands, forests, high mountain meadows, passes throughout state. Early April–October, some years exceedingly abundant, others absent.

Compton Tortoiseshell. *Nymphalis vaualbum.* Sporadic in forests of northeastern, southeastern Washington. Early April–October.

Mourning Cloak. *Nymphalis antiopa.* Woodlands, forest, riparian habitat throughout state, except wettest rain forest. Late March–October.

Milbert's Tortoiseshell. *Nymphalis milberti.* Occurs in all habitats with nettles from shrub-steppe to glaciated peaks. January–October.

American Lady. *Vanessa virginiensis.* Mostly in disturbed weedy areas, volcanic slopes, flower gardens, mostly southwestern Washington. August–October.

West Coast Lady. *Vanessa annabella.* Unpredictable. Cultivated areas, woodland edges throughout state. Late May–October.

Painted Lady. *Vanessa cardui.* Immigrant, in certain years extraordinarily abundant. Disturbed weedy areas, cultivated areas, woodlands, mountain meadows throughout state. April–October.

Red Admirable. *Vanessa atalanta.* Immigrant. Collected in all habitats throughout state, in certain years. April–October.

White Admiral. *Limenitis arthemis.* One record, probably an introduction. Kennewick.

Lorquin's Admiral. *Limenitis lorquini.* Woodlands, forests, parks, riparian habitat throughout state, except central Columbia Basin. Mid-May–early September.

Viceroy. *Limenitis archippus.* Lowland riparian fringes, willow groves along Columbia, Okanogan, Snake Rivers, tributaries. June–September.

California Sister. *Adelpha bredowii.* Accidental in southwestern Washington (five records). June–September.

Subfamily: Satyrinae: Satyrs, Browns, and Ringlets

Ochre Ringlet. *Coenonympha tullia.* Many grasslands, meadows through much of state, but unrecorded on Olympic Peninsula, Snohomish, Skagit, Whatcom Counties. April–early October.

Common Wood Nymph. *Cercyonis pegala.* Meadows, forest, edge grasslands at lower elevations both sides of Cascades. Also wet meadows in Columbia Basin. Late June–September.

Great Basin Woodnymph. *Cercyonis sthenele.* Most abundant in drier habitat of shrub-steppe of Eastern Washington. July–mid-August.

Dark Wood Nymph. *Cercyonis oetus.* Grassy shrub-steppe, pine woodlands of Eastern Washington. Late June–August.

Butler's Alpine. *Erebia epipsodea.* Openings in pine woodlands, Buckbrush, subalpine, lower alpine in Eastern Washington. Early June–mid-August.

Vidler's Alpine. *Erebia vidleri.* Wet subalpine meadows of North Cascades, Olympics. Mid-July–August.

Great Arctic. *Oeneis nevadensis.* Pine woodlands, forest openings, roads in Cascades. Common mid-May–July in even-numbered years.

Melissa Arctic. *Oeneis melissa.* Barren rock, talus in alpine heights of North Cascades (Slate Peak, Chopaka Mountain). Late June–August.

Chryxus Arctic. *Oeneis chryxus.* Two subspecies. One mostly in pine woodlands, high mountain meadows, subalpine summits across northern Washington. Second from alpine slopes of Olympics. Both mid-July–mid-August.

Subfamily Danaiinae: Milkweed Butterflies

Queen. *Danaus gilippus.* Several recent records around Tri-Cities, Tacoma. Unclear whether recent arrivals or introductions.

Monarch. *Danaus plexippus.* Breeds in Eastern Washington where milkweed abundant. Migrates mostly in river corridors, especially Okanogan, Snake, Columbia. Rare about Seattle. Early June–September.

DRAGONFLIES OF WASHINGTON

by Dennis Paulson

Abstracted from D. Paulson. 1999. *Dragonflies of Washington*. Seattle Audubon Society, Seattle.

Suborder Zygoptera:
Damselflies

Family Calopterygidae: Jewelwings

River Jewelwing. *Calopteryx aequabilis*. Lowlands, mainly south, more widespread in Eastern Washington. Slow warm-water streams, rivers in open or wooded country.

Family Lestidae: Spreadwings

California Spreadwing. *Archilestes californica*. Locally common in Eastern Washington lowlands, down Columbia River into Clark County. Slow streams, ponds.

Spotted Spreadwing. *Lestes congener*. Common in lowlands, mountains, often in larger water bodies than other spreadwings.

Common Spreadwing. *Lestes disjunctus*. Common in lowlands, mountains. Ponds, lakes.

Emerald Spreadwing. *Lestes dryas*. Common in mountains, local in lowlands. Often in temporary ponds with dense vegetation.

Sweetflag Spreadwing. *Lestes forcipatus*. Few localties in Pend Oreille, Okanogan, Kitsap, Clark Counties. Ponds, lakes.

Lyre-tipped Spreadwing. *Lestes unguiculatus*. Common in Eastern Washington lowlands, less common in mountains, Western Washington. Often in temporary ponds.

Family Coenagrionidae: Pond Damsels

Western Red Damsel. *Amphiagrion abbreviatum*. Locally common in lowlands, lower mountains. Marshy ponds, sloughs, typically in sedges.

Emma's Dancer. *Argia emma*. Common in Eastern Washington lowlands, also tributaries of Columbia River in Clark County. Rivers, streams, often rocky.

Vivid Dancer. *Argia vivida*. Common in Eastern Washington lowlands, local in Snohomish, Pierce Counties. Streams, springs, seeps.

Subarctic Bluet. *Coenagrion interrogatum*. Davis Lake (Ferry County). Dense bog vegetation.

Taiga Bluet. *Coenagrion resolutum*. Cascades, northeastern highlands. Dense sedge marshes.

Boreal Bluet. *Enallagma boreale*. Common from alkaline shrub-steppe ponds to boreal lakes, uncommon in Western Washington lowlands. Most abundant odonate in some parts of state, especially Columbia Basin ponds, lakes.

Tule Bluet. *Enallagma carunculatum*. Common throughout lowlands, lower mountains, often abundant at large lakes with beds of cattails, tules—a habitat shunned by other bluets.

Alkali Bluet. *Enallagma clausum*. Very local in Columbia Basin. Alkaline lakes—abundant at Soap Lake (Grant County).

Northern Bluet. *Enallagma cyathigerum*. Common in lowlands, lower mountains, except center of Columbia Basin. Less common than Boreal Bluet in Eastern Washington, more common west of Cascades. Ponds, lakes, slow streams.

Marsh Bluet. *Enallagma ebrium*. Locally common along northern tier of counties east of Cascades. Ponds, lakes.

Pacific Forktail. *Ischnura cervula*. Common lowlands, mountains: most ubiquitous species in state. Usually first odonate to appear in spring (as early as late March).

Swift Forktail. *Ischnura erratica*. Locally common west of Cascades in lowlands, also lower east side of Cascades. Ponds, especially Beaver ponds. Primarily spring species.

Western Forktail. *Ischnura perparva*. Common lowlands, mountains, usually less common than Pacific (except along streams where commoner). Marshy edges of ponds.

Sedge Sprite. *Nehalennia irene.*Cascades, highlands of Northeast; also Langendorfer Lake (King County). Dense sedge marshes.

Suborder Anisoptera:
Dragonflies Proper

Family Petaluridae: Petaltails

Black Petaltail. *Tanypteryx hageni*. Olympics, Cascades. Seeps, marshy stream edges on mountain hillsides, terrestrial larvae in burrows. Most primitive Northwest dragonfly.

Family Aeshnidae: Darners

California Darner. *Aeshna californica.* Common lowlands, lower mountains. Ponds, lakes. First dragonfly in spring (early April in south).

Canada Darner. *Aeshna canadensis.* Local throughout lowlands, lower mountains of northern half of state. Lakes, ponds.

Lance-tipped Darner. *Aeshna constricta.* Locally common in Eastern Washington lowlands, also recorded from Thurston, Clark Counties. Frequents small ponds, even temporary ones.

Lake Darner. *Aeshna eremita.* Local in northern half of state, lowlands, mountains. Lakes.

Variable Darner. *Aeshna interrupta.* Common in lowlands of Eastern Washington, locally common in western lowlands, also mountains. Lakes, ponds, also abundant in mountains away from water.

Sedge Darner. *Aeshna juncea.* Common Olympics, Cascades, highlands of Northeast. Ponds, small lakes.

Blue-eyed Darner. *Aeshna multicolor.* Common lowlands, mountains. Lakes, ponds.

Paddle-tailed Darner. *Aeshna palmata.* Common lowlands, mountains. Ponds, lakes.

Zigzag Darner. *Aeshna sitchensis.* Known from a few localities in Pend Oreille, Okanogan, Chelan Counties. Sedge meadows.

Subarctic Darner. *Aeshna subarctica.* Known only from Davis Lake (Ferry County), Fish Lake (Chelan County). Bog lakes.

Black-tipped Darner. *Aeshna tuberculifera.* Local, uncommon in Western, northeastern Washington, Cascades. Bog-margined lakes.

Shadow Darner. *Aeshna umbrosa.* Common in lowlands, mountains. Ponds, lakes, streams. Along with Yellow-legged Meadowhawk, last dragonfly in autumn.

Common Green Darner. *Anax junius.* Fairly common lowlands, lower mountains. Ponds, lakes, streams. Some populations migratory with spring immigrants from south, fall emigration of their offspring back to south.

Family Gomphidae: Clubtails

White-belted Ringtail. *Erpetogomphus compositus.* Known only from Crab Creek (Grant County), Yakima River (Benton County); not seen since 1972. Sandy streams, rivers.

Pronghorn Clubtail. *Gomphus graslinellus.* Known only from Stevens, Spokane Counties, but probably more widespread in Northeast. Lakes, streams.

Pacific Clubtail. *Gomphus kurilis.* Known only from Black Lake (Thurston County), Ice House Lake (Skamania County); old records from Seattle area. Lakes, possibly streams.

Columbia Clubtail. *Gomphus lynnae.* Yakima River Horn north of Benton City, perhaps more widespread. Shallow sandy, gravelly rivers.

Grappletail. *Octogomphus specularis.* Locally distributed in western lowlands, up Columbia River to Canyon Creek (Klickitat County). Small wooded streams.

Sinuous Snaketail. *Ophiogomphus occidentis.* Eastern lowlands, lower mountains. Also Chehalis River (Grays Harbor County). Muddy, rocky rivers.

Pale Snaketail. *Ophiogomphus severus.* Locally common in eastern lowlands. Also in Chehalis River drainage in Thurston, Grays Harbor Counties. Streams, rivers.

Olive Clubtail. *Stylurus olivaceus.* Local in Columbia Basin, tributaries of lower Columbia River in Western Washington. Sandy streams, rivers.

Family Cordulegastridae: Spiketails

Pacific Spiketail. *Cordulegaster dorsalis.* Local, uncommon in western lowlands, also southeast slopes of Cascades, Grande Ronde River area. Small wooded streams.

Family Macromiidae: Cruisers

Western River Cruiser. *Macromia magnifica.* Uncommon in lowlands of Eastern Washington; perhaps declining. Streams, rivers, sometimes lakes.

Family Corduliidae: Emeralds

American Emerald. *Cordulia shurtleffii.* Locally common in wooded lowlands, mountains, absent from Columbia Basin, not known from Blue Mountains. Ponds, lakes.

Beaverpond Baskettail. *Epitheca canis.* Local in western lowlands. Slow rivers, ponds in stream drainages.

Spiny Baskettail. *Epitheca spinigera.* Locally common in lowlands, lower mountains, quite local in Columbia Basin. Ponds, lakes; often seen away from water.

Ringed Emerald. *Somatochlora albicincta.* Common Olympics, Cascades; also Cedar Ponds Lake (Snohomish County). Ponds, lakes.

Ocellated Emerald. *Somatochlora minor.* Highlands of Northeast, also Stossel Creek (King County). Small, slow-moving streams through sedge meadows.

Mountain Emerald. *Somatochlora semicircularis.* Mountains except Blues. Local in western lowlands. Sedgy bogs, fens, lake margins.

Brush-tipped Emerald. *Somatochlora walshii.* Northeastern highlands, Cascades, also Langendorfer Lake (King County). Small streams flowing through sedge meadows.

Family Libellulidae: Skimmers

Western Pondhawk. *Erythemis collocata.* Common in eastern lowlands, more local but widespread in Western Washington. Ponds, marshy lakes.

Boreal Whiteface. *Leucorrhinia borealis.* Known only from near Molson (Okanogan County). Marshy ponds.

Crimson-ringed Whiteface. *Leucorrhinia glacialis.* Locally common in North Cascades, highlands of Northeast; also Langendorfer Lake (King County), Howell Lake (Mason County).

Hudsonian Whiteface. *Leucorrhinia hudsonica.* Locally common in wooded lowlands, more common in mountains. Ponds, bogs with dense emergent vegetation.

Dot-tailed Whiteface. *Leucorrhinia intacta.* Common lowlands, lower mountains, not known from Blue Mountains. Ponds, lake edges.

Red-waisted Whiteface. *Leucorrhinia proxima.* Common in highlands of Northeast, Langendorfer Lake (King County). Ponds, lake borders with much emergent vegetation.

Eight-spotted Skimmer. *Libellula forensis.* Common in lowlands. Ponds, lakes.

Chalk-fronted Corporal. *Libellula julia.* Locally common in northern, western lowlands. Lakes, ponds, bogs.

Widow Skimmer. *Libellula luctuosa.* Clark, Skamania Counties, rare north to Thurston County, east to Benton County; probably recent arrival from Oregon's Willamette Valley. Lakes.

Common Whitetail. *Libellula lydia.* Common in lowlands. Lakes, ponds, slow streams, typically muddy.

Twelve-spotted Skimmer. *Libellula pulchella.* Common in eastern lowlands. Few western records may not be established populations. Ponds, lakes.

Four-spotted Skimmer. *Libellula quadrimaculata.* Common in lowlands, mountains. Ponds, lakes with abundant vegetation.

Blue Dasher. *Pachydiplax longipennis.* Locally common in lowlands; more common in southern Washington. Ponds, lakes with emergent vegetation.

Wandering Glider. *Pantala flavescens.* Vagrant, records from Clark (several), Grant Counties. Usually seen away from water.

Spot-winged Glider. *Pantala hymenaea.* Scattered widespread records, especially southwestern lowlands. Possibly has bred in Benton County. Ponds, slow streams.

Variegated Meadowhawk. *Sympetrum corruptum.* Common in lowlands. Breeds in eutrophic ponds, lakes but can be seen anywhere, especially along coast or in Cascades, during August–September migration.

Saffron-winged Meadowhawk. *Sympetrum costiferum.* Common in lowlands, mountains. Ponds, lakes.

Black Meadowhawk. *Sympetrum danae.* Locally common in eastern lowlands, mountains; a few wander to west. Emergent vegetation in ponds, lakes.

Cardinal Meadowhawk. *Sympetrum illotum.* Common in western lowlands, local on southern edge of state on east side of Cascades, lower slopes of Blue Mountains. Ponds, lakes.

Cherry-faced Meadowhawk. *Sympetrum internum.* Locally common in eastern lowlands, sparingly higher; few records west may represent wanderers. Ponds, lakes, associated meadows.

Red-veined Meadowhawk. *Sympetrum madidum.* Local, uncommon in lowlands, into mountains. Temporary ponds host breeders, usually encountered away from water.

White-faced Meadowhawk. *Sympterum obtrusum.* Common in lowlands, mountains, not known from Blue Mountains. Ponds, associated meadows.

Western Meadowhawk. *Sympetrum occidentale.* Common in eastern lowlands, especially Columbia Basin. In west, resident near Randle, occasionally seen elsewhere. Often in pairs far from water.

Striped Meadowhawk. *Sympterum pallipes.* Common in lowlands, lower mountains. Ponds, lakes, associated meadows.

Yellow-legged Meadowhawk. *Sympetrum vicinum.* Locally common in forested lowlands in north, west; also in Blue Mountains foothills. Ponds, lakes with emergent vegetation. Latest-flying dragonfly (19 November).

Black Saddlebags. *Tramea lacerata.* Locally common in lowlands of Columbia Basin. Formerly rare, now annual in western lowlands; one breeding record. Ponds, lakes.

REFERENCES

Aitchison, C.J. (ed.). 2001. *The Birder's Guide to Vancouver and the Lower Mainland.* Vancouver Natural History Society. Whitecap Books, Vancouver, Toronto, and New York.

Alden, P.C. 1998. *National Audubon Society Field Guide to the Pacific Northwest.* Knopf, New York.

Alt, D.D., and D.W. Hyndman. 1984. *Roadside Geology of Washington.* Mountain Press, Missoula, Montana.

American Birding Association. 2002. *ABA Checklist: Birds of the Continental United States and Canada.* 6th ed. American Birding Association, Colorado Springs.

American Ornithologists' Union. 1998. *Check-list of North American Birds.* 7th ed. American Ornithologists' Union, Washington, DC. Supplements in *Auk* 117 (2000):847–858 and 119 (2002):897–906.

Campbell, R.W., N.K. Dawe, I. McTaggart-Cowan, J.M. Cooper, G.W. Kaiser, M.C.E. McNall, G.E.J. Smith, and A.C. Stewart. 1990–2001. *The Birds of British Columbia.* 4 vols. Royal British Columbia Museum, Victoria, and University of British Columbia Press, Vancouver and Toronto.

Cannings, R.A., R.J. Cannings, and S.G. Cannings. 1987. *Birds of the Okanagan Valley, British Columbia.* Royal British Columbia Museum, Victoria.

Cassidy, K.M. 1997. *Land Cover of Washington State: Description and Management.* Vol. 1 *in* Washington State Gap Analysis—Final Report (K.M. Cassidy, C.E. Grue, M.R. Smith, and K.M. Dvornic, eds.). Washington Cooperative Fish and Wildlife Research Unit, University of Washington, Seattle.

Cullinan, T. (compiler). 2001. *Important Bird Areas of Washington.* Audubon Washington, Olympia.

Dawson, W.L. 1909. *The Birds of Washington.* 2 vols. Occidental Publishing Company, Seattle.

Ennor, H.R. 1991. *Birds of the Tri-Cities and Vicinity.* Lower Columbia Basin Audubon Society, Richland.

Franklin, J.F., and C.T. Dyrness. 1973. *Natural Vegetation of Oregon and Washington.* Pacific Northwest Forest and Range Experiment Station, Forest Service, U.S. Department of Agriculture, Portland.

The Great Washington State Birding Trail Cascade Loop. 2002. Audubon Washington, Olympia. (Large folding map; other loops in preparation.)

Hunn, E.S. 1982. *Birding in Seattle and King County.* Seattle Audubon Society, Seattle.

Jewett, S.A., W.P. Taylor, W.T. Shaw, and J.W. Aldrich. 1953. *Birds of Washington State.* University of Washington Press, Seattle.

Kruckeberg, A.R. 1991. *The Natural History of Puget Sound Country.* University of Washington Press, Seattle and London.

Lewis, M.G., and F.A. Sharpe. 1987. *Birding in the San Juan Islands.* Mountaineers, Seattle.

MacRae, D. 1995. *Birder's Guide to Washington.* Gulf Publishing Company, Houston.

Marshall, D.B., M.G. Hunter, and A.L. Contreras (eds.). 2003. *Birds of Oregon: A General Reference.* Oregon State University Press, Corvallis.

Morse, B. 2001. *A Birder's Guide to Coastal Washington.* R.W. Morse Company, Olympia.

Morse, B., T. Aversa, and H. Opperman. 2003. *Birds of the Puget Sound Region.* R.W. Morse Company, Olympia.

O'Connor, G., and K. Wieda. 2001. *Northwest Arid Lands: An Introduction to the Columbia Basin Shrub-Steppe.* Battelle Press, Columbus, Ohio; distributed by University of Washington Press, Seattle.

Paulson, D. 1993. *Shorebirds of the Pacific Northwest.* University of Washington Press, Seattle and London, and Seattle Audubon Society, Seattle.

Smith, M.R., P.W. Mattocks, Jr., and K.M. Cassidy. 1997. *Breeding Birds of Washington State: Location Data and Predicted Distributions.* Volume 4 *in* Washington State Gap Analysis—Final Report (K.M. Cassidy, C.E. Grue, M.R. Smith, and K.M. Dvornic, eds.). Seattle Audubon Society, Seattle.

Stepniewski, A. 1999. *The Birds of Yakima County, Washington.* Distributed by Yakima Valley Audubon Society, Yakima.

Taylor, K. 2000. *The Birder's Guide Vancouver Island.* 5th ed. Steller Press, Vancouver.

Wahl, T.R. 1995. *Birds of Whatcom County Status and Distribution.* T.R. Wahl, Bellingham.

Wahl, T.R., and D.R. Paulson. 1991. *A Guide to Bird Finding in Washington.* rev. ed. T.R. Wahl, Bellingham.

Washington Department of Natural Resources. 2003. *State of Washington Natural Heritage Plan.* Washington State Department of Natural Resources, Olympia.

Zalesky, P.H. 2001. *Birding in Snohomish County.* rev. ed. Pilchuck Audubon Society, Everett.

WASHINGTON ORNITHOLOGICAL SOCIETY

*The Washington Ornithological Society was chartered in 1988
to increase knowledge of the birds of Washington
and to enhance communication among all persons interested in those birds.*

The Washington Ornithological Society (WOS) provides a forum for birders from throughout the state to meet and share information on bird identification, biology, population status, and birding sites. Over 400 enthusiastic birders—from backyard feeder watchers to professional ornithologists—belong to WOS. Membership is open to all persons interested in birds and birding.

WHAT WOS HAS TO OFFER:

• Members receive **WOSNews**, the bimonthly newsletter of the society, which features Washington Field Notes, a compilation of recent notable statewide bird sightings.

• **Washington Birds**, our scholarly journal, is published annually and is sent to all members.

• **WOS meetings** are held on the first Monday of each month (except July, August, and September) at the Center for Urban Horticulture on the University of Washington Seattle campus. An interesting program is presented and the meetings are open to the public.

• The **WOS Annual Conference**, open to all members, is held in a different part of the state each year. It includes speakers, workshops, and field trips.

• **Field trips** for members are held each month to different areas of the state.

• WOS operates the **Washington BirdBox**, a statewide rare bird alert, which can be reached by phoning 206-281-9172.

• WOS sponsors the **Washington Bird Records Committee**, which maintains the official state bird list and birding records that substantiate it. See next page.

• The **WOS website** provides the latest information for WOS members, plus bird lists, photos, and more: *http://www.wos.org*

• **Dues** are $20 for a single, $25 for a family membership. WOS is a non-profit organization under section 501(c)(3) of the Internal Revenue Code.

Washington Ornithological Society
P.O. Box 31783, Seattle, Washington 98103

WASHINGTON BIRD RECORDS COMMITTEE

Observations of species on the Washington Review List (common names italicized on the Annotated Checklist in this guide or not listed there at all) should be reported to the WBRC with written details and any supporting evidence such as photographs and sound recordings. Complete your report on-line or submit it to the WBRC at the address below. Documentation should include:

1. Species name.

2. Number of individuals seen.

3. Location.

4. Date.

5. Time and duration of sighting.

6. Observer's contact information.

7. Description of size, shape, and plumage. Describe in detail all parts of the bird, including the beak and the feet. Mention more than just the diagnostic characters, yet include only what was actually observed in the field.

8. Description of voice or call, if heard.

9. Description of behavior.

10. Habitat—general and specific.

11. Distance from you to the bird.

12. Optical equipment used (including binoculars, telescopes, cameras).

13. Light (sky condition, amount of light on bird, position of sun).

14. Similar-appearing species, which were eliminated by description, call, or behavior (7, 8, and 9 above). Explain.

15. Previous experience with this species and similar-appearing species.

16. Other observers.

17. Field guides, other books, articles, and advice consulted, and how these influenced your description.

18. Were field notes about the observation written during observation, immediately after, later, or not at all?

If you were able to take photos, make sound recordings, or draw sketches of the bird you observed, mail them to:

Washington Bird Records Committee

P.O. Box 31783, Seattle, Washington 98103

e-mail: *wbrc@wos.org*   web site: *www.wos.org/rarebird.htm*

AmericanBirding
A S S O C I A T I O N

Join the American Birding Association

When you become a member of the American Birding Association, you join tens of thousands of birders who are eager to improve their knowledge and skills to get the most out of their birding experiences.

✔ Network with friends and share the passion of birding.

✔ Learn more about birds and birding.

✔ Sharpen and augment your birding skills.

✔ Participate in workshops, conferences, and tours.

✔ Receive our full-color magazine, *Birding*, and our monthly newsletter, *Winging It*.

✔ Use our directory and catalogs to expand your birding horizons.

You don't have to be an expert birder to be a member of the American Birding Association. You're qualified simply by having a desire to learn more about birds, their habitats, and how to protect them.

ABA membership offers you the opportunity to meet and learn from experts and to improve your skills through our internationally attended conferences and conventions, Institute for Field Ornithology workshops, specialized tours, and volunteer opportunities. It is great way to get to know others who share your interests.

ABA Membership
P.O. Box 6599, Colorado Springs, CO 80934
Phone: 800-850-2473 * Fax: 719-578-1480
www.americanbirding.org

ABA Birdfinding Guide Series

A Birder's Guide to Alaska
George C. West
A Birder's Guide to the Rio Grande Valley
Mark W. Lockwood, William B. McKinney, James N. Paton, Barry R. Zimmer
A Birder's Guide to Metropolitan Areas of North America
Paul Lehman
A Birder's Guide to the Bahamas
Anthony R. White
A Birder's Guide to Virginia
David Johnston
A Birder's Guide to Southern California
Brad Schram
A Birder's Guide to Colorado
Harold R. Holt
A Birder's Guide to Florida
Bill Pranty
A Birder's Guide to New Hampshire
Alan Delorey
Birdfinder: A Birder's Guide to Planning North American Trips
Jerry A. Cooper
A Birder's Guide to Southeastern Arizona
Richard Cachor Taylor
A Birder's Guide to Arkansas
Mel White
A Birder's Guide to Eastern Massachusetts
Bird Observer
A Birder's Guide to the Texas Coast
Harold R. Holt
A Birder's Guide to Wyoming
Oliver K. Scott

New Guides in Progress
Michigan — Oregon — Belize

Other Recent ABA Publications
Birding on Borrowed Time   Attu: Birding on the Edge
Phoebe Snetsinger   *Charles E. Osgood*
ABA Checklist: Birds of the Continental United States and Canada
ABA Checklist Committee

ABA Sales — 800-634-7736
www.americanbirding.org/abasales

AMERICAN BIRDING ASSOCIATION
PRINCIPLES OF BIRDING ETHICS

*Everyone who enjoys birds and birding must always re-
spect wildlife, its environment, and the rights of others.
In any conflict of interest between birds and birders, the
welfare of the birds and their environment comes first.*

CODE OF BIRDING ETHICS

1. Promote the welfare of birds and their environment.

1(a) Support the protection of important bird habitat.

1(b) To avoid stressing birds or exposing them to danger, exercise restraint and caution during observation, photography, sound recording, or filming.

Limit the use of recordings and other methods of attracting birds, and never
use such methods in heavily birded areas or for attracting any species that is
Threatened, Endangered, or of Special Concern, or is rare in your local area.

Keep well back from nests and nesting colonies, roosts, display areas, and important feeding sites. In such sensitive areas, if there is a need for extended
observation, photography, filming, or recording, try to use a blind or hide, and
take advantage of natural cover.

Use artificial light sparingly for filming or photography, especially for
close-ups.

1(c) Before advertising the presence of a rare bird, evaluate the potential for disturbance to the bird, its surroundings, and other people in the area, and proceed
only if access can be controlled, disturbance can be minimized, and permission has been obtained from private land-owners. The sites of rare nesting
birds should be divulged only to the proper conservation authorities.

1(d) Stay on roads, trails, and paths where they exist; otherwise keep habitat disturbance to a minimum.

2. Respect the law and the rights of others.

2(a) Do not enter private property without the owner's explicit permission.

2(b) Follow all laws, rules, and regulations governing use of roads and public areas,
both at home and abroad.

2(c) Practice common courtesy in contacts with other people. Your exemplary behavior will generate goodwill with birders and non-birders alike.

3. Ensure that feeders, nest structures, and other artificial bird environments are safe.

3(a) Keep dispensers, water, and food clean and free of decay or disease. It is important to feed birds continually during harsh weather.

3(b) Maintain and clean nest structures regularly.

3(c) If you are attracting birds to an area, ensure the birds are not exposed to predation from cats and other domestic animals, or dangers posed by artificial hazards.

4. Group birding, whether organized or impromptu, requires special care.

Each individual in the group, in addition to the obligations spelled out in Items #1 and #2, has responsibilities as a Group Member.

4(a) Respect the interests, rights, and skills of fellow birders, as well as those of people participating in other legitimate outdoor activities. Freely share your knowledge and experience, except where code 1(c) applies. Be especially helpful to beginning birders.

4(b) If you witness unethical birding behavior, assess the situation and intervene if you think it prudent. When interceding, inform the person(s) of the inappropriate action and attempt, within reason, to have it stopped. If the behavior continues, document it and notify appropriate individuals or organizations.

Group Leader Responsibilities [amateur and professional trips and tours].

4(c) Be an exemplary ethical role model for the group. Teach through word and example.

4(d) Keep groups to a size that limits impact on the environment and does not interfere with others using the same area.

4(e) Ensure everyone in the group knows of and practices this code.

4(f) Learn and inform the group of any special circumstances applicable to the areas being visited (e.g., no tape recorders allowed).

4(g) Acknowledge that professional tour companies bear a special responsibility to place the welfare of birds and the benefits of public knowledge ahead of the company's commercial interests. Ideally, leaders should keep track of tour sightings, document unusual occurrences, and submit records to appropriate organizations.

PLEASE FOLLOW THIS CODE—
DISTRIBUTE IT AND TEACH IT TO OTHERS.

Additional copies of the Code of Birding Ethics can be obtained from:
ABA, PO Box 6599, Colorado Springs, CO 80934-6599.
Phone 800/850-2473 or 719/578-1614;
fax 800/247-3329 or 719/578-1480; e-mail: member@aba.org

7/1/96

INDEX

Rather than being listed alphabetically by name, several categories of index entries are grouped by type of site or facility: Dam; Ferry; Indian Reservation; Mountain passes; National Wildlife Refuge; Park (includes private, municipal, county, state, and national); Sewage treatment facilities; Wilderness Areas; Wildlife Area. If you can't find a site indexed under its proper name, look for it in one of these groups.

The **Abbreviated Table of Contents** boxes let you find the chapter location of any numeric index entry. For example, if you are on the Pacific Coast and wonder whether you can expect to find Brewer's Blackbird, you can quickly ascertain—by comparing the Abbreviated Table of Contents page-number range with the page numbers of the index entries—that this species is not mentioned in the text for this region. All ABA Birdfinding Guides use this time-saving feature.

A

Aberdeen 62-63
Accentor, Siberian 582
Admiralty Inlet 25, 27-28, 31, 81, 83, 192
Aeneas Valley Road 465
Albatross
 Black-footed 4, 66, 531, 549
 Laysan 14, 66, 531, 549
 Short-tailed 549
 Shy 1, 549
Alki Beach and Alki Point 162
Almira 396
Amazon Creek Marsh 478
American Birding Association 19, 614
American Camp 102
American Lake 202
Annas Bay 219
Ape Cave 242
Asotin 523
Asotin Slough Habitat Management Unit 523
Atkins Lake 384
Audubon Society chapters 19
Auklet
 Cassin's 5, 47, 66, 103, 109, 192, 539, 569
 Parakeet 569
 Rhinoceros 5, 14, 25, 27-29, 31-33, 47, 58, 66, 82-83, 89, 93, 96, 103, 109, 136-137, 145, 188, 197, 201, 214, 539, 569
 Whiskered 569

Avocet, American 11, 82, 159, 251, 317, 343, 345-346, 351, 356-357, 359, 362, 365-366, 368, 384, 393, 397, 403, 536, 562

B

Badger Mountain 381
Bainbridge Island 192
Balch Lake 333
Banks Lake 387
Barnaby Slough Fish Rearing Station 126
Bateman Island 347
Beezley Hills Preserve (TNC) 376-378
Bellingham 135-136
Bennington Lake 511
Benton City 346
Beth Lake 459
Bethel Ridge 328
Bickleton 340-341
Big Ditch (Skagit Wildlife Area) 189
Big Flat Habitat Management Unit 373
Big Meadow Lake 479-480
Bingen 332-333
Birch Bay 140
Bird Creek Meadows 262
BirdBox (rare bird alert) 20
Biscuit Ridge 513
Bittern, American 6, 34-36, 57, 63, 69, 115, 121, 147, 159, 172, 181, 211-212, 236, 240, 246, 252, 259, 317, 356, 364-365, 441, 478, 487-489, 501, 532, 551
Black River (Thurston County) 208
Black Rock Valley 316
Blackbird
 Brewer's 172, 279, 368, 426, 430, 435, 439, 466, 489, 547, 590
 Red-winged 6, 11, 100, 172, 214, 240, 279, 356, 375, 389, 415, 430, 466, 489, 491, 501, 546, 590
 Rusty 33, 113, 117, 137, 176, 181, 446, 500, 505, 507, 547, 590
 Tricolored 368, 387-389, 546, 590
 Yellow-headed 11, 137, 149, 159, 181, 205, 244, 253, 345, 349, 353, 355-356, 368, 375, 389, 391, 402-403, 429-430, 437, 439, 441, 444-445, 458, 475, 477, 501, 546, 590
Blackbird Island 412
Blaine 140-141, 143
Blue Mountains 513, 515, 519

Chumstick Mountain 418
Clallam Bay 44
Clarkston 521
Cle Elum 272-273, 277
Cliffdell 323
Climate and weather 13, 23, 78, 154, 233, 266, 351-352, 406, 462, 504
Cold Creek Road 310
Collared-Dove, Eurasian 414, 569
Colonial Creek Campground 129
Columbia Gorge 231-234, 243, 255, 257-259, 265-266, 332-333, 335-336
Columbia Hills 332, 335-336
Colville 475
Colville Valley 473-474
Commencement Bay 197-199, 201
Conboy Lake 338
Conconully 440, 449
Concrete 125
Condor, California 74, 231, 552
Conway 113, 115
Coot, American 6, 11, 146, 149-150, 240, 375, 446, 475, 501, 536, 561
Coppei Creek 514-515
Cormorant
  Brandt's 5, 28, 57, 74, 89, 96, 135, 145, 188, 197, 220, 532, 551
  Double-crested 5-6, 11, 57, 89, 92-93, 96, 145-146, 149-151, 201, 249, 291, 335, 358, 371, 393, 402, 488-489, 532, 551
  Pelagic 5-6, 14, 28, 31, 47, 54, 57, 74, 86-87, 89, 92-93, 96, 103, 135, 145, 151, 188, 191, 197, 201, 532, 551
  Red-faced 551
Coulee City 393
County Line Ponds (Grant/Adams Counties) 366
County Line Ponds (Skagit/Whatcom Counties) 127
Coupeville 83
Cowbird, Brown-headed 7, 279, 430, 498, 547, 590
Cowiche Canyon 319
Crab Creek (Lower) 359, 361-363, 388
Crane, Sandhill 6, 11, 14, 33, 62, 232, 243-244, 249, 285, 332, 338, 356-357, 359, 362-364, 366-370, 378, 384, 438, 536, 561
Creeper, Brown 8, 36, 51, 53, 81, 99-100, 105, 112, 122, 125, 166, 168, 201, 212, 221, 226, 240, 277, 279, 301, 339, 349, 420, 432, 448, 466, 478, 480, 498, 514, 524, 528, 543, 579
Crescent Lake 174
Crockett Lake 81
Crossbill
  Red 7, 9, 36, 39, 48, 50, 73, 86, 99, 102, 119, 123, 130, 201, 226, 269, 274, 277-279, 281-282, 293, 295, 299-302, 325, 328, 330, 339, 387, 394, 399-400, 403, 407, 409, 413, 416, 421, 429, 431-433, 438, 441, 448, 452, 456-457, 469-470, 475, 477-478, 490-491, 493-494, 496, 498-499, 501, 514, 528, 547, 592
  White-winged 8, 123, 129-130, 277, 325, 329, 400, 407, 433, 447, 450, 452, 455, 457, 469-470, 483-484, 498-499, 503, 528, 547, 592

Crow
  American 7, 161, 426, 435, 542, 577
  Northwestern 6, 50-51, 99-100, 107, 542, 577
Cuckoo
  Black-billed 487, 528, 570
  Yellow-billed 570
Curlew
  Bristle-thighed 55, 72, 563
  Far Eastern 143
  Little 72, 563
  Long-billed 11, 67, 284, 286, 303, 316-317, 343, 351, 356-357, 362, 365, 368-369, 371, 403, 439, 442, 444-445, 537, 563
Cusick 489

D

Dallesport 336
Dam
  Bonneville (Columbia River) 257
  Dry Falls (Snake River) 393
  Grand Coulee (Columbia River) 387, 395
  Ice Harbor (Snake River) 373, 505
  John Day (Columbia River) 340
  Lower Granite (Snake River) 520, 529
  Lower Monumental (Snake River) 374-375
  McNary (Columbia River) 342, 507
  North (Banks Lake) 395
  O'Sullivan (Potholes Reservoir) 357
  Rock Island (Columbia River) 376, 379
  Rocky Reach (Columbia River) 416
  Wanapum (Columbia River) 291, 361
  Wells (Columbia River) 435
Damon Point 59
Davenport 400
Deception Pass 79, 88-89
Deer Park 39, 41
Des Moines 197
Destruction Island 52
Devil's Gulch Roadless Area 414
Diamond Point 29, 31
Dickcissel 47, 589
Dipper, American 8, 32, 36, 52-53, 97, 111, 123, 129, 136, 171, 214, 221, 226-227, 238, 258, 270-271, 278, 281, 293, 315, 323-324, 328, 330, 337, 407, 409, 411, 419-420, 423, 427, 429, 431-432, 469, 475, 482-483, 489, 517, 543, 580
Discovery Bay 31
Dishman Hills Natural Area 495-496
Dixie 513
Dotterel, Eurasian 1, 59, 562
Douglas Creek 379-380

P

Storm-Petrel
  Fork-tailed 4-5, 47, 66, 109, 532, 550
  Leach's 5, 47-48, 66, 532, 551
  Wilson's 1, 550
Strait of Juan de Fuca 25, 28-29, 31, 33, 35, 37, 44, 47
Sullivan Lake 480
Sun Lakes 389, 391
Sunrise 228
Surfbird 5, 14, 25, 37, 44-45, 57, 65-66, 71-72, 74, 85, 103, 109, 537, 563
Swakane Canyon 416-418
Swallow
  Bank 11, 126, 139, 240, 291, 303, 347, 371, 410, 435, 441, 445, 529, 543, 578
  Barn 7, 365, 407, 435, 441, 543, 578
  Cliff 6, 11, 255, 293, 307, 313, 319, 355, 362, 365, 371, 380, 391, 393, 396-397, 435, 438, 441, 489, 493, 524, 543, 578
  Northern Rough-winged 6, 11, 104, 261, 296, 365, 414, 435, 441-442, 469, 489, 543, 578
  Tree 6, 11, 100, 161, 168, 181, 211, 241-242, 261, 271, 277, 303, 331, 340, 358, 409, 430-431, 441, 454, 457, 477, 480, 489, 542, 578
  Violet-green 7, 11, 93, 100, 129, 191, 261, 307, 313, 319, 323, 328, 331, 353, 355, 365, 393, 407, 409, 416, 423, 431, 435, 442, 446, 466, 496, 542, 578
Swan
  Mute 554
  Trumpeter 33, 53, 57, 69, 72, 77, 96, 104, 108, 113, 116-117, 121, 146, 186, 220, 285, 368, 423, 446, 533, 554
  Tundra 33, 57, 113, 116-117, 121, 139, 146, 235, 244, 249, 255, 285, 336, 338, 358, 368, 374, 385, 389, 393, 401, 446, 467, 488, 501, 507, 533, 554
Swanson Lakes 397
Swantown (Whidbey Island) 86
Swartz Bay (BC) 108
Swauk Creek Basin 281
Swift
  Black 39, 47, 122-123, 126-127, 129, 133, 159, 163, 165, 171, 181, 223, 270-271, 275, 277, 312, 325, 366, 409, 411, 415, 423, 429, 431, 467, 540, 571
  Vaux's 7, 47, 50-51, 111, 122-123, 125-127, 133, 159, 169, 171, 181, 215, 226, 229, 231, 240, 270-271, 273, 275, 279, 299-300, 324, 335, 337, 341, 409-410, 413-414, 478, 483, 487, 489, 495, 499, 508, 514, 540, 571
  White-throated 11, 290, 292, 295, 305, 307, 313, 319, 327-329, 353, 355, 362, 366, 375-376, 379, 383, 391, 394, 421, 427, 431, 442, 446, 465, 493, 495, 514, 540, 572

T

Table Mountain 283
Tacoma 197, 199
Tacoma Creek Road 479, 489
Takhlakh Lake 262
Tanager
  Summer 2, 586

Western 7-9, 53, 93, 96, 111, 122, 125, 129, 136, 151, 166, 173, 191, 207, 212, 217, 226, 261, 273, 278-279, 281-282, 286, 293, 295, 301, 306, 327-328, 330, 335, 337, 341, 347, 349, 375, 381, 400, 409-412, 418, 420, 423, 427, 430, 433, 441, 448, 466-467, 471, 477-478, 487, 494-495, 498, 517, 524, 528, 545, 586
Taneum Creek and Ridge 292
Tatoosh Island 47
Tattler
  Gray-tailed 72, 563
  Wandering 5, 37, 50, 57, 65, 74, 89, 111, 159, 180, 303, 536, 562
Teal
  Blue-winged 149, 159, 179, 211, 343, 355-356, 368, 393, 397, 403, 439, 441, 501, 533, 555
  Cinnamon 62, 93, 115, 149, 159, 179, 211, 278, 284, 343, 345, 349, 355-356, 368, 393, 397, 403, 431, 439, 441, 501, 533, 555
  Green-winged 104, 146, 174, 179, 187, 211, 315, 336, 355, 401, 439, 446, 501, 509, 533, 555
Teanaway River valley 279
Telegraph Slough 91
Tenino 207
Tennant Lake 139
Tern
  Arctic 5, 66, 145, 179, 182, 414, 508, 539, 568
  Black 11, 179, 246, 338, 347-348, 356, 399-400, 402-403, 415, 441, 459, 474, 489, 501, 539, 568
  Caspian 5, 11, 24, 49, 58, 75, 86, 91, 179, 182, 212, 214, 291, 343, 348, 356-357, 371, 393, 415, 441, 509, 539, 567
  Common 5, 32, 58, 65, 109, 141, 145, 150, 179, 192, 198, 201, 212, 214, 330, 347-348, 508, 539, 567
  Elegant 58, 539, 567
  Forster's 11, 179, 291, 343, 348, 356-357, 361, 371, 415, 437-438, 539, 568
  Least 568
Terrell (Lake) 139
Thirtymile Meadows 451
Thrasher
  Brown 47, 102, 370, 582
  Sage 10-11, 126, 150, 251, 265, 289, 292, 298, 304, 307, 309-312, 342, 345-346, 356, 358, 365-366, 378-380, 384-385, 389, 397-398, 405, 437-438, 443, 544, 582
Three Forks Natural Area 170
Thrush
  Dusky 1, 581
  Gray-cheeked 581

ABBREVIATED TABLE OF CONTENTS

Strait of Juan de Fuca and Pacific Coast

- 25 Indian / Marrowstone Islands
- 32 Sequim Bay / Dungeness
- 36 Ediz Hook
- 39 Hurricane Ridge / Deer Park
- 44 Tongue Point / Clallam Bay
- 46 Cape Flattery
- 48 La Push
- 50 Hoh Rain Forest
- 52 Lake Quinault
- 57 Ocean Shores
- 61 Bowerman Basin
- 62 Chehalis River Valley
- 65 Westport
- 67 Tokeland
- 68 Willapa NWR
- 71 Leadbetter Point
- 72 Fort Canby State Park

Northwest

- 81 Crockett Lake / Fort Casey
- 88 Deception Pass State Park
- 96 Orcas Island
- 101 San Juan Island
- 107 Sky Lark sites, BC
- 109 Victoria (BC)
- 113 Fir Island / Skagit Flats
- 117 Samish Flats
- 123 Rockport / Marblemount
- 129 Colonial Creek Campground
- 131 Mount Baker
- 135 Larrabee State Park
- 137 Lummi Flats
- 140 Drayton Harbor
- 146 Reifel Sanctuary (BC)
- 150 Stanley Park (BC)

Puget Sound

- 156 Discovery Park
- 162 Lake Sammamish
- 168 Rattlesnake Lake
- 172 Carnation Marsh
- 174 Crescent Lake Wildlife Area
- 177 Everett Ponds / Spencer Island
- 183 Stillaguamish River delta
- 186 Camano Island
- 192 Point No Point
- 198 Saltwater SP / Dash Point SP
- 199 Gog-Le-Hi-Te Wetland
- 200 Point Defiance
- 203 Fort Lewis Prairies

Puget Sound (continued)

- 207 Scatter Creek / Black River
- 210 Nisqually River delta
- 215 Totten Inlet / Kennedy Creek
- 216 Capitol State Forest
- 219 Annas Bay
- 221 Mount Walker
- 227 Paradise
- 228 Sunrise

Southwest

- 234 Julia Butler Hansen NWR
- 236 Hanaford Valley
- 240 Coldwater Ridge
- 241 Windy Ridge
- 243 Woodland Bottoms
- 244 Ridgefield NWR
- 246 Vancouver Lowlands
- 251 Steigerwald Lake NWR
- 255 Skamania / Wind River
- 261 Indian Heaven
- 262 Bird Creek Meadows

South Central

- 270 Commonwealth Basin / Hyak
- 275 Wish Poosh / Tucquala Lake
- 277 Cle Elum
- 278 Teanaway Road
- 281 Swauk Creek Basin
- 284 Kittitas Valley
- 289 Old Vantage Highway
- 290 Huntzinger Road
- 295 Buck Meadows
- 300 Wenas Campground
- 310 Cold Creek Road
- 319 Fort Simcoe State Park
- 324 Bumping Lake
- 327 Oak Creek Wildlife Area
- 328 Bethel Ridge
- 333 Lyle
- 336 Klickitat Wildlife Area
- 340 Rock Creek / Bickleton
- 342 Crow Butte State Park
- 347 Yakima River delta

Columbia Basin

- 353 Frenchman Coulee
- 357 Potholes Wildlife Area
- 359 Lower Crab Creek
- 369 Wahluke Slope / White Bluffs
- 373 Big Flat Habitat Mgt Unit
- 375 Palouse Falls SP, Lyons Ferry SP
- 376 Beezley Hills

Columbia Basin (cont'd)

- 378 Moses Coulee
- 381 Waterville Plateau
- 389 Lower Grand Coulee
- 393 Steamboat Rock / Northrup Cyn
- 397 Swanson Lakes
- 400 Reardan Ponds
- 403 Fishtrap Lake

Okanogan

- 407 Old Cascade Hwy / Union Gap
- 409 Lake Wenatchee / Fish Lake
- 414 Wenatchee Confluence SP
- 417 Swakane Canyon
- 418 Entiat River Basin
- 422 Stehekin
- 424 Chelan Ridge Hawkwatch
- 426 Methow Valley
- 433 Harts Pass
- 437 Timentwa Flats
- 440 Sinlahekin Wildlife Area
- 441 Similkameen River valley
- 444 Okanogan Valley (BC)
- 450 Roger Lake / Freezeout Pass
- 451 Long Swamp
- 452 Manning Provincial Park (BC)
- 455 Okanogan Highlands

Northeast

- 463 Sanpoil River Valley
- 466 Silver Creek Road
- 470 Togo Mountain
- 475 Little Pend Oreille NWR
- 479 Big Meadow Lake
- 480 Sullivan Lake
- 482 Salmo Pass
- 488 Calispell Lake
- 491 Spokane Canyons
- 495 Spokane Valley
- 498 Mount Spokane State Park
- 499 Turnbull NWR

Southeast

- 507 Burbank Slough
- 508 Walla Walla River Delta
- 513 Biscuit Ridge / Lewis Peak
- 519 Wenatchee Guard Station
- 520 Lower Granite Lake
- 523 Chief Joseph Wildlife Area
- 524 Fields Spring State Park
- 528 Kamiak Butte County Park

MAP KEY→